Kölner Schriften zum Friedenssicherungsrecht

Cologne Studies on International Peace und Security Law

Études colognaises sur le droit de la paix et de la sécurité internationales

Herausgegeben von/Edited by/Éditées par

Prof. Dr. Dr. h.c. Dr. h.c. Claus Kreß LL.M. (Cambridge)

Band/ Volume 16

Michael Riepl

Russian Contributions to International Humanitarian Law

A contrastive analysis of Russia's historical role
and its current practice

INSTITUTE FOR
INTERNATIONAL PEACE
AND SECURITY LAW

The Deutsche Nationalbibliothek lists this publication in the
Deutsche Nationalbibliografie; detailed bibliographic data
are available on the Internet at http://dnb.d-nb.de

a.t.: Köln, Univ., Diss., 2021

ISBN   978-3-8487-7307-7 (Print)
              978-3-7489-1321-4 (ePDF)

British Library Cataloguing-in-Publication Data
A catalogue record for this book is available from the British Library.

ISBN   978-3-8487-7307-7 (Print)
              978-3-7489-1321-4 (ePDF)

Library of Congress Cataloging-in-Publication Data
Riepl, Michael
Russian Contributions to International Humanitarian Law
A contrastive analysis of Russia's historical role and its current practice
Michael Riepl
447 pp.
Includes bibliographic references.

ISBN   978-3-8487-7307-7 (Print)
              978-3-7489-1321-4 (ePDF)

1st Edition 2022
© The Author

Published by
Nomos Verlagsgesellschaft mbH & Co. KG
Waldseestraße 3–5 | 76530 Baden-Baden
www.nomos.de

Production of the printed version:
Nomos Verlagsgesellschaft mbH & Co. KG
Waldseestraße 3–5 | 76530 Baden-Baden

ISBN   978-3-8487-7307-7 (Print)
ISBN   978-3-7489-1321-4 (ePDF)
DOI   https://doi.org/10.5771/9783748913214

Onlineversion
Nomos eLibrary

Preface

I did not write this thesis myself! Of course, I have signed the statement of authorship and I can assure you that – at least in a legal sense – the following thesis was authored, written, and reworked only by myself. However, I have felt that many eyes were looking over my shoulder. While every written work starts with a first word that hits the page, a first sentence that crystallises, a first chapter that emerges, we never start from zero.

My interest in the post-Soviet space came with my grandmother's heritage. Born in 1919 in a German village in today's Ukraine, she was one of a lucky few in her family to survive Stalin's purges. After an odyssey through a war-torn Europe she started her new life as a doctor in a small Bavarian village. Unfortunately, she never passed on the gift of the Russian language to my mother, but after all it was not her mother tongue either. The German immigrants in Ukraine had stubbornly clung to their language, custom, and religion. Thus, German was my grandma's native language and I must admit that speaking Russian in a Bavarian hamlet near the Iron Curtain at the height of the Cold War would not have been the brightest idea. Through my grandma's stories, however, I caught a keyhole glimpse of this strange land that lay to the east and about which I knew so little. Intrigued, the only thing I lacked was the key. So, I embarked on the tedious journey of studying Russian, and started to unlock the secrets of this mysterious region.

My grandma was not the only (imaginary) proof-reader of this thesis. From my mother, I have inherited a passion for history and languages. She was a teacher and – as all teachers do – she taught these subjects both in school and at home. From my father, I learnt about the beauty of words. His love for art and literature proved to me that language can do more than just convey cold facts. It is a warm, breathing, living organism that can tell a passionate story.

Hence, I would like to thank all my imaginary and actual proof-readers for their comments. I am grateful to my family, my friends (in particular Josef, who played a special role in all of this), and my colleagues for their input during our discussions. Equally, I would like to thank the scholars in this field, many of whom I have never met, but whose books, articles, and blog posts steered me through the endless sea of information. Likewise, I extend my gratitude to the people that I met in the course of my work and my travels in Russia, Ukraine, Azerbaijan, Armenia, Georgia, and the Baltic States, who helped me understand the similarities and differences in the post-Soviet region. And finally, I would like to thank my supervisor, Prof. Dr. Angelika Nußberger, who realised earlier than I that finding a topic – *this* topic – was as much a matter of the heart as it was a matter of the mind.

Yerevan, January 2020

Transliteration

I have chosen to render the Russian sources in Cyrillic script with the English translation in [brackets] rather than a transliteration in Latin script. For names and places, however, I have chosen the transliteration in Latin script. In instances where there are several versions of a transliterated name, for example, Kiev (Russian) or Kyiv (Ukrainian), I have chosen the transliteration according to the official local language. In the case of disputed territories, this inexorably contains a political statement, e.g. Donbass (Russian) or Donbas (Ukrainian), Lugansk (Russian) or Luhansk (Ukrainian). The battlefield of semantics was especially important for the war in eastern Ukraine. While I do not wish to bolster the ranks of these word-warriors, for reasons of practicality I had to settle for one transliteration. Dealing with the difficult questions of secession and annexation in this thesis, however, will at least allow me to provide the legal reasoning for my choice.

For the sake of readability, I have opted for a simplified transliteration that does not render all the special characters of the Cyrillic alphabet. Hence, I will refer to Pavel Felgengauer instead of Pavel Fel'gengauer, Donetsk instead of Donets'k etc.

Table of Contents

List of Abbreviations

AP I	Protocol Additional to the Geneva Conventions of 12 August 1949, and relating to the Protection of Victims of International Armed Conflicts (Protocol I) of 8 June 1977
AP II	Protocol Additional to the Geneva Conventions of 12 August 1949, and relating to the Protection of Victims of Non-International Armed Conflicts (Protocol II) of 8 June 1977
AP III	Protocol Additional to the Geneva Conventions of 12 August 1949, and relating to the Adoption of an Additional Distinctive Emblem (Protocol III) of 8 December 2005
APMBC	Anti-Personnel Mine Ban Convention
ARSIWA	Articles on State Responsibility for Internationally Wrongful Acts
Art	Article, Articles
ATT	Arms Trade Treaty
BBC	British Broadcasting Corporation
CA	Common Article
CCM	Convention on Cluster Munitions
CCRF	Criminal Code of the Russian Federation (1996)
CCW	Convention on Prohibitions or Restrictions on the Use of Certain Conventional Weapons Which May be Deemed to be Excessively Injurious or to Have Indiscriminate Effects
CERD	International Convention on the Elimination of All Forms of Racial Discrimination
CNN	Cable News Network
CRF	Constitution of the Russian Federation (1993)
DNR	Донецкая Народная Республика [Donetsk People's Republic]
DGO	Deutsche Gesellschaft für Osteuropakunde
ECHR	European Convention on Human Rights
ECtHR	European Court of Human Rights
EJIL	European Journal of International Law
et al	et alia
et seq	et sequitur
FRY	Former Republic of Yugoslavia

FSB	Федеральная служба безопасности [Federal Security Service]
GC I	Geneva Convention (I) for the Amelioration of the Condition of the Wounded and Sick in Armed Forces in the Field of 12 August 1949
GC II	Geneva Convention (II) for the Amelioration of the Condition of Wounded, Sick and Shipwrecked Members of Armed Forces at Sea of 12 August 1949
GC III	Geneva Convention (III) relative to the Treatment of Prisoners of War of 12 August 1949
GC IV	Geneva Convention (IV) relative to the Protection of Civilian Persons in Time of War of 12 August 1949
GGE	UN Group of Governmental Experts
GRU	Главное управление Генерального штаба Вооружённых Сил Российской Федерации [Main Directorate of the General Staff of the Armed Forces of the Russian Federation]
HJIL/ ZaöRV	Heidelberg Journal of International Law/ Zeitschrift für ausländisches öffentliches Recht und Völkerrecht
HR	Hague Regulations
HRW	Human Rights Watch
HVO	Croatian Defence Council
IAC	International armed conflict
ibid	ibidem
ICC	International Criminal Court
ICJ	International Court of Justice
ICL	International criminal law
ICRC	International Committee of the Red Cross
ICTR	International Criminal Tribunal for Rwanda
ICTY	International Criminal Tribunal for the Former Republic of Yugoslavia
IHFFC	International Humanitarian Fact-Finding Commission
IHL	International humanitarian law
IICI	Independent International Commission of Inquiry on the Syrian Arab Republic
IIFFMCG	Independent International Fact-Finding Mission on the Conflict in Georgia
ILC	International Law Commission
IMT	International Military Tribunal
ITLOS	International Tribunal for the Law of the Sea

JIT	Joint Investigation Team
KSSO	Командование сил специальных операций [Special Operations Forces Command]
LAWS	Lethal Autonomous Weapons Systems
LBU	Law of Burial and Undertaking
LNR	Луганская Народная Республика [Luhansk People's Republic]
MGIMO	Московский государственный институт международных отношений [Moscow State Institute of International Relations]
MP	Member of Parliament
MSF	Médecins sans frontières
n	Note; footnote
NATO	Northern Atlantic Treaty Organization
NGO	Non-governmental organization
NIAC	Non-international armed conflict
NKVD	Народный комиссариат внутренних дел [People's Commissariat for Internal Affairs]
ODIHR	Office for Democratic Institutions and Human Rights
OHCHR	Office of the United Nations High Commissioner for Human Rights
OMON	Отряд мобильный особого назначения [Special Purpose Mobile Unit]
ORF	Österreichischer Rundfunk
OSCE	Organization for Security and Co-operation in Europe
OSCE PA	Parliamentary Assembly of the Organization for Security and Co-operation in Europe
OSCE SMM	Organization for Security and Co-operation in Europe – Special Monitoring Mission (in Ukraine)
OTP	Office of the Prosecutor
OVV	Dutch Safety Board
p	Page
P5	The Five permanent members of the UN Security Council (China, France, Russia, UK, US)
PACE	Parliamentary Assembly of the Council of Europe
para	Paragraph
PDPA	People's Democratic Party of Afghanistan
PHR	Physicians for Human Rights
PMC	Private military company

PSC	Private security company
PMSC	Private military and security company
POW	Prisoner of war
PR	Public Relations
RF	Russian Federation
RSFSR	Russian Soviet Federative Socialist Republic
SBU	Служба безпеки України [Security Service of Ukraine]
SMM	Special Monitoring Mission
SOM	South Ossetian Militias
SWP	Stiftung Wissenschaft und Politik
TPNW	Treaty on the Prohibition of Nuclear Weapons
UDHR	Universal Declaration of Human Rights
UN	United Nations
UNCLOS	UN Convention for the Law of the Sea
UNESCO	United Nations Educational, Scientific, and Cultural Organization
UK	United Kingdom
US	United States
USSR	Union of Soviet Socialist Republics
UXO	Unexploded ordnance
VCLT	Vienna Convention on the Law of Treaties
VRS	Army of the Republika Srpska
v	versus
VDV	Воздушно-десантные войска России [Russian Airborne Forces]

Introduction

The topic for this thesis had lingered in my mind for a long time. I could not make sense of two contradicting narratives. They both concern Russia's influence on international humanitarian law (IHL).[1] One, however, is the tale of a sinner; the other the story of a saint.

On the one hand, we find what may be called the predominant "Western" narrative. It is exemplified by the following conversation that I had – in this or in a similar form – at various conferences, or family dinners, or over a glass of wine with my friends.
- "So, you are writing a PhD. What is your topic?"
- "Russia's contribution to the development of the laws of war."
- "Oh…, interesting!" My interlocutors would raise their eyebrows, smirk, and add hesitantly. "I can imagine their 'contribution.' Is there anything to write at all?"

I cannot blame my anonymised counterparts for their answer, because it corresponds to the mainstream Western narrative. Russia in not regarded as a nation that *makes* international law but rather *breaks* international law – both in the past and in the present.

In Russia, on the other hand, we find a completely different narrative. According to Russian scholars it is hard to "overstate […] the role of Russia in in the development of IHL."[2] They hail the role of Russian humanitarian pioneers like Nikolay Pirogov and Elena Pavlova and stress that these individuals acted as a precursor to the First Geneva Convention (1864).[3] Russian politicians often adopt the role of a strict schoolmaster,

---

1 Throughout this thesis, I will use IHL when referring to the laws applicable in armed conflict/laws of war. I am, however, aware that the term IHL is in fact much younger than the field of law that it describes and only dates back to the 1949 Geneva Conventions, see n 1923 and n 1924.

2 The reader can find the full text of the speech at: <https://www.icrc.org/ru/docume nt/gaagskie-mirnye-konferencii-1899-i-1907-godov-rossiyskaya-iniciativa-i-dalneyshe e-razvitie>.

3 И.И. Котляров [I.I. Kotlyarov], 'Вклад России в стоновление и развитие международного гуманитарного права [Russia's Contribution to the Formation and Development of IHL]' [2007] Российский Ежегодник Международного Права [Russian Yearbook of International Law] 62, 63. See also below n 83 and 'Хватит смотреть в рот Западу: Онищенко обвинил МККК в разведдеятельности на территории РФ и ДНР [Enough trying to appeal to the West! Onishchenko

reminding the US and other Western countries of their shortcomings in IHL, for example when Foreign Minister Sergey Lavrov accused NATO of violating the laws of war during the war in Serbia.[4]

This thesis tries to make sense of these two contradictory narratives. What *is* Russia? A sinner or a saint? Or perhaps both? Part I of this thesis will analyse Russia's historical contributions to the development of the laws of war. Part II will flesh out Russia's current approach to IHL. Finally, Part III will analyse and compare areas of continuity and change between Moscow's historical and current role.

At first glance, Russia seems to have undergone a spectacular transformation. The reader will discover that it made outstanding contributions to IHL. Historically, Russia was among the most important States – if not *the* most important State – in advancing, developing, and upholding IHL. However, Moscow's current contributions to IHL look rather bleak. Despite its legacy and its current involvement in numerous wars, Russia has done little to advance IHL since 1991. On the contrary, it has often undermined its own legacy in recent times.

This stark contrast between the past and the present reminded me of a famous biblical character who epitomises radical change: the story of Saul who was "breathing out murderous threats against the Lord's disciples" but later turns into Paul, one of the most devoted defenders of early Christianity.[5] Russia, it seems, has completed the inverse transformation. In terms of IHL, it turned from Paul into Saul.

---

accuses the ICRC of spying on the territory of RF and DNR]' (Federal News Agency, 5 December 2018) <https://prinmedia.ru/news/267/politics/politics/9840 -hvatit-smotret-v-rot-zapadu-onisenko-obvinil-mkkk-v-razveddeatelnosti-na-territo rii-rf-i-dnr?slug=hvatit-smotret-v-rot-zapadu-onisenko-obvinil-mkkk-v-razveddeatel nosti-na-territorii-rf-i-dnr>. For details on Nikolay Pirogov, Elena Pavlova, and the origins of the First Geneva Convention see below at pp 29 et seq.

4 Sergey Lavrov, Press Conference (16 February 2019) at the 2019 Munich Conference on Security Policy: "Of course, anyone can interpret IHL as he wishes. When during the bombardment of Belgrade a passenger train on a bridge or a TV station became targets, this was also regarded as normal. We are not willing to follow such an interpretation of IHL." Entire transcript available at <https://www.youtube.com /watch?v=ovDFn 8Ur_EA>.

5 See Acts 9:1–19. Saul of Tarsus is said to have persecuted the early disciples of Jesus. When Jesus appeared to him on the road to Damascus in a bright light, however, Saul was struck blind and only after three days his sight was restored. This revelation prompted Saul to convert to Christianity and he was thereafter commonly called Paul the Apostle. In Acts 13:9 the Bible refers to him as Paul for the first time. His story became a metaphor for radical betterment.

This question will form the centrepiece of my thesis. How did Russia shape IHL in the past and in the present and how can we explain the apparent contradiction which we find in Russia's relationship with IHL? Before I begin to explore this question, however, I would like to explain the scope of my research. First, you might ask: is it not madness to cover a time span of over 150 years? Analysing history and State practice in one thesis? I understand the reader's bewilderment. However, in my defence I would like to quote Lauri Mälksoo, one of the outstanding scholars studying Russia's legal history and current practice. He has embarked on the even more ambitious project of characterising Russian approaches to *general* international law including history, theorisation, and State practice in his recent book *Russian Approaches to International Law*. There, he answers his imaginary critic:

> *"It is a quite ambitious project to connect these three sub-areas – history, contemporary legal theory, and recent state practice – in one monograph on international law. It is possible to write monographs on each of these sub-areas of international legal research. However, my deep conviction is that the three sub-areas are interconnected and only when analysed together will they enable us to arrive at a holistic understanding of Russian approaches of international law in the past and in the present."[6]*

I absolutely share this view and believe that it holds equally true for Russian contributions to IHL. Hence, I ask the reader not to regard the historical chapter as a lengthy prelude. They may rather see it as a point of reference. It is important to know where Russia came from, to understand its current position, and to reconcile both narratives mentioned above.

Secondly, I would like to add a clarification. I have spoken of Russia's contributions to IHL. To be more precise, however, I should speak of the *Russias'* contribution to IHL, since we are dealing with one country that – like ice, water, and steam – exists in three different states of matter. My historical overview starts in 1850 when Russia was a mighty Empire ruled by its monarch, the Tsar. In 1917, the October Revolution laid the Empire to rest and replaced it with the Russian Soviet Federative Socialist Republic (RSFSR) which later became the centre of power in the Soviet Union (USSR) founded in 1922. Finally, after the collapse of the USSR in 1991, the Russian Federation emerged – a "democratic, federative State

---

6 Lauri Mälksoo, *Russian Approaches to International Law* (Oxford University Press 2015) 21.

of law with a republican form of government."[7] Thus, when I speak of "Russia" I refer to a country with a split personality. Nevertheless, I am convinced that there is a sense of continuity – and many Russians would share this belief. Vladimir Putin spoke for (and to) them in his famous speech at the Munich Conference on Security Policy (2007):

> *"Russia is a country with a history that spans more than a thousand years and has practically always used the privilege to carry out an independent foreign policy."*[8]

I will of course deal with the complex (legal) issue of State succession below.[9] For the purpose of my comparison, however, "Russia" shall encompass all three states of matter: the Empire, the USSR, and today's Russian Federation.

Finally, I would like to add two caveats. I am aware that comparing Russia's historical and current approach dances at the edge of simplicity. First, it risks "humanising" Russia by suggesting that any country has a core, a soul that either remains stable or alters in the course of history. I am aware that this would be utterly simplistic. No country, and no person, for that matter, has such an identity nucleus. Rather, I share the conviction with which Hermann Hesse confronts his protagonist Harry Haller in *Steppenwolf*:

> *"The mistaken and unhappy notion that a man is an enduring unity is known to you. It is also known to you that man consists of a multitude of souls, of numerous selves."*[10]

What is true for a person like Harry Haller, is even more true for a complex construct like a State. It does not have one steady core, but a "multitude of souls." At the same time, most would agree that countries do have their own ways. Their historical legacies shape their present. The revolutionary values of *liberté, égalité,* and *fraternité* still determine French identity and affect current policies, for example in the areas of immigra-

---

7 Art 1 of the 1993 Russian Constitution.

8 President of Russia, 'Speech and the Following Discussion at the Munich Conference on Security Policy' (10 February 2007) <http://en.kremlin.ru/events/presiden t/transcripts/24034>.

9 For the complex questions whether the RSFSR or the USSR succeeded the Russian Empire in legal terms, and whether the Russian Federation is the legal successor of the Soviet Union see below at pp 94 and 139.

10 Hermann Hesse, *Steppenwolf* (Creighton Basil tr, Bantham Books 1969) 218.

tion or religion (*laïcité*).[11] Germany's responsibility for the Second World War and the Holocaust continues to define its internal and foreign politics. Germany is still reluctant to use military force abroad and considers Israel's right to existence "*Staatsräson*."[12] Undoubtedly, a country's history defines its present. Often, the leaders themselves foster this narrative of continuity as Putin's reference to "a history that spans more than a thousand years" illustrates. Why should it be any different for IHL? *If* Russia was the driving force in developing this field of law in the 19th and 20th century, and *if* it took pride in this role, would it not be remarkable if it later completely reversed this legacy?

My second caveat concerns the pitfall of any historical comparison as such. Contrasting one aspect in the past and the present risks being simplistic if it disregards the changed context. We should be cautious in drawing obvious parallels since political ideas, legal concepts, and terms such as "humanity" or "sovereignty" might exist in both periods and yet have a completely different meaning. It is a truism that Russia's approach to IHL is not the only element to have changed over time. Warfare and international law itself have changed dramatically over the past 150 years. It would be foolish to ignore these changes. Hence, when I try to answer the overarching question of *if* and *why* Russia turned from Paul to Saul in Part III, I shall embed my assessment in today's altered context.

---

11 See e.g. ECtHR, *Affaire Dogru c France*, No 27058/05, 4 December 2008: "En France, l'exercice de la liberté religieuse dans l'espace public, et plus particulièrement la question du port des signes religieux à l'école, est directement lié *au principe de laïcité, principe autour duquel la République française s'est construite*" (emphasis added).

12 Angela Merkel, Speech in the Knesset (18 March 2008). See Bundeszentrale für politische Bildung, 'Israels Sicherheit als deutsche Staatsräson: Was bedeutet das konkret?' (30 January 2015) <https://www.bpb.de/apuz/199894/israels-sicherheit-als-deutsche-staatsraeson>.

Part I: Historical Development

This Part gives an account of Russian feats and failures in the sphere of IHL. It will take the reader back to the middle of the 19th century, to the birth date of the laws of war of our modern age.[13] I beg the reader not to regard these historical accounts as mere anecdotes. They will demonstrate why IHL is not just *any* sub-domain of international law in Russia. They will set the stage for the upcoming analysis of the current discourse in IHL, its implementation, and military practice. Readers will rediscover many of the historical protagonists in academic articles published in modern-day law journals. They[14] will spot their names in speeches delivered 150 years later, and they will even find their legacy in the IHL treaties themselves. The historical accounts will enable us to compare how Russia treated IHL in its infancy and how it does today. We will discover patterns of congruency, but also striking differences.

The structure of this chapter follows the chronology of events starting in 1850. While travelling forward in time, I will introduce the reader to outstanding Russian figures who left their imprint on IHL. For law is not made in a void, but is crafted by humans. Retelling the history of law also means retracing the lives of those who have shaped it. I will, for example, follow the fascinating character of Fyodor Fyodorovich Martens (1845–1909). Born at the fringe of the Russian Empire in a small Estonian village, he became an orphan at an early age. Despite that, he would grow

---

13 Most scholars place the origin of modern day IHL in the middle of the 19th century. Chris af Jochnick and Roger Normand, 'The Legitimation of Violence: A Critical History of the Laws of War' in Michael N Schmitt and Wolff Heintschel von Heinegg (eds), *The Development and Principles of International Humanitarian Law* (Routledge 2017) 62 et seq; Amanda Alexander, 'A Short History of International Humanitarian Law' (2015) 26 European Journal of International Law 109; Dietrich Schindler, 'International Humanitarian Law: Its Remarkable Development and Its Persistent Violation' in Michael N Schmitt and Wolff Heintschel von Heinegg (eds), *The Development and Principles of International Humanitarian Law* (Routledge 2017); of course there are many earlier examples of codification e.g. Hugo Grotius, *De Iure Belli Ac Pacis – Libri Tres*, vol 3 (1625). One of the oldest sources that contains rules for warfare is the 'Code of Hammurabi' by the King of Babylon (1728–1686 BC).

14 For the sake of gender equality, the author will use pronouns in their plural form when referring to an undefined addressee.

up to be an acclaimed law professor, a seasoned diplomat, and a passionate cosmopolitan that spoke six languages fluently. Above all, Martens would shape IHL like no other Russian before or after him.

Hence, it seems only just to end this introduction with one of his quotes. Martens was convinced that "even in times of war modern civilized nations recognize that they are bound by known custom and treaty law regulating their relations."[15] Advancing these laws of war became a project dear to him. In 1879 Martens expressed his dream of adopting the first comprehensive code of warfare:

> *"The country that successfully completes this matter [...] will not only earn the gratitude of the people, whose suffering it has attenuated, but also the right to call herself the first nation among all the States who understand the essence of civilization and value the legitimate desire of civilized peoples."[16]*

Was this a general Russian attitude, or Martens' personal belief? And why should Russia have been interested in elaborating the laws of war at all?

---

15 Ф.Ф. Мартенс [F.F. Martens], *Современное международное право цивилизованных народов [Contemporary International Law of Civilized Peoples]*, vol 1 (5th edn, Типография министерства путей сообщения [Printing House of the Ministry of Communication] 1904) 6–7.

16 Ф.Ф. Мартенс [F.F. Martens], *Восточная Война и Брюсселская Конферения 1874–1878 г [The Eastern War and the Brussels Conference 1874–1878]* (Типография министерства путей сообщения [Printing House of the Ministry of Communication] 1879) 76.

Chapter I: The Tsarist Era 1850–1917

1. The Crimean War 1853–1856 – the opening salvo?

In 1850 Russia seemed to be the dominant State of the European continent. Though under-industrialised, it possessed the largest land army.[17] The Empire had gradually expanded east- and southwards and it was virtually untouched by the revolts of 1848.[18] Then came what is sometimes called the "first modern war."[19] The Crimean War between Russia and a coalition of Britain, France, and the Ottoman Empire lasted from 1853–1856. It ended with a crushing defeat for the Tsar and temporarily halted Russian expansion into Ottoman lands. The conflict was fought with the latest deadly technology and claimed more than 250 000 casualties on either side.[20] However, it also brought about flickers of hope. On the British side, nurses like Florence Nightingale organised aid for wounded soldiers. In Russia Elena Pavlova, sister of Tsar Nicolas I, founded the Order of the *Сёстры Милосердия* [Sisters of Mercy] in 1854 and assisted the wounded on the battlefield.[21] Her compatriot Prince Anatoly Demidov, a Russian industrialist and philanthropist, organised humanitarian

---

17 For a detailed analysis of the Imperial Army see William C Fuller Jr, 'The Imperial Army' in Ronald Grigor Suny (ed), *The Cambridge History of Russia*, vol 2 (Cambridge University Press 2006) 545. Already in 1825 Russia had the largest standing army in Europe with around 750 000 men.

18 David Schimmelpenninck van der Oye, 'Russian Foreign Policy: 1815–1917' in Ronald Grigor Suny (ed), *The Cambridge History of Russia*, vol 2 (Cambridge University Press 2006) 558.

19 See e.g. Alexis S Troubetzkoy, *The Crimean War: The Causes and Consequences of a Medieval Conflict Fought in a Modern Age* (Carroll & Graf 2006).

20 Günther Stökl, *Russische Geschichte* (Kröner Verlag 1983) 505–507. See also Encyclopædia Britannica, 'Crimean War' <https://www.britannica.com/event/Crimean-War>.

21 М.Д. Беляева [M.D. Belyaeva], 'Сёстры милосердия Крымской войны – основатели культурных традиций сестринского дела в России [The Sisters of Mercy of the Crimean War – Founders of the Cultural Tradition of Nursing in Russia]' (2015) 94 Молодой Учёный Научный Журнал [Young Scientist's Journal] 390, 390.

aid for French, English, and Italian soldiers held captive in Russia.[22] These admirable manifestations of humanity, however, were not backed up by any legal framework. There was no convention regulating the rights of wounded soldiers or protecting those who came to their aid. Mary Seacole, a British nurse, was even refused passage by her own government.[23] The need for a humanitarian treaty was repeatedly raised – including by the famous Russian surgeon Nikolay Pirogov[24] – but these efforts never gained enough momentum to culminate in a treaty-making process.

The Treaty of Paris (1856), that marked the end of the Crimean War, did little in this respect. Its main purpose was to re-establish an acceptable balance of power. Admittedly, the treaty also contained the so-called Paris Declaration, which laid down rules for naval warfare. It abolished privateering,[25] specified which goods could be seized in war, and defined the conditions for a legitimate naval blockade that are still valid today.[26] This was remarkable, because for the first time modern nations agreed on rules applicable in armed conflict. Some scholars therefore consider the Declaration the "opening salvo [...] to codify the international law of warfare."[27] However, the Paris Declaration failed to address the central issue at stake in war: human suffering. The rules were not intended to relieve the hardship of those affected by armed conflict, but rather established a framework that limited economic warfare. In this sense, the Declaration was very different from the IHL to come. Not so much an opening salvo, but rather the faint sound of crackling fire.

---

22 See Jacques Meurant, 'Anatole Demidoff: Pionnier de l'assistance aux prisonniers de guerre' in Jacques Meurant and Roger Durant (eds), *Préludes et pionniers: Les précurseurs de la Croix-Rouge* (1991).

23 Encyclopædia Britannica, 'Mary Seacole' <https://www.britannica.com/biography/Mary-Seacole>.

24 И.И. Котляров [I.I. Kotlyarov] (n 3) 63.

25 A privateer is "a vessel armed and equipped by a person or persons, to the captain of which the Sovereign of a State at war, upon application of the owner, has issued a commission letter of marque and reprisals empowering him to levy war upon the enemy by capturing his property." See Thomas Gibson Bowles, *The Declaration of Paris of 1856* (Sampson Low 1900) 98.

26 Paris Declaration Respecting Maritime Law, Paris (16 April 1856) available at <https://ihl-databases.icrc.org/ihl/INTRO/105?OpenDocument>. For the current definition of blockade see ICRC Casebook, How Does Law Protect in War, 'Blockade' <https://casebook.icrc.org/glossary/blockade>.

27 Eric Myles, 'Humanity, Civilization and the International Community in the Late Imperial Russian Mirror – Three Ideas Topical for Our Days' (2002) 4 Journal of the History of International Law 310, 316–317.

In any case, the significance of the Treaty of Paris lay elsewhere for Russia. It sealed the crushing defeat which the Tsar's Army had suffered in the Crimean War. Russia was forced to cede Moldavia and Wallachia, which became part of the Ottoman Empire. The Black Sea was demilitarised, preventing Russia from building up a naval fleet.[28] The issue of humanising war was left for another occasion.

2. The First Geneva Convention 1864 – Russia, the sleeping giant

"Dunant [...] has always fascinated me most of all the Nobel laureates. Fascinated and annoyed me at the same time. For he is one of the most peculiar characters. [...] An absent-minded Don Quichote."[29]

Jaan Kross' fictitious F.F. Martens about Henry Dunant

The occasion to negotiate a binding humanitarian treaty presented itself roughly a decade after the Paris Declaration. As often in world history, at the origin of a good idea stood someone who was in the right place at the right time. Or rather, in the wrong place at the wrong time.

The impact of the Geneva Convention can hardly be over-estimated. As François Bugnion puts it: "no other legal text had ever brought such influence to bear on the relations between opposing parties in wartime."[30] The treaty owes its existence to the exceptional commitment and perseverance of the Swiss businessman Henry Dunant, who was on his way to France when he passed by the battlefield of Solferino (1859).[31] The bloodiest battle in Europe since Waterloo had just ended. It left 6 000 men dead and more than 40 000 wounded. Dunant was utterly shocked as he witnessed how the wounded soldiers dragged themselves off the battle ground and slowly perished without medical assistance. He interrupted his journey for several days and cared for the survivors together with local volunteers.[32]

In the aftermath of these tragic events, Dunant explored ways to institutionalise aid for those wounded in war. He dreamt of an international con-

---

28 Schimmelpenninck van der Oye (n 18) 560.
29 Jaan Kross, *Professor Martens Abreise: Roman* (Hanser 1992) 123–124. Henry Dunant, the founder of the International Committee of the Red Cross, received the Nobel Peace Prize in 1901 together with Frédéric Passy.
30 François Bugnion, *The International Committee of the Red Cross and the Protection of War Victims* (Macmillan Education 2003) 22.
31 Henry Dunant, *Un souvenir de Solférino* (1862).
32 Bugnion (n 30) 75.

vention and an organisation watching over its implementation. Together with four likeminded philanthropists, he founded the International Committee of the Red Cross (ICRC) in 1863. Thanks to their commitment and the support of the Swiss Confederacy, they accomplished an astonishing feat; only one year after its foundation, the International Committee managed to gather almost all central European powers in Geneva to discuss the fate of wounded soldiers. The conference culminated in the signature of the First Geneva Convention for the Amelioration of the Condition of the Wounded in Armies in the Field.[33] Art 6 of this Convention enshrined the principle that "wounded and sick combatants, to whatever nation they may belong, shall be collected and cared for." At the same time, the Convention protected those helping the wounded in various ways.[34] National Red Cross societies were founded to ensure its implementation.[35]

Russia played no role in this, since it chose not to take part in the conference. In a letter, the Russian Minister of War Dmitry Milyutin had expressed his "sympathy" for the proposals, but believed it "wiser to absolutely avoid any discussion of matters regarding international law and leave this aspect of the question to the initiative of the competent governmental bodies."[36] Nevertheless, Russia ratified the treaty fairly quickly in 1867.[37] In the same year the Tsar founded the Russian Red Cross Society and placed it under the aegis of his wife, Empress Maria Alexandrovna.[38] Soon, the society was to become highly active, well-organised, and it would play a crucial rule in the wars to come.[39]

---

33 François Bugnion, 'The International Committee of the Red Cross and the Development of International Humanitarian Law' (2004) 5 Chicago Journal of International Law 27, 191–193.

34 See e.g. Art 1–2 regulating the neutrality of medical aid, or Art 5 allowing for spontaneous individual help from the local population.

35 Bugnion (n 30) 23.

36 Société genevoise d'utilité publique, *Compte rendu de la Conférence internationale réunie à Genève les 26, 27, 28 et 29 octobre 1863, pour étudier les moyens de pourvoir à l'insuffisance du service sanitaire dans les armées en campagne* (Imprimerie Fick 1863) 30.

37 For an overview of IHL treaties that Russia has ratified see ICRC, 'Russian Federation – Historical Documents' <https://ihl-databases.icrc.org/applic/ihl/ihl.n sf/vwTreatiesHistoricalByCountrySelected.xsp?xp_countrySelected=RU&nv=8>.

38 André Durand, *From Sarajevo to Hiroshima: History of the International Committee of the Red Cross* (Henry Dunant Institute 1984) 79. See also Russian Red Cross, 'History' <http://www.redcross.ru/o-nas/istoriya>.

39 Bugnion (n 30) 38. Already in 1877, when war broke out between Russia and the Ottoman Empire the Russian Red Cross played a crucial role in treating and evacuating wounded and sick soldiers.

The success story of the Geneva Conventions proved to the world that it was possible to regulate humanitarian affairs on an international level. A new discipline of law began to emerge that would later be called international humanitarian law;[40] a domain in which Russia would soon excel, starting in 1868.

3. St Petersburg Declaration 1868 – closing Pandora's box

Retelling the story of the St Petersburg Declaration[41] means providing an answer to two puzzling questions: firstly, why was a weapon that had never been used on the battlefield prohibited on the initiative of the very State that had developed it?[42] Secondly, why is it still worth telling the story of this treaty today – more than 150 years later – if it only banned *one specific* type of projectile?

After being a bit late to the Geneva Convention, Russia decided to take the initiative. Tsar Alexander II found himself in constant conflict with the British Empire. The quest for territorial expansion in Central Asia – the so-called Great Game – pushed both powers towards an all-out open war.[43] With such gloomy prospects lurking ahead, the Tsar was deeply concerned that the next conflict would be fought using the latest deadly technology. He was specifically worried by a recent invention made by his own countrymen. Russian scientists had discovered exploding bullets with the primary object of blowing up munition wagons.[44] In the following years, these bullets were perfected to explode even on softer surfaces, such as the human body.[45] Soon it became clear that this ammunition would

---

40 For the shift of terminology from "the laws and customs of war" to "international humanitarian law" see n 1922 and n 1923.

41 Declaration Renouncing the Use, in Time of War, of Explosive Projectiles Under 400 Grammes Weight (29 November (11 December) 1868) available at <https://ih l-databases.icrc.org/ihl/full/declaration1868>.

42 Joshua F Berry, 'Hollow Point Bullets: How History Has Hijacked Their Use in Combat and Why It Is Time to Reexamine the 1899 Hague Declaration Concerning Expanding Bullets' (2010) 206 Military Law Review 88, 101.

43 Milton Bearden, 'Afghanistan, Graveyard of Empires' (2001) 80 Foreign Affairs 17, 17; see also Stökl (n 20) 531; Schimmelpenninck van der Oye (n 18) 563.

44 Georg Friedrich von Martens, 'Protocole I des Conférences militaires tenues à Saint-Pétersbourg Mémoire sur la suppression de l'emploi des balles explosibles en temps de guerre', *Nouveau recueil général de traités et autres actes relatifs aux rapports de droit international*, vol XVIII (Scientia Verlag 1873) 458.

45 ibid 459.

have horrific consequences for infantrymen, because the explosion could tear large wounds and cause great suffering.[46] Russia faced a dilemma. On the one hand it was at the forefront of the latest military technology. On the other hand, States such as Switzerland, Prussia, Austria, and Bavaria started to catch up and were testing similar projectiles.[47] It was only a matter of time before such bullets would become standard equipment in every European army. Therefore, any future war would expose Russian infantrymen to great suffering.

Hence Tsar Alexander II, known for his progressive thinking,[48] took a decision that seems quite remarkable from a modern-day perspective. In order to avoid an arms race, he strove to outlaw the use of these newly developed explosive projectiles. At the same time, his government worried about the decisive advantage that such bullets presented for other European armies. Hence, Russia pushed for the adoption of a multi-lateral treaty, banning the use of such weaponry altogether.[49] When consensus could not be reached in written negotiations,[50] the Tsar invited all European powers to his capital St Petersburg, where they were to hold three meetings.[51]

3.1 Proceedings at the conference and the final declaration

The Russian General and then Minister of War Dmitry Milyutin, who chaired the meeting, set the tone in his opening statement:

> *"Messieurs, nous sommes réunis pour délibérer sur la proposition [...] d'exclure certains projectiles de l'armement des troupes en temps de guerre. Il y a là d'abord une question de principe sur laquelle nous sommes tous*

---

46 ibid.
47 ibid 458.
48 See e.g. Larisa Zakharova, 'The Reign of Alexander II: A Watershed?' in Ronald Grigor Suny and William C Fuller Jr (eds), *The Cambridge History of Russia*, vol 2 (Cambridge University Press 2006).
49 Bugnion (n 33) 198–199.
50 von Martens (n 44) 464; Emily Crawford, 'The Enduring Legacy of the St Petersburg Declaration: Distinction, Military Necessity, and the Prohibition of Causing Unnecessary Suffering and Superfluous Injury in IHL' (2019) 20 Journal of the History of International Law 544, 548.
51 Discussions were held on 28 October and (9 November) and 1 November (13 November). The Declaration was finally signed on 4 November (16 November) 1868.

d'accord, un principe d'humanité qui consiste à limiter autant que possible les calamités de la guerre et à interdire l'emploi de certaines armes, dont l'effet est d'aggraver cruellement les souffrances causées par les blessures, sans utilité réelle pour le but de la guerre."[52]

It is this spirit of humanisation that permeates the diplomatic discussions. All participants seemed to accept that, in war, a State's right to hurt the enemy is not unfettered. Despite this general consensus, the conference did not lack controversies. While Prussia suggested broadening the discussion to all weapons,[53] Britain feared that such an approach might hamper its military development.[54] Other participants, such as the Netherlands, were only willing to sign a unanimously adopted document.[55] Finally, for the sake of consensus the scope of the treaty was limited to projectiles weighing less than 400 grams, since those were most likely to be used against humans. Additionally, the States included the so-called *clausula si omnes* – a legal novelty – in the declaration, which meant that the rules only applied if *all* warring parties on *both* sides were signatories.[56]

Despite these caveats, the outcome of the conference marked a turning point in international law. Seventeen States – including the sceptical British Empire – signed the Declaration in St Petersburg. Two States joined shortly afterwards.[57]

---

52 von Martens (n 44) 451.

53 ibid.

54 ibid 464, 466; see also Crawford, 'The Enduring Legacy of the St Petersburg Declaration: Distinction, Military Necessity, and the Prohibition of Causing Unnecessary Suffering and Superfluous Injury in IHL' (n 50) 548 et seq.

55 von Martens (n 44) 453.

56 The St Petersburg Declaration was the first recorded instance of the use of such a restriction. The clause was included in many of the subsequent IHL treaties such as the 1899 and 1907 Hague Conventions. It was not used any more after World War I, since it became apparent that in multi-party wars the clause could significantly hamper the application of the treaties. For example, Montenegro was not party to the 1906 Geneva Convention during World War I. Although the *si omnes* clause was never invoked during the war, technically it excluded the application of the treaty. Philippe Gautier, 'General Participation Clause (Clausula Si Omnes)', *Max Planck Encyclopedia of Public International Law* (Oxford University Press 2006); Jean Pictet, *The Geneva Conventions of 12 August 1949: Commentary on the Geneva Convention Relative to the Treatment of Prisoners of War* (International Committee of the Red Cross 1960) 21.

57 Brazil and the Grand Duchy of Baden. For a detailed list of ratifications see <https://ihl-databases.icrc.org/applic/ihl/ihl.nsf/States.xsp?xp_viewStates=XPages_NORMStatesParties&xp_treatySelected=130>.

3.2 Impact of the St Petersburg Declaration on IHL

The significance of the Declaration was twofold. Firstly, it banned the use of explosive bullets, averting the imminent danger of their use in battle. Secondly, it laid the foundation for the framework that governs the conduct of hostilities in general – a legacy that lives on in modern-day IHL.

The prohibition of explosive projectiles in the seventh paragraph of the Declaration may be called the obvious achievement of 1868. For the first time, States had agreed to ban a specific weapon, and successfully so. Despite occasional allegations that explosive bullets were used in the Franco-Prussian War (1870–1871) and the Boer War (1880–1881), there are no documented cases of their use.[58] The prohibition of exploding bullets has been reiterated in many other documents, such as the Brussels Declaration (1874),[59] the Oxford Manual (1880),[60] and the Oxford Manual of Naval War (1913).[61] By now, the rule is considered customary international law.[62] A violation of the rule may represent a war crime[63] which was already stated as early as 1919.[64]

Secondly, and far more importantly, the Declaration contained a subtle long-term achievement in its preamble. The introductory paragraphs planted the seed for today's framework governing the conduct of hostilities. It is for this reason that Robert Kolb and Momchil Milanov honour the Declaration as "establishing the very basis of IHL."[65] It is for the same

---

58 Robert Kolb and Momchil Milanov, 'The 1868 St Petersburg Declaration on Explosive Projectiles: A Reappraisal' (2019) 20 Journal of the History of International Law 515, 537.

59 Art 13(e), Project of an International Declaration concerning the Laws and Customs of War (27 August 1874) available at <https://ihl-databases.icrc.org/ihl/INTRO/135>.

60 Art 9, The Laws of War on Land, Oxford (9 September 1880) available at <https://ihl-databases.icrc.org/ihl/INTRO/140?OpenDocument>.

61 Art 17(2), Manual of the Laws of Naval War (9 August 1913) available at <https://ihl-databases.icrc.org/applic/ihl/ihl.nsf/INTRO/265?OpenDocument>.

62 ICRC, Customary IHL Database, Rule 78. The Customary IHL Database is available at <https://ihl-databases.icrc.org/customary-ihl/eng/docs/home>.

63 See Art 8 No 2(b)(xx) ICC Statute.

64 Preliminary Peace Conference, 'Commission on the Responsibility of the Authors of the War and on Enforcement of Penalties' (1920) 14 American Journal of International Law 95, 115.

65 Kolb and Milanov (n 58) 515. See also at p 524: "[…] the detailed and loftily worded preamble set out the general philosophy underlying the specific prohibition and has survived by far the latter […]."

reason that Gary Solis ranks the Declaration among the more important treaties relating to the law of war.[66] Scholars agree that the origins of the rules that regulate the conduct of hostilities today date back to the Declaration's preamble; the principle of military necessity, the principle of distinction, and the prohibition of causing unnecessary suffering or superfluous injury.[67] Hence, it is worth taking a look at the wording of the Preamble.

"That the only legitimate object which States should endeavour to accomplish during war is to weaken the military forces of the enemy;
That for this purpose it is sufficient to disable the greatest possible number of men;
That this object would be exceeded by the employment of arms which uselessly aggravate the sufferings of disabled men, or render their death inevitable;
That the employment of such arms would, therefore, be contrary to the laws of humanity."[68]

Each of these four paragraphs represents a central principle that still governs the conduct of hostilities today. The first paragraph lays down the principle of distinction by stating that the *"only* legitimate aim in war is to weaken the *military* forces of the enemy."[69] Thus, targeting civilians or civilian infrastructure is not permitted. The rule strikingly resembles Art 48 of Additional Protocol I (AP I) that was adopted in 1977 and enshrines the modern-day principle of distinction: "[...] the Parties to the conflict shall at all times distinguish between the civilian population and combatants and between civilian objects and military objectives [...]."

---

66 Gary D Solis, *The Law of Armed Conflict: International Humanitarian Law in War* (Cambridge University Press 2016) 53.

67 Crawford, 'The Enduring Legacy of the St Petersburg Declaration: Distinction, Military Necessity, and the Prohibition of Causing Unnecessary Suffering and Superfluous Injury in IHL' (n 50) 556; Kolb and Milanov (n 58) 529 et seq. See also Schindler (n 13) 249. For the codification of these principles in modern-day treaty law see e.g. Art 35 and Art 48–67 AP I.

68 Text of the Declaration is authentic only in its French version. For the purpose of discussion, however, I chose the English translation. The original reads: "Que le seul but légitime que les Etats doivent se proposer, durant la guerre, est l'affaiblissement des forces militaires de l'ennemi; Qu'à cet effet, il suffit de mettre hors de combat le plus grand nombre d'hommes possible; Que ce but serait dépassé par l'emploi d'armes qui aggraveraient inutilement les souffrances des hommes mis hors de combat ou voudraient leur mort inévitable; Que l'emploi de pareilles armes serait, dès lors, contraire aux lois de l'humanité."

69 Emphasis added.

Although the St Petersburg Declaration does not explicitly mention such a juxtaposition of civilian and military objectives, in essence, the restriction to military objectives acts as a precursor to the current rule in AP I.

The second paragraph lays the groundwork for the principle of military necessity. This principle is the centrepiece of the entire framework of the conduct of hostilities.[70] It permits only measures that are necessary to accomplish a legitimate military purpose and are not otherwise prohibited by international humanitarian law. In the case of an armed conflict the only legitimate military purpose is to weaken the military capacity of the other parties to the conflict.[71] This modern-day concept of necessity strikingly resembles the second paragraph of the Declaration which out-laws any belligerent action beyond those "sufficient to disable the greatest number of men." In other words: waging war is not prohibited. However, actions that are not aimed at subduing the enemy forces are illegal *per se*.

The third paragraph prohibits "uselessly" aggravating "the sufferings of disabled men." Thereby, it acts as a harbinger of the modern-day prohibition of inflicting unnecessary suffering or superfluous injury. This principle outlaws harm that is not justified by military considerations, either because it lacks even the slightest utility, or because the utility is consid-

---

70 On the one hand, it can be argued that the principles of distinction, proportionality, the prohibition of indiscriminate attacks, and the prohibition of inflicting unnecessary harm or superfluous injury stem from the principle of necessity. Such attacks are not necessary in military terms. The ICRC Casebook, however, describes the principle of necessity as the counterpart of the humanitarianism: "Military necessity generally runs counter to humanitarian exigencies. Consequently, the purpose of humanitarian law is to strike a balance between military necessity and humanitarian exigencies." See ICRC Casebook, How Does Law Protect in War, 'Military Necessity' <https://casebook.icrc.org/glossary/military-necessity>. For a detailed analysis of the under-explored principle of military necessity see e.g. Burrus M Carnahan, 'Lincoln, Lieber and the Laws of War: The Origins and Limits of the Principle of Military Necessity' (1998) 92 American Journal of International Law 213; GIAD Draper, 'Military Necessity and Humanitarian Imperatives Studies: Seminar on the Teaching of Humanitarian Law In Military Institutions, Sanremo, 6–18 November 1972' (1973) 12 Military Law and Law of War Review 129; Nils Melzer, 'Keeping the Balance between Military Necessity and Humanity: A Response to Four Critiques of the ICRC's Interpretive Guidance on the Notion of Direct Participation in Hostilities Forum: Direct Participation In Hostilities: Perspectives on the ICRC Interpretive Guidance' (2009) 42 New York University Journal of International Law and Politics 831.
71 See ICRC Casebook, How Does Law Protect in War, 'Military Necessity' <https://casebook.icrc.org/glossary/military-necessity>.

erably outweighed by the suffering caused.[72] Today, the prohibition of unnecessary suffering or superfluous injury is considered as a stand-alone rule and found its way into Art 23(e) of the Hague Regulations of 1899 and 1907.[73] It was confirmed in Art 35(2) AP I and has led to the adaption of a number of Conventions on specific weapons,[74] such as the Declaration Concerning Expanding Bullets 1899;[75] and the Geneva Protocol for the Prohibition of the Use in War of Asphyxiating, Poisonous, or Other Gases, and of Bacteriological Methods of Warfare 1925.[76]

Finally, the fourth paragraph introduces the notion of "humanity." More a vague idea than a concrete rule, this concept nevertheless set the tone for the future developments in IHL. The idea of humanity in war underpins the entire field of IHL and drives its development. Later treaties were to shape the contours of this vague concept, e.g. the so-called Martens Clause[77] in the Hague Regulations of 1899 and 1907, or the provisions relating to humane treatment in the Geneva Conventions of 1949.[78]

3.3 Russia's role – a pragmatic idealist?

In the light of all this, it is fair to say that the Declaration represented a milestone in IHL history. However, at this point I would like to take the reader back to the research question: what credit does Russia deserve for this?

---

72 Marco Sassòli, Antoine A Bouvier and Anne Quintin, *How Does Law Protect in War?* (3rd edn, ICRC 2011) 284.

73 Convention (II) with Respect to the Laws and Customs of War on Land and its Annex: Regulations concerning the Laws and Customs of War on Land (29 July 1899) available at <https://ihl-databases.icrc.org/ihl/INTRO/150>; Hague Convention (IV) respecting the Laws and Customs of War on Land and its Annex: Regulations concerning the Laws and Customs of War on Land (18 October 1907) available at <https://ihl-databases.icrc.org/ihl/INTRO/195>.

74 Sassòli, Bouvier and Quintin (n 72) 284.

75 Hague Declaration (IV,3) concerning Expanding Bullets (29 July 1899) available at <https://ihl-databases.icrc.org/applic/ihl/ihl.nsf/Treaty.xsp?documentId=D528A73B322398B5C12563CD002D6716&action=openDocument>.

76 Protocol for the Prohibition of the Use of Asphyxiating, Poisonous or Other Gases, and of Bacteriological Methods of Warfare (17 June 1925) available at <https://ihl-databases.icrc.org/applic/ihl/ihl.nsf/INTRO/280?OpenDocument>.

77 For a detailed discussion of the Martens Clause see below at p 56.

78 Kolb and Milanov (n 58) 529. The relevant Provisions of the Geneva Conventions are Art 12 GC I, Art 12 GC II, Art 13 GC III, Art 27 GC IV.

The obvious answer is that, without Russia, the Declaration would not exist. It was a Russian idea that led to the Russian initiative which culminated in a conference that was held in St Petersburg and was chaired by a Russian minister. When looking at these facts, Russia's role seems quite remarkable. Furthermore, the document breathes the Russian – and general European – *zeitgeist* of the 19th century.[79] The reader can discern the legacy of the French revolution, the spirit of disarmament and the rise of pacifism that permeated the era.[80] Since the 1860s progressive lawyers and scientists like Johann Kaspar Bluntschli promoted an idea of an ever-progressing civilisation, where peace was a precious good and the injuries of war should be reduced to a bare minimum.[81] In Russia especially, this vague idea of introducing humanity into international law had prospered.[82]

Having said that, the conference was not a purely humanitarian enterprise. We should clearly distinguish between the outcome of the Conference and the reasons for convening it in the first place. And we should be wary of romanticising the Tsar's reasons for inviting all major European powers to his capital. It would fall short of the harsh reality of international politics to narrow down Russia's motives to an indistinct love for humanity – an image that some contemporary Russian authors like to paint.[83]

On the contrary, the main motive to hold the conference in the first place was rather mundane. As pointed out above, the Tsar wanted to limit the damage done to his infantry in a future war. Scott Keefer argues that the Russian initiative was "as much a reaction to the revolutionary changes in technology as a truly humanitarian gesture."[84] Some authors have even

---

79 ibid 516–517.

80 For the development of the international peace movement see Arthur Eyffinger, *The 1899 Hague Peace Conference: The Parliament of Man, the Federation of the World* (Kluwer Law International 1999) 45 et seq.

81 Arthur Eyffinger, 'The 1907 Hague Peace Conference: The Conscience of the Civilized World' [2007] Netherlands International Law Review 197, 200.

82 Myles (n 27) 331.

83 See e.g. Vladislav Tolstykh, 'International Humanitarian Law in Russia (1850–1917) (Transl.)' [2004] Russian Law 67, 71 who quotes Milyutin and his desire to make war "less cruel" as the only reason for the Conference; see also И.И. Котляров [I.I. Kotlyarov] (n 3) 64, who portrays Russia as the fighter for humanity while the US and Great Britain have boycotted the Conference (the latter being factually untrue).

84 Scott Keefer, '"Explosive Missals": International Law, Technology, and Security in Nineteenth-Century Disarmament Conferences' (2014) 21 War in History 445, 450.

argued that the Declaration was, in fact, drawn up as a document of military necessity rather than of humanity.[85] I believe this falls short of the truth, since the very concept of military necessity already contains an element of humanisation by limiting warfare to acts that have a military value. Furthermore, as shown above, the Declaration goes far beyond military necessity. In the end, it arguably comes down to a "strange mix of pure rationalism and humanitarian concerns that is hard to disentangle."[86]

In this context, we encounter a question that will resurface in many parts of this thesis: why would States sign *any* document that limits their sovereignty? In most cases the answer will be: the loss of sovereignty is compensated by a strategic advantage in the long run. This is a common pattern in international law. For example, many States ratified the European Convention of Human Rights after the Second World War, because they saw it as an insurance against the rise of a new dictatorial regime in other European countries. In addition, it was a way of making sure that your neighbour adhered to certain standards.[87]

Similarly, the Russian Empire decided to tackle its problems by means of international law. Leading politicians, such as Tsar Alexander II and Minister of War Milyutin recognised that promoting humanity was actually in the interest of the State. Banning exploding projectiles unilaterally would have done nothing to protect Russian infantrymen. Banning them only for others would have had no chance of success. What remained was banning them collectively. Hence, in 1868 the terms *realpolitik* and IHL were not contradictory – they were synonymous. Russia's true achievement lay in opening an alley where States could see the long-term benefit of limiting warfare. To a romantic this might sound disappointing. To a pragmatist this represents an outstanding achievement.

---

85 Raphael Schäfer, 'The 150th Anniversary of the St Petersburg Declaration: Introductory Reflections on a Janus-Faced Document' (2019) 20 Journal of the History of International Law 501, 507.

86 Kolb and Milanov (n 58) 517.

87 Angelika Nußberger, *The European Court of Human Rights* (Oxford University Press 2020) Chapter 1, page 8.

4. The Brussels Conference 1874 – a stillborn phoenix

"Государство, которое с успехом доведёт до конца дело Брюссельской Конференции будет иметь право не только на признательность народов, страдание которых оно облегчит, но также на первое место в среде государств, понимающих действительные цели современной цивилизации."[88]

["The country that successfully completes this matter of the Brussels Declaration will not only earn the gratitude of the people, whose suffering it has attenuated, but also the right to call herself the first nation among all the States who understand the essence of civilization and value the legitimate desire of civilized peoples."]

F.F. Martens on the Brussels Declaration, 1879

The St Petersburg Declaration having been a huge success, Russia seemed thereafter to take a more confident stance in international law. More and more scholarly works were published and many of them struck a pro-European and westernising tone.[89] In Lauri Mälksoo's words, Russia became an "integral part of the European tradition of international law."[90] Even internally, the giant Empire embarked on a path of transformation. Tsar "Liberator"[91] Alexander II pushed through important reforms.[92] He abolished serfdom, restructured the administrative and judicial system, reformed the Army, and abolished corporal punishment. While Alexander II changed course after a failed assassination attempt and took a more reactionary stance in internal matters, he continued his visionary politics in external affairs.[93]

---

88 Ф.Ф. Мартенс [F.F. Martens], *Восточная Война и Брюсселская Конференция 1874–1878 г [The Eastern War and the Brussels Conference 1874–1878]* (n 16) 76.

89 Mälksoo, *Russian Approaches to International Law* (n 6) 42. The most notable exception being Nikolay Yakovlevich Danilevsky. In 1869 he published his study "Russia and Europe" in which strongly rejected the idea that Russia should orient itself towards Europe.

90 Lauri Mälksoo, 'FF Martens and His Time: When Russia Was an Integral Part of the European Tradition of International Law' (2014) 25 European Journal of International Law 811.

91 He had earned this nickname by freeing the serfs in 1861.

92 See Zakharova (n 48) 599–608.

93 ibid 609 et seq.

4.1 Thinking big – a comprehensive code of war

In 1874 the Russian Emperor called upon all European States to gather in neutral Belgium for a conference.[94] It might have been the success of the St Petersburg Declaration that prompted the Tsar to take the initiative yet again, or perhaps it was also the desire to distract from internal turbulences and ensure stability in a time of inner turmoil. Jean Huber-Saladin, a member of the Committee of the French Aid Society for the Care of the Wounded, wrote in a letter to Gustave Moynier, the future President of the ICRC:

> *"Change is in the air, with threats from below, anarchy in the middle and moral and political disorder more or less everywhere. Russia needs peace and the opportunity to strengthen herself institutionally."*[95]

On the other hand, it might have been a genuine quest for peace and for the humanisation of wars that led the Tsar to take the initiative. Baron Antoine-Henri Jomini, the Swiss officer in charge of the Russian delegation, declared: "Russia is a great power [...] nevertheless she is sincerely committed to the interests of peace."[96]

Whatever was behind the initiative, the goal was audacious. In his invitation the Tsar referred to the need for solidarity and consensus among nations.[97] The news of such a conference produced genuine astonishment in Europe, which had barely emerged from the devastating Franco-Prussian War (1870–1871).[98] What could be discussed at such a venue, which would soon be nicknamed the Brussels Conference? In Russia an unknown, but ambitious 28-year-old lawyer named Fyodor Fyodorovich Martens submitted a draft convention on the laws of war. He had the backing of Minister

---

94 Danièle Bujard, 'The Geneva Convention of 1864 and the Brussels Conference of 1874' (1974) 14 International Review of the Red Cross 527, 528.
95 ibid 529.
96 Ф.Ф. Мартенс [F.F. Martens], *Восточная Война и Брюссельская Конференция 1874–1878 г [The Eastern War and the Brussels Conference 1874–1878]* (n 16) 134.
97 Letter No 7 from Prince Gortchakow to Count Brunnow (11 May 1874) published in: Tracey Leigh Dowdeswell, 'The Brussels Peace Conference of 1874 and the Modern Laws of Belligerent Qualification' (2017) 54 Oosgoode Hall Law Journal 805, 825.
98 Bujard (n 94) 529.

of War Milyutin. Alexander II picked up on the idea and made it a subject for discussion at the Conference.[99]

Since this is Martens' first decisive moment in IHL history, it is worth taking a detailed look at this fascinating character. It is safe to say that no single person before or after has shaped the Russian image in international law like him. This is not only true with regards to IHL, but many other fields of international law.[100] Martens was born on 15 August 1845 in the small city of Pernov, which then belonged to the Russian Empire and is situated in today's Estonia. He became an orphan at an early age, but his teachers soon discovered the young boy's bright mind and enabled him to go to a German boarding school.[101] He went on to study law in St Petersburg,[102] joined the Ministry of Foreign Affairs at the age of 23,[103] and became a law professor at his *alma mater* at the age of 25.[104] He was fluent in Russian, Estonian, German, French, Italian, and English, and was the epitome of a cosmopolitan. He would become the author of numerous books, such as the *Recueil de Traités*[105] or his textbook *Contemporary International Law of Civilized Peoples*.[106] And he would become the diplomatic mastermind behind many of the international conferences from 1874 until the Second Hague Peace Conference in 1907.[107]

---

99 VV Pustogarov, *Our Martens: FF Martens, International Lawyer and Architect of Peace* (William E Butler tr, Kluwer Law International 2000) 109.

100 For example, the Permanent Court of Arbitration was a dream long harboured by Martens that finally came true after the Hague Peace Conference of 1899. Even the building of the Peace Palace in The Hague only exists thanks to Martens. When the American entrepreneur Andrew Carnegie wanted to make a large donation in support of the idea of world peace he approached Martens, who suggested funding the building of the new Court. See ibid 328.

101 ibid 7.

102 ibid 14.

103 ibid 105.

104 ibid 23.

105 Ф.Ф. Мартенс [F.F. Martens], *Собрание трактатов и конвенций заключённых Россиею с иностранными державами [Collection of Treaties and Conventions Concluded by Russia with Foreign States)* (Типография министерства путей сообщения [Printing House of the Ministry of Communication] 1874).

106 Ф.Ф. Мартенс [F.F. Martens], *Современное международное право цивилизованных народов [Contemporary International Law of Civilized Peoples]* (1st edn, Типография министерства путей сообщения [Printing House of the Ministry of Communication] 1882). In the following, I will quote from the updated 1905 edition.

107 See below at pp 42, 51, 68.

Martens had set himself an ambitious goal as he drew up the original proposal for the Brussels Conference that was circulated among States beforehand. He envisaged a universal code of land warfare that would be adopted and enforced by all nations and should be respected "in the interest of their country and to preserve the integrity of their people's honour."[108] Martens himself describes the conference as the "most significant attempt" to codify the laws of war.[109] However, prospects looked rather bleak. The hostile atmosphere after the Franco-Prussian War weighed on the discussions. In the run-up, rumours circulated that the Russian proposal was really a *code d'invasion* drafted in Berlin, to allow Otto von Bismarck to annihilate France in another war.[110]

Martens' draft convention comprised 71 articles, subdivided into four parts. Regulating the rights of combatants, the rights of civilians, relations between warring parties, and reprisals.[111] Such an unheard-of regulation of warfare met with sharp resistance, especially from the newly constituted German Empire. The participants of the Conference haggled over one issue especially: the status of irregular forces.[112] The origin of the dispute dated back to the Franco-Prussian war, where France used irregular troops such as the *francs-tireurs*. These French fighters, while authorised by the government, were not part of the regular French army. On these grounds the Prussians did not consider them as combatants but "unlawful" fighters and often executed them upon capture.[113]

The draft set out that the laws of war would not only apply and protect members of the regular armed forces, but also irregular fighters, as long as they met certain criteria. So-called partisans would have received rights and duties under IHL.[114] Germany strictly opposed such an approach and demanded that all irregular forces be outlawed.[115] After all, the German Empire possessed the most modern land army in Europe and the victories of Prussia and its allies against Austria-Hungary and France had been an impressive show of force to the world. Germany was not willing to limit

---

108 Ф.Ф. Мартенс [F.F. Martens], *Восточная Война и Брюссельская Конферения 1874–1878 г [The Eastern War and the Brussels Conference 1874–1878]* (n 16) 89.
109 ibid 90.
110 ibid 118.
111 ibid 131.
112 Dowdeswell (n 97) 826.
113 ibid 808–809.
114 Pustogarov (n 99) 110.
115 Dowdeswell (n 97) 826.

its military power, knowing that for smaller countries it was impossible to maintain a regular standing army of that kind.[116]

Martens always fought against such an absolute and unfettered principle of military necessity.[117] However, at Brussels he had to admit defeat. In the end the differences were too great to surmount. Although all States signed the final document, they did not accept it as a binding treaty and refused to ratify it.[118] Martens himself considered the Conference at Brussels a complete failure.[119] Even worse, the idea itself of codifying the laws of war by mutual agreement of States was seriously called into question.[120] Suddenly, the euphoria of St Petersburg seemed far away.

4.2 The aftermath of the failed convention

However, what might have looked like an immediate failure from Martens' perspective in 1874, greatly changed the course of IHL later on. Already by the Russo-Turkish War (1877–1878), many judged the behaviour of the warring parties by the standards laid down in the Brussels Declaration.[121] To measure the long-term impact of the conference one only needs to compare the texts of the Brussels Declaration of 1874 with the Hague Regulations of 1907. There is virtually no difference. The Hague Regulations mirrors the Brussels Articles almost word for word. Only occasionally has a word been added here or there, for example "absolutely" necessary in Art 43 Hague Regulations (respectively Art 3 of the Brussels Declaration). The definition of combatants and status of irregular troops

---

116 ibid 833.

117 See Ф.Ф. Мартенс [F.F. Martens], *Восточная Война и Брюсселская Конференция 1874–1878 г [The Eastern War and the Brussels Conference 1874–1878]* (n 16) 51–55 in response to articles published by the German General von Hartmann in the Deutsche Wochenschau, where von Hartmann argued that the "realism of war made it absolutely impossible to establish any rules or law for armed conflict whatsoever"; see also Peter Holquist, *The Russian Empire as a "Civilized State": International Law as Principle and Practice in Imperial Russia, 1874–1878* (National Council for Eurasian and East European Research 2004) 7 <https://www.ucis.pitt.edu/nceeer/2004_818-06g_Holquist.pdf>.

118 See Project of an International Declaration concerning the Laws and Customs of War (27 August 1874) available at <https://ihl-databases.icrc.org/ihl/INTRO/1 35>.

119 Pustogarov (n 99) 113.

120 Dowdeswell (n 97) 841.

121 Pustogarov (n 99) 114.

– the most contentious issue in Brussels – was adopted in The Hague without any change of wording. The rules regarding the treatment of prisoners of war, the status of spies, sieges and bombardments, and prohibited methods of warfare read almost identically in both documents. In this sense, it is fair to say that the Brussels Declaration served as a blueprint for the much-hailed Hague Regulations of 1899 and 1907. Thus, Martens' vision of a comprehensive convention on warfare – his "beloved child" as he called it – was not stillborn, but only delayed.[122]

5. *The Russo-Turkish War 1877–1878 – the crucible*

The Russo-Turkish War, sometimes also called the Eastern War,[123] might be less known to the reader. It was no less cruel than other wars – quite on the contrary. With a death toll of 21 percent among soldiers it ranks among the deadliest of the 19th century.[124] The Ottoman Empire had crushed rebellions in Bulgaria and Bosnia-Herzegovina with an estimated death toll between 10 000 and 30 000.[125] The brutality with which the Turks quelled the uprising produced an outcry in the international community. Intellectuals, such as Victor Hugo, called upon Western governments to intervene:

> "*Il devient nécessaire d'appeler l'attention des gouvernements européens sur un fait tellement petit, à ce qu'il paraît, que les gouvernements semblent ne point l'apercevoir. Ce fait, le voici: on assassine un peuple. Où? En Europe.*"[126]

But England and France were allies of the Ottoman Empire and thus kept a low profile. Finally, Serbia and its ally Russia decided to intervene.[127]

The Russo-Turkish War illustrates how the previous Declarations, Conventions, and negotiations at Geneva, Brussels, and St Petersburg had

---

122 ibid 178.
123 See e.g. Ф.Ф. Мартенс [F.F. Martens], *Восточная Война и Брюсселская Конференция 1874–1878 г* [*The Eastern War and the Brussels Conference 1874–1878*] (n 16).
124 Pierre Boissier, *Histoire du Comité International de la Croix-Rouge* (Institut Henry-Dunant 1978) 406.
125 Encyclopædia Britannica, 'Bulgaria, National Revival' <https://www.britannica.c om/place/Bulgaria/The-national-revival#ref476500>.
126 Victor Hugo, *Actes et paroles – depuis l'exil 1876–1880* (J Hetzel 1880) 3.
127 Stökl (n 20) 518.

changed Russia's attitude towards warfare. For Russia the Russo-Turkish War marked a watershed in the observance of international law. Peter Holquist argues that the conflict was an opportunity for Russia to show that a State could both win a war and simultaneously observe IHL.[128]

From the very beginning, Russia remained faithful to its IHL obligations.[129] It even went beyond: in order to "lessen the scourge of war" an official Senate Decree of 12 May 1877 unilaterally imposed the (non-binding) Brussels Declaration of 1874 as binding law on the Russian Army.[130] When the Ottomans adopted the Red Crescent due to religious and practical reasons, Russia was the first nation to recognise it as analogous to the emblem of the Red Cross.[131]

Furthermore, the Imperial Army went to great lengths to instruct their own troops in the laws of war. A military manual was issued and distributed among the soldiers. The Russian Red Cross even published a commentary to the Geneva Convention – a remarkable initiative at that time. It made very clear in its preamble that the new law should be respected: "Everyone, should in their own interest [...] respect the rules mentioned hereafter. [...] Terrible punishments – *in heaven and on earth* – await those who do not obey by them."[132] The efforts paid off. In practice, Ottoman soldiers who were *hors de combat* enjoyed the same treatment as Russians.[133]

This humanitarian fervour seems even more remarkable, since the Ottomans largely refused to comply with their obligations under the Geneva Convention. International newspaper correspondents who arrived on the battlefields sent back reports of terrible atrocities committed against captured and wounded Russian soldiers. They found evidence of mutilation,

---

128 Holquist (n 117) 15–16.
129 Boissier (n 124) 403.
130 The decree is reprinted in the annexes to Ф.Ф. Мартенс [F.F. Martens], *Восточная Война и Брюссельская Конференция 1874–1878 г [The Eastern War and the Brussels Conference 1874–1878]* (n 16) 37; the reference to the Brussels Declaration can be found in para XII of the decree.
131 Holquist (n 117) 15.
132 Boissier (n 124) 404. The decree is originally in Russian. This translation is based on the author's French translation (emphasis added).
133 ibid 403–404.

torture, and summary executions.[134] This was a clear violation of the Geneva Convention, which the Sultan had ratified in 1865.[135]

That being said, the Russians certainly committed cruelties as well, mostly against civilians. Cossacks and irregular Bulgarian troops especially tended to indiscriminate acts of violence.[136] The US historian Justin McCarthy claims that Russian soldiers, especially Cossacks together with Bulgarian revolutionaries carried out massacres against civilians.[137] Furthermore, the Russian Army caused a vast flow of refugees during its march on Constantinople which led to widespread starvation and disease among the civilian population.[138]

Yet, unlike the Turkish killings of wounded combatants, these acts did not constitute violations of IHL *stricto sensu* – however atrocious they may have been. It is important to recall, that the existing legal instruments, i.e. the Geneva Convention and the Declarations of St Petersburg and Brussels, only regulated the fate of combatants. The 1864 Geneva Convention applied to wounded *soldiers*. The St Petersburg Declaration prohibited using a certain bullet against *combatants*. The term "civilian" only features a single time in the entire Brussels Declaration.[139] Only the regime on occupation[140] – along with very few other provisions[141] – can be interpreted as *indirectly* protecting civilians. It was not until the Fourth Geneva Convention of 1949 that civilians as a group were explicitly and amply protected by the laws of war. Until then war was considered an affair between States in which civilians had no role to play and therefore enjoyed no protection. Hence, the Russians did not break the letter of the law when they displaced the civilian population on their way to Constantinople. Additionally, many cruelties were committed by irregular forces, for which Russia had no responsibility. The cruel acts did, however, contradict

---

134 ibid 405.

135 For a detailed list of ratifications see <https://ihl-databases.icrc.org/applic/ihl/ihl .nsf/States.xsp?xp_viewStates=XPages_NORMStatesParties&xp_treatySelected=1 20>.

136 Holquist (n 117) 17.

137 Justin McCarthy, *The Ottoman Peoples and the End of Empire: Historical Endings* (Arnold 2001) 48.

138 Dowdeswell (n 97) 844.

139 Art 22 of the Declaration states that civilians, tasked with delivering dispatches openly, are not to be considered spies.

140 Art 1–8 of the Brussels Declaration.

141 The prohibition of bombarding undefended localities in Art 15 of the Brussels Declaration; the prohibition of pillage in Art 18 of the Brussels Declaration.

the principle of humanity enshrined in the preamble of the St Petersburg Declaration.[142]

In other areas, Russia's efforts led to an improvement for civilians. As mentioned above, civilians did enjoy some form of protection under the rules applicable to occupied territory contained in the Brussels Declaration. While non-binding in nature, Russia had voluntarily accepted the Declaration as hard law for its soldiers at the outset of the war. When Russian troops occupied Bulgaria and parts of eastern Turkey these self-imposed obligations suddenly became extremely relevant. The Declaration's section on occupation contains rules on restoring public order and safety, tax collection, and basic rights of citizens.[143]

Did Russia respect these guarantees? In his textbook, Martens praises the behaviour of Russian troops in the occupied territories during the Eastern War and points out the stark contrast to the conduct of the Prussians in occupied France 1870–1871.[144] To a large extent, this corresponds to the truth. Admittedly, Russia changed Bulgarian laws and the administration in an attempt to groom Bulgaria for its nearing independence from the Ottoman Empire. This was formally prohibited under Art 3 and Art 4 of the Brussels Declaration. Furthermore, there are reports of Russian troops standing by while irregular units or civilian mobs took revenge against Muslims. However, in many instances Russian troops upheld law and order.[145] Looting was prohibited and punished, military courts were set up and delivered swift justice. In occupied eastern Turkey, the administration system was left intact.[146] Given the ethnically and religiously charged situation, this seems quite remarkable and was certainly much better than Russian behaviour in occupied Galicia during the First World War.[147]

---

142 The spirit of humanity that was invoked in the St Petersburg Declaration as well as the narrow definition of military necessity were at odds with such conduct. The reader may remember from above, that the preamble to the St Petersburg Declaration only permitted acts aimed at weakening the force of the enemy army. In the light of this, deliberate massacres against civilians were contrary to the *spirit* of IHL even at the time. In this respect, Russia did not live up to its pledges, at least where its own troops (and not ethnic mobs) committed massacres against civilians.

143 See Art 1–8 Brussels Declaration as well as Art 36–39.

144 Ф.Ф. Мартенс [F.F. Martens], *Современное международное право цивилизованных народов [Contemporary International Law of Civilized Peoples]* (n 15) 557–560.

145 Holquist (n 117) 24.

146 ibid 25–26.

147 ibid 17, 25.

In Adrianople (modern Edirne) Russia even took care of 45 000 Muslim refugees and repatriated them after the cessation of hostilities.[148] This was an act of humanity that went beyond any IHL convention in force.

Despite all this humanitarian commitment, the Russo-Turkish War did not pay off in political terms. The treaty of San Stephano ended the fighting on 3 March 1878 and seemed to mark a Russian victory. However, most of the Russian gains were undone in the same year by the Treaty of Berlin, where Russia found itself diplomatically isolated.[149] Politically speaking, the war had been a failure. But what is the legal legacy of the Russo-Turkish conflict? War itself can, of course, never be a humanitarian enterprise. However, Russia demonstrated in 1877–1878 that it was possible to win a war and at the same time respect IHL. Had it thereby become the "first among the civilized nations?"[150] That would go too far, but Russia felt the burden of a self-imposed responsibility and lived up to it. In order to remain a credible international actor, it had to practice what it preached. All the talk about humanity would have appeared hypocritical, if Russia had thrown overboard the rules it had solemnly proclaimed in St Petersburg and Brussels. In the long run, however, the war and its subsequent events forced Russia to lay aside any further diplomatic Conferences on IHL.[151] The next attempt to advance the laws of war through a convention would have to wait for more than 20 years.

6. The Hague Peace Conference of 1899 – the Parliament of Man

"The good seed is sown. Let the harvest come."[152]

Conference Chairman Egor de Staal in his concluding remarks at The Hague, 1899

In her speech delivered at a round table in 2018 Olga Glikman, lecturer at the prestigious Institute of International Relations in Moscow (MGIMO), argued that it is hard to "overstate the importance of the Hague Peace Conferences and as a consequence the role of Russia in in the development

---

148 ibid 24.
149 Schimmelpenninck van der Oye (n 18) 566.
150 Ф.Ф. Мартенс [F.F. Martens], *Восточная Война и Брюсселская Конференция 1874–1878 г [The Eastern War and the Brussels Conference 1874–1878]* (n 16) 76.
151 Dowdeswell (n 97) 841.
152 James Brown Scott, *The Proceedings of the Hague Peace Conferences: Translation of the Official Texts*, vol 1 (Oxford University Press 1920) 225.

of IHL."[153] What sets the Hague Conference apart from other diplomatic conferences? Why is it still praised as the "Parliament of Man?"[154] And why was it so significant for the development of IHL?

Interestingly, it was not the desire to further regulate the laws of war that sparked the idea for the Hague Conference. Rather, the original goal was to conclude a treaty on disarmament.[155] Europe found itself in troubled waters. The era of peace that followed the Congress of Vienna crumbled. In the last third of the 19th century, the balance of power in Europe began to shift. A decisive victory in the Franco-Prussian war had paved the way for the unification of Germany in 1871, thereby dramatically changing the map of Europe. France had been humiliated and plunged into political chaos. The 1878 Congress of Berlin asserted Germany's strong position and started the Scramble for Africa.[156] Among European powers, there reigned a general climate of distrust.[157] In addition, Russia faced internal strife. Severe unrest had shaken Russia and culminated in the assassination of Tsar Alexander II in 1881.

At the same time, Russia followed a path of industrialisation and had launched an ambitious railway programme.[158] In general, technological development continued at a breath-taking pace, especially in the military sector. Rather than sheer numbers, technology became increasingly decisive in wars.[159] New rifles, such as the needle gun, allowed for faster reloading. They were first issued to Prussian soldiers in 1848 and used extensively during the Austro-Prussian War 1866.[160] Thanks to the growing railway system, troops could be deployed much quicker than before. Field

---

153 The reader can find the full text of the speech (18 May 2018) at <https://www.icrc.org/ru/document/gaagskie-mirnye-konferencii-1899-i-1907-godov-rossiyskaya-iniciativa-i-dalneyshee-razvitie>.

154 Eyffinger (n 80).

155 The Tsar's circular that convened all countries to The Hague read: "The maintenance of general peace, and a possible reduction of excessive armaments which weigh upon all nations, present themselves in the existing condition of the whole world as the ideals towards which the endeavours of all Governments should be directed." Reprinted in Arthur Eyffinger, *The 1899 Hague Peace Conference: 'The Parliament of Man, the Federation of the World'* (Kluwer Law International 1999), 17.

156 Eyffinger (n 80) 10.

157 ibid 14.

158 ibid 7–8.

159 Fuller Jr (n 17) 539, 549.

160 Bastian Mehn, *Waffentechnische Innovationen in der ersten Hälfte des 19. Jahrhunderts und ihre Umsetzung in der bayerischen Armee (Master's Thesis)* (University of Würzburg 2011) 1, 54.

guns equipped with a hydraulic recoil mechanism revolutionised artillery warfare by allowing targeted shelling at a fast rate of fire.[161]

Thus, the question to which Russia sought an answer was not primarily how to behave in wars. It was rather how to *prevent* wars altogether by means of alliances or disarmament. In this, they were not alone. Britain, too, feared soaring military expenses and made a first demarche to initiate a Conference as early as 1894, shortly before the Death of Alexander III.[162] The British Prime Minister wrote in a letter to the Russian ambassador:

> *"I am quite clear that there is one person who is preeminently fitted to summon such a gathering. The Emperor of Russia by his high, pure character, and his single-minded desire for peace is the Sovereign who appears to me to be marked out as the originator of such a meeting."*[163]

The Tsar declined, but the vague idea of a pan-European conference on disarmament remained.[164] On 1 November 1894, with the ascension of Tsar Nicholas II, a man rose to power who was not only the cousin of the British King George V and the German Emperor Wilhelm II, but who was also eager to fill the shoes of his father who had earned the nickname *"Миротворец"* [Peacemaker] by bringing peace to Europe.[165] Indeed, the entire dynasty of the Romanovs had a "curious missionary ambition."[166]

The trigger, however, for initiating a peace conference turned out to be rather mundane: reports suggested that Germany, France, and Austria had developed a new rapid-firing field gun that would have represented a considerable military advantage.[167] At the same time Nicholas II decided to invest 90 million Rubles in the Russian fleet.[168] The then Russian Minister of Finance, Sergey Witte, and the Minister of War, Aleksey Kuropatkin, faced the choice of investing a considerable sum in the development of similar arms or finding another solution for the emerging arms race. Russia, suffering from inner turmoil, was simply not able to cope with

---

161 HCB Rogers, *A History of Artillery* (Citadel Press 1975) 115 et seq.
162 Thomas K Ford, 'The Genesis of the First Hague Peace Conference' (1936) 51 Political Science Quarterly 354, 360.
163 Aleksandr Feliksovich Meyendorff, *Correspondance diplomatique de M de Staal (1884–1900)*, vol 2 (M Rivière 1929) year 1894, No 9.
164 Ford (n 162) 355–357.
165 ibid 382.
166 Eyffinger (n 80) 19.
167 Rogers (n 161) 115 et seq.
168 Ford (n 162) 363.

the racing pace of technological development.[169] At the same time, it wanted to pursue its expansion in the east.[170] A conference on disarmament seemed like a good idea to free the necessary funds and bring prosperity to all the regions, as Witte put it:

> *"Suppose Europe could contrive to disband the bulk of her land forces, do with a mere nominal army, and confine her defences to warships, would she not thrive in an unprecedented way and guide the best part of the globe?"*[171]

At first, the idea of a disarmament deal only concerned Russia and Austria, but eventually the concept was broadened to achieve disarmament on a global scale.[172] Foreign Minister Nikolay Muravyov drew up a circular note that was handed to all foreign diplomats present in St Petersburg. All of them were taken by surprise.[173] No one had expected such a daring attempt to counter the arms race. Many governments, however, remained distrustful, and the agenda and the prospects of the conference remained murky.[174] Only one thing was clear from the outset: the conference would not take place in St Petersburg unlike its precursor of 1868. The Tsar deemed it more auspicious to hold it on neutral ground and chose a city that came as a surprise to many:[175] The Hague.

The conference would mark the beginning of the city's ascension as a popular international venue and "judicial capital of the world." Why Russia chose The Hague in the first place remains unclear. Most probably, it was the lack of a viable alternative. The Netherlands was a neutral power, and The Hague was easily accessible by rail and steamer. Other options like Berne and Geneva were ruled out due to "prevailing anarchy"

---

169 ibid 362.
170 ibid 365.
171 Emile J Dillon, *The Eclipse of Russia* (George H Doran 1918) 276.
172 Ford (n 162) 368–370.
173 ibid 376.
174 Pustogarov (n 99) 157.
175 Ford (n 162) 361; see also Pustogarov (n 99) 163. According to Pustogarov, Martens later advocated to hold the Conference in St Petersburg but his proposal was rejected. Martens claimed that the Russian Foreign Minister Count Lamsdorf wanted to avert damage from Russian diplomacy. He was afraid that the Conference would not yield tangible results and that the Russian public and the press would begin to proclaim its downfall. He thus preferred to hold it abroad where a meagre declaration of intent could be sold better to his own people. In his diary Martens reacted bitterly to such defeatism: "And for this an international conference? – How ridiculous."

in Switzerland. Finally, the governments of Denmark and Belgium had signalled no interest in holding a conference in their countries.[176]

You may wonder, why the name of Martens has not come up so far. The man who was to become the "soul of the Hague Conference"[177] had been completely left out of the loop until the circulation of the invitation. The reader should know that Martens could never penetrate the inner circles of the Russian government.[178] He was not of noble descent, neither was he ethnically Russian, but Estonian-born and of humble origins. Despite his undisputed brilliance and his professional achievements, the inner circles of power cultivated a certain degree of distrust towards him. He had not been consulted about The Hague and the news of a world-conference fell on him like "snow on the head."[179] When he returned to St Petersburg in September 1898, he found out that to his dismay there was no agenda for the conference whatsoever. So far, the Tsar's proposal was just hot air. And nobody in the Russian government was competent or experienced enough to fill this void, so it became his task. With amazing speed, Martens submitted a memorandum outlining the main objectives for the conference.[180] It was also Martens who had the idea to narrow down the scope of the conference in a certain respect and broaden it in another. On the one hand, he strictly excluded any kind of political questions, such as the status of Alsace-Lorraine and similar border disputes.[181] On the other hand, Martens added two new aspects to the agenda: instead of just focusing on disarmament he aimed to strengthen inter-State arbitration and mitigate the horrors of war by further advancing IHL.[182]

This broadened agenda was circulated, again to the great surprise of all States.[183] As a seasoned diplomat, Martens knew that a "quick success" regarding disarmament was utopian. Adding arbitration and IHL to the agenda was more likely to lead to a broad consensus among States.[184] There was already an extensive practice of arbitration and the codification

---

176 Eyffinger (n 80) 4, 39–40.
177 Pustogarov (n 99) 173.
178 See for this Kross (n 29). Kross describes Martens' humble origins in his book. Of course, this fictitious account should not be mistaken for an accurate historical source, but it nevertheless gives an impression of Martens' upbringing.
179 Pustogarov (n 99) 158 quoting from Martens' diary.
180 ibid 162.
181 ibid 164.
182 ibid 171, 164.
183 Second circular note reprinted in Eyffinger (n 80) 36.
184 Pustogarov (n 99) 164.

of the laws of war had enjoyed great success at Geneva and St Petersburg. Furthermore, regarding IHL, there was already a concrete proposal to be discussed: The Brussels Declaration. While it had never achieved the status of a binding treaty, Martens hoped that the Hague Conference could change that.[185] Thus, only thanks to Martens, the Hague Peace Conference of 1899 became what it would be remembered as by future generations: a milestone in the development of IHL.

6.1 Proceedings at the Conference

To Martens' bitter disappointment he was not appointed head of the Russian delegation. The Tsar chose Egor Staal, the Russian ambassador in London, a man who had never participated in an international conference in his life.[186]

The Conference was the largest international gathering of its kind so far: twenty-one European and six non-European States (China, Japan, Mexico, Persia, Siam, and the US) participated. An impressive number, given that the colonial powers still represented vast parts of Africa and Asia. Truly, it was a "Parliament of Man." The head of the Russian delegation Staal was elected as chairman, but it quickly became apparent that Martens pulled the strings. He assisted Staal in chairing the meetings, prepared drafts, and even directed the work in the different Commissions.[187]

The second Commission dealt exclusively with IHL issues. It deliberated on the adoption of a convention on the laws and customs of warfare. The Brussels Declaration with its 56 articles served as a starting point. Martens faced the difficulty of overcoming the scepticism of smaller States, who had opposed the Declaration in 1874 because it did not foresee the general right of the population to rise up against an occupant and withheld the combatant status from irregular *francs-tireurs*.[188] Rather, belligerent occupation was accepted as a given in modern wars. To satisfy the camp of smaller countries – who feared that this rule would leave them at the mercy of strongly militarised powers such as Germany – Martens suggested inserting a special clause in the preamble:

---

185 ibid 166.
186 ibid 169.
187 ibid 172–173.
188 ICRC Casebook, How Does Law Protect in War, 'Martens Clause' <https://caseb ook.icrc.org/glossary/martens-clause>.

"In instances not provided for by provisions adopted by them [i.e. the Convention States] the population and the belligerents remain under the protection and operation of the principles of international law insofar as they derive from customs established between civilized nations, from the laws of humanity, and the requirements of the public conscience."[189]

The paragraph would later be known as "Martens-Clause" and was received with great enthusiasm by all delegations. It paved the way for the adoption of the first unified code of war.[190]

6.2 Influence of the Conference on IHL

Thanks to Martens efforts the Conference adopted five binding treaties with regards to IHL.

– The Hague Convention II with respect to the Laws and Customs of War on Land, which in its annex contained 60 Articles regulating many aspects of warfare. In the following this annex will be called the <u>Hague Regulations (HR)</u>. The Hague Regulations represent the first comprehensive code of warfare in modern times.
– The Hague Convention III for the Adaptation to Maritime Warfare of the Principles of the Geneva Convention of 22 August 1864;
– The Hague Declaration IV,1 concerning the Prohibition of the Discharge of Projectiles and Explosives from Balloons or by Other New Analogous Methods;
– The Hague Declaration IV,2 concerning the Prohibition of the Use of Projectiles with the Sole Object to Spread Asphyxiating Poisonous Gases;
– The Hague Declaration IV,3 concerning the Prohibition of the Use of which can Easily Expand or Change their Form inside the Human Body Bullets [so-called dumdum bullets][191] such as Bullets with a Hard Covering which does not Completely Cover the Core, or Containing Indentations.

---

189 Pustogarov (n 99) 176.
190 ibid 177.
191 These were bullets designed to expand on impact thus causing horrible wounds. Their name is derived from the British Dum Dum Arsenal near Calcutta in India, where an early version of this bullet was produced.

To the major disappointment of many, States did not reach consensus with regards to disarmament.[192] In terms of IHL, however, the conference was a clear success. It is telling that only one out of the six final documents did not concern the laws of war: the First Hague Convention of 1899 for the Pacific Settlement of International Disputes, which *inter alia* established the Permanent Court of Arbitration in The Hague.

While some regarded the creation of the Court as the most spectacular achievement of the conference,[193] the sheer number of IHL rules adopted is also impressive. Arthur Eyffinger agrees that the codification of IHL "was considered by many contemporary observers the most thorough and respectable result of the ten weeks of debate."[194] Each treaty represented an achievement of its kind. First and foremost, the Hague Convention II was a huge victory for Martens and all those who had aimed to advance and systematise IHL. It represents the first comprehensive treaty governing various aspects of warfare, such as occupation, sieges, conduct of hostilities, and spies. The Convention was ratified by all participants except China, the US, and Switzerland. Even the latter three were to accede later.[195] In addition, Hague Convention III extended the rules of the 1864 Geneva Convention to maritime warfare, providing better protection to wounded seamen. This had previously been attempted in 1868, but had failed.[196] Finally, the three Hague Declarations (IV 1–3) added certain projectiles to the list of prohibited weapons.

In a broader context, The Hague Conference laid the foundations of modern IHL. Before 1899, binding treaty law only consisted of provisions regarding wounded combatants and the isolated ban of certain projectiles of St Petersburg. The latter formulated some general principles in its preamble but did not elaborate on them. Now, The Hague Regulations

---

192 Randall Lesaffer, 'Peace through Law: The Hague Peace Conferences and the Rise of the Ius Contra Bellum' in Maartje Abbenhuis, Christopher Ernest Barber and Annalise R Higgins (eds), *War, Peace and International Order? The Legacies of the Hague Conferences of 1899 and 1907* (Routledge 2017) 31.

193 Eyffinger (n 80) 440; Lesaffer (n 192) 31.

194 Eyffinger (n 80) 439.

195 The US in 1909, Switzerland in 1910, and finally China in 1917, see <https://ihl-databases.icrc.org/applic/ihl/ihl.nsf/States.xsp?xp_viewStates=XPages_NORMStatesParties&xp_treatySelected=195>.

196 The Additional Articles were adopted at a Conference in 1868 but never entered into force, because they could not secure enough ratifications. See ICRC, 'Additional Articles relating to the Condition of the Wounded in War. (20 October 1868)' <https://ihl-databases.icrc.org/applic/ihl/ihl.nsf/Treaty.xsp?documentId=ECB39EA050F80A5DC12563CD002D6624&action=openDocument>.

had codified rules on humanitarian aid, occupation, spies, flags of truce, capitulations, pillage, sieges, bombardments, and much more. Most importantly, it defined who qualified as a combatant and a prisoner of war.[197] The latter was hotly debated at the Conference of Brussels in 1874 and in the end prevented an agreement. While the issue was still contentious in 1899,[198] this time States managed to settle their differences. In return, smaller States overcame their misgivings about legalising belligerent occupation partly thanks to the Martens Clause.[199]

The Clause that immortalised Martens became one of the corner stones of IHL. It underlined that persons affected by armed conflict should never find themselves completely deprived of protection – even in cases not covered by IHL treaties *stricto sensu*. As a minimum they were protected by the principles of the law of nations, the laws of humanity, and the dictates of public conscience.[200] The reader may, for example, remember the events during the Russian advance on Constantinople 1878 that I have described in the previous section. While the forcible displacement of civilians was not illegal *per se*, the Martens Clause now provided the international community and lawyers with much better arguments to condemn such behaviour. Today, the Martens Clause is abundantly referenced in many of the IHL treaties, such as the 1949 Geneva Conventions,[201] their Additional Protocols,[202] and the UN Convention on Conventional Weapons of 1980.[203] It has found its way into the military manuals of

---

197 Art 1 and 4 of the Hague Regulations. The Hague Regulations still use both terms – "belligerents" and "combatants". Later States would settle for "combatant."

198 See e.g. Eyffinger (n 80) 305.

199 Pustogarov (n 99) 177.

200 For a detailed discussion of the significance of the Martens Clause and its development over time see Theodor Meron, 'The Martens Clause, Principles of Humanity, and Dictates of Public Conscience' (2000) 94 American Journal of International Law 78; Antonio Cassese, 'The Martens Clause: Half a Loaf or Simply Pie in the Sky?' (2000) 11 European Journal of International Law 187.

201 Art 63 GC I, Art 62 GC II, Art 142 GC III, Art 158 GC IV.

202 Art 1(2) AP I and in the preamble of AP II in para 4.

203 Convention on Prohibitions or Restrictions on the Use of Certain Conventional Weapons Which May be Deemed to be Excessively Injurious or to Have Indiscriminate Effects (CCW) 10 October 1980. The Clause is mentioned in the CCW preamble, para 5.

many States, such as the US[204] and Germany.[205] Moreover, the Clause is part of customary law and thus binding on all States.[206]

In the field of naval warfare (Hague Convention III) Russia had scored a surprise victory. It is likely that Martens originally included naval warfare in the agenda, because he expected a quick consensus and thus a positive ripple effect regarding other more contentious issues.[207] Nevertheless, the issue was highly controversial in a time, when Germany and England found themselves engaged in a naval arms race. So far, the ICRC and Switzerland had failed to extend the Geneva Convention of 1864 to sea warfare.[208] Thus, Russia was not just "plucking low hanging fruit to fill The Hague's basket."[209]

In addition, Russia had challenged the role of Switzerland (and the ICRC) as the "humanitarian number one" by including the Geneva Conventions in the agenda of a Russian-led conference. The Russians had briefed neither ICRC nor the Swiss government beforehand.[210] Was this diplomatic cunning or simply uncouth? In any case, it placed pressure on the ICRC and its supporters to modernise a 25-year-old treaty. The competition between Russia and Switzerland that had been created by the success of this conference revived the fading Swiss interest in the Geneva Conventions and forced them to develop their *own* version of IHL that would set it apart from "the Hague law."[211]

---

204 US Department of Defence, 'DoD Law of War Manual Updated Version 2016' (2015) 19.8.3.

205 Deutsches Bundesministerium der Verteidigung, 'Zentrale Dienstvorschrift (Dv) 15/2 Humanitäres Völkerrecht in bewaffneten Konflikten – Handbuch' (2016) para 140.

206 ICRC Casebook, How Does Law Protect in War, 'Martens Clause' <https://caseb ook.icrc.org/glossary/martens-clause>.

207 Neville Wylie, 'Muddied Waters: The Influence of the First Hague Conference on the Evolution of the Geneva Conventions of 1864 and 1906' in Maartje Abbenhuis, Christopher Ernest Barber and Annalise R Higgins (eds), *War, Peace and International Order? The Legacies of the Hague Conferences of 1899 and 1907* (Routledge 2017) 52.

208 See n 196.

209 Wylie (n 207) 56.

210 ibid 59.

211 ibid 52–53. Switzerland initiated a Conference in 1906 that led to an updated Geneva Convention, available at <https://ihl-databases.icrc.org/ihl/INTRO/180 ?OpenDocument>. The rivalry between the Hague and the Geneva branch of IHL existed for years to come. Only with the adoption of the 1949 Geneva Conventions and the 1977 Additional Protocols the distinction became obsolete, see

7. Analysing the bigger picture – why Russia?

At this point we should ask ourselves two questions. First, did Martens act as a representative of Russia or as a self-employed agent of peace? And secondly, why did Russia display such strong interest in advancing IHL?

The first question may be answered more easily. It is undisputed that the humanisation of warfare reflected the personal tenets of Martens.[212] At the same time, Martens was not only a humanitarian. Despite all his ambition for peace, he remained a member of the Russian diplomatic corps. Martens managed to reconcile both roles, as Vladimir Pustogarov describes in his book *Our Martens*:

> *"The members of all delegations acted at the Conference as the representatives of their countries. Martens was no exception. But if in such statement there is an allusion that Martens' actions were determined by some sort of mercenary interest of Russia, this must be resolutely refuted. A study of the open and closed materials (…) discloses not a single instance when Martens singled out some sort of special interest of Russia at the Conference."*[213]

Martens inspired the discussions at The Hague with his diplomatic skills, his personal charisma, and his profound knowledge of international law. However, the Conference was not his personal crusade. He remained an agent of the State. Russia had identified a stable European peace as its vital interest and acted accordingly.[214] Hence, it would be a mistake to ascribe the successful outcome of the Peace Conference to Martens alone.

This brings us to our second question: why did *Russia* want to advance IHL in the first place? We have come a long way from Crimea to The Hague. As we are approaching the zenith of Russia's IHL patronage, we should take a step back and glance at the bigger picture. How can we explain Russia's fervour for advancing the laws of war? In the following, I will provide five reasons: idealism, diplomatic pride, military strategy, economic self-interest, and Russian ingenuity. I will explain each one in turn.

Idealism seems to be the obvious motivation behind advancing IHL. Eyffinger considers the initiative for The Hague "another token of that

---

ICRC Casebook, How Does Law Protect in War, 'Law of The Hague' <https://casebook.icrc.org/glossary/law-hague>; see also below at p 67.

212 Eyffinger (n 80) 269.
213 Pustogarov (n 99) 191.
214 See Schimmelpenninck van der Oye (n 18) 554.

curious missionary ambition of the Romanovs."[215] Their dynasty had freed the serfs, modernised Russia, and genuinely believed that providence imposed the honourable task on them to establish a lasting peace in Europe. This quest for peace also struck the *zeitgeist*. We have seen that the idea of advancing humanity was very much *en vogue* in 19th century Russia.[216] Even the writings of a level-headed jurist like Martens had a missionary touch, when they predicted that the State that establishes a comprehensive code of war would take the first place among all civilised nations.[217]

Secondly, promoting IHL had become a Russian trademark. It justified Russia's presence in international diplomacy. In humanitarian matters the Tsar excelled among his European peers. Russia suffered from an inferiority complex in this respect. For a long time, scholars debated whether Russia could boast an international law tradition that was as old as the central European legacy, or whether Russia was a *parvenu*.[218] Martens himself, for example, argued that Russia's foreign relations were merely factual before Peter the Great (1682–1725) turned westwards and downplayed earlier treaties that Russia had concluded with China and Persia.[219] Even though by now Russia had become an integral member of the concert of European powers, Napoleon's derogatory phrase lingered on: *"Grattez le russe et vous trouverez un tartare."*[220] In 1868, when Russia started its IHL-offensive, it had conquered vast territories stretching from today's Poland and Lithuania to the west, the Pamir mountains in Central Asia, and remote Siberia to the east.[221] Nevertheless the humiliating diplomatic defeat at Paris in 1856 had been etched in its memory. Expanding the Empire was not enough to compensate for the psychological wounds in-

---

215 Eyffinger (n 80) 35.

216 Myles (n 27) 331.

217 Ф.Ф. Мартенс [F.F. Martens], *Восточная Война и Брюссельская Конферения 1874–1878 г [The Eastern War and the Brussels Conference 1874–1878]* (n 16) 76.

218 Mälksoo, *Russian Approaches to International Law* (n 6) 36 et seq; see also Angelika Nußberger, 'Russia', *Max Planck Encyclopedia of Public International Law* (Oxford University Press 2009) para 77.

219 Mälksoo, *Russian Approaches to International Law* (n 6) 43–45 with further sources.

220 See e.g. Schimmelpenninck van der Oye (n 18) 572. He argues that Russians were occasionally branded as "Asiatic" in the West despite their scrupulous observance of diplomatic protocol. Furthermore, the European Powers were often bewildered by the concentration of authority in the hands of the Tsar and considered this trait of Russian governance somewhat archaic.

221 ibid 561–563.

flicted in Crimea.[222] Even worse, at the Conference of Berlin (1878) Russia suffered another diplomatic setback, losing most of its territorial gains from the Russo-Turkish War.[223] The Tsars wanted their place *at the head* of the diplomatic table and IHL was their place card. The Hague Conference illustrates this well: the Russians included the Geneva Convention in the agenda without even consulting the Swiss or the ICRC.[224] Later they would attempt to subordinate the Geneva Convention to "their" Hague Convention.[225]

Thirdly, a limitation of the means and methods of warfare also served the military interest of the Tsar. With over 125 million inhabitants, Russia could boast the largest population on the European continent, by far exceeding its rivals Germany and France.[226] Thus, it is not surprising that Russia also possessed the largest land army. While other countries struggled to find fresh recruits, Russia had more men than they could train.[227] In 1881 the active army already comprised 84 400 soldiers. In addition, there was a large pool of reservists ever since Milyutin had reformed military service in 1874.[228] At the turn of the century, experts estimated that Russia could draw on the incredible number of 3.5 million professional soldiers and reservists.[229] To compare: even in 1914 the German Army only counted 800 000 men – and only after the Empire had invested huge sums in a military build-up.[230] The Russian Army had crossed this hallmark 30 years earlier. All these figures make one thing very clear: numerical superi-

---

222 See for this Dietrich Geyer, *Russian Imperialism: The Interaction of Domestic and Foreign Policy, 1860–1914* (Yale University Press 1987) 205.

223 See above and Schimmelpenninck van der Oye (n 18) 566.

224 Wylie (n 207) 59 et seq.

225 ibid 62. See also below at p 67.

226 The first and only census in the Russian Empire was carried out in 1897. Russia's total population amounted to 125 640 021 which by far exceeded the population of Germany, metropolitan France, or metropolitan Britain. The results of the census are available online at <https://archive.org/details/Statisticso fthe1897AllRussiaCensus>.

227 Gerhard von Pelet-Narbonne, 'Die neueren Tendenzen der Militärpolitik' (1909) 2 Zeitschrift für Politik 440, 442.

228 Fuller Jr (n 17) 545; see also 531: Already in 1825 Russia had the largest standing army in Europe with around 750 000 men.

229 Guido von Frobel, *Von Löbell's Jahresberichte über das Heer- und Kriegswesen XXXVI Jahrgang: 1909* (ES Mittler & Sohn 1910) 207. The report estimates that in 1909 the size of the standing Imperial Army amounts to 1 254 000 active soldiers. The rest is made up of reservists, Cossacks, and the Gendarmerie.

230 Karl-Volker Neugebauer, *Grundzüge der deutschen Militärgeschichte: Historischer Überblick*, vol 1 (Rombach Verlag 1993) 212.

ority was the ace up the Tsar's sleeve. Therefore, it is only understandable that he wanted rules that conferred certain rights on his soldiers when they were in captivity or wounded. It was even more understandable that he feared the rapidly advancing development of weaponry that decreased the value of the individual infantryman and therefore sought to outlaw certain means of warfare.

Fourthly, the Tsarist government had strong economic motives to oppose an arms race, let alone an unfettered war against which IHL was considered a remedy. Russia was late to industrialisation and chronically under-developed. It had to pay for a railway system, a brand-new fleet, and the exploration of the eastern part of its territory – all while struggling with internal reforms.[231] Limiting military expenses and ensuring a stable peace in Europe was the best way of guaranteeing prosperity. Hence, after the Russo-Turkish War military expenditures continuously dropped and they remained below a 20 percent threshold until 1905.[232] Sergey Witte's statement that I have quoted above sums up this rationale. The Russian Minister of Finance dreamt of a de-mobilised Europe that would "thrive in an unprecedented way and guide the best part of the globe."[233] Witte was not a soldier, but an economist. To him war, especially a total war, must have seemed an utterly pointless investment. Historian Thomas Ford even argues that "the Russian move was primarily the result of economic necessity; only secondarily did the elements of altruism [...] enter into it."[234]

While Ford is certainly right about Russia's economic motives, I disagree with his juxtaposition of self-interest and altruism as the two opposite ends of a spectrum. Rather, I believe that Russian ingenuity helped to overcome this contradiction. Imagine bending this straight-line spectrum into a circle so that the two opposite tips meet and welding them together. In essence, that is what Russia did, at the St Petersburg Conference, at Brussels, and at The Hague. Caught up in an arms race that was impossible to win, Russia managed to open up an alley, where all States could see the long-term benefit of limiting their sovereignty.

---

231 Ford (n 162) 361 et seq; Fuller Jr (n 17) 551; see also William C Fuller Jr, *Civil-Military Conflict in Imperial Russia, 1881–1914* (Princeton University Press 2014).
232 Fuller Jr (n 17) 549–550.
233 Dillon (n 171) 276.
234 Ford (n 162) 381.

Of course, we should be careful to ascribe the success of Russia's initiative to a "master plan" of the Tsar, the Russian government, or Martens. For example, the fact that there was no clear concept for the Hague Conference before Martens took over, shows that Russian leaders only harboured a vague hope that something would come of it. They took a shot in the dark.[235] In the end, however, the Conference *did* yield tangible results and represented a milestone in international legal history. It was a curious Russian mix of pragmatism, naïve foolhardiness, and idealism that made these achievements possible. The Hague Conference of 1899 especially represents a tremendous contribution to IHL; probably the single most significant contribution that Russia has ever made.

8. The Russo-Japanese War 1904–1905 – a war waged by the books

The Russo-Japanese war – a humane war? Is that a contradiction in terms? Does it not border cynicism to award this title to a war, whose final land battle at Mukden alone killed and maimed nearly 150 000 men on both sides?[236] Whilst the Russo-Japanese war seems on one level to have conformed to the new standards of "humane warfare", the immense number of casualties at the Battle of Mukden raises the question of how far IHL could ever be more than an exercise in mitigation. Nevertheless, the Russo-Japanese War illustrates how Russia's humanitarian initiatives impacted the reality on the battlefield.

In 1904, there were many IHL rules to be respected. The Hague Regulations were only five years old when the conflict erupted. The St Petersburg Declaration was in its late thirties, the Geneva Convention in its early forties. Together they formed an impressive compendium of rules in warfare. This time, unlike in the Russo-Turkish War, both sides – Japan and Russia – were eager to respect the new rules to gain credibility on the international stage.

At the outbreak of war Russia issued an updated IHL handbook to its soldiers, that *inter alia* reiterated the protection for the wounded, rights of

---

235 See e.g. Eyffinger (n 80) 35; see in general Jost Dülffer, *Regeln gegen den Krieg? die Haager Friedenskonferenzen von 1899 und 1907 in der internationalen Politik* (Ullstein 1981).

236 Encyclopædia Britannica, 'Russo-Japanese War' <https://www.britannica.com/ev ent/Russo-Japanese-War>.

POWs, and contained a general prohibition on targeting civilians.[237] The Russian Red Cross spent considerable funds that allowed it to maintain a chain of field hospitals reaching from St Petersburg to Harbin in China to evacuate and treat soldiers. It is striking that in this war both sides went to great lengths to respect IHL. A Times war correspondent reported that wounded and captured Russian soldiers were treated with utmost care. The same was true for Japanese soldiers.[238] Martens was personally in charge of the office that communicated lists with names and details of Japanese POWs to Tokyo – a procedure not even prescribed by law at the time. This good practice would soon be included in the 1906 Geneva Convention.[239] The Russian Red Cross furthermore sent two fully equipped hospital ships to accompany its battle fleet, in conformity with the Hague Convention III on Naval Warfare.[240] The following anecdote, taken from Martens diary, illustrates well how eager both sides were to respect IHL:

> *"In March 1905 he was invited to the General Headquarters of the Russian Army and informed that in Autumn 1904 when sending Japanese prisoners of war home who had been confined in the Far eastern village of Medved, one of the Japanese military servicemen gave to a Russian officer a petition in which he thanked Russia for humane treatment and requested a gift be accepted of 150 rubles which he had earned while imprisoned. The Japanese servicemen requested that the money be divided as follows: 50 rubles to the village of Medved, 50 rubles to the Russian Red Cross, and 50 rubles to the famous Professor Martens. The latter wish of the prisoner was based on the fact that thanks to international law and the labours of Martens in this domain the prisoners of war were treated humanely. In a conversation the prisoner of war explained that he had suited international law according to the cours of Martens."*[241]

---

237 'Наказ Русской армии о законах и обычаях сухопутной войны' ['Instruction of the Russian Army Concerning the Laws and Customs of Land Warfare'] 14 July 1904. The referenced rules can be found in 1.4), 1.5), and 2.1); the document is available at <http://lepassemilitaire.ru/istoricheskij-arxiv-111/>.

238 Boissier (n 124) 434–435.

239 ibid 436. Today, rules on the transfer of information can be found in Art 69 and 123 of the Third Geneva Convention of 1949.

240 ibid 437. See the Convention (III) for the Adaptation to Maritime Warfare of the Principles of the Geneva Convention of 22 August 1864 (29 July 1899).

241 Archive of the Foreign Policy of Russia, opis 787, delo 9, ed khr 6, 1.85; cited in Pustogarov (n 99) 184.

Russia lost the war due to severe strategic blunders and the inner turmoil that followed the revolution of 1905. The defeat demoralised the Imperial Army and made painfully clear that Russia was ill-prepared to confront a highly industrialised nation such as Japan.[242] It also ended Russian dreams of further expansion in the east. Russia only escaped harsh reparations thanks to the brilliant diplomacy of Sergey Witte, and the Treaty of Portsmouth (23 August 1905) imposed a relatively lenient penalty.[243] In terms of IHL, however, the Russo-Japanese war can be seen as a sequel to the Russo-Turkish War. Russia continued to hold IHL in high regard and applied it on the battlefield.

9. The revision of the Geneva Convention 1906 – who is the better humanitarian?

The Hague Peace Conference 1899 acted as a stimulus to the development of IHL. Russia had not consulted with anybody before convening States to The Hague. The fact that this impulse came from the Tsar took the guardians of the Geneva Convention – the ICRC and Switzerland – by surprise and forced them to articulate their ideas for developing IHL.[244] From 1899 onwards IHL developed in two separate branches: the "Hague branch" initiated by Russia and the "Geneva branch" based on the work of the ICRC.[245]

The ICRC and Switzerland entered this contest for humanity by launching a joint initiative to revise the 1864 Geneva Convention. Such a revision had already been agreed at the Hague Conference of 1899, but Russia attempted to delay or even prevent the conference.[246] This shows how competitive IHL had become. Russia had adopted IHL as its trademark and was not willing to share the brand. When the Swiss finally succeeded and managed to convene the conference, the Russian delegation attempted to "subordinate" the Geneva branch to the Hague branch by adding a reference to the rules of the Hague Regulations. However, this attempt

---

242 Fuller Jr (n 17) 542–543.
243 Schimmelpenninck van der Oye (n 18) 569.
244 See Wylie (n 207) 59 et seq.
245 See n 211.
246 Wylie (n 207) 61–62.

to side-line the Swiss was unsuccessful.[247] On 6 July 1906, States agreed on a revised Geneva Convention, further expanding the protections of IHL.[248] For instance, Art 10 recognised voluntary aid societies for the first time and vested them with certain rights and prerogatives. Art 4 regulated the transmission of information on the wounded and dead according to the model of the Russian agency headed by Martens during the Russo-Japanese war.[249]

Aside from the substantial additions to IHL, this episode shows that developing the laws of war was more than a humanitarian enterprise to Russia. It was also a struggle for recognition, power, and influence in international circles.

10. The Second Hague Peace Conference of 1907 – the calm before the storm

> *"Often ignored and ridiculed, the Second Hague Peace Conference was a unique exchange of views at a moment of paramount interest for the history of Europe. [...] 1907 proved the last stop of the nations on their headlong race for Verdun. At The Hague, the dice was cast."*[250]

> *Arthur Eyffinger on the Second Hague Peace Conference*

Martens had envisaged the Hague Conference 1899 as the opening salvo to a series of periodic gatherings. Unlike the first edition, the Second Hague Conference was originally an American initiative. The Russians, however, had asked for the conference to be postponed due to their war with Japan. After the end of the war the Tsar felt confident enough to take over the initiative and the Conference was scheduled for 1907.[251] By then, Martens was 62 years old and he might have expected that this was his last big appearance on the international stage. He had drafted the circular that was sent to all participating States laying down the objectives for the

---

247 ibid 62. Not all parties to the 1864 Geneva Convention had signed the Hague Regulations (or only with certain reservations). Hence, they did not support such a cross-reference.

248 Convention for the Amelioration of the Condition of the Wounded and Sick in Armies in the Field (6 July 1906) available at <https://ihl-databases.icrc.org/ihl/I NTRO/180>.

249 See above at p 65.

250 Eyffinger (n 81) 228.

251 ibid 204.

gathering. The proposal foresaw *inter alia* additions to the conventions on land warfare, and a comprehensive convention on sea warfare.[252]

While it was clear that States wanted to discuss IHL at the Conference, opinions differed with regards to disarmament. Downsizing the bloated armies of all European nations had been the primary motive for convening the first Hague Conference. The idea had since won important supporters, such as Great Britain. On the other hand, powerful States, such as the German Empire still opposed the idea.[253] Even Russia itself – militarily crippled after the Russo-Japanese War – had turned its back on the project.[254] Hence the proposal only foresaw the discussion of measures to improve the peaceful settlement of disputes.

With regards to IHL, the task of this edition of the Hague Conference was to be both easier and harder than in 1899. Easier, because there was already a precedent. Bringing States together had worked once, why should it not work a second time? On the other hand, consensus seemed harder to reach in certain respects. Questions, such as the inviolability of private property in sea warfare, were left open in 1899 because they were especially controversial.[255] An easy success was far from likely, especially since the overall political climate in Europe had not improved in the past years; nationalism was on the rise.

44 States heeded the call of The Hague, including 19 States from Latin America as well as China, Japan, Persia, and Siam.[256] Participation was even more diverse than in 1899 and in this sense, Martens was right in calling the gathering a "truly International Parliament."[257] For the second time, the Tsar did not appoint Martens head of the Russian delegation, but the Russian diplomat Alexandr Nelidov. However, for the second time Martens played an enormously important role behind the scenes. In addition, he chaired the Maritime Commission which had the task of agreeing on more detailed IHL rules in sea warfare. Martens considered this to

---

252 The circular is reproduced in A Pearce Higgins, *The Hague Peace Conferences and Other International Conferences Concerning the Laws and Usages of War* (Cambridge University Press 1909) 53.

253 Pustogarov (n 99) 311, 316.

254 Eyffinger (n 81) 203.

255 Pustogarov (n 99) 304.

256 Betsy Baker, 'Hague Peace Conferences (1899 and 1907)', *Max Planck Encyclopedia of Public International Law* (Oxford University Press 2009) para 22.

257 Pustogarov (n 99) 315.

be the "most difficult" task, especially due to the notorious reluctance of Great Britain.[258]

The Conference managed to advance IHL in numerous areas:[259]

– The Hague Convention II concerning land warfare was confirmed with slight modifications
– Conventions V–XIII contained elaborate rules on sea warfare. Most notably, the Geneva Convention of 1906 was extended to naval warfare, thus acting as a precursor of the Second Geneva Convention of 1949.
– Convention III laid down the need to declare war or provide some sort of "warning" before opening hostilities. Although strictly a *ius ad bellum* issue, this also had an effect on IHL[260]

Of course, the Second Hague Conference had its shortcomings. The Russians had proposed to draft a comprehensive convention on sea warfare. This initiative failed. Instead, the rules were scattered across various instruments.[261] Martens had furthermore envisaged the creation of an international prize court settling disputes about confiscated ships and cargo during naval warfare. This idea was torpedoed by his own government.[262] The Convention on a prize court was adopted, but it never achieved binding status, since it was only ratified by Nicaragua.[263]

Nevertheless, the Second Hague Conference advanced IHL in various ways. Art 3 of the Hague Regulations now foresaw that States were liable to pay compensation for IHL violations. The 1906 Geneva Convention henceforth applied to naval warfare. Means and methods of warfare, such as submarine contact mines, were regulated. And above all, the Hague Regulations were submitted to a much larger group of 44 States, which added to their universal acceptance.[264] Therefore, Martens was right in concluding that "all the same much has been done which will remain a

---

258 ibid 316–317.
259 Advancements in other areas of international law included the Hague Convention I on the Pacific Settlement of International Disputes and Hague Convention II Respecting the Limitation of the Employment of Force for Recovery of Contract Debts (so-called Drago-Porter Convention). For a detailed list of all Conventions adopted in 1907 see Higgins (n 252) 63–64.
260 Baker (n 256) paras 23 et seq.
261 Pustogarov (n 99) 326.
262 ibid 318; for a detailed examination why the prize court never came into existence see Eyffinger (n 81) 210 et seq.
263 Hague Convention (XII) relative to the Creation of an International Prize Court (18 October 1907) available at <https://ihl-databases.icrc.org/applic/ihl/ihl.nsf/States.xsp?xp_viewStates=XPages_NORMStatesParties&xp_treatySelected=235>.
264 Eyffinger (n 81) 205.

forever precious contribution to the treasury of progress of the international community."[265]

The Second Hague Peace Conference was Martens last major appearance on the international stage. Being a visionary, he seemed to have a premonition of what lay ahead: "The Second Peace Conference has ended, and in all likelihood, there will not be a third."[266] Martens died on 7 June 1909 at the age of 64.[267] With his death, the sun also set on an era of peaceful cooperation between States. Within half a century international law had greatly progressed. While war was not absent from international relations, conflicts were fought with increasing respect for IHL as shown by the examples of the Russo-Turkish War and the Russo-Japanese War. This success story was about to change, starting with a tragic summer morning in Sarajevo.

11. The First World War 1914–1918 – the great seminal catastrophe

"Our disillusionment on account of the uncivilized behaviour of our fellow citizens of the world during the war were unjustified. They were based on an illusion to which we had given way. In reality our fellow-citizens have not sunk so low as we feared because they had never risen so high as we believed."[268]

Sigmund Freud on the First World War, 1915

Pointing out that the First World War brought terrible bloodshed and carnage would be stating the obvious. Modern technology led to the erosion of well-established standards of humanity. While the famous English poet Sir Henry Newbolt compared war to a rugby match, the reality could not be further from this romantic image of a chivalrous standoff:[269] soldiers

---

265 Pustogarov (n 99) 324; for a contemporary Russian perspective on the outcome of the Conference see Vladlen Vereshchetin, 'Some Reflections of a Russian Scholar on the Legacy of the Second Peace Conference' in Yves Daudet (ed), *Actualité de la Conférence de la Haye de 1907, deuxième Conférence de la Paix* (Martinus Nijhoff Publishers 2008).

266 Pustogarov (n 99) 327.

267 ibid 338.

268 Sigmund Freud, *Civilisation, War and Death: Selections from Three Works by Sigmund Freud* (Hogarth Press and the Institute of Psycho-analysis 1939) 11.

269 His famous war poem 'Vitai Lampada' finishes on the line "Play up! play up! and play the game!".

crouched in the muddy trenches of Verdun searching for cover from endless artillery salvoes. While men were on the frontline, women and children were raped and killed in occupied territories, such as Galicia.[270] Destruction seemed omnipresent. Air warfare and submarines extended the battlefield to spheres that were unthinkable only a few years ago. The human cost was immense. Tragic peaks that continue to haunt our conscience even today include the Armenian Genocide and the first use of poisonous gas on the battlefields of Ypres. Nearly nine million dead combatants and probably as many dead civilians[271] – these figures truly stand for "*the* great seminal catastrophe" of the twentieth century.[272]

I would like to draw the spotlight to two specific issues during World War I that are of special relevance to Russia and IHL and will be the focus of the present investigation: the treatment of POWs and the use of chemical weapons. I have made this selection, because these issues have a special link to Russia and they were already regulated in IHL at the time, while other phenomena – such as the extremely high number of dead combatants and the suffering of civilians – fell outside of the protective scope of the laws of war. IHL remained incomplete, and the First World War was painfully suited to demonstrate this. There are some things from which IHL did not *yet* protect in 1914, and there are things from which even the most perfect IHL framework could *never* offer protection.

The first category, i.e. persons IHL did not *yet* protect, concerns civilians. At the outbreak of World War I, there was still no effective protection of civilians in wartime. It would take another 30 years for the 1949 Fourth Geneva Convention to see the light of day. Only then would the essential safeguards be extended to non-combatants. This, of course, does not mean that the First World War was less cruel on civilians. Although often ignored by history, civilians suffered greatly, especially in occupied territories where they were at the mercy of foreign troops. For example,

---

270 See for this Omer Bartov and Eric D Weitz, *Shatterzone of Empires: Coexistence and Violence in the German, Habsburg, Russian, and Ottoman Borderlands* (Indiana University Press 2013).

271 Encyclopædia Britannica, 'World War I – Killed, wounded, and missing' <https://www.britannica.com/event/World-War-I/Killed-wounded-and-missing>.

272 The expression was coined by George Frost Kennan, *The Decline of Bismarck's European Order: Franco-Russian Relations 1875–1890* (Princeton University Press 1979) 3.

the Russian soldiers who invaded eastern Prussia and the Balkans initiated pogroms and committed atrocities.[273]

Some of these acts were already illegal under IHL, which provided some sort of minimal protection to civilians under occupation. Other indirect effects of conflict, such as starvation were still blank spots in IHL even though they were among the main death causes.[274] Some hardships, such as the systematic internment of civilians, had not even appeared on the radar of international lawyers before. Gustav Ador the then President of the ICRC stressed in one of his speeches: "Civilian internees are an innovation of this war; the international treaties did not foresee it."[275]

The second category, i.e. persons IHL could *never* protect, concerns the soldiers that fell at Verdun, Ypres, Tannenberg, and on many other battlegrounds. IHL was never *made* to protect these young men.[276] Since it accepts war as a given, it must accept the possibility of targeting soldiers.[277] This inherent pragmatism has rarely been questioned ever since the 1864 Geneva Convention.[278] So, even if it sounds cynical, most of the nine

---

273 Annette Becker, 'The Great War: World War, Total War' (2015) 97 International Review of the Red Cross 1029, 1036–1038.

274 Encyclopædia Britannica, 'World War I – Killed, wounded, and missing' <https://www.britannica.com/event/World-War-I/Killed-wounded-and-missing>.

275 Gustav Ador, speech at the International Conference of the Red Cross on the issue of civilian prisoners: ICRC Archives, 411/10, "Introduction sommaire à la question concernant les civils" (September 1917) 1.

276 Lindsey Cameron, 'The ICRC in the First World War: Unwavering Belief in the Power of Law?' (2015) 97 International Review of the Red Cross 1099, 1100. According to Cameron "it seems astonishing that it was not somehow illegal to plan battles in which 10,000 casualties per day – for one's own side alone – were expected."

277 Of course, IHL imposes restrictions on *how* combatants can be targeted. The St Petersburg Declaration banning exploding bullets is a prime example for illegal means and methods or warfare. While there are other important restrictions on how combatants can be targeted, IHL still rests on the assumption that combatants represent legitimate targets in war.

278 One of the few instances in history, where the very existence of IHL was called into question, was after the Second World War. Art 2(4) of the UN Charter enshrined the prohibition of the use of force. Some authors argued that IHL had no place in a world that had outlawed war: Quincy Wright, 'The Outlawry of War and the Law of War' (1953) 47 American Journal of International Law 365, 370; Georges Scelle, 'Quelques réflexions sur l'abolition de la compétence de guerre' (1954) 25 Revue Générale de Droit International Public 18; Georg Schwarzenberger, *International Law as Applied by International Courts and Tribunals: Volume II: The Law of Armed Conflict* (Stevens and Sons 1968); see also

million dead soldiers in the First World War were killed in conformity with the law. They were combatants that became victims of conventional weapons such as artillery shells or machine guns.[279] Actually, overall IHL compliance during World War I can be considered "fairly good."[280] Hence, if we want to explore how Russia shaped IHL during the First World War, we should focus on the following two issues: poisonous gas and POWs.

11.1 Chlorine gas – a horror made in Germany

Did Russia violate the Hague law when its troops used poisonous gas? One thing is for sure: it was not Russia who used chemical weapons first. On the contrary, in 1914 Russia's chemical production was exclusively in the hands of German industrialists. When the war broke out, production sites were shut down for obvious reasons.[281] Contrary to the popular belief that poisonous gas was used for the first time on the Western Front, the weapon had its premiere against the Russian Empire. German troops deployed it in late January 1915 in Poland. However, the cold temperature greatly reduced its effect and made the attack go by almost unnoticed.[282] On 22 April 1915 Germany used Chlorine gas for the first time in a

---

the letters exchanged between William C Chandler and Prof Glueck, reprinted in Jonathan A Bush, 'The Supreme Crime and Its Origins: The Lost Legislative History of the Crime of Aggressive War' (2002) 102 Columbia Law Review 2324, 2402; The ILC refused to codify IHL, because it would send the wrong political sign after the adoption of the UN-Charter, see ILC, *Yearbook of the International Law Commission 1949 – Summary Records and Documents of the First Session Including the Report of the Commission to the General Assembly* (United Nations 1956) 281.

279   Becker (n 273) 2034. The author speaks of "10 million dead in four and a half years. Unlike in previous wars, very few died of disease; almost all were killed in the fighting. The survivors did not fare much better. Nearly 50 percent of all those who fought were wounded, whether seriously or not, and often more than once. Shells were the main cause; poison gas, though a new terror, caused far fewer casualties."

280   Cameron (n 276) 1119.

281   Maria Grigoryan and Oleg Yegorov 'How Russia countered Germany's chemical weapons in WWI' (Russia Beyond, 8 August 2018) <https://www.rbth.com/history/328927-russia-chemical-weapon-wwi>.

282   Ulrich Trumpener, 'The Road to Ypres: The Beginnings of Gas Warfare in World War I' (1975) 47 The Journal of Modern History 460, 462–463; 469.

large-scale operation in Ypres.[283] Later, its enemies – including Russia – would retaliate. Overall both sides used 110 000 tonnes of poisonous gas during the war, killing 91 000 and wounding 1.3 million more.[284]

However atrocious the consequences, the legal prohibition of poisonous gas was not as clear as many claimed at the time. The Geneva Protocol for the Prohibition of the Use in War of Asphyxiating, Poisonous or other Gases was only adopted in 1925 – and thus long after the war. At the time of the First World War the only existing framework was the Hague Declaration IV-2 of 1899 prohibiting "the use of *projectiles* the sole object of which is the diffusion of asphyxiating or deleterious gases."[285] The reader might notice that the provision does not ban gas itself, but only *projectiles* containing such gas. The second relevant norm was Art 23(a) and (e) of the Hague Regulations (1907). It prohibited the use of "poison" and arms that cause "unnecessary suffering." However, the wording remained very vague. None of the existing treaties contained a blanket and explicit ban of poisonous gas.

The Germans tried to use this ambiguity to their advantage. According to them the use of Chlorine at Ypres did not violate the letter of the law, because the gas was released from canisters and not fired by projectiles. The canisters were opened manually, and the wind then carried the gas towards the French positions. Moreover, so the Germans argued, the injuries caused by gas weren't any more "superfluous" than those inflicted by ordinary shrapnel.[286] Finally, gas was not "poison" in the sense of Art 23 Hague Regulations. While this question was discussed at the first Hague Peace Conference, the delegates did not reach consensus on it.[287]

Whether a violation of the strict letter of the law or a grey area case, the community of States unanimously condemned the German use of chlorine

---

283 M Girard Dorsey, 'More than Just a Taboo: The Legacy of the Chemical Warfare Prohibitions of the 1899 and 1907 Hague Conferences' in Maartje Abbenhuis, Christopher Ernest Barber and Annalise R Higgins (eds), *War, Peace and International Order? The Legacies of the Hague Conferences of 1899 and 1907* (Routledge 2017) 86.

284 ibid 90.

285 Declaration (IV,2) concerning Asphyxiating Gases (29 July 1899, emphasis added), available at <https://ihl-databases.icrc.org/applic/ihl/ihl.nsf/Article.x sp?action=openDocument&documentId=2531E92D282B5436C12563CD005161 49>.

286 Dorsey (n 283) 90–91.

287 ibid 89.

gas as a violation of international law.[288] Hence, MP Harold Tennant struck a point when he declared in the House of Commons in 1915:

> *"The actual terms of The Hague Declaration forbid only the use of projectiles the sole object of which is to diffuse asphyxiating or deleterious gases. Obviously, the diffusion of the gases was the object of the prohibition rather than the means by which they were diffused."*[289]

From today's perspective this position seems reasonable and in line with Art 31(1) of the Vienna Convention on the Law of Treaties (VCLT) which encourages us to interpret a treaty in the light of its "object and purpose." This also includes "subsequent practice."[290] After such a unanimous condemnation it was difficult to argue that the existing norms did not cover poisonous gas.

Condemning the German violation of IHL did not prevent Russia and its allies from resorting to the use of poisonous gas themselves.[291] Russia, for its part, managed to develop its own chemical weapons within a year's time. The Imperial Army used them for the first time in March 1916 during the offensive of Lake Naroch, in today's Belarus.[292] Was this a clear violation of IHL? Based on what has been said above, the reader might conclude that Russia's use of poisonous gas would equally violate Hague law.

The answer to this question, however, should not be rushed. You might remember your childhood days when you haggled with your siblings. When your parents intervened, you would defend yourself by resorting to the compelling argument: "But *they* started!". This intuitive defence also exists in international law in the form of reprisals. A belligerent reprisal describes a breach of IHL that would otherwise be unlawful, but in exceptional cases is considered lawful as an enforcement measure in response to a previous breach of IHL by the enemy.[293] Today, reprisals

---

288 ibid 91.
289 H Tenant (18 May 1915) House of Commons Debates Hansard Millbanks Series 5 Vol 71cc, 2119–2120 (emphasis added), available at <https://api.parliament.uk/historic-hansard/commons/1915/may/18/asphyxiating-gases-hague-convention>.
290 See Art 31(3)(b) VCLT.
291 Dorsey (n 283) 92–93; Durand (n 38) 73.
292 Maria Grigoryan and Oleg Yegorov 'How Russia countered Germany's chemical weapons in WWI' (Russia Beyond, 8 August 2018) <https://www.rbth.com/history/328927-russia-chemical-weapon-wwi>.
293 ICRC Casebook, How Does Law Protect in War, 'Reprisals' <https://casebook.icrc.org/glossary/reprisals>.

are only allowed under very strict conditions and there is a trend in IHL towards outlawing them completely.[294] However, in 1914–1918 countries were still free to retaliate – including by using poisonous gas. The Hague Conventions of 1899 and 1907 did not touch upon the issue of reprisals for fear of legitimising their use.[295] According to the (non-binding) Oxford Manual of 1880, belligerent reprisals were explicitly allowed "if the injured party deem the misdeed so serious in character as to make it necessary to recall the enemy to a respect for law, [and] no other recourse than a resort to reprisals remains."[296] Even after the First World War, reprisals were far from illegal. When signing the 1925 Geneva Protocol, many States retained the right to use poisonous gas to retaliate against a breach of the protocol by the enemy. While many States have withdrawn their reservation today, certain countries – including the US, China, and Syria – have not.[297] Christopher Greenwood and Shane Darcy argue that the use of gas (against combatants) could even be one of the few remaining examples of legal belligerent reprisals today.[298]

In the light of this, the Russian use of poisonous gas could be justified as a reprisal. Of course, every instance would have had to be proportional and aimed at ending the enemy's violation.[299] This would require a detailed analysis of each and every attack and therefore falls outside of the scope of this thesis. However, it is safe to say that Russia did not commit a large-scale violation of IHL by using gas *per se*.

---

294 ibid.

295 Frits Kalshoven, *Belligerent Reprisals* (A W Sijthoff 1971) 67.

296 Art 84 of the Oxford Manual on the Laws of War on Land.

297 Countries that maintain their reservation include: Algeria, Angola, Bahrain, Bangladesh, Cambodia, China, Fiji, India, Iraq, Israel, Jordan, Democratic People's Republic of Korea, Republic of Korea, Kuwait, Libya, Nigeria, Papua New Guinea, Serbia, Solomon Islands, Syria, Thailand, the US, and Vietnam. See <https://www.nti.org/learn/treaties-and-regimes/protocol-prohibition-use-war-asphyxiating-poisonous-or-other-gasses-and-bacteriological-methods-warfare-geneva-protocol/>.

298 Christopher Greenwood, 'The Twilight of the Law of Belligerent Reprisals' (1989) 20 Netherlands Yearbook of International Law 35, 54; Shane Darcy, 'The Evolution of the Law of Belligerent Reprisals' (2003) 175 Military Law Review 244, 212–213.

299 ICRC Casebook, How Does Law Protect in War, 'Reprisals' <https://casebook.icrc.org/glossary/reprisals>.

11.2 Prisoners of war in Russia – lost in the taiga

By 1917 Russia had over two million prisoners of war in custody.[300] In theory, Russia had the necessary legal framework to cope with such an astronomical number of people. At the outbreak of the war, the government had published a voluminous code regarding the rights and the treatment of POWs.[301] In practice, however, the Russian Empire was ill-prepared for such an influx. Whenever they captured a large number of POWs, the detainment system failed, and they could neither provide for them in the combat zone nor transport them to the rear. This involuntary chaos resulted in many deaths.[302] Eventually, most surviving prisoners were sent to Siberia, where they lived in poor conditions and fell victims to diseases. During the early stages of the war, thousands died of epidemics.[303] The Russians themselves were short of food and winter apparel. Thus, they did not issue any to the POWs.[304] Overall more than 400 000 prisoners perished which constituted one of the highest death rates for detention powers in the First World War.[305]

The massive influx of POWs painfully showed the difference between law and reality. While the Hague Regulations *did* set out fundamental protections for POWs, they did not provide any guidance how to cope with the huge numbers the detention powers were facing. Nobody had any experience in dealing with millions of detainees. Well-intended initiatives, such as the communication through neutral States, were ineffective due to practical difficulties. For example, the US (during its period of neutrality) represented German and Austro-Hungarian interests in Russia. However, many of the consular staff spoke little Russian or German, thus greatly complicating any intervention.[306]

---

300 Gerald H Davis, 'The Life of Prisoners of War in Russia 1914–1921' in Samuel R Jr Williamson and Peter Pastor (eds), *War and Society in East Central Europe Vol V – Essays on World War I: Origins and Prisoners of War* (Brooklyn College Press 1983) 163.
301 Durand (n 38) 70–75.
302 Davis (n 300) 165.
303 Reinhard Nachtigal, 'Seuchen unter militärischer Aufsicht in Rußland: Das Lager Tockoe als Beispiel für die Behandlung der Kriegsgefangenen 1915/16' (2000) 48 Jahrbücher für Geschichte Osteuropas 363, 367–368.
304 Davis (n 300) 168.
305 Reinhard Nachtigal and Lena Radauer, 'Prisoners of War (Russian Empire)', *International Encyclopedia of the First World War 5.*
306 Davis (n 300) 170.

In addition, the Russians did not react well to criticism. When an American Red Cross officer denounced the appalling conditions in the Siberian camp of Sretensk, where countless POWs had succumbed to a Typhus epidemic, he was recalled under the pressure from the Russian military.[307] The refusal to improve the appalling conditions clearly violated Art 4 of the Hague Regulations, which guaranteed POWs humane treatment. Russia furthermore forced many POWs to work in connection with military operations, building fortifications or roads within occupied territories. This constituted a clear violation of Art 6 of the Hague Regulations.[308] The country that had done so much to protect prisoners during the Russo-Turkish and the Russo-Japanese War now failed to live up to its responsibility.

It is difficult to say whether Russia neglected its obligations due to incompetence or whether the shortage of food, medicine, clothes, and accommodation was intended. It makes little difference legally, since the Hague Regulations do not set out any subjective element. What counts is the objective violation of minimum guarantees. Most likely, however, the Russians were simply overwhelmed and ill-prepared, as the number of POWs exceeded the local population in some places of detention.[309] This theory also finds support in accounts of more fortunate POWs who managed to benefit from the chaotic conditions. The absence of a strong governmental authority brought about a degree of freedom to self-organise. POWs founded papers, theatre groups, schools, colleges, labour unions, elected their leaders and even held a nationwide all-Russian prisoner of war congress. Many of the prisoners worked on farms, integrated themselves into everyday life and even decided to stay after the war.[310] Such "success stories" would have been impossible if the Russian State had followed a regime of calculated deprivation.

In the turmoil of the October Revolution most POWs were freed and received full citizen rights of the Soviet Union. However, they were still stranded in remote areas of Siberia and Turkestan, and many of them depended on the government-funded camp system.[311] While the negotiations with Germany at Brest-Litovsk proceeded, the prisoners were stuck in the taiga. In the long run, the political chaos would greatly hamper

---

307   ibid 172.
308   ibid 174.
309   Nachtigal and Radauer (n 305) 4.
310   Davis (n 300) 175–181.
311   ibid 181–182.

their homecoming.[312] While the repatriation of POWs had been one of the core tasks of the Red Cross, the 1917 revolution obliterated the old structures of the Russian Empire. This affected the work of the ICRC as well as of the Russian Red Cross. Even though the Bolsheviks vowed to honour the obligations under the Geneva Conventions in a decree signed by Lenin himself, relations with the ICRC gradually deteriorated.[313] It is emblematic that the position of the ICRC delegate in Russia remained vacant up to 1921.[314]

The delay in repatriations was aggravated by the decline of the Russian Red Cross. Founded in 1867, it had been an active and well-organised national society with good ties to the ruling circles. It will come as no surprise to the reader that the Bolsheviks completely changed, suspended, and finally tried to replace the national society.[315] A new Soviet Red Cross was created, while the old Imperial Red Cross re-founded itself in areas controlled by the "Whites"[316] and abroad.[317] This left the ICRC without a national counterpart which created an even worse situation: any sign of recognition of one society would be perceived as partial by the other. In addition, the allies opposed a quick exchange of POWs between Russia and Germany after the armistice in 1918 for fear of bolstering the Red Army in a crucial phase of the Russian Civil War.[318] Hence, Art 20 of the Hague Regulations that foresaw that "[a]fter the conclusion of a peace, repatriation of prisoners of war shall be carried out as quickly as possible" remained but an illusion. The last POWs only returned in 1922, four years after the armistice of 1918.[319]

---

312 Nachtigal and Radauer (n 305) 7–8.
313 The Decree can be found in Durand (n 38) 81.
314 ibid 87.
315 ibid 79, 85.
316 The term Белая Армия [White Army] describes a loose confederation of anti-communist forces that fought against the Red Army in the Russian Civil War (1917–1923).
317 Durand (n 38) 85.
318 Jean-François Fayet, 'Le CICR et la Russie: Un peu plus que de l'humanitaire' (2015) 1 Connexe: les espaces postcommunistes en question 55, 60.
319 Durand (n 38) 89.

12. Conclusion

In terms of IHL, the First World War is a mixed bag. On the one hand, Russia still went to great lengths to respect IHL. For example, it agreed to return a certain percentage of medical personnel among Austro-Hungarian POWs.[320] In 1915 it supported the ICRC's appeal for a ceasefire, so that nurses could collect the wounded.[321] Furthermore, Russia did not violate the Hague law *per se* by using chemical weapons. On the other hand, the poor treatment of POWs taints the Russian IHL record.

Hence, World War I constitutes the first instance, where Russia disregarded IHL norms on a large scale. Admittedly, Russia was no worse than other European powers and most of the violations occurred because the country was overwhelmed and manifestly ill-prepared for war.[322] However, none of this can justify the suffering of many individuals that should have been protected by IHL.

In this sense, the First World War marks a watershed in Russia's attitude to IHL. The "golden age" of Russia's humanitarianism began to fade.[323] The War ended the most productive period of Russia's IHL patronage (1868–1914) during which the Empire promoted humanity in warfare. As is well known, the February Revolution (1917) also put an end to the Russian Empire altogether. While the poor treatment of POWs during the First World War foreshadowed violations in future conflicts, the most fundamental changes were of another kind. As the Bolsheviks took power in 1917, they vowed to break with the past. How would this radical change affect Russia's attitude towards IHL?

---

320 Cameron (n 276) 1116.
321 Rapport Général du Comité International de la Croix Rouge sur son activité de 1912 à 1920 (Geneva 1921) 75–76.
322 See for this Fayet (n 318) 58.
323 See ibid 56. Fayet uses the term to refer to the period of 1867–1917, but mainly with reference to the relations between Russia and the ICRC.

Chapter II: The Soviet Era 1917–1991

1. Introduction

When the British historian Eric Hobsbawn coined the term of "the long 19th century" he referred to the period from the French Revolution up to the outbreak of the First World War.[324] This era that brought relative peace and prosperity to Europe found an abrupt end in 1914. For Russia, the turning point was more precisely 1917, when Tsar Nicolas II abdicated after the February Revolution. After nearly 200 years the Russian Empire, the third largest Empire in world history, ceased to exist. Shortly afterwards, three other long-standing European monarchies – the Austro-Hungarian, the German, and the Ottoman Empire – would also disappear. 1917 also marked the beginning of the first large-scale communist experiment on a State level. Ironically, it was not one of the highly industrialised nations of Western Europe, but a largely agrarian Russia that became the breeding ground for the workers' revolution. Ahead of us lies the "short twentieth century" spanning from 1914 to 1991, which Eric Hobsbawn also called "the age of the extremes."[325]

If the Soviet intermezzo were a picture, it would be framed by two events that took place in the Belarusian city of Brest. In 1918 Bolshevik Russia and the German Empire concluded the treaty of Brest-Litovsk ending the First World War and paving the way for the consolidation of Bolshevik rule. In 1991 it was again near Brest where three signatures put an end to another conflict. In the idyllic setting of Belovezhskaya Pushcha National Park, Russian, Ukrainian, and Belarusian representatives concluded the Belovezha Accords that started with the laconic phrase: "the Soviet Union ceases to exist as a subject of international law and as a geopolitical reality."[326] The Cold War was over.

---

324 His analysis consists of three volumes: Eric Hobsbawm, *Age of Revolution: 1789–1848* (Hachette UK 2010); Eric Hobsbawm, *Age of Capital: 1848–1875* (Hachette UK 2010); Eric Hobsbawm, *Age of Empire: 1875–1914* (Hachette UK 2010).

325 Eric J Hobsbawm and Marion Cumming, *Age of Extremes: The Short Twentieth Century, 1914–1991* (Abacus London 1995).

326 Treaty on the Creation of the Commonwealth of Independent States (8 December 1991). The Russian original reads: "Мы, Республика Беларусь, Российская Федерация (РСФСР), Украина как государства – учредители Союза ССР,

The following chapter will focus on the seven decades that lie in between these two historical events. Did the Soviet Union cherish IHL in the same way as Imperial Russia? How did the pragmatic field of IHL sit with Marxist ideology? And what convinced Stalin – one of the bloodiest tyrants of modern times – to sign the Geneva Conventions of 1949? I will structure my analysis of the Soviet reign thematically, rather than chronologically. In legal terms, IHL faced certain structural difficulties in Soviet times. There are four reasons why an overarching analysis is more suitable, than proceeding war by war, conference by conference.

Firstly, any account of the bloody 20th century risks escalating into an endless list of IHL violations. You might remember my enthusiastic accounts of how IHL was valued and implemented during the Russo-Turkish and Russo-Japanese war. You might remember my apologetic approach to Russia's violations during the First World War, which occurred to a large extent – especially with regards to POWs – due to incompetence and lack of resources rather due to bad faith. The Second World War was different. IHL violations were premeditated, endemic, and systematic – especially on the eastern front.[327] Both Stalin and Hitler waged an ideologically motivated total war which had a disastrous effect on IHL. I will not conceal these violations from the reader but examining them in detail would be a Sisyphean task.

Secondly, the Soviets did not attach as much value to IHL as imperial Russia had – or to law in general for that matter. Marxism-Leninism, the official State ideology of the USSR, saw its main priority as paving the way to a communist society. Law was never a central concern of Marxists. Their ideology rather focusses on the development of economic infrastructure and the organisation of power in a community. While law comes in as one sub-factor, it is doomed to remain merely tangential.[328] In addition, *international* law was the product of negotiations of bourgeois governments and thus always carried a counter-revolutionary smell.

Thirdly, after the end of World War II many of the conflicts with Soviet involvement were fought as proxy wars, the only notable exception being

---

подписавшие Союзный Договор 1922 года, далее именуемые Высокими Договаривающимися Сторонами, констатируем, что Союз ССР, как субъект международного права и геополитическая реальность, прекращает свое существование."

327 See below at pp 103 et seq.
328 Hugh Collins, *Marxism and Law* (Oxford University Press 1984) 9.

the Afghan War (1979–1989).[329] While it was an open secret that the Soviet Union provided support to warring parties in Korea, Vietnam, and to various African and Latin American guerrilla movements, the Red Army avoided directly participating in hostilities.[330] This strategy of outsourcing warfare to proxy actors, makes it much harder to establish genuine Soviet practice. The phenomenon of delegating warfare is highly interesting and – as we shall see later – a tradition that lives on in modern-day Russia. However, a comprehensive analysis of such support would go beyond the scope of this thesis and would not yield much with regards to IHL.

Fourthly, the Soviets came up with several new legal concepts that were at odds with the established framework of international law. Can you imagine acceding to a treaty without signing it? Can you imagine a different *system* of international law that applies only to socialist States? Legally speaking, these were truly revolutionary concepts worthy of a State that had sworn to change all aspects of rotten capitalist society. We shall have a look at these concepts in the following section. However, when the Soviet Union was laid to rest near Brest in 1991, most of these revolutionary ideas were buried with it. Thus, they have less relevance for the upcoming analysis of Russia's present-day approach to IHL.

What *can* we say about seven decades of Soviet reign? In the first part, I will tackle the idiosyncrasies of the Soviets' mindset with regards to international law and how they affected IHL. In the second part, I would like to highlight certain moments when the USSR managed to "shine" with regards to IHL, notably the International Military Tribunal at Nuremberg and the 1949 Diplomatic Conference for the revision of the Geneva Conventions. However, I will also point out Soviet misconduct, notably during the Second World War (1941–1945) and the Afghan War (1979–1989).

---

329 See below at p 131. Also, we shall briefly consider the rare instances in which the Soviet troops overtly engaged in combat outside Soviet territory. There are only five cases: The invasions in East Germany (1953), Hungary (1956), and Czechoslovakia (1968); the Sino-Soviet Border Conflict (1969); and the Afghan War (1979–1989). All of them – with the exception of Hungary and Afghanistan – resulted in little casualties, see below at p 128.

330 A notable exception is the participation of Soviet pilots in aerial combat during the Korean War and in the Middle East. However, their participation was not openly acknowledged until many years later, see Mark Kramer, 'Russia, Chechnya, and the Geneva Conventions, 1994–2006' in Matthew Evangelista and Nina Tannenwald (eds), *Do the Geneva Conventions Matter?* (Oxford University Press 2017) 179.

Finally, the overall impact of the Soviet Union on the structures of IHL will be examined.

2. Soviet peculiarities – breaking with the past

The October Revolution drastically changed Russia's approach to international law.[331] When the Bolsheviks emerged as the winner from the struggle for power, legal scholars began to rethink the very foundations of the international legal order. In particular, IHL came under fire from three sides. First, the traditional concept of universality in international law was shaken to the core as the idea of a separate legal order – "socialist international law" – emerged. The Soviet Union claimed that international relations of socialist States should be governed by a separate body of international law. What did this fragmentation mean for IHL (see 2.1)?

Secondly, the Soviets displayed a tendency to cast aside any legal rule, if it furthered their ideological aims. If such an ideological mindset extended to the rules of warfare it would not sit well with the pragmatic foundations of IHL that rests on the equality of belligerents. Was anything permitted in a war that served the creation of a communist society (see 2.2)?

Thirdly, the IHL treaties themselves faced a technical difficulty: was the Soviet Union bound by the treaties that the Russian Empire had signed at The Hague and Geneva? Or was the USSR a new subject of international law? The latter would imply a fresh start, a clean slate with no inherited obligations (see 2.3).

2.1 "Socialist international law" – the fragmentation of international law

Is international law a universal order for all humankind? In the 19th century we often find the restriction to "civilized nations", for example in Martens' textbook *Contemporary International Law of Civilized Peoples*.[332] In the early 20th century, however, we note a trend towards the universalisation of international law.[333] This is not to say that all States were bound

---

331 Mälksoo, *Russian Approaches to International Law* (n 6) 3 et seq.

332 Ф.Ф. Мартенс [F.F. Martens], *Современное международное право цивилизованных народов [Contemporary International Law of Civilized Peoples]* (n 15).

333 Mälksoo, *Russian Approaches to International Law* (n 6) 5.

by the same rules. Treaty obligations are restricted to the signatories and take effect *inter partes*. A State only carries the obligations which it has chosen to impose on itself.[334] However, according to the classic logic of the 20th century, States were like the stars of the Milky Way. While treaties sculpted them into different constellations, they all remained part of the same galaxy ("universal international law").

Today, the myth of absolute universality has crumbled. There is more than one galaxy. Certain scholars provide proof of a fragmented regime[335] and concepts like regional international law have gained acceptance.[336] However, the opposition to universality in international law is not all that recent. Shortly after the October Revolution the Soviets started to ask themselves: is there a regime of socialist international law that exists in complete separation from "universal international law?"[337]

This idea was first advanced by Andrey Sabanin, then director of the Soviet Foreign Ministry, in 1922. According to him, universal international law continued to regulate relations between Socialist and bourgeois States. In this respect, Soviet Russia would continue to shape universal international law as a global order. In addition, however, he envisaged a new legal order between socialist States.[338] In essence, Sabanin argued in favour of a fragmentation of international law, a division based on a State's political system. Other scholars, such as Evgeny Korovin came to a similar conclusion: international law was fragmented from now on. Korovin called his book *International Law of the Transitional Period* and argued that there were three distinct legal orders for inter-State relations: socialist–socialist relations, bourgeois–bourgeois relations, as well as mixed relations between bourgeois and socialist States.[339]

---

334 At least according to the doctrine of positivism, see James Leslie Brierly and Andrew Clapham, *Brierly's Law of Nations: An Introduction to the Role of International Law in International Relations* (7th edn, Oxford University Press 2012) 49. See also Permanent Court of International Justice, *France v Turkey (Lotus Case)*, 7 September 1927, 1927 PCIJ (Ser A) No 10, para 46.

335 See e.g. Anthea Roberts, *Is International Law International?* (Oxford University Press 2017).

336 Mathias Forteau, 'Regional International Law', *Max Planck Encyclopedia of Public International Law* (Oxford University Press 2006).

337 For an in-depth analysis see Theodor Schweisfurth, *Sozialistisches Völkerrecht? Darstellung, Analyse, Wertung der sowjetmarxistischen Theorie vom Völkerrecht 'neuen Typs'* (Springer 1979).

338 ibid 183–184.

339 Е.А. Коровин [E.A. Korovin], *Международное право переходного времени [International Law of the Transitional Time]* (1971) 6.

In the interwar period these ideas never really made it beyond the walls of the ivory tower. Soviet Russia was a war-torn country and isolated in international relations. When the Soviet Union was created in 1922, there were no socialist brethren to which the new body of socialist international law could be applied apart from underdeveloped Mongolia.[340] Consequently, the idea of a body of socialist international law only became relevant after the Second World War, when States like Yugoslavia, Poland, or Czechoslovakia became or were made socialist.[341] Around twenty years later it had found general acceptance by many leading scholars like Igor Blishchenko,[342] Grigory Tunkin,[343] and Gennady Ignatenko[344] and was referenced abundantly by the Soviet authorities.[345]

What was the importance of this new legal order between socialist States for IHL? For this, we have to distinguish two scenarios: socialist-socialist relations and socialist-bourgeois relations. Between socialist States, socialist international law introduced a new set of rules.[346] They regulated the question of military cooperation in case of attack,[347] an obligation of mutual help,[348] and a principle of fraternal friendship.[349] IHL – previously Russia's favourite child – did not feature among them. Certain authors

---

340 Schweisfurth (n 337) 182.
341 ibid 198–200. It was above all the conflict between Stalin and the free-minded Yugoslavian leader Tito that created the urge to formalise the relations between the USSR and other socialist States. The need to bring rebellious Tito back in line and give the USSR the last say in matters regarding the community of socialist States sped up the development of a separate concept of socialist international law.
342 И.П. Блищенко [I.P. Blishchenko], *Антисоветизм и международное право [Antisovietism and International Law]* (Международные отношения 1968) 62.
343 Г.И. Тункин [G.I. Tunkin], 'XXII съезд КПСС и международное право [XXII Congress of the Communist Party of the Soviet Union]' [1961] Советский ежегодник международного права [Soviet Yearbook of International Law] 15, 27.
344 Г.В. Игнатенко [G.I. Ignatenko], *Международное право и общественный прогресс [International Law and the Progress of Society]* (Международные отношения [International Relations] 1972) 99.
345 See e.g. UN General Assembly Resolution, UN Doc A/PV 1679 (3 October 1968) 7. Foreign Minister Gromyko invoked the "own socialist principles" to justify the Soviet invasion of the ČSSR after the Prague Spring 1968.
346 Admittedly, the new socialist principles had a much greater influence on *ius ad bellum* than *ius in bello*. See e.g. Edgar Tomson, *Kriegsbegriff und Kriegsrecht der Sowjetunion* (Berlin-Verlag 1979).
347 Schweisfurth (n 337) 402.
348 ibid 414.
349 ibid 420.

such as Fyodor Kozhevnikov even argued that the laws of war had no place in socialist international law at all:[350]

> *"It is evident that the concepts of bourgeois international law that relate to the domain of coercion, inequality, the use of armed force etc. do not exist in this system. Thus, for example, all norms that are directly related to the 'laws of war' are completely excluded from the socialist system of international legal relations."*[351]

Thus, IHL became a tainted field of international law and its universalism, once a ground-breaking asset, suffered a serious setback. In simple terms: in case of a war between socialist States IHL would not apply, because war between two like-minded socialist States seemed inconceivable.

Secondly and to a lesser extent, socialist international law also affected socialist-bourgeois relations, in the sense that it could serve as an excuse to disregard traditional (universal) international law. Well-known Soviet authors such as Grigory Tunkin argued that in case of collision, the socialist principles should take precedence over general international law.[352] Not all scholars agreed with this radical reading pointing out that universal international law was not inferior to the socialist order.[353] However, even if socialist international law were on equal footing with universal international law (and thus IHL), this would mean that the latter loses importance, because it receives a rival.

The legal debate simmered on throughout seven decades of Soviet rule.[354] The Soviets readily used their new socialist principles when accused of violating universal international law. Mostly, however, this concerned *ius ad bellum* issues, such as the concept of sovereignty during interventions.[355] Soviet Foreign Minister Andrey Gromyko, for example, tried to justify the Soviet invasion of the ČSSR – which under normal circumstances amounted to a breach of Art 2(4) UN Charter – by resorting

---

350 See also Jiří Toman, *L'Union Soviétique et le droit des conflits armés* (PhD 1997) 7.

351 Ф.И. Кожевников [F.I. Kozhevnikov], 'Вопросы международного права в свете новых трудов И.В. Сталина [Issues Regarding International Law in the Light of the Latest Works of I.V. Stalin]' (1951) 6 Советское Государство и Право [Soviet State and Law] 25, 30.

352 Г.И. Тункин [G.I. Tunkin], *Теория международного права [Theory of International Law]* (Международные отношения [International Relations] 1970) 25.

353 For a detailed analysis see Schweisfurth (n 337) 438–443.

354 For a concise description of the development see Nußberger, 'Russia' (n 218) paras 110–119.

355 ibid para 120.

to the socialist principle of "brotherly assistance." In 1968 he declared in the UN General Assembly that "socialist countries have their own vital interests, their own obligations [...] and their own socialist principles of mutual relations based on brotherly assistance."[356]

With regards to IHL, however, the fragmentation of international law turned out to have little practical impact. Firstly, a large-scale war between socialist States never occurred. Hence, the deletion of IHL from socialist international law never became relevant.[357] Secondly, with regards to socialist-bourgeois relations, the Soviets continued business as usual. In practice, they developed and used universal international law without modifications, despite the vivid theoretic debate that socialist international law could take precedence.[358] When Jiří Toman published his PhD *L'Union Soviétique et le droit des conflits armés* in 1981 he still saw the need to start off with a lengthy disclaimer explaining the concept of socialist international law. However, he concluded that it does not "change the reality of the facts" that the USSR stuck to universal international law in socialist-bourgeois relations.[359] Thus, IHL was spared. The hot revolutionary rhetoric cooled off in practice. As Angelika Nußberger puts it:

"The main characteristic of the socialist doctrine of international law was its ideological underpinning, although, after a comparatively short truly revolutionary period many questions continued to be solved in a rather pragmatic way."[360]

---

356 UN General Assembly Resolution, UN Doc A/PV 1679 (3 October 1968) 7.

357 Of course, the USSR intervened in the GDR, Hungary, and the ČSSR. IHL, however, was of limited relevance in these cases, since the actual problem revolved around the issue of sovereignty. For the IHL-related issues of these invasions see pp 128 et seq.

358 see Toman (n 350) 10.

359 ibid 7–10. The PhD thesis is among the few works written on this topic and I will repeatedly refer to Toman's findings. Toman argues that the official Soviet doctrine refused to recognise that the USSR applied universal international law in socialist-bourgeois relations, because this would have limited the influence of socialist international law in this sphere. In practice, however, the Soviets did apply universal international law in socialist-bourgeois relations.

360 Nußberger, 'Russia' (n 218) para 110.

2.2 Political justifications – renaissance of the just war theory?

> *"By 'defensive' war Socialists always meant a 'just' war in this sense. [...]*
> *For example, if tomorrow, Morocco were to declare war on France, India*
> *on England, Persia or China on Russia, and so forth, those would be 'just',*
> *'defensive' wars, irrespective of who attacked first; and every Socialist would*
> *sympathize with the victory of the oppressed, dependent, unequal States*
> *against the oppressing, slaveowning, predatory 'great' powers."*[361]

Lenin on war, 1915

Lenin wrote these lines during the First World War. According to him all wars against the "oppressor" were just.[362] And Marxism defined who was an oppressor and who was not. Thus, Lenin revived a theory long believed dead. A theory that may be called the sworn enemy of IHL: the idea of a "just war."[363]

In Roman times the idea of a *bellum iustum* allowed the Empire to resort to all necessary means once the cause of war was considered just.[364] A just war meant doing the will of the gods and could not be waged unjustly. With an increasing secularisation of law and the recognition that war can be perceived as just on both sides the importance of a strong

---

361 Vladimir Ilich Lenin, *Collected Works*, vol 21 (Progress Publishers Reprint 2011) 300. The original full quote in Russian reads: "Социалисты всегда понимали под 'оборонительной' войной 'справедливую' в этом смысле войну (В. Либкнехт однажды так и выразился). Только в этом смысле социалисты признавали и признают сейчас законность, прогрессивность, справедливость 'защиты отечества' или 'оборонительной' войны. Например, если бы завтра Марокко объявило войну Франции, Индия – Англии, Персия или Китай – России и т. п., это были бы 'справедливые', 'оборонительные' войны, независимо от того, кто первый напал, и всякий социалист сочувствовал бы победе угнетаемых, зависимых, неполноправных государств против угнетательских, рабовладельческих, грабительских 'великих' держав."

362 See e.g. Tomson (n 346) 19–22; Boris Meissner, *Sowjetunion und HLKO – Hektographierte Veröffentlichungen der Forschungsstelle für Völkerrecht und ausländisches öffentliches Recht der Universität Hamburg* (1950) 28–29.

363 For a detailed analysis of the Soviet just war doctrine see Johannes Socher, 'Lenin, (Just) Wars of National Liberation, and the Soviet Doctrine on the Use of Force' (2017) 19 Journal of the History of International Law 219.

364 Arthur Nussbaum, *A Concise History of the Law of Nations* (Macmillan 1947) 9 et seq.

and independent *ius in bello* grew.[365] In the Westphalian system, the right to wage war became an expression of State sovereignty.[366] At the same time, this made *ius in bello* indispensable.[367] If everyone has the right to wage war, certain rules must regulate the conduct of belligerents. In other words: "It is perfectly possible for a just war to be fought unjustly and for an unjust war to be fought in strict accordance with the rules."[368] This separation of *ius ad bellum* and *ius in bello* remains a fundamental principle of international law up to this day.

Just war theories, however, display a tendency of mixing the fields *ius ad bellum* and *ius in bello*. This often represents the first step towards a complete abrogation of IHL. "When fighting the bad guys everything should be allowed!" Even today, politicians and lawyers yield to the temptation of justifying IHL violations for a good cause. We find this sledgehammer approach in the words of Pavel Leptev the Russian representative at the Council of Europe reacting to the *Kononov* judgement of the European Court of Human Rights (ECtHR):[369] Leptev deemed it legal to strip the aggressor (in this case the Nazis and their supporters) of their protection under IHL.[370] We also find it in the concept of "unlawful combatants" that the Bush administration devised in the aftermath of 9/11. It deprived "terrorist" fighters of IHL protection by creating a third category between civilians and combatants.[371] As is well known, this concept led straight to the isolation cells of Guantanamo. Finally, we can find the approach in Donald Trump's bold statement that the Geneva Conventions are "the

---

365 Theodor Meron, 'Common Rights of Mankind in Gentili, Grotius and Suarez' in Theodor Meron (ed), *War Crimes Law Comes of Age: Essays* (Oxford University Press 1998) 122.

366 Sassòli, Bouvier and Quintin (n 72) 114.

367 Robert D Sloane, 'The Cost of Conflation: Preserving the Dualism of Jus Ad Bellum and Jus in Bello in the Contemporary Law of War' (2009) 34 Yale Journal of International Law 47, 59.

368 Michael Walzer, *Just and Unjust Wars*, vol 158 (Basic Books 2003) 21.

369 ECtHR, *Kononov v Latvia*, No 36376/04, 17 May 2010.

370 'Павел Лаптев: срок жизни Европейского суда может быть сокращен [Pavel Laptev: The Days of the European Court May Be Numbered]' (Kommersant, 31 May 2010) <https://www.kommersant.ru/doc/1378599>.

371 ICRC Casebook, How Does Law Protect in War, 'Unlawful Combatants' <https://casebook.icrc.org/glossary/unlawful-combatants>.

problem" when fighting the Islamic State, because "we can't waterboard, but they can chop off heads."[372]

IHL's very basis, however, remains reciprocity which presupposes that both belligerents are equal, no matter what they fight for. It is this spirit that permeates the treaties, and it is understood that reciprocity offers the best chance for the effective implementation of IHL. At times, this means "fighting with one hand tied behind [your] back", even if you are convinced to fight for the right cause.[373]

If many States continue to conflate *ius in bello* and *ius ad bellum*, why was there a special danger of undermining IHL in the Soviet Union? Simply, because Lenin's just war theory had the potential to become the official State doctrine, and thus leading to an abrogation of IHL as a whole. Indeed, the just war doctrine was not confined to Lenin's short rule 1917–1924, but was taken up by subsequent leaders, especially by Khrushchev and Brezhnev with regards to national liberation movements.[374] Did this render the laws of war superfluous?

According to some authors this could well have been the fate of IHL. Evgeny Korovin suggested that there were two different legal regimes in IHL – one for the aggressor and one for the aggressed State. Even if the aggressor were to respect IHL, the conduct could not be seen as legal, for the aggressor's aims were illegitimate. Killing an enemy combatant would not be justified by military necessity but constitute murder.[375] It is needless to say that, according to Lenin, the Soviet Union could *never* be the aggressor, when fighting against an "oppressing, slave-owning, bourgeois State."[376]

In the long run, however, this is not the development that we have seen. Let us interrogate Korovin's argument that IHL does not protect the aggressor. Other Soviet authors were not as quick to ring the death knell of

---

372 Ben Schreckinger, 'Trump Calls Geneva Conventions the Problem' (Politico, 3 March 2016) <https://www.politico.com/blogs/2016-gop-primary-live-updates-and-results/2016/03/donald-trump-geneva-conventions-221394>.

373 In allusion to the dictum of Aharon Barak, former President of the Israeli Supreme Court, who used this wonderful metaphor in HCJ 5100/94, *The Public Committee Against Torture v The Government of Israel*, 6 September 1999, para 39 and in the famous "targeted killing judgment" HCJ 769/02, *The Public Committee against Torture in Israel et al v The Government of Israel et al*, 13 December 2006, para 64.

374 Socher (n 363) 228–229.

375 Е.А. Коровин [E.A. Korovin], 'Международное право на современном этапе [International Law at a Current Stage]' (1961) 7 Международная жизнь [International Life] 2.

376 See again Lenin (n 361) 300.

IHL. In their 1976 textbook, Poltorak and Savinskiy rejected this reasoning because it would end any effective implementation of IHL.[377] The official Soviet Doctrine also rejected Korovin's approach.[378] Even Korovin himself was not completely consistent. In his 1944 textbook, he had claimed that the Soviet Union was bound by the Hague Regulations, albeit with certain reservations. He argued that the Soviet Union can and *must* apply IHL in order to minimise the suffering of workers in war.[379]

Remarkably, the Soviet Union even tried to reconcile its just war theory with existing IHL by granting "national liberation wars" a special status. At the International Conference drafting the Additional Protocols of 1977, the Soviet Union managed to insert Art 1(4) AP I.[380] The provision qualified *internal* "armed conflicts in which peoples are fighting against colonial domination, and alien occupation and against racist régimes in the exercise of their right of self-determination" as *international* armed conflicts. The rationale behind this was that international armed conflicts attracted more political attention and fighters and civilians enjoyed better protection: freedom fighters were now considered lawful combatants and enjoyed POW status when captured. Soviet scholars had long argued along these lines.[381]

Once again things were not as revolutionary as they seemed at first glance. Occasionally, scholars like Korovin argued in favour of a complete abrogation of IHL. Lenin's just war doctrine could have supported such an approach. In the end, however, none of this happened. The Soviet Union continued to regard IHL as a valuable field of law that continued to apply between socialist and bourgeois States. It even managed to embed their

---

377 А.И. Полторак [A.I. Poltorak] and Л.И. Савинский [L.I. Savinskiy], *Вооружённые конфликты и международное право [Armed Conflicts and International Law]* (Наука 1976) 81 et seq.

378 Toman (n 350) 20.

379 Е.А. Коровин [E.A. Korovin], *Краткий курс международного права – часть II [Brief Course on International Law – Part II]* (Военно-юридическая академия РККА [Military-legal Academy of the Red Army] 1944) 10 et seq.

380 Toman (n 350) 74; for a detailed account of this very contentious issue at the Conference see Giovanni Mantilla, 'The Origins and Evolution of the 1949 Geneva Conventions and the 1977 Additional Protocols' in Matthew Evangelista and Nina Tannenwald (eds), *Do the Geneva Conventions Matter?* (Oxford University Press 2017) 57–58.

381 А.И. Полторак [A.I. Poltorak] and Л.И. Савинский [L.I. Savinskiy] (n 377) 150 et seq, especially at 160–161; see also Г.И. Тункин [G.I. Tunkin], *Вопросы теории международного права [Questions Regarding the Theory of International Law]* (Gosyurisdat 1962) 47; Л.А. Моджорян [L.A. Modzhoryan], *Субъекты международного права [Subjects of International Law]* (Gosyurisdat 1958) 14.

"just war" concept in the existing framework of IHL. Instead of abrogating IHL as a whole the Soviets chose to develop it in their interest.

Yet, this brings us to our third issue: we have established that IHL applies *in principle*. But what treaties were binding on the Soviet Union? Let's not forget that when the USSR was founded many IHL treaties were already advanced in age. The Soviet Union, however, had just been born. Was it born free, or "into the chains" of the IHL treaties?

2.3 The Soviet Union and the Russian Empire – continuity or reset button?

What *was* the Soviet Union? This question plunges us deep into one of the most obscure fields of international law: State succession. The term describes the process by which one State replaces another with regards to its rights and the responsibilities.[382] What sounds easy at first, is murky water for international lawyers. State practice is scarce, it lacks uniformity, and it is heavily influenced by political considerations given that examples of State succession often occur in a conflict-ridden environment.[383] In a nutshell, succession regulates the entirety of obligations and rights that are passed on from one State to another. The details, however, are very controversial. Are all debts passed on? Even so-called "odious debts" that were imposed by illegitimate rulers in contradiction to State interest?[384] Does the successor inherit the membership status in international organisations? If a State disintegrates completely, which of the new sub-States becomes the "heir" to the previous State? Contentious examples include the breakup of Yugoslavia in the 1990s and the succession of the Ottoman Empire.

Amidst all this legal mist, it comes as no surprise that there is no easy answer to the following question: was the Soviet Union the legal successor

---

382 Art 2(1)(b) Vienna Convention on Succession of States in Respect of Treaties (23 August 1978).

383 Andreas Zimmermann, 'State Succession in Treaties', *Max Planck Encyclopedia of Public International Law* (Oxford University Press 2015).

384 Robert Howse, 'The Concept of Odious Debts in Public International Law (UNCTAD/OSG/DP/2007/4)' (United Nations Conference on Trade and Development 2007) which on page 11 also details the Soviet attitude towards Tsarist debts.

of the Russian Empire? Things were far from obvious.[385] But before we wade out into the murky waters of legal theory, I would like to quickly run the reader through the turbulent events in Russia from 1917 to 1922. On 15 March 1917, the February Revolution toppled Tsar Nicolas II. A provisional government was established, but it never managed to restore order. Finally, the Bolsheviks took over in the October Revolution and founded the Russian Soviet Federative Socialist Republic (RSFSR) in November 1917. On 20 December 1922, the RSFSR joined up with the Ukrainian, Belorussian, and Transcaucasian Soviet Republics to form the Union of Soviet Socialist Republics (USSR) – the Soviet Union was born.[386] This leaves us with the following picture:

15 March 1917
End of **Imperial Russia**
after February
Revolution

7 November 1917
Foundation of **RSFSR**
after October
Revolution

March - November 2017
Russian Provisional
Government

30 December 1922
Creation of Soviet Union by the
Russian, Ukrainian, Belorussian,
and Transcaucasian Soviet
Republics

When the Bolsheviks came to power in 1917, they broke with the imperial heritage. In his 'Decree on Courts No 1' Lenin ordered the dissolution

---

385 For a Russian perspective on the issue see e.g. Исаев М.А. [Isaev M.A.], *История Российского государства и права: Учебник [The History of the Russian State and Law: A Textbook]* (Statut 2012) chapter X, § 3; Г.М. Вельяминов. [G.M. Velyaminov], *Международное право: опыты [International Law: Essays]* (Statut 2015). Isaev writes that the chaotic 20th century was bound to lead to confusion with regards to the issue of State succession. He discusses the question of succession in detail under the subheading "Российская Федерация – продолжатель СССР и правопреемник Российской империи" [The Russian Federation – Continuator State of the USSR and Successor of the Russian Empire] (*nota bene*: e-book does not contain page numbers).

386 For a detailed account of events see Stephen Anthony Smith, 'The Revolutions of 1917–1918' in Ronald Grigor Suny (ed), *The Cambridge History of Russia*, vol 3 (Cambridge University Press 2006); Alan Ball, 'Building a New State and Society: 1921–1928' in Ronald Grigor Suny (ed), *The Cambridge History of Russia*, vol 3 (Cambridge University Press 2006); Donald J Raleigh, 'The Russian Civil War, 1917–1922' in Ronald Grigor Suny (ed), *The Cambridge History of Russia*, vol 3 (Cambridge University Press 2006).

of all Tsarist courts.[387] They annulled all debts.[388] The Bolsheviks deemed that the proletariat had no nation and certainly no affiliation with the Russian Empire.[389] Art 1(2) of the RSFSR Constitution adopted in 1918 reads like a fresh start: "The Russian Soviet Republic is established on the basis of the *voluntary union* of *free nations* as a federation of Soviet National Republics."[390] Despite this revolutionary rhetoric the RSFSR remained the legal successor of its Imperial ancestor.[391] Russia as a subject of international law did not cease to exist. Most Imperial treaties with non-Western countries stayed in force.[392]

Things changed more radically in 1922, when the Soviet Union was founded by the RSFSR and three other Soviet States – the Ukrainian, Belorussian, and Transcaucasian Republic. They did so to found a new subject of international law that did not exist before.[393] After an initial

---

387 Декрет 'О суде' [Decree 'On the Court'] 22 November 1917 (5 December 1917); available at <http://law.edu.ru/norm/norm.asp?normID=1119194>.

388 Декрет 'Об аннулировании государственных займов' [Decree 'On the Annulment of State Loans'] 21 January 1918 (3 February 1918) declares: "Все государственные займы, заключенные правительствами российских помещиков и российской буржуазии [...] аннулируются (уничтожаются) с декабря 1917 г." [All governmental loans that were taken out by the governments made up of Russian landowners and the Bourgeoisie are annulled effective as of December 1917.]; available at <http://www.hist.msu.ru/ER/Etext/DEKR ET/borrow.htm>.

389 Исаев М.А. [Isaev M.A.] (n 385) chapter X, § 3. Isaev argues that the Bolsheviks initially claimed that the proletariat had no fatherland and could thus not be confined to a State. Hence, they rejected all Imperial obligations.

390 Конституция (Основой Закон) РСФСР [Constitution (Fundamental Law) of the RSFSR], 10 July 1918. Art 1(2) reads: "Российская Советская Республика учреждается на основе свободного *союза свободных* наций как федерация Советских национальных республик" (emphasis added). Full text available at <http://www.hist.msu.ru/ER/Etext/cnst1918.htm>.

391 Nußberger, 'Russia' (n 218) para 78.

392 Г.М. Вельяминов. [G.M. Velyaminov] (n 385) 247–248. The author argues that border treaties with Turkey, Iran, Afghanistan, and Japan stayed in force.

393 The treaty text emphasises that the USSR represents a new union of three independent States, see Договор об образовании СССР [Treaty on the Creation of the USSR] 30 December 1922. The first paragraph reads: "Российская Социалистическая Федеративная Советская Республика (РСФСР), Украинская Социалистическая Советская Республика (УССР), Белорусская Социалистическая Советская Республика (БССР) и Закавказская Социалистическая Федеративная Советская Республика (ЗСФСР – Грузия, Азербайджан и Армения) заключают настоящий Союзный договор об объединении в одно союзное государство – Союз Советских Социалистических Республик – на следующих основаниях." [The RSFSR,

reluctance, the major European nations gradually started to recognise this new union. Germany and Poland did so in 1923, France in 1924.[394] Finally, in 1933, even the US established diplomatic relations.[395] Delicate questions such as the fate of the Tsarist debts were resolved bilaterally.[396] The Soviet Union had stressed from the beginning that it was not the legal successor of the Russian Empire. Notable jurists like Evgeny Korovin and Evgeny Pashukanis argued that the question of succession into the treaties signed by the Tsar could not be answered – as usual – collectively, but had to be solved on a case-by-case basis.[397] The statement of the USSR to the *Institut Intermédiare International* on 2 April 1924 illustrates this well:

"La rupture extraordinairement prolongée des relations politiques avec tous les Etats du monde, qui suivit la révolution de 1917, et les changements survenus entre le temps dans tout l'ensemble des engagements internationaux, ne permettraient certainement pas une reconstitution pure et simple de l'ensemble de traités des anciens gouvernements russes. Peu d'entre eux pourraient, en effet, être mis en exécution sans qu'il s'en suivit une collision avec le règlement ultérieur des mêmes questions qui survint après 1917 sans la participation de l'une des parties engagées dans ces traités. (...) C'est donc une question à résoudre dans chaque cas séparé. (...) Une abrogation générale de tous les traités de tous les traités conclus par la Russie sous l'ancien régime et sous le gouvernement provisoire n'eut jamais eu lieu. Mais il ne s'ensuit pas que tous les traités soient susceptibles d'être reconfirmés, et

---

USSR (Ukrainian Socialist Soviet Republic), and ZSFSR (Transcaucasian Socialist Federal Soviet Republic) conclude the following union treaty about the unification into one single, united State – the Union of Soviet Socialist Republics – on the following grounds].

394 Germany had previously entered into relations with the RSFSR by concluding the treaty of Rapallo (16 April 1922). English text available at <https://avalon.la w.yale.edu/20th_century/rapallo_001.asp>.

395 US Department of State, Office of the Historian, 'Recognition of the Soviet Union' <https://history.state.gov/milestones/1921-1936/ussr>.

396 Исаев M.A. [Isaev M.A.] (n 385) chapter X, § 3. Isaev explains that the issue was gradually resolved bilaterally. In 1922 the Bolsheviks signed the Treaty of Rapallo with Germany which annulled all Russian debts with regards to Germany. In 1924 the Soviet Union signed a treaty with Great Britain on the same issue. Certain aspects, however, were not regulated until very late in history. Only in 1996, for example, Russia concluded a treaty with France on its remaining Tsarist debts.

397 As quoted in Meissner (n 362) 7.

> *il y aurait lieu d'examiner cette question du point de vue de la clause 'rebus sic stantibus' pour chaque Etat et chaque traité séparément.*"[398]

According to this reasoning, the Soviet Union *did* start with a clean slate.[399] The idea of universal succession with regards to all obligations – "*une reconstitution pure et simple de l'ensemble de traités des anciens gouvernements russes*"– was rejected outright. However, the Soviets did not slam the door of succession completely. Whenever they wished, they could confirm a treaty: "*[...] examiner cette question [...] pour chaque Etat et chaque traité séparément.*" This "cherry-picking approach" was to decide the fate of the IHL treaties signed in St Petersburg, The Hague, and Geneva. The Soviet Union could confirm them on a case-by-case basis. It should be noted that confirming a treaty did not necessarily mean signing it, as will be explained below. Confirmation could also be the expression of approval through a competent organ, e.g. the Council of People's Commissars.[400]

Initially, the USSR only decided to confirm some less important IHL treaties, such as the Hague Convention for the adaptation of the principles of the Geneva Convention to maritime warfare[401] or the Hague Convention on hospital ships.[402] It did not, however, confirm the two major treaties: The Hague Convention IV of 1907, which contained a comprehensive code on land warfare (Hague Regulations) and the Geneva Convention in its updated 1906 version.[403] Maybe the Soviets were reluctant to sign due to their general scepticism towards international law that I have outlined above or perhaps they simply did not see the need to sign in the interwar period. Whatever the reason, at the eve of the Second World War, it was still unclear whether the Soviet Union was bound by the two most important IHL treaties.

Today, most argue that these treaties did in fact bind the Soviets. Scholars arrive at this conclusion in two ways. First, by resorting to customary international law. If treaty rules have crystallised into custom, it does not matter whether a State has signed the treaty itself. Customary law

---

398 Bulletin de l'Institut Intermédiaire International, Vol XI (1925) 155.

399 If we leave aside the issue of customary international law, see below at n 404.

400 For a discussion which Soviet organ had the authority to confirm a treaty see Meissner (n 362) 13; Tomson (n 346) 197.

401 George Ginsburgs, 'Laws of War and War Crimes on the Russian Front during World War II: The Soviet View' (1960) 11 Soviet Studies 253, 254.

402 Confirmed through a decree of the Sovnarkom (16 June 1925).

403 The Soviets did not sign the 1929 Geneva Convention. For an accession through verbal "approval" see below at n 417.

binds all States – new or old.[404] Boris Meissner, one of the leading experts in this field, argues that the Soviets had a concept – albeit a strange one[405] – of international customary law and that the Hague Regulations would have fallen under it.[406] Even high-ranking Soviet officials stressed that Hague Conventions represent universally recognised rules that were binding on all nations irrespective whether they had signed them or not.[407] The same would be true for the Geneva Convention, which was by then also customary law.

The second line of argument claims that the Soviet Union was in fact bound by IHL treaties themselves, because they had verbally "confirmed" them. Does accession not presuppose written ratification? Generally, the answer would be yes, as stated in Art 30 of the 1906 Geneva Convention and in Art 7 Hague Convention IV 1907.[408] It seems, however, that the USSR did not deem the act of ratification necessary to accede to treaties signed by Imperial Russia. This is in line with their "cherry-picking" approach mentioned above. A statement by Foreign Minister Vyacheslav Molotov on 25 November 1941 – i.e. shortly after Germany attacked Russia – illustrates this well. He declared that the Soviet Union does not intend to use reprisals against German POWS, because it remains faithful to the obligations "which the Soviet Union *assumed* under the Hague Conventions of 1907."[409] Scholars like Boris Meissner and Edgar Tomson

---

404 With the exception of persistent objectors, see Tullio Treves, 'Customary International Law', *Max Planck Encyclopedia of Public International Law* (Oxford University Press 2015).

405 According to Western scholars custom and treaty law are on the same level, while the Soviets gave absolute precedence to treaty law, see Meissner (n 362) 18.

406 ibid 6, 17–18.

407 Ginsburgs (n 401) 255.

408 It is worth noting that the Hague Convention IV (1907) foresees adherence without formal ratification, see Art 6. "Non-Signatory Powers may adhere to the present Convention. The Power which desires to adhere notifies in writing its intention to the Netherland Government, forwarding to it the act of adhesion, which shall be deposited in the archives of the said Government. This Government shall at once transmit to all the other Powers a duly certified copy of the notification as well as of the act of adhesion, mentioning the date on which it received the notification." The Soviet Union, however, did not follow this procedure.

409 Vyacheslav Molotov, *Soviet Government Statements on Nazi Atrocities* (Hutchinson 1946) 50 (emphasis added); see also Meissner (n 362) 6.

argue that this could be seen as a formal recognition of the Regulations.[410] This finds support in subsequent statements by Soviet leaders.[411] With regards to the Geneva Convention, we can turn to a decree signed by Lenin himself declaring that the Soviets vowed to honour the obligations under the Geneva Conventions.[412] In a similar manner the Soviet government also recognised the Geneva Convention of 1906 in 1925.[413]

So, why did the Soviet Union not formally ratify the treaties? With regards to the treaties "inherited" from Imperial times, the Soviet Union may have been too isolated or focussed on interior reforms to do so.[414] At the same time, this attitude also reflects an experimental approach to international law as a whole. The Bolsheviks argued that the proletariat was not confined to a State.[415] Treaties express the will of the ruling class – which in the case of the Soviet Union is the people in its entirety.[416] If the people have already consented, why bother with ratification? Take the following example of the updated 1929 Geneva Convention. When it was negotiated, the Soviet Union already existed as a subject of international law. Hence, we are not dealing with a problem of State succession, but accession to a treaty that should follow the usual rules. The 1929 Convention foresees ratification as the only means of accession in Art 92, which means: ratify to be in, or stay out. The USSR refused to ratify. However, in 1931 the Soviet Foreign Minister Maxim Litvinov issued the following decree:

---

410 Meissner (n 362) 13; Tomson (n 346) 197. Tomson points out that Foreign Minister Molotov was not necessarily the competent organ for such recognition. Meissner, however, describes this counterargument as *"formaljuristisch"* [formalistic]. In the same vein, Tomson argues that high-ranking persons generally had the authority to confirm or assume obligations in the name of the Soviet Union. Personally, I think that subsequent practice has shown that Foreign Ministers are generally authorised to conclude (or recognise) a treaty. Art 7(2)(a) VCLT, for example, explicitly mentions Foreign Ministers.

411 When Molotov accused the Germans of committing war crimes, he explicitly referred to the Hague Regulations. This argument only makes sense, if the Soviet Union regarded itself as bound, see Ginsburgs (n 401) 257–258.

412 Durand (n 38) 81.

413 Meissner (n 362) 11.

414 Исаев М.А. [Isaev M.A.] (n 385) chapter X, § 3, penultimate para.

415 ibid chapter X, § 3. See also n 389.

416 Toman (n 350) 7.

"The People's Commissar for foreign Affairs of the USSR declares that the USSR accedes to the [Geneva] Convention [...] the accession is final and does not require further ratification."[417]

This verbal "accession" was reaffirmed on various occasions, for example in a note by the People's Commissariat for foreign affairs to the German Foreign Office on 9 August 1941:

"The Soviet Government will respect in the course of the War [...] the Geneva Convention of 27 July 1929 [...]." They stressed however, that they *regarded themselves bound only "insofar as Germany herself respects [the rules].*"[418]

To conclude, Soviet practice was novel and improvised. The underlying question of who succeeded the Russian Empire remains a subject of debate even today.[419] For the narrow purpose of IHL, however, things are clearer. Russian law professor Igor Isaev argues that the IHL treaties – unlike treaties of a "political" nature – were undoubtedly confirmed.[420] It seems fair to agree with George Ginsburgs, who argues that the USSR was bound in *some way* by IHL, even if it is hard to understand why they did

---

417 ЦГАОР СССР [State Archive of the USSR] fond 9501, opis 5, ed khran 7 list dela 22. The full decree reads: "Нижеподписавшийся народный комиссар по иностранным делам Союза Советских Социалистических Республик настоящим объявляет, что Союз Советских Социалистических Республик присоединяется к конвенции об улучшении участи военнопленных, раненых и больных в действующих армиях, заключенной в Женеве 27 июля 1929г. В удостоверение чего народный комиссар по иностранным делам Союза Советских Социалистических Республик должным образом уполномоченный для этой цели подписал настоящую декларацию о присоединении. Согласно постановлению Центрального исполнительного комитета Союза Советских Социалистических Республик от 12 мая 1930 года настоящее присоединение является окончательным и не нуждается в дальнейшей ратификации."

418 Diplomatic note from USSR to the German Foreign Office transmitted through the Protecting Power Bulgaria (9 August 1941) cited in Durand (n 38) 437.

419 See e.g. a letter from the Russian Ministry of Interior (6 April 2006) No 3/5862, para 1(e). It answers a question posed by the Member of the State Duma A. N. Saveleva about State succession. The letter arrives at the cautious conclusion that "one can claim that the Russian Federation really is the successor State of the Russian Empire in a strictly legal sense. However, this legal fact warrants further explanation [...]." Available at <https://ru.wikisource.org/wiki/%D0%9F%D0%B8%D1%81%D1%8C%D0%BC%D0%BE_%D0%9C%D0%92%D0%94_%D0%A0%D0%BE%D1%81%D1%81%D0%B8%D0%B8_%D0%BE%D1%82_6.04.2006_%E2%84%96_3/5862>.

420 Исаев М.А. [Isaev M.A.] (n 385) chapter X, § 3.

not simply follow the usual process of ratification.[421] Sadly, the peculiar practice of verbal confirmation created a certain degree of uncertainty.[422] This circumstance was later exploited by Nazi jurists, who argued that IHL did not apply to the Soviet Union.[423] In reality, however, judging by the comments of Foreign Minister Molotov and the People's Commissariat, there can be no doubt than the Soviets regarded the essential rules of IHL as binding.

2.4 Conclusion – IHL through a Soviet lens

The Soviet mindset permeated all parts of society including international legal scholarship and doctrine. The peculiarities above show that the Bolsheviks wanted to break with old traditions. This also included breaking with the high value that the Imperial Russia attached to the law of war. IHL suffered numerous blows. It ceased to be Russia's "favourite child." Furthermore, the strange policy of verbally confirming treaties created a degree of uncertainty, hampering IHL implementation during World War II. The emergence of socialist international law created a rivalling regime of rules, and Lenin's renaissance of the just war concept could have eradicated IHL completely.

However, IHL was able to recover from these attacks. The early Soviet years were also a laboratory for new ideas. Many radical concepts turned out to be more moderate in practice. In the end the Soviets made it clear that they accepted the major IHL treaties as binding norms. As we shall see below, they would even ratify the updated version of the Geneva Conventions 1949, thus ending any discussion about their *de jure* applicability to the USSR. Furthermore, the argument that a just socialist war prevailed over IHL never became the mainstream narrative in the Soviet Union. Rather, the Soviets managed to insert their ideas into the framework of

---

421 Ginsburgs (n 401) 257.

422 Some authors, for example, still argue that the Soviet Union was not "formally" bound by the Geneva Convention, because it has never ratified the treaty. See e.g. Catherine Rey-Schyrr, *From Yalta to Dien Bien Phu – History of the International Committee of the Red Cross, 1945 to 1955* (ICRC 2007) 209; Durand (n 38) 448.

423 The Nazis argued that IHL did not protect Soviet POWs because the USSR had not ratified the treaties. Bearing in mind the above arguments, this was overly formalistic and also completely disregarded the question of customary international law, see for this Ginsburgs (n 401) 254.

IHL. Finally, socialist international law turned out to have little effect on the relations between bourgeois and socialist States.

Nevertheless, IHL had lost one of its major advocates. For decades Russia had been the spokesman of humanity in war. Now, the USSR was a country like many others in this respect. As we proceed to the major events of the 20th century, we shall see that the Soviet IHL record is a mixed bag with both high and low points. And we shall start with rock bottom – the Second World War.

3. *The Second World War on the eastern front – obliteration of IHL*

> *"La guerre n'est donc point une relation d'homme à homme, mais une relation d'Etat à Etat, dans laquelle les particuliers ne sont ennemis qu'accidentellement, non point comme hommes, ni même comme citoyens mais comme soldats."*[424]
>
> Jean-Jacques Rousseau on war, 1782

> *"Войну с фашистской Германией нельзя считать войной обычной. Она является не только войной между двумя армиями. Она является вместе с тем великой войной всего советского народа против немецко-фашистских войск."*[425]
>
> *[The war between fascist Germany cannot be considered an ordinary war. It is not only a war between two armies. It is a great war of the entire Soviet people against the Germano-fascist troops.]*
>
> Stalin, speech after the beginning of the German invasion, 3 July 1941

> *"Die Frage ist also nicht die, ob die Methoden, die wir anwenden, gut oder schlecht sind, sondern ob sie zum Erfolge führen. [...] Ich frage euch: Wollt ihr den totalen Krieg? Wollt ihr ihn, wenn nötig, totaler und radikaler, als wir ihn uns heute überhaupt noch vorstellen können?"*[426]

---

424 Jean-Jacques Rousseau, *Collection complète des œuvres*, vol 1 (1782) 198.

425 Stalin's speech (3 July 1941) is available in the English translation at <https://www.jewishvirtuallibrary.org/stalin-speaks-to-the-people-of-the-soviet-union-on-german-invasion-july-1941>.

426 Joseph Goebbels' speech at the Sportpalast (18 February 1943) is available in the English translation at <https://research.calvin.edu/german-propaganda-archive/goeb36.htm>.

> *[The question is not, whether the methods that we apply are good or bad, but whether they help us to succeed. [...] I ask you: Do you want total war? Do you want a war, if necessary, more total and radical than we could even imagine today?]*
>
> Joseph Goebbels, speech at the Sportpalast, 18 February 1943

The development of IHL is closely related to Jean Jacques Rousseau's idea that war is *"une relation d'Etat à Etat."* The two quotes by Stalin and Goebbels, however, make painfully clear why the rules of IHL were doomed to fail in the Second World War, at least on the eastern front. In Stalin's words this was no "ordinary" war between armies, but a war between two peoples. A war in which according to Goebbels the ends could justify all means. The Nazis considered the Slavs sub-humans and propagated a total war. Both sides threw Rousseau's civilising idea overboard that war was not an affair between individuals or peoples. This ideological thrust had a huge impact on IHL observance on the eastern front. Violations occurred on a massive scale – both against combatants and civilians.

As noted above, most of the victims of the First World War fell in line with IHL: they were combatants that died in battle. This fact may serve to draw a comparison to the Second World War. Especially on the eastern front (1941–1945), the victims were mainly civilians or soldiers *hors de combat*. The US historian Timothy Snyder speaks of the "Bloodlands" referring to the area between Berlin and Moscow that today comprises Poland, Belarus, the Baltic States, Ukraine and Western Russia. This region was the site of the most gruesome killings in the 20th century. Snyder estimates that Hitler and Stalin murdered fourteen million people in this area. *Not a single one* of them was killed in combat.[427] Many of the victims were Jewish. Over six million were gassed, shot, or perished in concentration camps. However, it is less well known that Soviet POWs also made up a large share of the victims. 5.7 million Red Army soldiers fell into German captivity. Two thirds of them – more than three million – were executed, beaten to death, or starved in the miserable conditions of the German camps.[428]

---

[427] Timothy Snyder, *Bloodlands: Europe between Hitler and Stalin* (Vintage Books 2011) viii.

[428] Christian Streit, *Keine Kameraden: Die Wehrmacht und die sowjetischen Kriegsgefangenen 1941–1945* (Dietz 1991) 130–131; Snyder (n 427) x.

3.1 IHL violations by Nazi Germany on the eastern front

Were most of these heinous crimes not committed by the Nazis? The systematic extermination of the Jews? The calculated starvation of Soviet POWs, sometimes called "one of the greatest crimes of the Second World War and surpassed only by the murder of the Jews?"[429] Was it not Hitler that had a *"Hunger-Plan"* that foresaw the death by starvation of tens of thousands of Slavs and Jews in the winter of 1941–1942?[430]

Indeed, the Nazis seem to have acquired a darker record during World War II. However, we have to consider that the Soviet Union had committed a large share of its killing *before* the war even started. Stalin set out to modernise the Soviet Union by force, which included the collectivisation of farming land as foreseen in his first Five Year Plan. He eliminated whomever stood in his way – or was suspected of standing in his way. First, he targeted prosperous peasants, so-called *Kulaks*, who allegedly resisted collectivisation.[431] Nearly two million were deported to Siberia.[432] When farmers in Ukraine and elsewhere still failed to meet grain quotas, the Soviets ruthlessly confiscated their remaining grain and livestock. The result was the *Holodomor*, an artificial famine that killed around 3.3 million in Soviet Ukraine.[433] Later, during the "Great Terror", Stalin liquidated hundreds of thousands of his own citizens in paranoia.[434] Those who

---

429 Bob Moore, 'Prisoners of War' in Evan Mawdsley and John Ferris (eds), *The Cambridge History of the Second World War – Fighting the War*, vol 1 (Cambridge University Press 2015) 681.

430 Snyder (n 427) xiv.

431 Stalin believed that the rich *Kulaks* formed a homogenous group that posed a serious threat to the Soviet Union, see David R Shearer, 'Stalinism, 1928–1940' in Ronald Grigor Suny (ed), *The Cambridge History of Russia*, vol 3 (Cambridge University Press 2006) 194–195; Snyder, however, shows that this was an illusion: "The attempt to 'liquidate the kulaks' during the first Five-Year Plan had killed a tremendous number of people, but it created rather than destroyed a class: those who had been stigmatized and repressed, but who had survived. The millions of people who were deported or who fled during collectivization were forever after regarded as kulaks, and sometimes accepted the classification." Snyder (n 427) 79.

432 Shearer (n 431) 195–196.

433 The exact number of deaths is still disputed. Official Soviet records speak of 2.4 million, while a demographic calculation carried out on behalf of the authorities of independent Ukraine suggests 3.9 million, Snyder (n 427) 53; Shearer even mentions 5 million casualties, but he refers to the whole of Ukraine, North Caucasus, and central Russia, Shearer (n 431) 196.

434 Shearer (n 431) 212–216; Snyder (n 427) 49 et seq.

were not executed were sentenced in sham trials and left to rot in Siberian Gulags. Minorities were systematically deported. Forcible resettlement of Poles, Germans, Fins, Koreans and later Chechens and Crimean Tatars started as early as 1932 and continued throughout Stalin's rule.[435] Overall, the death toll of Stalinism was immense. It was, however, not a concern of IHL, because the indiscriminate killing concerned Stalin's *own* people and happened in peacetime.

The Germans, in turn, committed most of their crimes in war or during belligerent occupation. Of course, the Nazis started to persecute the Jews, other minorities, and political opponents in Germany from the day Hitler came into power in 1933. Yet, in terms of sheer numbers this despicable internal persecution was dwarfed by Stalin's purges.[436] The scale of Nazi crimes, however, exploded abruptly on 1 September 1939, when the Wehrmacht invaded Poland. Soldiers that surrendered were stripped of their uniform, branded as partisans, and shot on the spot. First aid stations treating wounded combatants were targeted.[437] Bloodshed completely escalated after 22 June 1941, when the Nazis attacked the USSR. The POWs who were not shot upon their capture were deliberately starved to death or died from hard labour.[438] In total, Hitler's ruthless policy killed more than three million Soviet POWs making them the second largest group of victims during World War II, only to be surpassed by the Holocaust.[439] The high death toll was not due to negligence or mismanagement; it was cold-blooded murder. This becomes clear when we compare it with the fate of POWs on the western front. As many Soviet POWs died on a *single* day in autumn 1941 as did British and American POWs during the entire war.[440] Torture and summary executions were not only widely practiced, but explicitly ordered. Hitler's *Kommissarbefehl* [Order regarding Commissars] prescribed in dehumanising language that all Soviet political commissars – formally part of the Red Army and thus entitled to POW

---

435 Shearer (n 431) 202. Stalin deported the entire Chechen and Crimean Tatar people during the Second World War fearing that they might side with the Nazis.

436 Snyder (n 427) x.

437 ibid 121.

438 For a detailed account see Moore (n 429) 674 et seq.

439 ibid 681; Snyder (n 427). Exact numbers are controversial: Moore speaks of 2.5 million, Snyder of more than 3 million deaths.

440 Snyder (n 427) 182.

status – should be separated and liquidated: *"Sie sind nach durchgeführter Absonderung zu erledigen."*[441]

The Nazis were equally merciless towards civilians. In occupied[442] Poland Hitler's secret police showed for the first time what it was truly capable of: *Einsatzgruppen* hunted down and killed Jews, Polish intellectuals, and other groups.[443] They would later continue their murderous work in the occupied parts of the USSR. Needless to say, many of these acts constituted flagrant violations of IHL, which by now foresaw detailed rights for POWs, wounded soldiers, and civilians in occupied territory. The International Military Tribunal at Nuremberg would later state that the Nazis committed barbaric acts on a "vast scale, never before seen in the history of war."[444]

3.2 IHL violations by the Soviet Union on the eastern front

Even if the record of the Nazis was far worse during the war, we should not ascribe this to a humane streak in the Soviets. While Hitler's racial ideology pushed the Germans eastwards, Stalin simply saw the urgent need to purge his State from the inside. Furthermore, Soviet war crimes *did* happen on a large scale. Addressing this question remains a taboo in Russia up until today. The victory against fascist Germany became the unifying myth of Soviet and post-Soviet society.[445] Thus, mentioning, let alone condemning Soviet war crimes means humanising the Nazis and risks belittling the 25 million people the Soviet Union lost in defeating fascism.[446] In

---

441 Befehl vom 6 Juni 1941 WFST/Abt L (IV/Qu) Nr 44822/41, available at <https://www.ns-archiv.de/krieg/1941/kommissarbefehl.php>.

442 Poland could be legally considered occupied even though parts of the country (e.g. Wartheland and Danzig-Westpreußen) were officially incorporated into the German Reich according to German domestic law. The International Military Tribunal, however, explicitly rejected the defence that the regime of occupation ceased to apply after these territories were "incorporated", see S Paul A Joosten (ed), *Trial of the Major War Criminals before the International Military Tribunal*, vol 22 (IMT 1948) 497.

443 Snyder (n 427) 126.

444 Joosten (n 442) 469.

445 David R Stone, 'Operations on the Eastern Front 1941–1945' in Evan Mawdsley and John Ferris (eds), *The Cambridge History of the Second World War – Fighting the War*, vol 1 (Cambridge University Press 2015) 356–357.

446 25 million is only a rough estimate. The exact number remains unclear, since most of the fatalities went unreported. Hence, scholars are forced to estimate

2017, for example, the Russian schoolboy Nikolay Desyatnichenko was hit by a wave of indignation from the Russian media when he spoke in the German *Bundestag* and equated the fate of German POWs in Siberia to the hardships of Soviet internees in German camps.[447]

Desyatnichenko was right. Only half of the around 3.2 million Germans that fell into captivity returned after the war. The incredible number of 1.3 million is still missing.[448]The high death toll suggests flagrant disregard for the Hague Convention. While with POWs, much of the discussion revolves around the question of whether such a high death rate was intentional or due to mismanagement,[449] there are instances where Soviet IHL violations were clearly intended. The most obvious example is the massacre of Katyn, where 20 000 Polish officers were executed between April and May 1940.[450] The mass killing represented a war crime against protected POWs, because the Polish officers were protected under the

---

the total number of deaths by comparing it to normal peacetime mortality. In any case, the Soviet death toll was huge. In comparison, the United States suffered 400 000 war deaths, Britain 350 000, see John Barber and Mark Harrison, 'Patriotic War, 1941–1945' in Ronald Grigor Suny (ed), *The Cambridge History of Russia*, vol 3 (Cambridge University Press 2006) 225; see also Michael Ellman and Sergei Maksudov, 'Soviet Deaths in the Great Patriotic War: A Note' (1994) 46 Europe-Asia Studies 671.

447 'Russian School Director Reprimanded for Student's Anti-War Speech in Germany' (The Moscow Times, 12 December 2017) <https://www.themoscowtimes.com/2017/12/12/russian-school-director-reprimanded-for-students-anti-war-speech-in-germany-a59911>; 'Russian boy's WW2 speech to German MPs stirs web anger' (BBC, 21 November 2017) <https://www.bbc.com/news/world-europe-42066335>.

448 Moore (n 429) 681; for a more detailed examination of the fate of German POWs see Klaus-Dieter Müller, Konstantin Nikischkin and Günther Wagenlehner, *Die Tragödie der Gefangenschaft in Deutschland und in der Sowjetunion 1941–1956* (Bohlau Verlag 1998).

449 Legally, the issue of intent only makes a difference with regards to the *mens rea* of a potential war crime. The unintentional starvation of POWs would still constitute a violation of the Hague Regulations, since they set out objective criteria and do not formulate a subjective requirement.

450 For a detailed historical account see Wojciech Materski, *Katyn: A Crime Without Punishment* (Anna Cienciala and Natalia Lebedeva eds, Yale University Press 2007); Gerhard Kaiser, *Katyn: das Staatsverbrechen, das Staatsgeheimnis* (Aufbau Taschenbuch 2002); Franz Kadell, *Katyn: das zweifache Trauma der Polen* (Herbig 2011); Victor Zaslavsky, *Klassensäuberung: Das Massaker von Katyn* (Rita Seuß tr, 2nd edn, Wagenbach 2008).

Hague Convention.[451] Nevertheless, they were separated from the other internees, handed over to the NKVD,[452] and shot on the direct order of Stalin.[453]

The massacre represented such an obvious and flagrant violation of IHL that the Soviets made a substantive effort to cover it up. The situation became especially awkward, when Germany invaded the Soviet Union in summer 1941 and the Polish government in exile suddenly became a Soviet ally. They, too, noticed that their entire officer corps was missing.[454] As the Nazis advanced eastwards they discovered the Soviet mass graves and hastily shot a propaganda film to show how barbaric their enemy truly was.[455] The Soviets, in turn, tried to blame the massacre on the Nazis. At the International Military Tribunal at Nuremberg, Roman Rudenko, the chief prosecutor for the USSR, accused the Nazis of the very crime that his own State had committed. When the Soviets could not produce sufficient evidence to convince the Western allies, every mention of Katyn was deleted from the final verdict.[456] Nevertheless, it left a bitter aftertaste that at Nuremberg the murderers became judges of their own crime.[457]

This is but one tragic episode where Soviet disregard for IHL came at the cost of human lives. There were many others: the deportation of civilians that had fled Nazi-occupied Poland to the part occupied by the USSR;[458] the sacking of cities like Mukden (modern Shenyang, China),

---

451 More specifically, it constituted a violation of Art 4(1) HR. The Regulations applied ever since the eastern part of Poland had been invaded by Soviet Union following the Molotov-Ribbentrop Pact. For the question, whether the Soviet Union was bound by the Hague Regulations see above at pp 94 et seq. The violation of Art 4(1) HR also constituted a war crime at the time as Art 6(b) of the 1945 IMT Statute points out ("murder or ill-treatment of prisoners of war").

452 The *Народный комиссариат внутренних дел* [People's Commissariat for Internal Affairs] was the Interior Ministry of the Soviet Union.

453 Kaiser (n 450) 49 et seq. The official orders are reprinted on pp 252 et seq. Many controversial legal questions remain, e.g. whether Katyn represented an act of genocide or whether the insufficient investigations by the Russian Federation violated the ECHR. It is, however, generally accepted that the killings at Katyn violated IHL.

454 Snyder (n 427) 151.

455 The film is available at <https://www.youtube.com/watch?v=U_02PrLPYaE>.

456 Kaiser (n 450) 228–229.

457 Of course, the IMT as a whole represented a milestone in legal history – also in terms of IHL. It established an effective accountability mechanism for IHL violations. See below at pp 115 et seq.

458 Snyder (n 427) 126.

that sparked orgies of rape, murder, and pillaging;[459] the widespread rape of millions of women and children as the Red Army advanced onto Berlin;[460] the havoc that Soviet partisan groups wreaked in the Baltic States.[461] This list could go on and on, but for the purpose of this thesis there is little value in establishing every detail of the gruesome crimes both the Nazis and the Soviets committed during the Second World War. This important task is better left to historians. Already by now it is clear that not only did Hitler and Stalin violate IHL, they did so deliberately, systematically, and on a scale never seen before or after.[462] It is safe to say that on the eastern front, IHL was helpless, worthless, and superfluous.

The absurd culmination of this ideological war was that neither Hitler nor Stalin wanted their *own* troops to be protected under IHL, because it could make surrender a tempting option. For example, the initiative of the ICRC to give out typhus shots to their own soldiers was boycotted from both the German and the Soviet side for this very reason. They had essentially written off their troops as soon as they were captured.[463] Stalin issued his famous order No 270 as early as 16 August 1941, only two months into the war. It stigmatised the soldiers who fell into German captivity as traitors and imposed penalties on their families. In 1942, Stalin's order No 227 proclaimed a "not one step back" policy and sent out special units to

---

459 Francis Clifford Jones, *Manchuria since 1931* (Royal Institute of International Affairs 1949) 224–225.

460 Miriam Gebhardt, *Als die Soldaten kamen: Die Vergewaltigung deutscher Frauen am Ende des Zweiten Weltkriegs* (DVA 2015). The author claims, however, that contrary to popular belief rape was a common phenomenon not only in the Soviet sector. Both in the French and in the US sector rape occurred on a comparable scale (data from the British sector is not available).

461 See e.g. Rain Liivoja, 'Competing Histories: Soviet War Crimes in the Baltic States' in Kevin Jon Heller and Gerry J Simpson (eds), *The Hidden Histories of War Crimes Trials* (First edition, Oxford University Press 2013) 260. Especially the case of *Kononov*, a Soviet partisan commander in 1944, became known to a wider public when the defendants appealed to the European Court of Human Rights. The facts of the case go back to an incident in 1944, when Soviet partisans entered a Latvian village, shot a number of civilians, and burned down several farmhouses thereby killing the people remaining inside. See ECtHR, *Kononov v Latvia*, No 36376/04, 17 May 2010.

462 Generally speaking, the Soviet Union could not justify its violations as reprisals for the atrocities committed by the Nazis. While reprisals against civilians were still lawful at that time, it is hard to argue that the above mentioned violations acted as an enforcement measure aimed at ending this unlawful behaviour. For the concept of reprisals, see n 293.

463 Moore (n 429) 675.

shoot retreating officers.[464] In such a war IHL – whose implementation at that time essentially depended on reciprocity and the good will of the parties – was doomed to fail. It was simply crushed amidst the onslaught. The ICRC was equally powerless, since from the outset of the war the USSR refused to cooperate with the Swiss-based organisation, and from 1943 onwards even boycotted it completely.[465] After a golden age in the 19th century, the development of IHL had hit rock bottom.

4. The Soviets at Nuremberg – third wheel or driving force?

After night comes day. While half of Europe lay in ruins, the year of 1945 ended with what can be considered one of the greatest steps ahead in IHL implementation: the International Military Tribunals (IMT) of Nuremberg[466] and Tokyo.[467] Already after World War I, Russia had pushed to prosecute German war criminals. A special commission of inquiry concluded that German soldiers had violated IHL and that they should be punished for it.[468] This approach was reflected in the Treaty of Versailles, which foresaw an international tribunal for German Emperor Wilhelm

---

464 Barber and Harrison (n 446) 231.
465 Fayet (n 318) 65, 69; Durand (n 38) 450; even after the war ended the ICRC had very limited access to the POWs that remained in the USSR, see Rey-Schyrr (n 422) 121; things were better in the other theatres of the war. For a detailed account of the ICRC's efforts to mitigate suffering during and after the Second World War see Durand (n 38) 336 et seq; Rey-Schyrr (n 422) 113 et seq.
466 On the importance of the IMT at Nuremberg see Antonio Cassese and Paola Gaeta, *Cassese's International Criminal Law* (3rd edn, Oxford University Press 2013) 257–258; Matthew Lippman, 'Nuremberg: Forty Five Years Later' (1991) 7 Conneticut Journal of International Law 1, 37 et seq.
467 For reasons of continuity, I will focus on the Nuremberg Tribunal rather than on the Tokyo Tribunal, because the former addresses the crimes committed by the Nazis on the eastern front that I have discussed above; also history's verdict of the Tokyo Tribunal was less favourable, see Kirsten Sellars, 'Imperfect Justice at Nuremberg and Tokyo' (2010) 21 European Journal of International Law 1085, 1093; for more details on the Tokyo Tribunal see Neil Boister and Robert Cryer, *The Tokyo International Military Tribunal: A Reappraisal* (Oxford University Press 2008); for more information how the Tribunal was received in Japan see Philipp Osten, *Der Tokioter Kriegsverbrecherprozeß und die japanische Rechtswissenschaft* (BWV 2003).
468 Toman (n 350) 644–645.

II as well as the right to try German soldiers before military tribunals.[469] However, the outcome was rather bleak. The provisions of the Treaty of Versailles remained largely a dead letter.[470]

4.1 Run-up to Nuremberg – trial or execution?

This time the stakes were even higher. The Nazi atrocities were too egregious to go unpunished. The prevailing opinion was that those who were responsible should be made to pay, but the world's leaders disagreed on what exactly that entailed. Initially, Britain and the US favoured a swift execution of the Nazi leaders without trial.[471] Stalin, too, had expressed a desire for executing not only the German high command, but also 50 000 officers.[472] In the end, this option was discarded, although Britain only changed its approach very late, in April 1945.[473] The second possibility was an international tribunal that would try the leading figures – military and civilian – of the Third Reich.

Considerable preparatory work had been done during the war, especially by the Soviets. Eminent Soviet jurists such as Aron Traynin wrote a book on the *Hitlerite Responsibility under Criminal Law* (1944).[474] His work was translated into English, German, French, and received great attention worldwide. It contributed significantly to the development of international legal doctrine.[475] In his work, Traynin called for a criminal prosecution

---

469 Treaty of Peace between the Allied and Associated Forces and Germany (28 June 1919) Art 227–230.

470 Cassese and Gaeta (n 466) 64. See also Claus Kreß, 'The Peacemaking Process After the Great War and the Origins of International Criminal Law Stricto Sensu' (2021) 62 German Yearbook of International Law 163.

471 Bradley F Smith, *The Road to Nuremberg* (Basic Books 1981) 46–47.

472 At the Conference of Teheran, Stalin allegedly proposed a swift liquidation of 50 000 German officers and the entire German higher command through summary executions. The other Allies opposed this radical project, see Toman (n 350) 649–650.

473 Lippman (n 466) 20–21.

474 Aron Traynin, *Hitlerite Responsibility under Criminal Law,* (Hutchinson & Co, Ltd 1945); The original Russian edition was called А.Н. Трайнин [A.N. Traynin], *Уголовное ответственность гитлеровцев [The Criminal Responsibility of the Hitlerites]* (Юридическое Издательство НКЮ СССР [Legal Publishing House NKYu USSR] 1944).

475 Francine Hirsch, 'The Soviets at Nuremberg: International Law, Propaganda, and the Making of the Postwar Order' (2008) 113 The American Historical Review 701, 705–708.

of Nazi leaders *inter alia* for war crimes.[476] Furthermore, high-ranking Soviet officials, such as Foreign Minister Molotov, had denounced German war crimes throughout the war and left no doubt that the Nazis leaders were responsible for them.[477] His call for justice was heeded. At the Conference of St James, 13 January 1942, the Allies recognised criminal justice as one of their main war aims.[478] Molotov made clear that the Soviet Union wanted to place the Nazi leaders before an international tribunal and try lesser war criminals before national courts.[479] In theory, the Allies agreed with this approach, but they wanted to wait until the end of the war.[480]

The Soviets, however, did not wish to sit idle until the war was over. As early as April 1943, they issued a decree that allowed for the prosecution of war criminals before national courts.[481] In July 1943 the first trial was held in Krasnodar District.[482] Even though the defendants were all Soviet citi-

---

476 Besides the obvious charge of war crimes, Traynin also advocated to prosecute the Nazis for crimes against peace, see А.Н. Трайнин [A.N. Traynin] (n 474) 41.

477 Ginsburgs (n 401) 257–258 who cites a declaration by Foreign Minister Molotov. Molotov spoke of violations of the Hague Conventions of 1907 by the Nazis, particularly of Art 7 Hague Regulations which were "recognized both by the Soviet Union and Germany." He also accused the German authorities of mass executions of prisoners of war, of the use of captive Red Army-men for military work in violation of the Hague principles, of looting their personal belongings, of torturing them and systematically starving them to death. Already at this point, the Soviet leadership made clear that it laid "all the responsibility for these inhuman actions of the German military and civil authorities on the criminal Hitlerite Government."

478 ibid 260–261.

479 ibid 261–262.

480 At the conference of Moscow in autumn 1943 the Allies agreed to postpone such trials to the moment of an "armistice to any government which may be set up in Germany." Thus, the trials were only envisaged after the end of the war. The Moscow Declaration is available at <http://avalon.law.yale.edu/wwii/mosco w.asp>.

481 Ginsburgs (n 401) 263; the decree was never officially published, but is mentioned in А.Н. Трайнин [A.N. Traynin] (n 474) 90. Furthermore, on page 87 Traynin cites a decree (11 May 1943) by Molotov which stresses that German "private individuals carry the responsibility for the immeasurable hardship and suffering of Soviet citizens caused by them."

482 Судебный процесс по делу о зверствах немецко-фашистских захватчиков и их пособников на территории города Краснодара и Краснодарского края в период их временной оккупации [Proceedings concerning the cruelties of the German-fascist invaders and their helpers on the territory of the city of Krasnodar and the Krasnodar District in the period of the temporary occupation], available at <https://www.e-reading.club/chapter.php/1019465/82/Sbornik

zens and stood trial for treason and not for war crimes, the Soviets showed the world that they took the issue delivering justice for Nazi crimes very seriously. The Krasnodar trials also made clear that the Soviets would not content themselves with collaborators and small fish, but intended to go after the German superiors who had given the orders.[483] The first Germans were tried in Kremenchug and Kharkov as early as December 1943.[484] This time, the accused were convicted for war crimes and sentenced to death by hanging.[485]In the beginning, the trial was publicly hailed as a monumental step towards criminal justice. A propaganda movie was produced.[486] Later in the war the Soviets stopped mentioning the incident, probably for the fear of inciting German reprisals against their POWs.[487] Trials resumed shortly after the German capitulation with tribunals in Kyiv, Minsk, Riga, Leningrad (modern St Petersburg), Smolensk, Bryansk, Velikiye Luki, and Nikolayev.[488] The atmosphere of the trials was of course ideologically charged and the proceedings did not to correspond to current standards of criminal procedure. Nevertheless, they were not mere sham trials, but conducted in accordance with existing Soviet legal norms of the period.[489]

_materialov_Chrezvychaynoy_Gosudarstvennoy_Komissii_po_ustanovleniyu_i_
rassledovaniyu_zlodeyaniy_nemecko-fashistskih_zahvatchikov_i_ih_soobschnik
ov.html>.

483 Ginsburgs (n 401) 265.

484 Судебный процесс по делу о зверствах немецкого-фашистских захвачиков на территории города Харькова и Харьковской края в период их временной оккупации [Proceedings concerning the cruelties of the German-fascist invaders on the territory of the city of Kharkov and the Kharkov District in the period of the temporary occupation], available at <https://www.e-reading.club/chapter.php/1019465/83/Sbornik_materialov_Chrezvychaynoy_Gosudarstvennoy_Komissii_po_ustanovleniyu_i_rassledovaniyu_zlodeyaniy_nemecko-fashistskih_zahvatchikov_i_ih_soobschnikov.html>.

485 Ginsburgs (n 401) 267.

486 The film was entitled 'Суд идёт' ['The Court is in session'] and is available at <https://www.youtube.com/watch?v=XZRE1CrByOo>.

487 Ginsburgs (n 401) 270.

488 ibid; see also Alexander Victor Prusin, '"Fascist Criminals to the Gallows!": The Holocaust and Soviet War Crimes Trials, December 1945–February 1946' (2003) 17 Holocaust and Genocide Studies 1; Tanja Penter, 'Local Collaborators on Trial. Soviet War Crimes Trials under Stalin (1943–1953)' (2008) 49 Cahiers du monde russe 341.

489 Prusin (n 488) 1.

4.2 The work of the Nuremberg Tribunal

The IMT represented the first joint effort of the Allies to render justice. The Tribunal took up its work in November 1945 and delivered its judgements in October 1946. Three defendants were acquitted,[490] seven sentenced to prison terms ranging from ten years to life,[491] and twelve were sentenced to death by hanging.[492] The count of war crimes made up the backbone of the charges. Today – at least in Western literature[493] – the trials are often remembered as an "Anglo-American tale of liberal triumph" while the role of the Soviet Union is often downplayed as "regrettable but unavoidable."[494] This account falls short of the truth. Admittedly, the Soviets had enormous problems matching the American PR machine. They never managed to control the flow of information or shape international public opinion.[495] In substantial terms, however, the Soviets contributed a lot to the success of the Nuremberg trials.

First of all, the USSR had supported the idea of prosecuting the leaders while States like Britain were still opposed to it. This allowed the "Big Four" to find common ground and create the political momentum to

---

490 Hans Fritzsche, Hjalmar Schacht, and Franz von Papen were acquitted, see Lippman (n 466) 27.

491 Rudolf Hess, Walther Funk, and Erich Raeder were sentenced to life in prison. Albert Speer and Baldur von Schirach were sentenced to 20 years, Konstantin von Neurath to 15 years, and Karl Dönitz to 10 years, see ibid.

492 Herrmann Göring, Martin Bormann, Hans Frank, Wilhelm Frick, Alfred Jodl, Ernst Kaltenbrunner, Wilhelm Keitel, Joachim von Ribbentrop, Alfred Rosenberg, Fritz Sauckel, Arthur Seyss-Inquart, and Julius Streicher were sentenced to death by hanging, see ibid.

493 The current Russian narrative is quite different. It praises the role of the USSR and insists that criminal prosecution was only possible, because the Soviets insisted on it, see Mälksoo, *Russian Approaches to International Law* (n 6) 139.

494 For this see Hirsch (n 475) 701. Hirsch herself challenges this view and argues that the Soviets made significant contributions to the IMT at Nuremberg, see also her recently published book Soviet Judgment at Nuremberg: A New History of the International Military Tribunal after World War II (Oxford University Press 2020).

495 ibid 722–726. While the Soviets sent many journalists, cartoonists, writers, and filmmakers to Nuremberg they failed to seize the opportunity to shape public opinion. A senior official complained that Soviet personnel left a bad impression, that the Soviet interpreters were incompetent and the "clothing of our female personnel is so bad and looks so poor that the Americans and English make fun of them." The Russian documentary on Nuremberg called 'Суд народов' ['Tribunal of the Peoples'] and it is available at <https://www.you tube.com/watch?v=vShbwjnqG94>.

tackle such a historic task.[496] Secondly, the work of their scholars such as Traynin – who also worked as an adviser to the Soviet prosecution at Nuremberg – greatly influenced the legal work of the tribunal.[497] Finally, we should not forget that the Soviets could also draw on their own experience of war crime trials during the war. These foundations were a valuable test run for Nuremberg and parts of the Soviet practice was later picked up by the criminal provisions of the Geneva Conventions of 1949.[498]

Critics often denigrate the IMT as victor's justice.[499] This is not entirely wrong, since no Allied leader had to answer for his crimes at Nuremberg. This misbalance became painfully apparent, when the Soviets accused the Nazis of organizing the Katyn massacre which they had committed themselves.[500] The tendency to overlook their own wrongdoings was, however, not a Soviet phenomenon. In this respect the Soviets were no worse than their Western Allies. The latter simply managed to keep the delicate questions, such as the obliteration of Hiroshima and Nagasaki or the carpet bombing of German cities, out of the courtroom. The Soviets, again, failed at this PR campaign.[501]

---

496 ibid 730.

497 ibid 708, 727.

498 See Ginsburgs (n 401) 280. He writes that it "should be noted, in closing, that in many respects Soviet views expressed during World War II subsequently found general acceptance and were embodied in the Geneva Conventions of 1949. In addition, the Soviet attitude with regard to the applicability of the 1949 Geneva rules to war criminals is more consonant with the precedents established in the post-war trials of war criminals than the revised stipulations finally inserted into the Conventions themselves. In some instances, therefore, Soviet views have clearly exceeded the bounds of generally recognized international law, in some others they seem to be a more correct interpretation of norms developed during World War II than the versions presently expounded by some non-Communist Governments and jurists, and, finally, in a third category of cases the formerly novel Soviet contentions have since found international recognition."

499 See e.g. Sellars (n 467) 1089–1090; Herbert Wechsler, 'The Issues of the Nuremberg Trial' in Guénaël Mettraux (ed), *Perspectives on the Nuremberg Trial* (Oxford University Press 2008) 319; Telford Taylor, *Nuremberg and Vietnam: An American Tragedy* (Bantam Books 1971) 82; Bernard D Meltzer, 'Note on Some Aspects of the Nuremberg Debate, A' (1946) 14 University of Chicago Law Review 455, 469.

500 See above at n 450.

501 Hirsch (n 475) 717–719, 725. There even existed a "gentlemen's agreement" between the Soviets and the Western allies to keep certain questions, such as the Molotov-Ribbentrop pact and "Soviet-Polish" relations, out of the courtroom. In the end, this could not prevent these issues from surfacing.

Despite this justified criticism, Nuremberg is widely recognised as a crucial turning point in international law.[502] When IHL's traditional implementation mechanisms – reciprocity and *bona fide* – broke down, the international community created another: effective criminal prosecution of military and civilian individuals. If we accept that Nuremberg was a giant leap ahead, we must also accept that the Soviets contributed to it. It is not easy to resist the Cold-War-reflex of downplaying their role as the "Achilles' heel" of the trials.[503] Yet, Soviet legal theory and practice has shaped international criminal law in many respects.[504] The fault of Nuremberg and Tokyo was rather, that all efforts of international criminal justice were discontinued during the Cold War. Only in 1993 did the world witness the sequel to Nuremberg, when the UN Security Council established the International Criminal Tribunal for the Former Yugoslavia (ICTY) in Resolution 827.[505] The spectacular eruption of international criminal justice in 1945 catapulted IHL into the 20th century – only to remain dormant for over 40 years.[506]

5. The Geneva Conventions of 1949 – the Soviet Union as "scum of the earth" or "great humanitarian?"[507]

The gruesome events during the Second World War made it very clear that the Geneva Conventions had to be updated. The civilian population

---

502 Cassese and Gaeta (n 466) 64.

503 Quote from Christopher J Dodd, *Letters from Nuremberg: My Father's Narrative of a Quest for Justice* (Three Rivers Press 2008) 341.

504 Ginsburgs (n 401) 280.

505 UN Security Council Resolution 827, UN Doc S/RES/827 (25 May 1993): "The Security Council [...] decides hereby to establish an international tribunal for the sole purpose of prosecuting persons responsible for serious violations of international humanitarian law committed in the territory of the former Yugoslavia between 1 January 1991 and a date to be determined by the Security Council upon the restoration of peace and to this end to adopt the Statute of the International Tribunal annexed to the above-mentioned report."

506 Admittedly, the prosecution of Nazi criminals did not end in Nuremberg. Under the 'Control Council Law No 10' many more Nazis criminals were prosecuted in Germany before domestic courts. However, it would take more than 45 years for another international court to rule on war crimes.

507 "Scum of the earth" is an allusion to the famous caricature by David Low published in the Evening Standard on 20 September 1939 after the partition of Poland, available at <https://archive.cartoons.ac.uk/record.aspx?src=CalmV iew.Catalog&id=LSE2692>. The expression "great humanitarian" is borrowed

especially needed more effective protection. Previous attempts of the ICRC to enhance civilian protection in the inter-war period had failed. For example, the 15th Conference of the Red Cross (1934) produced the so-called Tokyo Draft which could have become the first comprehensive convention protecting civilians. However, by the time States agreed to discuss the proposal, it was too late: war had already broken out in Europe.[508]

5.1 A Soviet boycott

After the end of the Second World War, most States saw the need for an enhanced IHL Convention. However, they had to overcome a monumental stumbling stone: The Soviets categorically refused to participate and boycotted the preparatory Conference of Government Experts and all preliminary meetings that worked on the so-called Stockholm Draft.[509] The latter was to serve as a basis for discussion at the Diplomatic Conference scheduled for 1949.[510]

The Soviets were sceptical for two reasons: first of all, they were unhappy to see fascist States, such as Spain, at the negotiating table.[511] Secondly – and more importantly – the Soviets refused to engage with the ICRC after the Second World War. The difficult relationship dates back to the days of the October Revolution. The Bolsheviks mistrusted the Swiss-led Committee. While the ICRC and Soviet Russia still cooperated in the early 1920s amidst a bloody civil war and the ongoing repatriation of POWs,[512]

---

from the very insightful article by the historian Boyd van Dijk, '"The Great Humanitarian": The Soviet Union, the International Committee of the Red Cross, and the Geneva Conventions of 1949' (2019) 37 Law and History Review 209.

508 Rey-Schyrr (n 422) 210–211.
509 ibid 218.
510 van Dijk (n 507) 213.
511 ibid.
512 The reader may remember that the Bolsheviks had created their own Soviet Red Cross, while the old Imperial Red Cross was re-founded in counter-revolutionary circles in areas controlled by the "Whites" and abroad. The ICRC faced the dilemma that the recognition of one would antagonise the other. The ICRC therefore avoided the *de jure* recognition of any society, *de facto* cooperating with both. This approach, however, failed at international conferences, because the Soviet Red Cross refused to participate if representatives of the Tsarist organisation were equally invited. Hence, relations were always tense, and it is telling that the position of the ICRC delegate in Russia remained vacant

the Soviets quickly lost interest in the organisation after that. The ICRC's reputation was further damaged when Swiss-Soviet relations hit an all-time low after the assassination of the Soviet diplomat Vatslav Vorovsky in Lausanne in 1923.[513] In addition, Stalin was notoriously paranoid about anything foreign. To him the ICRC – an association under Swiss law with a directorate of "capitalist" businessmen – must have been the epitome of a bourgeois, foreign, and thus a suspicious actor.[514] The last straw that broke the camel's back, however, was the abominable condition in which Russian POWs were kept by the Nazis during the Second World War. As mentioned above, more than three million POWs perished behind German barbed wire fences. The Soviets held the ICRC responsible for failing to prevent these crimes against Red Army soldiers.[515]

States tried hard to overcome this obstacle. Several options were on the table. Some of them included internationalising the ICRC, subordinating it to another body, or completely eliminating it from the revision process of IHL. It was suggested that the future Conference could be held on neutral ground – in Prague or Paris. In the long run, this would have dramatically changed the role of the ICRC. We would probably speak of the First Prague or Paris Convention now. But in the end, the Soviets did not take the bait and rejected all *démarches*.[516]

In 1949, as the beginning of the Conference neared, prospects looked rather bleak. The Soviet Union was not just any State. It was one of the four victorious powers of the Second World War; it was a colossal country stretching from Lviv to Vladivostok; and it exerted significant

---

up to 1921, see above at pp 78 et seq. Even before the Revolution, however, relations were not always easy. Already in 1887 the Russians proposed to change the composition of the ICRC in order to make it an international instead of a Swiss-led organisation, see Bugnion (n 30) 70; for a detailed account of the relations between the ICRC and Russia see Fayet (n 318).

513 Alfred Erich Senn, 'The Soviet Union's Road to Geneva, 1924–1927' [1979] Jahrbücher für Geschichte Osteuropas 69, 69. Interestingly, Switzerland only recognised the Soviet Union after the Second World War, long after the US who did so in 1933.

514 For a detailed account of the decline of relations between Russia and the ICRC see van Dijk (n 507) 213–215.

515 Catherine Rey-Schyrr, 'Les Conventions de Genève de 1949 : une percée décisive – première partie' (1999) 833 Revue internationale de la Croix-Rouge 209, at n 59; for the ICRC's effort to improve the conditions of Soviet prisoners see Durand (n 38) 439 et seq. The ICRC made several attempts to provide assistance to Soviet prisoners of war, but the German authorities did not grant the organisation access.

516 van Dijk (n 507) 216–220.

influence on its proxies. The absence of the USSR would have completely undermined the acceptance of an updated Geneva Convention. Many diplomats believed that any revision process without Soviet participation was not even worth the effort.[517] To everyone's surprise, however, the USSR *did* confirm its participation on 15 April 1949, only days before the Conference started.[518] Finally, the Soviets were on board.

What does this interlude to the 1949 Conference tell us? On the one hand, it shows us how divided the Soviet Union was on IHL. While Tsarist Russia used to initiate conferences on the laws of war, now a landmark conference almost failed due to a potential Soviet boycott. On the other hand, the Soviets had not completely given up on IHL and finally chose to participate in the Conference. There was no apparent reason for the USSR's sudden change of heart. In the end it simply opted for a "rather-in-than-out" approach, because IHL could offer certain advantages. The Soviets saw IHL as a means of winning the global struggle for "hearts and minds."[519] Furthermore, they also welcomed the idea of imposing binding restrictions on the highly militarised West which could turn into a battlefield advantage in a future war that already loomed on the horizon.[520] In short, the Soviet Union still attached importance to this field of law. Shortly after confirming its participation in the Conference, the Soviet delegate in the International Law Commission stressed that the "laws of war should be retained as a necessary or desirable subject for codification."[521]

However, the episode also illustrates how deeply sceptical the Soviets were of all international organisations in general, and the ICRC in particular. David Forsythe, author of the comprehensive analysis of the ICRC's work over time, wrote: "the Soviets never cooperated with the ICRC in meaningful ways on humanitarian protection during the Cold War proper."[522] Indeed, this scepticism towards international interference is

---

517 ibid 222.
518 Telegram of the Swiss delegation in Moscow (15 April 1949) E2001E#1967/113#16123/BD874, SFA.
519 Mantilla (n 380) 42.
520 ibid 42–43.
521 ILC, *Yearbook of the International Law Commission 1949 – Summary Records and Documents of the First Session Including the Report of the Commission to the General Assembly* (n 278) 51.
522 David P Forsythe, *The Humanitarians: The International Committee of the Red Cross* (Cambridge University Press 2005) 53.

characteristic for this chapter and it continues to exist in modern day Russia as we shall see below.[523]

5.2 Soviet contributions to the Conference

After such a nerve-racking lead-up, it comes as no surprise that the discussions at the Conference were controversial. The Soviet Delegates did not mince their words and used the Geneva Conference as a forum to advance communism as the truly humanitarian and anti-colonialist ideology.[524] Furthermore, they wanted to embarrass States like the US and the UK by exposing their questionable behaviour during the Second World War, such as carpet bombing or the nuclear destruction of Hiroshima and Nagasaki.[525] Ironically, this meant that they supported the progressive Stockholm Draft to which they had not contributed due to their absence in previous meetings. Even more ironically, this brought the Soviet position in line with the position of the ICRC.[526]

Concerning legal substance, the Soviets contributed immensely to the protection of civilians in occupied territory. Furthermore, they pushed for an Article that would become *the* single most important provision of the Geneva Conventions: Common Article 3. In the following, I will explain the significance of these two aspects.

The reason why the USSR advocated for better protection of civilians during occupations is evident. The Soviets were still influenced by the Nazi atrocities in occupied Eastern Europe. The Stockholm Draft foresaw a convention entirely dedicated to civilian protection.[527] Even though largely forgotten today, it was thanks to the Soviets that this audacious project bore fruit.[528] Claude Pilloud, the then director of the ICRC responsible for law and policy, admitted that he "hardly dared to think what would have

---

523 For today's relationship between Russia and the ICRC see p 160. For Russia's general resistance to any external compliance mechanism see pp 153 et seq.
524 Mantilla (n 380) 42.
525 van Dijk (n 507) 227–228.
526 ibid 223, 227.
527 ICRC, 'Draft Revised or New Conventions for the Protection of War Victims [Stockholm Draft]' (Geneva 1948) 153 et seq. This would later become the Fourth Geneva Convention Relative to the Protection of Civilian Persons in Times of War (GC IV).
528 van Dijk (n 507) 229.

become of the Civilian Convention without the presence of [the Soviet] delegation."[529]

Thanks to the Soviet support the delegates finally adopted the Fourth Geneva Convention[530] which is still in force today. It explicitly prohibits rape,[531] extermination, murder, torture, mutilation, scientific experiments,[532] racial discrimination,[533] collective penalties or terrorism[534] as well as reprisals against protected civilians or their property.[535] The latter especially was crucial. The reader may remember the issue of reprisals from the discussion of the use of poisonous gas during the First World War.[536] During the Second World War the Germans tried to justify the extermination of entire villages as "reprisals" for partisan attacks.[537] Thus the explicit prohibition of reprisals against protected civilians in 1949 was a major step ahead.[538] The Soviets used their considerable voting power to push for these changes that also went against Western interests.[539] The USSR would have envisaged an even more ample protection of civilians that included limitations for the conduct of hostilities, but in this respect they did not get their way.[540] Hence, when signing the Fourth Convention, the Soviet Union declared that it did so even though "the present

---

529 Rapport Spécial Etabli par Claude Pilloud (16 September 1949) No CR-254-1, AICRC.
530 Fourth Geneva Convention of 12 August 1949 Relative to the Protection of Civilian Persons in Times of War.
531 Art 27(2) GC IV.
532 Art 32 GC IV.
533 Art 13.
534 Art 33(1).
535 Art 33(3).
536 See above at n 293.
537 See e.g. Christopher Neumaier, 'The Escalation of German Reprisal Policy in Occupied France, 1941–42' (2006) 41 Journal of Contemporary History 113.
538 Please note, however, that Art 33(3) GC IV only concerns protected persons, i.e. persons "who at a given moment and in any manner whatsoever, find themselves, in case of a conflict or occupation, in the hands of persons a Party to the conflict or Occupying Power of which they are not nationals" (see Art 4 GC IV). Reprisals against "other" civilians, such as bombing and destroying a city from the air (e.g. Dresden in 1945) could still be justified as reprisals even after the 1949 Convention. Reprisals against civilians were only outlawed completely by Art 52 No 1 AP I (1977). The Soviet Union was pushing for a complete ban of reprisals at the 1949 Conference, but it could not break the resistance of its former Western allies that had practiced "carpet bombing" throughout the Second World War, see Mantilla (n 380) 46.
539 van Dijk (n 507) 231.
540 Mantilla (n 380) 46.

Convention does not cover the civilian population in territory not occupied by the enemy and does not, therefore, completely meet humanitarian requirements."[541]

Secondly, the Soviets pushed for an even more revolutionary change in IHL by widening its scope of application. Up to 1949, IHL only applied to clashes between States, i.e. international armed conflicts (IAC). Its application required one State army facing another. The 1949 Conventions broke with this dogma. The four Conventions (GC I–IV) start with three identical Articles, the so-called Common Articles (CAs). While CA 1 outlines the obligation to respect and ensure respect, CA 2 defines the field of application in armed conflicts between two States. CA 3, however, introduced an absolute novelty: it extends the application of IHL to armed conflicts "not of an international character" (NIAC), i.e. wars between a State and an armed group (or two or more such groups).[542] It protected all persons not taking part in hostilities. This includes members of the armed forces that have laid down their arms as well as guerrilla fighters that have surrendered and ordinary civilians. CA 3 lays down certain minimum standards, such as the prohibition of torture and the obligation to care for the wounded and sick. In a way, it represents a little "condensed" convention of its own.[543]

---

541 Final Record of the Diplomatic Conference of Geneva of 1949 (Vol I) Federal Political Department, Berne, 355–356. The declaration is also available at <https://ihl-databases.icrc.org/applic/ihl/ihl.nsf/Notification.xsp?action=openDocument&documentId=48D358FE7D15CA77C1256402003F9795>.

542 For details on the distinction between IACs and NIACs and the relevance of conflict classification, see below at pp 263 et seq.

543 Due to its fundamental importance literature on CA 3 is abundant, see e.g. Jelena Pejic, 'The Protective Scope of Common Article 3: More than Meets the Eye' (2011) 93 International Review of the Red Cross 189; Andrew Clapham, Paola Gaeta and Marco Sassòli (eds), *The 1949 Geneva Conventions – A Commentary* (Oxford University Press 2015) Part I, subsection 3; Knut Dörmann and others (eds), *Commentary on the First Geneva Convention: Convention (I) for the Amelioration of the Condition of the Wounded and Sick in Armed Forces in the Field* (Cambridge University Press 2016) 351 et seq; Michael A Newton, 'Contorting Common Article 3: Reflections on the Revised ICRC Commentary' (2016) 45 Georgia Journal of International and Comparative Law 513. Of course, many legal questions regarding CA 3 were only solved long after the provision was drafted. For example, CA 3 defines a non-international armed conflict by the absence of the characteristics that would make it an IAC, which means that every armed conflict that is not international is non-international. It does, however, not provide any guidance how to distinguish a non-international armed conflict from situations of mere unrest. The definition of NIAC in use today dates back

Today, 90 percent of conflicts are non-international in character.[544] Classic wars between two State armies, such as the Falklands War and the First Gulf War have become a rare event. Despite this sharp increase in non-international armed conflicts, treaty rules regulating this type of war remain scarce. This underlines the tremendous and continuing importance of CA 3. For many States, such as the US, Syria, Iraq, Iran, and Israel, who have not ratified Additional Protocol II of 1977,[545] CA 3 remains the *only* treaty rule applicable to NIACs.

Whether the Soviets foresaw this development when they pushed for CA 3 or not, their contribution turned out to be extremely significant for modern day IHL. Initially, the US, France, Britain, and China opposed CA 3. Only smaller States such as Switzerland and Norway favoured the proposal. The unremitting support of the Soviet Union was crucial in bringing around the other big powers.[546] One cannot help but agree with the historian Boyd van Dijk:

> *"It remains ironic that the Soviets, as one of the major violators of civil rights in the twentieth century, played such a prominent role in the effort to push for greater civilian protection and rights in times of armed conflict."*[547]

---

to a decision of the ICTY in 1995. The Court ruled that a NIAC exists if there is "protracted armed violence between governmental authorities and organized armed groups or between such groups within a State." (ICTY, *The Prosecutor v Duško Tadić* (IT-94-1-T), Decision on the Defence Motion for Interlocutory Appeal on Jurisdiction, 2 October 1995, para 70).

544 The 2018 War Report identifies seven active international armed conflicts and 69 non-international armed conflicts. In addition, there are 18 scenarios of ongoing occupation, which according to CA 2(2) count as international armed conflicts, see Annyssa Bellal, 'The War Report – Armed Conflicts in 2018' (Geneva Academy of International Humanitarian Law and Human Rights 2019). For even more detailed figures on current armed conflicts see the Uppsala Conflict Data Program <https://ucdp.uu.se/>.

545 In addition, AP II has a higher threshold of application than CA 3, see Art 1 No 1 AP II. It only applies to armed conflicts "which take place in the territory of a High Contracting Party between its armed forces and dissident armed forces or other organized armed groups which, under *responsible command, exercise such control over a part of its territory as to enable them to carry out sustained and concerted military operations and to implement this Protocol*" (emphasis added).

546 Mantilla (n 380) 43–45. States opposed the proposal for different reasons. France and Britain feared unrest in their colonies, China had just emerged from a bloody civil war, and the US generally had a conservative attitude towards IHL.

547 van Dijk (n 507) 231.

At the same time, the 1949 Geneva Conference revealed a domain where the Soviets categorically refused to advance IHL. They had an almost fetishistic obsession with State sovereignty.[548] Hence, the USSR put up sharp resistance against a strong implementation mechanism for IHL. The Soviet delegates displayed little sympathy for proposals to give the ICRC a mandate to visit prisons where captured insurgents were held; they rejected a proposal to strengthen the role of the Protecting Powers;[549] they opposed the creation of a criminal court for war crimes; and they deleted a reference to better implementation in CA 3.[550] It seems that they "understood, better than most other imperial powers, that they could accept virtually any text as long as it did not infringe upon their sovereign discretion to refuse outside supervision when waging war against anti-Soviet insurgents."[551] As we shall see later this Soviet tradition lives on in today's Russia.[552]

This fierce resistance to any sort of effective oversight dealt a serious blow to IHL. As we have seen above, the Second World War called the traditional implementation mechanisms into question. The principle of reciprocity and good faith fails to work, if an ideological abyss gapes between the warring parties. If you truly hate your enemies and believe them inferior or evil, why should you respect IHL? If you don't care about the well-being of your own troops, why should you care about your enemy's soldiers? Humanitarian law was in dire need of a new, more robust implementation tool. Nuremberg was an attempt to answer this call, but the spark of the IMT was put out by the Cold War. None of the allied

---

548 Bill Bowring, *Law, Rights and Ideology in Russia: Landmarks in the Destiny of a Great Power* (Routledge 2013) 83. Bowring explains the Soviets' "rigid insistence" on sovereignty as well as the most prominent exception in favour of peoples fighting for national liberation.

549 A Protecting Power is a neutral State or a State not a party to the conflict which has been designated by a party to the conflict and accepted by the enemy party and has agreed to carry out the functions assigned to a Protecting Power under international humanitarian law. During the Second World War, Sweden and Switzerland represented many warring States in matters of IHL, see ICRC Casebook, How Does Law Protect in War, 'Protecting Powers' <https://caseboo k.icrc.org/glossary/protecting-powers>. See also below at p 157.

550 van Dijk (n 507) 233; Mantilla (n 380) 47.

551 van Dijk (n 507) 234.

552 See below at pp 153 et seq. In 2015, Russia successfully boycotted the introduction of a new implementation mechanism for the Geneva Conventions and its Additional Protocols at the 32nd International Conference of the Red Cross and the Red Crescent.

powers – neither the Soviet Union nor the US, nor the UK, nor France – wanted to see their own people in the dock. IHL's best chance for effective implementation during the Cold War and after was missed in 1949. It could have taken the form of a robust right of oversight of the ICRC or another international organisation; an effective fact-finding commission;[553] or a similar inter-State tool. Yet, the Soviets were not willing to go down this route.

The USSR signed the Convention in 1949. It ratified it in 1954[554] after the end of the Korean War that broke out in summer 1950 just months after the international delegates had left Geneva. While it declared certain reservations,[555] none of them challenged any fundamental provisions of the Convention.[556]

In conclusion, the role of the Soviet Union at the 1949 Conference remains ambiguous. On the one hand we have seen a super-power that wanted to participate in the process of shaping international law. To this end, the USSR was ready to forget its differences with the ICRC and even forged a strategic alliance with the organisation. It greatly advanced the cause of a civilian convention and it pushed to extend IHL to the realm of non-international armed conflicts. On the other hand, the Soviet Union

---

553 Such fact-finding commission (the International Humanitarian Fact-Finding Commission – IHFFC) was later established pursuant to Art 90 AP I, see below at p 157.

554 For a complete list of all ratifications see <https://ihl-databases.icrc.org/applic/ih l/ihl.nsf/States.xsp?xp_viewStates=XPages_NORMStatesParties&xp_treatySelecte d=380>.

555 Final Record of the Diplomatic Conference of Geneva of 1949 (Vol I) Federal Political Department, Berne, 355–356. The declaration is also available at <https://ihl-databases.icrc.org/applic/ihl/ihl.nsf/Notification.xsp?action=openDo cument&documentId=48D358FE7D15CA77C1256402003F9795>.

556 One of the most significant reservations was that the Soviet Union refused to extend the rights of the Third Convention (concerning POWs) to soldiers that had committed war crimes. According to the Soviet view, these soldiers should rather be subjected to the domestic law of the State, where they had committed their crimes. Hence, the USSR made a reservation to Art 85 GC III: "The Union of Soviet Socialist Republics does not consider itself bound by the obligation, which follows from Art 85, to extend the application of the Convention to prisoners of war who have been convicted under the law of the Detaining Power, in accordance with the principles of the Nuremberg trial, for war crimes and crimes against humanity, it being understood that persons convicted of such crimes must be subject to the conditions obtaining in the country in question for those who undergo their punishment." Available at <https://ihl-databases.icr c.org/applic/ihl/ihl.nsf/Notification.xsp?action=openDocument&documentId=4 8D358FE7D15CA77C1256402003F9795>.

strongly opposed any effective implementation mechanism other than reciprocity. This remains one of the major faults of IHL that continues to exist even today.[557]

In hindsight, however, it is staggering that Stalin's USSR made a significant contribution to IHL *at all*: a notoriously paranoid, cruel, and unpredictable dictator agreeing to such an ample protection of fundamental values in armed conflict at a time where tensions ran high. One should not forget the tense circumstances of the time. The Cold War had begun. During the negotiations in Geneva, the Soviets continued the Berlin Blockade, forcing the Allies to re-supply civilians in the German capital via airplanes. Shortly after the Conference, the Korean War broke out. The newly created UN Security Council found itself paralysed and the General Assembly had to resort to desperate measures adopting its "Uniting for Peace" Resolution.[558]

Despite this deepening divide between East and West, there was little evidence of such "block-mentality" at the Conference. The American delegation even occasionally voted for Soviet proposals and vice versa. In addition, the Western Europeans frequently voted against their Anglo-American allies. Van Dijk ascribes these patterns to the effective Soviet-ICRC cooperation and the initially close cooperation between Eastern and Western powers at the conference.[559] In the end, States that had little in common managed to agree on new limits of warfare. The Soviets could have thwarted the entire project. They chose to advance it instead.

---

557 Stefan Oeter, 'Civil War, Humanitarian Law and the United Nations' (1997) 1 Max Planck Yearbook of United Nations Law 195, 215. The author argues that the decline of reciprocity needs to be compensated by a strong compliance mechanism.

558 See UN General Assembly Resolution 377, UN Doc A/RES/377(V) A (3 November 1950): "The General Assembly [...] [r]esolves that if the Security Council, because of lack of unanimity of the permanent members, fails to exercise its primary responsibility for the maintenance of international peace and security in any case where there appears to be a threat to the peace, breach of the peace, or act of aggression, the General Assembly shall consider the matter immediately with a view to making appropriate recommendations to Members for collective measures, including in the case of a breach of the peace or act of aggression the use of armed force when necessary, to maintain or restore international peace and security."

559 van Dijk (n 507) 232.

6. Overt military operations during the Cold War – the denial of IHL

While the Tsarist period provided us with ample examples to study the impact of IHL on Russian military operations, such practice is scarce in Cold War era. A series of swift invasions and short-lived skirmishes aside, the Red Army only fought one overt campaign abroad: the Afghan War (1979–1989). Conflicts were increasingly delegated to proxies, e.g. in Vietnam, Korea, or various Latin American and African countries. The rare instances in which the USSR used armed force openly, however, share a common feature: the Soviets stubbornly denied the applicability of IHL.

6.1 From Berlin to Zhenbao

Between 1945 and 1979, the Red Army engaged in overt military operations abroad in only four instances: The interventions in East Germany (1953), Hungary (1956), Czechoslovakia (1968); and the Sino-Soviet Border Conflict (1969). These hostilities broke out in different countries, at different times, for different reasons. However, they all had something in common. The period of hostilities was short, the level of violence rather limited; fighting occurred between socialist States; and above all, the Soviets simply chose to ignore the applicability of IHL.

The clash with China over the disputed Damansky Island [*Zhenbao*] was mostly limited to skirmishes on the border. Nevertheless, more than 50 Soviet soldiers died in the main battle, when Chinese troops ambushed Soviet border guards in March 1969.[560] China had ratified the Geneva Conventions in 1956,[561] which meant that the situation represented an international armed conflict under CA 2(1). However, due to its brevity the application of IHL was never discussed – neither in the Soviet Union nor abroad.[562] The incident did not even make it into the ICRC's annual report.[563]

---

560 Kramer (n 330) 182.
561 For a complete list of ratifications see <https://ihl-databases.icrc.org/applic/ihl/ihl.nsf/States.xsp?xp_viewStates=XPages_NORMStatesParties&xp_treatySelected=380>.
562 Kramer (n 330) 182.
563 ICRC, 'Annual Report 1969' (1969).

Similarly, IHL was given little attention during the interventions in East Germany (1953) and Czechoslovakia (1968).[564] While these operations involved a large number of Soviet troops, casualties remained low and overall the soldiers behaved in a rather disciplined manner.[565] If the world's leaders were in shock, it was not out of concern for IHL. Both socialist and Western States heavily criticised the violation of Czechoslovakia's sovereignty.[566] The Soviets replied by invoking socialist international law and stressed that they considered the invasion as assistance against antisocialist forces.[567]

Crushing the Hungarian Revolution in 1956, however, was a somewhat different story. It was by far the bloodiest of all interventions. More than 100 000 Soviet troops participated in the operation nicknamed "Whirlwind." It killed 2 500, wounded 19 000, and displaced 200 000."[568] The images broadcast from the streets of Budapest brought to mind memories of the battle for Berlin. This time the ICRC reminded the warring parties of "fundamental principles of the Geneva Conventions by which all the peoples are bound."[569] The Red Cross delivered large amounts of medicine, blood plasma, and blankets to besieged Budapest via airplanes. The UN Security Council noted the "grave situation has been created by the use of Soviet military forces" but remained paralysed because of the Soviet Union's veto right.[570]

Mark Kramer argues that the "invasion of Hungary was notable mostly for the USSR's failure to comply with key provisions of the Geneva Conventions."[571] The General Assembly deplored in an emergency session

---

564 ICRC, 'Annual Report 1968' (1968) 44. The report briefly mentions the "events which took place in Czechoslovakia," but only to state that the "the ICRC made contact with the country's National Society to ask it whether it had any need of aid."

565 Kramer (n 330) 179–181.

566 See e.g. Gerhard Hafner, 'The Intervention in Czechoslovakia – 1968' (2019) 21 Austrian Review of International and European Law Online 27.

567 Schweisfurth (n 337) 1–12.

568 György Dalos and Elsbeth Zylla, *1956: Der Aufstand in Ungarn* (Bundeszentrale für politische Bildung 2006) 184–186. The Soviet Union lost 669 soldiers, which was the highest loss in a military operation between 1945 and 1979.

569 ICRC, 'Annual Report 1956' (1956) 5–6. The ICRC dedicated almost 20 pages to the Hungarian crisis.

570 UN Security Council Resolution 120, UN Doc S/RES/120 (4 November 1956) was adopted with 10 votes to 1. The Soviet Union voted against the resolution which convened an emergency session of the General Assembly that was held on the same day.

571 Kramer (n 330) 180.

that the "intervention of Soviet forces has resulted in grave loss of life."[572] Yet, it could do nothing to end the invasion.[573] Later the UN set up a Special Committee[574] that, *inter alia*, criticised flagrant IHL violations. It spoke of indiscriminate shooting, deliberate targeting of civilians and aid workers, and wanton destruction of private property. Furthermore, it reminded the Soviet Union that these acts amounted to violations of the Geneva Conventions.[575] The Soviets, however, adopted a strategy of absolute denial. They refused to answer to the allegations in the General Assembly and finally the matter was removed from the agenda.[576]

Things were to be solved under the radar of international humanitarian law. As I have outlined in my section on socialist international law, Moscow categorically opposed the application of IHL in a socialist-on-socialist war. Moscow wanted to avoid the impression that it was waging war against ideological brethren. This resulted in the negation of IHL. The non-application had little practical consequences in the cases of Germany, Czechoslovakia, and China. The invasion in Hungary, however, claimed numerous victims. Even if the fighting only lasted a week, IHL should have protected the civilian population and wounded combatants. The situation showed that the USSR was not willing to follow the rules to which it had recently agreed in 1949. On the contrary, Moscow chose to cast the veil of silence over IHL and completely ignored its application. It is worth bearing in mind this strategy of denial. We will encounter it again in the following section on the Afghan War and – in a more sophisticated manner – in Part II of this thesis dealing with Russia's current military practice.

---

572 UN General Assembly Resolution 1004 (ES-II), UN Doc A/RES/1004(ES-II) (4 November 1956).

573 The fighting lasted from 4–10 November 1956. For a timeline of the events see György Dalos, 238.

574 UN General Assembly Resolution 1132/XI, UN Doc A/RES/1132/XI (10 January 1957). The UN Special Committee on the Problem of Hungary consisted of five member States (Australia, Denmark, Ceylon, Tunisia, and Uruguay). It collected evidence by conducting witness hearings, following media coverage, and drawing upon official diplomatic correspondence. The material is available at <http://www.osaarchivum.org/digital-repository/osa:693f36ae-56a5-4564-89ee -0bc7b20eb414>.

575 UN General Assembly, 'Report of the Special Committee on the Problem of Hungary: General Assembly Official Records, 11th Session, Supplement No 18 (A3592)' (UN 1957) 231–232.

576 Kramer (n 330) 181.

6.2 Afghanistan 1979–1989 – the Russian Vietnam

The Cold War seemed to have frozen the enthusiasm for IHL that the Soviet Union had displayed at Geneva in 1949. This was illustrated by the proceedings at the Diplomatic Conference (1974–1977) which was tasked with adopting Additional Protocols to the Geneva Conventions. Again, Moscow strongly opposed the idea of external monitoring by the ICRC or any other organisation.[577] It suggested inserting a clause in the Protocol's preamble establishing an exception to IHL in "aggressive" wars. This plan was thwarted by the US, but it demonstrated the lurking danger of the Soviet Union's just war theory.[578] Finally, when States adopted the Protocols in 1977, the Soviets refused to sign.[579] Was this because the Soviet leaders did not see the need? Indeed, since 1945 the USSR had not been involved in a full-scale war. Apart from several proxy wars and the limited interventions described in the previous section, Moscow had no reason to draw upon IHL. This, however, was about to change in 1979.

In the Afghan War the USSR underwent a tragic transformation. The tables had turned. The Soviets had always claimed to defend the rights of the colonised peoples against their oppressors. Now, they would become colonisers themselves.[580] Moscow had long advocated the legalisation of partisan warfare.[581] Now, it would find itself entangled in a bloody confrontation with Mujahideen guerrillas.

Historically, the USSR maintained friendly relations with Afghanistan.[582] A simple glance at the map reveals the strategic importance of the country. It bordered the Soviet Republics of Turkmenistan, Uzbekistan, and Tajikistan and for a long time acted as a buffer zone between British India and the Soviet Union. In the 1970s, Afghanistan underwent a period of instability with leftist parties and Islamic movements competing for influence. In 1978, the leftist People's Democratic Party of Afghanistan (PDPA) seized power in a coup d'état. Despite the lack of popular support, the regime pushed ahead with ambitious reforms to modernise Afghan

---

577 Mantilla (n 380) 61.
578 ibid 63.
579 They acceded much later, in 1989. For a complete list of ratifications see <https://ihl-databases.icrc.org/applic/ihl/ihl.nsf/States.xsp?xp_viewStates=XPages_NOR MStatesParties&xp_treatySelected=475>.
580 See Stephen E Hanson, 'The Brezhnev Era' in Ronald Grigor Suny (ed), *The Cambridge History of Russia*, vol 3 (Cambridge University Press 2006) 312.
581 Toman (n 350) 506 et seq.
582 Hanson (n 580) 311.

society. Soon, however, the government met with fierce resistance from conservative circles in the Afghan society and increasingly lost control as the country descended into civil war.[583]

Initially, the Soviets were unwilling to send troops into Afghanistan: Aleksey Kosygin, Chairman of the Council of Ministers, turned down an invitation by the PDPA in a friendly, but determined way:

> *"The deployment of our forces in the territory of Afghanistan would immediately arouse the international community [...] One cannot deny that our troops would have to fight not only with foreign aggressors, but also with a certain number of your people. And people do not forgive such things."*[584]

In hindsight these words sound almost prophetic. The Soviet officials changed their mind as they gradually lost trust in the unpredictable PDPA leader Hafizullah Amin.[585] On Christmas Eve 1979, they decided to invade. The Soviets met with the resistance of loyal Afghan troops, but quickly overpowered them. Only three days after the beginning of the invasion, the Red Army took the palace where Amin was holding out and killed the PDPA leader. They then installed a puppet government under Babrak Karmal.[586]

The reaction of the West was swift. Jimmy Carter identified the intervention as the "most serious threat to world peace since the Second World War"[587] and annulled a number of agreements with the Soviet Union. Most Western countries boycotted the Olympic Summer Games 1980 in Moscow.[588] Most importantly, the CIA started to covertly support the Afghan mujahedeen in their fight against the Soviet occupants.[589] Instead

---

583 For a detailed account of the events leading up to the war see Odd Arne Westad, 'Prelude to Invasion: The Soviet Union and the Afghan Communists, 1978–1979' (1994) 16 The International History Review 49; William Maley, 'Afghanistan: An Historical and Geographical Appraisal' (2010) 92 International Review of the Red Cross 859, 859–865.

584 James G Hershberg, 'New Evidence on the Soviet Intervention in Afghanistan' (1996) 8 Cold War International History Bulletin 128, 147.

585 Hanson (n 580) 311.

586 W Michael Reisman and James Silk, 'Which Law Applies to the Afghan Conflict?' (1988) 82 American Journal of International Law 459, 466–474.

587 Gabriella Grasselli, *British and American Responses to the Soviet Invasion of Afghanistan* (Dartmouth Publishing Group 1996) 121.

588 Nicholas Evan Sarantakes, 'Jimmy Carter's Disastrous Olympic Boycott' (Politico, 9 February 2014) <https://www.politico.com/magazine/story/2014/02/carter-olympic-boycott-1980-103308>.

589 Bearden (n 43) 19–20.

of a quick expeditionary campaign, the Soviets were sucked into an all-out war. By 1985, 120 000 Red Army soldiers opposed 250 000 mujahedeen backed and equipped by the West. In the beginning they received rifles, later also mortars and Stinger anti-aircraft missiles.[590] The mujahedeen were never able to hold major cities, but they harried the Red Army very effectively throughout most of the countryside.[591]

The conflict came at a great cost. Even though the Afghan government continuously downplayed involvement of a "small contingent of Soviet forces" it was clear who actually did the fighting.[592] Overall, more than one million Soviet men would serve in Afghanistan.[593] Tens of thousands of Soviet soldiers would die.[594] Above all, however, it was the civilian population that suffered. Experts estimate that the war killed between one and two million civilians.[595] To compare, a recent report estimated that the US-led wars in Afghanistan, Iraq, and Pakistan *combined* produced a civilian death toll of 500 000.[596] Even by conservative estimates this amounts only to half of the casualties of the Soviet campaign. In the beginning of 1990, almost half of Afghanistan's pre-war population was living abroad as refugees.[597]

Given these figures it will not surprise the reader that the Soviet IHL performance in Afghanistan was very poor. Among scholars and practitioners there was a legal debate about whether the conflict was of an international or non-international character.[598] This largely depended on whether the new puppet government under Babrak Karmal could "invite" the Soviets to stay.[599] Given the political delicacy of this issue, it is not

---

590 ibid 21.
591 Maley (n 583) 866.
592 Quote from Felix Ermacora, 'Report on the Situation of Human Rights in Afghanistan Prepared in Accordance with Commission on Human Rights Resolution 1985/38 (UN Doc E/CN.4/1986/24)' (1986) 5.
593 Rafael Reuveny and Aseem Prakash, 'The Afghanistan War and the Breakdown of the Soviet Union' (1999) 25 Review of International Studies 693, 696.
594 Bearden (n 43) 21.
595 Noor Ahmad Khalidi, 'Afghanistan: Demographic Consequences of War, 1978–1987' (1991) 10 Central Asian Survey 101, 101.
596 Neta C Crawford, 'Human Cost of the Post-9/11 Wars: Lethality and the Need for Transparency' (Watson Institute for International & Public Affairs 2018) 1.
597 Maley (n 583) 868.
598 See e.g. Reisman and Silk (n 586).
599 If it could do so, we should classify the Afghan War as a non-international armed conflict between Afghan/Russian State forces and several armed groups. If Karmal's invitation was null and void, we would face an international armed conflict, see ibid 481.

surprising that the neutral ICRC did not want to position itself, but simply reminded the USSR of its obligations under the Geneva Conventions.[600] Similarly, the UN special rapporteur Felix Ermacora considered that "at least" CA 3 applied.[601] Ironically, the Soviet had shot themselves in the foot by pushing for CA 3 that extended minimum guarantees to people in non-international armed conflicts. In any case, the debate about the correct classification of the conflict had little relevance for assessing Soviet IHL violations, because most acts were clearly illegal under both regimes.

There were many such violations. The NGO Helsinki Watch document-ed that "Russians systematically entered all the houses executing the in-habitants including women and children often by shooting them in the head."[602] Rape and murder of civilians occurred on a large scale.[603] The ICRC had immense difficulties in carrying out its protection activities and received virtually no support from the Soviets.[604] The UN Commission on Human Rights, Human Rights Watch, and the UN Special Rapporteur Ermacora denounced grave violations of IHL and human rights,[605] for example bombardments with heavy civilian losses, indiscriminate high-al-titude bombings, and the use of certain incendiary weapons.[606] Ermacora's report furthermore reveals that Soviet troops massacred entire villages and went as far as using trained dogs to kill civilians.[607]

It is interesting to note that the Soviet Union never engaged in any legal dialogue on its IHL obligations. Moscow simply chose to ignore all allega-tions. During an entire decade of war Moscow denied all charges. When the ICRC reminded Moscow of its obligations under IHL a spokesman of the Foreign Ministry replied that these problems should rather be

---

600 Hans-Peter Gasser, 'Internationalized Non-International Armed Conflicts: Case Studies of Afghanistan, Kampuchea, and Lebanon Conference: The American Red Cross-Washington College of Law Conference: International Humanitarian and Human Rights Law in Non-International Armed Conflicts (12–13 April 1983)' (1983) 33 American University Law Review 145, 150–151.

601 Ermacora (n 592) 16.

602 Quoted in Reuveny and Prakash (n 593) 702.

603 Elaine Sciolino, '4 Soviet Deserters Tell of Cruel Afghanistan War' (The New York Times, 3 August 1984) <https://www.nytimes.com/1984/08/03/world/4-soviet-deserters-tell-of-cruel-afghanistan-war.html>.

604 ICRC Annual Report 1980, 44.

605 See e.g. Commission on Human Rights Resolution 1985/38 (13 May 1985); Ermacora (n 592); Amnesty International, 'Annual Report 1982 (POL 10/0004/1982)' (1983) 181.

606 Ermacora (n 592) 17–18.

607 ibid 19.

discussed with the Afghan authorities, because the USSR does not participate in combat.[608] Even under Gorbachev, the Kremlin did not formally respond to the charges.[609] Just like in Hungary in 1956, but on a much larger scale, we see a strategy of absolute denial, not just of the violations, but of the very application of IHL.

This strategy, however, backfired as the rumours of atrocities slowly but surely discredited the Red Army. Not only had it lost its moral credibility. It also lost the nimbus of invincibility: the army that had once defeated Nazi Germany could not quell an insurgency of ragtag guerrilla fighters. War weariness spread especially through many of the non-Russian Soviet Republics.[610] When Soviet forces withdrew in 1989, they left a war-torn country that became the breeding ground for many more conflicts to come.

---

608 ICRC, 'Annual Report 1980' (1980) 45; see also ICRC, 'Annual Report 1981' (1981) 37.
609 Kramer (n 330) 183.
610 Reuveny and Prakash (n 593) 698.

Conclusion Part I: Russia's Long Way from the "Golden Age" to the "Grey Age"

We have come a long way from Crimea to the Afghanistan, and we are at the verge of crossing the threshold into modern-day Russia. In what respect did the Soviet Union treat IHL differently than Imperial Russia? In a nutshell, we can distinguish three different ages: the "golden age", the "dark age", and the "grey age."

The contributions of Imperial Russia to IHL described in Part I were truly remarkable and probably only rivalled by one other State: Switzerland. There is no doubt that this period represented the "golden age" of Russian contributions to IHL.[611]

When the Bolsheviks rose to power, a period of insecurity ensued. The interwar years resembled a giant experiment. Anything seemed possible, even the total abrogation of IHL through novel legal concepts such as Lenin's just war theory. IHL was not only under attack from legal scholars. During the Second World War, its practical implementation hit an all-time low on the eastern front. While many crimes were committed by the Nazis, the Soviets also catapulted their IHL record back into a "dark age."

Around 1945, we see the beginning of what can be described as the "grey age." The Soviet Union continued to influence IHL, especially at the Nuremberg Tribunal and at the 1949 Geneva Conference. However, at no point did it assume the role of a driving force that the Tsars had cherished so much. In terms of IHL, the Soviet Union had become a State like any other. While it was both powerful and influential, it did not initiate change, it *reacted* to change. The USSR lacked the visionary character of the Russian Empire which associated advances in IHL with the progress of humanity itself. In addition, the Soviets developed a dangerous tendency of denying uncomfortable facts and even the very applicability of IHL. In light of the foregoing, I would like to return to Jiři Toman who concludes his voluminous study on the USSR's impact on IHL as follows:

> *"In my opinion, the application of IHL by the USSR and its proxies depends – more than it is the case for any other country – on the evaluation of its*

---

611 See Fayet (n 318) 56 who uses this term to refer to the period of 1867–1917. He, however, mainly focusses on the relations between Russia and the ICRC.

political interest. If the application of IHL can serve the 'final cause' of the USSR [...] it will develop, affirm, and apply the law. However, it will not hesitate to abandon it, if the application of IHL constitutes an obstacle to achieving its objectives."[612]

In 1991, the Cold War had been simmering for more than 40 years. Most Western scholars had long forgotten about the respectable contributions to IHL of the Russian Empire. They ignored the merits the Soviets had earned in Nuremberg and Geneva. Russia was now associated with Stalin, the *Gulag Archipelago*, and Chernobyl. Now, it was Russia, that had to learn Western lessons of liberalism.[613] In light of this, who would have thought in 1991 that roughly one hundred years before, the English Prime Minister Archibald Primrose suggested the Tsar as the obvious choice for the host of an international peace conference?

"I am quite clear that there is one person who is preeminently fitted to summon such a gathering. The Emperor of Russia by his high, pure character, and his single-minded desire for peace is the Sovereign who appears to me to be marked out as the originator of such a meeting."[614]

In 1991, modern-day Russia faced an uncertain future and had little time to contemplate its past. The following chapters analyse how the continuator State[615] of the Soviet Union re-oriented itself with regards to IHL. Did it see itself as the torchbearer of an Imperial IHL tradition? Did it continue to play the mediocre role of the Soviet Union? Or is its role perhaps even worse?

---

612 Toman (n 350) 736.
613 See Mälksoo, *Russian Approaches to International Law* (n 6) 8.
614 Meyendorff (n 163) 1894, No 11.
615 See for this n 616.

Part II: Russia's Contemporary Approach to IHL

Part I of this thesis dealt with Russia's historical role in shaping IHL. Part II will analyse the current state of affairs. How does Russia contribute to IHL today? I will tackle this question from three angles: First, let us talk about humanitarian diplomacy: does Russia still use its diplomatic weight to develop IHL and ensure compliance (Chapter I)? Secondly, let us look inwards: how has Russia implemented IHL into national law (Chapter II)? Thirdly, let us zoom in onto the battlefield: how has Moscow applied IHL in wars since 1991 (Chapters III–V)?

Chapter I: IHL in International Diplomacy – A Lost Russian Art?

"Diplomacy is the art of letting someone else have your way", a famous proverb goes. But what is Russia's way? Is IHL still an objective of Russian diplomacy? To find out, we will examine as a first step how Russia contributed to the developments in IHL treaty law since 1991. Secondly, we will analyse Moscow's position regarding compliance mechanisms in IHL. The reader will find that in both areas, Russia is a stumbling stone, rather than a driving force. Finally, to balance this assessment, we will look at a field where Russia still proactively engages in humanitarian diplomacy: the delivery of humanitarian aid.

1. Advancing IHL treaty law – Russia, the eternal sceptic

The main pillars of IHL were erected before 1991: The weight of humanitarian law rests on the various Hague Declarations, the Geneva Conventions of 1949, and their Additional Protocols of 1977. The Soviet Union was party to all these treaties and the Russian Federation – as the continuator State of the USSR – inherited all treaty obligations from the Soviets.[616] Regarding IHL, Moscow explicitly embraced this succession in a formal note to the ICRC: "The Russian Federation continues to exercise the rights and carry out the obligations resulting from the international agreements signed by the Union of Soviet Socialist Republics."[617]

Until today, the pillars supporting the protective roof of IHL remain unchanged. Nevertheless, States have advanced IHL in certain specialised

---

616 The transition from the Soviet Union to the Russian Federation is not a classic case of State succession. I follow the predominant view that the Russian Federation is the continuator State [государство продолжатель] of the USSR, which means that the Russian Federation did not automatically (i.e. *de jure*) succeed the Soviet Union, but consciously (i.e. *de facto*) accepted the rights and obligations of the USSR, see Nußberger, 'Russia' (n 218) paras 92–108, especially at 105.

617 Note from the Permanent Mission of the Russian Federation in Geneva transmitted to the ICRC on January 15 1992, available at <https://casebook.icrc.org/case-study/russian-federation-succession-international-humanitarian-law-treaties>.

areas since the end of the Cold War. Notably, in the field of weapons regulations, we have seen significant progress.[618] States agreed on treaties that either regulate the *use* of specific weapons or *banned* certain weapons altogether. Just like the St Petersburg Declaration of 1868, such treaties belong to the realm of IHL, because they regulate the means and methods of warfare. The list of noteworthy treaties includes:[619]

- The Convention on Certain Conventional Weapons (CCW) Protocol IV that banned blinding laser weapons. It was adopted in 1995 and is effective since 1998.[620]
- The so-called Ottawa Treaty or Anti-Personnel Mine Ban Convention (APMBC) outlawing *inter alia* using, producing, and stockpiling anti-personnel mines. It was signed in 1997 and entered into force in 1999.
- The Convention on Cluster Munitions (CCM) that outlawed *inter alia* using, producing, and stockpiling such weapons. It was signed in 2008 and entered into force 2010.
- The Arms Trade Treaty (ATT) which regulates the trade in conventional weapons. It also contains a prohibition against transferring arms in the knowledge that they will be used to commit war crimes.[621] It was adopted in 2013 and entered into force in 2014.
- Several treaties concerning nuclear weapons, especially the 2017 Treaty on the Prohibition of Nuclear Weapons (TPNW) which outlawed *inter*

---

618 In the following, I will refer to multilateral treaties instead of the bi-lateral US-Russian disarmament treaties. The latter, however, recently lost one of its main pillars when the US pulled out of the Intermediate-range Nuclear Forces Treaty (INF) claiming that Russia failed to respect its limitations.

619 Other recent treaties on IHL include: The Third Additional Protocol (AP III) to the Geneva Conventions (2005) that introduced the Red Crystal as a third protective emblem, Amended CCW Protocol II Prohibiting Mines, Booby-Traps, and Other Devices, and CCW Protocol V on Explosive Remnants of War. I have chosen not to include these treaties in the above list for the following reasons. AP III is of limited relevance. The Amended CCW Protocol II has largely been deemed inefficient and was soon surpassed by the Ottawa Treaty as I will explain below. CCW Protocol V applies to post-conflict situations, see Art 1(1), and thus falls outside of my strict focus on IHL.

620 The following dates and facts are taken from <https://treaties.un.org/>.

621 See Art 6(3) ATT: "A State Party shall not authorize any transfer of conventional arms covered under Art 2(1) or of items covered under Art 3 or Art 4, if it has knowledge at the time of authorization that the arms or items would be used in the commission of genocide, crimes against humanity, grave breaches of the Geneva Conventions of 1949, attacks directed against civilian objects or civilians protected as such, or other war crimes as defined by international agreements to which it is a Party."

alia using, producing and stockpiling such weapons. It has entered into force on 22 January 2021.[622]

Out of this list, Russia has only joined one single instrument: The CCW Protocol IV on Blinding Laser Weapons. This attracts criticism in two respects. First, in comparison with other States, Russia's number of ratified treaties is very low. To compare: Germany, France, and the UK have signed and ratified four out of five of the above-mentioned treaties.[623] Even the US has ratified two of the above and for a long time *de facto* adhered to a third.[624] Among the P5-States, only China has the same poor record as Russia.[625] Secondly, the only treaty that Moscow ratified has a very limited scope: While the CCW Protocol IV does represent an important addition to IHL, it also concerns a weapon that has never been used in combat.[626] On the other hand, Moscow refused to sign important treaties on anti-personnel mines (APMBC) and cluster munitions (CCM). These are weapons that continue to take a high civilian toll on modern-day battlefields. In the following, I will analyse Russia's sceptical attitude towards the regulation of existing and emerging weapon systems. Has the State that once initiated the very first weapons treaty of modern day IHL – the St Petersburg Declaration – turned its back on weapons regulation?

1.1 The APMBC – resisting the regulation of anti-personnel mines

The APMBC saw the light of day thanks to a joint effort of international diplomacy and civil society. It represents a milestone in weapons regulation. In the late 90s, experts estimated that between 60 and 200 million

---

622 The treaty entered into force recently, 90 days after the 50th ratification was deposited.

623 Germany, France, and the UK have not acceded to the TPNW.

624 The US has ratified the Fourth CCW Protocol and the ATT, although the latter has been called into question by the Trump Administration. Washington also banned the use of landmines everywhere but on the Korean Peninsula, where it uses them in the demilitarised zone. This *de facto* adherence, however, was recently reversed by the Trump Administration, see 'Trump Lifts Restrictions on US Landmine Use' (BBC, 31 January 2020) <https://www.bbc.com/news/world-us-canada-51332541>.

625 China has only ratified CCW Protocol IV.

626 In fact, this marked the second instance after the St Petersburg Declaration 1868 that a weapon was banned *before* it was widely used on the battlefield. For the history of CCW Protocol IV see Louise Doswald-Beck, 'New Protocol on Blinding Laser Weapons' (1996) 36 International Review of the Red Cross 272.

mines had been dug into the ground around the world. These ticking timebombs claimed tens of thousands of casualties every year. The wider impact went far beyond that. Thousands of villages were abandoned, arable land left behind, entire communities uprooted.[627] In 1996, the CCW failed to prohibit landmines due to the lack of consensus. While CCW Amended Protocol II imposed some technical restrictions on anti-personnel mines, it failed to introduce a blanket ban.[628] Meanwhile, however, the scourge of landmines and their civilian toll had caught the media's attention. Princess Diana became one the most vocal advocates of a ban. In a memorable moment in 1997, she strode on a mine field in Angola, a gesture that touched millions around the world.[629] To break the stalemate in the consensus-based CCW, States embarked on the "Ottawa Process" that culminated in the conclusion of the APMBC.[630] The treaty represented an example of how successful advocacy in the interests of war victims can be carried out in the post-Cold War environment.[631] Today, 164 countries have ratified the APMBC.[632] Despite all these efforts, anti-personnel mines remain a lurking danger. Landmine Monitor recorded more than 7 000 casualties in 2017.[633] The number of unreported cases is likely to be higher.

Russia was only an observer at the Ottawa Conference and has still not acceded today. Moscow continuously stresses the utility of anti-personnel mines and the lack of viable alternatives.[634] It used mines in Chechnya, Dagestan, Tajikistan, and on the border with Georgia. Russian-manufac-

---

627 International Campaign to Ban Landmines, 'Landmine Monitor 1999' (1999) 13.

628 For example, Art 4 bans non-detectable anti-personnel mines and Art 5 introduces a series of very technical rules.

629 'Diana's Support was "Turning Point" in Landmine Ban Effort' (BBC, 31 August 2017) <https://www.bbc.com/news/uk-england-cumbria-41111012>.

630 See Stuart Maslen and Peter Herby, 'An International Ban on Anti-Personnel Mines: History and Negotiation of the "Ottawa Treaty"' (1998) 38 International Review of the Red Cross 693.

631 ibid.

632 United Nations Treaty Collection, 'Convention on the Prohibition of the Use, Stockpiling, Production and Transfer of Anti-Personnel Mines and on their Destruction' <https://treaties.un.org/Pages/ViewDetails.aspx?src=IND&mtdsg_no=XXVI-5&chapter=26&clang=_en>.

633 International Campaign to Ban Landmines, 'Landmine Monitor 2018' (2018) 50. This number includes around 2 700 casualties through improvised mines.

634 Interview with Georgy Todua, Minister Counsellor of the Russian Embassy in Colombia (4 December 2009), available at <http://www.the-monitor.org/en-gb/reports/2018/russian-federation/mine-ban-policy.aspx#ftn2>.

tured mines have also appeared in Ukraine.[635] Over the years, Russia has been stressing that it does not exclude accession to the treaty and that a mine-free world remains a shared goal.[636] So far, however, this remains diplomatic lip service. Russia still possesses the largest stockpile of land-mines in the world. In 2018, it owned 26.5 million out of 45 million anti-personnel mines worldwide.[637]

1.2 The CCM – resisting the regulation of *"de facto* mines"

The genesis of the CCM reads like the sequel to the APMBC. Cluster munitions may be called *de facto* mines. A cluster bomb opens in mid-air to release tens or hundreds of submunitions. The small bomblets can saturate an area up to the size of several football fields. The submunitions are supposed to explode when they hit the ground. Often, however, they fail to detonate (so-called "duds") and remain on the ground as unexplod-ed ordnance (UXO).[638] Experts estimate that the average dud rate ranges from 10 to 30 percent.[639] The unexploded bomblets turn into *de facto* landmines and remain active for decades. In addition, cluster munitions have a wide-area-effect, which makes it especially difficult to distinguish between military and civilian persons and objects.[640]

A large portion of the international community became frustrated be-cause States could not agree on a prohibition of cluster munitions in the CCW. States like Russia and China strongly opposed the idea.[641] There-fore, following an invitation from Norway, several States embarked on the

---

635 Land Mine & Cluster Munition Monitor, 'Russian Federation' <http://www.the -monitor.org/en-gb/reports/2018/russian-federation/mine-ban-policy.aspx#ftn2>.

636 Statement by Vladimir Yermakov, UN General Assembly First Committee De-bate on Conventional Weapons (20 October 2017): "We do not exclude our possible accession to Ottawa Convention in the future. In the meantime, Russia continues work to address a number of technical, organizational and financial issues related to implementation of Ottawa Convention."

637 International Campaign to Ban Landmines (n 633) 16.

638 Cluster Munition Coalition, 'What is a Cluster Bomb?' <http://www.stopcluster munitions.org/en-gb/cluster-bombs/what-is-a-cluster-bomb.aspx>.

639 Mark Hiznay, 'Operational and Technical Aspects of Cluster Munitions', *Disar-mament Forum* (2006) 22.

640 Daryl Kimball, 'Cluster Munition at a Glace' <https://www.armscontrol.org/fact sheets/clusterataglance>.

641 Gro Nystuen and Stuart Casey-Maslen (eds), *The Convention on Cluster Muni-tions: A Commentary* (Oxford University Press 2010) 27.

"Oslo Process" that led to the adoption of the CCM in 2008.[642] Today, the CCM can boast 110 State parties.[643] While Russia recognises the risks of cluster munitions, it does not want to give up the military advantage that the weapon represents. For this very reason, Moscow had already blocked regulation in the CCW.[644] Later it spoke out against the "Oslo Process" that sought a ban outside the CCW system and chose not to participate in the final Conference.[645] In a letter to Human Rights Watch, Deputy Minister of Foreign Affairs Sergey Ryabkov explained that Russia "cannot agree to the classifications and restrictions of cluster munitions outlined in [the CCM] because they were established with disregard for the input from the Russian Federation. Therefore, we are not considering the ratification."[646]

This continues to be the Russian position. Moscow calls the CCM an "illusionary" and "political" agreement with little "impact on the ground."[647] In 2016, Russian Foreign Minister Sergey Lavrov defended the use of cluster munitions by the Russian Air Force in Syria calling cluster munitions an "entirely legal means of warfare."[648] Today, Russia continues to be a major producer and exporter of cluster munitions and stockpiles the weapon.[649] And indeed, as I will show below in the chapters on military

---

642 The Convention on Cluster Munitions, 'History' <https://www.clusterconventio n.org/the-convention/history/>.

643 United Nations Treaty Collection, 'Convention on Cluster Munitions' <https://t reaties.un.org/Pages/ViewDetails.aspx?src=TREATY&mtdsg_no=XXVI-6&chapt er=26&clang=_en>.

644 Mines Action Canada, 'Banning Cluster Munitions – Government Policy and Practice' (2009) 3.

645 Statement by Ambassador Anatoly I Antonov at the 2008 Meeting of the States Parties to the CCW (13 November 2008). As cited in ibid 230–232.

646 Letter from Sergey Ryabkov, Deputy Minister of Foreign Affairs, to Human Rights Watch (20 March 2009), reproduced in Mines Action Canada, 'Cluster Munition Monitor' (2010).

647 Statement of Russia, CCW Group of Governmental Experts on Cluster Munitions (1 September 2010), as quoted in Mines Action Canada, 'Cluster Munition Monitor' (2011) 299.

648 Letter of Sergey Lavrov to Human Rights Watch (6 December 2018), available at <https://www.hrw.org/sites/default/files/supporting_resources/pdf_for_publicati on_0.pdf>.

649 Mines Action Canada, 'Banning Cluster Munitions – Government Policy and Practice' (n 644) 233–234. See also Landmine & Cluster Munition Monitor, 'Russian Federation' <http://www.the-monitor.org/en-gb/reports/2018/russian-fe deration/cluster-munition-ban-policy.aspx#ftn6>.

practice, it made frequent – and indiscriminate – use of it in recent conflicts such as Syria and Georgia.[650]

1.3 Nuclear weapons – reversing Martens

Russia is one of nine States worldwide that own nuclear weapons and is very sceptical towards any regulation of them. Most recently, this was illustrated by Moscow's attitude to the Treaty on the Prohibition of Nuclear Weapons (2017). The TPNW is a treaty born out of frustration. The nuclear powers and their allies had been blocking any meaningful regulation process for years, despite the loud calls of many States and myriads of civil society groups.[651] Their joint efforts finally culminated in the adoption of the TPNW (2017).[652] In its preamble the treaty solemnly declares that

> *"any use of nuclear weapons would be contrary to the rules of international law applicable in armed conflict, in particular the principles and rules of international humanitarian law."*

From the beginning, Russia opposed the treaty making process and called the TPNW a "mistake."[653] It found itself in good company: All nine nuclear powers and several allied States boycotted the initiative.[654] In 2017, this opposition came as no surprise, since Russia's resistance to any restriction of nuclear weapons under IHL dates back to the early 90s.

Moscow spelled out its position in clear terms for the first time in the proceedings of the *Advisory Opinion on the Legality of the Threat or Use of Nuclear Weapons* before the International Court of Justice (ICJ).[655] In 1994, the General Assembly had referred the following question to the ICJ: "Is the threat or use of nuclear weapons in any circumstance permitted under

---

650 See below at pp 373 et seq.

651 Dan Joyner, 'The Treaty on the Prohibition of Nuclear Weapons' (*EJIL Talk!*, 26 July 2017) <https://www.ejiltalk.org/the-treaty-on-the-prohibition-of-nuclear-weapons/>.

652 UN General Assembly, Treaty on the Prohibition of Nuclear Weapons, UN Doc A/CONF.229/2017/8 (7 July 2017).

653 'Treaty on Prohibition of Nuclear Weapons "a Mistake" – Russian Foreign Ministry' (Tass, 3 May 2019) <https://tass.com/politics/1056868>.

654 Joyner (n 651).

655 ICJ, *The Legality of the Threat or Use of Nuclear Weapons*, Advisory Opinion, ICJ Reports (1996) 226 [hereinafter *Nuclear Weapons Advisory Opinion*].

international law?"[656] To provide an answer, the Judges in The Hague had to deal with IHL, especially the requirements of distinction, proportionality, and unnecessary suffering. Can a weapon that harms everything in its huge perimeter be in line with these fundamental principles?

The Court confirmed that IHL applied to nuclear weapons. At the same time, it added a caveat by ruling that nuclear weapons may not violate IHL "in any circumstance" especially when a State's "survival is at stake."[657] Ever since, scholars have been trying to decipher what this bail-out clause means in practice.[658]

While this thesis cannot provide an answer to the ongoing discussion, it is worth looking at the Russian position during the proceedings. In a letter to the Court, the Russian ambassador Leonid Skotnikov explained that IHL knows no prohibition of nuclear weapons. Furthermore, he argued that such weapons can be used in line with the principles of the conduct of hostilities.[659] This provides a much broader range of circumstances for use than the ICJ's exception of a State's "survival at stake." Most remarkably, however, Skotnikov's letter tries to evade Russia's most famous legacy – the Martens Clause. This clause stipulates that in case of a lacuna in IHL, individuals shall still be protected by "the laws of humanity and the requirements of the public conscience."[660] This safety net immortalised the name of the great Russian diplomat and lawyer Fyodor Martens whose legacy I have described in detail in the first part of this thesis. It was considered a monumental step and has since been reiterated in many

---

656 UN General Assembly Resolution 49/75 K, UN Doc A/RES/49/75K (15 December 1994).

657 *Nuclear Weapons Advisory Opinion* paras 95 and 96 (n 655).

658 See Louis G Maresca, 'Nuclear Weapons: 20 Years since the ICJ Advisory Opinion and Still Difficult to Reconcile with International Humanitarian Law' (*Humanitarian Law & Policy*, 8 July 2018) <https://blogs.icrc.org/law-and-policy/2016/07/08/nuclear-weapons-20-years-icj-opinion/>; Hisakazu Fujita, 'The Advisory Opinion of the International Court of Justice on the Legality of Nuclear Weapons' (1997) 37 International Review of the Red Cross 56; Winston Nagan, 'Simulated ICJ Judgment: Revisiting the Lawfulness of the Threat or Use of Nuclear Weapons' (2012) 1 Cadmus 93; Claus Kreß, 'The International Court of Justice and the Law of Armed Conflicts' in Christian J Tams and James Sloan (eds), *The Development of International Law by the International Court of Justice* (Oxford University Press 2013).

659 Letter from the Ambassador of the Russian Federation, together with Written Comments of the Government of the Russian Federation (19 June 1995), 11-14, 18.

660 See in detail at p 56.

treaties. The Russian letter, however, made clear that in today's world, the Martens clause had no more role to play:

> *"As to nuclear weapons the 'Martens clause' is not working at all. A 'more complete' code of the laws of war mentioned there as a temporal limit was 'issued' in 1949–1977 in the form of Geneva Conventions and Protocols thereto, and today the 'Martens clause' may formally be considered inapplicable."*[661]

Even today, Russia resists the increasingly loud call that nuclear weapons cannot be used in line with IHL. More strikingly, in doing so it even dismantled its most famous legacy: the Martens Clause.

1.4 The Arms Trade Treaty – unchecked exports

In addition, Moscow refused to join the Arms Trade Treaty (ATT). From an IHL perspective the treaty's greatest achievement lies in Art 6(3). The provision prohibits the transfer of arms in the knowledge that they will be used to commit war crimes. This controversial clause represents a powerful addition to IHL enforcement, because it tackles the root causes of violations.[662] It is supposed to curb the flow of weapons into conflict areas with a known record of war crimes. The provision thus represents the "heart" of the ATT, because it contains the legal imperatives that led to the campaign to regulate arms transfers in the first case.[663] So far 130 States have signed and 110 have ratified the treaty.[664]

At the first UN Conference in 2012, Moscow blocked the treaty at the last minute to the surprise and irritation of many.[665] At the second Conference (2013), Russia abstained, which allowed the treaty to pass the

---

661 Letter from the Ambassador of the Russian Federation, together with Written Comments of the Government of the Russian Federation (19 June 1995), 13.
662 See for this Laurence Lustgarten, 'The Arms Trade Treaty: Achievements, Failings, Future' (2015) 64 International & Comparative Law Quarterly 569, 588.
663 Stuart Casey-Maslen and others, *The Arms Trade Treaty: A Commentary* (Oxford University Press 2016) 178.
664 United Nations Treaty Collection, 'Arms Trade Treaty' <https://treaties.un.org/Pages/ViewDetails.aspx?src=TREATY&mtdsg_no=XXVI-8&chapter=26&clang=_en>.
665 Casey-Maslen and others (n 663) 11.

consensus-based working modalities.[666] Moscow, however, refused to join and stressed that the "list of the treaty's drawbacks is [...] pretty long."[667] Mikhail Ulyanov, in charge of weapons control in the Russian Ministry of Interior, called the ATT "a weak treaty that still remains a certain burden for its participants."[668]

Today, Russia remains the second largest arms exporter worldwide and escapes the limitations of Art 6(3) ATT regarding the transfer of weapons that might be used for IHL violations.[669]

1.5 Ongoing processes of regulation – no laws for LAWS?

Apart from its resistance to these existing treaties, Russia also opposes ongoing initiatives to regulate weapons. Most notably, this concerns the UN process to regulate autonomous weapons systems. These are systems that can select and attack targets without human interference.[670] Russia both develops and produces such weapons. It has tested them in combat, such as the Uran-9 robotic tank in Syria.[671] The emergence of systems that autonomously select and kill human beings has sparked an intense ethical

---

666 Iran, North Korea, and Syria voted against the treaty. 23 States abstained, see Brian Wood and Rasha Abdul-Rahim, 'The Birth and the Heart of the Arms Trade Treaty' (2015) 12 The SUR File on Arms and Human Rights 15, 17.

667 Daryl G. Kimball, 'Russia Undecided on Arms Trade Treaty' (Arms Control Association, June 2014) <https://www.armscontrol.org/act/2014-06/news-briefs/r ussia-undecided-arms-trade-treaty>.

668 'Russia Refuses to Join Major Arms Trade Treaty Citing Document's Weakness' (RT, 18 May 2015) <https://www.rt.com/russia/259625-russia-arms-treaty-weak/ >.

669 'USA and France Dramatically Increase Major Arms Exports; Saudi Arabia is Largest Arms Importer, Says SIPRI' (SIPRI, 9 March 2020) <https://www.sipri.o rg/media/press-release/2020/usa-and-france-dramatically-increase-major-arms-exp orts-saudi-arabia-largest-arms-importer-says>.

670 The debate about the legality of such systems starts with a battle over terminology. I have chosen to follow the ICRC definition that defines autonomous weapons as "any weapon system with autonomy in its *critical functions* – that is, a weapon system that can select (search for, detect, identify, track or select) and attack (use force against, neutralize, damage or destroy) targets without human intervention" (emphasis added). See Davidson, 5. Such weapons already exist and have been tested on the battlefield.

671 Sebastien Roblin, 'This Is the Robot Tank Russia Used in Syria' (The National Interest, 21 October 2019) <https://nationalinterest.org/blog/buzz/robot-tank-rus sia-used-syria-89866>.

and legal debate. A civil society campaign supported by actors such as Human Rights Watch calls for a ban of "killer robots."[672] An increasing number of States are calling for a ban or a least the regulation of such systems.[673] The UN Group of Governmental Experts (GGE) on Lethal Autonomous Weapons Systems (LAWS) has been debating this issue since 2014.

Since the very beginning, Russia openly questioned "the wisdom of continuing the discussion work on this topic" in the GGE.[674] A working paper that Moscow submitted to the GGE in 2019 illustrates the fundamental opposition towards any regulation. The paper highlights the positive aspects of LAWS which may be "more efficient than a human operator in addressing the tasks by minimizing the error rate."[675] At the same time, it concludes that "concerns regarding LAWS can be addressed through faithful implementation of the existing international legal norms." While "human control" over such systems is important, Russia believes that "specific forms and methods of human control should remain at the *discretion of States*."[676] In other words, Moscow is against any international provision that limits States' discretion to develop and use such weapons. Recently, Time Magazine accused Moscow of "sabotaging the talks."[677] The International Committee for Robot Arms Control believes that Russia is "trying to waste time" in order to "steamroll the process."[678]

This scepticism towards new regulations also concerns other weapon systems. For example, Russia opposes stricter rules on the use of white phosphorous. White phosphorus ignites when it reacts with oxygen, pro-

---

672 See e.g. the campaign "Stop Killer Robots" <https://www.stopkillerrobots.org/>.

673 PAX, 'Crunch Time – European Positions on Lethal Autonomous Weapon Systems' (2018) 5.

674 Statement by the Russian Federation at the Meeting of the High Contracting Parties to the CCW (13 November 2014), as quoted in Vincent Boulanin and Lina Grip, 'Humanitarian Arms Control' in SIPRI (ed), *Yearbook 2017: Armaments, Disarmament and International Security – Summary* (Stockholm International Peace Research Institute Solna 2017) 594.

675 Russian Working Paper for the Group of Governmental Experts of the High Contracting Parties to the CCW (8 March 2019), UN Doc CCW/GGE.1/2019/WP.1, para 2.

676 ibid paras 7 and 10 (emphasis added).

677 Melissa K Chan, 'China and the US Are Fighting a Major Battle Over Killer Robots and the Future of AI' (Time, 13 September 2019) <https://time.com/5673240/china-killer-robots-weapons/>.

678 As quoted in Melissa K Chan, 'China and the U.S Are Fighting a Major Battle Over Killer Robots and the Future of AI' (Time, 13 September 2019) <https://time.com/5673240/china-killer-robots-weapons/>.

ducing thick clouds of white smoke and reaching temperatures high enough to burn through metal.[679] It continues to burn until it disappears and cannot be put out. For this reasons it causes terrible injuries that literally "burn right to the bone."[680] Nevertheless, white phosphorous falls outside the scope of the CCW Protocol III on Incendiary Weapons (1980) because it is not "primarily designed to set fire to objects."[681] Like with LAWS, a growing number of States speaks out for a prohibition of phosphorus. At the annual meeting of the CCW in November 2018, however, it was Russia that prevented consensus on a widely supported proposal to continue discussions on a prohibition in 2019.[682] Moscow insisted that the existing framework is adequate.[683]

1.6 Conclusion

For the sake of fairness, I must stress that Russia is not alone in its opposition to new weapon treaties. The US never signed the CCM and insists on

---

679 Matthew J Aiesi, 'The Jus in Bello of White Phosphorus: Getting the Law Correct' (*Lawfare*, 26 November 2019) <https://www.lawfareblog.com/jus-bello-white-phosphorus-getting-law-correct>.

680 Charlie Dunlap, 'White Phosphorus Sometimes Can Be Lawfully Employed as an Anti-Personnel Weapon...but Should It Ever Be Used That Way? (Probably Not, but Maybe.)' (*Lawfire*, 29 September 2016) <https://sites.duke.edu/lawfire/2016/09/29/white-phosphorus-sometimes-can-be-lawfully-employed-as-an-anti-personnel-weaponbut-should-it-ever-be-used-that-way-probably-not-but-maybe/>.

681 See Art 1 CCW Protocol III. Furthermore, the Protocol does not ban such weapons but only imposes limitations, see n 683.

682 'Russia: Don't Block Action on Incendiary Weapons!' (Human Rights Watch, 11 November 2019) <https://www.hrw.org/news/2019/11/11/russia-dont-block-action-incendiary-weapons>.

683 This did not hinder several States to condemn reports on the use of incendiary weapons in Syria and to call for Protocol III to be put back on the CCW agenda. However, Russia and the US succeeded in blocking such efforts, arguing that Protocol III adequately defined incendiary weapons and that no separate agenda item was needed. See 'Incendiary Weapons Draw Widespread Condemnation – Russia, US Block Opening Up Discussions on Restrictions' (Human Rights Watch, 18 November 2019) <https://www.hrw.org/news/2019/11/18/incendiary-weapons-draw-widespread-condemnation>. The existing framework consists of CCW Protocol III which prohibits the use of "incendiary weapons," but contains a series of caveats. Notably, it only covers weapons that are "primarily designed to set fire to objects" (Art 1) and it does not cover weapons which may have similar secondary effects. See Aiesi (n 679).

using white phosphorous.[684] Recently, Donald Trump vowed to withdraw the US' signature from the ATT and lifted the *de facto* ban on anti-personnel mines.[685] China has signed neither the APMBC nor the CCM and while it officially supports a ban on LAWS, it also develops its own systems at amazing speed.[686] Finally, virtually all Western States refused to join the TPNW, because they are either nuclear powers themselves or close allies.[687]

It is, however, striking that Russia is always among the most vocal critics of new weapons treaties. Among the great powers it is – together with China – the country with the most sceptical attitude. Often, it spearheads the opposition against new regulation, such as in the case of LAWS. At this point I may remind the reader, that this thesis does not aim to analyse Russia's behaviour in comparison to its fellow States. It aims to contrast Russia's historical and current attitude towards IHL. In this sense, the above resistance is remarkable. The fundamental principles of the St Petersburg Declaration are considered Russia's "enduring legacy" that lives on in numerous weapon treaties.[688] The Martens Clause is enshrined in the preamble to the CCM and many other weapon treaties.[689] Against this background, it is surprising that the initiator of the St Petersburg Declaration and the Martens Clause now features among the main sceptics of further regulation.

---

684 US Department of Defence (n 204) para 6.14.1.3.
685 'Trump Lifts Restrictions on US Landmine Use' (BBC, 31 January 2020) <https://www.bbc.com/news/world-us-canada-51332541>.
686 Elsa Kaina, 'China's Strategic Ambiguity and Shifting Approach to Lethal Autonomous Weapons Systems' (*Lawfare*, 17 April 2018) <https://www.lawfareblog.com/chinas-strategic-ambiguity-and-shifting-approach-lethal-autonomous-weapons-systems>.
687 Among the few exceptions are Austria, San Marino, and the Vatican.
688 Crawford, 'The Enduring Legacy of the St Petersburg Declaration: Distinction, Military Necessity, and the Prohibition of Causing Unnecessary Suffering and Superfluous Injury in IHL' (n 50) 564.
689 While the APMBC also mentions the "public conscience in furthering the principles of humanity", it does not reproduce the Martens Clause in its entirety.

2. Advancing IHL compliance – "we are free like birds"[690]

While adopting new IHL rules meets with resistance from Russia and other States, few would subscribe to Cicero's famous aphorism *"silent enim leges inter arma."*[691] Virtually all States have accepted that there are basic rules in armed conflict even if they disagree on the details.[692] However, applying these rules poses a much larger challenge. What is Russia's attitude towards strengthening compliance with IHL through new and existing mechanisms?

States and organisations alike have long identified that compliance with IHL – or rather the lack thereof – represents the key problem.[693] The lack of compliance mechanisms may be called the congenital disease of IHL. The former President of the ICRC Jakob Kellenberger describes this chronic deficiency in the following terms:

> *"Despite the continuously evolving nature of armed conflict, the biggest threat or challenge to IHL remains the same. It is the too limited respect and compliance its rules and norms enjoy by parties to armed conflict all around the world."*[694]

The reasons for this are manifold. War means chaos, and chaos is not conducive to the rule of law. Instead of a judge, or the police, IHL largely depends on the faithful application by the parties. While this is true for many areas of international law, armed conflict represents a situation

---

690 In allusion to the third stanza of A.S. Pushkin's famous poem "The Prisoner" (1822):*"Мы вольные птицы; пора, брат, пора! Туда, где за тучей белеет гора, Туда, где синеют морские края, Туда, где гуляем лишь ветер... да я!"*.

691 In times of war, the laws fall silent (Cicero, 'Pro Milone' 52 BC).

692 The Geneva Conventions of 1949, for example, can boast 196 ratifications.

693 See 32nd International Conference of the Red Cross and Red Crescent, Resolution on Strengthening the Compliance with International Humanitarian Law, 32IC/15/R2 (10 December 2015), 1. The Resolution stresses "that the imperative need to improve compliance with IHL was recognized by all States in the consultation process facilitated by the ICRC and Switzerland as a key ongoing challenge, and that more can be done to address the current weaknesses and gaps in the implementation of IHL, including by non-State parties to armed conflict."

694 ICRC, 'Sixty years of the Geneva Conventions and the decades ahead' <https://www.icrc.org/en/doc/resources/documents/statement/geneva-convention-statement-091109.htm>.

where not only vital interests, but sometimes the very existence of the warring parties is at stake.[695]

What can help to ensure compliance in the fog of war? More than in other fields of international law, prevention becomes a crucial factor.[696] Prevention, in turn, largely depends on the national implementation of IHL. For example, has a State disseminated the rules to its armed forces? Do national courts know about IHL? Are political circles sensitive to IHL issues? I will analyse these questions with regards to Russia's in the subsequent chapter on *national* implementation. This chapter, however, focusses on the *international* component of compliance. What mechanisms are there to prevent or repress IHL violations on an inter-national level?

As I have just mentioned, IHL suffers from a shortage of gritty compliance tools. Nevertheless, IHL has been equipped with certain compliance mechanisms. Firstly, the prosecution of war crimes addresses IHL compliance from an individual angle. Today, the main actor on the international stage is the International Criminal Court (ICC), which can build on the legacy of several special Tribunals such as the International Criminal Tribunal for the Former Yugoslavia (ICTY), the International Criminal Tribunal for Rwanda (ICTR), and the Military Tribunals at Nuremberg and Tokyo.[697] Secondly, IHL has several non-judicial mechanisms to ensure compliance.

- The Geneva Conventions foresee the use of Protecting Powers.[698]
- Additional Protocol I to the Geneva Conventions introduced meetings of the High Contracting Parties that can be set up once approved by the majority of State parties.[699]
- In addition, Additional Protocol I introduced a fact-finding commission to investigate IHL violations: The International Humanitarian Fact-Finding Commission (IHFFC).[700]

---

695 Marco Sassòli, 'The Implementation of International Humanitarian Law: Current and Inherent Challenges' (2007) 10 Yearbook of International Humanitarian Law 45, 48–49.

696 See for this ibid 46.

697 Domestic courts play an increasingly important role in the prosecution of war crimes as I will discuss in the subsequent chapter on national implementation in Russia, see p 201.

698 The Geneva Conventions define the tasks of Protecting Powers in numerous Articles, e.g. Art 126 GC III and 76 GC IV. The concept of a Protecting Power is defined in Art 2(c) AP I.

699 Art 7 AP I.

700 Art 90 AP I.

– The ICRC may act as an (indirect) compliance tool through its interaction with warring parties and the affected population[701]

Finally, *de lege ferenda*, the ICRC and Switzerland have been pushing for a new periodic review mechanism. Such a mechanism already exists in human rights law in the form of the Universal Periodic Review in the Human Rights Council. So far, however, these efforts have been unsuccessful.

How does Russia position itself concerning the existing compliance tools? And what is its attitude towards strengthening compliance in IHL through a new reporting mechanism?

2.1 International criminal law – leaving the ICC

International criminal law received a boost after the end of the Cold War. Most importantly, the creation of the ICTY (1993) represented a huge leap forward for the prosecution of war crimes. Russia, however, has been watching the developments in international criminal law from a cautious distance. Being a close ally of Serbia, Moscow repeatedly questioned the Tribunal's impartiality and usefulness.[702] While the ICTY officially terminated its work in 2017, States had agreed on establishing a permanent International Criminal Court in 1998. Russia signed the founding document of the ICC – the so-called Rome Statute – in 2000, but it repeatedly postponed the ratification necessary for the treaty to take effect. Nevertheless, scholars and practitioners did not abandon hope that the Kremlin would ratify the Rome Statute in the long run.[703]

In a symbolic gesture of disapproval, however, Russia withdrew its signature in 2016 by a Presidential Order[704] reasoning that the Court

---

701 Steven R Ratner and Rotem Giladi, 'The Role of the International Committee of the Red Cross' in Andrew Clapham, Paola Gaeta and Marco Sassòli (eds), *The 1949 Geneva Conventions – a Commentary* (Oxford University Press 2015) para 37.

702 Gennady Esakov, 'International Criminal Law in Russia' (2017) 15 Journal of International Criminal Justice 371, 376.

703 See e.g. Bakhtiyar Tuzmukhamedov, 'The Implementation of International Humanitarian Law in the Russian Federation' (2003) 85 International Review of the Red Cross 385, 391.

704 More precisely, it was decided that Russia should "not become a member of the ICC", i.e. it should not ratify the Rome Statute, see Распоряжение Президента Российской Федерации, 16.11.2016, N 361-рп 'О намерении Российской Федерации не стать участником Римского Статута Международного Уголовного Суда' [Decree of the President of the Russian Federation, 16

"did not live up to its expectations and never became an independent, authoritative organ of international jurisprudence."[705] Russia did not withdraw out of the blue. Rather it decided so following two key events: On 27 January 2016, the ICC Pre-Trial Chamber authorised an investigation linked to crimes during the Russo-Georgian War (2008).[706] Later in the same year, the Office of the Prosecutor qualified the situation in Donbas as an international armed conflict and called Crimea "occupied."[707] Even though Russia had not ratified the Statute, the Court could also exercise its jurisdiction if crimes were committed on the territory of a State party – which was the case for both Georgia and Ukraine.[708] In other terms, the ICC could pronounce itself on possible war crimes by Russian nationals or Russian allies during the Russo-Georgian War, the occupation of Crimea, and the war in Donbas.

Thus, Russia's "un-signing" is partly symbolic. It cannot shield Russian nationals from prosecution before the ICC in the ongoing investigations regarding Ukraine and Georgia.[709] However, it *does* mean that Russian war crimes could not be prosecuted if they have taken place in countries that are also not party to the Rome Statute – such as Syria.[710] In addition, it

---

November 2016, No 361-rp 'On the Intention of the Russian Federation Not to Become a Party to the Rome Statute of the ICC'].

705 'МИД объяснил отказ России ратифицировать Римский статут МУС [The Ministry of Foreign Affairs Announced the Refusal of Russia to Ratify the Rome Statute of the ICC]' (Tass, 16 January 2016) <https://tass.ru/politika/3788778>. Moscow had previously criticised the Court because the ICC Pre-Trial Chamber authorised an investigation of alleged crimes during the Russo-Georgian War 2008, see ICC, *Situation in Georgia* (ICC-01/15–12), Pre-Trial Chamber I, 27 January 2016.

706 ICC, *Situation in Georgia* (ICC-01/15–12), Pre-Trial Chamber I, 27 January 2016.

707 The Office of the ICC Prosecutor, 'Report on Preliminary Examination Activities 2016' (2016) paras 158, 169.

708 See Art 12(a), 13(a) and (c), 14, 15 of the ICC Statute. Georgia ratified the Statute in 2003. Ukraine has lodged a declaration under Art 12(3) accepting the jurisdiction of the Court as a non-State-party.

709 Sergey Sayapin, 'Russia's Withdrawal of Signature from the Rome Statute Would Not Shield Its Nationals from Potential Prosecution at the ICC' (*EJIL Talk!*, 21 November 2016) <https://www.ejiltalk.org/russias-withdrawal-of-signature-from-the-rome-statute-would-not-shield-its-nationals-from-potential-prosecution-at-the-icc/>.

710 Unless there were a referral by the UN Security Council. This is highly unlikely because of Russia's veto, see Matt Killingsworth, 'Justice, Syria and the International Criminal Court' (Australian Institute of International Affairs, 13 March 2019) <https://www.internationalaffairs.org.au/australianoutlook/justice-syria-international-criminal-court/>.

sent a strong political sign that Russia is not willing to cooperate in any manner with the Court.[711] The precise moment of Russia's withdrawal after the announcement of an investigation in Georgia and Ukraine suggests that any external interference in terms of IHL compliance is unwanted. In a wider sense, the withdrawal dealt a blow to the ICC as an institution and shattered all hopes that Russia's deficient war crimes legislation would improve after a ratification.[712]

2.2 Other compliance mechanisms – three sleeping beauties

The family of non-judicial compliance mechanisms consists of Protecting Powers, the meeting of the High Contracting Parties under Art 7 AP I, and the IHFFC. All these institutions, however, may be called the "sleeping beauties" because their use in recent conflicts is extremely limited.[713]

A Protecting Power is not party to the conflict but fulfils certain functions under IHL that contribute to compliance. For example, it has the right to carry out visits to POW camps, pass on information on the wounded, or verify the food supply in occupied territories.[714] Protecting Powers were of major importance during the two World Wars. Swiss delegates, for instance, carried out visits to POW camps and dealt with accusations of ill-treatment.[715] After 1945, the use of Protecting Powers fell into desuetude. While the 1949 Geneva Conventions still placed emphasis on the role of Protecting Powers, they have only been used in five conflicts since the Second World War. The last recorded use dates back more than 35 years to the Falkland War (1982).[716] The record of the Meeting of High Contracting Parties under Art 7 AP I looks even bleaker. Not once has

---

711 Esakov (n 702) 378.
712 See for this Tuzmukhamedov (n 703) 391. For a detailed analysis of the deficiencies of the Russian war crimes legislation see below at pp 184 et seq.
713 For the IHFFC see Catherine Harwood, 'Will the "Sleeping Beauty" Awaken? The Kunduz Hospital Attack and the International Humanitarian Fact-Finding Commission' (*EJIL Talk!*, 15 October 2015) <https://www.ejiltalk.org/will-the-sleeping-beauty-awaken-the-kunduz-hospital-attack-and-the-international-humanitarian-fact-finding-commission/>.
714 See Art 16 GC I, Art 126 GC III, and Art 55 GC IV.
715 Dörmann and others (n 543) Art 8, paras 1012, 1016–1022; Alfred M De Zayas, *The Wehrmacht War Crimes Bureau, 1939–1945* (University of Nebraska Press 1989) 82–83.
716 Dörmann and others (n 543) Art 8 para 1115.

such meeting been convened.[717] Hence, neither the institute of Protecting Powers nor the meeting under Art 7 AP I play a significant role in the current struggle for IHL compliance.[718] This is true not just for Russia, but for the entire international community.

Arguably the most relevant "dormant" mechanism is the IHFFC. The Commission was established in 1991 pursuant to Art 90 AP I. It is a permanent body that consists of 15 independent experts. Its main purpose is to contribute to the respect of IHL by clarifying the facts on the ground. Any State party can refer a situation to the Commission on the condition that all parties to the conflict have recognised its competence.[719] The UN General Assembly[720] and the UN Security Council[721] repeatedly called upon States to accept the competence of the IHFFC. The Commission itself offered its services in various conflicts.[722] Despite that, its overall record is poor. Despite having existed for almost 30 years, it has exercised its statutory functions only once.[723]

Russia recognised the Commission when acceding to AP I in 1989.[724] Yet, to everyone's surprise, Moscow withdrew from the IHFFC in October 2019. Shortly before, the Commission had carried out its first investigation which happened to be in Russia's "backyard." The mission concerned a

---

717 Sofia Poulopoulou, 'Strengthening Compliance with IHL: Back to Square One' (*EJIL Talk!*, 14 February 2019) <https://www.ejiltalk.org/strengthening-compliance-with-ihl-back-to-square-one/>.

718 Robert Kolb, 'Protecting Powers' in Andrew Clapham, Paola Gaeta and Marco Sassòli (eds), *The 1949 Geneva Conventions – a Commentary* (Oxford University Press 2015) 559–560.

719 See <https://www.ihffc.org/index.asp?page=home>.

720 UN General Assembly Resolution 63/125, UN Doc A/RES/63/125 (11 December 2008); UN General Assembly Resolution 65/29, UN Doc A/RES/65/29 (10 January 2011).

721 UN Security Council Resolution 1894, UN Doc S/RES/1894 (11 November 2009); UN Security Council Resolution 1265, UN Doc S/RES/1265 (17 September 1999).

722 IHFFC, 'Report on the Work of the IHFFC on the Occasion of Its 20th Anniversary Constituted in 1991 Pursuant to Article 90 of Protocol I Additional to the Geneva Conventions' (2011) 15.

723 See e.g. ibid 18. At the time of the report (2011) there was not a *single* example of an investigation.

724 When ratifying AP I on 29 September 1989 the Soviet Union declared that the "State recognized the competence of the International Fact-Finding Commission in cases where international humanitarian law is violated." The declaration is available at <https://ihl-databases.icrc.org/applic/ihl/ihl.nsf/Notification.xsp?action=openDocument&documentId=74BABBD71087E777C1256402003FB5D4>.

tragic incident in eastern Ukraine in 2017. An OSCE observer was killed and two more wounded when their vehicle hit a mine. Following a memorandum of understanding between the OSCE and IHFFC, the Commission's first ever investigation took place.[725] It found that the explosion was caused by a Russian-manufactured anti-tank mine which had been laid very recently. At the same time, the mine had not been aimed at the OSCE vehicle which had taken an unplanned route.[726] Shortly after this investigation, the IHFFC offered its services to Ukraine and Russia with regards to the clash in the Kerch Strait (2018).[727] This offer, however, was rejected.[728]

In October 2019, Moscow revoked its recognition of the IHFFC arguing that "the commission has not functioned effectively during its existence." It went on to state that the IHFFC "was not used for its designated purpose" and that the majority States "have not recognised the commission's competence." In a way, the Russian position makes a compelling point. For a long time, the Commission had remained a dead letter. Nevertheless, Moscow's decision came as a surprise. On the one hand, its withdrawal is noteworthy precisely *because of* the Commission's weak record. It would have been easy to reject any inconvenient offers in the future, but Russia seemed eager to eliminate any possible leverage of external compliance. On the other hand, the timing of Russia's withdrawal is telling. Just before, the IHFFC had finally carried out its first mission. Moscow withdrew shortly after the successful investigation in eastern Ukraine – a conflict with Russian involvement – and after receiving another offer regarding the clash in the Kerch Strait. Some commentators already predicted the

---

725 Authors disagree over the fact whether this investigation was within the mandate of Art 90 AP I or merely constituted a provision of good offices, see Poulopoulou (n 717).

726 OSCE/IHFFC, 'Executive Summary of the Report of the Independent Forensic Investigation in Relation to the Incident Affecting an OSCE Special Monitoring Mission to Ukraine Patrol on 23 April 2017' (2017) <https://www.osce.org/home/338361?download=true>.

727 For details on the clash see below at pp 272 et seq.

728 Normally the Commission does not publish its offers. However, its website informs us that on 29 January 2019 "the International Humanitarian Fact-Finding Commission (IHFFC) has proposed its services to the governments of both the Russian Federation and the Ukraine through identical letters dated 4 December 2018. The IHFFC stands ready to assist both the Ukraine and the Russian Federation with regard to the situation relating to the incident, which occurred in the Kerch Strait on 25 November 2018." This statement is available at <https://www.ihffc.org/index.asp?page=news>.

"awakening" of the "sleeping beauty."[729] The course of events suggests that the Kremlin did not approve of such a sudden awakening. Rather, much like in the case of the ICC, it perceived any external compliance mechanism as a possible threat.

2.3 The ICRC – behind the veil of confidentiality

Finally, the ICRC may be called an indirect compliance mechanism. The organisation acts as the "guardian of IHL" and works to promote compliance with the law.[730] Despite this, it resorts to public legal judgments mostly as a last resort, preferring to emphasise pragmatic service.[731] On top of this the organisation conducts its work based on strict confidentiality which makes it difficult to assess the impact of the ICRC with regards to Russia. It does not publish its correspondence with the authorities and it rarely denounces violations. All this makes the organisation's impact "difficult to gauge" and "impossible to determine robustly."[732] For this reason, I will rather deal with its work in Chapters III, IV, and V, when analysing Russia's practice on the battlefield.

Suffice it to say that, while the ICRC certainly carries out compliance work in Russia, the actual impact remains unclear. On the one hand, the diplomatic channels between the ICRC and the Kremlin are functioning. In the past, for example, Vladimir Putin has received the current President of the ICRC, Peter Maurer.[733] The ICRC delegation in Moscow is very active and organises numerous events on IHL.[734] On the other hand, external observers remain sceptical about how much influence the ICRC *really* exerts on the Kremlin. Marco Sassòli argues that the ICRC could

---

729 Cristina Azzarello and Matthieu Niederhauser, 'The Independent Humanitarian Fact-Finding Commission: Has the "Sleeping Beauty" Awoken?' (*Humanitarian Law & Policy*, 9 January 2018) <https://blogs.icrc.org/law-and-policy/2018/01/09/the-independent-humanitarian-fact-finding-commission-has-the-sleeping-beauty-awoken/>.

730 Ratner and Giladi (n 701) 537.

731 Forsythe (n 522) 281.

732 Ratner and Giladi (n 701) 542.

733 President of Russia, 'Meeting with President of the International Committee of the Red Cross (ICRC) Peter Maurer' (24 February 2015) <http://en.kremlin.ru/events/president/news/47734>.

734 ICRC, 'Where we work' <https://www.icrc.org/en/where-we-work/europe-central-asia/russian-federation>.

never gain much leverage on Russia.[735] It may serve as proof, that the organisation recently had to close its offices in and around Chechnya. While the Russian Ministry of Foreign Affairs thanked the ICRC for its efforts in the Northern Caucasus, it stressed that "a cardinal change of the situation allows us to reorient the efforts of the ICRC to States in need, especially those caught up in armed conflicts."[736] In some cases, the ICRC and Russia even clashed publicly, for instance, on the question of an enhanced compliance mechanism, as I will explain in the following section.

2.4 The ICRC-Swiss-led compliance initiative – good intentions, bad prospects

So far, I have described *existing* compliance mechanisms. Recently, however, the call for an enhanced compliance mechanism gained traction. In the run-up to the 32nd International Conference of the Red Cross and the Red Crescent (2015), a consultation process led by the ICRC and Switzerland pushed for the creation of a new compliance mechanism. It envisaged an obligation for States to periodically report on IHL compliance, similar to the Universal Periodic Review in the Human Rights Council that scrutinises their human rights records at regular intervals. However, the idea met with fierce resistance from certain States. Russia was among the most vocal critics.[737] Prior to the 32nd Conference, the idea of a compulsory reporting mechanism was watered down to a forum for voluntary reporting and thematic discussions.[738]

In the end, States did not even manage to agree on these limited functions. According to the official ICRC report, a "very small number of States" managed to prevent agreement.[739] While the report does not name

---

735 Sassòli (n 695) 53.

736 Press statement 'О сотрудничестве Российской Федерации с Международным комитетом Красного Креста (МККК) [About the Cooperation Between the Russian Federation and the ICRC]' (Russian Ministry of Foreign Affairs, 28 December 2018) <https://www.mid.ru/mezdunarodnyj-komitet-krasnogo-kresta-mkkk-/-/asset_publisher/km9HkaXMTium/content/id/3468164>.

737 As cited in Emanuela-Chiara Gillard, 'Promoting Compliance with International Humanitarian Law' (Chatham House 2016) 4.

738 ibid 5.

739 ICRC/Swiss Federal Department of Foreign Affairs, 'Strengthening Compliance with International Humanitarian Law – Concluding Report of the 32 International Conference of the Red Cross and Red Crescent (32IC/15/19.2)' (2015) 17.

the sceptics, other sources describe that Russia submitted an alternative resolution a few days before the International Conference that torpedoed the process. In it, Moscow objected to any reporting – be it voluntary, or compulsory. It rather proposed to enhance the role of the International Conference in hosting State-led thematic discussions on IHL, strengthening States' bilateral confidential dialogue with the ICRC, and regional discussions between States and the ICRC.[740] In other words, it argued for leaving everything as it was.

Hence, the ICRC, Switzerland, and like-minded States had to abandon the idea of a reporting procedure. The final resolution at the 2015 Conference settled for an empty formula. It recommended the "continuation of an inclusive, State-driven intergovernmental process [...] to find agreement on a [...] potential forum of States and to find ways to enhance the implementation of IHL."[741] Until today States have not managed to overcome these differences. The stalemate continues and the process of enhanced compliance is back to "square one."[742]

2.5 Conclusion

Russia has successfully slipped away from the all international compliance mechanisms in IHL. It remained wary of the ICTY, turned its back on the ICC, and left the IHFFC. Furthermore, it took the lead role in stalling the initiative for an enhanced compliance mechanism at the 32nd International Conference. All this suggests that Russia regards any international external compliance mechanisms as a threat to its autonomy that needs to be neutralised.

3. *Humanitarian aid – from Russia with love?*

Admittedly, the above analysis paints a bleak picture of Russian IHL diplomacy. In one field, however, Moscow plays a more proactive – if not less controversial – role in diplomatic circles: humanitarian relief. In 2017,

---

740 Gillard (n 737) 4.
741 32nd International Conference of the Red Cross and Red Crescent, Resolution on Strengthening the Compliance with International Humanitarian Law, 32IC/15/R2 (10 December 2015).
742 Poulopoulou (n 717).

Vasiliy Nebenza, the Russian representative in the UN Security Council solemnly declared:

> *"In the past 10 years our country has provided humanitarian aid in the form of food deliveries in more than 100 States, all in all sending more than 650 thousand tons of humanitarian cargo. In the past years Russia has daily carried out more than 45 humanitarian operations to deliver humanitarian relief worth the overall sum of around 120 million Dollars."*[743]

Is this evidence of a true humanitarian credo or merely a diplomatic lip service? First, I will briefly highlight some legal issues that are necessary to understand the challenges that humanitarian relief schemes face in current wars. Then, I will use two major Russian relief operations – Syria and eastern Ukraine – to illustrate Moscow's diplomatic efforts to deliver aid in armed conflict.[744]

3.1 The legal framework of humanitarian relief – examining the care package

"Humanitarian relief" describes physical aid to the population affected by armed conflict, for example in the form of medicine, food, or water.[745] In order to be labelled "humanitarian", it needs to fulfil four basic principles:

---

743 'Постпред при ООН: Россия за 10 лет отправила 650 т гуманитарной помощи в 110 стран [Ambassador to the UN: Russia Has Sent 650 Tonnes of Humanitarian Aid in the Past 10 Years to 110 Countries]' (Tass, 13 October 2017) <https://t ass.ru/obschestvo/4641966>.

744 The events following the so-called 44-day War over Nagorno-Karabakh (2020) might serve as another example for Russia's humanitarian efforts. They will not be discussed in this chapter, since they took place after the finalization of the doctoral thesis on which this book is based. Russia not only brokered an effective cease-fire between Armenia and Azerbaijan in November 2020, but also deployed around 2 000 peace keepers that frequently engaged in humanitarian activities. Furthermore, Russia distributed humanitarian aid in Nagorno-Karabakh through its own agents and funded aid organizations operating in the region.

745 "Humanitarian relief" is the term used in the Geneva Conventions and their Additional Protocols. It designates assistance in the context of an armed conflict. Thus, the term is narrower than "humanitarian assistance" which, for example, also encompasses aid after natural disasters. See Flavia Lattanzi, 'Humanitarian Assisstance' in Andrew Clapham, Paola Gaeta and Marco Sassòli (eds), *The 1949 Geneva Conventions – a Commentary* (Oxford University Press 2015) 232.

humanity, neutrality, impartiality, and independence.[746] Humanitarian relief may be delivered by specialised neutral actors such as the ICRC, but States play an increasingly active role in delivering humanitarian aid directly.[747] Early examples range from the Belgian support of the operation "Lifeline Sudan" (1989), or US relief programmes in eastern Congo in the 90s.[748] More recent examples include Russian aid in Syria and Ukraine, which I will further discuss below.

---

746 ICRC, '20th International Conference of the Red Cross, "Proclamation of the Fundamental Principles of the Red Cross"' (1965) 5 International Review of the Red Cross 567, 573–574; Jean Pictet, *The Fundamental Principles of the Red Cross* (Henry Dunant Institute 1979) 14–45. The four terms have a distinct meaning:
Humanity is the concept "from which all the other principles flow" and means valuing every single human life.
Neutrality dictates not to take sides in a conflict. It concerns the greater picture (as opposed to impartiality). Humanitarian actors may not stand on the side of one party to the conflict – be it ideologically or militarily. For example, delivering military material under the guise of humanitarian aid would be a violation of this principle.
Impartiality is neutrality on a micro level. For instance, aid may not be distributed in a discriminatory way, according to political allegiance or religious belief.
Independence refers to the lack of influence from governmental, religious, or other bodies.

747 The Conventions and their Additional Protocols mostly speak about neutral "relief societies." This goes back to the original idea of the First Geneva Convention 1864, according to which national (and later international) relief societies should take care of those in need without distinction. Only one article in the Geneva Conventions, Art 59 GC IV, refers to humanitarian relief delivered *by States* and the provision only applies during occupation – and even then, only under very specific conditions. IHL regards States primarily as potential belligerents and not as humanitarian actors in their own right. In the system of the Geneva Conventions humanitarian relief is provided by international organisations such as the ICRC and domestic entities such as the National Red Cross and Red Crescent Societies. The reality on the ground, however, is quite different. States have long played an important role in delivering humanitarian supplies. See Kubo Mačák, 'A Matter of Principle(s): The Legal Effect of Impartiality and Neutrality on States as Humanitarian Actors' (2015) 97 International Review of the Red Cross 157, 168; Lattanzi (n 745) 238–239.

748 Organisation for Economic Co-operation and Development, 'Civilian and Military Means of Providing and Supporting Humanitarian Assistance during Conflict: A Comparative Analysis Note by the Secretariat (DCD/DAC(97)19/REV1)' (1998) 7.

The Geneva Conventions and their Additional Protocols regulate humanitarian relief in great detail.[749] In a nutshell, the primary responsibility for meeting the needs of civilians lies with their home State (in the following, I will refer to it as the "Territorial State"). If this State is unwilling or unable to do so, for example, because it has lost control of a certain region or has limited resources, external actors may offer their services.[750] This can lead to controversies regarding consent. Let's assume the relief actor A wants to deliver aid to the population in country B. Can A do so without the consent of B?

Humanitarian law foresees such consent in both IAC and NIAC. Not only must the Territorial State agree prior to any operation, it has a certain margin of discretion to withhold its consent.[751] Art 70(1) AP I represents the pivotal norm for humanitarian relief in IAC. The provision urges States to undertake relief actions if civilians are not "adequately provided" with essential goods. However, it also emphasises that such external relief is "subject to the *agreement* of the Parties concerned." Other provisions use a similar language. Art 10 GC IV, for instance, requires the "the consent of the Parties to the conflict" for any relief action.

In NIAC, Art 18(2) AP II represents the most important treaty provision. It resembles Art 70(1) AP I. While urging States to provide humanitarian relief, the provision insists on the Territorial State's consent. Even if "the civilian population is suffering undue hardship" relief actions "shall be undertaken subject to the *consent* of the High Contracting Party concerned."[752] Similarly, customary IHL – which applies both in IAC and NIAC – strikes the same balance. While States must "allow and facilitate

---

749 The main provisions can be found in Art 23, 59 GC IV, Art 69–71 AP I, CA 3, and Art 18 AP II.

750 See Emanuela-Chiara Gillard, 'The Law Regulating Cross-Border Relief Operations' (2013) 95 International Review of the Red Cross 351, 355.

751 The only exception to this is Art 59 GC IV. According to the provision the occupying power "shall agree relief schemes [...] and facilitate them by all means at its disposal." This represents a hard law obligation to negotiate relief schemes and to follow through. Providing aid is considered an obligation of result. This stems from the underlying rationale of occupation that obliges the occupying power to uphold law and order and imposes a series of positive obligations, see Lattanzi (n 745) 242.

752 Art 18(2) AP II (emphasis added). In a NIAC that falls below the threshold of application spelled out in Art 1 AP II only CA 3 applies. CA 3 foresees a right of initiative for humanitarian actors: "An impartial humanitarian body, such as the International Committee of the Red Cross, may offer its services to the Parties to the conflict [...]."

rapid and unimpeded passage of humanitarian relief" this is subject to the consent of the Party concerned.[753]

Of course, consent may be abused as an "escape clause" to keep out foreign aid.[754] The ICRC commentary argues that the discussions at the drafting conferences clearly showed that the parties must not refuse aid "for arbitrary or capricious" reasons.[755] While this formula is well intended, it does little to clarify the exact limits of the Territorial State's discretion. Furthermore, neither customary law, nor treaty law establish a procedure to substitute consent, even if the Territorial State acts "capriciously." This may lead to unsatisfactory results. Trucks containing precious cargo such as medicine, food, and water may be blocked at the border for months while the beneficiaries suffer on the other side.

Recently, some authors have challenged the consent-based view, but it is too early to say whether this trend will prevail.[756] However, even if consent were to become obsolete as a legal criterion in the long run, the practice on the ground would not necessarily change. Most humanitarian actors are not willing or able to engage in relief schemes without the consent of the Territorial State due to security concerns.[757]

To sum up, the issue of consent in relief schemes remains controversial. As of today, it represents a prerequisite for any relief action, even if this might lead to unsatisfactory results. An unauthorised relief operation would violate the sovereignty and integrity of the Territorial State.[758] At the same time, the usual exceptions apply. Notably, the UN Security Council may authorise relief operations against the will of the Territorial State as I shall explain in the following case of Syria.

---

753 ICRC, Customary IHL Database, Rule 55.

754 Yves Sandoz, Christophe Swinarski and Bruno Zimmermann (eds), *Commentary on the Additional Protocols of 8 June 1977 to the Geneva Conventions of 12 August 1949* (Martinus Nijhoff Publishers 1987) Art 70 paras 2805–2808.

755 ibid Art 70 paras 2805-2808.

756 For a very progressive view that opposes the traditional requirement of consent – at least for IACs – see Lattanzi (n 745) 242–246.

757 The ICRC, for example, will never work in a country without the consent of the central power.

758 Gillard (n 750) 370.

3.2 Russian humanitarian relief in Syria – aide sans frontières?

Russian relief in Syria has two dimensions: First, aid provided directly by *Russia* in government-controlled areas. Secondly, Russia's attitude towards relief delivered by *third parties* (i.e. States or humanitarian organisations) in rebel-controlled areas, notably the so-called "cross-border aid."

Russia has been running its own relief programmes in government-controlled areas for years. It represents a classic example of aid provided *with* the consent from the Territorial State. The relief aims at winning the "hearts and minds" of the population and is "designed to significantly improve Russia's image in the Middle East and the Arab World as a whole, to show that Russia also cares about the population."[759] Some Russian organisations were specifically created for the Syrian context. The head of the Chechen Republic Ramzan Kadyrov, for example, initiated a foundation that has provided aid in Damascus, Aleppo, Deir al-Zour, and eastern Ghouta. These organisations can rely on Russian military infrastructure in Syria.[760] Another major humanitarian hub is the Russian Centre for the Reconciliation of Opposing Sides in the Syrian Arab Republic – an entity created by the Ministry of Defence.[761] According to its own information, it has carried out more than 2 000 humanitarian actions delivering over 3 000 tonnes of aid.[762] In delivering humanitarian aid, Russia has even cooperated with members of the US-led coalition, such as France.[763]

The other side of humanitarian aid in Syria is the so-called "cross-border aid," i.e. relief schemes in rebel-controlled areas coming from third parties *without* the consent from Damascus. In this respect, Russia's attitude is most remarkable. It allowed the free flow of aid shipments against the explicit will of its close ally Syria.

---

759 'Russia Tries to Win Hearts and Minds with Aid in Syria' (Financial Times, 12 August 2018) <https://www.ft.com/content/e034bdde-96f0-11e8-b747-fb1e803ee 64e>.

760 ibid.

761 Russian Ministry of Defence, 'Peacemaking Bulletins' <https://syria.mil.ru/peace making_bulletins.htm>.

762 Briefing by Russian Centre for Reconciliation of Opposing Sides in Syria (13 April 2019) <http://syria.mil.ru/en/index/syria/peacemaking_briefs/brief.htm?id= 12225367@egNews>.

763 'France and Russia to Jointly Deliver Humanitarian Aid to Syria' (France 24, 20 July 2018) <https://www.france24.com/en/20180720-france-russia-jointly-deliver -humanitarian-aid-syria-eastern-ghouta-refugees>.

Why was there a need for cross-border aid in the first place? The Syrian government prohibited humanitarian organisations from working in rebel-controlled areas. If they did, they were banned from working in government-controlled territory. At the same time, there was and is no real alternative to these cross-border operations, because access to rebel-controlled areas from the hinterland would require crossing many frontlines and *de facto* render humanitarian relief impossible.[764]

To solve this conundrum, the UN Security Council adopted Resolution 2165 (14 July 2014) which established the regime of cross-border aid.[765] Russia chose not to block the resolution and essentially helped to override Damascus' resistance.[766] The resolution set up a monitoring mechanism which allowed for humanitarian relief from Syria's neighbouring countries through designated checkpoints. Syria was to be notified about each shipment and the cargo was to be checked in order to confirm its humanitarian nature.[767] Following the Resolution, UN agencies such as UNHCR launched large-scale relief schemes aimed at helping the population in rebel-controlled territory. More than four million beneficiaries depended on these shipments.[768]

On 13 December 2018, the contentious issue of cross-border aid was put on the agenda for a re-vote in the Security Council. The renewed success of the resolution was certainly not a given. The Assad regime had reconquered large parts of its territory and it wanted to clamp down on the aid organisations that operated in the remaining rebel-controlled areas. In public, Russia backed its ally.[769] However, when the UN Security

---

764 Somini Sengupta, 'Russia Balks at Cross-Border Humanitarian Aid in Syria' (The New York Times, 6 December 2017) <https://www.nytimes.com/2017/12/0 6/world/middleeast/syria-russia-humanitarian-aid.html>.

765 UN Security Council Resolution 2165, UN Doc S/RES/2165 (14 July 2014).

766 While the Resolution does not clearly state whether it falls under Chapter VII of the UN Charter, certain provisions of the Resolution aim to impose binding obligations on the parties to the conflict in Syria and other relevant States, see Gillard (n 750) 380–381.

767 UN Security Council Resolution 2165, UN Doc S/RES/2165 (14 July 2014).

768 'Security Council Beats Midnight Deadline, Renews Syria Cross-border Aid in Contentious Vote' (UN News, 10 January 2020) <https://news.un.org/en/story/2 020/01/1055181>.

769 Somini Sengupta, 'Russia Balks at Cross-Border Humanitarian Aid in Syria' (The New York Times, 6 December 2017) <https://www.nytimes.com/2017/12/0 6/world/middleeast/syria-russia-humanitarian-aid.html>.

Council voted on the extension of cross-border aid, Moscow did not use veto-power but rather abstained.[770]

Only in January 2020, Russia did change course. When the Security Council voted on the same issue again, Moscow used the threat of its veto power to significantly reduce the volume of cross-border aid.[771] The watered-down UN Security Council Resolution 2504 only allowed for two instead of four border crossings into Syria.[772] This had tragic effects, because even in 2020, cross-border aid remained vital for Syrian civilians.[773] Russia's efforts to downsize the operation mark the sad ending of a successful chapter of joint humanitarian relief. However, we should acknowledge that Moscow has allowed the flow of goods for nearly six years against the explicit will of its close ally in Damascus. Thanks to this, international organisations could supply aid to more than four million Syrians.[774]

3.3 Russian humanitarian relief in Ukraine – Trojan aid?

While Russia facilitated UN-led aid in Syria, it acted unilaterally in eastern Ukraine, installing its own relief scheme. I will elaborate on the conflict in eastern Ukraine (2014–today) at page 255. For the purpose of humanitarian relief, suffice it to say that the humanitarian situation in eastern Ukraine looked dire. From the very beginning, civilians were cut off from relief shipments. The self-proclaimed People's Republics of Luhansk and Donetsk controlled large chunks of the Donbas area in eastern Ukraine and categorically rejected humanitarian aid from international organisations.[775] The *de facto* authorities in Donetsk, for instance, declared that "despite the growing humanitarian catastrophe, the people of DNR [Donetsk People's Republic] will not take so-called humanitarian aid from Ukraine,

---

770 UN Security Council Resolution 2449, UN Doc S/RES/2449 (13 December 2018).

771 Russia and China first vetoed a draft Security Council resolution in December 2019 and then watered down UN Security Council Resolution 2504, UN Doc S/RES/2504 (10 January 2020).

772 UN Security Council Resolution 2504, UN Doc S/RES/2504 (10 January 2020).

773 Edith M Lederer, 'Russia Scores Victory for Ally Syria in UN Vote Cutting Aid' (AP News, 11 January 2020) <https://apnews.com/b2e6f5bb76ba00f6fbc3a4c32c2c2c9b>.

774 ibid.

775 Sabine Fischer, 'The Donbas Conflict – Opposing Interests and Narratives, Difficult Peace Progress' (Stiftung Wissenschaft und Politik 2019) 29.

even if it is cynically concealed as an ICRC mission."[776] Slamming the door in the face of the international community opened the gates for a Russian-led initiative.

Moscow could position itself as a mediator. In a television interview in 2015, Sergey Lavrov called upon the separatist authorities to "continue to coordinate with the UN humanitarian organisations and non-governmental organisations, that provided humanitarian aid to the population, in order to see in which way this work can continue."[777] In reality, there was little to coordinate. International organisations had great difficulties in accessing the rebel-controlled areas at all.

In this humanitarian vacuum, Russia launched its own aid scheme. The first Russian trucks arrived in August 2014 before the eyes of the world. Russia openly used the assistance to win over the local population. Many of the trucks bore the Russian Flag and Coat of Arms as well as the slogan: "Humanitarian aid from the Russian Federation." Originally, Moscow suggested a relief scheme "under the aegis of the ICRC"[778] which was to check the cargo, accompany the convoy, and distribute the aid. In the end, however, this plan failed. Ukraine categorically opposed the idea of Russian relief and the ICRC was not ready to take the responsibility for a convoy without special assurances. Finally, the convoy changed its course and crossed the border into Donbas through a rebel-controlled checkpoint without any international checks.[779] In the four following years up to the summer of 2018, nearly 80 convoys have crossed the border from Russia into separatist territory. These convoys range from as few as 10, to more than 40 trucks.[780]

---

776 'Власти ДНР отказались от украинской гуманитарной помощи [The Authorities of DNR Refuse Ukrainian Humanitarian Aid]' (Interfax, 21 August 2014) <https://www.interfax.ru/world/392604>.

777 The interview is available at <https://www.youtube.com/watch?time_continue=6&v=LFaq-hdDoRI>, quoted from minute 2:35.

778 'Москва предложила направлять российскую гуманитарную помощь на Украину под эгидой МККК – Чуркин [Moscow Suggested to Send Humanitarian Aid into Ukraine under the Aegis of the ICRC]' (Interfax, 6 August 2014) <http://www.interfax-russia.ru/South/special.asp?id=527431&sec=1724>.

779 Moritz Gathmann, 'Russischer Hilfskonvoi in der Ukraine – Putins taktischer Punktsieg' (Der Spiegel, 22 August 2014) <https://www.spiegel.de/politik/auslan d/ukraine-russischer-hilfskonvoi-als-mittel-im-propagandakrieg-a-987604.html>.

780 OSCE SMM, 'Spot Report by OSCE Observer Mission: Seventy-Sixth Russian Convoy of 17 Vehicles Crossed into Ukraine and Returned through Donetsk Border Crossing Point' (2018) <https://www.osce.org/observer-mission-at-russian-checkpoints-gukovo-and-donetsk/386142>.

There is an ongoing debate about the content of Russia's "care package." How much of the cargo constitutes humanitarian aid and how much military or dual use equipment is hard to say.[781] Ukrainian officials claim Russia is really importing arms and military goods. The Ukrainian foreign ministry repeatedly called on Russia to stop the violation of Ukraine's sovereignty.[782] The EU called the convoys illegal.[783] On several instances the OSCE Special Monitoring Mission has observed suspicious cargo loads and observers believe that the convoys also resupply fighters.[784] NATO secretary Rasmussen warned of a Russian attack "under the guise of a humanitarian operation."[785] Despite these allegations, the true nature of the cargo remains unclear. It is beyond doubt that Russia supports the separatists in various ways as I will explain at page 255. However, so far, nobody has managed to present irrefutable proof that this support was channelled through the said humanitarian convoys.

---

781 See e.g. Б.Е. Немцов [B.E. Nemtsov], 'Независимый Экспертный Доклад: Путин – Война [Independent Expert Report: Putin – War]' (2015) 27.

782 'Russia to Resume Sending "Humanitarian Convoys" to Occupied Donbas' (UNIAN, 24 July 2019) <https://www.unian.info/war/10629585-russia-to-resume -sending-humanitarian-convoys-to-occupied-donbas.html>.

783 'ЕС назвал незаконным второй российский гуманитарный конвой на Украину [The EU Called the Second Russian Humanitarian Convoy into Ukraine Illegal]' (Interfax, 15 September 2014) <https://www.interfax.ru/world/396875>.

784 See the following OSCE SMM report: "OSCE [...] observed a convoy of cargo trucks from the Russian Federation. In Luhansk city, the SMM saw five white cargo trucks in a compound known to us as used by the armed formations at 2a Rudnieva Street and that they were being unloaded by men in blue work uniforms without visible insignia, but could not see the cargo. One of the trucks was labelled 'Humanitarian Aid from the Russian Federation', the other trucks were not labelled. The SMM saw three armed men in military-type clothing standing around the perimeter of the compound. At the entrance of the compound, an armed man in military-type clothing told the SMM that it could not enter and that none of the people traveling with the convoy could speak to the SMM without permission from the armed formations in Luhansk. Later the same day, the SMM observed a convoy of 11 white covered cargo trucks exiting Ukraine at the border crossing point in Izvaryne (52km south-east of Luhansk)." OSCE SMM, 'Latest from the OSCE Special Monitoring Mission to Ukraine, Based on Information Received as of 19:30, 24 May 2018' (2018) <https://www.osce.org/special-monitoring-mission-to-ukraine/382531>.

785 Mark Galeotti, *Armies of Russia's War in Ukraine* (Osprey Publishing 2019) 35; Б.Е. Немцов [B.E. Nemtsov] (n 781) 27. See also Alex Luhn and Luke Harding, 'Russian Aid Convoy Heads for Ukraine Amid Doubts over Lorries' Contents' (The Guardian, 12 August 2014) <https://www.theguardian.com/world/2014/au g/12/russian-aid-convoy-ukraine-humanitarian>.

A steady flow of Russian goods still trickles across the border today.[786] The relief scheme raises a series of questions. First of all: can this be called a humanitarian operation at all, if Russia stands accused of resupplying the rebels under the guise of a humanitarian operation? As I have mentioned, the facts are murky. However, it is undisputed that civilians *also* benefited from the shipments. Any effort to relieve the suffering amidst armed conflict should be welcomed, even if it does not comply with the humanitarian criteria of neutrality, impartiality, and independence.[787] For those affected, "unhumanitarian" relief is better than no relief.

Secondly, the Russian convoy raises questions about Russia's take on the issue of consent as a precondition for humanitarian relief. Even though Ukraine rejected Russian aid, Moscow delivered it anyway. Russia's former UN ambassador Victor Churkin openly admitted that "we found ways and means in order to deliver humanitarian assistance to people in need."[788] The Kremlin never provided any legal arguments for its position and *de lege lata* the operation certainly violated Ukraine's sovereignty. On the other hand, advocates of "consent-free relief" may now point to Moscow's aid scheme as State practice in their support.[789] This thesis cannot solve the complex legal question of consent in relief schemes. However, whatever the outcome of the ongoing debate may be, the Russian

---

786 In early 2019 the humanitarian relief shipments were put on hold. The Kremlin was eager to stress that this was done in order to reassess the needs. Others, however, speculated that the interruption of aid occurred due to a change of leadership in the separatist republics and because Moscow was unhappy with the diversion of humanitarian aid for private purposes. The aid shipments resumed in summer 2019, see 'Another Russian "Humanitarian" Convoy Arrives in Occupied Donbas' (UNIAN, 17 October 2019) <https://www.unian.info/war/10722990-another-russian-humanitarian-convoy-arrives-in-occupied-donbas.html>.

787 See the ICRC Commentary that argues that this "in no way excludes the possibility [...] of unilateral actions undertaken for the benefit of only one party to the conflict. In particular, an unilateral action cannot be considered as indicating a lack of neutrality. It is important to emphasize this point, as traditional links, or even the geographical situation, may prompt a State to undertake such actions, and it would be stupid to wish to force such a State to abandon the action", Sandoz, Swinarski and Zimmermann (n 754) Art 70 para 2803.

788 'Russia Says Humanitarian Aid in Ukraine Is Example for UN in Syria' (The Moscow Times, 17 June 2014) <https://www.themoscowtimes.com/2014/06/17/russia-says-humanitarian-aid-in-ukraine-is-example-for-un-in-syria-a36451>.

789 For the highly controversial question when unauthorised relief is possible see Gillard (n 750) 369–373.

convoys in eastern Ukraine represent one of the rare cases where Moscow has taken the initiative in humanitarian affairs.

4. Conclusion

In diplomatic circles, Russia has turned from a driving force into a stumbling stone in IHL. Russia categorically refuses to sign important treaties such as the APMBC and the CCM. At various instances Russia opposed important treaty making processes. In crucial moments, Russia even commanded the "army of the sceptics" and managed to stall the process. For example, it currently blocks any regulation of LAWS and it played the lead role in preventing the IHL reporting mechanism at the 2015 International Conference of the Red Cross and Red Crescent.

Russia's attitude towards humanitarian aid represents a rare exception to this rule. In this respect, Russia is still willing to use its diplomatic weight. In Syria, Russia agreed to cross-border aid that supplied millions in need. In eastern Ukraine, Russia's role was more active – albeit more controversial. Relief from Moscow was tainted by allegations of secret support for the rebels and was largely condemned by the international community. For this reason, humanitarian relief only represents a limited exception. In all other areas of IHL diplomacy, however, Moscow represents the eternal sceptic.

Chapter II: IHL Implementation in the Domestic Russian Legal System – A Difficult Marriage?

"If you are failing to prepare, you are preparing to fail." The quote commonly ascribed to Benjamin Franklin holds true for most aspects of life – including IHL. While IHL regulates conduct in war time, States need to take steps in peace time to ensure that the law is respected. Have the armed forces been trained in the rules of war? Are politicians, administrative personnel, and courts aware of IHL when taking decisions related to war? Have fundamental rules of IHL been transformed into national law and how does IHL apply in the domestic legal system? These and other questions will have a tremendous effect on the respect for the law. Hence, one might call the incorporation of IHL into the national system (in the following "implementation") the *national* counterpart of the *international* compliance mechanisms described in the previous chapter.[790]

The duty to implement already flows from the Geneva Conventions. They contain a general rule to "respect and ensure respect" as well as specific obligations, for example, concerning the dissemination of IHL or the repression of certain IHL violations ("grave breaches").[791] How has Russia complied with these obligations?

As in any country, the constitution forms the very basis for incorporating international law into the legal system. Hence, I will start by examining the relevant provisions of the Constitution of the Russian Federation before moving on to selected acts of legislation that touch upon IHL. In a second step, I will scrutinise the case law of Russian courts: did they

---

790 Marco Sassòli, for example, identifies three ways to ensure respect with IHL. Prevention, measures during armed conflict, and repression. While the latter two refer to the mechanisms that I have described at pp 153 et seq, the former relies on the implementation in domestic law, see Sassòli (n 695) 46.

791 The obligation to "respect and ensure respect" can be found in CA 1, see n 1775 for further references. The obligation to disseminate the Conventions can be found in Art 67 GC I, Art 48 GC II, Art 127 GC III, and Art 144 GC IV. The obligations with regards to grave breaches can be found in Art 49–52 GC I, Art 50–53 GC II, Art 129–131 GC III, and Art 146–149 GC IV. See also Andreas R Ziegler and Stefan Wehrenberg, 'Domestic Implementation' in Andrew Clapham, Paola Gaeta and Marco Sassòli (eds), *The 1949 Geneva Conventions – a Commentary* (Oxford University Press 2015) 648.

take IHL into consideration whenever appropriate? In this, I will analyse ground-breaking judgments like the *Chechnya Decision* of the Russian Constitutional Court. Also, I will explore why Russian courts have never convicted anyone for war crimes despite Russia's frequent involvement in armed conflicts.

1. The Russian Constitution of 1993

The current Constitution of the Russian Federation (CRF) was adopted by national referendum on 12 December 1993. It echoed the ideas of the radical reformers headed by Boris Yeltsin who had won the power struggle against more conservative forces.[792] Many hailed the CRF as the "complete departure from the Communist dictatorship and a passage to democratic government."[793] The new Constitution contains numerous references to international law, e.g. in Art 46(3), 55(1), 62(1)(3), 67(2), 69, and its preamble. Already in its first chapter it addresses the issue of the interplay of international and national law, notably in Art 15(4) and 17(1). The status of IHL as a sub-branch of international law hinges upon these norms.

1.1 Art 15 – great expectations

Art 15(4) CRF is the main provision that regulates the interrelation of Russian law and international law. For the sake of the discussion I have divided it into two sub-paragraphs.

> *(i) "The universally-recognised principles and norms of international law and international treaties of the Russian Federation shall be a component part of its legal system.*
> *(ii) If an international treaty or agreement of the Russian Federation fixes other rules than those envisaged by law, the rules of the international agreement shall be applied."*

The application of any norm of international law in the Russian domestic system relies on this provision. In the following, I will explore the pivotal

---

792 See Angelika Nußberger (ed), *Einführung in das russische Recht* (Beck 2010) 22.
793 Gennady M Danilenko, 'The New Russian Constitution and International Law' (1994) 88 The American Journal of International Law 451, 451.

provision in detail. What does Art 15(4) mean when it speaks about "universally recognised norms"? Do international norms take precedence over national law? And what does Art 15(4) entail for IHL in concrete terms?

1.1.1 Art 15(4)(i) – Russia's gateway to international law

Art 15(4)(i) is the pivotal norm for the incorporation of international law. "Treaties" and "universally recognised principles and norms" automatically become part of the national "legal system" of Russia without any further act of implementation. Whether this makes Russia a monist or dualist country is still subject to debate, even though the majority of scholars interprets Art 15(4) as "moderate dualism."[794] The question of monism or dualism, however, has little practical relevance.[795] The debate also carries a significant historical burden, because "monism" in Russia is historically understood as a tainted concept that allows for excessive interference in internal affairs.[796] Whatever one might call it, the Constitution displays remarkable openness towards international law which stands in stark contrast to the strict dualist doctrine of the Soviet Union.[797] The

---

794 Some authors argue in favour of monism, see Ilya Levin and Michael Schwarz, 'At a crossroads: Russia and the ECHR in the aftermath of Markin' (*Verfassungsblog*, 30 January 2015) <https://verfassungsblog.de/crossroads-russia-echr-aftermath-markin-2/> ; Tarja Långström, *Transformation in Russia and International Law* (Martinus Nijhoff Publishers 2003) 375; the majority, however, argues in favour of dualism: В.Д. Зоркин [V.D. Zorkin], *Комментарий к конституции Российской Федерации [Commentary to the Constitution of the Russian Federation]* (3rd edn, Norma 2013) 158; Angelika Nußberger and Yury Safoklov, 'Artikel 15' in Bernd Wieser (ed), *Handbuch der russischen Verfassung* (Verlag Österreich 2014) para 21; Julia Haak, *Die Wirkung und Umsetzung von Urteilen des Europäischen Gerichtshofs für Menschenrechte: ein Rechtsvergleich zwischen der Bundesrepublik Deutschland und der Russischen Föderation* (Lit 2018) 146; for an extensive overview over the different opinions of Russian scholars on this issue see Bogdan Zimnenko, *International Law and the Russian Legal System* (William E Butler tr, Eleven International Publishing 2007); А.А. Ковалев [A.A. Kovalev] and С.В. Черниченко [S.V. Chernichenko], *Международное право [International Law]* (3rd edn, Омега-л 2008) 80–82.
795 Långström (n 794) 436–437.
796 Mälksoo, *Russian Approaches to International Law* (n 6) 112–113.
797 The Soviets agreed neither with "Western" monist nor dualist theories but adopted an approach that resembled a strict dualism, Långström (n 794) 348–351.

latter foresaw a rigid separation of the two fields with limited possibilities for incorporation.[798]

This gives Art 15(4)(i) a twofold effect: First of all, it automatically incorporates all "international *treaties*" on the condition that they have been ratified.[799] The Federal Law 'On International Treaties of the Russian Federation' reiterates this and clarifies that there is no further need for "interior acts for the application" of the treaty.[800] Secondly, Art 15(4)(i) also incorporates all "*universally recognised principles and norms*" into the national legal system. What does this include? The Constitution itself does not define the term "universally recognised principles and norms." In 1995, however, the Russian Supreme Court published a resolution in which it advises Russian courts on how to deal with this provision.[801] While the resolution is non-binding, its guiding principles are widely regarded as authoritative and they have been confirmed by the Russian Constitutional Court.[802] The Supreme Court argues that "universally recognised norms" refers to treaty law such as the ICCPR and ICESCR. In addition, it also includes "other documents" such as the Universal Declaration of Human Rights (UDHR)."[803] The UDHR is not a treaty but originated as a non-

---

798 Nußberger, *Einführung in das russische Recht* (n 792) 61; Tuzmukhamedov (n 703) 386.

799 Постановление Пленума Верховного Суда Российской Федерации, 10.10.2003, N 5 'О применении судами общей юрисдикции общепризнанных принципов и норм международного права и международных договоров Российской Федерации' [Resolution of the Plenum of the Supreme Court of the Russian Federation, 10 October 2003, No 5 'On the Application of Universally Recognized Principles and Norms of International Law and International Treaties by Lower Instance Courts'] para 3.

800 Art 5(3) of the Федеральный закон, 15.07.1995, N 101-ФЗ 'О международных договорах Российской Федерации' [Federal Law, 15 July 1995, No 101-F3 'On International Treaties of the Russian Federation'].

801 Постановление Пленума Верховного Суда Российской Федерации, 31.10.1995, N 8 'О некоторых вопросах применения судами Конституции Российской Федерации при осуществлении правосудия' [Resolution of the Plenum of the Supreme Court of the Russian Federation, 31 October 1995, No 8 'On Certain Questions of the Application of the Constitution of the Russian Federation by Courts when Adjudicating'].

802 Tuzmukhamedov (n 703) 388 with further sources at n 8.

803 Постановление Пленума Верховного Суда Российской Федерации, 31.10.1995, N 8 'О некоторых вопросах применения судами Конституции Российской Федерации при осуществлении правосудия' [Resolution of the Plenum of the Supreme Court of the Russian Federation, 31 October 1995, No 8 'On Certain

binding Resolution of the UN General Assembly before it crystallised into customary law.[804]

It may surprise the reader that the resolution of the Russian Supreme Court does not explicitly mention customary international law. At first glance, this might seem counterintuitive. What is custom, if not a "universally recognised norm?" Why did the Russian Supreme Court not mention this fundamental component of international law? The omission of custom may be attributed to the traditional scepticism that Russian jurists have harboured against this concept since Soviet times.[805] Nevertheless, most current authors argue that Art 15(4)(i) also covers customary international law.[806] This seems convincing, because treaty law is *explicitly* mentioned in Art 15(4). The additional element of "universally recognised norms" would be deprived of its independent meaning if it were only limited to treaties. In another resolution (2003) the Supreme Court seems more open to the concept of customary international law. The Court argued that 15(4) includes all "rules that are accepted and recognised as legally binding by the international community as a whole."[807] This comes close to a description of *consuetudo* ("accepted") and *opinio iuris* ("recognized as legally binding"), i.e. the two elements that form the basis of customary law. Hence, it is safe to say that not only treaty law, but also customary international law is automatically incorporated into the Russian legal system thanks to Art 15(4)(i).

Questions of the Application of the Constitution of the Russian Federation by Courts when Adjudicating'] para 5.

804 Hilary Charlesworth, 'Universal Declaration of Human Rights (1948)', *Max Planck Encyclopedia of Public International Law* (Oxford University Press 2008) paras 1, 16.

805 Nußberger, *Einführung in das russische Recht* (n 792) 62.

806 Nußberger and Safoklov (n 794) para 24; А.А. Ковалев [A.A. Kovalev] and С.В. Черниченко [S.V. Chernichenko] (n 794) 111; Haak (n 794) 138; Zimnenko (n 794) 171.

807 Постановление Пленума Верховного Суда Российской Федерации, 10.10.2003, N 5 'О применении судами общей юрисдикции общепризнанных принципов и норм международного права и международных договоров Российской Федерации' [Resolution of the Plenum of the Supreme Court of the Russian Federation, 10 October 2003, No 5 'On the Application of Universally Recognized Principles and Norms of International Law and International Treaties by Lower Instance Courts'.

1.1.2 Art 15(4)(ii) – establishing a hierarchy

Art 15(4) does more than just open the national legal system to international law. The second part of the provision also assigns international law its place in the national legal hierarchy. In case of collision between an international "treaty" and a national "law", the treaty rule shall prevail. This does not mean that the national law is permanently invalid, but rather temporarily pushed aside.[808]

It is important to note that international treaties only take precedence over *ordinary* national law. International law remains subordinated to the Constitution. While, Art 15(4) does not state this subordination in explicit terms, this is evinced from other constitutional norms: Art 15(1), for example, declares that the Constitution "shall have the *supreme* juridical force." The Russian Constitutional Court has always used this provision to argue that international law may not contradict the Constitution.[809] Scholars also point to Art 125(2)(d) and (6) CRF, which give the Court the power to review the constitutionality of international treaties before their entering into force, thus subordinating international law to the CRF.[810]

It may strike the reader that the second sentence of 15(4) does not address "universally recognised norms," let alone customary law. While customary norms are automatically incorporated by virtue of 15(4)(i), they do not enjoy the same privileged status as treaty rules under 15(4)(ii). In a similar vein, the Federal Law 'On International Treaties of the Russian Federation' mentions "adherence to customary norms" in its preamble, without any further guidance, as to what rank such norms should hold in the national system.[811] Angelika Nußberger ascribes this difference to the general scepticism towards customary law that dates back to Soviet times.[812] Consequently, customary law finds itself on the same level as or-

---

808   А.А. Ковалев [A.A. Kovalev] and С.В. Черниченко [S.V. Chernichenko] (n 794) 109.

809   Постановление Конституционного Суда Российской Федерации, 09.07.2012, N 17-П 'По делу о проверке конституционности не вступившего в силу международного договора Российской Федерации' [Ruling of the Constitutional Court of the Russian Federation, 9 July 2012, No 17-P 'On the Issue of the Constitutional Review of Treaties of the Russian Federation that Have not yet Entered into Force'] para 3.

810   See Haak (n 794) 142 with further sources.

811   Федеральный закон, 15.07.1995, N 101-ФЗ 'О международных договорах Российской Федерации' [Federal Law, 15 July 1995 No, 101-FZ 'On International Treaties of the Russian Federation'].

812   Nußberger, *Einführung in das russische Recht* (n 792) 62.

dinary national law, which means that it can be easily derogated, deleted, or pushed aside according to the *lex posterior* principle.[813]

This reluctance to give customary law an equal status to treaty law creates tension with regards to IHL. Even today, after 150 years of codification, certain domains of IHL heavily depend on customary international law. The framework of non-international armed conflicts (NIACs) in particular relies heavily on custom, because treaty law remains underdeveloped.[814] For example, while in international armed conflicts (IACs) States have agreed on ample treaty rules on the conduct of hostilities, the treaties that apply in NIAC do not even touch upon this issue.[815] The fundamental principles that govern hostilities – distinction, proportionality, and precautions – have never been codified for NIACs. Nevertheless, it is universally accepted that the IAC treaty rules apply in NIACs by virtue of their customary nature.[816] The ICRC Customary Law Study has identified, written down, and thus "quasi-codified" all customary norms in IAC and NIAC. This entire body of law would not enjoy the elevated status of treaty law in Russia. I will explain below what this means in concrete terms using the example of war crimes.

1.2 Art 17(1) – a heart for humanity?

If Art 15(4)(ii) denies customary norms the privileged status under the Russian Constitution, is there another way to achieve such privilege under the CRF? Some argue that Art 17 CRF may elevate the status of certain customary norms. It reads:

> *"In the Russian Federation recognition and guarantees shall be provided for the rights and freedoms of man and citizen according to the universally recognised principles and norms of international law and according to the present Constitution."*

---

813 А.А. Ковалев [A.A. Kovalev] and С.В. Черниченко [S.V. Chernichenko] (n 794) 111.

814 See e.g. Blank, 223. Generally, CA 3 applies to all non-international armed conflicts. In addition, AP II applies provided that the threshold of Art 1(1) AP II is met.

815 See Art 48–60 AP I.

816 Theodor Meron, 'The Geneva Conventions as Customary Law' (1987) 81 American Journal of International Law 348, 348–349. See also ICRC, Customary IHL Database, Rules 1, 14, 15, and in a wider sense Rules 1–24.

The language of the Article is somewhat cryptic. Yet, certain scholars think that it places "rights and freedoms of man" on the same rank as the Constitution[817] or even above.[818] Others vehemently oppose this view and regard Art 17(1) as a mere "general political statement."[819] The majority of scholars, however, acknowledge that Art 17(1) elevates the "rights and freedoms of man" beyond ordinary law, but stress that these rights take a rank below the Constitution.[820] In essence, this would equate the status of such "rights and freedoms" to the status of international treaties – above ordinary law and below the Constitution. If one accepts this finding, the elevated status under Art 17(1) would not only apply to treaties, but also to customary norms. After all, Art 17(1) mentions the "universally recognised principles" which – as I have shown above – include treaties and custom. It would seem only logical to interpret the term in the same way as in Art 15(1).[821] Could this also elevate customary IHL to a status above ordinary national law? Or in other words: Does IHL fall under the "rights and freedoms of man?"

Historically, IHL was perceived as classic inter-State law that protected individuals without granting them individual rights. This is a fundamental difference when compared with Human Rights Law. The past decades, however, may have changed this inter-State nature of IHL turning it into a field that also confers rights on individuals.[822] This change is controversial

---

817 See e.g. И.И. Лукашук [I.I. Lukashuk], *Нормы международного права в правовой системе России [Norms of International Law in the Legal Sytem of Russia]* (Спарк 1997) 39–40.

818 See e.g. В.П. Звеков [V.P. Zvekov], Б. И. Осминин [B.I. Osminin], *Комментарий к Федеральному закону 'О международных договорах Российской Федерации' [Commentary to the Federal Law 'On international Treaties of the Russian Federation']* (Спарк 1996) 17.

819 Manja Hussner, *Die Übernahme internationalen Rechts in die russische und deutsche Rechtsordnung: eine vergleichende Analyse zur Völkerrechtsfreundlichkeit der Verfassungen der Russländischen Föderation und der Bundesrepublik Deutschland* (Ibidem 2005) 94.

820 Gennady M Danilenko, 'Implementation of International Law in CIS States: Theory and Practice' (1999) 10 European journal of international law 51, 64; Nußberger, *Einführung in das russische Recht* (n 792) 63; И.И. Лукашук [I.I. Lukashuk] (n 817) 39–40; Haak (n 794) 139; Igor Lukashuk, 'Das neue russische Gesetz über internationale Verträge und das Völkerrecht' (1997) 43 Osteuropa-Recht 182, 183.

821 Rainer Arnold and Anastasia Berger, 'Artikel 17' in Bernd Wieser (ed), *Handbuch der russischen Verfassung* (Verlag Österreich 2014) para 9.

822 See Lawrence Hill-Cawthorne, 'Rights under International Humanitarian Law' (2017) 28 European Journal of International Law 1187, 1215. Hill-Cawthorne

and ongoing.[823] In scholarly literature on Art 17(1) the scope of "rights and freedoms of man" is limited to human rights law.[824] None of the authors addresses the question whether "the rights and freedoms of man" could include IHL norms. Bakhtiyar Tuzmukhamedov who has published one of the most comprehensive articles on IHL implementation in Russia does not even mention Art 17(1).[825] This avenue appears to be unchartered terrain, unexplored by Russian or international scholars alike. Hence, it would be premature to draw any conclusions at this point. While Art 17(1) might include IHL in the future, it is currently restricted to human rights law and similar norms.

1.3 Conclusion

Scholars agree that Russia's Constitution is open to international law. Bakhtiyar Tuzmukhamedov speaks of a text that is "conducive" to the incorporation of international norms.[826] Nußberger commends its "openness to international law."[827] Gennady Danilenko regards the Constitution as proof of the "desire of democratic Russia to become an open and law-abiding member of the international community."[828] William E Butler hails the "considerable innovation" of Art 15(4) that embraces international law as an integral part of the Russian legal system.[829] Indeed, Art 15(4) demonstrates that the Russian Constitution holds international law in

---

retraces the development towards granting individual rights. He argues that "early support for the individual rights perspective appeared to be superseded by practice relating to war reparations over much of the 20th century, only to re-emerge again in recent practice that, in part, reflects a more legalized (and individualized) approach to reparations for violations of IHL. The inclusion in the Rome Statute of the International Criminal Court of the power to award reparations to victims of international crimes is indicative of this more recent trend."

823 ibid 1211–1212.
824 Arnold and Berger (n 821) para 9; Nußberger, *Einführung in das russische Recht* (n 792) 63.
825 Tuzmukhamedov (n 703).
826 ibid 396.
827 Nußberger, *Einführung in das russische Recht* (n 792) 62.
828 Danilenko (n 793) 452.
829 William E Butler, 'Foreign Policy Discourses as Part of Understanding Russia and International Law' in P Sean Morris (ed), *Russian Discourses on International Law: Sociological and Philosophical Phenomenon* (Routledge 2018) 194.

high regard. It stands in stark contrast to the isolationist approach of the Soviet Union and even grants international treaty law priority over national law. Unfortunately, this privilege does not extend to customary international law, which still plays an important role in IHL.

At the moment of writing, however, the Constitution's remarkable openness faces an uncertain future. On 15 January 2020 Vladimir Putin delivered an address to the Federal Assembly. In it he announced an extensive reform of the 1993 Constitution. The centrepiece of the reform lifts the restriction of two consecutive terms in office and allows him to stay President until 2036.[830] On another note, the reform also touches upon the status of international law in the Russian legal system. According to Putin

"the requirements of international law and treaties as well as decisions of international bodies can be valid on the Russian territory only to the point that they [...] do not contradict our Constitution."[831]

This clause might surprise the reader, because such constitutional supremacy already exists under the 1993 Constitution. While it gives international law precedence over *ordinary* national law, it subordinates it to the Constitution. However, by such a pointed re-iteration of the *status quo* Putin's statement signals to the international community that any external interference by means of international law is unwanted and will be met with fierce resistance.[832]

The constitutional reforms have already passed Parliament and were confirmed by a popular vote with an approval rate of 79 percent.[833] While Art 15 CRF remained unchanged, the reforms modified Art 79 CRF which now stipulates that "decisions by international organs [...] that contradict the Constitution [...] are not subject to implementation in the Russian

---

830 For details on the reform see Thielko Grieß, 'Verfassungsänderungen in Russland: Der Plan des Autokraten' (Deutschlandfunk, 20 April 2020) <https://www.deutschlandfunk.de/verfassungsaenderungen-in-russland-der-plan-des-autokraten.724.de.html?dram:article_id=475021>.

831 President of Russia, 'Presidential Address to the Federal Assembly' (15 January 2020) <http://en.kremlin.ru/events/president/news/62582>.

832 Yulia Ioffe, 'The Amendments to the Russian Constitution: Putin's Attempt to Reinforce Russia's Isolationist Views on International Law?' (*EJIL Talk!*, 29 January 2020) <https://www.ejiltalk.org/the-amendments-to-the-russian-constitution-putins-attempt-to-reinforce-russias-isolationist-views-on-international-law/>.

833 Amy Mackinnon, 'Putin's Russia Gets Voters' Rubber Stamp' (Foreign Policy, 3 July 2020) <https://foreignpolicy.com/2020/07/03/putin-russia-voter-rubber-stamp-approval-constitutional-referendum-2036/>.

Federation."[834] Putin's constitutional "corrections"[835] will not put an end to the Constitution's openness towards international law on paper. They will, however, reinforce a tendency that we have already seen in practice over the past years; a trend of growing isolationism and scepticism towards international law.[836]

2. Other selected acts of implementation

The Order of the Ministry of Defence of the Soviet Union (16 February 1990) transformed the Geneva Conventions and its Additional Protocols into national law.[837] It is still in force today. Since then, Russia has enacted a plethora of instruments that deal with IHL. In the following, I will present the most important aspects of this legislation and analyse its impact.

2.1 Criminal law – Russian minimalism

International Criminal Law (ICL) has become a central pillar in the implementation of IHL. National courts play an increasingly important role

---

834 For a comparative table highlighting all changes in the Russian Constitution see <http://duma.gov.ru/media/files/WRg3wDzAk8hRCRoZ3QUGbz84pI0ppmjF.pdf>.

835 In Russian: "поправки."

836 Recently, this scepticism surfaced with regards to the implementation of judgments of the ECtHR. The Russian Constitutional Court, for example, opposed the implementation of the judgments ECtHR, *Anchugov and Gladkov v Russia*, Nos 11157/04 and 15162/05, 9 December 2019 and ECtHR, *OAO Neftyanaya Kompaniya Yukos v Russia*, No 14902/04, Judgment Just Satisfaction, 31 July 2014. This trend, however, is not confined to the case law of the ECtHR, but it affects international law in a wider sense and thus also IHL. For details see Bill Bowring, 'Russian Cases in the ECtHR and the Question of Implementation' in Lauri Mälksoo and Wolfgang Benedek (eds), *Russia and the European Court of Human Rights: the Strasbourg Effect* (Cambridge University Press 2017); Mälksoo, *Russian Approaches to International Law* (n 6) 121; Ioffe (n 832).

837 USSR Ministry of Defence, 16 February 1990, Order No 75 promulgating the Geneva Conventions on the Protection of Victims of War of 12 August 1949 and their Additional Protocols. Such an implementing act was necessary, because the Soviet Constitution did not contain a clause like 15(4) CRF that would have given treaties immediate effect in the domestic system.

in this process.[838] Russian scholars have always taken specific interest in the issue of war crimes.[839] Maybe the reasons for this curiosity lie in Russia's history. Long before the emergence of modern-day ICL, the Russian Empire criminalised violations of the laws of war.[840] At Nuremberg, the Soviets played a crucial role, and Soviet Scholars like Aron Traynin contributed immensely to the breath-taking development of ICL after the Second World War.[841] Today, there are several Russian textbooks on ICL[842] which is part of Russian curricula, and Russian scholars debate world events such as the wars in former Yugoslavia under the angle of individual criminal responsibility.[843]

How did the Russian government translate this enthusiasm into national law? First of all, the criminalisation of war crimes is not a voluntary act. States have a hard-law obligation to make certain violations of IHL crimes under domestic law. The Geneva Conventions of 1949 introduced the concept of "grave breaches."[844] The term describes acts of such gravity that States have an obligation to "enact legislation necessary to provide effective penal sanctions."[845] In addition, it is widely recognised that serious violations *other* than "grave breaches" may represent war crimes.[846] States need to repress such violations of IHL effectively and have a legal

---

838 Barbora Holá, Róisín Mulgrew and Joris van Wijk (eds), 'Special Issue: National Prosecutions of International Crimes: Sentencing Practices and (Negotiated) Punishments' (2019) 19 International Criminal Law Review 1.

839 See e.g. Esakov (n 702).

840 ibid 372. The author quotes Art 267 and Art 273–275 of the Войнский устав о наказаниях [Military Law on Punishments] of 1868 that foresaw a punishment for imposing an unauthorised indemnity on residents of localities occupied by the army, robbing dead or wounded soldiers, and pillaging.

841 А.Н. Трайнин [A.N. Traynin] (n 474). For the Soviets' role at Nuremberg see above at p 111.

842 А. В. Наумов [A.V. Naumov], *Международное уголовное право [International Criminal Law]* (2nd edn, Юрайт 2014).

843 See Е.Ю. Гуськова [E.Yu. Guskova], А.Б. Мезяев [A.B. Mezayev] and А.И. Филимонова [A.I. Filimonova] (eds), *Международный трибунал по бывшей Югославии: Деятельность. Результаты. Эффективность. [The International Tribunal for the Former Yugoslavia: Actions. Results. Effectiveness.]* (Индрик 2012).

844 For the criminalisation of grave breaches see Knut Dörmann and Robin Geiß, 'The Implementation of Grave Breaches into Domestic Legal Orders' (2009) 7 Journal of International Criminal Justice 703.

845 Art 49–52 GC I, Art 50–53 GC II, Art 129–131 GC III, Art 146–149 GC IV; see also Art 85 AP I.

846 See ICRC, Customary IHL Database, Rule 156 and Cassese and Gaeta (n 466) 67–70.

framework in place that allows for criminal prosecution.[847]Usually, this requires – even in monist countries – some sort of implementation into criminal law, in order to observe the principle *nulla poena sine lege*.[848]

The Soviet Union ratified the Geneva Convention in 1954. Shortly afterwards, the Criminal Code of the RSFSR (1960) was adopted and translated some of the grave breaches into national law. It criminalised violence against POWs,[849] the civilian population, and civilian property.[850] It also banned the misuse of the Red Cross emblem.[851] After the fall of the Soviet Union, the Russian Federation adopted a new Criminal Code in 1996 (CCRF) which is still in force today. Unfortunately, the CCRF only contains one provision that directly refers to war crimes – Art 356.[852] It reads:

> "*Cruel treatment of prisoners of war or civilians, deportation of civilian populations, pillage of national property in occupied territories, and use in a military conflict of means and methods of warfare prohibited by an international treaty of the Russian Federation, shall be punishable by deprivation of liberty for a term of up to 20 years.*"

The provision has three major weaknesses. The first shortcoming of Art 356 is obvious. It is simply too short. Tuzmukhamedov argues that the Russian legislator "squeezed the whole body of international humanitarian law into a single sentence."[853] Unsurprisingly, this was doomed to fail. Art 356 does not even cover all grave breaches the criminalisation of which is explicitly prescribed by the Geneva Conventions. While open terminology like "cruel treatment of civilians or POWs" could be stretched to include many acts, it could hardly cover "compelling a protected civilian or a POW to serve in the forces of a hostile power; wilfully depriving a protected civilian or POW of the right to a fair trial; taking hostages; and destruction

---

847 See e.g. ILC, 'The Obligation to Extradite or Prosecute (Aut Dedere Aut Judicare) – Final Report' (2014) para 18.
848 Sassòli, Bouvier and Quintin (n 72) 360–361.
849 Art 268 of the Criminal Code (1960) of the RSFSR.
850 Art 266 and Art 267 of the Criminal Code (1960) of the RSFSR.
851 Art 202 and Art 269 of the Criminal Code (1960) of the RSFSR. While the misuse of the emblem does not amount to a grave breach, the First Geneva Convention obliges States to prevent such conduct, see Art 54 GC I and Art 45 GC II, see n 859.
852 There are other provisions that deal with related issues, such as ecocide (Art 358), mercenarism (Art 359), and the use of a weapon of mass destruction (Art 356(2)).
853 Tuzmukhamedov (n 703) 390.

of property not justified by military necessity."[854] All of them, however, are listed as grave breaches in the Geneva Conventions. On top of that, Art 356 does not criminalise many "other serious violations of IHL" despite the fact that they are widely accepted as war crimes.[855] To compare: The Rome Statute lists 26 such violations. They are not grave breaches, but nevertheless war crimes.[856] Many of them will fall outside the scope of Art 356.[857] Finally, Art 356 falls short in other aspects. It does not contain a clause on command responsibility,[858] and it does not criminalise the misuse of the Red Cross or Red Crescent emblem.[859] The latter is especially surprising, because the previous Criminal Code of the RSFSR (1960) contained such a provision.[860]

In theory, the prevalence clause of Art 15(4)(ii) CRF could fill these gaps. Is this not a classic case, where ordinary law (i.e. the Criminal Code) contradicts international treaties (i.e. the Geneva Conventions)?[861] This

---

854 See Art 148 GC IV and Art 132 GC III.

855 Cassese and Gaeta (n 466) 67–70. For NIAC, treaty law does not define grave breaches at all. Yet, it is widely accepted that war crimes are not restricted to grave breaches and that such crimes may also occur in NIAC, see n 846.

856 See Art 8 No 2(b) ICC Statute.

857 See e.g. Art 8 No 2(b)(xiv) ICC Statute: "declaring abolished, suspended or inadmissible in a court of law the rights and actions of the nationals of the hostile Party"; Art 8 No 2(b)(xxiii) ICC Statute: "utilizing the presence of a civilian or other protected person to render certain points, areas or military forces immune from military operations"; Art 8 No 2(b)(xxv) ICC Statute: "intentionally using starvation of civilians as a method of warfare by depriving them of objects indispensable to their survival, including wilfully impeding relief supplies as provided for under the Geneva Conventions"; Art 8 No 2(b) (xxvi) ICC Statute: "conscripting or enlisting children under the age of fifteen years into the national armed forces or using them to participate actively in hostilities."

858 Esakov (n 702) 382. See also Art 86 AP I.

859 While the misuse of the emblem does not amount to a grave breach, the Geneva Conventions oblige States to prohibit such conduct under Art 54 GC I and 45 GC II; see also Art 6 AP III which Russia, however, has not ratified. Only the *perfidious* misuse of the emblem represents a grave breach under Art 85(3)(f).

860 Art 202 Criminal Code of the RSFSR (1960).

861 See also the 2003 Resolution of the Supreme Court which argues that in the case of Art 356 international treaty law could be applied directly to criminalise a certain act, Постановление Пленума Верховного Суда Российской Федерации, 10.10.2003, N 5 'О применении судами общей юрисдикции общепризнанных принципов и норм международного права и международных договоров Российской Федерации' [Resolution of the Plenum of the Supreme Court of the Russian Federation, 10 October 2003, No 5 'On the Application of

approach, however, encounters two problems. First, what penalty would a court give for a violation? The Geneva Conventions do not provide any guidance in this respect but leave it up to the legislator.[862] Secondly, it is very unlikely that a Russian court would have recourse to international law in order to introduce a crime that is not part of the criminal code. Unlike other treaties, the Criminal Code does not even reproduce the prevalence clause.[863] Furthermore, experience shows that judges concern themselves chiefly with national law. For these reasons, Anatoly Naumov even deems the direct application of international crimes by Russian courts "practically impossible."[864]

The second shortcoming of Art 356 CCRF lies in its blatant disregard for customary law. The provision refers to "means and methods of warfare prohibited by *treaties* of the Russian Federation" and thereby completely excludes custom.[865] As I have explained above, this is highly problematic, because the entire framework of the conduct of hostilities depends on customary rules in NIAC. No treaty rules enshrine the principles of distinction, proportionality and precautions in NIAC – yet they form the central pillars of any military attack. It is widely accepted among scholars, States, and international organisations that an intentional violation of these principles in NIAC constitutes a war crime.[866] Since their application entirely depends on customary international law, they fall outside the scope of Art 356. Interestingly, some Russian scholars seem to overlook this deficiency. Kuznetsovoy writes in his commentary that

---

Universally Recognized Principles and Norms of International Law and International Treaties by Lower Instance Courts'].

862 See Tuzmukhamedov (n 703) 391.

863 ibid 390–391.

864 A. B. Наумов [A.V. Naumov] (n 842) 57. Naumov argues that Decision No 5 (10.10.2013) of the Supreme Court does not foresee a direct application of international law through the courts. Rather, the State is bound to implement international law. Whatever the merit of this argument, the ruling of the Supreme Court makes it highly unlikely that any lower court will go against it.

865 Leaving aside IHL, Art 356 CCRF may also violate the principle of *nullum crimen sine lege certa*. However, since Art 356 has never actually been applied by Russian courts – as I will explain below – no one has ever challenged it before the Constitutional Court, see Esakov (n 702) 380.

866 ICTY, *The Prosecutor v Duško Tadić* (IT-94-1-T), Decision on the Defence Motion for Interlocutory Appeal on Jurisdiction, 2 October 1995, paras 135–136; ICTY, *The Prosecutor v Tihomir Blaškić* (IT-95-14), Trial Chamber Judgment, 3 March 2000, para 176; ICRC, Customary IHL Database, Rule 156; see also Art 8(2)(e) (i)-(iv) ICC Statute.

> *"As is well known the rules of war are not only regulated in international treaties, but also in custom. [...] However, the most serious war crimes with respect to the conduct of war have been codified in international instruments. The reference to international treaties in Art 356 means that it must be a treaty which is ratified and in force."*[867]

The author thus excludes customary law from the scope of Art 356, but claims that treaty law enshrines the most "serious war crimes." For NIAC, however, such treaty law simply does not exist.

Art 356 gives us no leeway to close this gap. While the Criminal Code states in Art 1(2) that it is based on the "generally recognised principles and norms of international law" this is hardly enough to introduce a reference to customary law *against* the strict wording of Art 356. Even the Russian Constitution cannot fix this problem, because its prevalence clause of Art 15 (4)(ii) CRF does not apply to customary law. It only elevates treaty law to a status above ordinary legislation. Finally, the Russian Supreme Court is openly sceptical of a direct application of international law in domestic criminal proceedings. It argues that international law which provides "elements of criminally punishable actions cannot be directly applied by the courts."[868] In any case, national judges are unlikely to deduce a criminal provision directly from international law in practice, as I have pointed out above.

In sum, Russian penal legislation contains numerous lacunas with regards to war crimes. There is no prospect for quick remedy. The faults have existed since 1996. In 2003 Tuzmukhamedov still hoped that they could be repaired as soon as Russia ratified the ICC Statute which it had signed in 2000.[869] Today, this has become a distant dream after Moscow publicly

---

867   Н.Ф. Кузнецовой [N.F. Kuznetsovoy], *Комментарий к уголовному кодексу Российской Федерации [Commentary to the Criminal Code of the Russian Federation]* (2nd edn, Зерцало 1998) 784.

868   While the Supreme Court cites Art 356 as an exception to this rule (because it explicitly refers to the treaties of the Russian Federation) this exception would only apply to treaty law – not customary law, see Постановление Пленума Верховного Суда Российской Федерации, 10.10.2003, N 5 'О применении судами общей юрисдикции общепризнанных принципов и норм международного права и международных договоров Российской Федерации' [Resolution of the Plenum of the Supreme Court of the Russian Federation, 10 October 2003, No 5 'On the Application of Universally Recognized Principles and Norms of International Law and International Treaties by Lower Instance Courts'] para 3.

869   Tuzmukhamedov (n 703) 391.

withdrew its signature in 2016.[870] What remains is a deficient framework. While Russian scholars seem to share the general enthusiasm for legislation concerning war crimes, and their recognition as such, Moscow does not like to "consider that international criminal law could play a certain role in Russia's own historical and political contexts."[871] We find evidence for this bias not only in the sloppy wording of Art 356 CCRF, but also in the attitude concerning the prosecution of war criminals before Russian courts, as I will explain below at page 207.

2.2 Legislation concerning the armed forces – Russian abundance

Unlike in the sphere of war crimes, there is no shortage of IHL legislation in military law. A number of instruments spell out the rights and obligations of Russian soldiers under IHL. Firstly, the 'Law on the Status of Military Service Personnel' (1998) contains a reference that soldiers need to observe the "universally recognised principles and norms of international law and the international treaties of the Russian Federation."[872] The wording is identical to Art 15(4)(i) CRF which suggests that the reference comprises treaty and customary law.

Secondly, the 'Service Regulation of the Armed Forces of the Russian Federation' (2007) urges Armed Forces to "know and respect the norms of international humanitarian law, the rules on the treatment of the wounded and sick, shipwrecked persons, medical and spiritual personnel, civilians in the zone of military operations as well as prisoners of war."[873]

---

870 Распоряжение Президента Российской Федерации, 16.11.2016, N 361-рп 'О намерении Российской Федерации не стать участником Римского Статута Международного Уголовного Суда' [Decree of the President of the Russian Federation, 16 November 2016, No 361-rp 'On the Intention of the Russian Federation Not to Become a Party to the Rome Statute of the ICC']; see also above at p 155.

871 Mälksoo, *Russian Approaches to International Law* (n 6) 136.

872 Федеральный закон, 27.05.1998, N 76-ФЗ 'О статусе военнослужащих' [Federal Law, 27 May 1998, No 76-F3 'On the Status of Military Service Personnel'] Art 26.

873 'Устав внутренней службы Вооруженных Сил Российской Федерации' утвержден указом Президента Российской Федерации, 10.11.2007, N 1495 ['Service Regulation of the Armed Forces of the Russian Federation' Confirmed by Presidential Decree of 10 November 2007 No 1495] para 22.

Thirdly, the 'Ministry of Defence Order No 333' (1999) regulates the education of soldiers in IHL.[874] It was later replaced by 'Order No 878' (2013) according to which education plays an important role to "realize the obligations of the Russian Federation concerning dissemination of IHL"[875] The Order foresees IHL training for all soldiers, the dissemination of the laws, and considers education in IHL an "integral part of the preparation for military service."[876] Legal training furthermore became mandatory for officers and may be a prerequisite for receiving a promotion in the Army.[877] At this point, it is worth noting that Russia has always been very progressive in terms of IHL education – not only with regards to its armed forces. After the fall of the USSR, Moscow allowed the ICRC to introduce a subject called "humanitarian values" in schools. It included elements of IHL and other humanitarian subjects. Students in higher classes even had to take a written IHL exam. The programme reached around 20 million school children between the ages of 11 and 17 before it was phased out.[878]

Fourthly, Russia issued a military manual in 2001.[879] This voluminous document contains 182 paragraphs that summarise the central elements of IHL such as the rules governing the conduct of hostilities, the rules in occupied territories, naval and aerial warfare, and the dissemination of IHL. It can be considered as very progressive and is partly based on the German military manual.[880]

Finally, Russia has made numerous references to the importance of international law in general. Moscow's 'Foreign Policy Conception' (2016),

---

874 Приказ, 29.05.1999, N 333 'О правовом обучении в Вооруженных Силах Российской Федерации' [Order No 333, 29 May 1999 'On the Legal Training of the Armed Forces of the Russian Federation'].

875 See the introductory paragraph of Приказ, 07.12.2013, N 878 'О правовом обучении в Вооруженных Силах Российской Федерации' [Order No 878, 7 December 2013 'On the Legal Training of the Armed Forces of the Russian Federation'].

876 ibid para 2.

877 ibid para 9; see also 'Наставление по международному гуманитарному праву для Вооруженных Сил Российской Федерации', 08.08.2001 ['Manual on International Humanitarian Law for the Armed Forces of the Russian Federation', 8 August 2001] para 182.

878 Matthew Evangelista, 'How the Geneva Conventions Matter' in Matthew Evangelista and Nina Tannenwald (eds), *Do the Geneva Conventions Matter* (Oxford University Press 2017) 340.

879 'Наставление по международному гуманитарному праву для Вооруженных Сил Российской Федерации', 08.08.2001 ['Manual on International Humanitarian Law for the Armed Forces of the Russian Federation', 8 August 2001].

880 Tuzmukhamedov (n 703) 394.

for instance, is "based on the generally accepted norms of international law."[881] The 2015 'Decree on the Strategy of National Security' used a similar formula and holds international law in high regard.[882]

2.3 Conclusion

On the one hand, the Russian war crimes framework remains painfully incomplete. Some even call the 1996 Criminal Code a "step back" compared with the legislation of Soviet times.[883] On the other hand, Russia can boast an impressive compendium of legal instruments that refer to the laws of war. To some degree, this shows that Russia remains genuinely committed to the implementation of IHL. Yet, the question remains *if and how* this framework is applied in practice. Tuzmukhamedov suggests that there might be a discrepancy between law and life:

"The legal framework is there. All members of the armed forces are aware that they are bound by international humanitarian law and that violators will be punished. They are under orders to study international humanitarian law and their knowledge is tested periodically. Promotion within the armed forces could depend in part on the results of those tests. What is not so clear is how that law would be enforced, should the need arise."[884]

---

881 Para 23 of Foreign Policy Concept of the Russian Federation (approved by President of the Russian Federation Vladimir Putin on 30 November 2016); an English translation is available at <https://www.mid.ru/en/foreign_policy/officia l_documents/-/asset_publisher/CptICkB6BZ29/content/id/2542248>; for details on the current Foreign Policy Concept and the role of Foreign Policy Concepts in Russia see Butler (n 829).

882 "Российская Федерация сосредоточивает усилия на укреплении [...] обеспечении стратегической стабильности и верховенства международного права в межгосударственных отношениях." [The Russian Federation focusses its efforts on strengthening the strategic stability and primacy of international law in international relations], taken from Указ Президента Российской Федерации, 31.12.2015, N 683 'О Стратегии национальной безопасности Российской Федерации' [Decree of the President of the Russian Federation, 31 December 2015, No 683 'On the Strategy of National Security of the Russian Federation'] available in Russian at <http://kremlin.ru/acts/bank/40391>; an updated security doctrine is expected for 2020.

883 Бахтияр Тузмухамедов [Bakhtiyar Tuzmukhamedov] 'Как воевать по правилам? [How to Wage War by the Rules?]' (Nezavisimaya Gazeta, 15 February 2010) <http://www.ng.ru/dipkurer/2010-02-15/11_wars.html>.

884 Tuzmukhamedov (n 703) 395–396.

Indeed, what if the need arises? Are these military regulations only empty words? At this point we leave the sphere of implementation and risk delving into Russia's conduct in recent wars. I will treat this subject extensively in Chapters III, IV, and V. But before that, I would like to shed light on another aspect of implementation: what role do Russian courts play in translating IHL into the domestic system? Do they refer to IHL when dealing with issues related to armed conflict?

3. IHL before Russian courts

Domestic courts play a crucial role in the implementation of IHL. On the one hand, they contribute to IHL by interpreting and developing the law in concrete cases. On the other hand, they can impose judicial review on the executive branch.[885] Yet, analysing the implementation of IHL through the Russian judiciary often means listening to the sound of silence. While William E. Butler highlights that courts have played a "veritably revolutionary role" in the implementation of international law in general, IHL has not received a lot of attention.[886] There is one notable exception: the Chechnya Decision (1995) of the Constitutional Court. It represented a landmark ruling and could have strengthened respect for IHL in the long run.[887] However, ever since then, a strange silence has come upon Russian courts. Judges (and prosecutors) have ignored IHL in cases where it should have played a leading role.

---

885 Laurie R Blank, 'Understanding When and How Domestic Courts Apply IHL' (2011) 44 Case Western Reserve Journal of International Law 205, 224.

886 Butler (n 829) 195.

887 Постановление Конституционного Суда Российской Федерации, 31.07.1995, N 10-П [Ruling of the Constitutional Court of the Russian Federation, 31 July 1995, No 10-P] in the following *Chechnya Decision*; an unofficial English translation of the decision is available at <https://ihl-databases.icrc.org/applic/ihl /ihl-nat.nsf/caseLaw.xsp?documentId=B0DD23E1E049B402C1257EF2005B87ED &action=openDocument&xp_countrySelected=RU&xp_topicSelected=GVAL-9 92BUA&from=state&SessionID=DNLLK0ZN62>.

3.1 The *Chechnya Decision* – a wake-up call?

Paola Gaeta, one of today's leading experts in the field of IHL and ICL,[888] commented on the *Chechnya Decision* in 1996. According to her, the decision of the Constitutional Court

> *"[...] must be commended for the strongly internationalist outlook it reflects. The Court has given pride of place to international law [...] The Court proves to be fully conscious that even the highest bodies of the Russian Federation must comply not only with constitutional provisions, but also with international rules whenever such rules impinge upon the conduct of State organs at home or abroad."*[889]

What prompted the Italian scholar to sing such praise unto the Constitutional Court of the Russian Federation? Undoubtedly, the Chechnya ruling is the single most important decision with regards to IHL in Russia. The Court had to assess the constitutionality of certain decrees passed by President Yeltsin during the First Chechen War.[890] I will explain the legal and practical issues of the Chechen Wars in great detail below at page 279. Nevertheless, the Court's ground-breaking decision must be understood against its historical background. For this reason, I would like to provide the reader with the context. The First Chechen War lasted from 1994–1996. Moscow aimed to quash separatist tendencies in the self-proclaimed independent Chechen Republic which was officially part of the Russian Federation. In many respects, the conflict can be called "Yeltsin's war." It was waged without the approval of Parliament and based on the decrees of a single man: President Yeltsin.[891] He called the fully-fledged war in Chechnya a "fight against bandits" and considered it a law enforcement operation outside the scope of IHL.[892]

---

888 See e.g. Cassese and Gaeta (n 466); Clapham, Gaeta and Sassòli (n 543).

889 Paola Gaeta, 'The Armed Conflict in Chechnya before the Russian Constitutional Court' (1996) 7 European Journal of International Law 563, 570.

890 It concerned the Presidential Decrees No 2137 (30 November 1994), No 2166 (9 December 1994), No 1360 (9 December 1994), and No 1833 (2 November 1993).

891 Matthew Evangelista, *The Chechen Wars: Will Russia Go the Way of the Soviet Union?* (Brookings Institution Press 2002) 11 et seq; for the divide between the Parliament, the Constitutional Court and the President see also Мемориал [Memorial], 'Правовые аспекты чеченского кризиса [Legal Aspects of the Chechen Crisis]' (1995).

892 See for this p 288.

A group of deputies challenged his decrees in front of the Constitutional Court. They argued that they contradicted Art 15(4) CRF, because the military operation in Chechnya systematically violated IHL.[893] The Judges did not follow this argument. They rather held that the review of concrete IHL violations "cannot be subject for consideration by the Constitutional Court and such should be performed by other competent organs."[894] It did not directly pronounce itself on the question of whether Yeltsin's decrees violated Art 15(4) CRF.

The Constitutional Court *did*, however, make three crucial statements with regards to IHL. Firstly, it clarified that the situation in Chechnya represented an armed conflict under IHL and that the rules of Additional Protocol II – i.e. the framework applicable in NIAC[895] – applied. In other words, the Judges contradicted Yeltsin's reading that he was conducting a law enforcement operation against bandits and fanatics outside the scope of IHL. The Court explicitly stated that the provisions of AP II were "binding on *both* parties to the armed conflict."

Secondly, the Court criticised the government for not having sufficiently implemented IHL into national law after the Geneva Conventions and its Protocols were promulgated in 1990. While the Supreme Soviet had instructed the Council of Ministers to do so, "that instruction was not followed."[896]

Thirdly, the Court explained in textbook-like language why the implementation of IHL is not a mere formality but affects the behaviour of soldiers on the battlefield. It is worth citing the paragraph in its entirety:

> *"At the same time improper consideration of these provisions in internal legislation has been one of the reasons of non-compliance with the rules of the above-mentioned additional protocol whereby the use of force must be*

---

893 Gaeta (n 889) 566–567.
894 *Chechnya Decision* (n 887) para 5; the Court did not specify who would be the competent for such a task.
895 The Russian Constitutional Court did not pronounce itself on the applicability of CA 3. However, applying AP II automatically means applying CA 3. According to Art 1(1) AP II the Protocol "develops and supplements" CA 3. CA 3 applies in *all* NIACs, whereas AP II only applies if the *additional* threshold of Art 1(1) AP II is met, i.e. if there is a NIAC between a State and an armed group which has "control over a part of its territory as to enable them to carry out sustained and concerted military operations."
896 *Chechnya Decision* (n 887) para 5.

> *commensurate with the goals and every effort must be made to avoid causing damage to civilians and their property.*"[897]

Thus, the judgment represented a strong pleading in favour of IHL and international law in general. Certainly, it would have been even more desirable if the Constitutional Court had reviewed concrete IHL violations instead of limiting itself to abstract statements. However, in the light of the narrow mandate of the Court, its judicial restraint is understandable.[898]

What is much more tragic for IHL, is that the Court's call for a better implementation remains unheeded until today.[899] Art 356 CCRF exemplifies this failure. The provision was adapted only one year after the ruling but lagged far behind effective implementation. Even more unfortunately, Yeltsin did not change course, but simply disregarded the judgment. To him, the Chechen War remained outside the scope of IHL. For this very reason, Mark Kramer, who has analysed Russia's attitude in the Chechen Wars for many years, even considers the judgment counter-productive, because it "gave the government precisely what it wanted: *de facto* authorisation for federal forces in Chechnya to continue disregarding the Geneva Conventions."[900] We shall see below that this attitude of denial remained unchanged during the Second Chechen War (1999–2009) under Vladimir Putin. While we cannot blame the Court for the fact that the President refused to abide by a binding decision, it hampered the enthusiasm of Russian courts to apply IHL in other instances. In the following cases IHL should have played the lead role, but rather found itself downgraded to a background actor.

---

897   ibid para 5.
898   See Angelika Nußberger, Carmen Schmidt and Tamara Morščakova (eds), *Verfassungsrechtsprechung in der Russischen Föderation: Dokumentation und Analyse der Entscheidungen des Russischen Verfassungsgerichts 1992–2007* (Engel 2009) 27–28.
899   Tuzmukhamedov (n 703) 395. See also Бахтияр Тузмухамедов [Bakhtiyar Tuzmukhamedov] 'Как воевать по правилам? [How to Wage War by the Rules?]' (Nezavisimaya Gazeta, 15 February 2010) <http://www.ng.ru/dipkurer/2010-02-1 5/11_wars.html>.
900   Kramer (n 330) 186–187.

3.2 The Law on Cultural Objects – the beginning of a long silence

The issue of "looted art" has long haunted German-Russian relations.[901] In 1998, the Russian Constitutional Court pronounced its decision on the constitutionality of a Federal Law (in the following 'Law on Cultural Objects') that gave Russia a right to retain artefacts which it had brought back from occupied Germany after the end of the Second World War.[902] The Court had to rule in an extremely tense political context. While the Germans called these objects "looted", the Russian law spoke of "cultural objects relocated to the USSR as a result of the Second World War and currently located on the territory of the Russian Federation."[903] Does this constitute stolen art, or legitimate spoils of war?

Works of art were taken both from public museums and private collections.[904] The German Ministry of Culture estimates that the Russian law concerns around 200 000 art objects as well as 3.6 million books.[905] The dispute touched upon IHL, because the Hague Regulations of 1907 protected property in occupied territories. The Soviet Union had acceded to

---

901 Judy Dempsey, 'How Looted Art Haunts German-Russian Relations' (Carnegie Europe, 24 June 2013) <https://carnegieeurope.eu/strategiceurope/52181>.

902 See Art 6 of the Федеральный закон, 15.04.1998, N 64-ФЗ 'О культурных ценностях, перемещенных в Союз ССР в результате Второй мировой войны и находящихся на территории Российской Федерации' [Federal Law, 14 April 1998, No 64-F3 'On Cultural Objects Relocated to the USSR as a Result of the Second World War and Currently Located on the Territory of the Russian Federation]; see also Susanne Schoen, *Der rechtliche Status von Beutekunst: eine Untersuchung am Beispiel der aufgrund des Zweiten Weltkrieges nach Russland verbrachten deutschen Kulturgüter* (Duncker & Humblot 2004) 104–106.

903 Постановление Конституционного Суда Российской Федерации по делу о проверке конституционности Федерального закона, 15.04.1998, 'О культурных ценностях, перемещенных в Союз ССР в результате Второй мировой войны и находящихся на территории Российской Федерации' [Ruling of the Constitutional Court of the Russian Federation Concerning the Constitutionality of Federal Law, 15 April 1998, 'On Cultural Objects Relocated to the USSR as a Result of the Second World War Currently Located on the Territory of the Russian Federation'].

904 Kerstin Holm, 'Großzügiges Russland' (Frankfurter Allgemeine Zeitung, 8 February 2019) <https://www.faz.net/aktuell/feuilleton/debatten/russland-erklaert-beutekunst-diskussion-fuer-beendet-16029668.html>.

905 Deutsches Ministerium für Kultur und Medien, 'Rückführung von Beutekunst' <https://www.bundesregierung.de/breg-de/bundesregierung/staatsministerin-fuer-kultur-undmedien/kultur/rueckfuehrung-von-beutekunst>.

the Hague Regulations before the Second World War.[906] Hence, any legal analysis of the constitutionality of the Law on Cultural Objects should have considered Art 15(4) CRF and the relevant rules of the Hague Regulations. The Constitutional Court, however, argued that the objects were "seized legally", because Germany represented an "aggressor State that was responsible for unleashing the Second World War."[907] While the latter is of course true, the connection between the two is flawed.[908] The Court mixed *ius in bello* and *ius ad bellum* which constitutes a deadly sin under IHL. The laws of war guarantee the equality of belligerents, no matter their motives for waging war.[909]

If the Judges had considered IHL, they would have found it difficult to justify the Law on Cultural Objects. Already in 1945, the Hague Regulations guaranteed the right to private property in occupied territory. Art 46 explicitly declared that "private property cannot be confiscated." Art 47 adds that "pillage is formally forbidden." This means that the seizing of *private* collections violated IHL, which corresponds to the position of the German government.[910] In addition, Art 56 prohibits confiscating "works of art and science" even if they are *State* property. Hence, none of the objects were "legally seized" under IHL. Quite on the contrary: there was a clear prohibition in both in treaty and customary law.[911] Russian and international scholars like Sergey Marochkin, Vladimir Popov, and Susanne

---

906 For a discussion whether and how the Soviet Union had ratified the existing IHL treaties see pp 94 et seq.

907 Постановление Конституционного Суда Российской Федерации по делу о проверке конституционности Федерального закона, 15.04.1998, 'О культурных ценностях, перемещенных в Союз ССР в результате Второй мировой войны и находящихся на территории Российской Федерации' [Ruling of the Constitutional Court of the Russian Federation Concerning the Constitutionality of Federal Law, 15 April 1998, 'On Cultural Objects Relocated to the USSR as a Result of the Second World War Currently Located on the Territory of the Russian Federation'] para 4.

908 I will limit myself to the aspects relevant to IHL. For a comprehensive analysis of the decision see Schoen (n 902) 108 et seq.

909 See above at p 90.

910 Deutsches Bundesministerium für Kultur und Medien, 'Rückführung von Beutekunst' <https://www.bundesregierung.de/breg-de/bundesregierung/sta atsministerin-fuer-kultur-undmedien/kultur/rueckfuehrung-von-beutekunst>.

911 The Hague Regulations had crystallised into customary law before the Second World War, see above at n 406. Schoen proves the customary status of the norms applicable to works of art, see Schoen (n 902) 43–45.

Schoen arrive at the same conclusion.[912] The decision of the Constitutional Court is flawed through its mixture of *ius ad bellum* and *ius in bello*, and thus completely disregards IHL.[913]

3.3 The Burial Law – thou shalt not mourn

The Russian Federal Law 'On Burial and Undertaking'[914] (LBU) received wide media attention after, in 2002, an amendment inserted Art 14(1) LBU. According to the provision, the bodies of persons, who have participated in terrorist acts and died therein, shall neither be handed over to their families nor shall their place of burial be communicated to their relatives.[915] The provision sparked an intense discussion about ethics in war. While its constitutionality was confirmed by the Russian Constitutional

---

912 Sergey Marochkin and Vladimir Popov, 'International Humanitarian and Human Rights Law in Russian Courts' (2012) 2 Journal of International Humanitarian Legal Studies 216, 224; Schoen (n 902) 43–45.

913 For the sake of completeness, I should add: This does not preclude that Germany has forgone these rights by including the works of art in its reparation payments to the Soviet Union. While scholars like Schoen challenge this view the question lies beyond the scope of IHL; see for this Schoen (n 902) 51–53. The Constitutional Court treats this issue in para 4 of its judgment. The Judges drew parallels to peace treaties of the Soviet Union with the former German allies Italy, Hungary, Bulgaria, Romania, and Finland arguing that the Treaty on the Final Settlement with Respect to Germany (12 September 1990) put an end to all German claims to the works of art. See Постановление Конституционного Суда Российской Федерации по делу о проверке конституционности Федерального закона, 15.04.1998, 'О культурных ценностях, перемещенных в Союз ССР в результате Второй мировой войны и находящихся на территории Российской Федерации' [Ruling of the Constitutional Court of the Russian Federation Concerning the Constitutionality of Federal Law, 15 April 1998, 'On Cultural Objects Relocated to the USSR as a Result of the Second World War Currently Located on the Territory of the Russian Federation'] para 4. The German government rejects the view that the works of art were included in the reparation payments, see Deutsches Bundesministerium für Kultur und Medien, 'Rückführung von Beutekunst' <https://www.bundesregierung.de/breg-de/bundesregierung/staatsministerin-fuer-kultur-undmedien/kultur/rueckfuehrung-von-beutekunst>.

914 Федеральный закон, 08.12.1995, N 8-ФЗ 'О погребении и похоронном деле' [Federal Law, 8 December 1995, N 8-F3 'On burial and Undertaking'].

915 The amendment was inserted by Федеральный закон, 11.12.2002, N 170-ФЗ [Federal Law, 11 December 2002, No 170-F3].

Court,[916] the ECtHR ruled that 14(1) LBU violated the right to family life.[917] Nevertheless, Russia has not amended the relevant provision so far.

The dispute also touches upon IHL which concerns certain rules on the treatment of the dead.[918] In addition, the law was tailored to the Chechen terrorists, whose acts – whether lawful or not – took place in the context of the armed conflict in the Northern Caucasus. The Second Chechen War still raged on when Art 14(1) LBU was inserted in 2002.[919] Nevertheless, the Constitutional Court did not address IHL, not even to discard its application. The majority vote completely ignored the hint of Judge Kononov in his dissenting opinion that the Geneva Conventions contained relevant rules concerning the respect of the dead. Kononov was outraged that the Court chose to "ignore these highly important norms of international law."[920] Marochkin and Popov ascribe this silence to the "deeply seated tradition of courts deciding with reference only to internal legislation [...] and the contemporariness of the current Constitution and the legal system to which courts are not yet accustomed."[921]

The Court need not have feared the application of IHL, because Art 14(1) LBU does not contradict the laws of war. Admittedly, States have a

---

916 Постановление Конституционного Суда Российской Федерации, 28.06.2007, N 8-П по делу о проверке конституционности статьи 14(1) Федерального закона 'О погребении и похоронном деле' [Ruling of the Constitutional Court of the Russian Federation, 28 June 2007, No 8-P Concerning the Constitutional Review of 14(1) of the Federal Law 'On Burial and Undertaking'].

917 ECtHR, *Sabanchiyeva and Others v Russia*, No 38450/05, 6 June 2013; ECtHR, *Maskhadova and Others v Russia*, No 18071/05, 6 June 2013; ECtHR, *Kushtova and Others v Russia*, No 21885/07, 16 January 2014; ECtHR, *Arkhestov and Others v Russia*, No 22089/07, 16 January 2014; ECtHR, *Zalov and Khakulova v Russia*, No 7988/09, 16 January 2014.

918 See ICRC, Customary IHL Database, Rules 112–116; see also See Art 17 GC I, Art 120 GC III, Art 130 GC IV.

919 The open battle phase had already ended, but it was followed by a vicious period of guerrilla warfare. The last Russian troops withdrew in 2009, see below at p 279.

920 The Court did, however, mention other international instruments, such as the UDHR. For the dissenting judgement of Judge A.L. Kononov see: Постановление Конституционного Суда Российской Федерации, 28.06.2007, N 8-П по делу о проверке конституционности статьи 14(1) Федерального закона 'О погребении и похоронном деле' – Особое Мнение А.Л. Кононова [Ruling of the Constitutional Court of the Russian Federation, 28 June 2007, No 8-P Concerning the Constitutional Review of Art 14(1) of the Federal Law 'On Burial and Undertaking' – Separate Opinion of Judge A.L. Kononov].

921 Marochkin and Popov (n 912) 235–236.

customary obligation to "endeavour to facilitate the return of the remains of the deceased [...] upon the request of their next of kin."[922] This customary rule is based on several treaty rules in the Geneva Conventions.[923] However, States are only obliged to *"endeavour to facilitate"* the return of the dead. This indicates a weak obligation of means, from which certain exceptions can be made. In addition, even the ICRC Customary Law Study admits that the rule only exists in IACs.[924] The Chechen War, however, qualified as a NIAC as I will explain below at page 283. Finally, courts in other countries found provisions like Art 14 LBU to be in line with IHL. The Israeli Supreme Court, for instance, confirmed that the State may hold back the bodies of deceased terrorists.[925]

In conclusion, while Art 14(1) LBU violates the right to family life under the European Convention on Human Rights (ECHR) it does not contradict IHL. However, what is striking is that the Russian Constitutional Court avoided any discussion of IHL in its ruling. This is all the more surprising, because Judge Kononov published a separate opinion, which suggests that the issue of IHL was raised in discussions but left out on purpose. The Court's silence stands in stark contrast to its *Chechnya Decision* and tells us about the low current standing of IHL in Russia.

3.4 War crime trials – living up to Nuremberg?

I have already explained why Art 356 CCRF is a deficient provision. In a way, it is also a dead provision. There have been no registered convictions under Art 356 since its introduction in 1996.[926] Why is that so? In many cases, the criminal investigations are already deficient. An act that might constitute a war crime never reaches the stage of judicial review.[927] In the rare exceptions where an investigation takes place, courts do not refer to Art 356, but rather sentence the accused for ordinary crimes. In the

---

922   ICRC, Customary IHL Database, Rule 114.
923   See Art 17 GC I, Art 120 GC III, Art 130 GC IV. The treaty rules would only apply in an IAC. However, the customary rules are virtually identical.
924   ICRC, Customary IHL Database, Rule 114.
925   Heba Nasser and Shatha Hammad, 'Supreme Court Allows Israel to Continue Holding Bodies of Killed Palestinians' (Middle Eastern Eye, 9 September 2019) <https://www.middleeasteye.net/news/supreme-court-allows-israel-withhold-bodies-palestinians>.
926   Esakov (n 702) 380 at n 23.
927   For the deficiencies of the criminal investigations see below at 204.

following, I will explain both phenomena in detail drawing on examples from Russia's recent wars in Chechnya, Georgia and Ukraine.

3.4.1 Criminal convictions for Russian wartime crimes – a handful of nothing

The rare convictions that Russian courts handed down for wartime crimes concern Chechnya. The killing of Kheda Kungaeva, a Chechen teenager who had been abducted, beaten, raped, and murdered by a Russian officer on duty, represented the first case in which the Russian authorities successfully prosecuted a wartime crime.[928] The case is also known under the name of the perpetrator – Yuri Budanov. His actions clearly violated Common Article 3 of the Geneva Conventions which protects persons not taking part in the hostilities against murder, cruel treatment and outrages on personal dignity. The Rostov Military Court, however, "only" convicted the officer for "abuse of power, abduction and murder."[929] These are all peacetime crimes.

While the prosecution of Yuri Budanov as such should be welcomed, it is hard to understand why the Court avoided Art 356 CCRF. The provision would have covered the crime. The murder of Kheda Kungaeva concerned the mistreatment and killing of a civilian at the hands of a Russian soldier which would qualify as "cruel treatment of [...] civilians" under Art 356. Not only did the Court refuse to call the act a war crime, but its verdict also failed to reflect the gravity of the deed. Budanov was sentenced to 10 years' imprisonment and conditionally released in 2009.[930]

There are a few other instances where Russian courts dealt with the killing of civilians during the Chechen Wars. None of them entailed convictions under Art 356, even though the crimes were committed by Russian soldiers in an armed conflict. For example, Eduard Ulman and three of his subordinates stood accused of having killed six civilians. In July 2007, a Military Court convicted Ulman and three other culprits

---

928 Human Rights Watch, 'Backgrounder on the Case of Kheda Kungaeva – Trial of Yuri Budanov Set for February 28' (2001) 1 <https://www.hrw.org/legacy/backgrounder/eca/chech-bck0226.htm>.

929 See Военная Коллегия Верховного Суда Российской Федерации, 06.10.2003, N 5–072/02 [Military Division of the Supreme Court of the Russian Federation, 6 October 2003, No 5–072/02].

930 Esakov (n 702) 383. After his release, Budanov was murdered in the streets of Moscow by a Chechen in an act of retaliation.

to long prison sentences.[931] However, they were not there to hear their verdict. Ulman and two other accused had gone into hiding. Only the fourth defendant appeared in court. The other three were sentenced in absentia and up to this day remain on the run.[932] In another trial, the Russian servicemen Evgeny Khudiakov and Sergey Arakcheev were accused of having killed three Chechen civilians. Khudiakov was sentenced to 17 and Arakcheev to 15 years of imprisonment. Again, only one defendant was there to hear the verdict. Arakcheev escaped justice and is still on the loose today.[933]

Four out of seven criminals on the run; this lax enforcement is another setback for the effective punishment of war crimes in Russia. In addition, *none* of the accused were convicted of violations of IHL, but only for ordinary crimes. What is truly shocking, however, is the absence of convictions in relation to the number of victims. The First Chechen War (1994–1996) claimed between 60 000 and 100 000 deaths, most of them civilians.[934] The Second Chechen War cost the lives of 14 000 civilians during the active battle phase alone (1999–2002).[935] Many more died due to the repressions in the ensuing guerrilla warfare. There are countless cases of torture, rape, and enforced disappearances.[936]

The stark contrast between the tens of thousands of dead civilians and the handful of convictions is painfully obvious.[937] What are the reasons

---

931   ibid. Unfortunately, the final judgment of the Supreme Court is not available online. While the defendants were first acquitted by a military Court, the Constitutional Court ordered a retrial without the participation of a jury. Finally, the Supreme Court quashed the acquittals and ordered a retrial by professional judges of the Military Court of Northern Caucasus without the participation of laymen. See Постановление Конституционного Суда Российской Федерации, 06.04.2006, N 3-П [Decision of the Constitutional Court of the Russian Federation, 6 April 2006, No 3-P].

932   See e.g. 'Где сейчас находится капитан Ульман? [Where is Captain Ulman Now?]' (Yandex Zen, 5 February 2019) <https://zen.yandex.ru/media/faculty_of_history/gde-seichas-nahoditsia-kapitan-ulman-5c58363c18d56e00ae42e423>.

933   Amnesty International, 'Europe and Central Asia Summary of Amnesty International's Concerns in the Region, July–December 2007 (EUR 01/001/2008)' (2008) 72.

934   Emil Souleimanov, *An Endless War: The Russian-Chechen Conflict in Perspective* (Peter Lang 2007) 125.

935   ibid 171.

936   See for this below at pp 288 et seq.

937   Civilian deaths may be justified under IHL as proportional "collateral damage", see Art 51(5) AP I and ICRC, Customary IHL Database, Rule 14. However, the numbers in Chechnya point to an absolutely disproportionate death rate among

for this judicial silence? It may be the lack of political willingness to admit that Chechnya constituted an armed conflict under IHL. It may be the abstract wording of Art 356 which deters courts and prosecutors for venturing into unchartered terrain. It may be the lack of precedents.[938] Whatever the reasons, the result is clear: perpetrators enjoy impunity for their war crimes in Chechnya.

3.4.2 Ignoring Strasbourg – from silence to defiance

Pressure on Russia to prosecute the culprits of the Chechen War increased when the ECtHR issued its first judgment *Isayeva and Others v Russia* in February 2005.[939] More than 250 decisions would follow. The Strasbourg case law was truly ground-breaking. For the first time in its history, it dealt with an active large-scale conflict.[940] When *Isayeva* was decided, the Second Chechen War was still ongoing.[941] Furthermore, the Court found extremely grave violations:[942] extrajudicial killings,[943] torture,[944] enforced disap-

---

civilians. In addition, direct and intentional violence against civilians, such as rape, murder, or torture may never be justified under IHL.

938 Esakov (n 702) 384.

939 ECtHR, *Isayeva v Russia*, No 57950/00, 24 February 2005.

940 While the Court did not directly apply IHL, it made an important contribution to the protection of war victims, see William Abresch, 'A Human Rights Law of Internal Armed Conflict: The European Court of Human Rights in Chechnya' (2005) 16 European Journal of International Law 741.

941 Michael Schwirtz, 'Russia Ends Operations in Chechnya' (The New York Times, 17 April 2009) <https://www.nytimes.com/2009/04/17/world/europe/17chechny a.html>.

942 For a detailed thematic overview see Philip Leach, 'The Chechen Conflict: Analysing the Oversight of the European Court of Human Rights' [2008] European Human Rights Law Review 732; Philip Leach, 'Egregious Human Rights Violations in Chechnya: Appraising the Pursuit of Justice' in Lauri Mälksoo and Wolfgang Benedek (eds), *Russia and the European Court of Human Rights: the Strasbourg Effect* (Cambridge University Press 2017); Abresch (n 940).

943 See e.g. ECtHR, *Amuyeva and Others v Russia*, No 17321/06, 25 November 2010.

944 See e.g. ECtHR, *Khadisov and Tsechoyev v Russia*, No 21519/02, 5 February 2009; ECtHR, *Sadykov v Russia*, No 41840/02, 7 October 2010; ECtHR, *Gisayev v Russia*, No 14811/04, 20 January 2011.

pearances,[945] indiscriminate aerial bombardments, and artillery shelling.[946] In many instances, the Court found substantial as well as procedural violations of Convention rights, because Russia had not investigated the alleged crime. Authorities failed to question the applicant, carry out an autopsy, or look for evidence. Often, no investigation at all took place, which represents the very root cause for the absence of convictions for war crimes.[947] How did Moscow react to this criticism?

Art 46 ECHR obliges all member States to abide by the final judgments of the ECtHR. In most cases, Russia paid the pecuniary and non-pecuniary damages.[948] However, implementing a judgment may also include changing the legal framework or practice in order to improve the standards of investigation and deter future violations.[949] In this respect, the Russian government has done almost nothing to ensure accountability for the abuses of security forces and prevent similar cases in the future. Philip Leach has represented several Chechen claimants before the ECtHR and extensively written on the issue. He argues that "although there have now been in excess of 250 judgments since 2005, finding the Russian authorities responsible for such breaches, there has been little or no political will to respond."[950] Initially, Russia took some steps such as setting up a special investigations unit. However, it quickly became obvious that this

---

945 See e.g. ECtHR, *Malika Dzhamayeva and Others v Russia*, No 26980/06, 21 December 2010; ECtHR, *Aslakhanova and Others v Russia*, No 2944/06 et seq, 18 December 2012; ECtHR, *Turluyeva v Russia*, No 63638/09, 20 June 2013; ECtHR, *Yandiyev and Others v Russia*, Nos 34541/06, 43811/06, and 1578/07, 10 October 2013; ECtHR, *Akhmatov and Others v Russia*, Nos 38828/ 10, 2543/11, 2650/11 et al, 16 January 2014.

946 See e.g. ECtHR, *Umayeva v Russia*, No 1200/03, 4 December 2008; ECtHR, *Abuyeva and Others v Russia*, No 27065/05, 2 December 2010; ECtHR, *Esmukhambetov and Others v Russia*, No 23445/03, 29 March 2011; ECtHR, *Kerimova and Others v Russia*, No 17170/04 et al, 3 May 2011; ECtHR, *Khamzayev and Others v Russia*, No 1503/02, 3 May 2011; ECtHR, *Damayev v Russia*, No 36150/04, 29 May 2012; ECtHR, *Abdulkhanov and Others v Russia*, No 22782/06, 3 October 2013; ECtHR, *Mezhidov v Russia*, No 67326/01, 25 September 2008; ECtHR, *Taysumov and Others v Russia*, No 21810/03, 14 May 2009.

947 See for this with further references to ECtHR case law: Leach, 'The Chechen Conflict: Analysing the Oversight of the European Court of Human Rights' (n 942) 750–755.

948 ibid 758.

949 See e.g. ECtHR, *Abakarova v Russia*, No 16664/07, 15 October 2015, para 112.

950 Philip Leach, 'The Continuing Utility of International Human Rights Mechanisms?' (*EJIL Talk!*, 1 November 2017) <ejiltalk.org/the-continuing-utility-of-international-human-rights-mechanisms/>.

would not yield tangible results.[951] Human Rights Watch laments that not a single perpetrator in the Chechen cases decided by the ECtHR has been held criminally accountable and provides a detailed account of the evidence that the Russian investigators ignored.[952]

Similarly, PACE[953] Rapporteur Dick Marty speaks of the "near-total impunity" of Russian servicemen. The rare convictions are almost exclusively for petty theft, traffic violations, or disorderly conduct.[954] Where new investigations were opened, the old flaws persisted. This is exemplified by three consecutive judgments that regarded the same shelling of the village Katr-Yurt in 2000.[955] The first case – *Isayeva and Others v Russia* (2005) – stated that the investigation of the bombardment was delayed and totally ineffective.[956] Five years later, in the case *Abuyeva and Others v Russia* the ECtHR held that "all the major flaws in the investigation indicated in 2005 persisted throughout the second set of proceedings."[957] Another five years later, but still concerning the same attack, the Court rendered a third judgement: *Abakarova and Others v Russia*. There, it criticised the fact that nothing had changed:

> *"The inadequacy of the investigation into the deaths and injuries of dozens of civilians, including the deaths of the applicant's family, was not the result of objective difficulties that can be attributed to the passage of time or the loss of evidence, but rather the result of the investigating authorities' sheer unwillingness to establish the truth and punish those responsible."[958]*

Such insufficient investigations not only violate the procedural limb of the right to life under the ECHR, but also the obligation under IHL to account for civilian deaths. In addition, States have the duty to prosecute and punish war crimes.[959] Hence, the reluctance to investigate the Chechen

---

951 PACE, 'Legal Remedies for Human Rights Violations in the North-Caucasus Region: Report of the Committee on Legal Affairs and Human Rights to the PACE' (2010) para 29.
952 Human Rights Watch, '"Who Will Tell Me What Happened to My Son?" Russia's Implementation of European Court of Human Rights Judgments on Chechnya' (2009) 11 et seq.
953 Parliamentary Assembly of the Council of Europe.
954 PACE (n 951) 25.
955 See for this in detail, Leach 283 et seq.
956 ECtHR, *Isayeva v Russia*, No 57950/00, 24 February 2005, paras 214–225.
957 ECtHR, *Abuyeva and Others v Russia*, No 27065/05, 2 December 2010, para 210.
958 ECtHR, *Abakarova v Russia*, No 16664/07, 15 December 2015, para 98.
959 ICRC, Customary IHL Database, Rule 117; see also Art 33 AP I, Art 8 AP II, and ICRC, Customary IHL Database, Rule 158.

cases not only constitutes a failure to comply with the ECHR, it also violates IHL. This is the root cause of the absence of a single conviction for war crimes delivered by a Russian court.

3.4.3 Critical assessment – ICL in Russia: a selective application

Apart from the few cases mentioned above at page 202, the Russian authorities have not investigated, let alone convicted Russian citizens for crimes committed during armed conflict. After the Russo-Georgian conflict, Moscow declared that "during the hostilities, no crimes were perpetrated against civilians by any military personnel" and there were "no instances where Russian military personnel were involved in crimes against citizens of other countries including Georgia."[960] In Syria, there are no known prosecutions.[961]

It is telling that Russian prosecutors are even reluctant to use Art 356 CCRF against citizens of "enemy-States." Following the Russo-Georgian War, Russian investigators opened criminal cases against Georgian citizens. Georgia had allegedly targeted the Russian peacekeeping contingent when it launched its offensive to win back South Ossetia in the 2008 war. If one accepts that these personnel were present as genuine peacekeepers, this might amount to a war crime.[962] Yet the Russian prosecution "only" investigated the "murder of two or several persons in the line of duty using socially dangerous means" according to Art 105(2) CCRF.[963] No mention of Art 356 CCRF. In another case, the Ukrainian pilot Nadiya Savchenko stood accused of murdering two Russian TV journalists. Instead of Art 356, the prosecution charged her with "ordinary" murder.[964] The only possible exception to this rule could have been the work of the Investigative Com-

---

960 IIFFMCG, 'Report of the Independent International Fact-Finding Mission on the Conflict in Georgia (Tagliavini Report) Volume III – Views of the Sides on the Conflict, Chronologies and Responses to Questionnaires' (2009) 489.
961 See, however, the interesting case of Slavonic Corpus where two CEOs of a private military company were convicted for mercenarism under Art 359 of the Russian Criminal Code, below at p 311.
962 Art 8(2)(b)(iii) ICC Statute.
963 IIFFMCG, 'Report of the Independent International Fact-Finding Mission on the Conflict in Georgia (Tagliavini Report) Volume III – Views of the Sides on the Conflict, Chronologies and Responses to Questionnaires' (n 960) 488.
964 Initially, Savchenko was also charged with war crimes and genocide, but these charges were later separated. The reason for this was not communicated, see Esakov (n 702) 386. In any case, Savchenko was later released in a prisoner swap

mittee of the Russian Federation (Sledkom), the main investigative agency in Russia. In 2014, it set up a special department to investigate alleged war crimes by the Ukrainian military in Donbas. Sledkom issued a strong statement stressing that it "will be working until all Ukrainian militants and individuals committing crimes against civilians have been prosecuted for them."[965] Nevertheless, its work remains purely symbolic. None of the investigations has ever made it to a trial stage.[966]

In this sense, Art 356 can be called dead letter law. In most cases, the criminal proceedings are already stalled at the investigative stage. The poor implementation of the ECtHR decisions has made it very clear that Russia is not interested in improving this. When violations of IHL actually make it to court, Art 356 is consistently ignored. While Russian legislation embraces the concept of war crimes in *theory*, the idea of prosecuting Russian citizens in *practice* meets with opposition from jurists, politicians, and certain scholars. Professor Irina Umnova heavily criticised the recommendation by the PACE[967], which called for the establishment of an international tribunal for Chechnya, as a "grave violation of political ethics."[968] Such misgivings against ICL even concern events that predate the Russian Federation. Classifying the massacre of Polish officers at Katyn or the deportation of civilians from the occupied Baltic States as a war crime breaks a Russian taboo.[969] International case law that dealt with these incidents, such as *Kononov v Latvia*, comes under heavy fire from Russian politicians.[970] Pavel Leptev, the Russian representative at the Council of Europe reacted sharply to the ECtHR's ruling and argued that war crimes

---

in 2016. For details on her case and for the question whether she was a POW see below at p 271.

965 'Russia's Investigative Committee Sets up Special Unit to Investigate International Crimes in Ukraine' (Sledkom, 4 June 2014) <https://en.sledcom.ru/news/item/517777/>.

966 Esakov (n 702) 386.

967 See PACE, 'Recommendation 1600 (2003) – The Human Rights Situation in the Chechen Republic' (2003) para 3.5.

968 Quoted in Mälksoo, *Russian Approaches to International Law* (n 6) 137.

969 Lauri Mälksoo, 'Soviet Genocide? Communist Mass Deportations in the Baltic States and International Law' (2001) 14 Leiden Journal of International Law 757; Mälksoo, *Russian Approaches to International Law* (n 6) 138.

970 ECtHR, *Kononov v Latvia*, No 36376/04, 17 May 2010. The case concerned Vasiliy Kononov, a former Soviet partisan fighter who had been convicted by Latvian courts for killing civilians during the Second World War. The Grand Chamber of the ECtHR ruled that this conviction did not violate the prohibition of retrospective punishment under Art 7 ECHR.

could not be committed in a war against the aggressor.[971] In sum, this proves a sad truth: not only is Art 356 a deficient and dead provision, but also the very idea of international criminal law meets heavy resistance when it is supposed to be applied to Russians.

At the same time, ICL still receives much interest from Russian scholars. My take on Russian implementation would be incomplete, if I did not honour their valuable – and highly critical – contributions: Gennady Esakov has published an article that denounces the "deplorable" current Russian framework and points out ways to mend the deficiencies.[972] Bakhtiyar Tuzmukhamedov, who has served as the Russian Judge at the ICTR from 2009–2015, has been lamenting the faulty implementation of war crimes in international[973] and domestic fora.[974] Even at the height of the Chechen War, voices like Vladimir Galitsky's penetrated the veil of indifference. Galitsky, who was at the time a professor at the Military Academy, criticised that Russia's Army waged war "in a legal vacuum."[975] Despite these persistent calls, however, the discussion has never gained enough momentum in political circles. Esakov concedes that the "rising interest in international criminal law and a cognizance of the need for reforms" is confined to the "theoretical level."[976] At the same time, he argues that the debate could reach far beyond the ivory tower and ends his article with a plea: "Now, many Russians are involved in the armed conflict on Ukraine's territory and to dismiss their possible unlawful acts is a wanton disregard of reality. It is necessary to bring justice to our courts, if not today, then certainly tomorrow."[977] The hearing of his plea would prove a great step forward for the Russian implementation of IHL.

---

971 'Павел Лаптев: срок жизни Европейского суда может быть сокращен [Pavel Laptev: The Days of the European Court May be Numbered]' (Kommersant, 31 May 2010) <https://www.kommersant.ru/doc/1378599>.

972 Esakov (n 702).

973 Tuzmukhamedov (n 703).

974 Бахтияр Тузмухамедов [Bakhtiyar Tuzmukhamedov] 'Как воевать по правилам? [How to Wage War by the Rules?]' (Nezavisimaya Gazeta, 15 February 2010) <http://www.ng.ru/dipkurer/2010-02-15/11_wars.html>.

975 Владимир Галицкий [Vladimir Galitsky], 'Война в правовом вакууме [War in a Legal Vacuum]' (Nezavisimaya Gazeta, 16 June 2000) <http://nvo.ng.ru/concept s/2000-06-16/4_vacuumwar.html?id_user=Y>.

976 Esakov (n 702) 371.

977 ibid 392.

4. Conclusion

> "A farmer went out to sow his seed. [...] Some fell on rocky places, where it
> did not have much soil. It sprang up quickly, because the soil was shallow.
> But when the sun came up, the plants were scorched, and they withered
> because they had no root. [...] Still other seed fell on good soil. It came
> up, grew and produced a crop, some multiplying thirty, some sixty, some a
> hundred times."
>
> *Mark 4:2–8 (New International Version).*

Judging by the Russian Constitution, one could argue that the seed of
IHL fell on "good soil." Art 15(4) CRF displays a laudable openness to
international law; but did IHL spring up too quickly and wither? The
Constitutional Court voiced its enthusiasm for IHL in its *Chechnya Decision* (1995) and reminded the government that war should not be waged
outside the law. This marked a glorious moment of judicial oversight
and IHL implementation. Unfortunately, the Court has fallen silent ever
since and the Kremlin successfully ignored its wake-up call during both
Chechen Wars.[978]

Similarly, IHL did not thrive in other respects. Today, the Russian
framework is deficient concerning the criminalisation of war crimes.
Worse, even the *existing* framework is not applied by the judiciary. Either
the law enforcement organs already fail to investigate, or courts are reluctant to apply Art 356 CCRF. Other efforts to implement IHL, notably the
plethora of laws concerning the military are laudable, but it remains to
be seen what impact they have on the practice of Russian warfare. As I
will show in the following chapters on Russia's practice on the battlefield,
Moscow often denies the very application of IHL. It thereby sidelines
its own implementation mechanisms, turning them into mere decoration
with no substance.[979] Due to these shortcomings, Russia has implemented
IHL only to a minor extent. Most of the good seed fell on barren land.

---

978 See Lauri Mälksoo, 'Case Law in Russian Approaches to International Law'
in Anthea Roberts and others (eds), *Comparative International Law* (Oxford University Press 2018) 347. The author argues that in "politically important cases,
especially in foreign affairs, Russian courts and judges do not seem to claim the
role of counterweight to the executive and the legislative powers."

979 For the difference between implementation and internalisation see Evangelista
(n 878) 323–324.

Chapter III: Evading IHL on the Battlefield – Denying the Existence of an Armed Conflict ("The Paintbrush")

Does Russia turn IHL into a nice "car that never leaves the garage?"[980] Despite IHL's chronic enforcement problem, many would consider that IHL *did* in fact leave the garage many times. However, when studying Russia's behaviour in recent wars, one cannot overlook that Moscow is keen on evading IHL, turning it into a showcase car. Moscow rarely challenges existing IHL norms directly. Rather, it uses a toolbox of evasion tactics. What does it contain? I contend that Russia mainly uses three tools to produce the intended result: waging war without incurring restrictions under IHL. Firstly, the "paintbrush." By blurring legal lines Russia already denies the very existence of an armed conflict – and thus the applicability of IHL. Secondly, the "apprentice." By outsourcing warfare to a certain type of proxy, Russia seeks to avoid responsibility for its actions. Thirdly, the "sledgehammer." If neither the paintbrush nor the apprentice work, Russia resorts to a crude denial of facts concerning the IHL violation of which it stands accused.

Of course, these three methods do not exist in complete separation. In the same way a mechanic might loosen a stuck screw with a hammer before using the screwdriver, the three approaches can be combined. In eastern Ukraine, Russia both denies the existence of an armed conflict and outsources warfare to proxies. In Syria, Russia uses outsourcing while denying the violations of its own troops. Yet, what is evinced from all the following examples is a strong desire to sideline IHL – a field of law which Russia has once influenced like no other State.

---

980 Sir Ian Brownlie, 'Comment' in Antonio Cassese and Joseph Weiler (eds), *Change and Stability in International Law-making* (De Gruyter 2010) 110. Brownlie's original quote did not refer to IHL, but *ius cogens*.

1. *The threshold of application – the Achilles' heel of IHL*

Let us turn to the first tool – the "paintbrush." Denying the very application of the law strikes the Achilles' heel of IHL. Unlike human rights treaties that – at least within a State's jurisdiction – apply at any time, in any place, IHL is the framework tailored to armed conflict and belligerent occupation.[981] For it to apply, violence must reach the threshold of either an international or non-international armed conflict. This may present a weak spot, because denying the existence of such a conflict can be used to discard the entire framework of IHL altogether.

In 1949 the term of "armed conflict" was meant to introduce an "objective and factual" criterion that excluded any subjectivity, formalism, and evasion.[982] At the time the drafters wanted to exclude the argument that an undeclared war did not trigger the application of the Conventions.[983] Against this background, it was a huge achievement to clarify that the Conventions apply to "all cases of declared war or of *any other* armed conflict which may arise between two or more of the High Contracting Parties." However, closing one loophole opened others. We shall see how Russia uses and abuses these gaps to prevent the application of IHL:

- Moscow tries to avoid the IHL framework governing belligerent occupation by resorting to a mix of legal arguments and factual denial. I will deal with these cases under point 2 using the examples of Crimea, Transdniestria, Abkhazia, and South Ossetia.
- In other situations, Moscow simply denies the involvement of its soldiers in a very crude way. This will be discussed under point 3, using the example of eastern Ukraine.
- Finally, Moscow has "rebranded clashes" portraying them as "military" but falling outside the scope of IHL. I will address this under point 4 using the examples of the Chechen Wars and the recent clash in the Sea of Azov.

---

981 See e.g. Art 2 International Covenant on Civil and Political Rights, Art 1 European Convention on Human Rights, Art 1 American Convention on Human Rights, Art 1 African Charter on Human and Peoples' Rights, Art 2 Arab Charter on Human Rights.

982 Dörmann and others (n 543) Art 2 para 209.

983 Jean Pictet, *The Geneva Conventions of 12 August 1949: Geneva Convention for the Amelioration of the Condition of the Wounded and Sick in Armed Forces in the Field* (International Committee of the Red Cross 1952) 28.

2. Avoiding occupation – ceci n'est pas une occupation

Belligerent occupation[984] has been a bone of contention in the development of IHL. It was among the reasons that led to the failure of the Brussels Declaration.[985] Later, however, States regulated the issue in great detail in the Hague Regulations of 1899 and 1907 – Martens' *chef d'oeuvre*. 14 out of 56 articles were dedicated to occupation.[986] In 1949, the Fourth Geneva Convention added another 100 Articles.[987] This makes occupation one of the most regulated situations in armed conflict.

In Russia, the issue of occupation is a highly sensitive topic. To Russians, it is more than a legal term, and it evokes memories of the gruesome crimes that the Nazis committed against the citizens of the Soviet Union. I have detailed these crimes at page 105, and they remain beyond comprehension and comparison. It goes without saying, that I will be using the term occupation in a strictly legal sense stripped of its historical burden.

Firstly, I will briefly outline the concept of belligerent occupation. When is territory considered occupied and what protection does IHL offer? In the second part we will look at the case study of Crimea, where Russia consistently evades the application of the occupation regime. In the second case study, we will look at Transdniestria, South Ossetia, and Abkhazia. There, too, Russia rejects the role of the occupant, though with an entirely different reasoning. I will argue that in Crimea – and to a lesser extent also in Transdniestria, South Ossetia, and Abkhazia – Russia tries to outmanoeuvre the framework of occupation with arguments that are at odds with international law.

---

984 The term belligerent occupation is the literal translation of the Latin term *occupatio bellica*. Since the term occupation is also used in other fields of international law, I would like to point out that the following analysis only deals with occupation under IHL. See also Yoram Dinstein, *The International Law of Belligerent Occupation* (2nd edn, Cambridge University Press 2019) 35.

985 See above at n 189 and pp 43 et seq.

986 See Art 42–56 HR.

987 See Art 27–34 GC IV, i.e. the common provisions that apply to all protected persons. Art 47–78 GC IV are tailored to occupation and Art 79–141 GC IV apply both in occupied territories and to aliens in the territory of a party to the conflict.

2.1 Occupation under IHL – an elaborate framework

Occupation is a frequent phenomenon in armed conflict. Yoram Dinstein, a distinguished expert in this field, writes:

> "The most persistent myth is that the occurrence of belligerent occupation is an anomaly or even an aberration. In reality, when an international armed conflict breaks out, armies tend to be on the move on the ground whenever they have an opportunity to do so. Each Belligerent Party usually spares no effort to penetrate, and if possible take possession of the territory of the enemy."[988]

The application of the full framework of occupation hinges upon one article: Art 42 HR.[989] The provision considers territory occupied "when it is actually placed under the *authority* of the hostile army." The treaty, however, does not define what it means by "authority". Throughout history, this vague provision has often caused uncertainty.[990] Today, however, there is consensus that a State needs "effective control" over territory in order to have authority in the sense of Art 42 HR.[991]

Before clarifying what "effective control" means, I would like to flag that the term is used in other contexts as well. This sometimes leads to unfortunate, but avoidable confusion. The ICJ used "effective control" in its Nicaragua judgment.[992] There, the Court refers to control over *groups or individuals* as a standard of *attribution* under today's Art 8 ASRIWA. Furthermore, the ECtHR uses "effective control" in its case law. There, it refers to *jurisdiction* under Art 1 ECHR.[993] Under belligerent occupation, however, "effective control" simply describes the level of factual control a

---

988 Dinstein (n 984) 1.

989 The Fourth Geneva Convention does not contain its own definition of occupation, but rather refers to the Hague Regulations, see Art 154 GC IV. Nevertheless, GC IV is wider than the HR and protects individuals beyond the scope of Art 42 HR, for example during the invasion phase, see below at n 1006.

990 Eyal Benvenisti, *The International Law of Occupation* (2nd ed, Oxford University Press 2012) 44–47.

991 See ibid 47–48 with further sources.

992 ICJ, *Military and Paramilitary Activities in and against Nicaragua (Nicaragua v United States of America)*, Merits Judgment, ICJ Reports (1986) 14 [hereinafter *Nicaragua Case*] para 115. I will deal with the ICJ judgment when addressing the issue of occupation by proxy at p 238.

993 See e.g. ECtHR, *Güzelyurtlu and Others v Cyprus and Turkey*, No 36925/07, 29 January 2009, paras 191–197. Sometimes, the ECtHR also uses the term "effective overall control" leading to further confusion. Unfortunately, the Court does

foreign army needs to have over *territory* in order to be called an occupying power.

Scholars, States, and courts have rallied around two criteria that characterise effective control under IHL:

- The former government does not exercise authority over the territory anymore (1)
- The occupying power now exercises such authority, which means that it can enforce its will on the population (2).[994]

Effective control is thus a matter of fact.[995] But what does this mean in concrete terms? How many men, how much military equipment is needed to have effective control? Quite clearly, this depends on the country and the circumstances. The standard will change from case to case, based on population density, terrain, and other factors.[996] The ICTY developed the formula that "the occupying power has a sufficient force present, or the capacity to send troops within a reasonable time to make the authority of the occupying power felt."[997] Certainly, control over territory does not necessarily mean that the army manages to control the entire population.

---

not always distinguish clearly between the issues of jurisdiction under Art 1 ECHR and State attribution, see n 1701.

994 Tristan Ferraro, 'Determining the Beginning and End of an Occupation under International Humanitarian Law' (2012) 94 International Review of the Red Cross 133, 141–143 with further sources; See also Robert Kolb and Sylvain Vité, *Le droit de l'occupation militaire: perspectives historiques et enjeux juridiques actuels* (Bruylant 2009) 143 et seq; Dinstein (n 984) 48; (n 72) 21; for military manuals see Deutsches Bundesministerium der Verteidigung (n 205) para 5.4; UK Ministry of Defense, 'The Joint Service Manual of the Law of Armed Conflict (Joint Service Publication 383)' (2004) para 11.3; US Department of Defence (n 204) para 11.2.2. For evidence of these conditions in case law see ICJ, *Armed Activities on the Territory of the Congo (Democratic Republic of the Congo v Uganda)*, Judgment, ICJ Reports (2005) 168 [hereinafter *Armed Activities Case*] para 172; ICJ, *Legal Consequences of the Construction of a Wall in the Occupied Palestinian Territory*, Advisory Opinion, ICJ Reports (2004) 13 [hereinafter *Wall Opinion*] para 78; Permanent Court of Arbitration, *Eritrea-Ethiopia Claims Commission (ECC) Partial Award: Central Front – Eritrea's Claim 2*, April 28 2004, para 29; ICTY, *The Prosecutor v Mladen Naletilić and Vinko Martinović* (IT-98-34-T), Trial Chamber Judgment, 31 March 2003, paras 216 et seq.

995 Dinstein (n 984) 43.

996 ibid 43–44. See also ICTY, *The Prosecutor v Mladen Naletilić and Vinko Martinović* (IT-98–34-T), Trial Chamber Judgment, 31 March 2003, para 218.

997 ICTY, *The Prosecutor v Mladen Naletilić and Vinko Martinović* (IT-98–34-T), Trial Chamber Judgment, 31 March 2003, para 217.

Personal control over *each* citizen is not necessary. Art 42 HR merely requires *territorial* control.[998]

At the same time, occupation needs some amount of "boots on the ground."[999] According to the position of the ICRC, the occupying power has to enforce its will *by virtue* of the presence of its troops.[1000] Mere influence through other channels – be it political or economic – does not suffice.[1001] The ECtHR has endorsed this position in *Sargsyan v Azerbaijan* where it argued that "occupation is not conceivable without boots on the ground."[1002] This does not preclude ruling through a local civil administration as long as the military retains the ultimate authority.[1003] A possible exception to the "boots-on-the-ground-rule" is the delicate issue of "occupation by proxy", which I will discuss extensively below using the examples of Transdniestria, Abkhazia, and South Ossetia. Finally, it is worth noting that effective control may exist only in certain parts of a country. The Geneva Conventions speak of *"partial* or total occupation" and do not require the occupant to take control of the entire territory.[1004]

In addition to having "effective control" through its soldiers, the occupying power will have to be present against the will of the sovereign.[1005] Consensual occupation does not trigger the application of IHL. In turn, non-consensual belligerent occupation always constitutes an international armed conflict. IHL keeps applying to the situation of occupation even if hostilities have long died down. This is true even if the invasion does not meet with armed resistance as clarified by CA 2(2). The above said leaves us with three conditions for belligerent occupation:[1006]

---

998   Benvenisti (n 990) 51–53.

999   Dinstein (n 984) 50.

1000   Ferraro (n 994) 144; ICRC, 'Expert Meeting, Occupation and Other Forms of Administration of Foreign Territory' (2012) 17–19.

1001   For the issue of "virtual occupation" see Benvenisti (n 990) 53–54.

1002   See ECtHR, *Sargsyan v Azerbaijan*, No 40167/06, 16 June 2015, para 94; see also para 144 of the same judgment: "The Court finds that Gulistan is not occupied by or under the effective control of foreign forces as this would require a presence of foreign troops in Gulistan."

1003   Dinstein (n 984) 65.

1004   See CA 2(2).

1005   Dinstein (n 984) 39.

1006   Finally, it is worth noting that civilians are not completely without protection during the invasion phase, i.e. before a State establishes effective control under 42 HR. The protection under GC IV is wider than under the Hague Regulations. As Jean Pictet writes in his 1958 Commentary: "So far as individuals are concerned, the application of the Fourth Geneva Convention does not depend upon the existence of a state of occupation within the meaning of the

1. The former government has lost its authority over the territory
2. The occupying power replaced this authority in the sense that it can enforce its will
3. This substitution of power was non-consensual

As mentioned above, occupation is one of the most regulated areas of IHL. Detailed rules set out the rights and duties of the occupying power. Generally speaking, it has to take necessary steps to restore law and order and public life, and maintain them as far as possible while respecting the laws in force, unless absolutely prevented from doing so.[1007] Some have compared this position to being the "trustee" for the occupied territory.[1008] The regime of occupation contains both positive and negative obligations for the occupant. On the positive side, the occupying power must restore public order (Art 43 HR) and is responsible for the treatment of the

---

Art 42 referred to above. The relations between the civilian population of a territory and troops advancing into that territory, whether fighting or not, are governed by the present Convention. There is no intermediate period between what might be termed the invasion phase and the inauguration of a stable regime of occupation. Even a patrol which penetrates into enemy territory without any intention of staying there must respect the Conventions in its dealings with the civilians it meets." Jean Pictet, *The Geneva Conventions of 12 August 1949: Geneva Convention Relative to the Protection of Civilian Persons in Time of War* (International Committee of the Red Cross 1958) 60. Therefore, individuals are protected as soon as they fall into the hands of the enemy. Note, however, that this neither turns the invader into an occupant nor the invaded territory into occupied territory. It merely extends the protection of GC IV to individuals in the hands of the enemy. There is still a major difference between the invasion phase and occupation under 42 HR. In the former, a State is only responsible for the conduct of its own troops. In the latter, States also have numerous positive obligations to uphold law and order. For example, if a soldier kills a civilian during the invasion this would violate Art 27 GC IV. If a (non-attributable) militiaman kills a civilian this would not violate Art 27 GC IV. If the State, however, already exercises effective control as an occupying power, the killing by a third actor may constitute a failure to uphold law and order. Another major difference is that GC IV only protects persons during the invasion phase. The protection of property requires effective control under 42 HR. See Benvenisti (n 990) 52–53; M Milanović, 'Al-Skeini and Al-Jedda in Strasbourg' (2012) 23 European Journal of International Law 121, 122. See also ICTY, *The Prosecutor v Mladen Naletilić and Vinko Martinović* (IT-98–34-T), Trial Chamber Judgment, 31 March 2003, para 221.

1007 ICRC Casebook, How Does Law Protect in War, 'Occupation' <https://casebook.icrc.org/glossary/occupation>.

1008 Allan Gerson, 'Trustee-Occupant: The Legal Status of Israel's Presence in the West Bank' (1973) 14 Harvard International Law Review 1.

protected persons[1009] in its hand (Art 29 GC IV). It has an obligation to let in humanitarian relief (Art 59 GC IV), and to maintain the supply of food and medical items, as well as public health (Art 55 and 56 GC IV).

Moreover, the occupying power has numerous negative obligations. The following may only serve as examples. Generally, the occupant must treat protected persons with "respect for their honour, their family rights, their religious convictions and practices, and their manners and customs. They shall at all times be humanely treated, and shall be protected especially against all acts of violence or threats thereof and against insults and public curiosity" (Art 27(1) GC IV). Furthermore, IHL formulates special prohibitions against hostage-taking (Art 34 GC IV), pillage and reprisals (Art 33 GC IV), corporal punishment, torture (Art 32 GC IV), and deportation (Art 49 GC IV). The protections of civilian internees especially are regulated in great detail (Art 79–141 GC IV). In addition, the Hague regulations protect private and other types of property (Art 47–56 HR), and family life (Art 46 HR). Finally, Art 49 GC IV prohibits forcible transfer and deportation.

2.1.1 The case of Crimea – belligerent occupation or mending a "historical injustice"?

Bearing in mind the above, we will turn to the case of Crimea where Russia has successfully ignored the framework of occupation for the past years. Firstly, I will retrace the events on the peninsula in 2014. Then, I will apply the three conditions of belligerent occupation as outlined above to the Crimean case. Finally, I will show how Russia has repeatedly rebuffed calls to respect specific IHL provisions and explain what this means for Russia's attitude to IHL in general.

2.1.2 The events in Crimea in 2014 – arrival of the "little green men"

In the early morning hours of 27 February 2014, armed individuals seized government institutions on the Crimean Peninsula including the regional Parliament in Simferopol.[1010] The media quickly called them "little

---

1009 Art 4 GC IV defines who is a protected person.
1010 For a detailed chronology of events see Lawrence Freedman, *Ukraine and the Art of Strategy* (Oxford University Press 2019) 82–90.

green men" because they wore modern camouflage uniforms without insignia.[1011] Although they called themselves "Crimea's armed self-defence force" it turned out that they actually belonged to the KSSO, Russia's newly formed Special Operations Command.[1012] They were supported by Russian airborne forces (VDV).[1013] In the following days their units managed to take control over the entire peninsula. On 1 March, the Russian Federation Council officially approved the use of Russian troops in Crimea.[1014]

Events unfolded at an amazing speed. On 11 March, the Republic of Crimea issued a declaration of independence which foresaw a referendum on this question. The popular vote was originally scheduled for 25 May, but then hastily moved forward to 16 March.[1015] It produced an overwhelming, yet internationally contested majority of 95 percent in favour of independence and reunification with Russia.[1016] On 18 March, two days after the referendum, Putin signed the Accession Treaty. Two days later the Russian State Duma ratified the treaty, retroactively declaring the

---

1011 A Finnish military magazine identified the soldiers' uniforms and equipment because it was only used by the Russian Federation at that time, Arto Pulkki, 'Crimea Invaded By High Readiness Forces Of The Russian Federation' (Suomen Sotilas, 3 March 2014) <https://web.archive.org/web/20150330124704/http://www.suomensotilas.fi/en/artikkelit/crimea-invaded-high-readiness-forces-russian-federation>. The rest of the media quickly picked up the term "little green men", see e.g. Vitaly Shevchenko, "Little Green Men" or "Russian Invaders"? (BBC, 11 March 2014) <https://www.bbc.com/news/world-europe-26532154>; Steve Pifer, 'Watch Out for Little Green Men' (Der Spiegel, 07 July 2014) <https://www.spiegel.de/international/europe/nato-needs-strategy-for-possible-meddling-by-putin-in-baltic-states-a-979707.html>. People sympathetic to the Russian intervention called the unmarked soldiers "polite people" in allusion to their disciplined behaviour.

1012 Galeotti, *Armies of Russia's War in Ukraine* (n 785) 11.

1013 Mark Galeotti, *Spetsnaz: Russia's Special Forces* (Osprey Publishing 2015) 50.

1014 'Federation Council Approves Putin's Request for Troop Deployment in Ukraine' (The Moscow Times, 1 March 2014) <https://www.themoscowtimes.com/2014/03/01/federation-council-approves-putins-request-for-troop-deployment-in-ukraine-a32583>.

1015 'Аксенов: перенос референдума в Крыму связан с тем, что конфликт вышел за пределы разумного [Aksenov: Postponing the Referendum in Crimea is Linked to the Fact that the Conflict Left the Limits of Reason]' (Interfax, 1 March 2014) <https://www.interfax.ru/world/362023>.

1016 'Crimea Referendum: Voters Back Russia Union' (BBC, 16 March 2014) <https://www.bbc.com/news/world-europe-26606097>.

accession valid from 18 March onwards.[1017] Within only three weeks, the Ukrainian Republic of Crimea had been dismantled and incorporated into Russia. On 24 March, all Ukrainian troops that had not defected to Russia withdrew to the Ukrainian mainland.[1018]

Although Ukraine had 22 000 soldiers stationed in Crimea – more than a tenth of its then military strength[1019] – there was virtually no resistance. This was partly due to the turbulent events in Kyiv after the Maidan revolution. The new government was in chaos. Ukraine did not even have a Minister of Defence when the first "green men" crossed the border on 27 February.[1020] Furthermore, the troops were not in a high state of readiness and the invasion simply took them by surprise. As there were no orders from Kyiv, they did nothing.[1021] Due to the Ukrainian apathy and the disciplined behaviour of the Russian special forces, there were virtually no casualties when the Ukrainian troops withdrew on 24 March.[1022]

2.1.3 Classifying Crimea – Russia vs the rest of the world

By now, scholars have produced abundant legal literature on the case of Crimea.[1023] The following will not – and cannot – be an in-depth analysis

---

1017 Kremlin, 'Agreement on the Accession of the Republic of Crimea to the Russian Federation Signed' <http://en.kremlin.ru/events/president/news/20 604>. The treaty bears the name Договор между Российской Федерацией и Республикой Крым о принятии в Российскую Федерацию Республики Крым и образовании в составе Российской Федерации новых субъектов [Treaty between the Russian Federation and the Republic of Crimea about the Accession of the Republic of Crimea to the Russian Federation and the Formation of New Subjects within the Russian Federation] 18 March 2014.

1018 'Ukrainian Forces Withdraw from Crimea' (BBC, 24 March 2014) <https://www.bbc.com/news/world-europe-26713727>. Reports suggest that around half of the Ukrainian troops stationed in Crimea defected to the Russian side.

1019 Galeotti, *Armies of Russia's War in Ukraine* (n 785) 7.

1020 ibid 11.

1021 ibid 7.

1022 Marie-Louise Gumuchian and Victoria Butenko, 'Ukraine Orders Crimea Troop Withdrawal as Russia Seizes Naval Base' (CNN, 25 March 2014) <https://edition.cnn.com/2014/03/24/world/europe/ukraine-crisis/index.html>.

1023 The following section can only summarise what others have analysed in much greater detail. For an extensive analysis of the legal status of Crimea see Thomas D Grant, *Aggression against Ukraine: Territory, Responsibility, and International Law* (First edition, Palgrave Macmillan 2015); Christian Marxsen, 'The Crimea Crisis – an International Law Perspective' (2014) 74 ZaöRV/HJIL

of all arguments that Russia has put forward in the Crimean case. For instance, Russia has argued that the military intervention was necessary to protect its nationals and the Russian-speaking population abroad.[1024] Or that the annexation of Crimea constituted "historical justice."[1025] Whatever the bearing of such arguments, they exclusively concern the violation of Ukraine's sovereignty and thus belong to the realm of *ius ad bellum*.[1026]

Instead, I will limit myself to the issue of occupation under *ius in bello*. The question of whether territory is occupied under IHL does not depend on the lawfulness of the occupation under *ius ad bellum*.[1027] This allows us to restrict ourselves to the application of the criteria outlined above, i.e. the substitution of authority ("effective control") by the occupying

---

367; Władysław Czapliński and others, *The Case of Crimea's Annexation under International Law* (Scholar 2017); Bill Bowring, 'Who Are the "Crimea People" or "People of Crimea"? The Fate of the Crimean Tatars, Russia's Legal Justification for Annexation, and Pandora's Box' in Sergey Sayapin and Evhen Tsybulenko (eds), *The Use of Force against Ukraine and International Law: Jus Ad Bellum, Jus In Bello, Jus Post Bellum* (Springer 2018); Juan Francisco Escudero Espinosa, *Self-Determination and Humanitarian Secession in International Law of a Globalized World: Kosovo v Crimea* (Springer Berlin Heidelberg 2018); for a Russian perspective see Vladislav Tolstykh, 'Three Ideas of Self-Determination in International Law and the Reunification of Crimea with Russia' (2015) 75 ZaöRV/HJIL 119; Anatoly Kapustin, 'Crimea's Self-Determination in the Light of Contemporary International Law' (2015) 75 ZaöRV/HJIL 101.

1024 Putin wrote in his letter to the Federation Council: "In connection with the extraordinary situation in Ukraine, the threat to the lives of citizens of the Russian Federation, our compatriots, the personnel of the military contingent of the Armed Forces of the Russian Federation deployed in the territory of Ukraine (Autonomous Republic of Crimea) in accordance with an international treaty, and pursuant to Art 102–1(d) of the Constitution of the Russian Federation, I hereby submit to the Federation Council of the Federal Assembly of the Russian Federation a letter on the use of the Armed Forces of the Russian Federation in the territory of Ukraine pending normalization of the public and political situation in that country." The letter is available at <https://tass.com/russia/721586>.

1025 See e.g. address by President Putin on 18 March 2014: "In people's hearts and minds, Crimea has always been an inseparable part of Russia. This firm conviction is based on truth and justice and was passed from generation to generation, over time, under any circumstances, despite all the dramatic changes our country went through during the entire 20th century." The address is available at <http://en.kremlin.ru/events/president/news/20603>.

1026 For a comprehensive analysis of these arguments see Marxsen (n 1023).

1027 Daniel Thürer, 'Current Challenges to the Law of Occupation' in Mark Vuijlsteke and Floricica Olteanu (eds), *Proceedings of the Bruges Colloquium* (Collegium 2006) 10.

power against the will of the sovereign. However, we cannot completely ignore considerations of general international law. In this respect, Russia advanced two counterarguments that could exclude occupation. Firstly, Moscow claimed that Crimea had a right to secede from Ukraine. Secondly, the Kremlin argued that Ukrainian President Yanukovych sent an invitation for Russian troops to intervene. If accurate, these arguments would not only exclude a violation under *ius ad bellum*. They would also preclude the presence of troops *against* the will of the (Crimean or Ukrainian) sovereign – one of the three conditions of belligerent occupation.

2.3.1.1 The element of "substitution of effective control" in Crimea

During the pre-incorporation phase (27 February–18 March), we see Russia assuming control over all centres of power – both political and military – thanks to the coordinated and decisive actions of its special forces. While Moscow initially denied that these were on-duty soldiers, Putin later admitted that as early as February he had given the order to deploy special forces, naval infantry, and paratroopers in Crimea.[1028] These highly trained and well-equipped soldiers occupied central political institutions such as the Parliament.[1029] Without orders, the Ukrainian soldiers stood by while Russian soldiers gradually took their bases one by one.[1030] While

---

1028 Freedman (n 1010) 90. Russia's official position changed over time. Initially, the Kremlin denied all ties to the "little green men." Sergey Lavrov declared on 3 March 2014 that the armed men were "self-defence units" while Putin suggested these units could have bought the uniforms (that bore a striking resemblance with official Russian Army gear) in any store. Later, in April 2017 Putin admitted that Russian troops "stood behind Crimea's defence forces." See, for example, 'The Changing Story Of Russia's 'Little Green Men' Invasion' (Radio Free Europe/Radio Liberty, 25 February 2019) <https://www.rferl.org/a/russia-ukraine-crimea/29790037.html>; 'Putin Admits Russian Forces Were Deployed to Crimea' (Reuters, 17 April 2014) <https://www.reuters.com/article/russia-putin-crimea/putin-admits-russian-forces-were-deployed-to-crimea-idUSL6N0N921H20140417>.

1029 Harriet Salem, Shaun Walker, and Luke Harding, 'Crimean Parliament Seized by Unknown Pro-Russian Gunmen' (The Guardian, 27 February 2014) <https://www.theguardian.com/world/2014/feb/27/crimean-parliament-seized-by-unknown-pro-russian-gunmen>.

1030 Simon Shuster, 'Ukraine Troops in Crimea Face Dilemma: To Defect, Flee or Fight' (Time, 4 March 2014) <https://time.com/17356/ukraine-troops-in-crimea-face-dilemma-to-defect-flee-or-fight/>.

the Russian forces amounted to no more than 2 000 in the first few days, their number rose to over 20 000 before the legal incorporation date of 18 March.[1031]

Since the incorporation (18 March–present), Russia exercises absolute control over the Crimean Peninsula. Crimea and the City of Sevastopol are now listed as two new subjects in the Russian constitution.[1032] The Ruble has become the only official currency.[1033] Everyone automatically became a Russian citizen unless they explicitly objected within a one-month period.[1034] The accession agreement foresaw that the laws of the Russian Federation would apply from 18 March onwards.[1035] In July 2015, Medvedev deemed Crimea "fully integrated" into the Russian Federation.[1036] In sum, it is safe to say that from the invasion in late February 2014 until today, Russia exercises "effective control" over Crimea in the sense of Art 42 HR and thus substituted the authority of the Ukrainian sovereign.

2.3.1.2 The element of "against the will of the sovereign" in Crimea

This substitution of authority happened against the will of the sovereign. The fact that there was no armed resistance has no bearing according to CA 2(2). Furthermore, we are not dealing with an "intervention on invitation", which would exclude the framework of occupation. Moscow suggested that former President Viktor Yanukovych had invited Russian

---

1031 Galeotti, *Armies of Russia's War in Ukraine* (n 785) 11.

1032 Art 65(1) Constitution of the Russian Federation.

1033 'Russian Ruble Becomes Only Legal Currency in Crimea' (AA, 1 June 2014) <https://www.aa.com.tr/en/world/russian-ruble-becomes-only-legal-currency-in -crimea/154839>.

1034 The Office of the ICC Prosecutor (n 707) 35.

1035 See Art 9(1) of the Договор между Российской Федерацией и Республикой Крым о принятии в Российскую Федерацию Республики Крым и образовании в составе Российской Федерации новых субъектов [Treaty between the Russian Federation and the Republic of Crimea about the Accession of the Republic of Crimea to the Russian Federation and the Formation of New Subjects within the Russian Federation] 18 March 2014. However, Art 9(2) foresaw a transition period for the old laws in force.

1036 Jess McHugh, 'Putin Eliminates Ministry Of Crimea, Region Fully Integrated Into Russia, Russian Leaders Say' (International Business Times, 15 July 2015) <https://www.ibtimes.com/putin-eliminates-ministry-crimea-region-fully-integr ated-russia-russian-leaders-say-2009463>.

troops to intervene after the "coup" in Kyiv.[1037] Seeing his power slip away, Yanukovych had fled Ukraine on 21 February.[1038] The next day the Parliament voted to remove him, but did not reach the necessary majority.[1039] Elections were scheduled anyway. A week later in a UN Security Council meeting, the Russian representative Vitaly Churkin presented a letter. In it, Yanukovych begged Putin to intervene militarily in Crimea to "re-establish the rule of law, peace, order, stability and to protect the people of Ukraine." The letter dated from 1 March.[1040]

Yanukovych, so went Russia's argument, remained the *de jure* President of Ukraine and could thus consent to the invasion in Crimea.[1041] This view, however, ignores a major aspect. Yanukovych was not in a position to invite anybody, because he no longer possessed any real power having fled the country days before the letter. Authors like Christian Marxsen and Gregory Fox argue convincingly that only the *effective* government could have invited foreign troops.[1042] Traditionally, consent must be expressed by the effective government. This is to avoid a battle of competing legal claims. While the legitimacy of a leader's claim plays an increasing role, it is not the primary criterion.[1043] Marxsen argues that Yanukovych lost effective power when he fled the country. Furthermore, even in terms of legitimacy Yanukovych could not claim a better title than the democratically elected government after his ousting.[1044] Thus, he had no legal authority to invite the Russian forces.

Russia's second (and main) argument in favour of consensual occupation was the alleged secession of the Peninsula from Ukraine. Moscow

---

1037 UN Security Council, 7125th meeting, UN Doc S/PV.7125 (3 March 2014) 3.

1038 'Putin: Russia Helped Yanukovych to Flee Ukraine' (BBC, 24 October 2014) <https://www.bbc.com/news/world-europe-29761799>.

1039 Art 111 of the Ukrainian Constitution would have required a two thirds majority, while only 73 percent of the deputies were in favour of ousting the President, see Marxsen (n 1023) 375.

1040 Louis Charbonneau, 'Russia: Yanukovich Asked Putin to Use Force to Save Ukraine' (Reuters, 4 March 2014) <https://www.reuters.com/article/us-ukraine-crisis-un/russia-yanukovich-asked-putin-to-use-force-to-save-ukraine-idUSBREA2224720140304>.

1041 UN Security Council, 7125th meeting, UN Doc S/PV.7125 (3 March 2014) 3.

1042 Marxsen (n 1023) 375 et seq; Veronika Bílková, 'The Use of Force by the Russian Federation in Crimea' (2015) 75 ZaöRV/HJIL 27, 39 et seq; Gregory H Fox, 'Ukraine Insta-Symposium: Intervention in the Ukraine by Invitation' (*OpinioJuris*, 10 March 2014) <http://opiniojuris.org/2014/03/10/ukraine-insta-symposium-intervention-ukraine-invitation/>.

1043 Marxsen (n 1023) 377.

1044 ibid 379.

argued that, in the referendum, the people of Crimea had expressed their will to leave Ukraine and subsequently join the Russian Federation.[1045] This debate highlights the interface between *ius ad bellum* and *ius in bello* and shows that IHL is not a hermetically closed system. The occupying State can circumvent the application of GC IV by resorting to arguments outside IHL.

However, the overwhelming majority of States, international organisations, and scholars challenged Russia's view. They stated that Crimea had no right to secede – neither under national nor under international law.[1046] Under domestic law, the referendum violated the Ukrainian Constitution, because territorial changes could only be introduced by a nationwide referendum.[1047] The Ukrainian Constitutional Court and the Venice Commission confirmed this reading.[1048]

Similarly, Crimea could not avail itself of a right to secede under international law. Such a right may not be deduced from the principle of "self-determination of peoples" as enshrined in Art 2(2) UN Charter. First of all, the population of Crimea – with the arguable exception of the indigenous Tatars – does not constitute a "people" in the sense of international law.[1049] Even if they did, the principle of self-determination would not automatically confer on them a right to secession. According to UN General Assembly Resolution 2625 (1970), the right to self-determination should not be construed as "authorizing or encouraging any action which would dismember or impair, totally or in part, the territorial integrity of

---

1045　Bowring, 'Who Are the "Crimea People" or "People of Crimea"?' (n 1023) 35.

1046　For the international reactions to the events in Crimea see below at pp 229 et seq.

1047　Art 73 Constitution of Ukraine. In any case, the Venice Commission noted that the referendum was not "in line with European democratic standards", see Venice Commission, 'Opinion No 762/2014 on Whether the Decision Taken by the Supreme Council of the Autonomous Republic of Crimea in Ukraine to Organise a Referendum on Becoming a Constituent Territory of the Russian Federation or Restoring Crimea's 1992 Constitution Is Compatible with Constitutional Principles' (2014) para 28.

1048　Constitutional Court of Ukraine, Judgment No 2-rp/2014 (Case No 1–13/2014) 14 March 2014. The judgment is available at <https://mfa.gov.ua/en/news-fe eds/foreign-offices-news/19573-rishennya-konstituci>; see also Venice Commission, 'Opinion No 762/2014 on Whether the Decision Taken by the Supreme Council of the Autonomous Republic of Crimea in Ukraine to Organise a Referendum on Becoming a Constituent Territory of the Russian Federation or Restoring Crimea's 1992 Constitution Is Compatible with Constitutional Principles' (2014) para 27.

1049　Bowring, 'Who Are the "Crimea People" or "People of Crimea"?' (n 1023) 35.

political unity of sovereign and independent States."[1050] Thus, as a rule self-determination only confers a right to pursue its independent destiny *within* a State.

A controversial exception to this rule is the concept of "remedial secession." Can a people secede in reaction to gross violations of human rights perpetrated against it by the government?[1051] The answer to this question is highly disputed. Some see remedial secession as the last bastion against "subjugation and tyranny."[1052] Others call it a "myth."[1053] The issue has received much attention during the *Kosovo Advisory Opinion* before the ICJ.[1054] Contrary to popular belief, the Court never endorsed the principle of remedial secession. Only two Judges expressed sympathy for it in their separate opinions.[1055] States, too, are very divided on the issue. Western States pushed for an exception from the general rule of territorial integrity and subsequently recognised Kosovo as an independent State.[1056] Other nations including Russia fiercely opposed the concept.[1057] Ironically, Moscow's attitude radically changed with the events in Crimea. Vladimir Putin himself referred to Kosovo in his speech on 18 March 2014 – the day the Crimean referendum was held. He even mentioned the ICJ's Advisory Opinion arguing that if Kosovo's independence was in line with international law, so was Crimea's.

1050 UN General Assembly Resolution 2625 (XXV), Declaration on Principles of International Law Concerning Friendly Relations and Cooperation Among States in Accordance with the Charter of the United Nations, UN Doc A/RES/2625 (24 October 1970).

1051 Katherine del Mar, 'The Myth of Remedial Secession' in Duncan French (ed), *Statehood and Self-Determination: Reconciling Tradition and Modernity in International Law* (Cambridge University Press 2013) 79; an undisputed exception is the secession of a State under colonial rule, Antonio Cassese, *Self-Determination of Peoples: A Legal Reappraisal* (Cambridge University Press 1995) 332.

1052 ICJ, *Accordance with International Law of the Unilateral Declaration of Independence in Respect of Kosovo*, Advisory Opinion, ICJ Reports (2010) 403, Separate Opinion Judge Cançado Trindade, para 175.

1053 del Mar (n 1051) 79–80.

1054 ICJ, *Accordance with International Law of the Unilateral Declaration of Independence in Respect of Kosovo*, Advisory Opinion, ICJ Reports (2010) 403 [hereinafter *Kosovo Advisory Opinion*].

1055 ICJ, *Accordance with International Law of the Unilateral Declaration of Independence in Respect of Kosovo*, ICJ Reports (2010) 403, Separate Opinion Judge Cançado Trindade, para 175; and Separate Opinion Judge Yusuf, para 11.

1056 For an overview which countries have recognised Kosovo see <https://www.kosovothanksyou.com/>.

1057 Marxsen (n 1023) 387.

"We keep hearing from the United States and Western Europe that Kosovo is some special case. What makes it so special in the eyes of our colleagues? It turns out that it is the fact that the conflict in Kosovo resulted in so many human casualties. Is this a legal argument? The ruling of the International Court says nothing about this."[1058]

This reading, however, is incorrect.[1059] First of all, the ICJ never ruled on Kosovo's independence, but only on the limited question whether its declaration of independence violated international law.[1060] Secondly, Kosovo's statehood is still subject to great debate and not even all EU member States have managed to agree on it, let alone the international community as a whole. Recently, Ghana was the 16th State to withdraw its recognition showing that the issue is far from settled.[1061] Hence, it makes a weak precedent.[1062] Thirdly, in Kosovo, we have seen grave human rights violations and oppression over an extended period of time. Nothing of that kind happened in Crimea. On the contrary. The Ukrainian Constitution gave considerable freedom to the Peninsula granting it the status of an Autonomous Republic. Isolated events – which may well constitute human rights abuses – like the decision of the Ukrainian Parliament to

---

1058 Address by President Putin, 18 March 2014. Putin also explicitly refers to the *Kosovo Advisory Opinion*: "We keep hearing from the United States and Western Europe that Kosovo is some special case. What makes it so special in the eyes of our colleagues? It turns out that it is the fact that the conflict in Kosovo resulted in so many human casualties. Is this a legal argument? The ruling of the International Court says nothing about this. This is not even double standards; this is amazing, primitive, blunt cynicism. One should not try so crudely to make everything suit their interests, calling the same thing white today and black tomorrow. According to this logic, we have to make sure every conflict leads to human losses." The address is available at <http://en.kremlin.ru /events/president/news/20603>.

1059 Marxsen (n 1023) 387.

1060 *Kosovo Advisory Opinion* (n 1054) para 122.

1061 'Ghana is the 16th Country to Withdraw Recognition of So-called Kosovo, more to Follow by End of Year' (Telegraf, 11 November 2019) <https://www.tel egraf.rs/english/3120840-ghana-is-the-16th-country-to-withdraw-recognition-of-s o-called-kosovo-more-to-follow-by-end-of-year>.

1062 Marxsen (n 1023) 388.

repeal a language law[1063] or the deaths of nearly 50 pro-Russian protesters in Odessa[1064] could not justify secession as last resort.

Hence, Russia's effective control over the Peninsula goes against the will of the Ukrainian sovereign which means that Moscow's presence in Crimea represents a case of belligerent occupation under IHL. Virtually all international scholars, organisations, and States – with the exception of Russia – share this view.[1065] Many organisations such as the UN High Commissioner for Human Rights,[1066] UNESCO[1067] and the OSCE PA[1068]

1063 On 23 February 2014 the Ukrainian Parliament voted to repeal a law that allowed the use of minority languages in administration and schools where the minority exceeded ten percent of the population. Scrapping the law targeted the status of the Russian language in Ukraine. The decision, however, was vetoed by the new President Turchynov, see 'Ukraine's Parliament-appointed Acting President Says Language Law to Stay Effective' (Tass, 1 March 2014) <https://tass.com/world/721537>. Up to this day, language remains a divisive issue in Ukraine. President Poroshenko's election slogan in 2019, for example, read "Army, Language, Faith." Since 2014, Ukraine has passed a number of controversial language laws that attracted international criticism, see e.g. Council of Europe, 'Opinion on the Provisions of the Law on Education of 5 September 2017 Which Concern the Use of the State Language and Minority and Other Languages in Education (CDL-AD (2017) 030-e)' (2017); Venice Commission, 'Opinion No 902/ 2017 on the Provisions of the Law on Education of 5 September 2017 Which Concern the Use of the State Language and Minority and Other Languages in Education' (2017).

1064 In Odessa, 48 pro-Russian protesters died in clashes with pro-Ukrainian protesters and the security forces on 2 May 2014. The protesters had barricaded themselves in a trade union building when a fire broke out. Russia has called the events a "fascist massacre" and accused Ukraine of stirring anti-Russian sentiments, see Howard Amos and Harriet Salem 'Ukraine Clashes: Dozens Dead after Odessa Building Fire' (The Guardian, 2 May 2014) <https://www.th eguardian.com/world/2014/may/02/ukraine-dead-odessa-building-fire>; Shaun Walker, 'Tensions Run High in Odessa on Anniversary of Deadly Clashes' (The Guardian, 2 May 2016) <https://www.theguardian.com/world/2016/may/02/ode ssa-ukraine-second-anniversary-clashes>.

1065 Certain Russian scholars defended the Russian view in international academic circles. The most prominent example are the articles by Anatoly Kapustin and Vladislav Tolstykh that were published in the Heidelberg Journal of International Law, see Kapustin (n 1023); Tolstykh, 'Three Ideas of Self-Determination in International Law and the Reunification of Crimea with Russia' (n 1023).

1066 The reports of the OHCHR use the terminology "temporarily occupied by the Russian Federation." The reports are available at <https://www.ohchr.org/en/co untries/enacaregion/pages/uareports.aspx>.

1067 See e.g. UNESCO, Doc 204 EX/5 Part I.D (17 May 2018) 4.

1068 OSCE Parliamentary Assembly, Luxembourg Declaration AS (19) DE (July 2019) 3.

have condemned the occupation of Crimea. Even close Russian allies such as Belarus refused to recognise Crimea as a *de jure* subject of the Russian Federation.[1069]

2.1.4 Russian denial – what occupation?

How does Russia meet this criticism? The Kremlin has become very skilled at ignoring and avoiding the uncomfortable legal classification of belligerent occupation. We shall consider the following example: on 14 November 2016, the ICC classified the situation in Crimea as belligerent occupation. It stated that

> *"[t]he information available suggests that the situation within the territory of Crimea and Sevastopol amounts to an international armed conflict between Ukraine and the Russian Federation. This international armed conflict began at the latest on 26 February when the Russian Federation deployed members of its armed forces to gain control over parts of the Ukrainian territory without the consent of the Ukrainian Government. The law of international armed conflict would continue to apply after 18 March 2014 to the extent that the situation within the territory of Crimea and Sevastopol factually amounts to an on-going state of occupation."*[1070]

Two days later Russia refused to ratify the Rome Statute as a symbolic act of disapproval complaining that the ICC "did not live up to its expectations."[1071] But it was clear that the withdrawal from the ICC came as a reprisal against the Prosecution's report.[1072]

1069 Lukashenko called the annexation a "bad precedent", but recognised that Crimea from now on *"de facto"* belonged to Russia, see 'Belarusian President Says Crimean Annexation 'Bad Precedent' (Radio Free Europe/Radio Liberty, 23 March 2014) <https://www.rferl.org/a/belarus-lukashenka-crimea-precedent/25306914.html>.

1070 The Office of the ICC Prosecutor (n 707) 35.

1071 Распоряжение Президента Российской Федерации, 16.11.2016, N 361-рп 'О намерении Российской Федерации не стать участником Римского Статута Международного Уголовного Суда' [Decree of the President of the Russian Federation, 16 November 2016, No 361-rp 'On the Intention of the Russian Federation Not to Become a Party to the Rome Statute of the ICC']; see also 'МИД объяснил отказ России ратифицировать Римский статут МУС [Ministry of Foreign Affairs Announced the Refusal of Russia to Ratify the Rome Statute of the ICC]' (Tass, 16 January 2016) <https://tass.ru/politika/3788778>.

1072 See above at p 155.

Russia has ducked criticism in other fora such as the UN Security Council. When the German representative emphasised that "Crimea is still occupied" at the occasion of the fifth anniversary of the Minsk agreements (2019), Russia abstained from making any legal or even factual arguments but added rather sarcastically:

> *"It turns out that all of Ukraine's woes and misfortunes — not just of the past few years but the past three centuries — are the legacy of Russia's occupation of Ukraine. Under that lying paradigm, a new, falsified version of history is being created at accelerated speed, cobbled together from all the skeletons in its cupboard."*[1073]

The Kremlin not only ignores comments on the general status of Crimea, but also refuses to react to violations of specific provisions. There are many problematic issues with relation to Crimea, for example subjecting Crimeans to compulsory military service (Art 51 GC IV); Altering the status of judges (Art 56 GC IV); introducing the Russian administrative, penal, and tax system (Art 64 GC IV, Art 48 HR); imposing Russian citizenship (Art 45 HR); let alone the crackdown on the Crimean Tatars (Art 27, 71 GC IV).[1074] International pressure has done little to put an end to these violations. On 19 December 2016, the UN General Assembly adopted a resolution urging Russia to respect Art 51 of the Fourth Geneva Convention which prohibits compelling a protected person in occupied territory to serve in its armed forces.[1075] The General Assembly's resolutions 72/190 (19 December 2017) and 73/263 (22 December 2018) added that "the imposition and retroactive application of the legal system of the Russian Federation [...] is contrary to international humanitarian law, including the Geneva Conventions."[1076] Russia voted against each Resolution and did not further comment on its content.

In sum, the classification of Crimea as occupied is clear-cut. It follows the well-established definition of belligerent occupation that I have out-

---

1073 UN Security Council, 8461st meeting, UN Doc S/PV.8461 (12 February 2019) 8.

1074 OSCE/ODIHR, 'Report of the Human Rights Assessment Mission on Crimea (6–18 July 2015)' (2015) 82 et seq.

1075 UN General Assembly Resolution 71/205, UN Doc A/RES/71/205 (1 February 2017) 2.

1076 UN General Assembly Resolution 72/190, UN Doc A/RES/72/190 (19 December 2017) 2; UN General Assembly Resolution 73/263, UN Doc A/RES/73/263 (22 December 2018) 2. The prohibition to impose the legal system of the occupying power can be found in Art 47, 54, and 64 GC IV as well as in Art 43 HR.

lined above. However, Russia categorically rejects the application of IHL in Crimea, despite heavy, repeated, and virtually unanimous criticism from the entire international community. Meanwhile, the Crimean population does not benefit from the protection under IHL and Russia's blatant disregard for well-established norms risks eroding respect for the regime of occupation in the long run.

2.2 Occupation by proxy – the cases of Transdniestria, Abkhazia, and South Ossetia

Crimea is the most obvious example in which Russia challenges the application of belligerent occupation. There are other, more controversial examples. When walking the streets of Tbilisi, for example, one cannot help but notice the graffiti and stickers plastered over the old walls, pretty wooden balconies and lamp posts. In bold letters, they make a bold statement: "Russia is occupant."[1077] This is of course a reference to the situation in South Ossetia and Abkhazia, the two Georgian breakaway regions. Another analogous example is the Moldovan breakaway republic Transdniestria. What makes a good political slogan is, however, more difficult under IHL. Is Russia really an occupying power in these regions?

Scholars and practitioners are divided on these cases. Unlike in Crimea, Moscow does not exercise complete direct control over these regions by means of its armed forces and civilian administration. It only maintains a limited number of troops. Rather, the Kremlin finances, equips, and supports local authorities supportive to the Russian cause. The legal debate thus revolves about the issue of "occupation by proxy."

First, I will describe the degree of Russian influence over Transdniestria, South Ossetia, and Abkhazia (in the following, I will use "the Regions" when referring to these three regions collectively).[1078] Then, we will look at the concept of occupation by proxy and its legal intricacies. Finally,

---

1077 The slogan has been adopted by a civil society movement, see <https://1tv.ge/en /news/russia-is-occupant-demands-impeachment-of-president/>.

1078 One could argue that LNR and DNR also fit this pattern. I, however, have chosen not to treat Russia's relationship with the People's Republics in this sub-section because – unlike in Transdniestira, South Ossetia, and Abkhazia – Russia already *denies the presence* of its soldiers in these entities. I will deal with this strategy of denying the facts in the following sub-section starting at p 255. For those interested, a case study on occupation by proxy tailored to the Ukrainian context can be found in Alexander Gilder, 'Bringing Occupation

I will deal with Russia's attitude towards the alleged occupation in the Regions and clarify what this tells us about Moscow's approach to IHL.

2.2.1 Russia's influence in Transdniestria, South Ossetia, and Abkhazia

The three Regions have much in common.[1079] All of them emerged in the course of the dissolution of the Soviet Union and owe their existence to armed struggle against their respective central State – Moldova and Georgia. Both Moldova and Georgia were former Soviet Republics and gained independence when the USSR broke apart, while Abkhazia, South Ossetia, and Transdniestria did not enjoy this status. Hence, according to the *uti possidetis* doctrine the Regions should have remained part of the former Soviet Republics Georgia and Moldova.[1080] However, for various political, ethnic, and historical reasons, the Regions strove for independence and the ensuing hostilities lasted until 1992 (in South Ossetia and Transdniestria) and 1994 (in Abkhazia). Politically, the issue of secession remains unresolved even if the armed conflicts have been "frozen" since the mid-90s. In the case of Georgia, hostilities flared up again in the 2008 war. Despite these ongoing tensions, the Regions evolved into functioning *de facto* States with their own governments, administrations, and courts.

It is safe to say that the local authorities in all three regions only exist and survive thanks to Russian support. Transdniestria, for example, depends on Russia in economic, military, and political respects. It has massively benefited from free gas and Russian welfare programmes.[1081]

---

into the 21st Century: The Effective Implementation of Occupation by Proxy' (2017) 13 Utrecht Law Review 60, 79.

1079　The following paragraph is largely based on Angelika Nußberger, 'South Ossetia', *Max Planck Encyclopedia of Public International Law* (Oxford University Press 2013) paras 9–17; Angelika Nußberger, 'Abkhazia', *Max Planck Encyclopedia of Public International Law* (Oxford University Press 2013) paras 11–17. See also Encyclopædia Britannica, 'Transnistria' <https://www.britannica.com/place/Transdniestria>.

1080　For the doctrine of *uti possidetis* see Giuseppe Nesi, 'Uti Possidetis Doctrine', *Max Planck Encyclopedia of Public International Law* (Oxford University Press 2018). At p 279, I will describe in detail how this doctrine influenced the emergence of new States after the collapse of the Soviet Union.

1081　In 2012 the Russian government argued that it had delivered gas worth 1.5 billion US Dollars to Transdniestria, see for this ECtHR, *Catan and Others v Moldova and Russia*, Nos 43370/04, 8252/05 and 18454/06, 19 October 2012, para 99.

Key positions in the Transdniestrian administration are held by Russian citizens.[1082] The 14th Russian Army has played a decisive role both during the secession conflict and afterwards.[1083] Although Russia has reduced its troops, 1 500 Russian soldiers are still present in Transdniestria today.[1084] Russia's military, political, and economic influence led the ECtHR to conclude that the Moldovan Republic of Transdniestria (MRT) remains under "the effective authority, or at the very least under the decisive influence, of the Russian Federation, and in any event that it survives by virtue of the military, economic, financial and political support given to it by the Russian Federation."[1085] Recently, the Ukrainian crisis has led to economic decline in the breakaway region, thereby further increasing the dependence on Moscow.[1086]

We find a similar picture in Abkhazia. The popular tourist location lies between the Black Sea and the Great Caucasus with Sukhumi as a capital. During the 2008 war, Abkhazia enlarged its territory into the upper Kodori Valley.[1087] After the end of the war, Russia recognised Abkhazia as an independent State. Venezuela, Nicaragua, Nauru, and Syria followed suit.[1088] While Abkhazia was always a bit more advanced than

---

1082 Bogdan Ivanel, 'Puppet States: A Growing Trend of Covert Occupation' (2016) 18 Yearbook of International Humanitarian Law 43, 48–52.

1083 See for this В.Л. Полушин [V.L. Polushin], *Генерал Лебедь – загадка России [General Lebed – A Russian Enigma]* (Внешторгиздат 1997) 33 et seq.

1084 EU Parliament Subcommittee on Security and Defence, 'Russian Military Presence in the Eastern European Partnership Countries' (2016) 21.

1085 ECtHR, *Ilaşcu and Others v Moldova and Russia*, No 48787/99, 8 July 2004, para 392; see also paras 386–391. The Court has confirmed this dependence in ECtHR, *Ivanţoc and Others v Moldova and Russia*, No 23687/05, 15 November 2011, paras 116–120; ECtHR, *Catan and Others v Moldova and Russia*, Nos 43370/04, 8252/05 and 18454/06, 19 October 2012, paras 121–122; ECtHR, *Mozer v Moldova and Russia*, No 11138/10, 23 February 2016, paras 108–110; and ECtHR, *Mangîr and Others v the Republic of Moldova and Russia*, No 50157/06, 17 July 2018, para 28.

1086 'Transdniestria: My Head Is in Russia, My Legs Walk to Europe' (Carnegie Europe, 3 December 2018) <https://carnegieeurope.eu/2018/12/03/transdniestri a-my-head-is-in-russia-my-legs-walk-to-europe-pub-77843>.

1087 IIFFMCG, 'Report of the Independent International Fact-Finding Mission on the Conflict in Georgia (Tagliavini Report) Volume I' (2009) 22.

1088 Tuvalu and Vanuatu recognised Abkhazia, but later withdrew their recognitions. For the Russian recognition see also the decision by the Federal Council reprinted in IIFFMCG, 'Report of the Independent International Fact-Finding Mission on the Conflict in Georgia (Tagliavini Report) Volume III – Views of the Sides on the Conflict, Chronologies and Responses to Questionnaires' (n 960) 445.

South Ossetia in its state-building process, it still depends heavily on Russia. For instance, in 2008 most of the inhabitants in Abkhazia held a Russian passport. The Russians controlled political institutions and security forces.[1089] This dependence increased after the war. Many major economic assets are under Russian ownership.[1090] In 2014, Abkhazia and Russia signed the Treaty on Alliance and Strategic Partnership which includes closer cooperation in the areas of defence, customs, and border control. The treaty proclaims that Moscow and Sukhumi form a "common space of defence and security."[1091] Russia still maintains a large military base in Abkhazia.[1092] While the Treaty on Alliance and Strategic Partnership allows for some autonomy of the Abkhaz authorities, overall, their fate remains tied to Moscow.[1093] This is especially obvious in economic terms. A 2013 report estimated that Russian subsidies amounted to 70 percent of the Abkhazian annual budget.[1094]

Out of the three Regions, South Ossetia's[1095] dependence on Russia is the most evident.[1096] The smallest breakaway region occupies a neuralgic point on the map. Its south-eastern border is located only 50 km from Georgia's capital Tbilisi and almost touches the major Georgian East-West highway E 60. South Ossetia is home to around 50 000 peo-

---

1089 Nußberger, 'Abkhazia' (n 1079) para 27.
1090 Andre WM Gerrits and Max Bader, 'Russian Patronage over Abkhazia and South Ossetia: Implications for Conflict Resolution' (2016) 32 East European Politics 297, 301.
1091 Art 3 of the Договор между Российской Федерацией и Республикой Абхазия о союзничестве и стратегическом партнерстве [Treaty Between the Russian Federation and the Republic of Abkhazia on Alliance and Strategic Partnership] 24 November 2014.
1092 Gerrits and Bader (n 1090) 302. See also Соглашение между Республикой Абхазия и Российской Федерацией об объединенной российской военной базе на территории Республики Абхазия [Treaty Between the Republic of Abkhazia and the Russian Federation about the United Russian Military Base on the Territory of the Republic of Abkhazia] 17 February 2010.
1093 For the interesting drafting history of the Treaty see Thomas Ambrosio and William A Lange, 'The Architecture of Annexation? Russia's Bilateral Agreements with South Ossetia and Abkhazia' (2016) 44 Nationalities Papers 673, 683–684.
1094 International Crisis Group, 'Abkhazia: The Long Road to Reconciliation' (2013) 6.
1095 Since a referendum in 2017 the full name of South Ossetia reads: "Republic of South Ossetia – the State of Alania."
1096 Nußberger, 'South Ossetia' (n 1079) para 9; Ambrosio and Lange (n 1093) 688.

ple.[1097] Around 30 000 live in the capital Tskhinvali. Since the Russo-Georgian War, Russia recognises its independence alongside with Nicaragua, Venezuela, Nauru, and Syria.[1098] Angelika Nußberger argues that even before the war, Moscow had decisive control over the South Ossetians. Its policy of "passportisation" has turned most of them into Russian citizens, subjecting them to Russian jurisdiction. Furthermore, Moscow maintains *de facto* control over all political Ossetian institutions and maintains a tight grip on the security forces.[1099]

Since the end of the Russo-Georgian War, Tskhinvali's dependence on Moscow has continuously grown. In 2015, Russia and South Ossetia concluded a Treaty on Alliance and Integration.[1100] Just like in Abkhazia, the treaty advanced and consolidated the Russian influence in South Ossetia in numerous areas such as foreign policy, customs, transport, and above all in the security sector.[1101] In comparison with Abkhazia, however, it left the authorities in Tskhinvali with even less autonomy.[1102] This is demonstrated by the term "integration" (as opposed to "strategic partnership" in the Russo-Abkhaz treaty), because it may be read as a commitment to officially join the Russian Federation in the long run. However, in 2017, the referendum on the question of accession was postponed. Allegedly, this happened due to pressure from Moscow that has little to gain from such an initiative at the moment.[1103] Despite this aborted attempt at integration, South Ossetia's dependence on Russia remains obvious. Moscow maintains a large military presence including the 4th military base which

---

1097 'Окончательные данные переписи: в Южной Осетии живут 53 532 человека [Final Data of the Census: In South Ossetia Live 53 532 People]' (Sputnik, 11 August 2016) <https://sputnik-ossetia.ru/South_Ossetia/20160811/2874839.html>.

1098 Nußberger, 'South Ossetia' (n 1079) para 31; see also the decision by the Federal Council reprinted in IIFFMCG, 'Report of the Independent International Fact-Finding Mission on the Conflict in Georgia (Tagliavini Report) Volume III – Views of the Sides on the Conflict, Chronologies and Responses to Questionnaires' (n 960).

1099 Nußberger, 'South Ossetia' (n 1079) para 20.

1100 Договор между Российской Федерацией и Республикой Южная Осетия о союзничестве и интеграции [Treaty Between the Russian Federation and the Republic of South Ossetia on Alliance and Integration] 18 March 2015.

1101 For a detailed analysis of the treaty see Ambrosio and Lange (n 1093) 685–687.

1102 ibid 688.

1103 'Adjournment: South Ossetia Postpones Referendum' (RIAC, 6 June 2016) <https://russiancouncil.ru/en/analytics-and-comments/analytics/otkladyvanie-partii-yuzhnaya-osetiya-perenosit-referendum/>.

holds around 4000 troops.[1104] In 2017, parts of the South Ossetian armed forces were officially subordinated to Russian command.[1105] Finally, South Ossetia lacks an independent source of income and its budget almost entirely depends on Russian aid.[1106]

Does this considerable influence mean that Russia occupies the three Regions? In the following, I will explain the concept of so-called "indirect occupation" or "occupation by proxy," before drawing my legal conclusion and analysing Russia's position on this question.

2.2.2 Direct and indirect occupation

As I have explained above belligerent occupation under IHL requires the following criteria to be fulfilled:
1. The former government lost its authority over the territory
2. The occupying power replaced this authority in the sense that it can enforce its will
3. This substitution of power is non-consensual

The Russian forces in Georgia and Moldova are present against the will of the respective sovereign.[1107] However, direct occupation would require Russia administering the territory through its own institutions or its own armed forces. This is not the case. At the same time, a State's territory does not need to be occupied in its entirety. The Geneva Conventions explicitly foresee *partial* occupation.[1108] Therefore we can easily consider the areas occupied where Russian soldiers are stationed, i.e. mostly in and near the military bases.[1109] In addition, from August until October 2008 the

---

1104 Gerrits and Bader (n 1090) 302. See also Соглашение между Республикой Южная Осетия и Российской Федерацией об объединенной российской военной базе на территории Республики Южная Осетия [Treaty Between the Republic of South Ossetia and the Russian Federation on the United Russian Military Base on the Territory of the Republic of South Ossetia] 7 April 2010.

1105 Подписано соглашение о вхождении части подразделений армии Южной Осетии в ВС РФ [The Agreement of the Integration of Parts of the Units of the Army of South Ossetia and into the Armed Forces of the Russian Federation Has Been Signed]' (Tass, 31 March 2017) <https://tass.ru/armiya-i-opk/4143137 >.

1106 Gerrits and Bader (n 1090) 302.

1107 See for this below at pp 245 and 250.

1108 CA 2(2) uses the formula "in cases of partial or total occupation."

1109 The Tagliavini Report argues down these lines: "The extent of the control and authority exercised by Russian forces may differ from one geographical area to

so-called "buffer zone" in Georgia was under the effective control of the Russian Army.[1110] The zone was taken by Moscow during the 2008 War and lay beyond the borders of South Ossetia and Abkhazia on undisputed Georgian territory. In the buffer zone, Russian troops invaded, replaced the Georgian administration, and held the area for about two months.[1111]

Most of the Regions' territory, however, is administered by their own local authorities. Russian troops neither control nor interfere with the day-to-day administration.[1112] How should we classify these areas? At first sight, the above definition of belligerent occupation does not exclude occupation by proxy. Why should criteria No 1 and 2 (substitution of effective control) require the direct intervention of a State's official armed forces? Could proxy forces that are controlled by a State not exercise the same authority?[1113] In other words: even if occupation needs "boots on the ground," why should the boots not belong to a proxy?

Thus, the question is not *if* territory can be occupied by a proxy, but *what level of control* the State needs to exert over its proxy actor. In essence, the debate revolves around different ways of defining control over groups.[1114] This leads us to the issue of State responsibility and its most fundamental rule: States are only responsible for their own conduct, i.e. the conduct of persons acting – on whatever basis – on their behalf.[1115] If the acts of the local *de facto* authorities can be attributed to Russia, then it would be fair to speak of Russian occupation under IHL.

The rules of attribution have been codified in the Articles on State Responsibility for Internationally Wrongful Acts (ARSIWA) 4–11 which by

---

another. It was possibly looser in the territories of South Ossetia and Abkhazia administered by the *de facto* authorities. In the Kodori Valley, and in districts and villages in South Ossetia such as Akhalgori, where before the conflict the Georgian forces and administration had exercised control, the substitution is more evident." Taken from IIFFMCG, 'Report of the Independent International Fact-Finding Mission on the Conflict in Georgia (Tagliavini Report) Volume II' (2009) 311.

1110 ibid.

1111 Luke Harding, 'Russia Begins Final Pull-out from Georgia Buffer Zone' (8 October 2008) <https://www.theguardian.com/world/2008/oct/08/georgia.russia>.

1112 See e.g. Ivanel (n 1082) 55.

1113 See e.g. Ferraro (n 994) 160.

1114 Tom Gal, 'Unexplored Outcomes of Tadić: Applicability of the Law of Occupation to War by Proxy' (2014) 12 Journal of International Criminal Justice 59.

1115 ICJ, *Application of the Convention on the Prevention and Punishment of the Crime of Genocide (Bosnia and Herzegovina v Serbia and Montenegro)*, Judgment, ICJ Reports (2007) 43 [hereinafter *Bosnian Genocide Case*] para 406.

now constitute customary law.[1116] There are various ways of attributing the conduct of persons or groups to a State. I will extensively discuss them at page 342 when addressing Russia's outsourcing strategies in active warfare. For the context of occupation, suffice it to say that the most relevant provision is Art 8 ARSIWA. It requires a group to be under the "direction or control" of a State. What level of control would Russia need over the *de facto* authorities in the Regions to satisfy this criterion? There are two ways to answer this question. One I shall call the "narrow", the other the "wide" approach.

According to the narrow approach, occupation by proxy is possible, but only on the condition that the sponsor State has "effective control" over the proxy regime. Note that "effective control" in this context does not refer to Art 42 HR, i.e. control over territory. It rather refers to the rules of State responsibility as defined by the ICJ in the *Nicaragua Case* that I will explain in detail below. Thus, the narrow approach requires a *double* standard of effective control: A State having effective control over a *group* (ICJ standard) which effectively controls *territory* (Art 42 HR standard).

The broad approach, on the other hand, deems it sufficient that the sponsor State exercises *overall* control over local groups that exercise *effective* control over the territory.[1117] "Overall control" – a standard created by the ICTY[1118] – sets a lower threshold than the ICJ's effective control standard, as I will explain below.

2.2.2.1 The narrow approach – effective control (ICJ standard)

According to the ICJ case law, Art 8 ARSIWA sets a very high threshold. In its famous *Nicaragua* Decision, the Court required "effective control of the military or paramilitary operations in the course of which the alleged violations were committed."[1119] The Court ruled that this goes beyond merely financing, organising, training, and supporting a certain group.[1120]

1116 James R Crawford, 'State Responsibility', *Max Planck Encyclopedia of Public International Law* (Oxford University Press 2006) para 65.

1117 See e.g. Ferraro (n 994) 158.

1118 See ICTY, *The Prosecutor v Duško Tadić* (IT-94–1-T), Appeals Chamber Judgment, 15 July 1999, paras 146–160; ICTY, *The Prosecutor v Tihomir Blaškić* (IT-95-14), Trial Chamber Judgment, 3 March 2000, paras 117–118.

1119 *Nicaragua Case* (n 992) para 115. Of course, the ICJ judgment (1986) predated the ARSIWA (2001), but the issue at heart remains unchanged.

1120 See e.g. *Nicaragua Case* (n 992) paras 115–116.

The State needs to *specifically* plan the operation in question.[1121] The mere fact that a group displays a "high degree of dependency" does not suffice for attribution.[1122]

While the Regions heavily depend on Moscow, their dependence does not reach this ICJ standard of effective control. This would require the detailed planning of each and every of their actions. Bearing in mind the above facts, this seems unlikely at the present time.[1123] Thomas Ambrosio and William Lange have analysed the current status of the Regions in great detail. They argue that "neither South Ossetia nor Abkhazia should be considered mere appendages of Russia. There are internal political and identity-based processes in both territories that, while dominated by Russia, are not fully controlled by Moscow." At the same time, the Regions "should not be seen as fully independent political entities [...]. Instead they should be characterised as possessing a range of effective sovereignty, which has political and ideational substance, but is ultimately subordinated to Moscow."[1124] The same is true for Transdniestria.[1125]

This assessment may change in the future, e.g. with South Ossetia's integration process. However, we have seen that Moscow is deeply sceptical of extending its official rule to the Regions. The process has finally stalled. Thus, as long as the Regions are caught in a grey zone between dependence and autonomy, Russia's control falls short of the ICJ threshold of effective control.[1126]

1121 See *Bosnian Genocide Case* (n 1115) para 413.

1122 *Nicaragua Case* (n 992) para 115.

1123 The ECtHR also dealt with the issue of control in *Ilaşcu and Others v Moldova and Russia*, No 48787/99, 8 July 2004, paras 386–392. The Judges found that Russia "effectively controls" the Transdniestrian authorities. In this instance, however, the Court did not refer to the ICJ standard of effective control, but to its own standard of establishing attribution. The Court neither cited the ICJ case law, nor did it explain its own standard of effective control, see Ivanel (n 1082) 57. For the ECtHR's stance on attribution see also n 1701.

1124 Ambrosio and Lange (n 1093) 688.

1125 Ivanel (n 1082) 48–54.

1126 One limited exception could be the part of the South Ossetian armed forces that is now officially subjected to Russian command, see above n 1105.

2.2.2.2 The broad approach – overall control (ICTY standard)

Can there be occupation by proxy below the threshold of the ICJ standard? Certain scholars have come out in favour of this.[1127] Notably, Tristan Ferraro (ICRC) supported this idea in his 2012 article. He speaks of "indirect effective control" and argues that occupation

> *"may be exercised through surrogate armed forces as long as they are subject to the overall control of the foreign State. Thus, a State would be an occupying power for the purposes of IHL when it exercises overall control over de facto local authorities or other local organized groups that are themselves in effective control of a territory or part thereof."*[1128]

Ferraro does not deviate from the "effective control" standard under Art 42 HR. Rather, he uses a lower standard for attribution: overall control. This test was developed by the ICTY Appeals Chamber in 1999 and requires "coordinating or helping in the general planning" of the activities of a group.[1129] It goes beyond providing financial assistance, military equipment, or training. But it stays below the ICJ's threshold of planning *every specific* operation.[1130] The approach was also endorsed by the ICC in Lubanga.[1131] While the overall control standard was originally developed for classifying a conflict as international, the ICTY later explicitly used the test for *attributing* proxy occupation. In *Blaškić*, for example, the ICTY ruled that Croatia occupied parts of Bosnia and Herzegovina, because it supported a local *de facto* regime. The Tribunal reasoned that Croatia was an occupying power "through the overall control it exercised over

---

1127 Gal (n 1114) 64; Gilder (n 1078) 80; Amy Elizabeth Chinnappa, 'The United States and the Coalition Provisional Authority – Occupation by Proxy?' [2019] Leiden Journal of International Law 415, 433; Sylvain Vité, 'Typologie des conflits armés en droit international humanitaire: concepts juridiques et réalités' (2009) 91 Revue internationale de la Croix-Rouge 69, 74–75; Dapo Akande, 'Classification of Armed Conflicts: Relevant Legal Concepts' in Elizabeth Wilmshurst (ed), *International Law and the Classification of Conflicts* (Oxford University Press 2012) 18. See also Rulac, 'Military Occupation of Moldova by Russia' <http://www.rulac.org/browse/conflicts/military-occupation-of-moldova-by-russia#collapse2accord>.

1128 Ferraro (n 994) 158.

1129 See ICTY, *The Prosecutor v Duško Tadić* (IT-94–1-T), Appeals Chamber Judgment, 15 July 1999, para 131.

1130 ibid para 137.

1131 ICC, *The Prosecutor v Thomas Lubanga Dyilo* (ICC-01/04–01/06), Trial Chamber Judgment, 14 March 2012, para 541.

the HVO [Croatian Defence Council],[1132] the support it lent it, and the close ties it maintained with it."[1133] In the same decision, the ICTY provided concrete examples for overall control: paying salaries, taking decisions in meetings, and sharing troops or operational goals with an armed group.[1134]

This standard corresponds to Russia's influence in the Regions. I have detailed its economic, political, and military control above. The Regions heavily depend on Russia. The Kremlin is able to influence crucial political, military, and financial decisions in the breakaway republics. The Regions are "ultimately subordinated to Moscow."[1135]The Tagliavini Report[1136] seems to suggest that there are strong indicators for Russia's overall control of South Ossetia and Abkhazia.[1137] I am convinced that in each of the Regions, Russian influence reaches the ICTY's threshold of "coordinating and planning." Several scholars share this view.[1138]

The question remains, however, of whether overall control represents the right legal standard for attributing occupation. There are certain arguments in favour of such an assertion: Firstly, the ICTY explicitly recognised overall control as the right standard for attributing occupation in

---

1132 The Croatian Defence Council was the military wing of the unrecognised Croatian Republic of Herzeg-Bosnia that existed from 1991–1996 on the territory Bosnia-Herzegovina. It was supported by Croatia.

1133 ICTY, *The Prosecutor v Tihomir Blaškić* (IT-95-14), Trial Chamber Judgment, 3 March 2000, paras 149–150.

1134 ibid paras 101, 106, 108, 117–118.

1135 Ambrosio and Lange (n 1093) 688.

1136 The Report of the Independent International Fact-Finding Mission on the Conflict in Georgia, or short Tagliavini Report – named after the Swiss diplomat Heidi Tagliavini – was an EU sponsored report that brought together a group of renowned international and independent experts to shed light on the factual and legal aspects of the Russo-Georgian War. It was a bold attempt of the EU to establish the truth in the aftermath of a highly politicised conflict, see Thomas de Waal, 'The Still-Topical Tagliavini Report' (Carnegie, 30 September 2015) <https://carnegie.ru/commentary/61451>. I will rely on the three volumes of the report when dealing with the Russo-Georgian War.

1137 IIFFMCG, 'Report of the Independent International Fact-Finding Mission on the Conflict in Georgia (Tagliavini Report) Volume II' (n 1109) 303–304. Finally, the report leaves the question open because the framework for the conduct of hostilities is virtually the same in IAC and NIAC.

1138 For Transdniestria see e.g. Ivanel (n 1082); Kieran O'Reilly and Noelle Higgins, 'The Role of the Russian Federation in the Pridnestrovian Conflict: An International Humanitarian Law Perspective' (2008) 19 Irish Studies in International Affairs 57; for Georgia see e.g. Grazvydas Jasutis in Bellal (n 544) 54.

Blaškić and (implicitly) in *Tadić*.[1139] Secondly, extending the framework of occupation to situations of overall control would be in line with the protective nature of IHL.[1140] Otherwise States could avoid their obligations by outsourcing occupation. At the ICRC Meeting of Experts, many participants shared this protective view and stressed the need to "prevent any attempt by the occupying power to evade its duties under occupation law through the installation of a government by proxy, which would exert governmental functions on its behalf."[1141] Thirdly, the rationale of Art 47 GC IV speaks in favour of the broad approach. Art 47 intends to exclude the evasion of the occupation regime "in any case or in any manner whatsoever." Finally, the wording of Art 42 HR does not preclude the overall control test. It speaks of the "authority of the hostile army" without detailing what standard should be used.

There are, however, weighty arguments against widening the scope of attribution for proxy occupation. Firstly, State practice does not support the broad approach. All UN Security Council resolutions on situations that involve occupation by proxy, name the proxy actor as the occupier – not the sponsor State.[1142] Secondly, the approach has met with fierce resistance in academia. Renowned scholars such as Dinstein reject the broad approach and demand "a double requirement of effective control," i.e. effective control over the group and over the territory.[1143] Eyal Benvenisti also firmly opposes to deviation from the ICJ's standard.[1144] Thirdly, there is considerable case law in support of the narrow approach. The ECtHR ruled that the "physical presence of *foreign* troops is a *conditio sine qua*

1139 ICTY, *The Prosecutor v Tihomir Blaškić* (IT-95–14), Trial Chamber Judgment, 3 March 2000, paras 149–150. Furthermore, the ICTY implicitly recognised the overall control standard for occupation in *Tadić*. The Trial Chamber ruled that "the relationship of de facto organs or agents to the foreign Power includes those circumstances in which the foreign Power '*occupies*' or operates in certain territory *solely through the acts of local de facto organs or agents.*" The ICTY Appeals Chamber then clarified that the necessary relationship of a State and the *de facto* organ is "overall control" thereby deviating from the effective control test of the ICJ. See ICTY, *The Prosecutor v Duško Tadić* (IT-94-1-T), Trial Chamber Judgment, 7 May 1997, para 584 (emphasis added); ICTY, *The Prosecutor v Duško Tadić* (IT-94-1-T), Appeals Chamber Judgment, 15 July 1999, para 117.

1140 Gilder (n 1078) 62–63.

1141 ICRC, 'Expert Meeting, Occupation and Other Forms of Administration of Foreign Territory' (n 1000) 19.

1142 Ivanel (n 1082) 56.

1143 Dinstein (n 984) 50.

1144 Benvenisti (n 990) 61.

non for occupation."[1145] This formulation seems to exclude occupation by supporting local proxies. More importantly, the ICTY's case law – which is often cited in favour of the broad approach – is not consistent. In *Naletilić and Martinović*, for example, the Tribunal decided that

> "there is an essential distinction between the determination of a State of occupation and that of the existence of an international armed conflict. The application of the overall control test is applicable to the latter. A further degree of control is required to establish occupation"[1146]

The most important argument against the broad approach, however, is the case law of the ICJ. The Court developed its effective control standard in the *Nicaragua Case* (1986). Thirteen years later, in 1999, the ICTY Appeals Chamber challenged the test of effective control and replaced it with the lower threshold of overall control.[1147] The ICJ responded politely, but firmly in the *Bosnian Genocide Case* (2007).[1148] The Court explicitly rejected the ICTY standard for State attribution and upheld its own notion of effective control. The ICJ pointed to the ICTY's narrow mandate that only concerned individual crimes and did not include issues of State attribution.[1149] It reasoned that overall control may well be the test "applicable and suitable" for *classifying* an armed conflict, but for *State attribution* the test was "unsuitable, for it stretches too far, almost to breaking point, the

---

1145 ECtHR, *Sargsyan v Azerbaijan*, No 40167/06, 16 June 2015, para 94.

1146 ICTY, *The Prosecutor v Mladen Naletilić and Vinko Martinović* (IT-98–34-T), Trial Chamber Judgment, 31 March 2003, para 214 (emphasis added).

1147 See ICTY, *The Prosecutor v Duško Tadić* (IT-94–1-T), Appeals Chamber Judgment, 15 July 1999, paras 115–145, especially at para 137. The ICTY dealt with the question of attribution, because it had to classify the conflict at hand. It largely based its reasoning on the distinction between an *individual* and a highly *organised armed group*: "Where the question at issue is whether a single private individual or a group that is not militarily organized has acted as a de facto State organ when performing a specific act, it is necessary to ascertain whether specific instructions concerning the commission of that particular act had been issued by that State to the individual or group in question; alternatively, it must be established whether the unlawful act had been publicly endorsed or approved *ex post facto* by the State at issue. By contrast, control by a State over subordinate *armed forces or militias or paramilitary units* may be of an overall character" (para 137 of the judgment, emphasis in the original).

1148 Already in the earlier *Armed Activities Case* the ICJ had favoured its own Nicaragua standard, although it did not explicitly address the ICTY's decision in *Tadić*, see *Armed Activities Case* (n 994) paras 168, 226.

1149 ICTY, *The Prosecutor v Duško Tadić* (IT-94–1-T), Appeals Chamber Judgment, 15 July 1999, para 404.

connection which must exist between the conduct of a State's organs and its international responsibility."[1150] Since then, the issue seems settled, and it is hard to argue in favour of a lower threshold for Art 8 ARSIWA. James Crawford writes that "so far as the law of State responsibility is concerned, this determination effectively ends the debate as to the correct standard of control to be applied under Art 8."[1151] Admittedly, the *Bosnian Genocide Case* did not deal with occupation, but attribution in general. It would, however, seem logical to have a unified standard of attribution.[1152]

In conclusion, there is currently no consensus as to the concept of "occupation by proxy." Notably, the ICRC considers it sufficient that the sponsor State has "overall control" of the proxy. However, the predominant view – and above all the ICJ – rejects the idea of occupation by proxy below the threshold of effective control. To my mind, the question has been settled ever since the ICJ *Bosnian Genocide Case* where the Court clearly favoured the narrow view: *only* effective control can trigger attribution. Of course, this narrow view tears a hole into the occupation regime. Certain forms of occupation by proxy fall outside the scope of IHL, thereby creating a gap in protection for civilians.[1153]

1150 *Bosnian Genocide Case* (n 1115) para 407.

1151 James Crawford, *State Responsibility: The General Part* (Cambridge University Press 2013) 156.

1152 This clear rejection leaves little room for occupation by proxy through overall control. There is only one way to save the broad approach: by avoiding attribution altogether and equating occupation to ordinary conflict classification. In other words: isn't classifying a situation as occupation quite similar to classifying a conflict as international? It is undisputed that we may use the overall control test to classify a NIAC as an IAC because a State has control over an armed group (so-called "internationalisation" of a NIAC). Even the ICJ conceded that it "may well be that the test is applicable and suitable" for classifying an armed conflict (*Bosnian Genocide Case* (n 1115) para 407). Could occupation by proxy represent a special form of an internationalised conflict? After all, occupation is regulated in CA 2 – the main Article for conflict classification. It is, however, doubtful what would be the advantage of such "occupation without attribution." In concrete terms this would mean that Russia could be considered an occupying power in Georgia, but the actions of the local South Ossetian and Abkhazian authorities would not be attributable to Moscow. Gilder calls this protection gap a "get out of jail free card", because the State would be considered an occupying power, but at the same time it would always escape State responsibility, see Gilder (n 1078) 80; Ivanel (n 1082) 56–57; Gal (n 1114) 78.

1153 Gilder (n 1078) 61.

2.2.3 Russia's approach – between loopholes and denial

What does this mean for the Regions? It means that Moscow's strategy is extremely effective in avoiding the framework of occupation. Firstly, the Kremlin does not use too many of its own troops in order to avoid direct control over the entire territory. Secondly, it maintains its support of the proxies at a low enough level to avoid attribution through effective control. Thirdly, while its support *does* reach the threshold of overall control, Russia rejects using this standard for attribution. In this, it can refer to the case law of the ICJ that upheld the strict standard of effective control.

Based on this, Russia argues that it is not occupying *any* part of *any* of the Regions. In the following, I will analyse this position – first with regards to South Ossetia and Abkhazia, then with regards to Transdniestria.

On the one hand, Moscow resorts to sound legal arguments to reject proxy occupation in the Regions. Notably, it can cite the ICJ case law that I have outlined above in its support. On the other hand, Russia also denies crucial facts, especially with regards to Transdniestria which it has never officially recognised as a State. Furthermore, it challenges occupation even in the areas where it has "boots on the ground" through its own soldiers, namely on and near the military bases and the "buffer zone" during the 2008 War. In these respects, the Russian position rather resembles the obstinate, but untenable denial we have seen in Crimea.

2.3.2.1 Russia's attitude towards South Ossetia & Abkhazia – brothers in arms

Russia speaks openly about its support of South Ossetia and Abkhazia. Unlike in eastern Ukraine, the financial and military aid is not a state secret. Certainly, it is difficult to judge how much influence Russia wields via informal ways that are traditionally of great importance in the Caucasus.[1154] However, the formal support to the Georgian breakaway regions are public knowledge. The official budget details the aid to the breakaway republics;[1155] politicians sign contracts on military bases, and the President

---

1154 Ambrosio and Lange (n 1093) 689.
1155 Available at <https://www.zakonrf.info/doc-33132812/pril14.2/>.

promises military and financial support on camera.[1156] Nevertheless, Russia does not regard itself as an occupying power – neither direct, nor by proxy.[1157] In essence, Moscow relies on three arguments for challenging its occupation. I will present and comment on them in turn.

The first argument concerns statehood. Moscow recognises Abkhazia and South Ossetia as "subjects of international law endowed with a legal capacity to enter into international treaties."[1158] It portrays itself as the power protecting the Regions' right to self-determination thereby giving "two peoples the chance to evolve, rather than to be exterminated."[1159] According to this logic, the presence of Russian troops is covered by the consent of the sovereign.[1160] This justification is at odds with international law. A State needs territory, population, and effective government.[1161] While both Abkhazia and South Ossetia fulfil the first two requirements, neither of them meets the criteria of effective government.[1162] Their dependence on Russia prevents them from regulating their internal and external affairs independently. Furthermore, virtually no State has recognised these

---

1156 Ellen Barry, 'Putin Promises Abkhazia Economic and Military Support' (The New York Times, 12 August 2009) <https://www.nytimes.com/2009/08/13/worl d/europe/13russia.html>.

1157 IIFFMCG, 'Report of the Independent International Fact-Finding Mission on the Conflict in Georgia (Tagliavini Report) Volume II' (n 1109) 308.

1158 IIFFMCG, 'Report of the Independent International Fact-Finding Mission on the Conflict in Georgia (Tagliavini Report) Volume III – Views of the Sides on the Conflict, Chronologies and Responses to Questionnaires' (n 960) 431.

1159 The quote is taken from Dmitry Medvedev's statement during a meeting with the South Ossetian President Eduard Kokoity, 13 August 2010, available at <http://kremlin.ru/events/president/transcripts/8639>. See also the Appeal of the Federal Council of the Federal Assembly of the Russian Federation to Recognize the Breakaway Republics, 25 August 2008, reprinted in IIFFMCG, 'Report of the Independent International Fact-Finding Mission on the Conflict in Georgia (Tagliavini Report) Volume III – Views of the Sides on the Conflict, Chronologies and Responses to Questionnaires' (n 958) 446.

1160 IIFFMCG, 'Report of the Independent International Fact-Finding Mission on the Conflict in Georgia (Tagliavini Report) Volume III – Views of the Sides on the Conflict, Chronologies and Responses to Questionnaires' (n 960) 433.

1161 James Crawford, 'State', *Max Planck Encyclopedia of Public International Law* (Oxford University Press 2011) paras 13–24.

1162 Nußberger, 'Abkhazia' (n 1079) para 27; Nußberger, 'South Ossetia' (n 1079) para 20; IIFFMCG, 'Report of the Independent International Fact-Finding Mission on the Conflict in Georgia (Tagliavini Report) Volume II' (n 1109) 127.

entities.[1163] While recognition is not constitutive for statehood, it serves as a strong indicator.[1164]

Moscow's second argument against occupation concerns effective control under Art 42 HR – or rather the lack thereof. While Russia agrees that effective control is "the determining factor" for occupation it insists that it does not have enough soldiers in Abkhazia and South Ossetia to meet this standard.[1165] During the proceedings of the Tagliavini Report, Moscow argued that it only maintained a small presence of 3700 servicemen in each Georgian breakaway republic. This number was not enough to exercise effective control over the Regions.[1166] In support of its argument, Moscow referred to the case law of the ICTY which had ruled that the establishment of a "temporary administration" is one of the indicators for "authority" under Art 42 HR.[1167] In this respect, Moscow stressed that Abkhazia and South Ossetian had their own local authorities and that it did not interfere with any administrative issues.[1168]

Russia adopted the same line of argument in the proceedings of *ICJ, Application of the International Convention on the Elimination of All Forms of Racial Discrimination (CERD)*.[1169] Russia stated that its

> *"presence in either Abkhazia or South Ossetia cannot, even prima facie, be qualified as either one of belligerent occupation or as one of effective control*

1163 Since the Russo-Georgian War, Moscow recognises South Ossetia's independence alongside with Nicaragua, Venezuela, Nauru, and Syria. Abkhazia's statehood was recognised by Russia as well as Venezuela, Nicaragua, Nauru, and Syria.

1164 Crawford, 'State' (n 1161) para 44.

1165 IIFFMCG, 'Report of the Independent International Fact-Finding Mission on the Conflict in Georgia (Tagliavini Report) Volume III – Views of the Sides on the Conflict, Chronologies and Responses to Questionnaires' (n 960) 435; IIFFMCG, 'Report of the Independent International Fact-Finding Mission on the Conflict in Georgia (Tagliavini Report) Volume II' (n 1109) 304.

1166 IIFFMCG, 'Report of the Independent International Fact-Finding Mission on the Conflict in Georgia (Tagliavini Report) Volume III – Views of the Sides on the Conflict, Chronologies and Responses to Questionnaires' (n 960) 435.

1167 See ibid 435 at n 2. See also ICTY, *The Prosecutor v Mladen Naletilić and Vinko Martinović* (IT-98–34-T), Trial Chamber Judgment, 31 March 2003, para 217.

1168 IIFFMCG, 'Report of the Independent International Fact-Finding Mission on the Conflict in Georgia (Tagliavini Report) Volume III – Views of the Sides on the Conflict, Chronologies and Responses to Questionnaires' (n 958) 436.

1169 ICJ, *Application of the International Convention on the Elimination of All Forms of Racial Discrimination (Georgia v Russian Federation), Preliminary Objections, Judgment*, ICJ Reports (2011) 70 [hereinafter *Racial Discrimination Case*].

> *over the territories concerned, whether before, during or after the outbreak of hostilities."*[1170]

In the proceedings before the ICJ, the Russian team further elaborated on the issue of effective control under Art 42 HR. It stated that such control needs to "substitute" authority and "replace the former government,"[1171] and explained that this required a very high presence of troops like in *Loizidou v Turkey* that it called an "instructive precedent."[1172] In *Loizidou*, so the Russians stressed, the ratio of Turkish troops in Northern Cyprus was 20 times higher than the Russian presence in Georgia.[1173] That led the Russian legal team to conclude that their "presence at no point in time could be perceived as *[...]* constituting belligerent occupation"[1174]

In this respect, Russia's legal reasoning is flawed. The argument that there are not enough troops to occupy all of Abkhazia and South Ossetia is too simplistic. Occupation may concern parts of a territory.[1175] This is spelled out *expressis verbis* in CA 2 GC IV. Hence, Russia jumps the gun when it argues that it does not occupy *any* parts of Abkhazia and South Ossetia, because it does not have enough men to occupy the *whole* Region. As I have shown above, Russia did in fact have enough troops

---

1170 ICJ, *Application of the International Convention on the Elimination of All Forms of Racial Discrimination (Georgia v Russian Federation) – Preliminary Objections of the Russian Federation* (1 December 2009) at para 5.61; see also paras 5.73 and 5.65.

1171 ICJ, *Application of the International Convention on the Elimination of All Forms of Racial Discrimination (Georgia v Russian Federation) – Preliminary Objections of the Russian Federation* (1 December 2009) para 5.63.

1172 ICJ, *Verbatim Record of Public Sitting in the Case Concerning Application of the International Convention on the Elimination of All Forms of Racial Discrimination (Georgia v Russian Federation) Held on 10 September 2008 at 4.30 pm* (CR 2008/27) 12.

1173 ibid 13.

1174 ICJ, *Application of the International Convention on the Elimination of All Forms of Racial Discrimination (Georgia v Russian Federation) – Preliminary Objections of the Russian Federation* (1 December 2009) para 5.73; with regards to direct occupation, Russia argued that its troops were merely peacekeepers and – in any case – that their number was not sufficient to amount to effective control. As a comparison, Russia pointed to the 30 000 Turkish troops stationed in occupied Northern Cyprus (paras 5.65 – 5.69) and argued that today, the "number (approximately 2 500 in each Republic), functions and role of the Russian troops present exclude any ability of the Russian Federation to exercise overall effective control in either Abkhazia or South Ossetia" (para 5.72).

1175 See also IIFFMCG, 'Report of the Independent International Fact-Finding Mission on the Conflict in Georgia (Tagliavini Report) Volume II' (n 1109) 310.

in the "buffer zone" to replace the Georgian sovereign. The Tagliavini Commission, for example, found that "to a certain degree, Russian forces were in a position to ensure public order and safety in the territories they were *stationed* in."[1176] Admittedly, now the number of Russian troops is lower than during the war, but in and near its military bases, Russia continues to exercise enough authority through its troops. Despite that, Moscow's argument strikes a point. In a large chunk of Abkhazian and South Ossetian territory it does not meet the necessary threshold of control through its armed forces thanks to its effective outsourcing.

This brings us to Russia's third counterargument which concerns attribution. Moscow argues that its control over the Abkhazian and South Ossetian authorities stays below the ICJ's "strict view on attribution" adopted in the Genocide Case.[1177] Therefore, the acts of its proxies are not attributable to Moscow.[1178]

Russia's third argument concerning attribution is correct. We have to concede that the standard of the ICJ is indeed very strict and at the present time, Russia does not wield enough control over its proxies to meet this threshold. Finally, I have shown above that the concept of attributing occupation via overall control – a lower threshold – has met with the fierce resistance of States, scholars, and courts. Even its staunchest supporters concede that it is an emerging concept and does not necessarily correspond to current treaty law.[1179]

So, is Russia an occupying power?[1180] Yes, but only in small patches of the Georgian territory, namely its military bases and the former "buffer

---

1176 ibid 373.

1177 ICJ, *Verbatim Record of Public Sitting in the Case Concerning Application of the International Convention on the Elimination of All Forms of Racial Discrimination (Georgia v Russian Federation) Held on 8 September 2008 at 3 pm* (CR 2008/23) 17. For the relation between Russian and South Ossetian and Abkhaz forces see IIFFMCG, 'Report of the Independent International Fact-Finding Mission on the Conflict in Georgia (Tagliavini Report) Volume II' (n 1107) 433–434.

1178 IIFFMCG, 'Report of the Independent International Fact-Finding Mission on the Conflict in Georgia (Tagliavini Report) Volume II' (n 1107) 259; see also *Racial Discrimination Case* (n 1163) para 83.

1179 Gilder (n 1078) 61.

1180 Often, scholars and international organisations speak of Russian occupation in the Regions without going into the differences between occupation by proxy and direct occupation, see e.g. Rulac, 'Military Occupation of Georgia by Russia' <http://www.rulac.org/browse/conflicts/military-occupation-of-georgia-by-russia>; Human Rights Watch, 'Up in Flames – Humanitarian Law Violations and Civilian Victims in the Conflict over South Ossetia' (2019) 35; Bellal (n 544) 32.

zone."[1181] There, Russia's position of denying occupation simply contradicts the law and reminds us of the simple but effective strategy of denial that we have seen in Crimea. However, with regards to a large chunk of Georgian territory in Abkhazia and South Ossetia, Russia cannot be considered as a *de jure* occupying power. In this respect it has successfully used the loopholes of IHL to its advantage.

This mix of denial and legal chutzpah leaves a severe protection gap. For instance, most violations during the Russo-Georgian War occurred *after* the hostilities died down and were committed by *private* individuals, not Russian soldiers.[1182] Hence, the question was "actually one of policing and maintaining order to prevent or stop such violations."[1183] This is exactly the classic focus of the occupation regime which obliges a State to guarantee law and order and whose applicability Russia denied. Especially in the "buffer zone" – which became a hotbed of IHL abuses – civilians were left without the protective framework of IHL. Bandits and paramilitaries looted, kidnapped, and torched houses, while Russia denied its role as an occupant. The Tagliavini Report concludes that

> *"Russian forces were in a position to ensure public order and safety in the territories they were stationed in, and claim to have undertaken measures in this regard. This contrasts strikingly with what happened on the ground, where there was a serious lack of action by the Russian troops to prevent violations and protect ethnic Georgians."*[1184]

In the areas controlled by Russia's proxies, the population was equally deprived of protection under GC IV. Admittedly, slipping through a legal loophole by avoiding attribution is legitimate *per se*. It does, however, say much about Russia's desire to wage war below the radar of IHL.

2.3.2.2 Russia's attitude towards Transdniestria – brothers in denial

In Transdniestria, the Russian position is slightly different. First of all, unlike Abkhazia and South Ossetia, Russia has never recognised the

---

1181 The most recent institution to argue that the "buffer zone" was occupied by Russian troops was the ECtHR in its judgment on the merits of *Georgia v Russia*, No 38263/08, 21 January 2021, paras 145–222.
1182 IIFFMCG, 'Report of the Independent International Fact-Finding Mission on the Conflict in Georgia (Tagliavini Report) Volume II' (n 1109) 371.
1183 ibid.
1184 ibid.

breakaway region as an independent State.[1185] The presence of Russian troops can thus not be justified through the consent of the Transdniestrian sovereign. Rather, Moscow considers its remaining 1 500 troops as peacekeepers that are stationed in Transdniestria following a 1992 agreement with Moldova.[1186] Moldova, however, has repeatedly expressed its grievances against the peacekeepers, lamented their lack of neutrality, and rallied support to push out the Russian troops.[1187] In 2018, the UN General Assembly passed a resolution calling for the "complete and unconditional withdrawal" of Russian forces whose presence "on the territory of the Republic of Moldova, without its consent, violates its sovereignty and territorial integrity."[1188] Russia felt criticised unjustly and refused to withdraw the troops.[1189] In any case, it does not consider their presence as occupation.

Apart from the peacekeeping mission, Russia denies supporting Transdniestria in any exceptional way. This represents a striking difference to the Georgian scenario. Unlike in Abkhazia and South Ossetia, Russia is cautious about admitting its support to the Transdniestrian republic. On numerous occasions, it has denied providing *any* notable support to the entity, namely in several high-profile cases before the ECtHR. While these cases did not deal with belligerent occupation *per se*, they contain rare insights into the Russian position. The first of a series of cases was *Ilaşcu v Moldova and Russia* (2004). There, Russia denied that it

---

1185   Cristian Urse, 'Solving Transnistria: Any Optimists Left?' (2008) 7 Connections 57, 69–70. Nevertheless, Russia maintains a *de facto* consulate in Tiraspol which it calls Пункт выездного консульского обслуживания в Тирасполе [Tiraspol office for consular services concerning travels abroad]. The consulate is officially subordinated to the Russian embassy in Moldova. The Transdniestrian authorities also maintain an office in Moscow, see <https://moldova.mid.ru/punkt-vyezdnogo-konsul-skogo-obsluzivania-v-tiraspole>.

1186   Agreement on the Principles for the Friendly Settlement of the Armed Conflict in the Transdniestrian Region of the Republic of Moldova, 21 July 1992; for details on the agreement see ECtHR, *Ilaşcu and Others v Moldova and Russia*, No 48787/99, 8 July 2004, paras 87 et seq.

1187   ECtHR, *Ilaşcu and Others v Moldova and Russia*, No 48787/99, 8 July 2004, paras 92 et seq.

1188   UN General Assembly resolution 72/282, UN Doc A/RES/72/282 (22 June 2018); the Transdniestrian authorities appealed to Moscow to continue the mission, 'Transnistria's Leader Calls for Russian Peacekeepers' Continued Presence in the Region' (Tass, 25 June 2019) <https://tass.com/world/1065544>.

1189   Urse (n 1185) 69.

> *"exercised, or had exercised in the past, any control whatsoever over Trans-dniestrian territory and pointed out that the "MRT" had set up its own power structures, including a parliament and a judiciary. [...] The Russian Federation had never given the authorities of Transdniestria the slightest military, financial or other support."[1190]*

The strategy of factual denial continued in later cases. In *Mozer v Moldova and Russia* (2016) Moscow argued that "the territory was controlled by a *de facto* government which was not an organ or instrument of Russia and which *did not depend on Russia in any way.*"[1191] In *Catan v Moldova and Russia* (2012) Russia called its economic support to the MRT mere human-itarian aid that "could be compared with humanitarian aid provided by the European Union."[1192] It repeated that Transdniestria "did not depend on Russia in any way."[1193] Of course, this reading is at odds with the actual level of support that Russia provides to Transdniestria and that I have described at page 232.

At the same time, Moscow stresses the high threshold of direct or at-tributed occupation – just like in South Ossetia and Abkhazia. In *Catan*, for example, Russia argued that extraterritorial jurisdiction "might include cases where the State Party was in long-term settled occupation or where a territory was effectively controlled by a government which was properly regarded as an organ of the relevant State party, in accordance with the test applied by the International Court of Justice [in the Genocide Case]."[1194] It then argued that things were different for Transdniestria, because "the territory was controlled by a *de facto* government *which was not an organ or instrument* of Russia."[1195] In *Mozer*, Russia compared its influence to the US support to the Contras and argued that it had much less influence over the MRT authorities than the US had had over the rebels in Nicaragua, notably due to a lack of soldiers on the ground.[1196] In essence, the position

---

1190 ECtHR, *Ilaşcu and Others v Moldova and Russia*, No 48787/99, 8 July 2004, paras 354–357.

1191 ECtHR, *Mozer v Moldova and Russia*, No 11138/10, 23 February 2016, para 94.

1192 ECtHR, *Catan and Others v Moldova and Russia*, Nos 43370/04, 8252/05 and 18454/06, 19 October 2012, para 100.

1193 ECtHR, *Mozer v Moldova and Russia*, No 11138/10, 23 February 2016, para 94.

1194 ECtHR, *Catan and Others v Moldova and Russia*, Nos 43370/04, 8252/05 and 18454/06, 19 October 2012, para 96.

1195 ibid.

1196 ECtHR, *Mozer v Moldova and Russia*, No 11138/10, 23 February 2016, para 93.

is very similar to the Georgian cases: No troops, no attribution, no occupation by proxy below effective control.[1197]

To sum up, Russia does not regard itself as a direct occupying power in Transdniestria. In factual terms, it is striking that Moscow denies providing the "slightest support" to the Transdniestrian authorities.[1198] This sets the case apart from Georgia and is reminiscent of Crimea where Moscow tried to deny the obvious.

In legal terms, the line of argument resembles the position towards Abkhazia and South Ossetia. Moscow denies direct occupation and insists that occupation by proxy requires the strict effective control test established by the ICJ. Just like in Georgia, the Russian position is partly flawed. The presence of Russian troops without the consent of the Moldovan sovereign means that certain areas *are* under direct occupation. With regards to occupation by proxy, however, Russia succeeds in slipping through a legal loophole.

2.3 Conclusion

Crimea, Abkhazia, South Ossetia, and Transdniestria – these four regions show that occupation continues to be a bone of contention, and that Russia has chosen to operate below the radar of the protective framework provided by IHL. The fact that occupation sparks heated debates is nothing new. Controversies about the application of the framework are as old as the framework itself. In the beginning, the drafters feared that invading armies, seeking to benefit from the powers that the law granted to occupants, would declare occupation prematurely without actually controlling the area. Only when occupation became more of a "burden than a boon" did States shift to avoiding its application.[1199]

Such avoidance is not a specific Russian phenomenon either. Israel's occupation of the West Bank, Turkey's occupation in Northern Cyprus,

---

1197 In *Mozer* Russia explicitly refers to "overall control" without clarifying whether this could be a standard of attribution *in casu*: "The notion of 'overall control' had been further developed by the International Criminal Tribunal for the former Yugoslavia. The Court's interpretation of this notion differed from the interpretations of these [ICJ and ICTY] international tribunals." See ECtHR, *Mozer v Moldova and Russia*, No 11138/10, 23 February 2016, para 25.

1198 ECtHR, *Ilaşcu and Others v Moldova and Russia*, No 48787/99, 8 July 2004, paras 354–357.

1199 Benvenisti (n 990) 43.

and Morocco's presence in Western Sahara are other instances where States refuse to recognise the *de jure* applicability of the Geneva Conventions.[1200] Yet, it is striking that Moscow is involved in four, possibly five such scenarios if eastern Ukraine is included.[1201] The ICTY's vision of IHL as a "realistic body of law, grounded on the notion of effectiveness and inspired by the aim of deterring deviation from the standards to the maximum extent possible" disappears into the mist of a Russian smoke screen.[1202]

The fact that Russia deems IHL inapplicable thwarts any dialogue about specific violations and creates a double-standard. On the one hand, it allows Russia to endorse the framework of occupation when talking about the Golan heights[1203] or the American occupation of the eastern bank of the Euphrates in Syria.[1204] On the other hand, Russia believes it out of question to apply the framework to Russian actions abroad. In this sense, belligerent occupation truly has become a "car that never leaves its (Russian) garage."[1205]

1200 Bellal (n 544) 32. Israel, for example, applies certain rules of occupation to the West Bank *de facto*, but rejects their *de jure* application.

1201 For an extensive case study of the issue of occupation by proxy in eastern Ukraine see Gilder (n 1078). I will deal with the war in eastern Ukraine below, but not with regards to occupation by proxy for the reasons which I have explained in n 1078.

1202 ICTY, *The Prosecutor v Duško Tadić* (IT-94-1-T), Appeals Chamber Judgment, 15 July 1999, para 96.

1203 'Russia, Iran and Syria Slam Trump's Golan Heights Comments' (Deutsche Welle, 22 March 2019) <https://www.dw.com/en/russia-iran-and-syria-slam-trumps-golan-heights-comments/a-48016842>.

1204 'See Security Council Backsliding on Duty to Protect Syria's Civilians, Rights Advocate Stresses, amid Calls to Protect Hospitals, Review Deconfliction Accords' (UN, 30 July 2019) <https://www.un.org/press/en/2019/sc13903.doc.htm>.

1205 For the sake of completeness, I should point out that evading IHL does not produce a legal vacuum. Thanks to the progressive case law of the ECtHR, Russia faces legal responsibility under human rights law in all four Regions. While this is to be welcomed from a victim's perspective, it accentuates the decline of IHL. As Russia sidelines the laws of war, human rights law steps in – notably in the form of the ECHR as interpreted by the judgments of the ECtHR. However, it remains to be seen what the future holds for the implementation of these obligations given Russia's recent resistance in highly politicised cases such as ECtHR, *Anchugov and Gladkov v Russia*, Nos 11157/04 and 15162/05, 9 December 2019 and ECtHR, *OAO Neftyanaya Kompaniya Yukos v Russia*, No 14902/04, Judgment Just Satisfaction, 31 July 2014. For human rights law filling the protection gaps of IHL in situations of occupation by proxy see Ivanel (n 1082) 57; for Russia's difficult relationship with the ECtHR see Bowring,

3. Denying the involvement of Russian soldiers – phantoms of war in Donbas

While the Russian strategy of avoiding occupation has both a factual and legal component, we now enter the realm of absolute factual denial. The presence of Moscow's troops in eastern Ukraine is an open secret. Yet, the conflict has become the prime example of Moscow's readiness to deny undeniable facts. The first part of the following discussion will provide details on the Russian intervention in eastern Ukraine. I will place the emphasis on the use of Russian on-duty soldiers, since the outsourcing to proxy actors (Cossacks, militias, and private companies) will be dealt with in Chapter IV. In the second part, I will briefly outline the Russian version of events. Thirdly, I will apply the law to the facts. What does the direct involvement of Russian soldiers mean in terms of IHL? Finally, the last part will explain how the Russian strategy of denial affected the effective application of IHL.

3.1 Donbas – a beautiful battleground

Donbas has always enjoyed a special status in Ukraine. The soil is rich – both on the surface and below. In summer, a visitor might decipher the true meaning of the Ukrainian flag gazing at the endless sunflower and wheat fields against the blue sky. In the countryside, babushkas dry heaps of apricots on colourful cloths under the hot sun. At the same time, Donbas was always highly urbanised and industrialised. It is home to valuable resources such as high-quality coal (anthracite). Donetsk was a thriving city home to one million and Luhansk to half a million inhabitants. Its population is a wild mix of Russians, Ukrainians, and other ethnicities. Russian remains the predominant language. The Donbas was also Yanukovych's home base and the birth place of his Party of the Regions.[1206] Hence, it is not surprising that the people of Donbas remained sceptical of the government in Kyiv and maintained close ties to Russia.[1207] Nevertheless, when turmoil spilled over from Crimea in spring 2014, the locals did not greet the separatists with open arms. While the separatists managed to

---

'Russian Cases in the ECtHR and the Question of Implementation' (n 836); Mälksoo, *Russian Approaches to International Law* (n 6) 121; Ioffe (n 832).

1206 Jutta Sommerbauer, *Die Ukraine im Krieg: Hinter den Frontlinien eines europäischen Konflikts* (K&S 2016) 28–29.

1207 Fischer (n 775) 7.

establish two *de facto* regimes in Donbas – the Luhansk People's Republic (LNR) and the Donetsk People's Republic (DNR) – a survey in April 2014 showed that a majority of the population rejected the armed struggle for secession.[1208] DNR's Defence Minister Igor "Strelkov" Girkin famously complained that in Donetsk – a city of one million – he could not even find 1 000 men ready to take up arms against Kyiv.[1209] What caused the bloody war in Donbas which has been dragging on until today?

3.1.1 Chronology of a war – four phases

One may divide the first year of the war into three phases.[1210] The first phase (April 2014) concerns the "Donbas revolution." In Donetsk and Luhansk, local armed formations took control of public and administrative buildings.[1211] On 12 April, former GRU[1212] officer Igor Strelkov gathered a couple of dozens of men and seized local police and government buildings in Slovyansk.[1213] Even at this early moment, Russian special forces actively participated in the fight.[1214] The leading Russian military expert Pavel Felgengauer claims that they made up the "military nucleus of the fighters in Slovyansk." The special forces brought know-how and weapons no people's militia [*ополченцы*] could ever have, such as the use of the latest air defence systems against Ukrainian helicopters.[1215]

1208 Margarete Klein and Kristian Pester, 'Kiew in der Offensive – Die militärische Dimension des Ukraine-Konflikts' (Stiftung Wissenschaft und Politik 2014) 3.

1209 ibid.

1210 Nikolay Mitrokhin, 'Infiltration, Instruktion, Invasion: Russlands Krieg in der Ukraine' (2014) 64 Osteuropa 3.

1211 Galeotti, *Armies of Russia's War in Ukraine* (n 785) 14.

1212 GRU or GU stands for *Главное управление Генерального штаба Вооружённых Сил Российской Федерации* [Main Directorate of the General Staff of the Armed Forces of the Russian Federation]. It is Russia's military intelligence agency that also commands its own special forces.

1213 Galeotti, *Armies of Russia's War in Ukraine* (n 785) 14–15.

1214 Mitrokhin (n 1210) 5–6.

1215 The air defence systems in question were Manpads (man-portable air-defence systems). These are guided portable missiles that can be used against low flying aircraft. Felgengauer argues that the use of such weapons requires a specially trained soldier. Furthermore, the Ukrainian helicopter could not have been shot down by Manpads taken from Ukrainian stocks, because the device is equipped with a "friend or foe" identification (IFF) that blocks the use against friendly aircraft. See Журналист Павел Фельгенгауэр: использование ПЗРК доказывает, что боевое ядро в Славянске – это российский спецназ [Journal-

The Ukrainian army was too overwhelmed to react. When Kyiv launched the so-called "Anti-Terrorist Operation" in mid-April 2014, less than 10 percent of its soldiers were ready for combat.[1216] Their training was poor and their equipment outdated.[1217]

The second phase lasted from May 2014 to July 2014. The Ukrainians started to fight back. Poroshenko's "Anti-Terrorist-Operation" gained momentum, and the conflict entered a new level of intensity producing high casualties on both sides.[1218] During this time an influx of volunteers from Russia and other countries was seen. Cossacks, veterans from the wars in Afghanistan and Chechnya, Imperial nostalgists, members of Limonov's Natsbol Party,[1219] or simply soldiers of fortune came together to form an odd army.[1220] Most volunteers crossed the border into Ukraine through Rostov where they were equipped, trained, and briefed on Russian soil.[1221] I will analyse two types of volunteer battalions in detail below: Cossacks, and the private military company "Wagner Group." For now, suffice it to say that Russian special forces remained in eastern Ukraine as Russia facilitated the arrival of volunteer fighters.

During the third phase (August 2014–June 2015) the war escalated further. Regular Russian soldiers started to fight alongside insurgent militias. Lawrence Freedman writes that "the conflict became less of an externally sponsored insurgency [...] and more of a limited war between Ukraine and Russia."[1222] Despite heavy losses, Kyiv's soldiers gained ground and

---

ist Pavel Felgengauer: The Use of Manpads Proves that the Military Core in Slovyansk Consists of Russian Special Forces]' (Dozhd, 2 May 2014) <https://tvr ain.ru/teleshow/here_and_now/zhurnalist_pavel_felgengauer_ispolzovanie_pzr k_dokazyvaet_chto_boevoe_jadro_v_slavjanske_eto_rossijskij_spetsnaz-367872/ >.

1216 Of course, the name carried a political connotation, because it branded the separatists as terrorists. In 2018 Kyiv changed the name into Joint Forces Operation, see Adam Coffey, 'Ukraine Declares 'Anti-Terrorist Operation in the Donbas' Officially Over: What Does That Mean?' (RUSI, 16 May 2018) <https:// rusi.org/commentary/ukraine-declares-anti-terrorist-operation-donbas-officially -over-what-does-mean>.

1217 Klein and Pester (n 1208) 1.

1218 Freedman (n 1010) 111; Klein and Pester (n 1208) 1.

1219 Short for National Bolshevik Party [Национал-большевистская партия], a highly controversial political organisation in Russia that promotes a nationalistic version of Bolshevism. It was founded by the Russian writer and dissident Eduard Limonov.

1220 Mitrokhin (n 1210) 9.

1221 ibid 10.

1222 Freedman (n 1010) 110.

retook strategic cities like Slovyansk where Igor Strelkov had held his command centre.[1223] Then the Ukrainian Army closed in on Luhansk and Donetsk.[1224] In early August it managed to cut off the separatists' supply routes. At this moment, Russia decided to open the floodgates and send in scores of regular troops to avoid the rebels' certain defeat.[1225] Violence temporarily eased after the Minsk initiative (Minsk I) in September 2014, but from October 2014 onwards, more Russians soldiers and tanks crossed into Ukraine.[1226] Intense fighting followed and continued despite a second agreement in Minsk (Minsk II):[1227] The battle for Donetsk airport (September 2014–January 2014) and Debaltseve (January–February 2015), and Maryinka (June 2015). By June 2015 OCHA reported 6 500 deaths, 16 000 wounded, and 15 million in need of humanitarian aid.[1228]

After the first year, the war entered a fourth phase (July 2015–today). The Ukrainian Army steadily improved due to reforms, combat experience, as well as Western aid and training. The human cost of another large-scale Russian offensive would have been enormous.[1229] Hence, it never happened. Both parties started to fortify their positions along the so-called "contact line." There is no hope for quickly overpowering the enemy, but still shelling and shooting occurs on an almost daily basis. So far, the conflict refuses to "freeze" like those in Georgia and Transdniestria. This simmering conflict might attract less media attention, but it is no less lethal. From June 2015–February 2019, another 6 500 people died as the body count reached 13 000. Millions are still displaced.[1230] Russian troops are still present in LNR and DNR even though the times of large-scale offensives are long over.[1231]

1223   ibid 111.
1224   Galeotti, *Armies of Russia's War in Ukraine* (n 785) 17.
1225   Mitrokhin (n 1210) 14.
1226   Freedman (n 1010) 121.
1227   ibid 123. Minsk II was signed on 12 February 2015.
1228   ibid at n 109.
1229   ibid 127.
1230   OHCHR, 'Report on the Human Rights Situation in Ukraine: 16 February to 15 May 2019' (2019) at n 22.
1231   Tamila Varshalomidze, 'Poroshenko: Over 80,000 Russian Troops in and Around Ukraine' (Al Jazeera, 1 December 2018) <https://www.aljazeera.com/news/2018/12/poroshenko-80000-russian-troops-ukraine-181201164222788.htm l>.

3.1.2 Pointillism of war – individual stories painting a bigger picture

I have already mentioned that during all four phases, Russian soldiers were present in eastern Ukraine. During the third and fourth phase especially, this fact was impossible to hide. The following well-documented examples may serve as proof for the presence of on-duty personnel.

On 16 May 2015, the Russians Alexander Alexandrov und Yevgeniy Yerofeyev were caught during a reconnaissance mission near Shastya. They claimed to be on active duty carrying out orders.[1232] In an interview with Novaya Gazeta, Alexandrov dissipated any remaining doubts about his motivation:

> *"Tell me why am I in all this? I was just following orders! I am not a terrorist. It was an order! I mean, I swore an oath to my fatherland."*[1233]

A Ukrainian Court later found that both were "Russian servicemen that had been sent to the territory of Ukraine to commit acts involving weapons and military force."[1234]

There are other cases like Alexandrov's. In March 2015, Novaya Gazeta published an interview with the Buryat tank driver Dorji Batomunkuev. He was conscripted in 2013 in Siberia and later sent 6 000 kilometres westwards to fight in Donbas. When he was wounded during the battle of Debaltseve he was treated in a Donetsk hospital where journalists found him.[1235] Another highly publicised case concerns a group of Russian para-

---

1232 Sommerbauer (n 1206) 116.

1233 Павел Каныгин [Pavel Kanygin], 'Приказа применять оружие не было [There was No Order to Use Armed Force]' (Novaya Gazeta, 22 May 2015) <https://ww w.novayagazeta.ru/articles/2015/05/22/64226-171-prikaza-primenyat-oruzhie-ne -bylo-187>.

1234 Goloseevsky District Court (Kyiv), *Alexandrov and Yerofeyev*, No 752/15787/15- k, 18 April 2016, para 28. Both accused were finally convicted *inter alia* under Art 437(2) of the Ukrainian Criminal Code for waging an aggressive war. The judgment is highly problematic from the point of view of IHL because it mixes *ius ad bellum* an *ius in bello*. An ordinary combatant cannot be accused of waging an aggressive war, otherwise the entire concept of combatant immunity would crumble and every soldier in a State's army would be turned into a potential criminal. For detailed information on the trial see Sergey Sayapin, 'A Curious Aggression Trial in Ukraine: Some Reflections on the Alexandrov and Yerofeyev Case' (2018) 16 Journal of International Criminal Justice 1093.

1235 Елена Костюченко [Yelena Kostyuchenko], 'Мы все знали, на что идем и что может быть [We All Knew What We Were Getting Ourselves into and What Might Happen]' (Novaya Gazeta, 2 March 2015) <https://www.novayagazeta.ru /articles/2015/03/02/63264-171-my-vse-znali-na-chto-idem-i-chto-mozhet-byt-18

troopers who allegedly "lost their way" on patrol and ventured 20 kilometres into Ukrainian territory.[1236] We might also consider the Russian serviceman Vladimir Starkov, who really got lost and delivered the military supplies intended for the rebels directly to a Ukrainian checkpoint.[1237]

Certain analysts have combined these cases and composed the bigger picture. The Russian opposition politician Boris Nemtsov proved the Russian presence in eastern Ukraine by documenting the deaths of Russian soldiers. His report was published posthumously after his assassination in 2015 on a bridge in the centre of Moscow. He speaks of the "mass deaths of Russian soldiers connected to the escalation of the conflict" in summer 2014.[1238] Similarly, Novaya Gazeta also reported on the death of Russian servicemen.[1239] A steady stream of hundreds of coffins marked "Cargo 200" – the Russian military code for a dead soldier – trickled back into Russia.[1240]

Thus, it is clear that from early summer 2014, Russia was sending regular soldiers – not just Spetsnaz[1241] units – to fight in Ukraine. Soldiers came not as volunteers but "without any ideological motivation on the order of the high command."[1242] The Russian security expert Mark Galeotti claims that Russia provided a surge in troop numbers in decisive military moments to turn the tide. Overall, he argues, Moscow maintained about 10 000 servicemen in eastern Ukraine throughout the war.[1243] Other experts estimated that in March 2015, around 12 000 official troops were

---

7>. The interview was translated into English and published in The Guardian: Yelena Kostyuchenko, 'Invisible Army: The Story of a Russian Soldier Sent to Fight in Ukraine' (The Guardian, 25 March 2015) <https://www.theguardian .com/world/2015/mar/25/russia-ukraine-soldier>. See also Б.Е. Немцов [B.E. Nemtsov] (n 781) 22.

1236 Roland Oliphant, 'Russian Paratroopers Captured in Ukraine 'Accidentally Crossed Border' (The Telegraph, 26 August 2014) <https://www.telegraph.co.u k/news/worldnews/europe/ukraine/11056312/Russian-paratroopers-captured-in -Ukraine-accidentally-crossed-border.html>.

1237 Sommerbauer (n 1206) 117.

1238 Б.Е. Немцов [B.E. Nemtsov] (n 781) 23.

1239 Сергей Канев [Sergey Kanev], 'Лапочка из Кущевки [Sweetheart from Kushevki]' (Novaya Gazeta, 3 September 2014) <https://www.novayagazeta.ru/articles/ 2014/09/03/60980-lapochka-iz-kuschevki>.

1240 Б.Е. Немцов [B.E. Nemtsov] (n 781).

1241 Spetsnaz stands for *(Войска) специального назначения* [Special Purpose Forces], the umbrella term used for all Russian special forces.

1242 Mitrokhin (n 1210) 3.

1243 Galeotti, *Armies of Russia's War in Ukraine* (n 785) 34.

present in Ukraine. 50 000 reinforcements waited behind the border.[1244] Igor Sutyagin from the British Royal United Services Institute claims that since summer 2014, the presence of large numbers of Russian troops has "become a permanent feature of the conflict," with soldiers operating on the ground as early as mid-July 2014.[1245] In 2016, even the ICC Prosecutor endorsed this view and spoke of "direct military engagement between Russian armed forces and Ukrainian government forces" since July 2014.[1246] Up to this day, the OSCE keeps reporting on military convoys that enter separatist territory via the Russian border, bringing reinforcements[1247] and Russia continues to maintain its military presence in the LNR and DNR.[1248]

3.2 The Russian position – denying the obvious

Up to this date, Russia denies that its armed forces are present in eastern Ukraine, even though the position has changed a little over time. In April 2014, Putin answered on his show "Direct Line with the President": "I can tell you outright and unequivocally that there are no Russian troops in Ukraine."[1249] Later, on 4 July 2014 he reiterated:

1244 Maksymilian Czuperski, 'Hiding in Plain Sight: Putin's War in Ukraine' (The Atlantic Council of the United States 2015) 5.

1245 Igor Sutyagin, 'Russian Forces in Ukraine' (2015) 9 RUSI Briefing Paper 1.

1246 The Office of the ICC Prosecutor (n 707) para 169. The OTP identifies 14 July 2014 as the starting date of the international armed conflict with Russia: "Additional information, such as reported shelling by both States of military positions of the other, and the detention of Russian military personnel by Ukraine, and *vice-versa*, points to direct military engagement between Russian armed forces and Ukrainian government forces that would suggest the existence of an international armed conflict in the context of armed hostilities in eastern Ukraine from 14 July 2014 at the latest, in parallel to the non-international armed conflict."

1247 OSCE SMM, 'Latest from the OSCE Special Monitoring Mission to Ukraine, Based on Information Received as of 19:30, 8 August 2018' (2018) <https://www.osce.org/special-monitoring-mission-to-ukraine/390179>.

1248 Galeotti, *Armies of Russia's War in Ukraine* (n 785) 34–35.

1249 Kremlin, 'Direct Line with Vladimir Putin' (16 April 2015) <http://en.kremlin.ru/events/president/news/49261>.

> *"There were no, and there are no Russian military units or military instructors in the South-East of Ukraine. The Americans are lying. We have never been involved in the destabilization of Ukraine and we will never do so."[1250]*

Foreign Minister Lavrov confirmed this position in January 2015, long after the full-scale invasion of Russian troops in summer 2014 that helped to push back the Ukrainian army and retake strategic towns:

> *"I say every time: if you allege this so confidently, present the facts. But nobody can present the facts, or doesn't want to. So before demanding from us that we stop doing something, please present proof that we have done it."[1251]*

Finally, in December 2015, Putin raised some eyebrows when he admitted in his yearly press conference that special forces might be present on the ground, but at the same time denied that any regular Russian servicemen were present.

> *"We never said that there we don't have people there who resolve certain issues including in the military field. But this does not mean that regular soldiers of the Russian Army are present on the ground. Appreciate the difference!"[1252]*

While the President admits that there are special forces on the ground "resolving certain issues", Putin never admitted that they participated in hostilities. Also, his statement seemed surreal at a time where tens of *thousands* of regular troops had already fought in eastern Ukraine.

Even today, the official Russian position remains that the ongoing conflict is a non-international armed conflict between the Kyiv government and the forces of LNR and DNR.[1253] In the following, I will talk about the issue of the correct classification of the war in Donbas. I will also examine what effect the Russian denial had on the application of IHL. I aim to show that to some extent the Russian strategy succeeded in obfuscating

---

1250 Vladimir Putin in an interview on 4 July 2014 as quoted in Б.Е. Немцов [B.E. Nemtsov] (n 781) 17.

1251 Gabriela Baczynska, 'Russia Says No Proof it Sent Troops, Arms to East Ukraine' (Reuters, 21 January 2015) <https://www.reuters.com/article/us-uk raine-crisis-lavrov/russia-says-no-proof-it-sent-troops-arms-to-east-ukraine-idUSK BN0KU12Y20150121>.

1252 Kremlin, Большая пресс-конференция Владимира Путина [Big Press Conference of Vladimir Putin]' (17 December 2015) <http://kremlin.ru/events/preside nt/news/50971>.

1253 Czuperski (n 1244) 7.

the international legal discourse. This also affects the application of IHL on the ground, as in the case of the Ukrainian pilot Nadiya Savchenko. In a broader sense, Moscow degraded IHL to showcase-rules to which you can pay lip-service without restricting your behaviour in practice, because according to Moscow's logic, IHL did not apply to its actions in eastern Ukraine.

3.3 Applying the law to the facts – what type of conflict is the war in Donbas?

How should we classify the conflict in eastern Ukraine? Since this is the first time that I address the issue of conflict classification in detail, I would like to explain the legal framework. Then, I will classify the war in Donbas. Finally, I shall explain how Moscow's strategy of denial managed to undermine basic, clear-cut principles of conflict classification under IHL.

3.3.1 The framework of conflict classification

There are two ways of classifying a conflict: as an international armed conflict (IAC) and a non-international armed conflict (NIAC). While the Geneva Conventions of 1949 contain both the term IAC (in CA 2) and NIAC (in CA 3)[1254] the treaty text does not define these terms. In its famous *Tadić* decision, the ICTY offered a definition that has become commonly accepted: An IAC exists whenever "there is a resort to armed force between States." A NIAC exists whenever there exists "protracted armed violence between governmental authorities and organized armed groups or between such groups within a State."[1255]

   In a nutshell, this means that an IAC can only exist between States, while a NIAC may exist when violence occurs between States and/or armed groups that fulfil certain criteria. One of the key differences is that IAC requires a much lower threshold of armed violence than NIAC. Again, in *Tadić* the ICTY deemed *any* resort to armed force between States sufficient to trigger an IAC.[1256] This has been confirmed by subsequent

---

1254 Literally, CA 3 speaks of an "armed conflict not of an international character."
1255 ICTY, *The Prosecutor v Duško Tadić* (IT-94–1-T), Decision on the Defence Motion for Interlocutory Appeal on Jurisdiction, 2 October 1995, para 70.
1256 ibid para 70.

ICTY case law, as well as other international courts such as the ICC.[1257] Today, the conviction that even "minor skirmishes" between the armed forces of two States will trigger an armed conflict is firmly grounded in State practice and academia.[1258] For a NIAC on the other hand, violence needs to be "protracted" i.e. of certain intensity.[1259] While this is a case by case decision, the ICTY has fleshed out criteria that indicate such intensity: the kind of weapons used, the number of casualties, the number of soldiers engaged and the frequency of military operations, the number of refugees fleeing the combat zone.[1260] All in all, the threshold is – and should be – considerable in order to distinguish "war" from "internal turmoil."[1261]

To complicate things, a NIAC may be "internationalised" if a State has "overall control" over an armed group that is engaged in an armed conflict

---

1257 ICTY, *The Prosecutor v Zejnil Delalić et al* (IT-96–21-T), Trial Chamber Judgment, 16 November 1998, para 184; ICTY, *The Prosecutor v Vlastimir Đorđević* (IT-05–87/1-T), Trial Chamber Judgment, 23 February 2011; ICTY, *The Prosecutor v Fatimir Limaj et al* (IT-03–66-T), Trial Chamber Judgment, 30 November 2005; ICTY, *The Prosecutor v Ramush Haradinaj et al* (IT-04–84-T), Trial Chamber Judgment, 3 April 2008; ICTY, *The Prosecutor v Mile Mrkšić et al* (IT-95–13/1-T), Trial Chamber Judgment, 27 September 2007; ICC, *The Prosecutor v Thomas Lubanga Dyilo* (ICC-01/04–01/06–2842), Trial Chamber Judgment, 14 March 2012, para 506; ICC, *The Prosecutor v Jean-Pierre Bemba Gombo* (ICC-01/05–01/08), Decision Pursuant to Art 61(7)(a) and (b) of the Rome Statue on the Charges of the Prosecutor Against Jean-Pierre Bemba Gombo, 15 June 2009, para 220.

1258 Dörmann and others (n 543) Art 2, para 238; Djemila Carron, 'When Is a Conflict International? Time for New Control Tests in IHL' (2016) 98 International Review of the Red Cross 1019, 1030; Sassòli, Bouvier and Quintin (n 72) 22; for a differing view see ICRC, 'International Humanitarian Law and the Challenges of Contemporary Armed Conflicts (31IC/11/5.1.2)' (2011) 7.

1259 The ICTY interpreted the criterion of "protracted armed violence" as a threshold of intensity rather than of duration, although the latter may serve as an indicator for the former, see ICTY, *The Prosecutor v Ramush Haradinaj et al* (IT-04–84-T), Trial Chamber Judgment, 3 April 2008, para 49.

1260 ICTY, *The Prosecutor v Fatimir Limaj et al* (IT-03–66-T), Trial Chamber Judgment, 30 November 2005, para 90 et seq; see also ICTY, *The Prosecutor v Ljube Boškoski and Johan Tarčulovski* (IT-04–82-T), Trial Chamber Judgment, 10 July 2008, para 177; ICTY, *The Prosecutor v Ramush Haradinaj et al* (IT-04–84-T), Trial Chamber Judgment, 3 April 2008, para 49.

1261 See ICTY, *The Prosecutor v Duško Tadić* (IT-94–1-T), Trial Chamber Judgment, 7 May 1997, para 562. The Court reasoned that the two criteria (organisation and intensity) exist "solely for the purpose, as a minimum, of distinguishing an armed conflict from banditry, unorganized and short-lived insurrections, or terrorist activities, which are not subject to international humanitarian law."

with another State.[1262] Again, the concept was developed by the ICTY in *Tadić*. If State A is "coordinating or helping in the general planning" the activities of an armed group that fights against State B this leads to an IAC between State A and B.[1263] This approach was subsequently endorsed by the ICC in Lubanga.[1264] I have already discussed the exact criteria of overall control at page 240 when contrasting it with the ICJ's effective control test.

The dichotomy between IAC and NIAC is not confined to semantics. Historically, the laws of war were confined to inter–State conflicts.[1265] Hence, all treaties before 1949 only apply to IACs. Similarly, the 1949 Conventions – with the meagre exception of CA 1 & 3 – and AP I only apply in international armed conflicts. NIAC treaty law is confined to CA 1 & 3 and the 28 supplementary Articles of AP II. Admittedly, customary IHL applies in both scenarios and has done a lot to close protection gaps in NIAC.[1266] This is especially true with rules governing the conduct of hostilities where the rules are virtually the same. In certain aspects, however, the framework for NIAC continues to lag behind that of IAC, for example regarding the right of the ICRC to access places of detention or States' obligation to let in humanitarian aid.[1267] Furthermore, the concept

---

1262 For this and a typology of other "odd" NIACs see Pejic (n 543) 5–9; Vité (n 1127).

1263 ICTY, *The Prosecutor v Duško Tadić* (IT-94-1-T), Appeals Chamber Judgment, 15 July 1999, para 131.

1264 *The Prosecutor v Thomas Lubanga Dyilo* (ICC-01/04–01/06–2842), Trial Chamber Judgment, 14 March 2012, para 541.

1265 For the Soviets' efforts to include CA 3 in the 1949 Geneva Conventions see above at pp 121 et seq.

1266 The ICRC Customary Law Study details for every rule whether it applies in IAC, NIAC, or both. Most rules apply in both scenarios. See also IIFFMCG, 'Report of the Independent International Fact-Finding Mission on the Conflict in Georgia (Tagliavini Report) Volume II' (n 1109) 304. The Report underlines that "although the classification of an armed conflict as international or non-international is important in terms of the responsibilities of the various parties involved, when it comes to the effective protection by IHL of the persons and objects affected by the conflict it does not make much difference. Indeed, it is generally recognized that the same IHL customary law rules generally apply to all types of armed conflicts."

1267 In IAC, the ICRC must be granted access to POWs and civilian detainees, whereas in NIAC it may only offer its services, see Art 126 GC III, Art 76, 143 GC IV. See also Rule 124 of the ICRC Customary Law Study which also distinguishes between IACs and NIACs in this respect. Regarding humanitarian assistance, the right of access is stronger in IAC than in NIAC, see e.g. Lattanzi (n 745).

of combatants and POWs does not exist in NIAC and issues like detention are still under-regulated.[1268] Thus, classification is not a mere formality, but determines the level of protection. In addition, an IAC comes with a low, clear, and virtually undisputed threshold for classification. Either there *is* armed force between two States, or there is *not*. In this sense it leaves little room for States to outmanoeuvre IHL compared to the sophisticated threshold criteria necessary to classify a NIAC.

3.3.2 The war in Donbas as an international armed conflict

Applying the above to the war in Donbas should leave us with a clear picture. As Ilya Nuzov and Anne Quintin state: The framework of IAC applies "if even one Russian soldier is fighting against the Ukrainian army." I have shown that not just a handful of Russian troops fought in eastern Ukraine, but entire units. From July onwards, Russia had around 10 000 troops in the area and they participated in decisive battles such as Debaltseve. Whether or not they fought in joint units with the rebels or formed separate units does not matter at this point. It is possible for an IAC and a NIAC to exist in parallel.[1269]

In 2016, the ICC Office of the Prosecutor (OTP) was among the first major organisations to endorse this view. Based on the "direct military engagement between Russian armed forces and Ukrainian government forces" the OTP classified the conflict in eastern Ukraine as international "from 14 July 2014 at the latest."[1270] Already on 7 September 2014, Amnesty International put out a press statement that it considered the conflict international.[1271] Certain academics agreed and classified the conflict

---

1268 See Tilman Rodenhäuser, 'Strengthening IHL Protecting Persons Deprived of Their Liberty: Main Aspects of the Consultations and Discussions since 2011' (2016) 98 International Review of the Red Cross 941. Since 2011 the ICRC has been urging States to reinforce the protection of detainees in NIAC. So far, however, these attempts were not crowned with success.

1269 See e.g. Vité (n 1127) 90; Ilya Nuzov and Anne Quintin, 'The Case of Russia's Detention of Ukrainian Military Pilot Savchenko under IHL' (*EJIL Talk!*, 3 March 2015) <https://www.ejiltalk.org/the-case-of-russias-detention-of-ukrainian-military-pilot-savchenko-under-ihl/>.

1270 The Office of the ICC Prosecutor (n 707) para 169.

1271 Amnesty International, 'Ukraine: Mounting Evidence of War Crimes and Russian Involvement' (7 September 2014) <https://www.amnesty.org/en/latest/news/2014/09/ukraine-mounting-evidence-war-crimes-and-russian-involvement/>.

as international because Russian soldiers clashed with Ukrainian armed forces.[1272]

Surprisingly, this verdict was not unanimous. Given the straightforwardness of the IAC criteria – *any* resort to armed force between States – one would expect commentators to rally around the classification of an international armed conflict. Yet, this is not what happened. States, academics, and even the ICRC (at a certain point) qualified the conflict as a NIAC. They had different reasons for doing so and I will deal with them in turn. I would like to stress that I do not wish to criticise these actors for their classification. I, today, write with the benefit of hindsight, while most of the statements and articles were written in the period between 2014–2016.

This, however, does not mean that the correct information was not available at the time. Mitrokhin, on whom I heavily relied above, gave a detailed and well-founded account of Russia's direct involvement as early as summer 2014.[1273] Important newspapers like Novaya Gazeta and The Guardian, as well as distinguished experts like Pavel Felgengauer came out about the active involvement of regular Russian soldiers.[1274] Instead of criticising the following actors for their classification, I wish to show that Russia's strategy of obfuscation bore fruit and managed to mislead not only its own population, but also international institutions and academics thereby eroding a clear norm of IHL.

Several contributions by well-known scholars explicitly dealt with the classification of the conflict in eastern Ukraine.[1275] Robert Heinsch, for example, published an article (2015) in which he concluded that given "the uncertainties surrounding the nature of Russia's involvement, one should be hesitant in qualifying this as a classic international armed conflict."[1276]

1272 Agnieszka Szpak, 'Legal Classification of the Armed Conflict in Ukraine in Light of International Humanitarian Law' (2017) 58 Hungarian Journal of Legal Studies 261, 275–276.

1273 See Mitrokhin (n 1210).

1274 See in detail above at n 1215.

1275 Russian scholars have been avoiding this topic. Vladislav Tolstykh, for example, complains that despite "Russia's involvement in [...] conflicts on the territories of the former USSR (primarily the conflict in the southeast of Ukraine), there is no serious analysis of the regime of the use of force and current trends in the field." Taken from Vladislav Tolstykh, 'The Nature of Russian Discourses on International Law – a Contemporary Survey' in P Sean Morris (ed), *Russian Discourses on International Law: Sociological and Philosophical Phenomenon* (Routledge 2018) 19.

1276 Robert Heinsch, 'Conflict Classification in Ukraine: The Return of the "Proxy War"?' (2015) 91 International Law Studies 323, 355.

On the one hand, Heinsch doubted that on-duty Russian soldiers actually fought in Donbas. On the other hand, he argued that even if Russian soldiers were involved this would not make the situation an IAC.[1277] In support of his view he pointed to the (novel) criterion of "continuous direct involvement" of such forces citing the ICTY decision in *Rajić*.[1278] In this case, the ICTY had stated that only "the *significant and continuous* military action by the armed forces of Croatia in support of the Bosnian Croats against the forces of the Bosnian Government [...] was sufficient to convert the domestic conflict between the Bosnian Croats and the Bosnian Government into an international one."[1279]

Heinsch deduces from this that *any* involvement of a State on the side of a non-state actor needs to be "significant and continuous" to trigger an IAC. This novel criterion, however, is neither mentioned in the ICRC commentary nor in other works that deal with the threshold of IAC. It only appears in *one* isolated decision of the ICTY. Even if this were a hard criterion, Croatia's role in Bosnia was entirely comparable with Russia's involvement in eastern Ukraine: In *Rajić* the Court found that "between 5000 to 7000 members of the Croatian Army [...] were present in the territory of Bosnia and were involved, both directly and through their relations with HB and the HVO [the Croatian secessionist movement in Bosnia], in clashes with Bosnian Government forces."[1280] If you replace Bosnia with Ukraine, Croatia with Russia, and HB & HVO with LNR & DNR the decision might as well be written for eastern Ukraine.

In another article (2015), Shane R. Reeves and David Wallace argued that "there is overwhelming evidence showing the Russians actively equipping, training and *even fighting alongside* the separatists in eastern

---

1277 ibid 355, 357. In defence of the author, I have to stress the following: Heinsch *does* arrive at the conclusion that the conflict is international, because it has been internationalised through Russia's support to the rebels. However, this approach requires Russia to have overall control over the armed forces of LNR and DNR which is much more difficult to prove and represents an unnecessary threshold, if an IAC already exists due to direct clashes between Ukrainian and Russian soldiers.

1278 ICTY, *The Prosecutor v Ivica Rajić* (IT-95–12-R61), Review of the Indictment pursuant to Rule 61 of the Rules of Procedure and Evidence, 13 September 1996, para 13.

1279 ibid.

1280 ibid.

Ukraine."[1281] Yet the authors do not even mention the possibility that such direct clashes of Russian and Ukrainian soldiers might trigger an international armed conflict. Rather, they directly jump onto the issue of "internationalisation" of a NIAC. This is surprising, because such "internationalised" conflict requires much more evidence. There is a double threshold: One needs to meet the criteria of an ordinary NIAC and in addition the standard of "overall control" of a State over an armed group. The latter especially gives countries much leeway to downplay their influence. In other words: If there are direct clashes of government forces there is no need to fall back to an "internationalised" conflict. Under IHL, this already represents a classic IAC. Tellingly, Reeves and Wallace reject the existence of an "internationalised" conflict precisely because its threshold is too high:

> *"Without more evidence to clarify the Russian-separatist relationship, it is not known whether Russia is exercising a sufficiently high level of control over the separatists to internationalize the well-established non-international armed conflict."*[1282]

The confusion about the correct classification did not only affect academia. Even the ICRC qualified the conflict as a NIAC for a certain period. On 23 July 2014 amidst intensifying combat, the ICRC put out a press statement in which the Director of Operations Dominik Stillhart invoked IHL and reminded everybody that the "rules and principles apply to all parties to the *non-international* armed conflict in Ukraine, and impose restrictions on the means and methods of warfare that they may use."[1283] It is rare for the ICRC to put out a press statement in which it explicitly classifies the conflict. Often, the classification is only communicated bilaterally to the countries involved. While its assessment is not binding, it carries a lot of weight.[1284]

In October 2014 – several months after the massive influx of Russian troops into Donbas – the head of delegation in Ukraine, Michael Masson, reiterated this position:

1281 Shane Reeves and David A Wallace, 'The Combatant Status of the "Little Green Men" and Other Participants in the Ukraine Conflict' (2015) 91 International Law Studies 361, 382.

1282 ibid 381.

1283 ICRC, 'Ukraine: ICRC Calls on All Sides to Respect International Humanitarian Law (News Release 14/125)' (23 July 2014).

1284 Heinsch (n 1276) 326.

> *"According to international humanitarian law, there are several classifications of cases of violence. At the current moment we assess the situation in Donbass as a non-international armed conflict. With such classification the territory of conflict falls under the rule of the Third Article common, for all of the Geneva Conventions and other norms of the international humanitarian law are implemented."[1285]*

Later, the ICRC settled for the inconspicuous formulation of an "armed conflict" in Ukraine without classifying its nature.[1286]

Whilst the reasons for the ICRC's stance on the conflict in eastern Ukraine have not been made public, they were most likely operational. We should not forget that the ICRC has a dual function. It serves as guardian of IHL, but it is also one of the most important operational humanitarian actors on the ground.[1287] Openly admitting the involvement of Russian soldiers – especially at such an early stage – would have jeopardised the work of the organisation in the field. Usually, the ICRC is known to adopt a very diplomatic stance in its public statements. I have no knowledge what prompted the ICRC's classification in eastern Ukraine, but its attitude may have been an operational compromise like during the Afghan War (1979–1989) where it chose a middle way: It reminded the parties that at least CA 3 applied without explicitly classifying the conflict as international or non-international.[1288] Hans-Peter Gasser, at the time the head of the ICRC legal division, wrote in 1983 that rigidly applying all existing IHL norms (i.e. insisting on an IAC) would be "wishful thinking," and that in practice one had to find a compromise that provided "protection for all actual and potential victims of the conflict."[1289] In 2014, there was certainly no operational advantage to be gained by pushing for an IAC in Donbas. Ironically, however, this was precisely *because of* Russia's obstinate denial. By refusing to accept its presence in Donbas, Moscow had raised the stakes. Anyone who challenged the Russian position publicly could not do so without creating a huge diplomatic incident and implicitly accusing Moscow of lying. In this way, the lie became a weapon to silence the truth.

1285 'ICRC: Ukrainian Conflict is Not International' (Russian Peacekeeper, 10 October 2014) <http://peacekeeper.ru/en/?module=news&action=view&id=22517>.

1286 See ICRC, 'Ukraine Conflict' <https://www.icrc.org/en/where-we-work/europe-central-asia/ukraine/ukraine-conflict>.

1287 See above at p 160.

1288 Gasser (n 600) 150–152. See also above at n 600.

1289 ibid 152.

3.4 Conclusion

In sum, Russia was successful in obfuscating what used to be a crystal-clear norm: *Any* resort to armed force between two State armies results in an international armed conflict. Moscow denied its presence so stubbornly and effectively that many either lacked the evidence to classify the conflict as international, looked for novel legal methods, or could not speak their mind without upsetting the Kremlin. This concerned States, academics, and the ICRC.

As I have explained above, the question of classification is not confined to semantics. Firstly, IHL of IAC is simply more protective. Secondly, the low threshold of IAC should normally lead to legal clarity. The case of Nadiya Savchenko may serve as an example. The Ukrainian military pilot was captured in summer 2014 and brought to Russia.[1290] Savchenko should have been a POW but was denied this status. Rather she was sentenced to 22 years in prison for killing two Russian journalists.[1291] Whatever the basis of the accusations, POWs could only be tried for war crimes and only in front of the same courts as Russian soldiers.[1292]

In general terms, Russia's blatant disregard for the application of IHL could have long-term effects. If law is undermined in such a way, it becomes an empty shell.[1293] Russia's attitude of ignoring IHL might represent a short-term success for Russia. In the long run, it will lead to the erosion of even the most well-established rules of IHL and undermine the application of the laws of war for all States.

1290 Mark Feygin, 'Russia's Illegal Prisoners of War' (The Washington Post, 24 December 2014) <https://www.washingtonpost.com/opinions/russias-illegal-pri soners-of-war/2014/12/24/d68fc5ae-8ad7-11e4-9e8d-0c687bc18da4_story.html>.

1291 'Ukrainian Ex-military Navigator Savchenko Sentenced to 22 Years in Prison' (RAPSI, 22 March 2016) <http://www.rapsinews.com/judicial_news/20160322/275674213.html>.

1292 See Art 102 GC III and Nuzov and Quintin (n 1269).

1293 In practice, one violation risks being met with a counter-violation. Responding to the conviction of Savchenko, a Ukrainian court convicted Russian soldiers for their participation in hostilities. This judgment is at odds with the principle of combatant immunity in IAC, see Sayapin, 'A Curious Aggression Trial in Ukraine' (n 1234). See also ICRC Casebook, How Does Law Protect in War, 'Eastern Ukraine Disputed POW Status' <https://casebook.icrc.org/case-study/ea stern-ukraine-disputed-pow-status>.

4. Rebranding armed clashes – a war of words

Following the example of eastern Ukraine – where Moscow's denial was purely *factual* – we shall now address two case studies where Russia challenged well-established rules by *legal* rebranding. Both cases concern the issue of conflict classification. In both cases, Russia acknowledged the use of military force but refused to recognise that this military force triggered an armed conflict. Rather, Russia "rebranded" the armed clashes and thus evaded IHL. Apart from this, the two case studies do not have much in common. One concerns an IAC, the other a NIAC. One took place on the sea, the other within the boundaries of the Russian Federation. And while first incident only saw three wounded, the latter conflict claimed hundreds of thousands of lives.

4.1 The clash in the Kerch Strait (2018) – the art of euphemism

The recent escalation in the Sea of Azov serves as a good example for Russia's strategy of rebranding military clashes. First, I would like to give the reader the context. The Sea of Azov covers an area of 37 600 km² which is less than Lake Michigan.[1294] Not much of a sea, you might think. It is, however, of prime strategic importance. For the Ukrainian ports of Mariupol and Berdyansk it is the only connection to the Black Sea and international trading routes. All ships need to pass through the Kerch Strait, which is only 40 km wide and separates Crimea from the Russian peninsula Taman.[1295] Before the annexation of Crimea in 2014 on average 8 000 ships passed through the Kerch Strait every year. The conflict has seriously disrupted the flourishing trade and inflicted heavy financial losses on the Ukrainian side.[1296] Today, an 18 km long bridge stretches over the Kerch Strait and connects Crimea to the Russian mainland. This stunning technological feat further adds to the importance of the Strait, because it is Crimea's only land lifeline to Russia.

1294 Encyclopædia Britannica, 'Sea of Azov' <https://www.britannica.com/place/Sea -of-Azov>.

1295 Alexander Skaridov, 'The Sea of Azov and the Kerch Straits' in David D Caron and Nilufer Oral (eds), *Navigating Straits: Challenges for International Law* (Brill Nijhoff 2014) 221.

1296 Valentin J Schatz and Dmytro Koval, 'Russia's Annexation of Crimea and the Passage of Ships through Kerch Strait: A Law of the Sea Perspective' (2019) 50 Ocean Development & International Law 275, 277.

On the morning of 25 November 2018, three Ukrainian vessels – two artillery boats and a tugboat – sailed towards the Kerch Strait aiming to transit to the Ukrainian port Mariupol. They were intercepted by the Russian Coast guard. The Russians rammed the Ukrainian tugboat and tried to turn it away, but the Ukrainians did not give up.[1297] The standoff dragged on throughout the day until the Russian Coast Guard, assisted by special forces, pursued the Ukrainian Ships, fired upon them, boarded them, and took 23 seamen prisoner. In the course of the attack, at least three Ukrainian seamen were injured. The above facts are undisputed, Russia quickly confirmed the use of armed force.[1298]

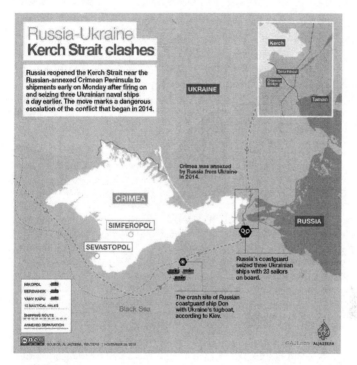

Map of the Kerch Strait incident (source Al Jazeera, Reuters)

1297 Michael Cruickshank, 'Investigating The Kerch Strait Incident' (Bellingcat, 30 November 2018) <https://www.bellingcat.com/news/uk-and-europe/2018/11/30/investigating-the-kerch-strait-incident/>.
1298 'Russia-Ukraine Tensions Rise after Kerch Strait Ship Capture' (BBC, 26 November 2018) <https://www.bbc.com/news/world-europe-46340283>.

What ensued was an intense debate about the right of Ukrainian ships to pass the Strait, and whether Ukraine sufficiently notified the port authorities of its passage.[1299] The incident shed the spotlight on highly complex issues related to maritime law. Much is controversial in this respect: the rights of passage, the proper procedure, and the status of the Sea of Azov itself.[1300]

Under IHL, however we have the luxury of leaving these questions unanswered, because what counts is the use of direct force between the armed forces of two States.

What was the significance of the Kerch Strait incident to IHL? I would like to remind the reader that the ICTY defined an IAC as any "resort to armed force between States" thus setting a very low threshold.[1301] It is generally accepted that this threshold is minimal.[1302] Often, we refer to the "first shot" theory.[1303] Jean Pictet – the author of the first commentary to the Geneva Conventions – even spoke of the first "captured" soldier.[1304] The IAC could also consist of a one-sided strike.[1305] Some have proposed to exclude insignificant border incidents,[1306] but this has not been accept-

---

1299 Schatz and Koval (n 1296) 289.

1300 See for this Valentin J Schatz and Dmytro Koval, 'Ukraine v. Russia: Passage through Kerch Strait and the Sea of Azov' (*Völkerrechtsblog*, 10 January 2018) <https://voelkerrechtsblog.org/ukraine-v-russia-passage-through-kerch-strait-and-the-sea-of-azov/>.

1301 ICTY, *The Prosecutor v Duško Tadić* (IT-94-1-T), Decision on the Defence Motion for Interlocutory Appeal on Jurisdiction, 2 October 1995, para 70.

1302 Dörmann and others (n 543) Art 2, para 238 with further sources. The commentary considers "even minor skirmishes" and "unconsented-to military operations" as IACs. See also n 1258. It is noteworthy that the ILC sets a slightly higher threshold by demanding "fighting of some intensity", see International Law Association (Committee on the Use of Force), 'Final Report on the Meaning of Armed Conflict in International Law' (2010) 2 and fn 7.

1303 Carron (n 1258) 1030; Sassòli, Bouvier and Quintin (n 72) 22.

1304 Pictet, *The Geneva Conventions of 12 August 1949* (n 1006) 23. Pictet argues that "if there has been no fighting, the fact that persons covered by the Convention are detained is sufficient for its application."

1305 International Law Association (Committee on the Use of Force), 'Final Report on the Meaning of Armed Conflict in International Law' (2010) 31.

1306 Maria-Daniella Marouda and Stelios Perrakis (eds), 'Application of International Humanitarian Law in Contemporary Armed Conflicts: Is It "Simply'a Question of Facts?"', *Armed Conflicts and International Humanitarian Law 150 Years after Solferino: Acquis and Prospects* (Edition Sakkoulas 2009) 205; Louise Arimatsu, 'Beginning of IHL Application: Overview and Challenges' (2013) 13 Proceedings of the Bruges Colloquium on the Scope of Application of International Humanitarian Law 71, 76–77.

ed by the majority of scholars and would go against the protective intention of the Geneva Convention. Any additional subjective threshold of significance bears the risk of evasion.[1307] In fact, the very reason for replacing the subjective term "war" with the notion of armed conflict was to avoid any ambiguities.[1308]

The assessment of whether armed force occurred is entirely factual. It does not matter what terminology the affected or third States use. The ICRC commentary emphasises this minimal threshold "must be based solely on the prevailing facts demonstrating the *de facto* existence of hostilities between the belligerents, even without a declaration of war."[1309] It goes on to state that "States might not publicly acknowledge such situations as armed conflicts and may describe them simply as 'incidents'." However, "[…] the fact that a State publicly uses a term other than 'armed conflict' to describe a situation involving hostilities with another State is not in itself determinative of the classification of that situation as an armed conflict."[1310]

Applying the law to the Kerch incident yields an obvious result: The events fulfil every element of an armed conflict. The Ukrainian boats belonged to the Ukrainian navy. Two of them were artillery boats. The third was an auxiliary tugboat, also a craft of the Ukrainian Navy. They were part of the armed forces and in terms of IHL all three of them represented legitimate military objectives.[1311] These boats were first rammed and then fired upon by the Russian Coast Guard. Neither side denies the use of force. The use of the coast guard – instead of the Russian navy – does not rule out the existence of an armed conflict.[1312] The fact that the coast guard is normally rather a law-enforcement organ is irrelevant

---

1307 See Dörmann and others (n 543) Art 2, para 239.

1308 Pictet, *The Geneva Conventions of 12 August 1949: Commentary on the Geneva Convention Relative to the Treatment of Prisoners of War* (n 56) 23.

1309 Dörmann and others (n 543) Art 2, para 211.

1310 ibid Art 2, para 243.

1311 James Kraska, 'The Kerch Strait Incident: Law of the Sea or Law of Naval Warfare?' (*EJIL Talk!*, 3 December 2018) <https://www.ejiltalk.org/the-kerch-strait-incident-law-of-the-sea-or-law-of-naval-warfare/>.

1312 Dörmann and others (n 543) Art 2, para 226. The commentary clarifies that "one should not discard outright the possibility that armed conflict within the meaning of Art 2(1) may come into existence even if the armed confrontation does not involve military personnel but rather non-military State agencies such as paramilitary forces, border guards or coast guards. Any of those could well be engaged in armed violence displaying the same characteristics as that involving State armed forces."

under IHL.[1313] Otherwise a State could simply evade its obligations by outsourcing the fighting to security forces other than the military. We shall see in a moment that even Russia itself qualifies the operation on 25 November as "military in nature."[1314]

Some commentators saw the clash as the dramatic transition from a hybrid conflict into an open Russo-Ukrainian war. Sergey Sayapin argues that the Kerch incident represented an "act of war, which was carried out openly, in full knowledge that it would be attributed to Russia as such." He then adds that "most importantly, now, Russia cannot deny the existence of an *international armed conflict* with Ukraine, in the sense of applicable international law."[1315] Other authors spoke out in favour of the application of the law of naval warfare – IHL's special branch tailored to the sea.[1316] Ukraine, too, jumped on the occasion and quickly classified the sailors as POWs. The Ukrainian Ombudswoman Lyudmyla Denisova called upon Russia to respect the Geneva Conventions.[1317] Indeed, the Kerch Strait incident could not be talked away. Russia had little room for evading the (politically uncomfortable) classification of an international armed conflict with Ukraine.

However, many seem to have underestimated Russia's legal creativity. The Foreign Ministry downplayed the incident as a "gross violation of the rules of peaceful passage [...] by Ukrainian naval ships."[1318] Not a word of an international armed conflict. Russia then went on to prosecute the sailors before an ordinary military court for violating the Russian

---

1313 Arimatsu (n 1306) 77.

1314 ILOTS, *Case concerning the detention of three Ukrainian naval vessels (Ukraine v Russian Federation) Request for the prescription of provisional measures (Case No 26)*, Order, 25 May 2019, para 51.

1315 Sergey Sayapin, 'The End of Russia's Hybrid War against Ukraine?' (*Opinio Juris*, 4 January 2019) <http://opiniojuris.org/2019/01/04/the-end-of-russias-hybrid-war-against-ukraine/> (emphasis added).

1316 Kraska (n 1311).

1317 'Уповноважений Людмила Денісова: Статус військовополонених передбачає особливу процедуру звільнення наших моряків [Commissioner Lyudmila Denisova: The Status of Prisoners of War Requires a Special Procedure for the Release of Our Sailors]' (3 December 2018) <http://www.ombudsman.gov.ua/ua/all-news/pr/31218-am-upovnovazhenij-lyudmila-denisova-status-vijskovopolonenix-peredbachaye/>.

1318 Ministry of Foreign Affairs of the Russian Federation, Foreign Ministry Statement (26 November 2018) <http://www.mid.ru/en/web/guest/maps/ua/-/asset_publisher/ktn0ZLTvbbS3/content/id/3420678>.

border.[1319] Under IHL they should rather have been considered prisoners of war,[1320] who cannot be prosecuted for their participation in hostilities except for international crimes.[1321]

Moscow reiterated this position before the International Tribunal for the Law of the Sea (ITLOS), where Kyiv accused Moscow of having violated the UN Convention for the Law of the Sea (UNCLOS). During the proceedings, Russia argued that the Kerch incident was "manifestly a dispute concerning *military* activities."[1322] Yet, it rejected the "categorization of the situation as an armed conflict for the purposes of international humanitarian law."[1323] A military clash between two States – and yet no armed conflict. Russia tried to square the circle.

This is surprising, because applying IHL could have offered several legal advantages to Russia. Under IHL, the Ukrainian boats represent legitimate military targets. Attacking them was perfectly in line with the laws of war. Furthermore, IHL supplants the UNCLOS framework and would allow Russia to legally implement stricter checks of Ukrainian vessels.[1324] Russia could thus use IHL to counter the accusations that blocking Ukrainian ships violates Kyiv's passage rights under the law of the sea.[1325]

1319 'Russia Starts Prosecuting Ukrainians after Sea Clash' (AP News, 28 November 2018) <https://apnews.com/b5777ee4495e4596bb0af533ed963c89>.

1320 See Art 4 (A)(1) GC III.

1321 This flows from the concept of combatant immunity which grants combatants immunity from the prosecution for the mere participation in hostilities, see Art 43(2) AP I: "Members of the armed forces of a Party to a conflict (other than medical personnel and chaplains covered by Art 33 of the Third Convention) are combatants, that is to say, they have the right to participate directly in hostilities."

1322 ITLOS, *Case concerning the detention of three Ukrainian naval vessels (Ukraine v Russian Federation) Request for the prescription of provisional measures (Case No 26)*, Order, 25 May 2019, para 51. The issue revolved around the applicability of the UNCLOS. Russia argued that the UNCLOS did not apply in the present case, because the incident concerned *military* activities for which it had excluded the Convention's application according to Art 298(1)(b) UNCLOS. Ironically, Ukraine found itself defending the opposite position. Hence, Kyiv argued that the incident did not represent a "military activity" even though it had previously called the captured sailors prisoners of war.

1323 ILOTS, *Case concerning the detention of three Ukrainian naval vessels (Ukraine v Russian Federation) Request for the prescription of provisional measures (Case No 26)*, Order, 25 May 2019, para 44.

1324 Kraska (n 1311).

1325 Schatz and Koval (n 1296) 15–16.

Yet, Moscow chose to reject the application of IHL. What is the significance of this limited incident and why is it important whether it represents an IAC? Are the ongoing occupation of Crimea and the war in Donbas not reason enough to speak of an armed conflict between Russia and Ukraine?

It is – and I have argued along these lines above. Both the conflict in eastern Ukraine and the occupation of Crimea represent IACs.[1326] However, Russia has never accepted this reading and justified its stance by pointing to the referendum and the peninsula's right to self-determination. In eastern Ukraine, it simply denied the facts. In this lies the significance of the Kerch incident. For the first time, factual denial was not an option because the events had unfolded in front of the eyes of the world. Also, there was little room for legal manoeuvre, because the low threshold of IAC represents a clear-cut rule.

In theory, this would make it harder to reject the correct conclusion, i.e. that the incident is part of an armed conflict. In practice, however, this is exactly what Russia did. It arrived at the untenable conclusion that the armed clash was "military" but not part of an armed conflict. This not only proves a high degree of brazenness, but it also shows that Russia wants to avoid applying IHL at all costs, even at the cost of undermining a well-established and crystal-clear rule. Finally, it shows that to Russia, political considerations are far more important than IHL, or legal coherence for that matter. James Kraska concludes:

> *"The incident demonstrates how adept Russia is at exploiting the seam between the contending peacetime and wartime legal dimensions of the Crimea conflict to create perceptions of a "gray zone" that effectively advance its geopolitical agenda while confusing and demoralizing its critics."*[1327]

1326 James Kraska, for example, argues that the law of naval warfare applied even *before* the Kerch incident due to the occupation of Crimea in February 2014, see Kraska (n 1311).

1327 ibid.

On a brighter note, however, I should add the following. The 24 sailors were released on 7 September 2019 in exchange for 35 Russian prisoners held in Ukraine.[1328] Their ships were returned in November 2019.[1329]

4.2 The Chechen Wars – Moscow's fight against "banditism"

Chechnya is a landlocked republic in Northern Caucasus roughly the size of Slovenia. In the course of two bloody wars (1994–1996 and 1999–2009) this tiny patch of land was turned into "a small corner of hell."[1330] It is impossible to understand the nature of the conflict without looking into the events that followed the break-up of the Soviet Union. Hence, I would like to provide the reader with the political context first. Why did violence in Chechnya descend into one of the bloodiest civil wars of recent times? Secondly, I will explain how to classify the two Chechen wars under IHL. Finally, we will examine Russia's attitude towards IHL during the Chechen conflict and how this affected the respect for the law on the ground.

4.2.1 Descent into war – "I will crush you"

In 1991, the Soviet Union consisted of 15 constituent republics, among which the RSFSR was *primus inter pares*. When the USSR was dissolved, all these republics achieved independence.[1331] Armenia, Azerbaijan, Belorussia, Estonia, Georgia, Latvia, Lithuania, Moldova, Kazakhstan, Kirgizstan, Russia, Tajikistan, Turkmenistan, Ukraine, Uzbekistan – an entire generation of new States was born or re-born. Parallel to that, another process took place that was commonly nicknamed the "parade of sovereign-

---

1328 Ivan Nechepurenko and Andrew Higgins, 'Russia and Ukraine Swap Dozens of Prisoners, in a 'First Step to Stop the War' (The New York Times, 7 September 2019) <https://www.nytimes.com/2019/09/07/world/europe/russia-ukraine-priso ner-swap.html>.

1329 'Russia Returns Navy Vessels Seized from Ukraine' (Deutsche Welle, 18 November 2018) <https://www.dw.com/en/russia-returns-navy-vessels-seized -from-ukraine/a-51286196>.

1330 Anna Politkovskaja, *A Small Corner of Hell: Dispatches from Chechnya* (University of Chicago Press 2007).

1331 Nußberger, 'Russia' (n 218) paras 92 et seq.

ties."[1332] *Within* the RSFSR, many ethnic Republics declared their independence and tried to achieve statehood.[1333] Chechnya was one of them.[1334] Virtually all ethnic Republics, however, later abandoned their quest for independence and signed the Federation Treaty that laid the foundation for today's Russian Federation.[1335]

Chechnya refused to sign the treaty for various reasons.[1336] First of all, it could boast being one of the most ethnically homogenous of all Russian republics. Furthermore, it had fought Russian rule for over a century since the first military encounter in 1722 and suffered from continued repression under the Tsars. Under Stalin, the entire Chechen people was deported from their native lands creating a collective trauma that persists until today.[1337] Against this background, the Chechens issued their declaration of sovereignty long before the dissolution of the USSR, in November 1990. On 6 September 1991, a newly elected parliament went on to proclaim an independent State. Finally, Chechnya refused to sign the above-mentioned Federation Treaty in 1992 and rather chose to adopt a Constitution for the Chechen Republic of Ichkeria.[1338] The name was derived from the traditional name of the southern Chechen highlands, the ancient land of the Chechens.[1339]

1332 See Bowring, *Law, Rights and Ideology in Russia* (n 548) 96. Note that the Baltic States are generally considered to have been occupied and annexed by the Soviet Union, therefore never losing their sovereignty in the first place.

1333 Not only in the RSFSR ethnic groups strove for independence, but to a lesser extent also in the other former Soviet Republics. See, for example, the cases of South Ossetia, Abkhazia, and Transdniestria above at p 231.

1334 For a complete list see Bowring, *Law, Rights and Ideology in Russia* (n 548) 99.

1335 Федеративный договор [Federation Treaty] 31 March 1992. Only Chechnya and Tatarstan refused to sign. Tatarstan, however, settled its differences with Russia peacefully and signed the договор о разграничении предметов ведения и взаимном делегировании полномочий между органами государственной власти Российской Федерации и органами государственной власти Республики Татарстан [Treaty on Delimiting the Subjects of Jurisdiction and Mutual Delegation of Powers between Agencies of State Power of the Russian Federation and Agencies of State Power of the Republic Tatarstan] 15 February 1994. See Nußberger, 'Russia' (n 218) paras 66–67.

1336 For a more detailed account see Bowring, *Law, Rights and Ideology in Russia* (n 548) 98–101.

1337 Evangelista (n 891) 3, 12 et seq.

1338 Nußberger, 'Russia' (n 218) para 68.

1339 Amjad M Jaimoukha, *The Chechens: A Handbook* (2012 edition, Routledge 2012) 22.

Formally, Chechnya did not have the right to secede. According to the doctrine of *uti possidetis* only former Republics of the Soviet Union could do so.[1340] The *uti possidetis* doctrine is originally derived from Roman property law, but today it describes a way of defining boundaries in international law. When a State or an Empire falls apart, new States emerge along the lines of the existing boundaries within the former entity.[1341] Thus, the principle does not take into account ethnic identity, homeland, or culture, but favours stability over material justice.[1342] According to 71(1) and 78(1) of the 1978 Constitution of the RSFSR, Chechnya had the Status of an Autonomous Socialist Soviet Republic *within* the RSFSR. It was not a Republic of the USSR and thus stayed with Russia when the Soviet Union disintegrated. The Russian Constitutional Court confirmed this reading in 1995.[1343]

Yet, despite all efforts from Moscow, Chechnya *de facto* managed to escape Russia's control in the years 1991–1994. Moscow was overwhelmed by the events following the dissolution of the Soviet Union and the little Republic of Ichkeria enjoyed *de facto* independence. Its President was Dzhokhar Dudayev, a former Soviet Air Force General. Negotiations between him and President Yeltsin took place but did not yield any tangible results.[1344] Finally, President Yeltsin issued the secret decree 2137 sanctioning the use of military force:[1345] In a famous last meeting between the Russian Minister of Defence Pavel Grachev and Dzhokhar Dudaev, the Chechen President refused to give in. Grachev is said to have replied with a threatening remark: "I will crush you."[1346] For the first time in its young history, the Russian Federation decided to go to war on its own territory.

The First Chechen War lasted from 11 December 1994 to 31 August 1996 and ended in a humiliation for the disorganised Russian Army. While the Russians managed to take control of most of the Chechen territory at a great human cost, they could not hold out. In the end,

---

1340 Nußberger, 'Russia' (n 218) para 72.

1341 Nesi (n 1080) paras 1–4.

1342 ibid paras 9–10.

1343 *Chechnya Decision* (n 887) para 2. Under the Constitution of the Russian Federation – just like under the previous Soviet Constitution of 1978 – subjects cannot change their status unilaterally, let alone may they secede from the Russian Federation without consent from Moscow.

1344 For the prelude to the First Chechen War see Evangelista (n 891) 20–33.

1345 Presidential Decree No 2137 (30 November 1994).

1346 Ю.М. Батурин [Y.M. Baturin] (ed), *Эпоха Ельцина: очерк политической истории [Yeltin's Epoch: An Essay of Political History]* (Vagrius 2001) 598.

the rebels retook Grozny and forced Moscow into peace negotiations. The parties finally concluded the Khasavyurt Agreement that postponed the decision about Chechnya's fate to 2001 and gave the rebel-region quasi-independence.[1347] The inter-war period was marked by "warlordism, rampant criminality, hostage-takings, chaotic violence, grisly attacks on foreign aid workers, and general lawlessness."[1348] Evangelista nicknamed the period "no war, no peace."[1349]

In this general lawlessness, radical Islamist elements gained strength. Fundamentalist leaders like Shamil Basayev and Ibn al-Khattab destabilised the region. They launched raids into neighbouring Dagestan and pledged to set up a Wahabist State in Caucasus.[1350] Finally, a series of terror attacks were the straw that broke the camel's back. When several apartment buildings were blown up in Buynaksk, Moscow, and Volgodonsk, suspicion fell on the Chechens.[1351] Putin describes his decision to go to war in his biography: "If we don't stop this now, Russia as we know it today will not exist."[1352]Thus, the Second Chechen War began in August 1999. A year-long battle phase was followed by a long period of bloody guerrilla

---

1347 See para 1 of the Khasavyurt Agreement which foresees that the question of Chechnya's status should "be solved by 31 December 2001 in accordance with universally recognized principles and norms of international law." Para 3 of the agreement implicitly gave the Chechen Republic the right to pass its own laws until such solution was found. It thus enjoyed quasi-independence. The agreement is available in English at <https://peacemaker.un.org/russia-khasavyo urtdeclaration96>.

1348 Mark Kramer, 'The Perils of Counterinsurgency: Russia's War in Chechnya' (2005) 29 International Security 5, 7.

1349 Evangelista (n 891) 46.

1350 Kramer (n 1348) 7; Evangelista (n 891) 64. Some say that Basayev's last invasion into Dagestan in August 1999 already marked the beginning of the Second Chechen War.

1351 Emil Pain, 'From the First Chechen War Towards the Second' (2001) 8 The Brown Journal of World Affairs 7, 10. Until today, it remains a mystery who was really behind the bombings. Some claim that the attacks were not carried out by Chechen terrorists, but rather by the Russian intelligence services in order to create a pretext for war. I will not delve into these speculations, because they do not influence the following analysis of IHL.

1352 Н. Геворкян [N. Gevorkyan], Н. Тимакова [N. Timakova] and А. Колесников [A. Kolesnikov], *От первого лица – разговоры с Владимиром Путиным [From a First Person Perspective – Interviews with Vladimir Putin] (electronic version)* (Vagrius 2000) 78.

warfare. The last Russian troops would only leave Chechnya ten years later.[1353]

4.2.2 The correct classification of the Chechen Wars – freedom fighters or terrorists?

Legally, there are four different possibilities to classifying a conflict such as the Chechen Wars.
1) as a classic international armed conflict
2) as a liberation war under Art 1(4) AP I
3) as non-international armed conflict
4) as internal disturbances outside the scope of IHL

The possibility of an IAC – an armed conflict between two States – must be discarded straight away, because Chechnya never achieved *de jure* independence. While it had issued a declaration of independence and adopted a Constitution prior to the war, Chechnya legally remained part of Russia.[1354] According to the black letter of the Constitution of the RSFSF and later the Russian Federation, Chechnya remained an integral part of the Russian Federation.[1355] The Khasavyurt Accords did nothing to alter this status. They stipulate that the "mutual relations between the Russian Federation and the Chechen Republic" should only be determined later on. In this, the Accord was deliberately vague.[1356] The Russians saw it as proof for Chechnya's autonomy within the Russian Federation, the Chechens as a reaffirmation of their independence.[1357] In reality, the Accords did nothing but buy time. While absolute independence could well have been the result of the negotiations, the Accords made clear that "concerning

---

1353 'Death Toll in Battles in Chechnya Put at 600' (The New York Times, 26 December 1995) <https://www.nytimes.com/1995/12/26/world/death-toll-in-battles-in-chechnya-put-at-600.html>.

1354 Evangelista (n 891) 141–142; not a single State recognized the independence of Chechnya. While recognition is not constitutive for a state, the lack of recognition serves as a strong indicator against the assumption of statehood, see Crawford, 'State' (n 1161) para 17.

1355 See Art 71(1) and 78(1) of the 1978 Constitution and Art 65 and 66(5) of the current Russian Constitution.

1356 Souleimanov (n 934) 119; Wendy Turnoff Atrokhov, 'The Khasavyurt Accords: Maintaining the Rule of Law and Legitimacy of Democracy in the Russian Federation amidst the Chechen Crisis' (1999) 32 Cornell International Law Journal 367, 380.

1357 Atrokhov (n 1356) 377–378.

mutual relations [...] a future negotiation process will be conducted."[1358] Until such settlement – which was of course never reached – Chechnya remained in a limbo.

The second possibility, i.e. the classification of the conflict as a "liberation war" found many supporters in Chechnya.[1359] The concept can be found in Art 1(4) AP I. It represents an "odd" rule in IHL, because it links *ius in bello* to *ius ad bellum* creating an exception from the strict separation of the two fields. The provision stipulates that an armed conflict is always an IAC, if a people fight "against colonial domination and alien occupation and against racist régimes in the exercise of their right of self-determination, as enshrined in the Charter of the United Nations [...]." In a nutshell, an ordinary NIAC is upgraded to an IAC because the armed group is fighting for a "respectable" reason. Ironically, the Soviet had once been the most fervent supporters of this provision and pushed for its adoption at the Diplomatic Conference of 1977.[1360] The norm corresponded to Lenin's anti-colonial rhetoric and was in line with Soviet Union's concept of a strong right to self-determination.[1361]

It is beyond doubt that the Chechens fought for self-determination. The concept even made it into the preamble of the Khasavyurt Agreement. However, did this right to self-determination grant them a right to secede from the Russian Federation turning the conflict into an IAC under Art 1(4) AP I?[1362] Or was this beyond the scope "enshrined in the Charter of the United Nations" as Art 1(4) requires? Once again, we return to the question of remedial secession that we have already addressed in the context of Crimea. Suffice it to say that the mere existence of such a concept is highly controversial, let alone the conditions under which the right can be exercised.[1363] The Chechen rebels certainly saw themselves within the scope of Art 1(4). The insurgents even issued a declaration

---

1358 The Chechens cited the reference to self-determination in the Agreement's preamble as evidence for their right to independence. The Russians, however, made clear that this had never been the intention of the Khasavyurt Agreement. It is true that the Agreement does not address secession, but only self-determination ("Proceeding from the universally recognized right of peoples to self-determination"). One does not necessarily imply the other, see for this ibid 379.

1359 Evangelista (n 891) 143. Chechen leaders such as Akhmad Kadyrov constantly stressed the anti-colonialist nature of Chechnya's struggle.

1360 Toman (n 350) 74.

1361 See above at p 90.

1362 Gaeta (n 889) 568.

1363 See above at pp 223 et seq.

under Art 96(3) AP I to the Swiss government as the depositary of the Geneva Conventions – something that has not happened before or since. Art 96(3) acts as the procedural counterpart to Art 1(4) and allows an armed group to be recognised as the "authority representing a people engaged against a High Contracting Party in an armed conflict" under Art 1(4). The insurgents declared that they would adhere to the Conventions and asked to be recognised as an official liberation movement. The Swiss, however, declined.[1364] Most States, organisations, and academics shared this view and did not consider the Chechen War as a "liberation war" in the sense of Art 1(4). I agree with this assessment, because the concept of self-determination could not – neither today nor at the time – justify remedial secession.

This, however, does not mean that IHL did not apply in Chechnya. I rather agree with the overwhelming majority of States and scholars that classified the situation as a non-international armed conflict.[1365] This also became the position of the ICRC.[1366] We have already touched upon the criteria of a NIAC at page 263. To reiterate, a non-international armed conflict exists whenever there is resort to armed force between States or protracted armed violence between governmental authorities and organised armed groups or between such groups within a State.[1367] Thus, unlike an

---

1364 Noëlle Quénivet, 'The Moscow Hostage Crisis in the Light of the Armed Conflict in Chechnya' (2001) 4 Yearbook of International Humanitarian Law 348, 353.

1365 Abresch (n 940) 754; Gaeta (n 889) 568; Quénivet (n 1364) 354; Мемориал [Memorial], 'Всеми имеющимися средствами: Операция МВД РФ в селе Самашки, 7–8 апреля 1995 года [All Necessary Means: the Operation of the Russian Ministry of Interior in the Village of Samashki, 7–8 April 1995]' (1995); Deutscher Bundestag, 'Drucksache 13/718 – Antwort der Bundesregierung, Verhalten der Bundesregierung zum russischen Vorgehen im Tschetschenien-Konflikt' (1995) 3; Human Rights Watch, 'Chechnya: Report to the 1996 OSCE Review Conference (D816)' (1996).

1366 ICRC, 'Annual Report 1995' (1995) 203. See also ICRC, Customary IHL Database, Rule 124 that argues: "On this basis, the ICRC systematically requests access to persons deprived of their liberty in connection with *non-international armed conflicts*, and such access is generally granted, for example, in relation to the conflicts in [...] Chechnya [...]." The ICRC was extremely cautious not to give the impression that Chechnya had any claim to sovereignty. Throughout its Annual Report (1995), for example, it used the cumbersome formula "Chechnya (southern Russia)."

1367 ICTY, *The Prosecutor v Duško Tadić* (IT-94–1-T), Decision on the Defence Motion for Interlocutory Appeal on Jurisdiction, 2 October 1995, para 70. *Tadić* was only decided in 1995, but similar definitions of NIAC existed before. While

IAC, the threshold of application for NIACs is considerable. Two criteria must be met: Sufficient intensity[1368] ("protracted armed violence") and sufficient level of organisation ("organised armed groups"). The double threshold is important to distinguish an armed conflict from mere internal disturbances.[1369] Hence, the distinction between the above categories 3) or 4) – and the very application of IHL itself – hinges upon the threshold criteria for which international jurisprudence has produced a list of indicators.

– The following factors point to sufficient intensity: the kind of weapons used, the number of casualties, the number of soldiers engaged, and the frequency of operations, the number of refugees fleeing the combat zone.[1370]

– Criteria that point to sufficient organisation of the armed group include: the existence of headquarters, designated zones of operation, and the ability to procure, transport, and distribute arms.[1371]

Both Chechen Wars clearly met this double threshold. The First War dragged on for two years and saw heavy fighting. On its first day, 11 December 1994, the Russian Army spearheaded into Chechnya with around 25 000 troops, 80 tanks and 200 armoured vehicles.[1372] By February 1995, the number of forces had swollen to 70 000.[1373] The Chechens

---

the ICTY contributed greatly to the present-day definition by channelling and clarifying the existing approaches, others had previously used similar criteria to define NIACs, see e.g. Pictet, *The Geneva Conventions of 12 August 1949* (n 983) 49–50.

1368 The ICTY interpreted the criterion of "protracted violence" as intensity rather than duration, although the latter may serve as an indicator for the former, see ICTY, *The Prosecutor v Ramush Haradinaj et al* (IT-04–84-T), Trial Chamber Judgment, 3 April 2008, para 49.

1369 ICTY, *The Prosecutor v Duško Tadić* (IT-94-1-T), Trial Chamber Judgment, 7 May 1997, para 562. The two criteria (organisation and intensity) exist "solely for the purpose, as a minimum, of distinguishing an armed conflict from banditry, unorganized and short-lived insurrections, or terrorist activities, which are not subject to international humanitarian law."

1370 See e.g. ICTY, *The Prosecutor v Fatimir Limaj et al* (IT-03–66-T), Trial Chamber Judgment, 30 November 2005, para 177; ICTY, *The Prosecutor v Ramush Haradinaj et al* (IT-04–84-T), Trial Chamber Judgment, 3 April 2008, para 49.

1371 ICTY, *The Prosecutor v Fatimir Limaj et al* (IT-03–66-T), Trial Chamber Judgment, 30 November 2005, para 90; see also ICTY, *The Prosecutor v Ramush Haradinaj et al* (IT-04–84-T), Trial Chamber Judgment, 3 April 2008, para 60.

1372 Souleimanov (n 934) 100.

1373 ibid.

could muster between 12 000 and 18 000 men.[1374] Hardly a skirmish, or a law-enforcement operation against criminal bands. Indiscriminate carpet bombings and artillery barrages were a common feature of the conflict. In one *hour*, Grozny saw three times more detonations than Sarajevo at the height of its siege during an entire *day*.[1375] At Grozny, Gudermes, and Samashki, scores of fighters and civilians perished.[1376] During the New Year's Eve attack on Grozny alone, Russia lost between 500 and 2 000 soldiers.[1377] Overall, the death toll estimates for the First Chechen War range between 60 000 and 100 000, with many more wounded.[1378] The ICRC spoke of an "escalation of hostilities" that warranted a "large-scale ICRC humanitarian mission."[1379]

Similarly, the Second Chechen War fulfils the double threshold of a NIAC. The first year saw fierce battles. At the height of the assault on Grozny in December 1999, Russia deployed 150 000 soldiers in Chechnya. Initially they were up against what experts believed to be 26 000 to 40 000 rebels.[1380] At the end of the active battle phase, Russia had suffered nearly 2 000 dead and 6 000 wounded, which came very close to the casualty numbers of the First Chechen War.[1381] Like in 1994–1996, the use of the air force and heavy artillery produced terrible civilian losses.[1382] More than 10 000 civilians were dead by 2002[1383] and the city of Grozny had been completely levelled by Russian air strikes.[1384] In the end, the Russian Army managed to control most of the Chechen territory, but could never take the impregnable rebel strongholds in the mountains. Open conflict faded into a vicious guerrilla war that lasted until 2009.[1385] The rebels still managed to inflict heavy casualties on the Russian forces. Countless civilians became victims of arbitrary killings, sweep-up operations (*zachistkas*), and

---

1374 ibid 103.

1375 David Remnick, *Resurrection: The Struggle for a New Russia* (Vintage Books 1998) 263–264.

1376 See, for example, 'Death Toll in Battles in Chechnya Put at 600' (The New York Times, 26 December 1995) <https://www.nytimes.com/1995/12/26/world/death-toll-in-battles-in-chechnya-put-at-600.html>.

1377 Souleimanov (n 934) 104.

1378 ibid 125 with further sources.

1379 ICRC, 'Annual Report 1995' (n 1366) 203.

1380 Souleimanov (n 934) 167–168.

1381 Evangelista (n 891) 84.

1382 Pain (n 1351) 11.

1383 Souleimanov (n 934) 171 with further sources.

1384 Kramer (n 1348) 8.

1385 Souleimanov (n 934) 164–189.

torture at the hands of Russian soldiers and Chechen security forces.[1386] Only in 2009, would Russia withdraw its last fighting troops.[1387]

In sum, both the threshold of organisation and intensity that define a NIAC were met in the Chechen Wars. Given the immense level of violence and the fierce and well-organised resistance of the rebels, it is out of question to call the conflict an "internal disturbance" beyond the scope of IHL. Rather, it is the exact situation that Common Article 3 had in mind when extending the protection of IHL to "conflicts not of an international character."

4.2.3 The Russian position – a fight against banditry

The Russian government, however, opted for an entirely different interpretation. According to Moscow, both Chechen Wars were nothing but a law enforcement operation against armed bands to which IHL did not apply.

4.3.2.1 Russia's approach to IHL in the First Chechen War (and its consequences)

From the very beginning, Russia refused to recognise the existence of an armed conflict in the Northern Caucasus. It portrayed the events as a fight against "banditry."[1388] This is shown by Presidential decree 2137. It authorised the use of force and marked the starting point of the First Chechen War. It speaks of the need to "restore constitutional legality and law and order" and "disarming and liquidating the armed formations." For the unsuspecting reader, this might evoke the image of a law enforcement campaign, not a full-scale war. The subsequent decrees used similar vocabulary.[1389]

1386 Marcel van Herpen, *Putin's Wars: The Rise of Russia's New Imperialism* (2nd edn, Rowman & Littlefield 2015) 187–199; for the disastrous effect of the war on civilians in general see Emma Gilligan, *Terror in Chechnya: Russia and the Tragedy of Civilians in War (e-Book)* (EBSCO Publishing 2014).

1387 Michael Schwirtz, 'Russia Ends Operations in Chechnya' (The New York Times, 17 April 2009) <https://www.nytimes.com/2009/04/17/world/europe/17chechnya.html>.

1388 Abresch (n 940) 754.

1389 See Decrees No 2166 (9 December 1994), No 1360 (9 December 1994), and No 1833 (2 November 1993).

Yeltsin himself was less tempered in his tone but played the same tune. In an interview he expressed his views on the Chechen fighters: "These are criminals […], professional bandits, fanatics."[1390] The Russian NGO Memorial writes in its report: "From the beginning of the armed conflict in the Chechen Republic the president and the government obstinately presented the events as a mere law enforcement operation aimed at disarming armed bands. They considered it an exclusively internal affair of Russia."[1391] For the government, applying IHL was out of question. Representatives of the ICRC raised the issue of the applicability of IHL during a visit to Minister of Foreign Affairs Andrey Kozyrev in 1995.[1392] Russia, however, formally notified the organisation that it did "not regard the current operation as coming under the auspices" of IHL, because it was "only a limited operation to cope with an internal disorder and to combat terrorists."[1393]

This simplistic narrative was challenged by the Russian Constitutional Court in July 1995.[1394] In its historic ruling, it classified the Chechen "situation" as a NIAC and declared that the provisions of IHL "are binding on both parties to the armed conflict."[1395] While the Judges did not provide any reasoning, they could not have been clearer in their conclusion. Yet, on the government's side, nothing changed. It clung to its position that the counterinsurgency operation in Chechnya fell outside the scope of IHL.[1396] The government also ignored the verdict in another respect. The Court had explicitly criticised the "improper consideration [of IHL] in internal legislation"[1397] and obliged the legislator to make amends.[1398]

1390 Available at <https://www.youtube.com/watch?v=DGPv8VzJ2S4>.

1391 Мемориал [Memorial], 'Россия – Чечня: цепь ошибок и преступлений [Russia – Chechnya: A Series of Mistakes and Crimes]' (1998) chapter 3.

1392 The ICRC managed to maintain its delegations in Northern Caucasus. Sometimes ICRC delegates were even allowed to visit places of detention. In general, however, their work was made very difficult and the organisation could never gain any real leverage on Moscow, see ICRC, 'Annual Report 1995' (n 1366) 203, 206; Sassòli (n 695) 53.

1393 Kramer (n 330) 189.

1394 *Chechnya Decision* (n 887); for an analysis how the *Chechnya Decision* influenced the implementation of IHL in Russia see above p 194.

1395 *Chechnya Decision* (n 887) para 5.

1396 Kramer (n 330) 187.

1397 *Chechnya Decision* (n 887) para 5.

1398 *Chechnya Decision* (n 887) para 8: "The Federal Assembly of the Russian Federation shall settle the legislation on the use of the armed forces of the Russian Federation, as well as on the regulation of other conflicts and issues arising out of extraordinary situations, including those falling under the additional

This never happened.[1399] The verdict did not lead to "concrete steps neither from the civilian nor from the military authorities with respect to the observation of IHL norms in Chechnya."[1400] Some even called the *Chechnya Decision* counterproductive, because "it gave the government precisely what it wanted: *de facto* authorization for federal forces in Chechnya to continue disregarding the Geneva Conventions and related documents."[1401]

How could the applicability of IHL be denied despite the clear finding of the Constitutional Court? One could call the First Chechen War "Yeltsin's war":[1402] a conflict started by *his* presidential decree 2137, led by *him* as the Commander in Chief. In many respects, the President was acting outside the law and continued to do so even after the ruling of the Constitutional Court.[1403] Ruslan Khasbulatov, Yeltsin's political adversary at the time and former speaker of the Supreme Soviet of the RSFSR, argued that Chechnya was

> *"[...] Yeltsin's private war, because the government did not declare war, and the parliament did not declare war. The entire war was carried out according to the commands and decrees of one political figure."[1404]*

Yeltsin's policy of denial led to severe IHL violations. I have described the human toll above. The First Chechen War claimed between 60 000 and 100 000 deaths, most of them civilians.[1405] The first assault on Grozny alone in winter 1994–1995 killed between 25 000 and 50 000 civilians.[1406] Disproportional attacks, arbitrary killings, and torture were commonplace.

---

protocol to the Geneva Conventions of 12 August 1949, concerning protection of the victims of armed conflicts of a non-international character (Protocol II)."

1399 Tuzmukhamedov (n 703) 395. See also Бахтияр Тузмухамедов [Bakhtiyar Tuzmukhamedov] 'Как воевать по правилам?' [How to Wage War by the Rules?] (Nezavisimaya Gazeta, 15 February 2010) <http://www.ng.ru/dipkurer/2010-02-15/11_wars.html>.

1400 Мемориал [Memorial], 'Россия – Чечня: цепь ошибок и преступлений [Russia – Chechnya: A Series of Mistakes and Crimes]' (n 1391) chapter 3.

1401 Kramer (n 330) 186–187.

1402 Evangelista (n 891) 11 et seq; for the divide between the Parliament, the Constitutional Court and the President see also Мемориал [Memorial], 'Правовые аспекты чеченского кризиса [Legal Aspects of the Chechen Crisis]' (n 891) 30.

1403 Мемориал [Memorial], 'Правовые аспекты чеченского кризиса [Legal Aspects of the Chechen Crisis]' (n 891) 8.

1404 Evangelista (n 891) 11.

1405 Souleimanov (n 934) 125.

1406 Gilligan (n 1386) 28.

To this day, places like Grozny, Gudermes, or Samashki remain associated with flagrant violations of the laws of war. The violations of international law have been well documented by organisations, journalists, and academics.[1407] In addition, most of the Russian media critically reported on the conflict to the point that President Yeltsin ordered them to cease by public proclamation.[1408]

Several sources have established a clear link between these atrocities on the ground and Moscow's refusal to apply IHL. The Constitutional Court itself ruled that the "improper consideration of these provisions in internal legislation has been one of the reasons of non-compliance with the rules."[1409] The NGO Memorial claims in one of their numerous reports:

> *"This legal nihilism by the Russian authorities had grave consequences. The war was fought without rules – both with respect to the conduct of hostilities and the conduct of Federal forces in the territory under their control."[1410]*

Mark Kramer – a specialist on Chechnya who has conducted over 100 interviews with Russian officers and servicemen – identifies a similar chain of cause-and-effect:

> *"Because the Russian government's official position during both wars was that the fighting in Chechnya was not covered by IHL, troops from the Russian army and the Russian MVD deployed in Chechnya were not given any training in the Geneva Conventions and were regularly given assignments that contravened basic principles of IHL."[1411]*

The entire Russian campaign contained a dangerous mix: the refusal to apply IHL paired with a lack of discipline and military incompetence. Not only were the Russian authorities denying that they were fighting an armed conflict under IHL, but their soldiers were not even aware of the rules, and in any case lacked the discipline to apply them. It is not hard to imagine that eighteen or nineteen-year-old conscripts with no experience in the army would perform poorly on the battlefield – both in terms

---

1407 President Yeltsin famously declared that the war "is also the journalists' fault, because they made a big deal out of it." Available at <https://www.youtube.com /watch?v=DGPv8VzJ2S4>.

1408 Pain (n 1351) 8.

1409 *Chechnya Decision* (n 887) para 5.

1410 Мемориал [Memorial], 'Россия – Чечня: цепь ошибок и преступлений [Russia – Chechnya: A Series of Mistakes and Crimes]' (n 1391) chapter 3.

1411 Kramer (n 330) 188.

of soldiery and IHL.[1412] The military experts Novichkov, Snegovsky, and Sokolov published an extensive report on the performance of the Russian Army in the First Chechen War. Their verdict is devastating. Soldiers were undisciplined, their equipment outdated. Only one out of five tanks actually made it to Grozny, because the rest of them broke down.[1413] The command structure had remained unchanged since the 30s.[1414] This Russian Army in disarray was bound to perform poorly in terms of IHL which depends on a disciplinary system to ensure compliance.[1415] Even worse, the Russian Army attempted to use tactics from the Afghan War that had already led to two million civilian deaths.[1416] Novichkov, Snegovsky, and Sokolov argue that in Chechnya the Afghan tactic of waging war in populated areas – blockading and liquidating villages with the help of air support – did not work.[1417] As in Afghanistan, the tactic did not only fail to work. It killed countless civilians.

4.3.2.2 Russia's approach to IHL in the Second Chechen War (and its consequences)

In political terms, the Second Chechen War was very different from the first one. In 1999, a political "parvenu" called the shots in the Kremlin: Prime Minister – soon to be President – Vladimir Putin.[1418] Secondly, the terror attacks on several apartment buildings had turned public opinion around. While many Russians had been critical of the first Chechen War, now 65 percent of the population were in favour of a military solution

---

1412 See e.g. van Herpen (n 1386) 161.
1413 Н.Н. Новичков [N.N. Novichkov], В.Я. Снеговский [B.Ya. Snegovsky] and А.Г. Соколов [A.G. Sokolov], *Российские вооруженные силы в чеченском конфликте: анализ. итоги. выводы [The Russian Armed Forces in the Chechen Conflict: An analysis. Results. Conclusions]* (Holweg Infoglob 1995) 25.
1414 ibid 183.
1415 See e.g. the definition of armed forces in Art 43 No 1 AP I: "Such armed forces shall be subject to an internal disciplinary system which, inter alia, shall enforce compliance with the rules of international law applicable in armed conflict."
1416 See above at p 131.
1417 Н.Н. Новичков [N.N. Novichkov], В.Я. Снеговский [B.Ya. Snegovsky] and А.Г. Соколов [A.G. Sokolov] (n 1413) 55.
1418 Yeltsin stepped down on 31 December 1999.

for the renegade Republic.[1419] In addition, the Russian press miraculously abandoned its critical attitude. Official news reports heralded the triumphant actions of the Russian Army and showed little compassion for the civilians killed. War became a dry, unavoidable everyday occurrence. Villages were not attacked, but "cleaned out." Grozny was not bombed and stormed but subjected to a "special action."[1420]

What did not change, was the attitude towards the application of IHL in governmental and military circles – or rather the *refusal* to accept its application. The official position remained firm: The situation was not an armed conflict, but a law enforcement operation.[1421] During the course of the Second Chechen War the government learned to place increasing emphasis on the prevention of terrorism, a keyword that flew particularly well with the West, especially after the attacks of 9/11.[1422] Depending on the occasion, the fighters were called terrorists, or bandits. Both terms implied the exclusion of IHL. Putin sent a grim warning to these fighters in his book (2000):

> *"You know what I can guarantee you? I will repeat: These bandits will be annihilated. Everyone who takes up arms will be annihilated."*[1423]

While the Russian authorities did acknowledge that the Second Chechen War had begun with a "military phase" they expressly denied that this operation was governed by IHL.[1424] Even Putin himself called Chechnya a "military operation" in his book.[1425] Yet, this did not trigger the application of IHL. This marks a striking parallel to the Russian line of argument in the Kerch Strait case: There too, Russia faced "a military operation," but stubbornly denied being involved in an armed conflict in the sense of IHL.

Like in the First Chechen War, the government's denial of IHL was mimicked by the military. Kramer quotes a colonel serving in Chechnya, with whom he had conducted an interview in 2006. The officer was convinced that "these sorts of international agreements [the Geneva Con-

---

1419 Emil Pain and RR Love, 'The Second Chechen War: The Information Component' (2000) 80 Military Review 59, 60.

1420 Pain (n 1351) 8.

1421 Abresch (n 940) at n 44 with further sources.

1422 Evangelista (n 891) 151.

1423 Н. Геворкян [N. Gevorkyan], Н. Тимакова [N. Timakova] and А. Колесников [A. Kolesnikov] (n 1352) 79–80.

1424 Kramer (n 330) 189.

1425 Н. Геворкян [N. Gevorkyan], Н. Тимакова [N. Timakova] and А. Колесников [A. Kolesnikov] (n 1352) 79–80.

ventions] do not apply here, not at all. We're dealing with terrorists. It's out of the question. This is a counterterrorist operation."[1426] Similarly, a Lieutenant Colonel, with whom Kramer conducted an interview in 2007 reacted with surprise when asked about the application of the Geneva Protocols: "We are in charge of a counterterrorist operation; this is not an international war."[1427]

Unlike in the First Chechen War, the Constitutional Court remained silent this time. In rare cases, however, Russian commentators dared to contradict the government's policy of denial. Captain Vladimir Galitsky – at the time a professor at the Military Academy – criticised that Russia's army waged war "in a legal vacuum" and that "neither the Constitutional Court, nor the Ministry of Justice reacts to this."[1428]

This vacuum became the ideal breeding ground for flagrant violations of IHL. I would like to highlight three aspects of this pattern. Firstly, the Russian aerial bombing campaign between September and June 2000 showed blatant disregard for all principles governing the conduct of hostilities. Russian military expert Pavel Felgengauer speaks of deliberate attacks on civilians and the use of indiscriminate fuel bombs prohibited by the CCW.[1429] Thousands of civilians died in Grozny alone during the bombardments, because the Russians had refused to carry out an effective evacuation. Emma Gilligan calls the operation a clear "war crime."[1430]

Secondly, Russia intensified its use of *zachistkas*. The word is derived from *зачистить* which may be translated as cleaning something up or out. Originally, these sweep-up operations were supposed to root out armed resistance in populated areas. In reality, the term became a euphemism for a collective punishment campaign against the Chechen civilian population.[1431] The searches went hand in hand with murder, torture, looting, and enforced disappearances. The Russian NGO Memorial esti-

---

1426 Kramer (n 330) 188.

1427 ibid.

1428 Владимир Галицкий [Vladimir Galitsky], 'Война в правовом вакууме [War in a Legal Vacuum]' (Nezavisimaya Gazeta, 16 June 2000) <http://nvo.ng.ru/conce pts/2000-06-16/4_vacuumwar.html?id_user=Y>.

1429 Pavel Felgengauer, 'The Russian Army in Chechnya' (2002) 21 Central Asian Survey 157, 158.

1430 Gilligan (n 1386) 29.

1431 ibid 31.

mates that around 5 000–10 000 people were killed in *zachistkas* between 2000 and 2004.[1432]

Thirdly, the use of "filtration points" created another area of lawlessness. In 2000, there were around 30 filtration points with 10 000 to 20 000 detainees.[1433] They were conceived as temporary detention centres to "filter" and weed out resistance fighters from the civilian population. Torture became widespread practice in detention centres like the infamous Chernokozovo filtration point. Detainees describe genital beatings, electro shocks, threats of castration, and even brandings.[1434] These IHL violations became known to a wider public through the case law of the ECtHR. The Court issued its first judgment in 2005.[1435] Since then, it found human rights violations *inter alia* due to extrajudicial killings,[1436] torture,[1437] enforced disappearances,[1438] indiscriminate aerial bombardments, and ar-

---

1432 Alexander Cherkasov, 'The Chechen Wars and the Struggle for Human Rights' in Richard Sakwa (ed), *Chechnya: from Past to Future* (Anthem Press 2005) 139–141. This number is even more shocking, because it is based on the data from only one third of Chechnya's territory to which the NGO had access.

1433 Martin Malek, 'Russia's Asymmetric Wars in Chechnya since 1994' (2009) 8 Connections 81, 93; Gilligan (n 1386) 34. Originally, the filtration centres were established on the basis of the Ministry of Interior Directive N 247 (1994) and later heavily used in the Second Chechen War.

1434 Gilligan (n 1386) 34–35.

1435 ECtHR, *Isayeva v Russia*, No 57950/00, 24 February 2005.

1436 See e.g. ECtHR, *Amuyeva and Others v Russia*, No 17321/06, 25 November 2010.

1437 ECtHR, *Khadisov and Tsechoyev v Russia*, No 21519/02, 5 February 2009; ECtHR, *Sadykov v Russia*, No 41840/02, 7 October 2010; ECtHR, *Gisayev v Russia*, No 4811/04, 20 January 2011.

1438 See e.g. ECtHR, *Dzhamayeva and Others v Russia*, No 26980/06, 21 December 2010; ECtHR, *Aslakhanova and Others v Russia*, No 2944/06, 18 December 2012; ECtHR, *Turluyeva v Russia*, No 63638/09, 20 June 2013; ECtHR, *Yandiyev and Others v Russia*, Nos 34541/06, 43811/06, and 1578/07, 10 October 2013; ECtHR, *Akhmatov and Others v Russia*, Nos 38828/ 10, 2543/11, 2650/11 et al, 16 January 2014.

tillery shelling.[1439] Thus, the ECtHR case law represents a cross-section of the violations described above.[1440]

Yet, none of this changed the Russian position on the inapplicability of IHL. The policy of denial did not end in 2009 when Russian troops pulled out. Until today, no one has been convicted for war crimes committed in Chechnya.[1441] Most cases were not even investigated, whereas the few cases that saw a judicial review totally excluded IHL.[1442]

4.3 Conclusion

It is not uncommon that States are reluctant to concede their involvement in an armed conflict. Recognising the existence of an IAC can be delicate in diplomatic relations. Recognising the existence of a NIAC may be seen as "upgrading" criminals to freedom fighters. Hence, States are prone to avoid facing this difficult truth.[1443] Having said that, Russia's position remains extreme. In the Sea of Azov, Moscow has shown that it is willing to go at great lengths to avoid IHL. It denied the applicability of IHL, despite the fact that the events unfolded before the eyes of the world; despite the very clear-cut (low) threshold of IACs that allows no room for legal manoeuvre; and despite the Ukrainian insistence that the sailors were POWs.

In Chechnya, Moscow rejected the existence of a NIAC for more than ten years. On the one hand, the threshold of NIAC is more difficult to

---

1439 See e.g. ECtHR, *Umayeva v Russia*, No 1200/03, 4 December 2008; ECtHR, *Abuyeva and Others v Russia*, No 27065/05, 2 December 2010; ECtHR, *Esmukhambetov and Others v Russia*, No 23445/03, 29 March 2011; ECtHR, *Kerimova and Others v Russia*, No 17170/04 et al, 3 May 2011; ECtHR, *Khamzayev and Others v Russia*, No 1503/02, 3 May 2011; ECtHR, *Damayev v Russia*, No 36150/04, 29 May 2012; ECtHR, *Abdulkhanov and Others v Russia*, No 22782/06, 3 October 2013; ECtHR, *Mezhidov v Russia*, No 67326/01, 25 September 2008; ECtHR, *Taysumov and Others v Russia*, No 21810/03, 14 May 2009.

1440 For a detailed analysis see Leach, 'Egregious Human Rights Violations in Chechnya: Appraising the Pursuit of Justice' (n 942); Abresch (n 940); Leach, 'The Chechen Conflict: Analysing the Oversight of the European Court of Human Rights' (n 942).

1441 For details on how Russia reacted to alleged war crimes see Evangelista (n 891) 150–164.

1442 See above pp 201 et seq.

1443 Other examples include Turkey's war against the PKK and the UK's attitude towards the "Troubles" in Ireland, Abresch (n 940) 754–756.

prove simply because it contains a double threshold subject to interpretation. On the other hand, the jurisprudence of the ICTY and other courts has fleshed out the criteria that separate disturbances from an armed conflict. There are, and there will always be contentious grey cases.[1444] The Chechen Wars, however, are not situated in this grey zone. They were – together with the Balkan Wars – the bloodiest armed conflict on the European continent since the end of the Second World War. There is no doubt that they met the threshold of a NIAC. Hence, the Russian denial of this legal fact was extreme in many ways: extreme, because it implicitly denied the deaths of thousands of soldiers and civilians; extreme, because the President ignored the ruling of its own Constitutional Court; extreme, because the narrative finally convinced most of the population.

There is one notable exception where Russia openly embraced the existence of an armed conflict. During the Russo-Georgian War, Russia acknowledged from the beginning that it was involved in an IAC.[1445] Yet, as the following two chapters will show Moscow attempted to find other ways of avoiding limitations on its conduct in war: outsourcing warfare and denying violations.

1444 For example, situations of intense violence in the absence of well-organised non-state actors (e.g. drug wars) or short-lived outbursts of armed violence (e.g. border skirmishes or a *coup d'état*), see Sven Peterke, 'Regulating "Drug Wars" and Other Gray Zone Conflicts: Formal and Functional Approaches' (Hasow 2012).

1445 IIFFMCG, 'Report of the Independent International Fact-Finding Mission on the Conflict in Georgia (Tagliavini Report) Volume III – Views of the Sides on the Conflict, Chronologies and Responses to Questionnaires' (n 960) 438.

Chapter IV: Evading IHL on the Battlefield – Outsourcing Warfare ("The Apprentice")

"Perhaps the US administration would be willing to inform the media about the number of US civilians in Iraq during its presence in that country, both in the form of US private military companies and other agencies? How many people died? I assure you, the numbers may be shocking. Mind your own business instead of spreading disinformation about Russia."[1446]

Spokesperson Maria Zakharova, Russian Ministry of Foreign Affairs, 2018

The idea of outsourcing warfare is not new. Private military actors were a common feature of most wars until the mid-nineteenth century.[1447] In classical times, hired Greek soldiers from the same *polis* often fought on both sides.[1448] Later, mercenarism became a thriving economic branch in certain European countries. The Swiss Guards and German *Landsknechte*[1449] competed both for contracts and on the battlefield.[1450] In fact, the idea of having a people's army is a by-product of the rise of the modern nation-State. According to Max Weber, a modern State is a community that "claims the monopoly of physical violence"[1451] and thus cannot tolerate private violence beyond its control. That explains why the term "mercenaries" became an insult, and their use an ostracised practice.[1452] In another

---

1446 Ministry of Foreign Affairs of the Russian Federation, 'Briefing by Foreign Ministry Spokesperson Maria Zakharova' (15 February 2018) <https://www.mid.ru/en/foreign_policy/news/-/asset_publisher/cKNonkJE02Bw/content/id/3077521#11>.

1447 Hannah Tonkin, *State Control over Private Military and Security Companies in Armed Conflict* (Cambridge University Press 2011) 6.

1448 Erika Calazans, *Private Military and Security Companies: The Implications under International Law of Doing Business in War* (Cambridge Scholars Publishing 2016) 8–9.

1449 A group of mostly German mercenaries in the 15th and 16th century.

1450 Calazans (n 1448) 12–13.

1451 From Max Weber's lecture 'Politik als Beruf' (28 January 1919): "Staat ist diejenige menschliche Gemeinschaft, welche innerhalb eines bestimmten Gebietes – dies: das Gebiet gehört zum Merkmal – das Monopol legitimer physischer Gewaltsamkeit für sich (mit Erfolg) beansprucht."

1452 See Art 47 AP I. For a historical account of the use of private military actors see Tonkin (n 1447) 8 et seq.; Calazans (n 1448) et seq.

guise, however, private actors started to re-appear in the post-colonial wars of the 1960s and have seen a boom since the 1990s.[1453] Today, they are again a common feature of most wars.

A State can outsource warfare to many actors such as volunteer corps, rebel movements, militias, and private military companies (PMCs). In literature the term "outsourcing" is sometimes limited to PMCs. I will use it in a broader sense which includes any armed formation that carries out duties that regular soldiers cannot or do not want to perform. Preventively, I would like to debunk two myths: Firstly, outsourcing warfare does not contravene international law *per se*. The use of militias and volunteer corps is even mentioned in the Geneva Conventions.[1454] The Montreux Document lays down rules for companies providing military and security services.[1455] Secondly, Russia is not alone in outsourcing warfare. Virtually all States that wage war do so. For a long time, Russia even lagged behind in this trend. The US and the UK had heavily relied on PMCs in Iraq and Afghanistan at a time where the Russian PMC industry was still in its infancy. In 2011, the US had more contractors in Afghanistan and Iraq than uniformed personnel (155 000 compared to 145 000).[1456]

If outsourcing is a common feature of war, why is it worth focussing on Russia's practice? While Moscow is neither a pioneer, nor one of the biggest economic players in the outsourcing business, it has developed its own approach – and it negatively affects IHL.[1457] Outsourcing happens in an under-regulated and opaque environment. The proxy actors only maintain loose ties to Moscow. These traits are not accidental, but deliberate. Remaining under the radar is crucial to Russia's proxies. Their missions, however, often involve active combat.

Russian volunteers – or rather non-state soldiers – come in all shapes and forms.[1458] For example, it is believed that 30 000 Russian volunteers

---

1453   Tonkin (n 1447) 12–13.

1454   Art 4(A)(2) GC III.

1455   Schweizerische Eidgenossenschaft/ICRC, 'The Montreux Document on Pertinent International Legal Obligations and Good Practices for States Related to Operations of Private Military and Security Companies during Armed Conflict' (2008). See also the section on under-regulation at pp 311 et seq.

1456   Moshe Schwartz and Joyprada Swain, 'Department of Defense Contractors in Afghanistan and Iraq: Background and Analysis' (Congressional Research Service 2011) 'Summary'.

1457   Big players in the private military industry include the US, the UK, Israel, and South Africa.

1458   See e.g. Mark Galeotti, *Russian Political War: Moving Beyond the Hybrid* (Routledge 2019) 80–85.

fought in eastern Ukraine alone.[1459] Many more volunteers participated in the Russo-Georgian War 2008 and in other conflicts such as Syria and Libya. Who were they and what was their connection to the Russian State? I will look at three examples of groups that fight for Russian interests in various conflicts around the world.

– The Russian PMCs "Wagner Group" and "Slavonic Corpus"
– Cossack units
– The South Ossetian Militias

I will acquaint the reader with each proxy in turn, before explaining how Russia uses them to evade IHL. In a nutshell, I will argue that Russia uses these proxies, because they cannot be attributed to the State. This allows Moscow to have boots on the ground without incurring responsibility for possible IHL violations.

1. Wagner's Valkyries – a new type of PMC?

As a contextual introduction, I will briefly acquaint the reader with the concept of a PMC and the evolution of this sector in Russia. Then, the chapter will zoom in on the infamous "Wagner Group" and its precursor "Slavonic Corpus." I argue that they represent a novel type of PMC with distinctive characteristics that set them apart from regular providers of private military force.

1.1 Defining PMCs – the commodification of armed conflict

Today, PMCs[1460] are a common appearance in any war zone. While the media likes to brand them "mercenaries" this is legally incorrect. Merce-

---

1459 Б.Е. Немцов [B.E. Nemtsov] (n 781) 25.

1460 Note on the terminology: Authors often draw a line between private military companies (PMC) and private security companies (PMS). While the former provide services of a military character such as combat support, maintenance of military equipment, or military advisory services, the latter focus on classic security tasks such as guarding objects or persons. In practice, however, this distinction is difficult to maintain, because one company may offer both military and security services in different countries or even the same country. Hence, other authors combine the two terms PMC and PSC into PMSC. For the purpose of this thesis, I will use the term PMC, because I will focus on the military services that Russian companies like Wagner provide.

naries have been defined and ostracised in Art 47 AP I.[1461] However, the provision remained a dead letter due to its extremely narrow wording. I recall my IHL professor stating that "whoever is stupid enough to fulfil it deserves to be called a mercenary."[1462]

For PMCs there is no universally recognised definition. Rather, the acronym describes what they are *not*. PMCs are not members of the armed forces and not mercenaries in the sense of Art 47 AP I, but lie on a spectrum in between these terms.[1463] At the fringes, notions might overlap. Sean McFate, a former US paratrooper who worked himself as private military contractor in Africa and Eastern Europe provides five criteria that define a PMC: They are profit-oriented (1) multinational corporations (2) that operate mostly abroad (3). They operate in a military manner (4), rather than in law enforcement and are "lethal and represent the commodification of armed conflict" (5).[1464] On the mercenary-end of the spectrum we find PMCs like Executive Outcomes and Sandline that fought fully-fledged wars in Angola, Sierra Leone, and Papua New Guinea in the 1990s. These were extremely strong actors that could raise considerable manpower and disposed of heavy weaponry. In essence, they represented

---

1461 A mercenary has no right to POW status. However, the person would still benefit from minimal guarantees. Art 47 AP I is a cumbersome rule. While it contains a definition of "mercenaries" it sets a very high threshold by enumerating six strict conditions: "A mercenary shall not have the right to be a combatant or a prisoner of war. A mercenary is any person who: a) is specially recruited locally or abroad in order to fight in an armed conflict; b) does, in fact, take a direct part in the hostilities; c) is motivated to take part in the hostilities essentially by the desire for private gain and, in fact, is promised, by or on behalf of a Party to the conflict, material compensation substantially in excess of that promised or paid to combatants of similar ranks and functions in the armed forces of that Party; d) is neither a national of a Party to the conflict nor a resident of territory controlled by a Party to the conflict; e) is not a member of the armed forces of a Party to the conflict; and f) has not been sent by a State which is not a Party to the conflict on official duty as a member of its armed forces."

1462 For the many loopholes of Art 47 AP I see Tonkin (n 1447) 29–30. In 2005, the UN established a Working Group on the Use of Mercenaries as a Means of Violating Human Rights and Impeding the Exercise of the Right of Peoples to Self-determination. The Working Group's mandate is not restricted to the narrow definition of Art 47 AP I, but also covers related issues such as foreign fighters and the regulation of private military and security companies in general. These actors will often not fulfil the narrow definition of Art 47 AP I.

1463 ibid 28.

1464 Sean McFate, *The Modern Mercenary: Private Armies and What They Mean for World Order* (Oxford University Press 2014) 13.

private armies for hire.[1465] Due to international pressure such PMCs are virtually absent from today's market.[1466] One of the rare exceptions are the Russian companies that I will address below.

With the wars in Afghanistan (2001) and Iraq (2003), another type of PMC started to dominate the scene. US Companies like Blackwater, Dyn-Corp, and Triple Canopy provided heavily armed security to politicians, diplomats, and premises.[1467] They do not normally participate in offensive combat missions, but may provide security in an extremely hostile environment in a military fashion.[1468] Furthermore, they offer high-level military advice, technological expertise, logistic support, and maintenance.[1469] Such PMCs have a number of advantages for States. They can be hired fast. They cost less. They provide expertise in specialised military fields.[1470] Finally, their deaths cause less public outrage compared to regular soldiers "when the body bags start coming home."[1471]

1.2 PMCs in Russia after 1991 – a late blossom

Russia was not among the pioneers in the privatisation of war. Despite the popular Hollywood image of Russian mercenaries, the reality was quite different. While security companies in Russia flourished during the "Wild Nineties" in a climate of crime and corruption, their tasks were restricted to guarding objects or persons in Russia.[1472] Only few Russians, let alone Russian companies, provided military services in war zones abroad, among them former Soviet pilots that were recruited by international

---

1465 ibid 14; Tonkin (n 1447) 41–44.
1466 McFate (n 1464) 14.
1467 Tonkin (n 1447) 49.
1468 ibid 50.
1469 ibid 40.
1470 ibid 45–52.
1471 Clive Walker and Dave Whyte, 'Contracting out War? Private Military Companies, Law and Regulation in the United Kingdom' (2005) 54 International and Comparative Law Quarterly 651, 660.
1472 Åse Gilje Østensen and Tor Bukkvoll, 'Russian Use of Private Military and Security Companies – the Implications for European and Norwegian Security' (Norwegian Defence Research Establishment 2018) 14.

companies.[1473] In 1996, for example, Angola purchased several Russian helicopters and fighter jets with Russian and Ukrainian personnel.[1474]

From the turn of the millennium, a few Russian companies started to offer concrete military services, such as Moran Security Group, RSB Group, and Antiterror Orel.[1475] Most of them are still in business today and mimicked their Western counterparts, such as Blackwater and DynCorp.[1476] They would not engage in active combat roles, but guard facilities or persons. Their clients were private and State-owned businesses, like Gazprom, Lukoil, and Tatneft.[1477] So far, Russia was neither a very influential actor in the PMC business, nor did it set itself apart by the type of services provided.

In 2013, the Russian renowned military analyst Vladimir Neelov wrote in one of his reports on PMCs: "According to the sources available today our government has not used PMCs for solving concrete [military] tasks."[1478] Some pages down, however, Neelov hints at rumours that a novel Russian company now operates in Syria: "If this is true, this can be called the first serious success of a Russian military company on this market."

These rumours proved to be right. The year 2013 marked a watershed in Moscow's use of PMCs. From then on, Russia was home to a more secretive class of private military companies. They are quite different from their Western counterparts, in the sense that they operate in a grey zone and fulfil active combat missions.[1479] It is these companies that we shall examine in detail.

1473 ibid 21.

1474 William Reno, 'African Weak States and Commercial Alliances' (1997) 96 African Affairs 165, 178.

1475 Владимир Неелов [Vladimir Neelov], 'Частные военные компании в России – опыт и перспективы использования [Private Military Companies in Russia – Experiences and Perspectives of Their Use]' (2013) 25.

1476 Nathaniel Reynolds, 'Putin's Not-So-Secret Mercenaries: Patronage, Geopolitics, and the Wagner Group' (Carnegie Endowment for International Peace 2019) 3.

1477 For example, Russians served as contractors in Iraq from 2004 onwards for Antiterror Orel providing security for facilities of Russian companies. Moran's website lists missions in Iraq, Nigeria, Kenya, and the Central African Republic including anti-piracy services and training for local forces. RSB calls itself a "military consulting group" and offers bodyguard services, demining, protection of industrial objects, and maritime security. For details see Владимир Неелов [Vladimir Neelov] (n 1475) 27–33.

1478 ibid 25.

1479 Reynolds (n 1476) 3.

1.3 Slavonic Corpus and Wagner Group – a new type of shadow warriors?

Who are these new players?[1480] In 2013, a group called "Slavonic Corpus" emerged. It was registered in Hong Kong but operated from Russia.[1481] Its first task was to win back the oil fields from ISIS.[1482] A bit later, the company "Wagner Group" [in the following Wagner] appeared on the radar in Ukraine, Syria, Libya, Sudan, and the Central African Republic. Rather than serving private businesses, Wagner and Slavonic Corpus seemed to work on behalf of the Kremlin in delicate missions and developed an infamous reputation.[1483]

Given the companies' delicate business, their work remains shrouded in secrecy. The scarce information available exists thanks to a handful of Russian and international investigative journalists. These include: Denis Korotkov who used to publish on the platform fontanka.ru and later worked for Novaya Gazeta; Vladimir Neelov who has written extensively on PMCs in Russia, and the journalists of the investigative networks The Bell[1484] and Bellingcat.[1485] Many of those who worked on the issue have received threats or suffered reprisals. Korotkov received a funeral wreath delivered to his office that bore the inscription "traitor of the mother-

---

1480 In the following, I will focus on the two most prominent actors: Slavonic Corpus and Wagner. However, they are not alone on the market. The organisational structures of these PMCs are fluid and new companies keep appearing on the radar. In 2018, the investigative news platform Dozhd discovered a new PMC called "Patriot" in Syria. The documentary is available at <https://www.youtube.com/watch?v=0fRhvWWVt_w>. Another PMC called "Turan" later turned out to be a sophisticated media hoax, see Østensen and Bukkvoll (n 1472) 27.

1481 ibid 25.

1482 Денис Коротков [Denis Korotkov], 'Последний бой "Славянского корпуса" [The Last Fight of the Slavonic Corpus]' *Fontanka.ru* (14 November 2013) <https://www.fontanka.ru/2013/11/14/060/>.

1483 I will cover Wagner's missions in Ukraine, Syria, and Libya in detail below at pp 304 et seq. For Wagner's activity in Sudan see '"Putin's Cook" Set Out to Mine Gold in Africa' (The Bell, 5 June 2018) <https://thebell.io/en/putin-s-cook -set-out-to-mine-gold-in-africa/>. For Wagner's activities in the Central African Republic see Tim Lister, Sebastian Shukla, and Clarissa Ward, 'Putin's Private Army' (CNN, August 2019) <https://edition.cnn.com/interactive/2019/08/africa /putins-private-army-car-intl/>.

1484 The network was founded by the Russian investigative journalist Yelizaveta Osetinskaya, see <https://thebell.io/>.

1485 <https://www.bellingcat.com/>.

land."[1486] Neelov was arrested for high treason.[1487] Others have died under mysterious circumstances.[1488] The following part will rely on their work as well as the research of international scholars, military analysts, and journalists.[1489] Despite this diligently researched information, it is in the nature of the topic that some aspects will remain in the dark.[1490]

Why is it worth the effort to describe these Russian PMCs in detail? Because there are three characteristics which set them apart from their international counterparts. In fact, some observers argue that they are not traditional PMCs at all.[1491] What makes them so different? Firstly, they fulfil an active combat role. Unlike most current PMCs they don't seem to be restricted to guarding and other auxiliary tasks. On the contrary, they serve as "shock troops." Secondly, there is an absolute lack of regulation in Russian national law. On paper PMCs are illegal and should not exist. Yet, they do. Thirdly, their purpose is to operate in absolute deniability. Their missions, their contracts, and above all their links to the Russian State remain unclear. I will detail each aspect in turn.

1486 'Автору расследования о "ЧВК Вагнера" прислали венок с надписью "предатель Родины" [The Initiator of the Investigation about the PMC Wagner Was Sent a Wreath with the Inscription "Traitor of the Motherland"]' (BBC, 18 October 2018) <https://www.bbc.com/russian/news-45906295>.

1487 It is not entirely clear whether this is connected to his work on PMCs, see Военный эксперт Владимир Неелов арестован по делу о госизмене. Он интересовался деятельностью ЧВК, в том числе "Вагнером" [Military Expert Vladimir Neelov on His Trial for High Treason. He Investigated the Activities of PMCs, Including Wagner]' (Meduza, 3 November 2018) <https://meduza.io/f eature/2018/11/03/voennyy-ekspert-vladimir-neelov-arestovan-po-delu-o-gosizm ene-on-interesovalsya-deyatelnostyu-chvk-v-tom-chisle-vagnerom>.

1488 In 2018, three Russian journalists were murdered in the Central African Republic while filming a documentary about Wagner's activities in the region. Furthermore, the investigative journalist Maksim Borodin, who reported on Russian PMCs in Syria, fell from his balcony, see Kimberly Marten, 'Russia's Use of Semi-State Security Forces: The Case of the Wagner Group' (2019) 35 Post-Soviet Affairs 181, 189.

1489 See e.g. Christopher Spearin, 'NATO, Russia and Private Military and Security Companies: Looking into the Dark Reflection' (2018) 163 The RUSI Journal 66; Christopher Spearin, 'Russian Military and Security Privatization: Implications for Canada' (2019) 19 Canadian Military Journal 4; Marten (n 1488); Reynolds (n 1476).

1490 Marten (n 1488) 189. She argues that "these semi-state Russian groups are shadowy and protean, it can be challenging to find reliable information about their activities. They are surrounded by rumours, and some of the prominent individuals involved with them have been caught in direct lies."

1491 Reynolds (n 1476) 13; Marten (n 1488) 183.

1.3.1 Offensive missions

Slavonic Corpus was the first Russian PMC to set foot on Syrian territory. When the investigative journalist Denis Korotkov interviewed ex Corpus members in Russia, he found out that around 2 000 contractors have been operating throughout Syria in 2013. Most were veterans from the Army, OMON,[1492] or the Spetsnaz.[1493] On arrival they were equipped with machine guns and grenade launchers – and then given the choice to "guard or fight."[1494] Slavonic Corpus participated in active combat, but mysteriously vanished from Syria in 2014.[1495] Before long, its CEOs Vadim Gusev and Yevgeniy Sidorov found themselves before a Moscow Court where they received a jail sentence for the crime of recruiting mercenaries.[1496] While the Corpus would later reappear, one of its former employees – an ex GRU officer called Dmitriy Utkin – founded a company that would enjoy a more long-lived success in the PMC business:[1497] Wagner Group [*Группа Вагнер*].

It is no coincidence that the name recalls Richard Wagner. Utkin is said to revere the German composer and chose "Wagner" as his *nom de guerre* in previous conflicts.[1498] After his career as a GRU officer, he served in the Slavonic Corpus in Syria and participated in anti-piracy missions on the high sea. This suggests that Slavonic Corpus and Wagner Group are connected on an organisational level.[1499] Observers are convinced that

---

1492 OMON stands for *отряд мобильный особого назначения* [Special Purpose Mobile Unit], the term used for special police units in Russia.

1493 Денис Коротков [Denis Korotkov], 'Последний бой "Славянского корпуса" [The Last Fight of the Slavonic Corpus]' (n 1482).

1494 ibid.

1495 It later reappeared, see Денис Коротков [Denis Korotkov], '"Славянский корпус" возвращается в Сирию [The Slavonic Corpus Returns to Syria]' *Fontanka.ru* (16 October 2015) <https://www.fontanka.ru/2015/10/16/118/>.

1496 'Славянский корпус вербовал боевиков для исламистов [Slavic Corpus Recruited Fighters for Islamists]' (Kommersant, 15 January 2015) <https://www.kommersant.ru/doc/2645963>. They were convicted under Art 359 of the Russian Criminal Code, see below at p 311.

1497 Денис Коротков [Denis Korotkov], '"Славянский корпус" возвращается в Сирию [The Slavonic Corpus Returns to Syria]' (n 1495).

1498 Денис Коротков [Denis Korotkov], 'Они сражались за Пальмиру [They Fought for Palmyra]' *Fontanka.ru* (29 March 2016) <https://www.fontanka.ru/2016/03/28/171/>.

1499 Денис Коротков [Denis Korotkov], 'За Башара Асада – без флага, без Родины [For Bashar Assad – without Flag and Motherland]' *Fontanka.ru* (22 October 2015) <https://www.fontanka.ru/2015/10/22/144/>.

certain parts of the disbanded Slavonic Corpus morphed into the newly founded Wagner Group.[1500]

The rise of Wagner is closely connected to the conflict in Ukraine. It first appeared in Crimea, and later also in Donbas.[1501] Wagner ran a training facility near the Russo-Ukrainian border that was later moved to Molkino in Krasnodar District. There, recruits were trained, briefed, and sent to their deployment in eastern Ukraine.[1502] As I have explained above, Russia steadily increased its military presence in Ukraine throughout 2014. What started as a trickle quickly turned into a torrent of regular soldiers and different types of "volunteers."[1503] Many of the latter were private contractors that bolstered the separatists' ranks in crucial moments of the war.

For instance, Wagner's contractors participated in the battle of Debaltseve (January 2015), one of the most decisive – and bloodiest – battles of the war.[1504] The city is located in between LNR and DNR, near the current front line, and represents a key road and rail hub.[1505] Kyiv lost the battle after 6 000 government troops were caught in a kettle. They finally withdrew having suffered heavy losses. Around 300 Ukrainian soldiers were killed and 700 wounded.[1506] Losses on the pro-Russian side are harder to estimate, but Korotkov documented that several Wagner contractors were among the victims.[1507] In the end, the city fell to the separatists and continues to be held by them today.

Besides engaging with Ukrainian government forces, Wagner's men were also tasked with maintaining order among the various factions fighting for the separatists. They were involved in killing several rebel comman-

---

1500 Marten (n 1488) 192.

1501 ibid.

1502 Rinat Sagdiev, Anton Zverev, and Maria Tsvetkova, 'Kids' Camp on a Defense base? How Russian Firms Masked Secret Military Work' (Reuters, 4 April 2019) <https://www.reuters.com/article/us-mideast-crisis-syria-russia-prigozhin/exclusi ve-kids-camp-on-a-defense-base-how-russian-firms-masked-secret-military-work-i dUSKCN1RG1QT>.

1503 See above at pp 256 et seq.

1504 Денис Коротков [Denis Korotkov], 'Они сражались за Пальмиру [They Fought for Palmyra]' (n 1498).

1505 Galeotti, *Armies of Russia's War in Ukraine* (n 785) 32–34.

1506 Amos C Fox, 'Battle of Debaltseve: The Conventional Line of Effort in Russia's Hybrid War in Ukraine' (*Benning*, 14 September 2016) <https://www.benning.army.mil/armor/eARMOR/content/issues/2017/Winter/1Fox17.pdf>.

1507 Денис Коротков [Denis Korotkov], 'Они сражались за Пальмиру [They Fought for Palmyra]' (n 1498).

ders that had become too independent-minded for Moscow's taste, such as the infamous Batman[1508] and Alexey Mozgovoy.[1509] They were behind disarming the notorious Odessa Brigade[1510] and helped in bringing the Cossacks back in line when they sought independence from *both* Kyiv *and* Moscow proclaiming their own State in Luhansk.[1511]

In 2015, Wagner entered Syria. Its contractors were in charge of maintaining Assad's military equipment, but they also engaged in active fighting and suffered heavy casualties.[1512] They participated, for example, in the 2017 Palmyra offensive serving as "shock troops" alongside the Syrian army supported by the Russian Airforce.[1513] The operation aimed at re-capturing the historic city of Palmyra and its surroundings from ISIS. Reuters reported around 18 Russian casualties in the ground assault.[1514] Korotkov mentions "dozens of deaths."[1515] Other sources speak of losses of up to 30 percent.[1516] Whatever the exact numbers, the offensive at Palmyra shows

---

1508 Alexander "Batman" Bednov was the commander of the Rapid Reaction Group "Batman" that fought on the side of LNR. He achieved notoriety for looting, organised criminality, and human rights abuses. In January 2015, he was killed in an ambush, see Galeotti, *Armies of Russia's War in Ukraine* (n 785) 29–30.

1509 Alexey Mozgovoy was the commander of the notorious *Призрак* [Ghost] Brigade – one of the most feared and effective units fighting on the side of LNR. His unit attracted numerous foreign volunteers and preserved a large degree of independence until Mozgovoy was killed in an ambush in May 2015, see ibid 28.

1510 The Odessa Brigade took part in several decisive battles before being disarmed in January 2015.

1511 Денис Коротков [Denis Korotkov], 'Расшифровка года – Вагнер [The Decryption of the Year – Wagner]' *Fontanka.ru* (3 January 2017) <https://www.fontanka.ru/2016/12/28/094/>; Денис Коротков [Denis Korotkov], '"Славянский корпус" возвращается в Сирию [The Slavonic Corpus Returns to Syria]' (n 1495).

1512 Денис Коротков [Denis Korotkov], 'Расшифровка года – Вагнер [The Decryption of the Year – Wagner]' (n 1511).

1513 'How "Wagner" Came to Syria' (The Economist, 2 November 2017) <https://www.economist.com/europe/2017/11/02/how-wagner-came-to-syria>.

1514 Maria Tsvetkova, 'Russia Underplayed Losses in Recapture of Syria's Palmyra' (Reuters, 22 March 2017) <https://af.reuters.com/article/worldNews/idAFKBN16T0S2>.

1515 Денис Коротков [Denis Korotkov], 'Они сражались за Пальмиру [They Fought for Palmyra]' (n 1498).

1516 Анна Долгарева [Anna Dolgareva], '"Люди должны знать правду": экс-боец рассказал о службе в "ЧВК Вагнера" [The People Have to Know the Truth: An Ex-Fighter about the Service in the PMC Wagner]' (Ridus, 20 February 2018) <https://www.ridus.ru/news/271195>.

that Wagner was embedded in an assault with regular Syrian soldiers assisted by the Russian Airforce. Such an active combat role lies far beyond the typical tasks of modern-day PMCs like Blackwater or DynCorp.

7 February 2018 marked the bloodiest day of Wagner's campaign in Syria. Around 500 pro-Syrian fighters attacked US-backed Kurdish troops near the town Khasham in the Deir al-Zour Governorate.[1517] The attackers had communicated with each other via radio before the battle. The radio chatter picked up by US surveillance was in Russian and many of the pro-Syrian fighters turned out to be Wagner contractors.[1518] The reasons for starting the battle remain clouded in mystery and I will come back to this incident when talking about Wagner's ties to the Kremlin. In any case, the fight raged on for hours. The Kurdish units returned fire and finally called in American airstrikes which promptly arrived.[1519] The New York Times described what happened next:

"The artillery barrage was so intense that the American commandos dived into foxholes for protection, emerging covered in flying dirt and debris to fire back at a column of tanks advancing under the heavy shelling. It was the opening salvo in a nearly four-hour assault in February by around 500 pro-Syrian government forces — including Russian mercenaries — that threatened to inflame already-simmering tensions between Washington and Moscow."[1520]

The US bombardment annihilated the Wagner contingent which – unlike at Palmyra – did not receive Russian air support. It is difficult to name the exact number of casualties. Estimates range from a handful to several hundred deaths. The New York Times spoke of "dozens" of dead contractors.[1521] Others sources speak of over 80 or 100 dead and

---

1517 Kimberly Marten, 'The Puzzle of Russian Behaviour in Deir Al-Zour' (*War on the Rocks*, 5 July 2018) <https://warontherocks.com/2018/07/the-puzzle-of-russian-behavior-in-deir-al-zour/>.

1518 Thomas Gibbons-Neff, 'How a 4-Hour Battle Between Russian Mercenaries and U.S. Commandos Unfolded in Syria' (The New York Times, 24 May 2018) <https://www.nytimes.com/2018/05/24/world/middleeast/american-commandos-russian-mercenaries-syria.html>.

1519 Marten (n 1517).

1520 Thomas Gibbons-Neff, 'How a 4-Hour Battle Between Russian Mercenaries and U.S. Commandos Unfolded in Syria' (The New York Times, 24 May 2018) <https://www.nytimes.com/2018/05/24/world/middleeast/american-commandos-russian-mercenaries-syria.html>.

1521 Ivan Nechepurenko, Neil Mac Farquhar and Thomas Gibbons-Neff, ' Dozens of Russians Are Believed Killed in U.S.-Backed Syria Attack' (The New York

many more wounded.[1522] Moscow denied any involvement and argued the numbers were exaggerated and "a classic case of misinformation."[1523] It merely admitted the deaths of five Russian citizens who were there in their private capacity,[1524] whereas most observers regard this as a drastic understatement.[1525] The full-scale battle not only sparked new tensions between the US and Russia, but also highlighted the active combat role of Wagner.

Today, Wagner is believed to employ around 5 000 fighters worldwide.[1526] Most recently, the media reported on Wagner's presence in Libya. In September 2019, more than 100 Wagner fighters assisted Khalifa Haftar in his assault on Tripoli, the capital of the UN-backed government.[1527] Haftar opposes the UN-backed administration and has long been supported by Russia.[1528] In the course of the attack, between 10 and 35 Wagner contractors were killed.[1529] Wagner personnel were also spotted in the Central African Republic and Belarus.[1530]

Times, 13 February 2018) <https://www.nytimes.com/2018/02/13/world/europe/russia-syria-dead.html?module=inline>.

1522   Maria Tsvetkova, 'Russian Toll in Syria Battle was 300 Killed and Wounded' (Reuters, 15 February 2018) <https://www.reuters.com/article/us-mideast-crisis-syria-russia-casualtie/russian-toll-in-syria-battle-was-300-killed-and-wounded-sources-idUSKCN1FZ2DZ>; Neil Hauer, 'Russia's Mercenary Debacle in Syria' (Foreign Affairs, 26 February 2018) <https://www.foreignaffairs.com/articles/syria/2018-02-26/russias-mercenary-debacle-syria>.

1523   Ministry of Foreign Affairs of the Russian Federation, Briefing by Foreign Ministry Spokesperson Maria Zakharova, (15 February 2018) <https://www.mid.ru/en/foreign_policy/news/-/asset_publisher/cKNonkJE02Bw/content/id/3077521#11>.

1524   ibid.

1525   Marten (n 1517).

1526   Neil Hauer, 'The Rise and Fall of a Russian Mercenary Army' (Foreign Policy, 6 October 2019) <https://foreignpolicy.com/2019/10/06/rise-fall-russian-private-army-wagner-syrian-civil-war/>.

1527   Samer Al-Atrush and Stepan Kravchenko, 'Putin-Linked Mercenaries Are Fighting on Libya's Front Lines' (Bloomberg, 25 September 2019) <https://www.bloomberg.com/news/articles/2019-09-25/-putin-s-chef-deploys-mercenaries-to-libya-in-latest-adventure>.

1528   Marten (n 1488) 182.

1529   'Dozens of Russian Mercenaries Killed in Libya' (The Moscow Times, 3 October 2019) <https://www.themoscowtimes.com/2019/10/03/dozens-of-russian-mercenaries-killed-in-libya-meduza-a67569>.

1530   'A Private Army for the President: The Tale of Evgeny Prigozhin's Most Delicate Mission' (The Bell, 31 January 2019) <https://thebell.io/en/a-private-army-for-the-president-the-tale-of-evgeny-prigozhin-s-most-delicate-mission/>; 'Belarus

This shows that Wagner – and previously Slavonic Corpus – are not restricted to guarding strategic persons, objects, and maintaining equipment in war zones. The above accounts – based on the painstaking work of investigative journalists and renowned analysts – paint a clear picture. These PMCs assume an active fighting role. The military analyst Christopher Spearin argues that it is precisely the "offensive character of their operations" that makes these companies special.[1531] Most PMCs have shifted away from providing active combat services since the scandals concerning the companies Sandline and Executive Outcomes in the 90s.[1532] Wagner's contractors, however, fight alongside Russian allies in Syria, Libya, and Ukraine. At times, they even fight side by side with regular Russian servicemen, for example when Russian fighter jets provided air-support during the battle of Palmyra, or in Ukraine where both Russian soldiers and Wagner contractors participated in the battle of Debaltseve.[1533] Hence, security analyst Kimberly Marten calls them "reliable providers of contract violence abroad" who at times work "directly alongside regular Russian military forces."[1534]

We now know *how* Wagner and Slavonic Corpus fight. But *why* and *for whom* do they fight? In my introduction I have already mentioned that these companies serve the interest of the Kremlin. While this is true in general terms, the full truth is more nuanced. To understand it, we must look at the second and third characteristic of Russia's shadow PMCs: The issue of under-regulation; and their loose and deniable ties to the Kremlin.

1.3.2 Under-regulation

The second and arguably most striking characteristic of PMCs like Wagner is their under-regulation. They represent a living paradox: While they are illegal under Russian domestic law, their business is thriving.

Russian legislation bans companies from providing active combat services. Art 13(5) of the Constitution forbids the creation of "armed forma-

---

Accuses 'Russian mercenaries' of Election Plot' (BBC, 31 July 2020) <https://www.bbc.com/news/world-europe-53592854>.

1531 Spearin, 'NATO, Russia and Private Military and Security Companies' (n 1489) 66.

1532 See above at n 1465 and Tonkin (n 1447) 17.

1533 For the participation of Russian on-duty soldiers in eastern Ukraine see above at pp 256 et seq.

1534 Marten (n 1488) 183.

tions" that would undermine the monopoly of force of the Russian State. It applies to any organisation that pursues political or other aims by means of a militarised character and has a very wide scope.[1535] Art 13(5) thus applies to PMCs like Wagner, and the Russian Cabinet of Ministers voiced its concern that a legalisation of such companies may violate the Constitution.[1536]

The Russian Criminal Code speaks in even more concrete terms. Art 359 CCRF criminalises the recruitment of "mercenaries" as well as their participation in an armed conflict [*Наемничество*]. The article also provides the following definition of a mercenary:

> *"A mercenary is considered a person who acts for the purpose of getting a material reward, and who is not a citizen of the State in whose armed conflict or hostilities he or she participates, who does not permanently reside on its territory, and also who is not a person fulfilling official duties."*

The definition is modelled after Art 47 AP I, although it is a bit broader in some respect.[1537] Unlike in international law, where Art 47 AP I has remained a largely dead provision due to its narrow scope, Russian courts did not hesitate to apply Art 359 CCRF. The Russian Supreme Court confirmed that the activities of Slavonic Corpus fulfilled the definition of mercenarism under Art 359 CCRF.[1538] There is no doubt that the same would be true for Wagner, a Slavonic Corpus spin-off whose operations go far beyond the scope of its predecessor. In this sense, Maria Zabolotskaya, a spokesperson from the Russian Ministry of Foreign Affairs, was absolutely

---

1535 В.Д. Зоркин [V.D. Zorkin] (n 794) 146.

1536 'Kremlin Blocks the Bill Legalizing Russian Private Military Companies' (Uawire, 28 March 2018) <https://uawire.org/russia-will-not-legalize-mercen aries>.

1537 See А.В. Наумов [A.V. Naumov], *Комментарий к уголовному кодексу Российской Федерации [Commentary to the Criminal Code of the Russian Federation]* (2nd edn, Юрист 1996) 805; Н.Ф. Кузнецовой [N.F. Kuznetsovoy] (n 867) 789. For example, the Russian definition does not include the aspect of Art 47(2)(a) AP I, which requires that the mercenary "is specially recruited locally or abroad in order to fight in an armed conflict."

1538 'Славянский корпус вербовал боевиков для исламистов [Slavic Corpus Recruited Fighters for Islamists]' (Kommersant, 15 January 2015) <https://www.ko mmersant.ru/doc/2645963>.

correct when she declared at an ICRC meeting (2016): "Under Russian law, it is not possible to set up a PMC or use one abroad."[1539]

This prohibition *on paper* has prevented any attempt to regulate the activities of PMCs *in reality*. Where can they operate? Whom can they hire? How should they conduct their business? How transparent should they be?[1540] These questions remain unanswered. The under-regulation is even more striking, because Russia chose to impose strict rules on private security companies providing services of a non-military kind, e.g. watchmen guarding premises or private detectives. Following the boom of private security firms in the 1990s, the State Duma passed, for example, the 'Law on Private Detective and Guarding Activities in the Russian Federation.' This legislation, however, neither covers the use of military force nor missions outside the Russian Federation.[1541]

There have been numerous attempts to regulate PMCs, but all of them stalled.[1542] The latest attempt in 2018 to elaborate a comprehensive law on PMCs was stalled by the Russian government that did not support the draft.[1543] There are different, sometimes contradictory explanations for this. Some claim that the FSB[1544] objects to a regulation of companies like Wagner.[1545] Others argue that Army and more specifically the GRU are not willing to tolerate a rival in military affairs.[1546] Certainly, the lack of regulation has a decisive advantage for Moscow: It comes in handy to point to the illegality of PMCs when confronted with allegations of

---

1539 ICRC, 'Russian Federation: Regulating Private Military and Security Companies' <https://www.icrc.org/en/document/russian-federation-regulating-private-military-security-companies>.

1540 Wagner and Slavonic Corpus are not officially registered in Russia. Slavonic Corpus was registered in Hong Kong, Wagner is not registered anywhere at all. Yet, both mainly operate(d) from Russia, see Marten (n 1488) 192; Østensen and Bukkvoll (n 1472) 25.

1541 See Art 1.1 and 16 of the Федеральный закон, 11.03.1992, N 2487–1 'О частной детективной и охранной деятельности в Российской Федерации' [Federal Law, 11 March 1992, No 2487–1 'On Private Detective and Guarding Activities in the Russian Federation'].

1542 Østensen and Bukkvoll (n 1472) 28–29.

1543 'Правительство РФ не поддержало законопроект о частных военных компаниях [The Government of the RF Does Not Support the Draft Law on Private Military Companies]' (Interfax, 27 March 2018) <https://www.interfax.ru/russia/605539>.

1544 FSB stands for *Федеральная служба безопасности* [Federal Security Service]. The FSB is the main internal intelligence service in Russia.

1545 Østensen and Bukkvoll (n 1472) 32–33.

1546 ibid 32.

their use abroad. In other words, what *should* not exist, *does* not exist. Furthermore, the lack of regulation makes it more difficult to pinpoint a concrete violation. How can these companies break any rules if there are none? The following statement by President Putin on Wagner during his yearly press conference (2018) illustrates this well:

> *"Everything must stay within the legal framework [...]. If Wagner violates the law the General Prosecutor's Office should deal with that. As far as their presence abroad is concerned – if they do not violate Russian laws they may work and pursue their business interests in every corner of the world."*[1547]

The absence of legal regulation appears especially stark in comparison with other countries. All big players in the PMC business – e.g. the US, the UK, and South Africa – have detailed legislation on military service providers. Even China has regulated PMCs.[1548] It is surprising that Russia – usually a State with a tight grip over its highly professionalised militaries – continues to tolerate unregistered and loosely controlled PMCs operating from its territory.[1549]

The lack of regulation does not only concern national law. Moscow also dodges international efforts to regulate PMCs. In 2008, a Swiss initiative brought together 17 of the most relevant States to elaborate rules on military and security companies. The States signed the so-called Montreux Document. It contains a non-binding collection of existing obligations, recommendations, and best practice regarding private military and security companies.[1550] Russia participated in the discussion, but refused to endorse the document.[1551] After almost three years of preparation, the Russian representative argued "somewhat apologetically" that the document contravened Russian legislation which prohibited the provision of private military services.[1552] Up to this date, Russia has not changed its mind. This is striking, because virtually *all* influential actors on the world scene

---

1547 'Путин прокомментировал деятельность ЧВК Вагнер [Putin Commented on the Activities of the PMC Wagner]' (Ria Novosti, 20 December 2018) <https://ria.ru/20181220/1548329637.html?in=t>.

1548 Marten (n 1488) 185.

1549 ibid 198.

1550 Schweizerische Eidgenossenschaft/ICRC (n 1455).

1551 James Cockayne, 'Regulating Private Military and Security Companies: The Content, Negotiation, Weaknesses and Promise of the Montreux Document' (2008) 13 Journal of Conflict and Security Law 401, 425.

1552 See ibid, where the author suggests that Russia's refusal might be linked to the outbreak of the Russo-Georgian War.

have joined the Montreux initiative. Certain key players in the industry like the US, the UK, France, China, South Africa, Afghanistan, Iraq, and Canada were among the original signatories. Others like Italy, Spain, and the Netherlands acceded later on. Today, 56 States support the Montreux Document.[1553] Russia is the only P5 State that has not embraced the initiative. Security analyst Kimberly Marten finds this very surprising:

> *"From a constructivist theoretical political science perspective, legalization should have been a preference for the status-conscious Russian state. The actions of other permanent members of the UNSC in signing the Montreux Document demonstrate that legalization is an appropriate action for powerful states to take. Legalization would therefore help emphasize that Russia is a member of the great-power club. [...] Moscow's long-standing decision not to legalize PMCs remains a puzzle from the perspective of state interests."[1554]*

Despite that, Russia's position remains firm. In 2016, Sergey Belokon from the General Staff of the Russian armed forces deemed a national law "premature." Russia should rather participate in negotiating a binding international treaty and only then enact national legislation in line with it.[1555] In the absence of any process, let alone momentum for such a treaty, Russian PMCs will remain unregulated for a long time.

1.3.3 Denial & deniability

PMCs like Wagner carry out highly delicate combat missions and they operate in a legal vacuum. But for *whom* do they fight? In all countries where Wagner and Slavonic Corpus have boots on the ground, strategic Russian interests are at stake. An operation in eastern Ukraine or government-controlled Syria, for example, would be impossible without the consent of the Kremlin. However, Russia does not comment on the combat-like character of these PMCs. It prefers blame-shifting and denies any affiliation

---

1553 Swiss Federal Department of Foreign Affairs, 'Participating States of the Montreux Document' <https://www.eda.admin.ch/eda/en/home/foreign-policy/international-law/international-humanitarian-law/private-military-security-companies/participating-states.html>.

1554 Marten (n 1488) 187.

1555 ICRC, 'Russian Federation: Regulating Private Military and Security Companies' <https://www.icrc.org/en/document/russian-federation-regulating-private-military-security-companies>.

with these private (illegal) entities.[1556] To Moscow, the contractors are not "Russian servicemen," but merely "citizens" who, for whatever reason, end up in a conflict region.[1557] However, there is sufficiently strong evidence that many of the missions of Wagner and Slavonic Corpus served genuine interests of the Kremlin. In the following, I will present the evidence that leaves no doubt that these companies – at least partially – operate on behalf of Russia. Secondly, I will show how Moscow challenges this truth by stubbornly denying any ties to the companies in question, and by giving them a lot of discretion in the execution of their operations. Some call this approach "plausible deniability,"[1558] others refer to it as "grey-zone approach."[1559]

Journalists and experts have collected proof that PMCs like Slavonic Corpus and Wagner maintain close ties to the Russian State. Korotkov describes how contractors from Slavonic Corpus arrived back in Moscow from their first mission in Syria and were greeted by FSB agents. They questioned the contractors, made them sign a declaration of confidentiality, confiscated their SIM cards, and handed them a ticket home.[1560] While the existence of Slavonic Corpus was short-lived, Wagner still operates and there is ample evidence that its founder Utkin maintains close ties to the Russian leading circles. He was spotted at the "reception for the heroes of the fatherland" hosted by the Kremlin in 2016. Putin's spokesman Dimitry Peskov admitted that Utkin was awarded the *Орден Мужества* [Order of Courage].[1561] The Order is awarded to citizens that have displayed "courageous and decisive actions in fulfilling a military duty."[1562] Other

---

1556 Ministry of Foreign Affairs of the Russian Federation, Briefing by Foreign Ministry Spokesperson Maria Zakharova, (15 February 2018) <https://www.mid.ru/en/foreign_policy/news/-/asset_publisher/cKNonkJE02Bw/content/id/3077521#11>.

1557 ibid.

1558 Marten (n 1488) 187.

1559 Spearin, 'NATO, Russia and Private Military and Security Companies' (n 1489) 68.

1560 Денис Коротков [Denis Korotkov], 'Последний бой "Славянского корпуса" [The Last Fight of the Slavonic Corpus]' (n 1482).

1561 Денис Коротков [Denis Korotkov], 'Расшифровка года – Вагнер [The Decryption of the Year – Wagner]' (n 1511).

1562 See the statute of the Order of Courage, Указ Президента, 07.09.2010, РФ N 1099 'О мерах по совершенствованию государственной наградной системы Российской Федерации' [Decree of the President of the Russian Federation, 7 September 2010, No 1099 'On the Means of Establishing a State Decoration System of the Russian Federation'].

Wagner fighters posthumously received similar medals for their heroic death in battle. Korotkov, for example, has researched the case of Wagner contractors who fell in battles at Debaltseve, Ukraine, and Syria.[1563] In battle, contractors are equipped with modern Russian weapons, vehicles, tanks, and artillery.[1564] The Russian State has covered the medical bills of wounded Wagner fighters.[1565] Finally, material uncovered by the investigative network Bellingcat suggests that the GRU aids Wagner in procuring international passports.[1566]

Another indicator for Wagner's close ties to the Kremlin is the involvement of Yevgeny Prigozhin in the company. Prigozhin has a typical oligarch's biography and made it from rags to riches in the wild 90s. He is known as "Putin's chef" because he owns a restaurant business and has excellent ties to the President.[1567] He is also the man behind Moscow's so-called "troll factory" – a Russian agency that influences public opinion on the internet and was accused of meddling with the 2016 US elections.[1568]

1563 Денис Коротков [Denis Korotkov], 'Они сражались за Пальмиру [They Fought for Palmyra]' (n 1498).

1564 Marten (n 1517).

1565 'Cossack Fighter Laments Russian 'Utilization' of Mercenaries in Syria' (Radio Free Europe/Radio Liberty, 22 February 2018) <https://www.rferl.org/a/syria-ru ssian-mercenaries-cossack-shabayev--interview/29056934.html>.

1566 'Wagner Mercenaries With GRU-issued Passports: Validating SBU's Allegation' (Bellingcat, 30 January 2019) <https://www.bellingcat.com/news/uk-and-europe /2019/01/30/wagner-mercenaries-with-gru-issued-passports-validating-sbus-alleg ation/>.

1567 Putin denied having close ties to Prigozhin in an interview with an Austrian TV station (4 June 2018): "You have just said that Mr Prigozhin is referred to as "Putin's chef". Indeed, he runs a restaurant business, it is his job; he is a restaurant keeper in St Petersburg. But now let me ask you: do you really think that a person who is in the restaurant business, even if this person has some hacking opportunities and owns a private firm engaged in this activity – I do not even know what he does – could use it to sway elections in the United States or a European country? Could it be that the media and political standards in the countries of the consolidated West have been driven down to such a low level that a Russian restaurant keeper can sway voters in a European country or the United States? Isn't it ridiculous?" Available at <http://en.kremli n.ru/events/president/news/57675>.

1568 'Powerful 'Putin's Chef' Prigozhin Cooks Up Murky Deals' (BBC, 4 November 2019) <https://www.bbc.com/news/world-europe-50264747>; Neil Mac-Farquhar, 'Inside the Russian Troll Factory: Zombies and a Breakneck Pace' <https://www.nytimes.com/2018/02/18/world/europe/russia-troll-factory.html>.

Besides that, he was involved in the founding and funding of Wagner.[1569] Kimberly Marten calls him "Wagner's patron."[1570]

For these reasons, there is no doubt that PMCs like Wagner are – at least in part[1571] – a tool of the Russian State. Mark Galeotti calls them "hybrid businesses," because they are technically private, but essentially acting as the arms of the Russian State.[1572] Other observers, such as Christopher Spearin and Nathaniel Reynolds agree with him.[1573] Reynolds argues that "Putin always looms above Prigozhin, presiding over the broader system of control. Wagner cannot exist without Putin's blessing, and Prigozhin probably needs the Kremlin's approval for strategic-level decisions, like where and when Wagner is deployed."[1574] Marten points out that Russia has consciously used Wagner in Ukraine and Syria, because in both contexts deniability was a key factor in the Kremlin's information policy. In Ukraine, Russia denied having boots on the ground at all. In Syria it was important to avoid media reports on Russian casualties in order to maintain public support for the war.[1575]

Despite this evidence, Moscow denies that it uses PMCs as a State tool. It denies the personal connections between PMCs and the Kremlin. Putin calls Prigozhin a "restaurant keeper" and claims not to "even know what he does" on the side.[1576] Moscow also denies that the contractors in war zones act on behalf of the Russian State. Putin's spokesperson Peskov broke it down to the simple formula: "If there are Russian citizens in Syria as volunteers, they have nothing to do with the State"[1577]

1569 'Частная армия для президента: история самого деликатного поручения Евгения Пригожина [A Private Army for the President: the History of the Most Delicate Mission of Yevgeny Prigozhin]' (The Bell, 29 January 2019) <https://th ebell.io/41889-2/>; Денис Коротков [Denis Korotkov] 'Повар любит поострее [The Cook Likes to Spice It up]' (Novaya Gazeta, 22 October 2018) <https://ww w.novayagazeta.ru/articles/2018/10/22/78289-povar-lyubit-poostree>.

1570 Marten (n 1488) 198.

1571 See below at p 320 how Wagner pursues its private business interests.

1572 Mark Galeotti, 'Moscow's Mercenaries in Syria' (*War on the Rocks*, 5 April 2016) <https://warontherocks.com/2016/04/moscows-mercenaries-in-syria/>.

1573 Spearin, 'NATO, Russia and Private Military and Security Companies' (n 1489) 67.

1574 Reynolds (n 1476) 5.

1575 Marten (n 1488) 198.

1576 Vladimir Putin, Interview with ORF (4 June 2018), available at <http://en.krem lin.ru/events/president/news/57675>.

1577 'Kremlin: Russian Private Citizens Fighting for Syria's Assad are Volunteers' (Reuters, 2 August 2017) <https://www.reuters.com/article/us-mideast-crisis-syri

This was also the line of defence adopted by the Russian Ministry of Foreign Affairs after scores of Russian contractors died in the battle of Deir al-Zour, Syria. A spokesperson admitted that "five people, presumably Russian citizens, died in an armed clash", but reiterated that "the issue is *not* about Russian servicemen." She then suggested that all the Wagner fighters were in Syria for personal reasons, with no connection to the Russian State whatsoever:

> *"There are large numbers of citizens in the conflict zones from all regions of the world, including Russia and the CIS countries. They have different reasons for being in these hot spots, including to engage in hostilities. Clearly, people leaving for warzones do not contact government authorities to notify them of their destinations. They make it to the combat zones in various ways, including illegal ones. Tracking them, or checking who does what, or their current status, is highly problematic."*

In 2019, Putin admitted for the first time that Wagner had men in Syria. However, he called Wagner a "private *security* company" [*частная охранная компания*][1578] that only engaged in guarding oil and gas facilities and had no ties to the Russian State.

> *"They are not Russian State actors. And they do not participate in hostilities – unfortunately or should I say fortunately. Of course, we admit that even working in this economic context they risk their lives. This is also a contribution to the fight against terrorism. From whom did they take the oil fields? From ISIS. But the Russian State and the Russian Army is not involved in this. That's why we don't comment on it."[1579]*

Denial also takes another dimension as laws are created that make it more difficult to unearth the truth. In 2018, Putin signed a decree that makes any information about those who cooperate with "intelligence services of the Russian Federation without being their official employees" a state secret.[1580] Andrey Soldatov, a Russian security expert, believes that this law

---

a-russia-casualtie/kremlin-russian-private-citizens-fighting-for-syrias-assad-are-vol unteers-idUSKBN1AI11Z>.

1578   As opposed to a private *military* company [частная *военная* компания] (emphasis added).

1579   'Они там действительно присутствуют: Путин о ЧВК в Сирии [They Are Really Present over There: Putin on PMCs in Syria]' (BBC, 20 June 2019) <https://www.bbc.com/russian/news-48708291>.

1580   Указ Президента Российской Федерации, 03.09.2018, N 506 'О внесении изменений в перечень сведений, отнесенных к государственной тайне' [De-

was tailored to the work of Wagner in countries like Syria and Ukraine. It is supposed to prevent "any question about who is working for the secret services."[1581] Betraying a state secret may entail a prison sentence up to 14 years.[1582]

Having said that, there are instances where PMCs like Wagner do not carry out orders from the Kremlin, but rather pursue their own *private* business interests by means of military force. In a way, this margin of discretion is another effective strategy of obfuscation, because it makes it even harder to identify who is behind a specific operation. In Syria, for example, Wagner was promised 25 percent of the revenues from each oil and gas field it managed to recapture.[1583] An odd public private partnership. Marten argues that Russia uses

> *"nebulous armed organizations that sometimes cooperate with the uniformed military on behalf of clear state interests, but at other times (and sometimes simultaneously) serve the interests of private Russian individuals who are closely connected to Putin's regime."*

Again, the carnage at Deir al-Zour in February 2018 illustrates this well. I have mentioned the incident which allegedly cost the lives of hundreds of Wagner contractors to underline the offensive character of its missions. The battle, however, also displays another characteristic feature of Wagner's *modus operandi*. Up to this day, it is not clear whether the attack was carried out *on behalf* of the Russian State, or because Wagner's patron Prigozhin wanted to push through *his* business interests and secure the nearby gas fields. The build-up before the battle seems to suggest the latter, but Prigozhin may also have become a victim of a payback scheme.

A close consideration of the events will prove instructive. In 2015, Russia and the US divided up the area around Deir al-Zour – rich in oil and gas – into their spheres of influence. However, on 18 February this delicate balance was tipped. Several hundred Wagner contractors attacked

---

cree of the President of the Russian Federation, 3 September 2018, No 506 'On the Introduction of an Amendment Concerning the List of Information Referring to State Secrets'].

1581 Алексей Никольский [Aleksey Nikolskiy] Светлана Бочарова [Svetlana Borcharova] 'Президент засекретил сведения о некадровых разведчиках [The President Classified Information about Non-official Employees of the Secret Service]' (Vedemosti, 4 September 2018) <https://www.vedomosti.ru/politics/articles/2018/09/04/779931-prezident>.

1582 Art 283 of the Russian Criminal Code.

1583 Galeotti, *Russian Political War* (n 1458) 77.

US backed Kurdish fighters that were guarding a natural gas plant in Deir al-Zour.[1584] The Kurds returned fire and called in American air support. In the ensuing battle tens, if not hundreds of Wagner contractors fell.[1585] Leaked US intelligence suggests that the Kremlin was aware of the attack beforehand. Shortly before the battle, Prigozhin had boasted to have secured permission from an unspecified Russian minister to move forward with a "fast and strong" initiative in February.[1586] However, this time the Russian Air Force did not support Wagner unlike in previous battles, e.g. during the 2017 Palmyra offensive.

On the contrary, the Kremlin claims to have been ignorant of the imminent attack. We know this from the communication between the Russian and US command. Before and even during the battle the US command was in direct contact with the Russian military over the so-called "deconfliction line" – a direct phone connection installed to prevent clashes between Russian and US troops in Syria. When the US asked Moscow to stop the attack, the Russian command denied any ties to this operation.[1587] Even after the attack, regular Russian soldiers stationed nearby were reluctant to collect the wounded and dead Russian contractors from the battlefield.[1588] Why did Moscow let down Wagner? To maintain plausible deniability? Or had it really not approved the attack?

Maybe Moscow first approved Prigozhin's attempt to snatch the gas plants but later changed its mind. Kimberly Marten goes even further and suggests that this episode might have been a trap to "send Prigozhin a message."[1589] Shortly before, the oligarch had fallen out of favour which

---

1584 Marten (n 1517).

1585 For casualty numbers see above at n 1514 et seq.

1586 Ellen Nakashima, Karen DeYoung and Liz Sly, 'Putin Ally Said to be in Touch with Kremlin, Assad before His Mercenaries Attacked U.S. Troops' (The Washington Post, 23 February 2018) <https://www.washingtonpost.com/world/natio nal-security/putin-ally-said-to-be-in-touch-with-kremlin-assad-before-his-mercen aries-attacked-us-troops/2018/02/22/f4ef050c-1781-11e8-8b08-027a6ccb38eb_stor y.html>.

1587 Mike Eckel, 'Pentagon Says U.S. Was Told No Russians Involved In Syria Attack' (Radio Free Europe/Radio Liberty, 23 February 2018) <https://www.rfer l.org/a/syria-deir-zor-attack-pentagon-russians-involved/29058555.html>.

1588 'Cossack Fighter Laments Russian 'Utilization' Of Mercenaries In Syria' (Radio Free Europe/Radio Liberty, 22 February 2018) <https://www.rferl.org/a/syria-r ussian-mercenaries-cossack-shabayev--interview/29056934.html>. Only long after the battle had ended the wounded were allegedly repatriated on Russian military planes.

1589 Marten (n 1488) 196.

negatively affected Wagner's cooperation with the Ministry of Defence.[1590] Moscow's message to Prigozhin might have been to "stay away from [the] battlefields" when he was not working for the government, or retribution for previous disputes about money.[1591]

In sum, one can only agree with US Secretary of Defence Jim Mattis that the Russian behaviour at the battle of Deir al-Zour remains "perplexing."[1592] It remains unclear whether Deir al-Zour was "the first direct battle between Washington's and Moscow's forces"[1593] or an ill-planned business enterprise. However, it clearly shows that Wagner pursues private business interests parallel to genuine State interests – or both simultaneously. It also illustrates that the Kremlin grants Wagner considerable discretion in their operations. At the end of the day, however, such PMCs depend on the Kremlin. They run the risk of being abandoned for the sake of deniability.

1.4 Conclusion

Russian PMCs like Wagner operate in a hazy environment. Illegal under domestic law, they should not exist and yet their business thrives. They fulfil delicate combat missions on behalf of the State but sometimes pursue private business interests in parallel. They dangle in a complicated web of dependence and independence. On the one hand, they are not independent private entities like most mainstream PMCs on the international market, but highly dependent on the Kremlin for contracts, arms, and mil-

---

1590 In 2016, there was very close cooperation on all levels: aviation-artillery support, weapons supplies, military hardware, ammunition, and evacuation of the wounded. At some point in 2017, the support suddenly dried up, especially when it came to weapons. See the interview with Denis Korotkov (30 August 2017), available at <https://meduza.io/en/feature/2017/08/30/people-think-it-doesn-t-affect-them-but-it-affects-everyone>.

1591 Marten (n 1488) 196.

1592 Ellen Nakashima, Karen DeYoung and Liz Sly, 'Putin Ally Said to be in Touch with Kremlin, Assad before His Mercenaries Attacked U.S. Troops' (The Washington Post, 23 February 2018) <https://www.washingtonpost.com/world/national-security/putin-ally-said-to-be-in-touch-with-kremlin-assad-before-his-mercenaries-attacked-us-troops/2018/02/22/f4ef050c-1781-11e8-8b08-027a6ccb38eb_story.html>.

1593 'Sponsor of Mercenary Army Boasted of Go Ahead from Moscow for Attack on U.S. Troops in Syria' (The Bell, 23 February 2018) <https://thebell.io/en/sponsor-mercenary-army-boasted-go-ahead-moscow-attack-u-s-troops-syria/>.

itary support. In addition, criminal prosecution for "mercenarism" looms over them like the Sword of Damocles that may be used arbitrarily, but effectively, as illustrated by the case of Slavonic Corpus.[1594] On the other hand, they enjoy significant freedom in their operations as Moscow trades off tight control in favour of plausible deniability. In sum, PMCs like Wagner operate in a world full of contradiction and opaqueness which is best summed up by the words of the man who first reported on them – Denis Korotkov: "They shouldn't exist, but they do."[1595]

We will see what effect this has on IHL below at page 339. First, however, I want to acquaint the reader with two other examples of Russian "apprentices": Cossacks and South Ossetian Militias. Despite considerable differences between these groups they operate in a similarly opaque framework to Wagner.

2. Cossacks – for faith, Tsar and fatherland[1596]

In 2014, sports enthusiasts from around the world flocked to the Olympic Summer Games in Sochi. To their surprise, among the men policing the streets were grim figures in fur hats and a leather whip (*Nagayka*) dangling on their belt. Russia had decided to include Cossack Units to guarantee public order at the international sports event.[1597] On the eve of the Olympic closing ceremony, news from Ukraine reached the Kremlin that Viktor Yanukovych had been ousted. This would trigger a series of events that would lead the Cossacks into their next mission, this time far away from the Olympic glamour of Sochi.

2.1 Historical context – born at the fringes of the Russian Empire

In modern-day Russia, Cossacks are more than just a historical phenomenon. However, if we want to understand Russia's present-day Cossackdom, we must examine its roots. Cossacks emerged in the 16th century

---

1594 Marten (n 1488) 199.
1595 Денис Коротков [Denis Korotkov], 'Они сражались за Пальмиру [They Fought for Palmyra]' (n 1498).
1596 In allusion to a famous saying among Russian soldiers in the 19th century.
1597 Gabriela Baczynska, 'Russian Cossacks Patrol Sochi Olympics' (Reuters, 9 January 2014) <https://www.reuters.com/article/us-olympics-cossacks-idusbrea0811 820140109>.

as "frontier-people" and made up the warrior class of Russia. They were former serfs that had broken their chains. They thus had a reputation of being freedom-loving and indeed enjoyed significant autonomy in their military communities in south-eastern Ukraine and southern Russia. Defending the fringes of Moscow's realm, they became known as ferocious warriors.[1598] Their relationship with the Russian State, however, was always ambiguous. Cossacks served the Empire as much as their own agenda and at times constituted a threat to the Tsar. At times they fought for the Emperor, at times they rebelled.[1599] Overall, however, they remained a useful military elite on which the Tsar could rely to push the Empire's boundaries into the Caucasus, Siberia, and central Asia.[1600] Their successful military campaigns gave them a near-mystical image of invincible and dreadful fighters. Mikhail Lermontov immortalised this lifestyle in his 'Cossack Lullaby' which he wrote in 1838 while exiled in the Caucasus.

"По камням струится Терек,
Плещет мутный вал;
Злой чечен ползет на берег,
Точит свой кинжал;
Но отец твой старый воин,
Закален в бою:
Спи, малютка, будь спокоен,
Баюшки-баю.
Сам узнаешь, будет время,
Бранное житьё;
Смело вденешь ногу в стремя
И возьмёшь ружьё.
Я седельце боевое
Шёлком разошью...
Спи, дитя моё родное,
Баюшки-баю."

"Muddy Terek River splashes
Boulders in the shade;
An Evil Chechen creeps ashore while
Sharpening his blade;
But your father is a warrior,
Battle-hardened, too:
Sleep, my son, and don't you worry,
Bayushki-bayu.
Soon enough there'll be a time to
Learn the soldier's way;
Bravely step into the battle,
Shoot while in the fray.
Your fine horse's saddle cloth
With silken thread I'll sew ...
Sleep, my dear, beloved baby,
Bayushki-bayu."[1601]

1598 van Herpen (n 1386) 143; Østensen and Bukkvoll (n 1472) 16–17.
1599 Encyclopædia Britannica, 'Cossack' <https://www.britannica.com/topic/Cossack>.
1600 Østensen and Bukkvoll (n 1472) 16.
1601 Mikhail Lermontov, 'Cossack Lullaby' (1838), translation (with minor changes) by David Mark Bennett.

Later, the Bolsheviks virtually eradicated many Cossack communities. This was part of the Soviets' social engineering, but it also constituted revenge for the Russian Civil war, where many Cossacks had fought for the "Whites" or in independent Cossack Armies.[1602] During this "decossackisation" hundreds of thousands were killed, starved, or deported.[1603] Despite that, around seven million Russians self-identify as Cossacks today.[1604] In many cases these people will not be biological descendants of the historical Cossacks, but feel affiliated to their values or attracted to their historical legacy. This explains why some call the Cossacks a "re-invented" community.[1605] Rather than ethnic features, the Cossack movement appears to be united under the umbrella of its common values: Orthodox faith, bravery, traditional family values, and patriotism.

2.2 Developments in Russia after 1991 – a Cossack renaissance

In 1991, the Supreme Council of the RSFSR passed a law that recognised the Cossacks as a persecuted people.[1606] One year later, the Russian Federation followed suit.[1607] From then on, their relationship with the State grew increasingly closer. In several decrees and regulations, Yeltsin shaped the Russian policy towards Cossack communities and created a national register for their organisations.[1608] Under Putin, the Cossack movement received a real boost. The mixture of patriotism, orthodox faith, and con-

---

1602 Østensen and Bukkvoll (n 1472) 16.

1603 Robert Gellately, *Lenin, Stalin, and Hitler: The Age of Social Catastrophe* (Alfred A Knopf Incorporated 2007) 70.

1604 Mark Galeotti, 'Living in Cossackworld' (*Jordan Russia Center*, 2 October 2012) <http://jordanrussiacenter.org/news/living-in-cossackworld/#.Xa8IBOgzaUk>.

1605 Galeotti, *Armies of Russia's War in Ukraine* (n 785) 19.

1606 See Art 2 of the Закон РСФСР, 26.04.1991, N 1107–1 'О реабилитации репрессированных народов' [Law of the RSFSR, 26 April 1991, No 1107–1 'On the Rehabilitation of the Repressed Peoples'].

1607 The Supreme Council of the Russian Federation adopted Постановление, 16.06.1992, N 3321–1 'О реабилитации казачества' [Regulation, 16 June 1992, No 3321–1 'On the Rehabilitation of the Cossackdom'].

1608 Указ, 09.08.1995, N 835, 'О государственном реестре казачьих обществ к государственной и иной службе' [Decree, 9 August 1995, No 835 'On the Register of Cossack Communities for State Service and Other Service']; Постановление, 22.04.1994, N 355 'О концепции государственной политики по отношению к казачеству' [Regulation, 22 April 1994, No 355 'On the Conception of a State Policy Concerning the Cossacks'].

servative values appealed to the new President who swore to restore the Russians' pride in their nation and put an end to a period of instability. In a television interview, Putin declared that "the Cossacks are a fascinating part of Russian culture. I don't only mean Cossack dances and songs, but their traditional patriotism [...]. In this sense the Cossacks play a uniquely positive role."[1609] Under Putin the Duma also passed the 'Law on the State Service of Russian Cossacks.'[1610] It stipulated that the former steppe-warriors could organise "military-patriotic education" for Russian conscripts, maintain law and order, and defend State borders.[1611] While the Cossacks were already used for vigilante duties in the 90s, their role in the security sector reached a whole new level and the law granted them privileged access to State service.[1612] Furthermore, there are eleven military Cossack societies [*войсковые казачьи общества*] in Russia, commonly referred to as the "Cossack troops."[1613] They can muster between 300 000 and 500 000 members and cultivate a close relationship to the Kremlin.[1614] Their leaders ("atamans") are often former members of Russian ministries, the army, or the police force, and the Cossack generals are appointed by the President of the Russian Federation.[1615]

It is important to bear in mind that only "registered" Cossacks are eligible for State service.[1616] Thus, the legislation also made certain Cossack organisations more dependent on the Russian State. The "Cossacks' superficial 'self-organisation' is controlled and maintained from the top down, and supported economically and ideologically by the Kremlin."[1617] The various organisations receive funding from both the federal and local

---

1609 Vladimir Putin, press conference (2013) available at <https://www.youtube.com/watch?v=oRQMWs9ezB8>.

1610 Федеральный закон, 05.12.2005, N 154-ФЗ 'О государственной службе российского казачества' [Federal Law, 5 December 2005, N 154-F3 'On the State Service of the Russian Cossacks'].

1611 Art 5 of the Федеральный закон, 05.12.2005, N 154-ФЗ 'О государственной службе российского казачества' [Federal Law, 5 December 2005, N 154-F3 'On the State Service of the Russian Cossacks'].

1612 van Herpen (n 1386) 144–145.

1613 Østensen and Bukkvoll (n 1472) 18.

1614 Jolanta Darczewska, *Putin's Cossacks. Folklore, Business or Politics?* (Center for Eastern Studies 2017) 24–25.

1615 ibid 26–27.

1616 See Art 6 of the Федеральный закон, 05.12.2005, N 154-ФЗ 'О государственной службе российского казачества' [Federal Law, 5 December 2005, N 154-F3 'On the State Service of the Russian Cossacks'].

1617 Darczewska (n 1614) 60.

budgets worth billions of Rubles.[1618] This trend to form an ever-closer relationship also determines Russia's latest 'Strategy for Cossackdom until 2020'[1619] which envisages the systemic integration of the Cossacks into the security and defence systems.[1620]

Given the Cossacks' free-spirited mindset, however, numerous organisations chose not to register but remain "free Cossacks." Many rejected the privilege of State service in favour of independence.[1621] The fact that they cannot be used for law enforcement duty, however, does not mean that they do not engage in paramilitary training. Quite the contrary, as we will see below, many of the Cossack groups that fought in Ukraine, for example, were unregistered. Take the example of the "Cossack National Guard." The group appeared in 2014 and recruited mostly unregistered Don Cossacks, moulding them into an army. They served under the loose command of Nikolai Kozitsyn, ataman of the "Great Don Army" [*Всевеликое войско Донское*].[1622] Kozitsyn is a highly decorated citizen of the Russian Federation. A knight under 28 State orders, he was elevated to the rank of a Cossack general by Vladimir Putin himself.[1623]

2.3 Fighting Russian wars – "Cossacks have no borders"[1624]

Already during the conflict in Transdniestria (1990–1992), Cossack units fought together with separatists and the 14th Russian Army against the

---

1618 ibid 49.

1619 Стратегия развития государственной политики Российской Федерации в отношении российского казачества до 2020 года [Strategy to Develop the State Policy of the Russian Federation in Relation to the Russian Cossackdom until 2020] 15 September 2002, available at <http://kremlin.ru/events/councils/16682>.

1620 Darczewska (n 1614) 64.

1621 Tomáš Baranec, 'Russian Cossacks in the Service of the Kremlin: Recent Developments and Lessons from Ukraine' (2014) 153 Russian Analytical Digest 9, 12.

1622 Александр Шаповалов [Alexandr Shapovalov], 'Казаки занимают Донбасс [Cossacks Seize the Donbas]' (Nezavisimaya Gazeta, 21 May 2014) <http://www.ng.ru/regions/2014-05-21/1_donbass.html>.

1623 Darczewska (n 1614) 21.

1624 This is a quote from an actual Cossack fighter in Ukraine: "'Cossacks have no borders,' said Nikolai Pervakov, the first deputy commander of Russia's Kuban Cossack legion, who is leading their mission to Crimea from his usual base of operations in the southern Russian city of Krasnodar." Quoted from Simon Shuster, 'Armed Cossacks Flock to Crimea to Help Russian Annexation Bid'

central government of Moldova. The Russian Army welcomed them and provided support and arms.[1625] During the Russo-Georgian War, Cossack units fought alongside Ossetian Militias and the Russian Army.[1626] After the South Ossetian Militias, they made up the second largest paramilitary force counting thousands of fighters.[1627] In the following, however, I shall focus on more recent events: The Cossacks played a crucial role in the annexation of Crimea.[1628] They manned checkpoints, guarded the headquarters of the new separatist government, patrolled the streets.[1629] Recruits came from both sides of the border.[1630] Many of them were local Crimean Cossacks, others arrived from neighbouring Cossack districts like Kuban.[1631]

In 2014, when inner turmoil in eastern Ukraine escalated into an armed conflict, the Cossacks jumped on the occasion. Cossack organisations – redolent of the Tsarist "golden age" – had long pushed Moscow to ignore the post-Soviet boundaries and re-establish the Imperial frontiers.[1632] Back then, Ukraine was an integral part of the Russian Empire and the sphere of Cossack influence would extend far beyond Russia's modern border with Ukraine. Around 30 Russian Cossack leaders came out in favour of

---

(Time, 12 March 2014) <https://time.com/22125/ukraine-crimea-cossacks-russia/>.

1625 ECtHR, *Ilaşcu and Others v Moldova and Russia*, No 48787/99, 8 July 2004, para 60.

1626 Human Rights Watch, 'Georgia/Russia: Use of Rocket Systems Can Harm Civilians' (2008) <https://www.hrw.org/news/2008/08/11/georgia/russia-use-rocket-systems-can-harm-civilians>; van Herpen (n 1386) 221.

1627 'Paramilitary: The Cossacks Return' (Strategy Page, 17 September 2010) <https://www.strategypage.com/htmw/htpara/articles/20100917.aspx>; Tom Parfitt, 'Armed Cossacks Pour in to Fight Georgians' (The Guardian, 9 August 2008) <https://www.theguardian.com/world/2008/aug/09/russia.georgia1>.

1628 Cossacks also fought on the Ukrainian side, but neither their numbers nor their contribution were comparable to the Cossacks fighting for LNR and DNR, see Østensen and Bukkvoll (n 1472) 19. In addition, Ukraine does not have a legal framework that is comparable to Russia's institutionalised system of Cossackdom. To most Ukrainians the Cossacks are above all a historical phenomenon.

1629 Simon Shuster, 'Armed Cossacks Flock to Crimea to Help Russian Annexation Bid' (Time, 12 March 2014) <https://time.com/22125/ukraine-crimea-cossacks-russia/>.

1630 ibid.

1631 ibid.

1632 Mark Galeotti, 'The Cossacks: A Cross-Border Complication to Post-Soviet Eurasia' [1995] IBRU Boundary and Security Bulletin 55, 59.

the separatist cause in Donbas.[1633] The ataman of the Great Don Army, Nikolay Kozitsyn, openly stated that its members would come to "the aid of our Cossack brothers" in Donbas.[1634] The newly created Cossack National Guard was quick to stake its territorial claims in eastern Ukraine:

> *"Historically, Lugansk and Donetsk oblast [district] are a part of the Don Army's oblast. Among its population we find around 80 % ethnic Cossacks who have been less affected by "decossackization" than their brothers in other regions. [...] Hence, the rule of ataman Kozitsyn is the only legitimate rule."[1635]*

Throughout the early stages of the war, the Cossacks wielded significant influence in eastern Ukraine. Radio Svoboda called the Cossacks "one of the main forces in the occupation of Donbass."[1636] Their exact numbers and the ratio of "registered" and "non-registered" Cossacks are unknown. It is clear, however, that Cossacks made up a large percentage of the fighters. Their influence was felt in LNR especially, where they formed their own units under the umbrella of Kozitsyn's Cossack National Guard.[1637] Some of LNR's most effective combat units such as Alexey Mozgovoy's notorious Ghost Brigade [*Бригада Призрак*] heavily relied on Cossack recruits.[1638] Mozgovoy even calls himself a hereditary Cossack.[1639] Cossack fighters such as Kasak Babay – the commander of the "Wolves Hundred" – became YouTube celebrities and conveyed an image of brave bearded frontiersmen fighting off the fascist invaders.[1640]

1633 Østensen and Bukkvoll (n 1472) 19.
1634 Information available on the website of the Cossack National Guard <http://xn--80aaaajfjszd7a3b0e.xn--p1ai/istoriya.html>.
1635 ibid.
1636 Як Росія використала донських "козаків" на Донбасі? Ексклюзивне інтерв'ю із учасником руху [How Did Russia Use the Don Cossacks in the Donbas? An Exclusive Interview with a Participant of the Movement] (Radio Svoboda, 24 December 2018) <https://www.radiosvoboda.org/a/donbass-realii/29672334.html>.
1637 Galeotti, *Armies of Russia's War in Ukraine* (n 785) 28; Richard Arnold, 'Whose Cossacks Are They Anyway? A Movement Torn by the Ukraine-Russia Divide' (*Ponars Eurasia*, January 2019) <http://www.ponarseurasia.org/memo/whose-cossacks-are-they-anyway-ukraine-russia-divide>.
1638 Galeotti, *Armies of Russia's War in Ukraine* (n 785) 28.
1639 Екатерина Сергацкова [Yekaterina Sergatskova], 'Очень краткий путеводитель по комбатам сепаратистов [A Short Who's Who of the Separatist Fighters]' (Colta, 16 March 2015) <https://www.colta.ru/articles/society/6649-ochen-kratkiy-putevoditel-po-kombatam-separatistov>.
1640 See <https://www.youtube.com/watch?v=plfDw1GC_hI>.

Later in the war the tide turned, and friends turned into foes. From the very beginning, the Cossacks had considered themselves allies of the separatists rather than subordinates to a central command.[1641] When the war started to fade into a stalemate, the Cossacks proclaimed their own republic within LNR. Nikolai Kozitsyn and Pavel Dryomov claimed to control 80 percent of the Luhansk region, including major towns, strategic roads, and border crossings to Russia.[1642] The free-spirited Cossacks suddenly became a threat to Moscow and other separatist groups.[1643] In a series of internal purges, Cossack units were disarmed and disbanded first in DNR, and later also in LNR.[1644] Aside from the *de facto* authorities of Luhansk and Donetsk, the Russian PMC Wagner played an important role in these operations.[1645] In allusion to Pierre Vergniaud's famous quote before his execution in 1793 – "*la Révolution est comme Saturne. Elle dévore ses propres enfants.*" – Nikolay Mitrokhin has called this process "when secession devours its parents."[1646]

2.4 An official order or the call of duty – who sent in the Cossacks?

It is undisputed that scores of Cossacks fought in wars with Russian involvement, such as in Moldova, Georgia, and especially eastern Ukraine. While a fair share of these fighters were local Cossacks that took up arms in the hope of more influence and recognition, Russian Cossacks – registered and unregistered – helped to bolster their ranks. In Crimea alone, more than 1 000 Cossacks came from across the border.[1647] In Donbas, all Cossacks units heavily relied on fighters from abroad – much more than the other separatist formations.[1648] But just like in the case of Wagner, it is

---

1641 Galeotti, *Armies of Russia's War in Ukraine* (n 785) 28.

1642 Andrew E Kramer, 'Cossacks Face Grim Reprisals From Onetime Allies in eastern Ukraine' (The New York Times, 4 August 2015) <https://www.nytimes.com/2015/08/05/world/europe/cossacks-face-reprisals-as-rebel-groups-clash-in-eastern-ukraine.html>.

1643 ibid.

1644 Nikolay Mitrokhin, 'Diktaturtransfer im Donbass – Staatsbildung in Russlands Volksrepubliken' (2017) 67 Osteuropa 41, 43–45.

1645 Денис Коротков [Denis Korotkov], 'Они сражались за Пальмиру [They Fought for Palmyra]' (n 1498).

1646 Mitrokhin (n 1644) 46.

1647 Igor Rotar, 'The Cossack Factor in Ukrainian War' (Jamestown Foundation 2014) <https://www.refworld.org/docid/53f49aeb4.html>.

1648 Galeotti, *Armies of Russia's War in Ukraine* (n 785) 21.

2. Cossacks – for faith, Tsar and fatherland

difficult to determine for *whom* they fought. Were they just "volunteers" or sent by the Kremlin?

Moscow never denied the presence of Cossacks in Ukraine. To the Kremlin, however, these were merely volunteers. Putin called them "people who listen to the call of their heart and fulfil their duty."[1649] However, things were not so simple. Firstly, there is evidence that *registered* Cossacks fought on Ukrainian battlefields. The Ukrainian intelligence services published a series of pictures portraying registered Cossacks participating in hostilities in Donbas.[1650] The news agency Reuters reported that some of the registered Cossacks guarding the fan zones during the FIFA World Cup 2018 had been fighting in eastern Ukraine.[1651] This establishes at least a financial link with the Kremlin, since registered Cossack organisations receive heavy funding from the State as I have explained above.

Secondly, there is sufficient evidence that *all* Cossack units in Ukraine – registered and unregistered – received support from the Kremlin from the moment they were recruited until the moment when they set foot on the battlefield. The recruitment of Cossack fighters was coordinated by the *военкоматы* [State military commissariats] in Russia.[1652] They were then trained and equipped at bases near Rostov-on-Don and received weapons and gear from the Russian State.[1653] Russian border guards would not stop Cossacks from crossing into Ukraine. In an interview with Time Magazine, a Cossack fighter recalls: "There's an open corridor for the Cossacks. [...]

1649 Б.Е. Немцов [B.E. Nemtsov] (n 781) 27.

1650 'Ukraine Crisis: What the 'Russian Soldier' Photos Say' (BBC, 22 April 2014) <https://web.archive.org/web/20140424025657/http://www.bbc.com/news/world-europe-27104904>; Mat Babiak, 'Insurgents Identified: The Green Men of VKontakte' (Ukrainian Policy, 2014) <https://web.archive.org/web/20140423233203/http://ukrainianpolicy.com/insurgents-identified-the-green-men-of-vkontakte/>.

1651 Maria Tsvetkova, 'Militias Guarding World Cup Have Links to Kremlin's Foreign Wars' (Reuters, 13 June 2018) <https://www.reuters.com/article/us-soccer-worldcup-russia-cossacks/militias-guarding-world-cup-have-links-to-kremlins-foreign-wars-idUSKBN1J928P>.

1652 The military commissariats are an administrative authority in Russia in charge of conscription, mobilisation, and managing the financial resources of the military.

1653 Б.Е. Немцов [B.E. Nemtsov] (n 781) 26. See also Як Росія використала донських "казаків" на Донбасі? Ексклюзивне інтерв'ю із учасником руху [How Did Russia Use the Don Cossacks in the Donbas? An Exclusive Interview with a Participant of the Movement] (Radio Svoboda, 24 December 2018) <https://www.radiosvoboda.org/a/donbass-realii/29672334.html>.

They didn't even stamp my passport."[1654] Finally, once in Ukraine, the Kremlin would help to coordinate their military efforts.[1655] Against this background, Boris Nemtsov concluded in his report on the war in eastern Ukraine:

> *"The collected evidence confirms that a considerable part of the Russian fighters in Donbas was sent into Ukraine in an organized fashion. They underwent relevant training and preparation, were provided material, and even 'volunteers' received a monetary compensation for their participation in hostilities.*[1656]

Given this evidence, there is no doubt that Moscow has been providing material support to the Cossacks that fought in Ukraine. However, there is no proof that Russia issued an order to *send* the Cossacks into Donbas. While this may represent a probable scenario, the Kremlin successfully maintained its deniability. The example of the Wolves Hundred [*Волчьей сотни*], an unregistered Cossack group that fought in eastern Ukraine, illustrates this grey area approach: The group had ties to the Kremlin, but at the same time maintained a large degree of autonomy. Time Magazine journalist Simon Shuster concludes that its links to Moscow are "just tenuous enough for Putin to deny having sent them, and these fighters in turn deny being paid, equipped or deployed by the Kremlin."[1657] Others called the Wolves Hundred "Russian citizens fighting in eastern Ukraine for the Kremlin's interests, even though without any evincible link to the Russian State."[1658] This is especially true for *un*registered Cossack units that cannot be traced back to the State. Jolanta Darczewska, author of a recent book on the Cossacks' role in Russia, writes:

1654 Simon Shuster, 'Meet the Cossack 'Wolves' Doing Russia's Dirty Work in Ukraine' (Time, 12 May 2014) <https://time.com/95898/wolves-hundred-ukraine-russia-cossack/>.

1655 Mark Galeotti suggested that this was done by the GRU from their headquarters in Rostov-on-Don, see Mark Galeotti, *Hybrid War or Gibridnaya Voina? – Getting Russia's Non-Linear Military Challenge Right* (lulu 2016) 59.

1656 Б.Е. Немцов [B.E. Nemtsov] (n 781) 27.

1657 Simon Shuster, 'Meet the Cossack 'Wolves' Doing Russia's Dirty Work in Ukraine' (Time, 12 May 2014) <https://time.com/95898/wolves-hundred-ukraine-russia-cossack/>.

1658 Baranec (n 1621) 11.

"Unregistered Cossack organisations are more useful when fulfilling the role of 'Russian fifth columns', as they can camouflage their ties with the Russian state more effectively."[1659]

Hence, Moscow would not have to give a "formal order" to deploy the Cossacks. By funding and strengthening Cossack organisations at home, it has revived a movement that takes pride in warfare. All it had to do, was open the borders and provide military training and material support.[1660]

The developments in DNR and LNR show that Moscow initially left the Cossacks with a lot of freedom. Cossack organisations clearly voiced their territorial ambitions in eastern Ukraine and wanted to reclaim what they believed to be their hereditary lands. Only when the Cossacks' call for an independent State became too loud, did Russia decide to disband their units.[1661] Simon Shuster describes this system of deniability with a hint of grudging respect:

"All of this points to the complicity, if not also the direct orders, of various branches of the Russian government [...] from Russian border guards all the way up to the Kremlin Council for Cossack Affairs. But it would be difficult to prove that the Russian government explicitly sent these fighters to wage a war in eastern Ukraine."[1662]

In this sense, Russia has developed an admirable model of deniability. The Cossacks represent a disciplined paramilitary group with its own incentive to wage war in Moscow's backyard – even without clear orders from the Kremlin.[1663]

1659 Darczewska (n 1614) 22.
1660 Time Magazine quotes a fighter who confirms that the Cossacks were allowed to pass the border uninhibited: "There's an open corridor for the Cossacks, for the Wolves," says Mozhaev. "They didn't even stamp my passport." Quoted from Simon Shuster, 'Meet the Cossack 'Wolves' Doing Russia's Dirty Work in Ukraine' (Time, 12 May 2014) <https://time.com/95898/wolves-hundred-ukrai ne-russia-cossack/>; see also Andrew E Kramer, 'Russians Find Few Barriers to Joining Ukraine Battle' (The New York Times, 9 June 2014) <https://www.nyti mes.com/2014/06/10/world/europe/russians-yearning-to-join-ukraine-battle-find -lots-of-helping-hands.html>.
1661 Mitrokhin (n 1644) 44, 55.
1662 Simon Shuster, 'Meet the Cossack 'Wolves' Doing Russia's Dirty Work in Ukraine' (Time, 12 May 2014) <https://time.com/95898/wolves-hundred-ukrain e-russia-cossack/>.
1663 Baranec (n 1621) 12.

3. South Ossetian Militias – experts for "dirty work"

Militias are my third example for Russia's outsourcing of warfare. More precisely, I will focus on the South Ossetian Militias during the Russo-Georgian War (2008). The term "militia" describes a military force that is not composed of professional soldiers, but of regular citizens with military training.[1664] They can be integrated into the armed forces of a State, such as in Switzerland. In other cases, they remain a separate force. Using militias does not contradict IHL *per se*. On the contrary, according to Art 4(A)(2) GC III militia members may even qualify as prisoners of war.[1665]

During the 2008 War, militias represented the bulk of the armed forces of South Ossetia. As South Ossetia did not have a regular army, most able-bodied men took up arms. Fighters were often referred to as militiamen [ополченцы] unless they could be directly attributed to the police or the Ministry of Interior.[1666] According to their own information, these militias numbered around 3500 men.[1667] This may not seem much at first glance. However, with a total population of 50 000, this means that nearly 15 percent of all South Ossetian males fought as militiamen.

I have chosen to present the example of the South Ossetian Militias (SOM) for two reasons. Firstly, their ties to Russia are well explored thanks to several international reports.[1668] Secondly, they have acquired a gruesome reputation for IHL violations. This makes the issue of attribution of their actions to Russia more than a mere hypothetical. When the

---

1664 Julia Gebhard, 'Militias', *Max Planck Encyclopedia of Public International Law* (Oxford University Press 2010) para 1.

1665 In order to benefit from POW status, militias need to "belong" to a conflict Party and fulfil the following four criteria: a) being commanded by a person responsible for his subordinates; b) having a fixed distinctive sign recognizable at a distance; c) carrying arms openly; d) conducting their operations in accordance with the laws and customs of war. Especially the latter is not the case for the SOM, since they acquired a gruesome reputation for systematic IHL violations.

1666 Human Rights Watch, 'Up in Flames – Humanitarian Law Violations and Civilian Victims in the Conflict over South Ossetia' (n 1180) 127.

1667 IIFFMCG, 'Report of the Independent International Fact-Finding Mission on the Conflict in Georgia (Tagliavini Report) Volume III – Views of the Sides on the Conflict, Chronologies and Responses to Questionnaires' (n 960) 520.

1668 See notably IIFFMCG, 'Report of the Independent International Fact-Finding Mission on the Conflict in Georgia (Tagliavini Report) Volume I' (n 1087); Human Rights Watch, 'Up in Flames – Humanitarian Law Violations and Civilian Victims in the Conflict over South Ossetia' (n 1180).

SOM stand accused of the "worst ethnic cleansing" in Europe since the Balkan Wars, this raises the delicate question of whether Russia incurred responsibility for their IHL violations.[1669]

3.1 The Russo-Georgian War – Georgia up in flames

Officially, the Russo-Georgian War only lasted from 7 to 12 August 2008 and was consequently nicknamed the 5-day war. Large-scale hostilities started on 7 August, just before midnight. Georgia launched an attack to retake the renegade province South Ossetia. Russia came to South Ossetia's aid and retaliated using its ground and air forces as well as the Black Sea Fleet.[1670] The Georgian military was no match for the combined power of Russian and Ossetian forces. Tbilisi encountered fierce resistance and was forced to withdraw from South Ossetia altogether on 10 August. The Russian forces then pushed on into territory that was undisputedly beyond the administrative boundaries of South Ossetia to create a so-called "buffer zone". They occupied a number of towns including Gori – the birthplace of Stalin and a city of strategic importance at the crossing of two major highways.[1671] Following the trail of the Russian Army, South Ossetian militiamen surged into the buffer zone. Heavy fighting ended on 12 August 2008 when Moscow and Tbilisi agreed on a ceasefire plan initiated by Nicolas Sarkozy.

However, the ceasefire failed to put an end to violence. Russian and Ossetian forces continued to advance into Georgia for several days.[1672] Both in South Ossetia and the buffer zone, ethnic Georgians found themselves at the mercy of the SOM that had followed the advancing Russian Army. Militiamen entered villages with covered license plates and started to kill, burn, and loot.[1673] Violence continued for weeks. Only in October 2008, the Russian and Ossetian troops withdrew to the positions they held at

---

1669 Luke Harding, 'Russia's Cruel Intention' (The Guardian, 1 September 2008) <https://www.theguardian.com/commentisfree/2008/sep/01/russia.georgia>.

1670 IIFFMCG, 'Report of the Independent International Fact-Finding Mission on the Conflict in Georgia (Tagliavini Report) Volume II' (n 1109) 209.

1671 ibid 211.

1672 IIFFMCG, 'Report of the Independent International Fact-Finding Mission on the Conflict in Georgia (Tagliavini Report) Volume I' (n 1087) 22.

1673 van Herpen (n 1386) 229.

the outbreak of hostilities.[1674] Human Rights Watch collected numerous eyewitness accounts and described the abuses by the SOM in its report:

> *"South Ossetian forces and militias embarked on a campaign of deliberate and systematic destruction of the Tbilisi-backed villages in South Ossetia, which involved the widespread and systematic pillage and torching of houses, and beatings and threats against civilians. In undisputed parts of Georgian territory, they conducted a campaign of deliberate violence against civilians, burning and looting their homes, and committing execution-style killings, rape, abductions, and countless beatings."[1675]*

Thus, the SOM earned a brutal reputation. Guardian journalist Luke Harding called their crimes "the worst ethnic cleansing since the war in former Yugoslavia [...] to create a mono-ethnic greater South Ossetia in which Georgians no longer exist."[1676] The Tagliavini Report confirmed these gruesome details. It accused the South Ossetian forces of "summary executions,"[1677] "ill-treatment and torture,"[1678] "arbitrary arrests, abduction and taking of hostages,"[1679] and a "systematic and widespread campaign of looting [...] against mostly ethnic Georgians."[1680]

3.2 Russia's control over the SOM – equal allies?

I have described Russia's influence on South Ossetia as a State-like structure at page 232 when dealing with occupation by proxy. The question in *this* section is related, but slightly narrower: To what degree did Russia exercise control over the militias during and directly after the Russo-Georgian War?

1674 Nußberger, 'South Ossetia' (n 1079) para 26.
1675 Human Rights Watch, 'Up in Flames – Humanitarian Law Violations and Civilian Victims in the Conflict over South Ossetia' (n 1180) 127.
1676 Luke Harding, 'Russia's Cruel Intention' (The Guardian, 1 September 2008) <https://www.theguardian.com/commentisfree/2008/sep/01/russia.georgia>.
1677 IIFFMCG, 'Report of the Independent International Fact-Finding Mission on the Conflict in Georgia (Tagliavini Report) Volume II' (n 1109) 355.
1678 ibid 359, 361.
1679 ibid 362.
1680 ibid 365.

South Ossetia highly depends on Russia. Prior to the conflict, Russia had trained and equipped the SOM.[1681] Furthermore, Moscow enabled a flow of volunteers through the Roki Tunnel and over the Caucasus range, bolstering their ranks.[1682] When the war broke out, Russian troops fought on the same side as the Ossetian Militias. Human Rights Watch suggests that their operations must have been coordinated, because the Ossetian Militias always arrived shortly after the Russian soldiers had moved through a village. In other cases, Russian soldiers even seemed to provide them with cover.[1683] This points to a "close cooperation" between the SOM and the Russian Army.[1684] The Tagliavini Report hints at the fact that Russia had considerable control over the SOM, much more than for example over the Abkhaz units.[1685] The report also suggests that Russian soldiers at least tolerated some violations related to ethnic cleansing. In certain cases, Russian personnel were present on the scene,[1686] or failed to prevent the violations of IHL.[1687]

During the proceedings of the Tagliavini Report, Moscow readily admitted that it fought alongside the South Ossetians, but it denied having any sort of control over them. When asked about the "formal and informal relationship" between the Russian military and South Ossetian forces it replied that *prior* to the war one could only speak of "cooperation" between Russia and the SOM. Moscow admitted that *during* the war there

---

1681 IIFFMCG, 'Report of the Independent International Fact-Finding Mission on the Conflict in Georgia (Tagliavini Report) Volume I' (n 1087) 20.

1682 ibid.

1683 Human Rights Watch, 'Up in Flames – Humanitarian Law Violations and Civilian Victims in the Conflict over South Ossetia' (n 1180) 9.

1684 ibid 128.

1685 IIFFMCG, 'Report of the Independent International Fact-Finding Mission on the Conflict in Georgia (Tagliavini Report) Volume II' (n 1109) 132, 304. The report claims that in "factual terms, one may have to draw a distinction with regard to the nature of the relationship between Russia and South Ossetia on the one hand, and between Russia and Abkhazia on the other. In the former, ties seem to be stronger. During the meeting between the IIFFMCG experts and the representatives of the Ministry of Internal Affairs of Georgia, the representatives stressed the political and economic links between Russia and South Ossetia. They also claimed that Russia exercises control over South Ossetia through various channels ranging from financial help to the presence of Russian officials in key military positions in the South Ossetian forces."

1686 See ibid 361 with regards to the ill-treatment of combatants.

1687 See ibid 365 with regards to looting.

was a "certain degree of interaction" between the two. Yet, it "came about as we understand in an ad-hoc fashion as the conflict evolved."[1688]

When confronted with the IHL violations (committed by the SOM) Russia clarified that

> *"Russia exercises control over the Armed Forces of the Russian Federation only. Russia exercises no degree of control (effective or actual) over South Ossetian military personnel, civilians or territory."*[1689]

South Ossetia categorically refused to answer any question about the relationship of its troops with Russia.[1690] It merely commented on the command structure:

> *"The Armed Forces of the South Ossetian Republic never conducted any joint military operations with [...] the Armed Forces of the Russian Federation and acted in accordance with instructions issued by their own command. It goes without saying that the need to organise a coordinated response against a common enemy was a factor and actions taken by selected units in carrying out specific missions regardless of their chain of command did not run contrary to those undertaken by other units."*[1691]

In short, South Ossetia's position on the issue resembles the Russian stance: Coordination yes; but no joint operations, and no Russian command. The latest institution to scrutinize Russia's control over the operations of the SOM was the ECtHR in *Georgia v Russia* (2021). It is telling that the Court skirted the issue and stated that it is not "necessary to provide proof of detailed control of each of those actions" for the purpose of its judgment.[1692]

1688 IIFFMCG, 'Report of the Independent International Fact-Finding Mission on the Conflict in Georgia (Tagliavini Report) Volume III – Views of the Sides on the Conflict, Chronologies and Responses to Questionnaires' (n 960) 433–434.

1689 ibid 440.

1690 Thus, the third volume of the Tagliavini Report only reproduces the questions, no answers see IIFFMCG, 'Report of the Independent International Fact-Finding Mission on the Conflict in Georgia (Tagliavini Report) Volume II' (n 1109) 525–526.

1691 IIFFMCG, 'Report of the Independent International Fact-Finding Mission on the Conflict in Georgia (Tagliavini Report) Volume III – Views of the Sides on the Conflict, Chronologies and Responses to Questionnaires' (n 960) 520.

1692 ECtHR, *Georgia v Russia*, No 38263/08, 21 January 2021, para 214. The Court argued that Russia could be held responsible for the ethnic violence, but it did not explain whether this was because the actions of the SOM were *attributable*

Of course, Russia and South Ossetia have a genuine interest in down-playing their relations. The evidence collected by Human Rights Watch and the Tagliavini Commission suggest that Moscow's influence over the SOM was considerable. However, apart from the rare cases where Russian personnel were present on the scene of the crimes, it appears to remain below the threshold of direct Russian command or genuine joint operations. Just like in the case of Wagner and the Cossacks, Moscow's loose coordination sufficed, because the SOM had its own incentive to join the fight.

4. The effects of outsourcing – flying below the radar of international law

PMCs like Wagner, Cossacks, and South Ossetian Militias (in the following: "Proxy Actors") demonstrate that Russia likes to outsource active combat to a special kind of proxy. Why is this problematic for IHL? On the one hand, I have explained that outsourcing *per se* is not illegal. On the other hand, Russia's approach challenges IHL, because it consists in maintaining deniability through loose control. This does not only create an ideal breeding ground for IHL violations. It also outmanoeuvres the protective framework of State responsibility, absolving Russia from any legal accountability and enabling it to wage war below the radar of IHL.

4.1 Avoiding State responsibility and the impact on IHL

> *"Каждый человек несёт ответственность перед всеми людьми за всех людей."*
>
> Fyodor Dostoyevsky, Brothers Karamazov (1879)

Fyodor Dostoyevsky's famous line from his work Brothers Karamazov translates into: "Everyone bears responsibility to all for all." The sentence represents the centrepiece of Dostoyevsky's doctrine of universal guilt and one of his most important contributions to the discussion of moral responsibility.[1693] His concept stands in stark contrast to the framework of State

---

to Russia or whether Russia violated its *positive* duty under the ECHR to protect the ethnic Georgians.

1693 James Patrick Scanlan, *Dostoevsky the Thinker* (Cornell University Press 2002) 104.

responsibility where it constitutes a fundamental rule that a State is only responsible for its own conduct.[1694]

In the following, I will explain how Russia's outsourcing policy outmanoeuvres the law of State responsibility. On the one hand, Moscow simply denies its ties to certain groups, as I have shown above for Wagner. On the other hand, it exploits the loopholes of the law of State responsibility which sets very strict conditions for attributing the behaviour of a proxy to a State. This approach negatively affects IHL, because the framework of State responsibility remains an important accountability mechanism. In sum, I will show that Russia's outsourcing is another step towards waging war below the radar of IHL.

4.1.1 Why State responsibility matters

At this point, we should be careful not to conflate the issues of State responsibility and individual responsibility. Unlike in human rights, it is universally accepted that IHL binds not only States, but also armed groups, and even individuals.[1695] A Cossack in Debaltseve, an Ossetian militiaman in Gori, or a Wagner contractor in Palmyra – they are all bound by IHL. It does not matter whether they are acting on behalf of a State, of an armed group, of an armed group that is controlled by a State, or on their own.[1696] Their IHL violations, however, may simultaneously entail both individual criminal responsibility and State responsibility.[1697] In fact, State responsi-

---

1694 *Bosnian Genocide Case* (n 1115) para 406.

1695 Jann K Kleffner, 'The Applicability of International Humanitarian Law to Organized Armed Groups' (2011) 93 International Review of the Red Cross 443, 433, 449 with further sources at n 21 and 22.

1696 Of course, their legal *status* will depend on the type of conflict, on their affiliation, and other factors. The concerned person could be a combatant or a civilian directly participating in hostilities. Even a civilian participating in hostilities, however, can commit war crimes. In this sense, everyone is bound by the same rules.

1697 See Art 58 ARSIWA which states that these "Articles are without prejudice to any question of the individual responsibility under international law of any person acting on behalf of a State." For the interplay of State responsibility and individual responsibility see André Nollkaemper, 'Concurrence between Individual Responsibility and State Responsibility in International Law' (2003) 52 International & Comparative Law Quarterly 615, 618–619; Shabtai Rosenne, 'War Crimes and State Responsibility' in Yoram Dinstein and Mala Tabory (eds), *War Crimes in International Law* (Nijhoff 1996); ILC, 'Draft Articles on

bility is the older, more traditional form of accountability in international law.[1698] It forms the link between a violation on the battlefield and the accountability of a State and thus fulfils a crucial role for IHL.

First, it gives teeth to a field of law that chronically lacks enforcement mechanisms, because it allows reprimanding the responsible State. One might call State responsibility the equivalent of a "civil law attachment to individual criminal responsibility" as it exists in many national legal systems.[1699] Let's assume an IHL violation were attributable to Russia. This means that Moscow can be successfully sued before the ICJ for a violation of international law. Furthermore, it may give individual victims a basis to claim compensation before national and international courts. While there is no special international court to rule on the IHL violations of a State, the ECtHR has tried to fill this gap and decides cases in the context of an armed conflict.[1700] The Strasbourg Court, too, takes into account the framework of State responsibility.[1701] In addition, the rules of State responsibility urge other States to become active. When the violation concerns a "serious breach", Art 40 and Art 41 ARSIWA prescribe that all States have an obligation to "cooperate to bring to an end" such a violation and may "not recognize" the situation as lawful.

Secondly, the law of State responsibility is well suited to address widespread violations of IHL. Rather than just addressing each individual case with regards to criminal guilt, State responsibility addresses the systemic

---

Responsibility of States for Internationally Wrongful Acts, with Commentaries' (2001) 2 Yearbook of the International Law Commission 30, Art 58 paras 1–2.

1698 Nollkaemper (n 1697) 616.

1699 ibid 622.

1700 See e.g. ECtHR, *Al Skeini and Others v The United Kingdom*, No 55721/07, 7 July 2011 and ECtHR, *Jaloud v The Netherlands*, No 47708/08, 20 November 2014. Both decisions dealt with events in Iraq. See also the ECtHR case law on Chechnya that I have described in detail above at p 204.

1701 The Court's stance on the framework on State responsibility remains unclear. In some cases, Strasbourg applies the general rules of State responsibility, in others it does not. With regards to attribution, the Court has never clarified, whether it applies the ARSIWA or whether it follows an ECHR-specific regime. The ECHR may contain rules on attribution that take precedence over the ARSIWA, but they would not exclude the application of the ARSIWA altogether, see James Crawford and Amelia Keene, 'The Structure of State Responsibility under the European Convention on Human Rights' in Anne van Aaken and Iulia Motoc (eds), *The European Convention on Human Rights and General International Law* (Oxford Scholarship Online 2018) 178–179; Marko Milanović and Tatjana Papić, 'The Applicability of the ECHR in Contested Territories' (2018) 67 International and Comparative Law Quarterly 779, at n 18 and 19.

causes. Would it not be strange to try Slobodan Milošević, but leave intact the State structures that enabled him to commit his crimes?[1702] Furthermore, it increases diplomatic pressure, because the violation becomes more than "just" an individual criminal act. For example, the criminal prosecution of the Libyan agent responsible for the Lockerbie bombing did not preclude UK and US claims against the Libyan State. On the contrary, such claims increased the pressure and shed spotlight on a specific violation of international law.[1703]

The object of this chapter is to show that Russia evades State responsibility for IHL violations by outsourcing to Proxy Actors. It uses a mix of denial of facts and loopholes in the legal framework to lead the rules of State responsibility into no man's land. While the individual fighters remain bound, Russia as a State is let off. In this sense, I regard outsourcing as yet another way to sideline IHL, and another way to turn it into a set of rules that do not apply to the Russian State.

4.1.2 The framework of State responsibility

In the following, we shall discuss three different ways of attributing the conduct of groups to a State. For each one, I will explain the difficulty of attributing PMCs like Wagner, the Cossacks, and the SOM to Russia.

In 2001, following three years of intense debate, the International Law Commission (ILC) adopted the Articles on State Responsibility for Internationally Wrongful Acts (ARSIWA).[1704] The document contains 59 Articles. While States never cast these rules into the form of a binding treaty, it is generally accepted that the majority of the Articles constitute customary law, especially the different ways of attribution which I will discuss below.[1705] The basic rule can be found in Art 1 ARSIWA. It stipulates that "every internationally wrongful act of a State entails the international responsibility of that State."

1702 Nollkaemper (n 1697) 625.
1703 See ibid 619–620.
1704 From the moment of its creation in 1947, the ILC considered the elaboration of rules on State responsibility as a priority. When codifying the ARSIWA (2001) the Commission could rely on the work of previous generations, e.g. on the 1961 Draft Convention on the International Responsibility of States for Injuries to Aliens, see Crawford, *State Responsibility* (n 1151) 35–44.
1705 Crawford, 'State Responsibility' (n 1116) para 65.

Such an "international wrongful act" must fulfil two criteria. The conduct must breach an international obligation – such as a rule of the Geneva Conventions – and it must be attributable to a State.[1706] It constitutes a fundamental rule of the ARSIWA that a State is only responsible for its own conduct, that is to say the conduct of persons acting – on whatever basis – on its behalf.[1707] Art 4–11 ARSIWA enumerate different ways of attributing conduct to a State. In the following, I will address the forms of attribution that are most relevant to Russia's armed proxies:[1708]

– Attribution of conduct of *organs* of a State (Art 4 ARSIWA);
– Attribution of conduct *directed or controlled* by a State (Art 8 ARSIWA)
– Attribution of conduct of entities exercising elements of *governmental authority* (Art 5 ARSIWA);

4.2.1.1 Article 4 ASRIWA

Art 4 regulates the default case of attribution, i.e. the conduct of State organs:

> *"The conduct of any State organ shall be considered an act of that State under international law, whether the organ exercises legislative, executive, judicial, or any other functions, whatever position it holds in the organization of the State."*

First of all, the wording covers what is called a *de jure* organ of a State. For the purpose of IHL, the classic example for a *de jure* organ would be

---

1706 See Art 2 ARSIWA.

1707 *Bosnian Genocide Case* (n 1115) para 406.

1708 Other ways of attribution include the acknowledgment of conduct (Art 11 ARSIWA) or conduct carried out in the absence or default of official authorities (Art 9 ARSIWA). Both, however, are not relevant to Russian proxies. On the contrary, Russia denies any affiliation and avoids "adopting [their] conduct as its own", as Art 11 ARSIWA would require. A prime example for such adoption would be Teheran's behaviour in the *Hostages Case*, where the Iranian Foreign Minister endorsed the occupation of the US Embassy by private actors as an act "done by our nation", see ICJ, *United States Diplomatic and Consular Staff in Tehran*, Judgment, ICJ Reports (1980) 3, para 74. Art 9 ARSIWA has an extremely narrow scope and does not apply when citizens have already succeeded in forming a *de facto* government, see Crawford, *State Responsibility* (n 1151) 167–168.

the armed forces.[1709] In addition, Art 4 ARSIWA also covers the actions of *de facto* organs.[1710] This describes an entity which is private, but acts *just like* a State organ despite not having this function under national law. The rationale behind this is that a State should not be able to avoid responsibility by denying an organ its official status under internal law.[1711]

Please note that the term *"de facto* organ" is used both in the context of Art 4 and Art 8 ARSIWA. In Art 4, it covers an entity that has *de facto* become part of the State, i.e. an organ *within* the State structure. In Art 8 it concerns a private entity that stands *outside* the State structure, but over which the State has "effective control."[1712] To avoid confusion, I shall use the term *"de facto* organ" only in the context of Art 4.[1713]

A *de facto* organ constitutes an exceptional case and the term should be construed narrowly.[1714] The ICJ dealt with this issue in *Nicaragua* (1986) and the *Bosnian Genocide Case* (2007). Both cases revolved around armed groups. In *Nicaragua*, the Judges had to decide whether the Contras constituted a *de facto* organ of the US. In the *Bosnian Genocide Case*, it addressed Serbia's relation with the Army of the Republika Srpska (VRS) – a Serbian secessionist group in Bosnia during the Bosnian War (1992–1995). The Court fleshed out the criteria of a *de facto* organ and set a very high threshold. The armed group must be in a relation of "complete dependence" on the State.[1715] This "requires proof of a particularly great degree of State control over them."[1716] The Judges gave particular importance to certain indicators of dependence, e.g. whether the State has created the organ, whether the State installed, selected, and paid the leaders of the group, and whether the aid went beyond mere training and funding.[1717] Despite the

---

1709 For the discussion whether Art 91 AP I represents *lex specialis* for attributing the conduct of the armed forces to a State in IAC see Tonkin (n 1447) 82 et seq.

1710 *Bosnian Genocide Case* (n 1115) para 397.

1711 ILC, 'Draft Articles on Responsibility of States for Internationally Wrongful Acts, with Commentaries' (n 1697) Art 4 para 11.

1712 I will discuss Art 8 ARSIWA extensively below at p 347.

1713 See for this Crawford, *State Responsibility* (n 1151) 125 at n 73. Crawford clarifies that the ICJ created *two* tests in Nicaragua, whereas international scholarship erroneously spoke of *one* unified test of attribution.

1714 ibid 125.

1715 *Nicaragua Case* (n 992) para 110 and *Bosnian Genocide Case* (n 1115) para 392.

1716 *Bosnian Genocide Case* (n 1115) para 393.

1717 *Nicaragua Case* (n 992) paras 107–112.

very close ties in both cases, neither the VRS nor the Contras met the high threshold of Art 4.[1718]

Thus, there are two ways in which the Russian Proxy Actors could fall under Art 4. Either Moscow officially includes them in their armed forces; or it incorporates them "*de facto*" by subjecting them to "complete dependence." Both scenarios do not correspond to what we have seen so far. An overt integration into the armed forces is out of the question. Let's not forget, for example, that Russia uses PMCs and Cossack units in countries like Ukraine, so that it can deny having any regular servicemen on the ground.[1719] While Russia has incorporated certain registered Cossacks into its armed forces,[1720] they were not the ones that fought in eastern Ukraine. Most of them belonged to unregistered Cossack associations. Even in Georgia, where Russian soldiers fought side by side with the SOM, the militiamen were not incorporated into the Russian Army, at least not in 2008. Only in 2015, the Treaty on Alliance and Integration foresaw the official merge of South Ossetian units into the Russian armed forces.[1721] To this day, this process is ongoing, the incorporation of the South Ossetian forces into the Russian Army has not been finalised, and it is questionable whether it will ever be.[1722]

Secondly, attributing Russia's proxies as *de facto* organs has little chance of success given the immense hurdle of "complete dependence." No armed group before an international tribunal has met this standard. Russia's proxies do not fulfil the ICJ criteria outlined above. For example, there

---

1718 *Nicaragua Case* (n 992) para 110; see also *Bosnian Genocide Case* (n 1115) para 394.

1719 See above p 261.

1720 See Art 5(2) of the Федеральный закон, 05.12.2005, N 154-ФЗ 'О государственной службе российского казачества' [Federal Law, 5 December 2005, N 154-F3 'On the State Service of the Russian Cossacks']: "The Russian Cossacks will serve in the armed forces of the Russian Federation [...]."

1721 See Art 2(2) of the Договор между Российской Федерацией и Республикой Южная Осетия о союзничестве и интеграции [Treaty between the Russian Federation and the Republic of South Ossetia on Alliance and Integration] 18 March 2015.

1722 Joshua Kucera, 'South Ossetia Keeps Its Military, For Now' (Eurasianet, 19 January 2017) <https://eurasianet.org/south-ossetia-keeps-its-military-now >; some Ossetian units, however, have been subjected to Russian command: 'Подписано соглашение о вхождении части подразделений армии Южной Осетии в ВС РФ [The Agreement of the Integration of Parts of the Units of the Army of South Ossetia and into the Armed Forces of the Russian Federation Has Been Signed]' (Tass, 31 March 2017) <https://tass.ru/armiya-i-opk/4143137 >.

is no proof that Russia *created* its Proxy Actors. With regards to Wagner and Slavonic Corpus, it rather used existing structures in what some call Moscow's famed "ad hoc decision-making."[1723] The same is true for Cossack associations, both registered and unregistered. While they heavily depend on Russian State support, Moscow lacks the "particularly great degree of State control" required by the ICJ. Instead of following a direct command, these actors operate under a *laissez-faire* regime that gives them substantial freedom as long as they do not cross certain boundaries. Both Wagner and the Cossacks have shown that they also pursue their own agenda, e.g. when Wagner was to receive 25 percent of the revenues of every captured gas field. In extreme cases, however, this *laissez-faire* regime may lead to strategic clashes between Moscow and its proxies. Wagner's private raid in Deir al-Zour and the Cossacks' self-proclaimed Republic in Ukraine illustrate this well. In the *Bosnian Genocide Case* such fundamental "strategic differences" between the State and its proxy – in this instance between Serbia and the Republika Srpska – led the ICJ to reject attribution under Art 4.[1724] The same would be true for Russian PMCs and Cossack units.

The Ossetian Militias are probably the most dependent group of all. Yet, they still fly below the radar of *"complete* dependence." The Tagliavini Commission concluded that the raids of Ossetian Militias – only weeks before the war – could not be attributed to Russia under Art 4.[1725] Admittedly, this assessment concerns actions *before*, and not during the war. Still, it seems difficult to imagine that in a matter of days the militia crossed the

---

1723 Reynolds (n 1476) 1. Both Wagner and the Slavonic Corpus are derivates of previous companies like Antiterror-Orel and Moran.

1724 *Bosnian Genocide Case* (n 1115) para 394 where the Court argues that: "While the political, military and logistical relations between the federal authorities in Belgrade and the authorities in Pale, between the Yugoslav army and the VRS, had been strong and close in previous years […], and these ties undoubtedly remained powerful, they were, at least at the relevant time, not such that the Bosnian Serbs' political and military organizations should be equated with organs of the FRY. *It is even true that differences over strategic options emerged at the time between Yugoslav authorities and Bosnian Serb leaders; at the very least, these are evidence that the latter had some qualified, but real, margin of independence"* (emphasis added).

1725 The Commission dealt with this question because it assessed whether the attacks by South Ossetian forces *before* the war constituted an "armed attack" by Russia in the sense of Art 51 UN Charter, see IIFFMCG, 'Report of the Independent International Fact-Finding Mission on the Conflict in Georgia (Tagliavini Report) Volume II' (n 1109) 258–261.

threshold to "complete dependence."[1726] The ICJ's decision in *Application of the International Convention on the Elimination of All Forms of Racial Discrimination* failed to shed light on this issue. The Court did not decide the question on attribution, since it found that it did not have jurisdiction.[1727] Given the above, however, Moscow's level of control would not fulfil Art 4.[1728]

4.2.1.2 Article 8 ARSIWA

The second possibility for attributing Russia's Proxy Actors is Art 8. Art 8 is a close relative of Art 4.[1729] While Art 4 covers private entities that have become *"de facto"* organs of a State, Art 8 deals with entities that remain private, but over which the State has certain influence.[1730] It reads:

> *"The conduct of a person or group of persons shall be considered an act of a State under international law if the person or group of persons is in fact acting on the instructions of, or under the direction or control of, that State in carrying out the conduct."*

Art 8 contains two alternatives: "instructions" or "direction or control." The first alternative – "instructions" – requires a clear manifestation of

---

1726 The Commission also rejected attribution under Art 8 ARSIWA, ibid 261.

1727 *Bosnian Genocide Case* (n 1115) para 187.

1728 Russia argued that neither Art 4 nor Art 8 ARSIWA applied because the threshold was not met. The South Ossetian organs did not constitute "mere instruments" of Russia, because they "conducted their own policy, have held elections, and have had independent governments." See ICJ, *Verbatim Record of Public Sitting in the Case Concerning Application of the International Convention on the Elimination of All Forms of Racial Discrimination (Georgia v Russian Federation) Held on 8 September 2008 at 3 pm* (CR 2008/23) 45. Similarly, Prof Zimmermann, who represented the Russian Federation in the proceedings, argued that neither Art 8 nor Art 4 ARSIWA were fulfilled because "those persons formed part of the South Ossetian authorities and exercised authority on its behalf", but not on behalf of Russia. See ICJ, *Verbatim Record of Public Sitting in the Case Concerning Application of the International Convention on the Elimination of All Forms of Racial Discrimination (Georgia v Russian Federation) Held on 10 September 2008 at 4.30 pm* (CR 2008/27) 18.

1729 At times, the different standards for Art 4 and Art 8 ARSIWA have been confused, see n 1713.

1730 Lindsey Cameron and Vincent Chetail, *Privatizing War: Private Military and Security Companies under Public International Law* (Cambridge University Press 2013) 144.

the will of the State which sets a high threshold and does not cover cases in which the State gives the private actor a lot of freedom.[1731] The ILC commentary gives the example of "groups of private individuals who, though not specifically commissioned by the State and not forming part of its police or armed forces [...] are *sent* as 'volunteers' to neighbouring countries."[1732] The State's instructions have to regard the commission of a *specific act* that breaches the international obligations, not just the operation as a whole.[1733] In addition, any unlawful behaviour that is "incidental" to the instructions would also fall under Art 8.[1734] In other terms: if a State gives vague instructions, and violations seem within the reasonable ambit of these instructions, they would be attributable. Everything beyond represents an *ultra vires* act that cannot be attributed.[1735]

The second alternative of Art 8 concerns attribution through "direction or control." According to the ILC, this requires a "real link" between the State and the armed group.[1736] In its famous *Nicaragua* decision (1986) the ICJ further fleshed out the exact conditions. The Judges found that the US participated in "financing, organizing, training, supplying and equipping of the contras, the selection of its military or paramilitary targets, and the planning of the whole of its operation."[1737] In short, the US influence on the Contras was considerable. Despite this, the Court rejected attribution under Art 8, because this would require *"effective control* of the military or paramilitary operations in the course of which the alleged violations were committed."[1738] While the Court did not further clarify the notion of "effective control", it became clear that this threshold was very high. Despite the "high degree of dependency" of the Contras their actions were not "imputable" to Washington.[1739]

Since 1986, this high threshold has been called into question. In *Tadić* (1999), the ICTY challenged the effective control test and replaced it with

---

1731 ibid 205.
1732 ILC, 'Draft Articles on Responsibility of States for Internationally Wrongful Acts, with Commentaries' (n 1697) Art 8 para 2.
1733 Cameron and Chetail (n 1730) 205.
1734 Crawford, *State Responsibility* (n 1151) 145; Cameron and Chetail (n 1730) 208.
1735 Cameron and Chetail (n 1730) 208.
1736 ILC, 'Draft Articles on Responsibility of States for Internationally Wrongful Acts, with Commentaries' (n 1697) Art 8 para 1.
1737 *Nicaragua Case* (n 992) para 115.
1738 ibid.
1739 ibid paras 115 and 116.

the lower threshold of "overall control."[1740] I may point the reader to the section on proxy occupation where I have already discussed the ensuing argument between the two The Hague Courts.[1741] Suffice it to say that the ICJ rejected the ICTY's approach in the *Bosnian Genocide Case* (2007), at least with regards to attribution.[1742] This ended the debate as to the correct standard of control to be applied under Art 8.[1743] Attribution needs "effective control [...] in respect of *each* operation."[1744]

Having settled this preliminary question, the ICJ applied its effective control test to the genocide in Srebrenica. It found that the killings committed by Serbian separatists were not attributable to Serbia. Belgrade's ample support to the VRS was not sufficient, because the decision to exterminate the male population at Srebrenica was taken by the VRS alone.[1745] The Court stressed that the standard of effective control had to be proved for *each operation*, not just overall.[1746] The ample support the Serbs had provided to the Republika Srpska changed nothing in this respect. Only the *specific* planning of the genocide from an office in Belgrade could have triggered attribution to Serbia under Art 8.[1747]

What does this mean for Russia's Proxy Actors? When applying Art 8 to Wagner, Cossacks, and the SOM, we encounter two obstacles: one practical, one legal. In practical terms, there is simply not enough evidence for Russia's influence. With regards to PMCs especially, much remains in the dark.[1748] This is the result of Russia's (successful) strategy of denial paired with under-regulation, and the use of oligarchs as front men. Often, Russia will not pose as the contracting State – if there even is a contract

---

1740 See ICTY, *The Prosecutor v Duško Tadić* (IT-94–1-T), Appeals Chamber Judgment, 15 July 1999, para 115 et seq. The ICTY dealt with the question of attribution because it had to classify the conflict at hand, see n 1147.

1741 See pp 238 et seq.

1742 Already in the *Armed Activities Case* (2005) the ICJ had confirmed its Nicaragua standard, albeit without explicitly discarding *Tadić*, see *Armed Activities Case* (n 994) paras 168 and 226.

1743 Crawford, *State Responsibility* (n 1151) 156.

1744 *Bosnian Genocide Case* (n 1115) para 400.

1745 ibid paras 411 and 413.

1746 ibid para 400.

1747 ibid para 413.

1748 See Kimberly Marten who argues that because "these semi-state Russian groups are shadowy and protean, it can be challenging to find reliable information about their activities. They are surrounded by rumours, and some of the prominent individuals involved with them have been caught in direct lies." Marten (n 1488) 189.

– but prefers to avoid any legal ties.[1749] In public discourse, it can always point to the illegality of the companies and prosecute them afterwards. We have witnessed this in the case of Slavonic Corpus. With regards to the Cossacks, Russia *has* enacted numerous laws tying them to the State. However, Moscow does not rely on these laws for using the Cossacks in war. Rather, the fighting is done by "unregistered" units or "registered" Cossacks posing as volunteers. Taking advantage of the Cossacks' extreme patriotism, Moscow engineered a self-powered recruitment system that works without direct orders and runs on anticipatory obedience: a *perpetuum mobile bellicum*.

Secondly, there is a legal reason why Russia's proxies are hard to attribute. Their very structure makes it difficult to ever fulfil the threshold of "effective control." This applies especially to the Cossacks and PMCs like Wagner. Moscow's proxies follow a "dual-use" strategy, serving both State and private interests. Take again Wagner's raid in Deir al-Zour or the Cossacks who went out of line in Ukraine. Russia's *laissez-faire* strategy departs from the traditional concept of how a State controls the use of force. It falls outside the scope of "effective control" which rests upon a traditional concept of the use of armed force: such force should be controlled by a strong State that issues orders and firmly holds the reigns in its hand. Russia, however, prefers to trade off tight command in favour of deniability. Kimberly Marten highlights this in her recent article on Wagner:

> *"While Wagner is sometimes used in the same ways that other rational states use PMCs, corrupt informal networks tied to the Russian regime have also used it in ways that are not typical of other strong states and that potentially undermine Russian security interests. [...] "Strong states" are not supposed to work with hazy, unregulated, semi-state security forces, either on their own territory or abroad, and Russia is doing both today."[1750]*

The same applies *mutatis mutandis* to the Cossack units. There, too, it is difficult to disentangle when they defend the Kremlin's interests and when they pursue their own goals. When the use of force is delegated to what Marten calls "corrupt informal networks", the threshold of effective control is the wrong tool. Both Cossacks and PMCs like Wagner have shown that they possess a structure that resembles organised crime rather

---

1749 Денис Коротков [Denis Korotkov], 'Они сражались за Пальмиру [They Fought for Palmyra]' (n 1498).
1750 Marten (n 1488) 181 and 188.

than classic paramilitary units.[1751] Mark Galeotti strikes a point when he argues that Russia "has traded off operational effectiveness for the sake of deniability."[1752]

Things are slightly different with regards to the SOM. Firstly, we find extensive evidence of Russian control over these Militias. Even before the war, Moscow had an iron grip on South Ossetia's security forces. The Tagliavini Commission noted that "decisive positions within the security structures of South Ossetia were occupied by Russian representatives, or by South Ossetians who had built their careers in Russia."[1753] During the war, it was impossible to overlook that Russia and the SOM fought side by side, coordinating their efforts. Secondly, the SOM's militia structure resembles a classic paramilitary proxy actor – like the Contras or the armed forces of Republika Srpska – that better allows for attribution through effective control.

Having said that, to a large extent, the cruelties of the SOM during the Russo-Georgian War are not attributable to Russia. In the ICJ *Racial Discrimination Case* (2011), Russia argued that the SOM could not be attributed according to Art 8, because the threshold was not met.[1754] I, too, believe that Russia's control stayed below effective control during the Russo-Georgian War – at least with regards to *most* operations of the SOM. According to the ICJ standard from the *Bosnian Genocide Case*, a State needs to control *each specific* operation.[1755] Thus, we must not simply rely on Russia's overall control over the security apparatus, which is undisputed. We need to prove that Russia "directed or controlled" the atrocities which the SOM committed in South Ossetia and the bordering buffer

---

1751 For the Cossacks see Mitrokhin (n 1644) 44; for PMCs see Marten (n 1488) 188, 196.

1752 Galeotti, *Armies of Russia's War in Ukraine* (n 785) 35.

1753 IIFFMCG, 'Report of the Independent International Fact-Finding Mission on the Conflict in Georgia (Tagliavini Report) Volume II' (n 1109) 133.

1754 ICJ, *Verbatim Record of Public Sitting in the Case Concerning Application of the International Convention on the Elimination of All Forms of Racial Discrimination (Georgia v Russian Federation) Held on 8 September 2008 at 3 pm* (CR 2008/23) 45–46; ICJ, *Verbatim Record of Public Sitting in the Case Concerning Application of the International Convention on the Elimination of All Forms of Racial Discrimination (Georgia v Russian Federation) Held on 10 September 2008 at 4.30 pm* (CR 2008/27) 18. In the end, the ICJ did not have to pronounce itself on attribution. The Court found that it had no jurisdiction, since the procedural requirements of the CERD were not fulfilled. Thus, it followed Russia's second preliminary objection, see *Racial Discrimination Case* (n 1169) para 187.

1755 *Bosnian Genocide Case* (n 1115) para 400.

zone. Moscow's involvement stayed below such a high level of control. Against this backdrop, it is understandable that the Tagliavini Commission refused to attribute South Ossetian raids into Georgia under Art 8, even though it had detailed Russia's high level of control over the SOM some pages before.[1756]

In addition, Moscow and the SOM followed a clear division of labour: Russian troops took a village, moved through, and left. Then, the SOM arrived to do the "dirty work."[1757] While this division of labour requires a degree of coordination, it does not necessarily point to effective control. On the contrary, it suggests coordination by broad strokes rather than tight control on the level of the individual soldier. The Tagliavini Commission appears to take the same stance. It only accuses the SOM – and not the Russian armed forces – of violations related to ethnic cleansing, such as summary executions,[1758] ill-treatment and torture,[1759] the taking of hostages,[1760] and looting carried out against the Georgian population.[1761] Had there been effective control, the Russian forces would be equally guilty of such acts.

Rare exceptions could be those cases where Russian on-duty soldiers stood by while IHL violations occurred, because this indicates a higher level of operational control.[1762] The ICJ missed an opportunity to shed light on these issues in the *Racial Discrimination Case*. The Court found

---

1756 The raids took place shortly before the war, in June 2008. However, there is no reason to believe that the Russian involvement suddenly rose to effective control when war broke out a month later, see IIFFMCG, 'Report of the Independent International Fact-Finding Mission on the Conflict in Georgia (Tagliavini Report) Volume II' (n 1109) 132, 261. The Tagliavini Report does not even reach a conclusion whether Russia fulfilled the (lower) standard of overall control of the South Ossetian forces. The Commission did not have to answer this question, because the rules for the conduct of hostilities are almost identical for IAC and NIAC, see ibid 304.

1757 van Herpen (n 1386) 229.

1758 IIFFMCG, 'Report of the Independent International Fact-Finding Mission on the Conflict in Georgia (Tagliavini Report) Volume II' (n 1109) 355.

1759 ibid 359, 361.

1760 ibid 362.

1761 ibid 365.

1762 In some cases, Russian soldiers were present on the scene and failed to prevent violations of IHL, see above at n 1686 and n 1687. Russia, however, has always denied that its troops witnessed violations by the SOM, see e.g. ICJ, *Verbatim Record of Public Sitting in the Case Concerning Application of the International Convention on the Elimination of All Forms of Racial Discrimination (Georgia v Russian Federation) Held on 10 September 2008 at 4.30 pm* (CR 2008/27) 17.

that it had no jurisdiction, because the procedural requirements of the CERD were not fulfilled.[1763] Therefore, it did not pronounce itself on the material question of attribution. However, given its strict standard and past case law, I believe that the Court would have rejected attribution under Art 8. Thus, even for the SOM, Russia's *laissez-faire* attitude bypasses the traditional standard of "effective control" although this conclusion is less evident than for Wagner and the Cossacks.

4.2.1.3 Article 5 ARSIWA

Finally, Art 5 covers the conduct of persons or entities exercising elements of governmental authority. Whereas Art 4 is a *structural* test for attribution, Art 5 – just like Art 8 – represents a *functional* test.[1764] It reads:

> "*The conduct of a person or entity which is not an organ of the State under article 4 but which is empowered by the law of that State to exercise elements of the governmental authority shall be considered an act of the State under international law, provided the person or entity is acting in that capacity in the particular instance.*"

The article sets two conditions that are critical with regards to proxies. They must "exercise elements of governmental authority" (I) and be "empowered by law" to do so (II).

The first element (I), i.e. the meaning of "governmental authority" gives rise to much debate. The interpretation will depend on the particular society, its history, and its traditions. The ILC commentary provides four indicators to identify governmental authority: The *content* of the power that is delegated (1); *how* it is delegated (2); for what *purpose* (3); and to what extent the entity is *accountable* to the government (4).[1765] Generally, most authors agree that the participation in hostilities constitutes an exercise of governmental authority. As a matter of fact, it represents the very core content of the term. Scholarship, for example, has extensively discussed PMCs as an example for the delegation of governmental author-

---

1763 *Racial Discrimination Case* (n 1169) para 187.
1764 Crawford, *State Responsibility* (n 1151) 127.
1765 ILC, 'Draft Articles on Responsibility of States for Internationally Wrongful Acts, with Commentaries' (n 1697) Art 5 para 6.

ity.[1766] Furthermore, courts have interpreted the notion of governmental authority in a way that encompasses the use of military armed force.[1767]

Thus, in principle, Russia's Proxy Actors exercise public authority in the sense of Art 5 ARSIWA. They wage war. It is no secret that they operate in regions where strategic Russian interests are at stake and I have provided ample evidence of their ties to the Kremlin. The far greater challenge, however, for attributing Russia's Proxy Actors under Art 5 is the element of "empowerment by law" (II). This criterion is generally interpreted in a wide way. The entity must be empowered "pursuant to some legal provision." That could be a law or a public contract.[1768] Certain authors even regard this wide reading as too formalistic and suggest eliminating it completely. Lindsey Cameron and Vincent Chetail, for example, highlight that the ICJ did not always expressly address "empowerment by law" when applying Art 5, for example in the *Armed Activities Case*.[1769]

While I agree that "empowerment by law" should be interpreted widely, I believe that we cannot disregard the criterion altogether. The ILC commentary to Art 5 places specific emphasis on the concept and limits Art 5

> *"to entities which are empowered by internal law to exercise governmental authority. This is to be distinguished from situations where an entity acts under the direction or control of the State, which are covered by Article 8."*[1770]

This view sits well with the system of attribution under the ARSIWA. Both Art 8 and Art 5 ARSIWA represent functional tests. The element of "empowerment by law" sets them apart and should not be overlooked. Finally, omitting the criteria of "empowered by internal law" would not only contradict the ILC commentary. It would contradict the clear wording of the provision itself.

Since "empowerment by internal law" is a hard criterion under Art 5, it does not cover Wagner, Cossacks, or the SOM – no matter how wide

---

1766 Cameron and Chetail (n 1730) 172; Crawford, *State Responsibility* (n 1151) 127.

1767 See ECtHR, *Olujic v Croatia*, No 22330/05, 5 February 2009, para 32.

1768 Crawford, *State Responsibility* (n 1151) 132.

1769 Cameron and Chetail (n 1730) 169–170. The authors cite the *Armed Activities Case* (n 994), para 160, in their support and argue that "national law is just a fact in the international legal order, and that a State cannot invoke the lacunae of its domestic order to escape the reality of the fact that it has outsourced governmental functions relevant to its international obligations."

1770 ILC, 'Draft Articles on Responsibility of States for Internationally Wrongful Acts, with Commentaries' (n 1697) Art 5 para 7.

we interpret the provision. Given the absolute absence of PMC legislation in Russia, Wagner & Co fall outside of the scope of Art 5. Moscow has *no* legislation whatsoever that regulates the use of force by PMCs. Quite to the contrary, the Kremlin frequently refers to the illegality of such companies. In addition, Russia does not pose as the contracting State, if there is any contract at all. The same is true for the SOM, for whom there is no law or contract.[1771]

As to the Cossacks, Russia has created an extensive legal framework. It regulated the rights and duties of Cossacks in the 'Law on the State Service of the Russian Cossackdom' and other instruments.[1772] *Inter alia*, registered Cossacks have an obligation to defend State borders and to fight terrorism.[1773] However, Russia does not rely upon these provisions when using the Cossacks abroad. The laws only apply to registered Cossacks in State service. Yet, most Cossacks in Ukraine were "unregistered" and the few "registered" fighters came as volunteers. Of course, they all received ample Russian support, but nevertheless they acted outside the legal framework, thus camouflaging their ties with the Russian State more effectively.[1774]

In sum, this shows that my three examples of Russian Proxy Actors – Wagner, Cossacks, and the SOM – fly below the radar of State attribution. This allows the Kremlin to wage war without incurring responsibility for IHL violations.[1775]

1771 This was true at least at the time of the Russo-Georgian War (2008), i.e. before the Treaty on Alliance and Integration spoke of the incorporation of the South Ossetian forces into the Russian Army. See above at n 1105 and Договор между Российской Федерацией и Республикой Южная Осетия о союзничестве и интеграции [Treaty between the Russian Federation and the Republic of South Ossetia on Alliance and Integration] 18 March 2015.

1772 See p 325.

1773 Art 5 No 4(3) of the Федеральный закон, 05.12.2005, N 154-ФЗ 'О государственной службе российского казачества' [Federal Law, 5 December 2005, N 154-F3 'On the State Service of the Russian Cossacks'].

1774 Darczewska (n 1614) 22.

1775 There exists a limited safety net: Under CA 1 States must "ensure respect" for IHL, which means that they "must exert their influence, to the degree possible, to stop violations of international humanitarian law", see ICRC, Customary IHL Database, Rule 144. This obligation, however, is not about *attributing* conduct of third actors to a State. Rather, CA 1 contains an obligation to react to conduct of third actors that are *not* attributable to a State. Hence, we can call it a due diligence obligation. Such an obligation, however, has several weaknesses. First, a CA 1 violation would carry less weight than directly attributing a substantial violation to Russia. Secondly, CA 1 only contains an

5. Conclusion

Russia's outsourcing policy contains an explosive mix. It includes highly violent non-state actors that fight for patriotism and personal gain. Their ties to the Kremlin are deliberately loose. The loss of effective command is a price Moscow is willing to pay for the sake of deniability. This *laissez-faire* approach flies below the radar of State attribution. On the one hand, Russia exploits the loopholes of the framework of State responsibility. On the other hand, the Russian policy of denial and obfuscation leads to a lack of evidence.

If there are gaps in the current legal framework that allow Russia to slip through the cracks of State attribution, we cannot blame Moscow for that. However, I revealed that Moscow's approach is not just based on exploiting lamentable loopholes. It includes cunning, factual denial, under-regulation, and sometimes blatant lies in order to avoid any possible ties with its proxies. More than anything else, this unveils an underlying desire to wage war without incurring tedious restrictions under IHL.

In addition, the proxy fighters would also fall outside the scope of any domestic IHL implementation mechanism Russia has in place for its armed forces which I have described at page 190. Even worse, Moscow's

---

obligation of means, which gives States more leeway to argue their way out. Thirdly, the exact scope of CA 1 is still under-explored, and the provision is rarely used in practice. It is seldom applied in international case law. A notable exception is the *Nicaragua Case*, where the ICJ ruled that the dissemination of a military manual to the Contras breached CA 1, because it must "be regarded as an encouragement, which was likely to be effective, to commit acts contrary to general principles of international humanitarian law reflected in treaties" (*Nicaragua Case* (n 992) para 255). For the scope of CA 1, especially the so-called "external dimension" (i.e. "ensure respect") see Robin Geiß, 'Common Article 1 of the Geneva Conventions: Scope and Content of the Obligation to "Ensure Respect" – "Narrow but Deep" or "Wide and Shallow"?' in Heike Krieger (ed), *Inducing Compliance with International Humanitarian Law* (Cambridge University Press 2015); Cameron and Chetail (n 1730) 247; Laurence Boisson de Chazournes and Luigi Condorelli, 'Common Article 1 of the Geneva Conventions Revisited: Protecting Collective Interests' (2000) 82 International Review of the Red Cross 67, 67; Luigi Condorelli and Laurence Boisson de Chazournes, 'Quelques remarques à propos de l'obligation des États de respecter et faire respecter le droit international humanitaire en toutes circonstances' in Christophe Swinarski (ed), *Études et essais sur le droit international humanitaire et sur les principes de la Croix-Rouge en l'honneur de Jean Pictet.* (Comité international de la Croix-Rouge 1984) 26; Dörmann and others (n 543) Art 1, para 120.

laissez-faire approach may also lead to low discipline which is known to have a knock-on effect on IHL compliance. Especially the case of the SOM has shown what loosening the reigns means in an ethnically charged context leading to "indiscipline and counter-productive brutality."[1776]

1776 Galeotti, 'Living in Cossackworld' (n 1604); see also Tonkin (n 1447) 23.

Chapter V: Evading IHL on the Battlefield – Denying Facts ("The Sledgehammer")

The third and last aspect of Russia's evasion strategy concerns situations in which it neither challenges the existence of an armed conflict (e.g. in Syria and Georgia), nor outsources the fighting to proxies (e.g. in aerial warfare). We will look at a worrying series of attacks on hospitals by the Russo-Syrian coalition (1) and the use of cluster munitions in Syria and Georgia (2) and see how Russia challenges well-established facts to stifle any discussion on the law. The logic is simple. A legal argument may be defeated. Challenging the facts, however, renders any legal debate on equal footing superfluous. The third case study (3) – the downing of flight MH17 – represents the odd one out. The plane was *not* shot down by Russian soldiers, but by Russian-*backed* rebels in eastern Ukraine. After the incident, however, Moscow launched an impressive barrage of alternative facts in order to hide its involvement in this IHL violation.

1. Targeting "errors" – healthcare in danger

> *"The Syrian and Russian Governments know the exact location of most health facilities, and yet they continue targeting them."*[1777]

This accusation by Susannah Sirkin, Director of Policy at the NGO Physicians for Human Rights (PHR), during her speech in the UN Security Council was grave: The respect for medical care in armed conflict already formed the centrepiece of the 1864 Geneva Convention. It continues to be one of the most important rules of IHL.[1778] Did Russia really violate this fundamental norm in a systematic manner?

1777 UN Security Council, 8589th meeting, UN Doc S/PV.8589 (30 July 2019) 6.
1778 See e.g. Art 1 of the 1864 Geneva Convention: "Ambulances and military hospitals shall be recognised as neutral, and as such, protected and respected by the belligerents as long as they accommodate wounded and sick. Neutrality shall end if the said ambulances or hospitals should be held by a military force."

1.1 Russia's war in Syria – a "Road to Damascus Experience"?

Moscow decided to intervene in Syria in late summer 2015. Its long-standing ally Bashar al-Assad had launched a formal request for Russian military aid. On 26 August 2015, both States signed a treaty that established the conditions of the use of the Syrian airport Khmeimim by the Russian Air Force.[1779] Russian airstrikes began on 30 September 2015. In addition, Russia deployed several warships and around 4 000 ground forces.[1780] Its primary objective was to re-establish the military and political capacities of the Assad regime – one of Moscow's most loyal and long-standing allies in the region. Besides, there was genuine concern that Assad's downfall would be exploited by radical Islamists. This would have threatened Russian security interests not just in Syria, but in Northern Caucasus and Central Asia.[1781] Moscow's involvement proved to be a game-changer. First, it made a large-scale Western intervention in Syria impossible.[1782] Secondly, Russian firepower tipped the scales in military terms. Already by October 2015 the Russian Air Force carried out around 50–60 attacks per day.[1783] According to the Russian chief of staff Valery Gerasimov, Russia conducted 19 000 combat missions and delivered 71 000 strikes in the first 18 months of the campaign.[1784] Even after Putin declared Russia's partial withdrawal from Syria on 14 March 2016, it maintained its military bases at Tartus and Khmeimim. From there it continues to provide logistics, ma-

---

1779 Соглашение между Российской Федерацией и Сирийской Арабской Республикой о размещении авиационной группы Вооруженных Сил Российской Федерации на территории Сирийской Арабской Республики [Agreement between the Russian Federation and the Syrian Arab Republic about the Deployment of an Aviation Group of the Armed Forces of the Russian Federation on the Territory of the Syrian Arab Republic] 12 November 2016.

1780 Joseph Daher, 'Three Years Later: the Evolution of Russia's Military Intervention in Syria' (Atlantic Council, 27 September 2018) <https://www.atlanticcoun cil.org/blogs/syriasource/three-years-later-the-evolution-of-russia-s-military-inter vention-in-syria>.

1781 Fiona Hill, 'The Real Reason Putin Supports Assad' (Foreign Affairs, 25 March 2017) <https://www.foreignaffairs.com/articles/chechnya/2013-03-25/real-reaso n-putin-supports-assad>; Nikolay Kozhanov, 'Main Drivers of Russian Military Deployment in Syria' (2017) 13 International Studies Journal 21, 22 and 25.

1782 ibid 26.

1783 Jonathan Marcus, 'Russian Firepower Ups the Stakes in Syria' (BBC, 15 October 2015) <https://www.bbc.com/news/world-middle-east-34522268>.

1784 As quoted in Oscar Jonsson, *The Russian Understanding of War: Blurring the Lines between War and Peace* (Georgetown University Press 2019) 44.

terial, and training to Assad's forces.[1785] Above all – and most relevant to my case study – Russian fighter jets continued their aerial bombardments of rebel-held territory until 2020.

The classification of the Syrian Conflict is highly complex. At the height of the war, several States fought against hundreds of armed groups and sub-factions whose allegiance often remained hazy. The intervention of a US-led coalition without Syrian consent further complicated the question of classification.[1786]

With regards to Russia, however, the question of classification is very simple. Moscow had entered a pre-existing NIAC. The hostilities have been taking place between Russian and Syrian forces on the one side, and various armed groups – such as the Free Syrian Army, the Islamic State and Jabhat Fatah al-Sham (formerly known as Jabhat al-Nusra) – on the other side. These armed groups are furthermore sufficiently organised.[1787] Major battles with Russian involvement included the siege of Aleppo that was taken back from the rebels in 2016 and more recently the battle for Idlib, the last rebel stronghold.[1788] Unlike the US-led Coalition, Russia operated in Syria with the consent of the sovereign. It supported the Assad regime in a NIAC with various armed groups by directly participating in hostilities.[1789] While Moscow never acknowledged that its ground troops engaged in active combat, it never denied providing air support

---

1785 Kozhanov (n 1781) 31–32.

1786 Particularly controversial is the question, whether the US-led coalition found itself in an IAC with Syria simply because it fought the Islamic State on Syrian territory without consent from Damascus. See for this Beth Van Schaack, 'Mapping War Crimes in Syria' (2016) 92 International Law Studies 282, 289–290; the ICRC, for example, holds the opinion that any unconsented intervention on foreign territory represents an IAC, Dörmann and others (n 543) Art 2 para 259.

1787 Annyssa Bellal, 'The War Report – Armed Conflicts in 2016' (Geneva Academy of International Humanitarian Law and Human Rights 2017) 36.

1788 ibid 34. See also Tom Perry and Orhan Coskun, 'Damascus Presses Idlib Attack, Artillery Hits Turkish Position' (Reuters, 4 May 2019) <https://www.reuters.co m/article/us-syria-security-northwest/damascus-presses-idlib-attack-artillery-hits -turkish-position-idUSKCN1SA0EG>.

1789 Since Russia directly takes part in hostilities there is no reason to resort to the so-called "support based approach." See Tristan Ferraro, 'The Applicability and Application of International Humanitarian Law to Multinational Forces' (2013) 95 International Review of the Red Cross 561.

to Assad.[1790] On the contrary, it extensively broadcast combat footage on state-owned TV channels.

This classification as a NIAC is shared by the vast majority of scholars.[1791] In legal terms, this means that Russia is bound by CA 3, AP II,[1792] and customary international law applicable in NIACs. In any case the following violations concern the conduct of hostilities for which the law of IAC and NIAC are virtually identical.

1.2 Protection of healthcare – firm rules, feeble respect

Under the framework of the conduct of hostilities, hospitals and other medical units[1793] enjoy extensive protection. They must be respected and protected at all times, by all belligerents. This protection is enshrined in both the Geneva Conventions and the Additional Protocols.[1794] Medical objects are protected unless the installations are used to commit acts harmful to the enemy outside of their humanitarian function.[1795] Such acts could consist in sheltering able-bodied combatants, storing ammunition, or serving as a military observation post.[1796] Treating *wounded* enemy fighters, however, has no impact on the protection of a hospital, because it falls

---

1790 'Ministarstvo odbrane Rusije: Nikakvih ruskih kopnenih snaga u Siriji nije bilo [Russian Ministry of Defense: There Were no Russian Ground Forces in Syria]' (Sputnik Srbija, 18 July 2019) <https://rs-lat.sputniknews.com/rusija/201907181 120390683-ministarstvo-odbrane-rusije-nikakvih-ruskih-kopnenih-snaga-u-siriji -nije-bilo/>.

1791 Bellal (n 544) 35; Van Schaack (n 1786) 288 et seq.

1792 AP II governs Russian operations despite the fact that Syria has not ratified the Protocol.

1793 The Geneva Conventions use the term "medical units" which encompasses more than just hospitals, see Art 8(e) AP I: "Medical units means establishments and other units, whether military or civilian, organized for medical purposes, namely the search for, collection, transportation, diagnosis or treatment – including first-aid treatment – of the wounded, sick and shipwrecked, or for the prevention of disease. The term includes, for example, hospitals and other similar units, blood transfusion centres, preventive medicine centres and institutes, medical depots and the medical and pharmaceutical stores of such units. Medical units may be fixed or mobile, permanent or temporary."

1794 Art 19, 33, 35 GC I; Art 22–27 GC II; Art 12(I) AP I; Art 9–11 AP II.

1795 Sassòli, Bouvier and Quintin (n 72) 201. See also Art 21 GC I; Art 34 GC II; Art 13(1) AP I; Art 11 AP II.

1796 Pictet, *The Geneva Conventions of 12 August 1949* (n 983) 200–201.

within the humanitarian scope of medical aid.[1797] Even if a medical unit is used outside its humanitarian function it may not be attacked straight away. Rather, its protection only ceases "after a warning has been given setting, whenever appropriate, a reasonable time-limit, and after such warning has remained unheeded."[1798] Deliberately attacking a hospital or other medical units may represent a war crime.[1799]

These principles exist in IAC and in NIAC alike.[1800] They are clearly spelled out in treaty law.[1801] In addition, there are corresponding customary rules to respect and protect medical units, medical transport, as well as people and objects displaying the protective emblem.[1802] States, too, have endorsed these principles in their military manuals.[1803] Russia's military manual, for example, clarifies that medical objects are not legitimate military targets and targeting them represents a prohibited method of warfare.[1804] Furthermore, it reiterates the rule that medical persons and objects may only be attacked after "warning has been given setting, whenever

---

1797 See for IACs Art 13(2)(d) AP I. There is no treaty rule for NIACs. The ICRC commentary, however, comes to the same conclusion that treating wounded enemy fighters has no impact on the protection of a medical unit, see Sandoz, Swinarski and Zimmermann (n 754) para 4723.

1798 Art 13(1) AP I; Art 11(2) AP II; See ICRC, Customary IHL Database, Rule 28: "It is further specified in State practice that prior to an attack against a medical unit which is being used to commit acts harmful to the enemy, a warning has to be issued setting, whenever appropriate, a reasonable time-limit and that an attack can only take place after such warning has remained unheeded."

1799 See e.g. Art 8(2)(b)(xxiv) ICC Statue for IAC and Art 8(2)(e)(ii) ICC Statute for NIAC. For the Syrian context see, for example, the statement of UN Special Rapporteur on the right to health, Dainius Puras (10 June 2016): "These incidents amount to *war crimes* and may constitute crimes against humanity, as well as a violation of the right to health, and those responsible must be brought to justice" (emphasis added). Statement available at <https://www.ohchr.org/EN/NewsEvents/Pages/DisplayNews.aspx?NewsID=20080&LangID=E>.

1800 ICRC, Customary IHL Database, Rules 28–30.

1801 See n 1794 and n 1795.

1802 ibid.

1803 Canada, Office of the Judge Advocate General, 'The Law of Armed Conflict at the Operational and Tactical Levels' (2001) para 447; Deutsches Bundesministerium der Verteidigung (n 205) paras 612–619; Israeli Military Advocate-General's Corps Command, 'Rules of Warfare on the Battlefield (2nd Edition)' (IDF School of Military Law 2006) 24.

1804 'Наставление по международному гуманитарному праву для Вооруженных Сил Российской Федерации', 08.08.2001 ['Manual on International Humanitarian Law for the Armed Forces of the Russian Federation', 8 August 2001] paras 1 and 7.

appropriate, a reasonable time-limit, and after such warning has remained unheeded."[1805]

While the legal principles of the protection of healthcare could not be clearer, challenges have arisen in practical respects. In recent conflicts like Syria and Yemen, we have seen a sharp increase of attacks on health workers and installations. The Red Cross and Red Crescent Movement launched the campaign "healthcare in danger"[1806] and the ICRC dedicated two special issues of its Review to these worrying incidents which have become part of the "contemporary reality of warfare" to the extent "that they barely stand out in the constant stream of news headlines."[1807] Recently, the UN Security Council passed Resolution 2286 (2016). It represents the first Resolution exclusively dedicated to the issue of violence against healthcare and met the unanimous approval of States. Russia, too, voted in favour.[1808] The resolution "strongly condemns acts of violence, attacks and threats against the wounded and sick, medical personnel and humanitarian personnel exclusively engaged in medical duties" and urges all warring parties to respect the rules of the Geneva Conventions and their Additional Protocols.[1809]

1.3 Targeting hospitals in Syria – "srabotalo"[1810]

On the one hand, States – including Russia – unanimously endorsed the protection of healthcare in armed conflict. On the other hand, harrowing reports of hospital bombings shocked the world from the very beginning of the war in Syria. The NGO Physicians for Human Rights corroborated

---

1805 ibid paras 58 and 83.

1806 <https://healthcareindanger.org/hcid-project/>.

1807 Vincent Bernard, 'Violence against Health Care: Giving in Is Not an Option' (2013) 95 International Review of the Red Cross 5, 5.

1808 UN Security Council, 7685th meeting, UN Doc S/PV.7685 (3 May 2016) 2.

1809 UN Security Council Resolution 2286, UN Doc S/RES/2286 (3 May 2016) paras 1 and 2.

1810 Russian for "it worked." It was this phrase a Russian pilot used after bombing a hospital near Idlib, Syria. The New York Times used the intercepted radio communication to prove that the Russian Air Force bombed several medical installations, see Christiaan Triebert et al, 'How Times Reporters Proved Russia Bombed Syrian Hospitals' (The New York Times, 13 October 2019) <https://www.nytimes.com/2019/10/13/reader-center/russia-syria-hospitals-investigation.html>.

578 attacks on at least 350 separate facilities from March 2011 to July 2019, killing at least 890 medical personnel.[1811]

Russia started to operate in Syrian airspace in autumn 2015. Since then, the disturbing attacks on hospitals and health workers have continued. Worse, they even intensified, as seen during the battles for Aleppo (2016)[1812] and Idlib (2019),[1813] where Russian and Syrian planes operated jointly. It quickly became obvious that the repeated attacks on health installations could not be a series of "targeting errors" but rather followed a systematic pattern. Amnesty International stated as early as 2016 that "wiping out hospitals" became a part of the Russo-Syrian military strategy.[1814]

Can we trust these statements? As is well known, the first casualty of war is truth.[1815] We should be careful in trusting any source, especially in Syria where major geopolitical interests are at stake. Having said that, evidence compiled by international organisations, NGOs, and journalists leaves no room for doubt that the Russo-Syrian coalition carried out numerous attacks on medical installations.

Bellingcat researchers, for example, used publicly available flight observation data, witness accounts, videos, imagery, and geolocation to analyse eight attacks on Syrian hospitals in 2017. The open source investigators found that the Syrian and Russian Air Force were responsible for *all* eight strikes.[1816] In the same vein, the Syrian American Medical Society claims that the Russian intervention in Syria led to a sharp rise of attacks

---

1811 UN Security Council, 8589th meeting, UN Doc S/PV.8589 (30 July 2019) 5.

1812 'Syrian and Russian Forces Targeting Hospitals as a Strategy of War' (Amnesty International, 3 March 2016) <https://www.amnesty.org/en/latest/news/2016/03/syrian-and-russian-forces-targeting-hospitals-as-a-strategy-of-war/>; see also UN Security Council, 8589th meeting, UN Doc S/PV.8589 (30 July 2019) 5.

1813 Josie Ensor, 'Syria and Russia Bomb Hospitals in Idlib after They Were Given Coordinates in Hope of Preventing Attacks' (The Telegraph, 30 May 2019) <https://www.telegraph.co.uk/news/2019/05/30/syria-russia-bomb-hospitals-idlib-given-coordinates-hope-preventing/>.

1814 'Syrian and Russian Forces Targeting Hospitals as a Strategy of War' (Amnesty International, 3 March 2016) <https://www.amnesty.org/en/latest/news/2016/03/syrian-and-russian-forces-targeting-hospitals-as-a-strategy-of-war/>.

1815 The origin of the quote is unknown, but it is commonly ascribed to US Senator Hiram Warren Johnson (1918).

1816 Syrian Archive & Bellingcat, 'Medical Facilities under Fire – Systematic Attacks during April 2017 on Idlib Hospitals Serving More than One Million in Syria' (2017).

on hospitals.[1817] Physicians for Human Rights, whose Director Susannah Sirkin I have quoted above, has been tracking attacks on healthcare installations with Russian and Syrian involvement for the past years. The data shows that Russo-Syrian forces carried out 240 attacks on healthcare installations.[1818] The numbers also highlight a sharp increase in such attacks during the Russo-Syrian assaults on Aleppo and Idlib.[1819]

The UN, too, voiced its grave concern about such violence against health workers. The bombing of hospitals during the battle for Aleppo – together with similar attacks in Yemen, Libya, and Afghanistan – prompted the Security Council to adopt Resolution 2286 (2016).[1820] While the Resolution remains neutral in its language and does not single out Russian violations, the UN Independent International Commission of Inquiry on the Syrian Arab Republic (IICI) was more direct in its findings. In several reports it *directly* accused the Russian and Syrian Air Forces of destroying medical infrastructure.[1821] The IICI was shocked to find that during the battle for Aleppo (2016), *not a single* hospital was left functioning, because all of them were destroyed by Russo-Syrian aerial attacks.[1822] It concluded that "the Syrian and Russian forces carried out daily air strikes, claiming hundreds of lives and reducing hospitals […] to rubble."[1823]

1817 Syrian American Medical Society, 'The Failure of UN Security Council Resolution 2286 in Preventing Attacks on Healthcare in Syria' (2017) 4.

1818 PHR, 'Illegal Attacks on Health Care in Syria' <https://syriamap.phr.org/#/en >; see also UN Security Council, 8589th meeting, UN Doc S/PV.8589 (30 July 2019) 5. At the time of the UN Security Council meeting the number of attacks was 224.

1819 UN Security Council, 8589th meeting, UN Doc S/PV.8589 (30 July 2019) 5–6.

1820 See e.g. the statement of the US and UK representatives in the Security Council: "If Russia genuinely believes in the commitment that we have all just made to protecting medical workers, it must bring its full influence to bear to restrain the Al-Assad regime and bring its merciless attacks to an end." UN Security Council, 7685th meeting, UN Doc S/PV.7685 (3 May 2016) 13, 15–17. See also the statement of the Russian representative Evgeniy Zagaynov who tried to counter the allegations of Russian misconduct: "We are not able to corroborate the accusations levelled against the Russian air force of violations of international humanitarian law in Syria", ibid 15.

1821 IICI, 'Report of the Independent International Commission of Inquiry on the Syrian Arab Republic (A/HRC/33/55)' (2016) 8–10; IICI, 'Report of the Independent International Commission of Inquiry on the Syrian Arab Republic (A/HRC/34/64)' (2017) 9–10.

1822 IICI, 'Report of the Independent International Commission of Inquiry on the Syrian Arab Republic (A/HRC/34/64)' (n 1822) 8.

1823 ibid 1, 7.

In 2019 the attacks on Idlib – the last pocket of resistance in the north-west of Syria – intensified. In and around the city, Russian and Syrian forces attacked 54 hospitals and clinics in opposition territory.[1824] The UN Security Council was alarmed and put the issue back on its agenda for its 8589th meeting. This time, the debate specifically revolved around the Russo-Syrian attacks. During the meeting, the UN Under-Secretary-General for Humanitarian Affairs, Mark Lowcock, and the US representative accused Russia of *directly* targeting hospitals.[1825] Following the motion of ten member States, Secretary General Guterres established a "board to investigate events in North-West Syria" under Art 97 UN Charter.[1826] While the final report failed to name Russia as a direct perpetrator, it accused "the Government of Syria and/or its allies" of attacks on healthcare installations.[1827]

Hence, there is ample proof that the Russo-Syrian coalition carried out attacks on medical installations. Furthermore, these attacks are not mere targeting errors, but follow a *systematic* pattern.[1828] This can be evinced from their sheer number. Destroying *every single* hospital in Aleppo cannot be ascribed to targeting errors. In addition, many of the hospitals were registered under the so-called "deconfliction mechanism." This OCHR initiative shares the coordinates of medical installations with all belligerents in order to avoid accidental targeting. Given the fact that many hospitals followed this standard procedure, it is hard to understand why they later became targets. During the Idlib offensive (2019) alone, 14 of the medical installations that were later targeted by the Russo-Syrian coalition had pre-

---

1824　The data refers to the period from April 2019 to September 2019, see Evan Hill and Christiaan Triebert, '12 Hours. 4 Syrian Hospitals Bombed. One Culprit: Russia.' (The New York Times, 13 October 2019) <https://www.nytimes.com/20 19/10/13/world/middleeast/russia-bombing-syrian-hospitals.html>.

1825　UN Security Council, 8589th meeting, UN Doc S/PV.8589 (30 July 2019) 2–5, 8.

1826　UN Press Release SG/SM/19685 (1 August 2019) 'Secretary-General Establishes Board to Investigate Events in North-West Syria since Signing of Russian Federation-Turkey Memorandum on Idlib' <https://www.un.org/press/en/2019/sgsm 19685.doc.htm>.

1827　Observers called it a "deliberately mealy-mouthed report" because it failed to detail the Russian responsibility, see Evan Hill, 'U.N. Inquiry Into Syria Bombings Is Silent on Russia's Role' (New York Times, 6 April 2020) <https://www.n ytimes.com/2020/04/06/world/middleeast/UN-Syria-Russia-hospital-bombings.h tml>. The report is available at <https://www.un.org/sg/sites/www.un.org.sg/file s/atoms/files/NWS_BOI_Summary_06_April_2020.pdf>.

1828　IICI, 'Report of the Independent International Commission of Inquiry on the Syrian Arab Republic (A/HRC/34/64)' (n 1822) 8, which also speaks of a pattern.

viously passed on their coordinates to all parties to the conflict – including Moscow and Damascus.[1829]

One evidentiary problem, however, remains. How can we attribute the strikes to either the Syrian or the Russian Air Force?[1830] You might have noticed that I spoke of "Russo-Syrian" attacks, or violations by "Russia and Syria." We find similar expressions in most reports.[1831] The reason for this is simple: In many instances, it is impossible to identify whether the pilot was Russian or Syrian. Both countries carry out joint operations, both use the same planes and weaponry. As a long-standing Russian ally, Syria's Air Force is largely composed of Soviet and Russian manufactured MiG and Sukhoi aircraft.[1832]

In certain cases, however, we have clear evidence that Russian planes, manned by Russian pilots bombed a specific health installation. The New York Times, for example, analysed previously unpublished radio recordings, plane spotter logs, and other witness accounts. The evidence allows us to attribute the bombings of four hospitals in May 2019 to Russian pilots.[1833] All four hospitals had previously communicated their coordinates

---

1829 Liz Sly, 'U.N. to Investigate Accusations that Russia, Syria are Deliberately Targeting Hospitals' (The Washington Post, 1 August 2019) <https://www.wash ingtonpost.com/world/middle_east/un-to-investigate-accusations-that-russia-syri a-are-deliberately-targeting-hospitals/2019/08/01/efa6461a-b478-11e9-acc8-1d847 bacca73_story.html>.

1830 Even if a specific attack cannot be attributed to the Russian Air Force, the Russian conduct still raises questions with regards to IHL. Robert Lawless argues that Moscow's systematic denial of Syrian war crimes could constitute a violation of IHL, because it makes Russia an accomplice to Syrian violations. In any case, under CA 1 Russia has a duty to use its influence on the Syrian government to end these bombings. This, however, would go beyond the scope of the present chapter, for details see Robert Lawless, 'A State of Complicity: How Russia's Persistent and Public Denial of Syrian Battlefield Atrocities Violates International Law' (2018) 9 Harvard National Security Journal 180.

1831 See e.g. Syrian Archive & Bellingcat (n 1816) 46, 54, 63, 79, 89, 98, 106; IICI, 'Report of the Independent International Commission of Inquiry on the Syrian Arab Republic (A/HRC/34/64)' (n 1822) 8. The report of the IICI claims that "either the Russian air force *or* the Syrian air force *or both*" carried out certain attacks (emphasis added).

1832 See World Directory of Modern Military Aircraft, <https://www.wdmma.org/sy rian-air-force.php>.

1833 Evan Hill and Christiaan Triebert, '12 Hours. 4 Syrian Hospitals Bombed. One Culprit: Russia.' (The New York Times, 13 October 2019). For their methodology see Christiaan Triebert et al, 'How Times Reporters Proved Russia Bombed Syrian Hospitals' (The New York Times, 13 October 2019) <https://www.nytim es.com/2019/10/13/reader-center/russia-syria-hospitals-investigation.html>.

to the Russian Air Force.[1834] This proves that Russia has directly targeted health installations. In addition, the IICI also blamed Russia for several direct attacks on health installations in a recent report. The Commission investigated two attacks on 22 July and 16 August 2019. They concluded that:

> *"Based on the evidence available, including witness testimonies, video footage, data imagery as well as reports by flight spotters, flight communication intercepts and early warning observation reports, the Commission has reasonable grounds to believe that a Russian aircraft participated in each incident described above. In both incidents, the Russian Air Force did not direct the attacks at a specific military objective, amounting to the war crime of launching indiscriminate attacks in civilian areas."[1835]*

In sum, this shows that the Russo-Syrian coalition systematically targeted health installations. While for many of the 240 attacks, we cannot establish beyond reasonable doubt whether the pilot belonged to the Russian or Syrian Airforce, we have enough evidence to attribute specific attacks to Moscow. The remaining attacks were carried out either by Russian or Syrian pilots – or by both in a joint operation. In any case, all of them suggest a systematic disregard for one of the most fundamental rules of IHL; that medical installations should be respected and protected.

1.4 Russia's denial – fake news?

Despite this overwhelming evidence, Moscow denies that its armed forces violate IHL. Instead of providing legal arguments, however, Moscow prefers to challenge the facts on which its critics base their legal conclusions. It thereby creates an alternative narrative that makes any discussion about the law superfluous, because Moscow has already undermined the factual grounds needed for any legal conclusion. We encounter this approach not only with regards to the above attacks on healthcare, but also with regards to the use of cluster munitions and the MH17 incident, both of which I will describe below. Moscow's strategy is not aimed at produc-

---

1834 Evan Hill and Christiaan Triebert, '12 Hours. 4 Syrian Hospitals Bombed. One Culprit: Russia.' (The New York Times, 13 October 2019) <https://www.nytimes.com/2019/10/13/world/middleeast/russia-bombing-syrian-hospitals.html>.

1835 IICI, 'Report of the Independent International Commission of Inquiry on the Syrian Arab Republic (A/HRC/43/57)' (2020) 6.

ing a single, coherent, and credible counter-narrative for an allegation. It rather uses diversion tactics in order to obfuscate the mainstream narrative as much as possible while insisting on the lack of reliable information.

When Russia supported SC Resolution 2286 (2016), it added a caveat by highlighting the need for verified and reliable information:

> *"It is unacceptable that unverified reports of attacks against hospitals taken from unreliable sources are fed to the media and then used for political pressure for short-term objectives."*[1836]

According to a spokesman of the Russian Foreign Ministry the "Russian Air Force carries out precision strikes only on "accurately researched targets."[1837] Any information that goes against this narrative is swept aside as being unreliable, fake, or polemicised. After an alleged Russian attack on a hospital on 10 February 2016, Russia accused the Western media of spreading the "fabrication" of the destruction of a MSF hospital in order to "achieve significant public response."[1838] Russia felt especially cornered when the Security Council discussed the Russo-Syrian bombardments during the battle for Idlib (2019). To remind the reader, during this session Susannah Sirkin accused Russia of knowing "the exact location of most health facilities, and yet [...] targeting them" anyway.[1839] The Russian representative outright rejected these allegations:

> *"As usual, today we heard another series of invectives against Syria and the Russian Federation. Colleagues spouted statistics, quotes and emotional testimony. Incidentally, we are well aware of the value of such emotionally charged testimony."*[1840]

The Russian representative also suggested that the information of PHR and other organisations is "fake" and showed concern that "the United Nations mechanism should be involved in the circulation of such fake information."[1841] Russia also strongly opposes the IICI and exerted pressure on the Secretary General's investigative board tasked to shed light

---

1836 UN Security Council, 7685th meeting, UN Doc S/PV.7685 (3 May 2016) 15.
1837 ibid.
1838 Statement available at <https://syria.mil.ru/en/index/syria/news/more.htm?id=1 2078613@egNews>.
1839 UN Security Council, 8589th meeting, UN Doc S/PV.8589 (30 July 2019) 6.
1840 UN Security Council, 7685th meeting, UN Doc S/PV.7685 (3 May 2016) 15.
1841 ibid 17.

on bombings in Western Syria.[1842] Finally, Moscow attempts to shift the blame. While rejecting any Russian IHL violation, Moscow deplored that hospitals were targeted in Afghanistan and Yemen and accused the UN Under-Secretary-General for Humanitarian Affairs Mark Lowcock of double standards by turning a blind eye to these violations.[1843]

It is true that attacks on healthcare are not limited to Syria. Saudi Arabia, and various armed groups are similarly accused of targeting health installations.[1844] The US, too, came under heavy criticism when it attacked a hospital in Kunduz. The US representative was forced to publicly apologise in the UN Security Council stressing that the "United States deeply regrets the tragic and mistaken attack on the Médecins Sans Frontières hospital in Kunduz."[1845] Whatever the basis of these alleged violations, Russia's *tu quoque* argument – using another's misconduct to justify your own – has no legal bearing under IHL. The laws of war must be respected regardless of possible violations of other States.[1846] In addition, the systematic nature of Russo-Syrian attacks on health installations truly stands out from a wider pattern of disrespect for healthcare in armed conflict worldwide.

While the rules of IHL remain crystal clear, Russia's obstinate factual denial renders any legal discussion superfluous. Russia likes to embrace the rules in abstract resolutions such as Security Council Resolution 2286 (2016) and readily invokes them when condemning the conduct of other States such as the US. However, it adopts a position of absolute factual denial when it comes to assessing its own conduct in Syria. This double

---

1842 Whitney Hurst and Rick Gladstone, 'U.N. Query on Syria Hospital Bombings May Be Undermined by Russia Pressure, Limited Scope' (The New York Times, 14 November 2019) <https://www.nytimes.com/2019/11/14/world/middleeast/russia-syria-hospital-bombing.html>.

1843 ibid 15.

1844 'Saudi Should be Blacklisted' over Yemen Hospital Attacks' (BBC, 20 April 2017) <https://www.bbc.com/news/world-middle-east-39651265>.

1845 ibid 16.

1846 In *Kupreškić* the ICTY clarified this point: "The Trial Chamber wishes to stress, in this regard, the irrelevance of reciprocity, particularly in relation to obligations found within international humanitarian law which have an absolute and non-derogable character. It thus follows that the *tu quoque* defence has no place in contemporary international humanitarian law", ICTY, *The Prosecutor v Zoran Kupreškić et al* (IT-95-16-T), Trial Chamber Judgment, 14 January 2000, para 511. See also ICTY, *The Prosecutor v Milan Martić* (IT-95-11-A), Appeals Chamber Judgment, 8 October 2008, para 61 and Roger O'Keefe, *International Criminal Law* (Oxford University Press 2015) 222.

standard degrades IHL to a showcase rule, a rule that may be paraded or turned against others but does not restrict one's own conduct in warfare.

2. Cluster munitions – denying the obvious

Cluster munitions describe an explosive weapon that opens up in mid-air to release tens or hundreds of submunitions. From a military perspective, cluster munitions offer a decisive advantage when attacking targets that are spread out over a wide area. At the same time, this wide-area-effect makes it difficult to distinguish between military and civilian objects. Furthermore, the high number of duds contaminates a vast area creating a lethal danger to the civilian population.[1847] I have already discussed cluster munitions above at page 144 when dealing with Russia's opposition to a prohibition treaty. In the following, I will briefly describe the legality of cluster munitions under IHL, before assessing how Russia used this weapon in Georgia (2008) and Syria (2015- today).

2.1 The legality of cluster munitions – barbaric bomblets?

The legal status of cluster munitions remains controversial. In 2008, a number of States signed the Convention on Cluster Munitions. The CCM outlawed *inter alia* using, producing, and stockpiling such weapons. To-day, 110 States have acceded.[1848] While the Convention represented a milestone in international arms law, Russia chose not to sign for reasons that I have outlined above.[1849] Other major producers of cluster munitions like the US also turned their backs on the treaty.

It is hotly debated whether there is a prohibition of cluster munitions under customary law. While the CCM only creates obligations for State parties, a customary norm would bind all States. Certain scholars argue that cluster munitions are *inherently* indiscriminate and thus illegal.[1850]

1847 Daryl Kimball, 'Cluster Munition at a Glace' <https://www.armscontrol.org/fac tsheets/clusterataglance>.

1848 For details see UNODA, 'Convention on Cluster Munitions' <http://disarmame nt.un.org/treaties/t/cluster_munitions>.

1849 See p 144.

1850 Jonathan Black-Branch, 'The Legal Status of Cluster Munitions under Interna-tional Humanitarian Law: Indiscriminate Weapons of War' (2012) 4 Journal of International Law of Peace and Armed Conflict 186; often the call for illegality

Most States and scholars, however, would not go so far. The ICRC customary study, for example, points out that there "is insufficient consensus [...] to conclude that, under customary international law [cluster munitions] violate the rule prohibiting the use of indiscriminate weapons."[1851]

This does not mean that cluster munitions fall outside the scope of the general rules governing the conduct of hostilities. Like any weapon, they must be used in accordance with the principles of distinction, proportionality, and precautions. Bearing in mind the wide-area-effect of cluster munitions, this seems difficult if military and civilian objects intermingle, let alone in a densely populated urban setting. Cluster munitions are an area-weapon and cannot be fired at one specific target.[1852] Furthermore, even if civilians temporarily left the target area, the remaining duds would pose a threat upon their return. Hence there is growing consensus that the weapon is unsuitable for areas populated by civilians.

In theory, Russia agrees that cluster munitions should only be used to "inflict casualties on the enemy and destroy military equipment in *open* spaces."[1853] Moscow has condemned the use of cluster munitions in populated areas by third States as "indiscriminate" such as in the case of South Sudan.[1854]

---

is paired with a caveat, see Virgil Wiebe, 'Footprints of Death: Cluster Bombs as Indiscriminate Weapons under International Humanitarian Law' (2000) 22 Michigan International Law Journal 85, 87. The author argues (already in 2000) that the "inherent nature of cluster bombs as wide-area munitions, at a minimum, should make their use illegal in *civilian* areas" (emphasis added).

1851 ICRC, Customary IHL Database, Rule 71.

1852 Most cluster bomblets are completely unguided. Recently, Russia has tested the bomb PBK-500U "Drill" that contains 15 submunitions each guided by an infrared or radar system, see 'Планирующая авиабомба ПБК-500У "Дрель" [Air Delivered Bomb PBK-500U is Being Planned]' (Armeysky Vestnik, 5 October 2018) <https://army-news.ru/2018/10/planiruyushhaya-aviabomba-pbk-500u-drel-zavershaet-ispytaniya/>.

1853 IIFFMCG, 'Report of the Independent International Fact-Finding Mission on the Conflict in Georgia (Tagliavini Report) Volume III – Views of the Sides on the Conflict, Chronologies and Responses to Questionnaires' (n 960) 484.

1854 Security Council Resolution 2155, UN Doc S/RES/2155 (27 May 2014) noted "with serious concern reports of the indiscriminate use of cluster munitions." Russia voted for the Resolution.

2.2 Russia's use of cluster munitions in Syria and Georgia

How does this position affect Russia's own use of cluster munitions on the battlefield? Moscow has been employing cluster munitions in various conflicts since 1991.[1855] When the Russo-Georgian War erupted in 2008, the international community was extremely sensitised to the issue. Only months before the war, more than 100 States had signed the CCM. Similarly, the use of cluster munitions remains a hot topic in the ongoing Syrian Conflict.[1856] Both in Syria and Georgia, Russia stands accused of the indiscriminate use of cluster munitions. Yet, both in Syria and Georgia, Russia denies having used the weapon at all.

There have been frequent allegations that Russia dropped cluster munitions in the Syrian campaign.[1857] Shortly after Moscow intervened in Syria, the latest cluster munitions "made in Russia" appeared on the battlefield. This suggests that Moscow either equipped its own planes with these weapons or supplied them to its Syrian ally – or both.[1858]

The Russian Ministry of Defence calls these allegations "fake information."[1859] However, cluster munitions were heavily used in all major military engagements that saw Russian involvement, such as the battle for Aleppo (July 2016–December 2016). At Aleppo, Russian and Syrian planes carried out daily air strikes. The IICI found "an alarming number of

---

1855 Russia used cluster munitions extensively during both Chechen Wars, often in an indiscriminate manner. For example, at Shali (3 January 1995) at least 55 civilians were killed when the Russian Air Force bombed the city using cluster munitions. Many more were wounded. Organisations and States condemned these indiscriminate bombings, yet without specifically focusing on cluster munitions as a weapon as such, see Wiebe (n 1851) 143.

1856 Cluster munitions were also used in eastern Ukraine. However, I chose to exclude this issue here, because Russia already denied its very *presence* in Ukraine, and did thus not comment on the use of specific weapons, see above at pp 255 et seq.

1857 See e.g. 'Russia/Syria: Widespread New Cluster Munition Use' (Human Rights Watch, 28 June 2016) <https://www.hrw.org/news/2016/07/28/russia/syria-wides pread-new-cluster-munition-use>.

1858 'Syria: New Russian-Made Cluster Munition Reported' (Human Rights Watch, 10 October 2015) <https://www.hrw.org/news/2015/10/10/syria-new-russian-ma de-cluster-munition-reported>.

1859 Минобороны: Россия не применяет кассетные боеприпасы в Сирии [Ministry of Defence: Russia Does not Employ Cluster Munitions in Syria]' (Ria Novosti, 23 December 2015) <https://ria.ru/20151223/1347566946.html>; Russian Ministry of Defence Briefing (23 December 2015) available at <http://eng.mil.r u/en/news_page/country/more.htm?id=12072315@egNews>.

incidents involving cluster munitions"[1860] and concluded that due to the high population density in Aleppo, the use of such weapon represented an indiscriminate attack and a war crime.[1861] In 2019, Human Rights Watch made similar accusations regarding the Russo-Syrian bombardments in the Idlib Region.[1862]

Neither Human Rights Watch nor the IICI specified whether the bombs were dropped by Russian or Syrian planes.[1863] As I have explained above, both countries use the same aircraft and weaponry which makes it difficult to attribute a specific attack to Russia.[1864] However, there is secondary evidence that Russia equips its planes in Syria with cluster bombs. During a visit of Foreign Minister Lavrov to Syria, the Russian TV-Station RT accidentally televised Russian planes at Khmeimim airbase that carried cluster munitions under their wings.[1865]

In the Russo-Georgian War, on the other hand, we find abundant evidence for Russia's use of cluster munitions. An OSCE report confirms that Russia readily used this weapon in the 2008 war.[1866] The Tagliavini Report goes even further. Not only did Russian forces resort to cluster munitions, but their use in populated areas also led to "indiscriminate attacks and the

---

1860 IICI, 'Report of the Independent International Commission of Inquiry on the Syrian Arab Republic (A/HRC/34/64)' (n 1822) 12.

1861 ibid.

1862 'Russia/Syria: Flurry of Prohibited Weapons Attacks' (Human Rights Watch, 3 June 2019) <https://www.hrw.org/news/2019/06/03/russia/syria-flurry-prohibited-weapons-attacks>.

1863 The IICI reports leave this question open, because this can almost never be assessed with certainty. Only in relation to chlorine bombs the report explicitly states that in "none of the incidents reviewed did information gathered suggest the involvement of Russian forces" and attributes them to the Syrian forces, see IICI, 'Report of the Independent International Commission of Inquiry on the Syrian Arab Republic (A/HRC/34/64)' (n 1822) 12.

1864 See above pp 363 et seq.

1865 Минобороны показало кассетные бомбы на выставке о войне в Сирии. Россия всегда отрицала их использование [Ministry of Defence showed cluster bombs at military exhibition in Syria. Russia had always denied their use]' (Meduza, 26 July 2019) <https://meduza.io/feature/2019/07/26/minoborony-pokazalo-kassetnye-bomby-na-vystavke-o-voyne-v-sirii-rossiya-vsegda-otritsala-ih-ispolzovanie>.

1866 OSCE/ODIHR, 'Human Rights in the War Affected Areas Following the Conflict in Georgia' (2008) 20.

violation of the principle of precaution."[1867] The Commission *inter alia* relied on data collected by Human Rights Watch that found

> *"overwhelming evidence that several villages in the Gori and Kareli Districts had been hit by air-dropped RBK-500s and RBK-250s carrying AO-2.5 RTM submunitions and by Hurricane missiles carrying 9N210 submunitions."*[1868]

All these weapon systems are of Russian origin. Unlike in Syria, the weapon here leads to the culprit, because Georgia did not stockpile these weapon systems.[1869] Furthermore, there are eyewitness accounts that corroborate the suspicion that Russia launched the attacks.[1870] Human Rights Watch concluded that at least three cluster munition strikes were "indiscriminate" and thus violated IHL. The attacks may even have violated the principle of distinction, because there were no military targets in the vicinity.[1871]

Further evidence that Russia used cluster munitions in the Georgian war comes from the Netherlands. After the Dutch cameraman Stan Storimans was killed on a central square in Gori, the Dutch Ministry of Foreign Affairs established a commission of inquiry. The investigators concluded that Storimans was killed by a cluster munition shrapnel and that "the cluster weapon must have been dropped by a tactical ballistic missile of the SS 26 type originating from the Russian Federation."[1872]

Despite the overwhelming evidence, Russia categorically denied the use of cluster munitions in Georgia.[1873] In response to a questionnaire for the Tagliavini Report it stated:

1867 IIFFMCG, 'Report of the Independent International Fact-Finding Mission on the Conflict in Georgia (Tagliavini Report) Volume II' (n 1109) 343.

1868 Human Rights Watch, 'Up in Flames – Humanitarian Law Violations and Civilian Victims in the Conflict over South Ossetia' (n 1180) 104.

1869 Human Rights Watch, 'A Dying Practice – the Use of Cluster Munitions by Russian and Georgia in August 2008' (2009) 40; Tweede Kamer der Staten-Generaal, 'Kamerstuk 2008–2009, 31595 Nr. 2: Verslag Onderzoeksmissie Storimans' (2008) 6. The report is available at <https://zoek.officielebekendmakingen.nl/kst-31595-2-b1>.

1870 Human Rights Watch, 'Up in Flames – Humanitarian Law Violations and Civilian Victims in the Conflict over South Ossetia' (n 1180) 104.

1871 ibid 105.

1872 Tweede Kamer der Staten-Generaal (n 1870).

1873 'Russia Denies Use of Cluster Bombs in Georgia' (Sputnik, 15 August 2008) <http://en.rian.ru/world/20080815/116065270.html>.

> *"Cluster munitions, though available to the strike units of the Russian Federation Air Force [...] have never been used."*[1874]

When Putin was confronted with the findings of the Storimans Report at a press conference in Amsterdam (2013), he countered that he "did not even know about this. But we will definitely look into it and investigate."[1875] Needless to say, that such investigation never took place.

As I have explained above, the use of cluster munitions is not illegal *per se*. Russia has not ratified the CCM and may use the weapon in line with the principle of distinction, proportionality, and precautions. Therefore, it is interesting that Russia prefers to deny the (well-documented) *fact* that it has used cluster munitions, instead of arguing that it has used them *in line* with IHL. It probably regards the latter as too "risky." A legal argument can be countered, while challenging the facts avoids any meaningful discussion on the law altogether. In Syria, such a denial is more feasible – if still not credible – because both Damascus and Moscow use the same planes and weaponry. In Georgia, Russia tries to hide the obvious which reminds us of the crude, but obstinate denial of the presence of on-duty soldiers in eastern Ukraine. In both cases, however, the limitations that IHL imposes on cluster munitions are degraded to a showcase rule – a rule that Russia can use against others, but which does not restrict its own conduct. This allows Moscow to condemn strikes in South Sudan as "indiscriminate" without applying the same restrictions to its operations in Georgia and Syria.

3. The MH17 incident – "and then, bodies just fell from the sky"[1876]

My third case study of Russia's factual denial concerns the downing of Malaysia Airlines flight MH17. This example may be called the odd one out, because the plane was not shot down by Russian soldiers – even

---

1874 IIFFMCG, 'Report of the Independent International Fact-Finding Mission on the Conflict in Georgia (Tagliavini Report) Volume III – Views of the Sides on the Conflict, Chronologies and Responses to Questionnaires' (n 960) 484.

1875 'Путин пообещал прояснить вопрос о гибели голландца в Грузии в 2008 г [Putin Promised to Shed Light on the Death of a Dutch Citizen in Georgia in 2008]' (Ria Novosti, 8 April 2008) <https://ria.ru/20130408/931601162.html>.

1876 Eye witness account from eastern Ukraine taken from the Vice News documentary 'Russian Roulette – Dispatch 60' (Vice News, 18 July 2014), available at <https://www.youtube.com/watch?v=Px2rfWBW4wg>.

though the Russian State provided generous aid to the perpetrators, namely separatist units in eastern Ukraine. Thus, it does not concern a violation *by* Russia, but by a close ally that acted with Russian *support*. At the same time, the incident is emblematic, for it shows how Moscow aims to stifle any meaningful discussion regarding accountability by burying the facts under a barrage of fake information.

3.1 The crash of MH17 – a tragic day in July

On 17 July 2014, Malaysia Airlines (MH) flight 17 from Amsterdam to Kuala Lumpur was shot down over eastern Ukraine. The crash left all 298 passengers and crew members dead. The wreckage site of nearly 50 km² covered the fields around the village of Hrabove in rebel-controlled territory.[1877] The first journalists to arrive on site reported from a surreal scene. Shocked locals and fighters in ragtag uniforms swarmed through a sea of debris, personal belongings, and body parts.[1878]

OSCE observers arrived the next day, followed by international investigators.[1879] As most victims were of Dutch origin, the Netherlands headed a Joint Investigation Team (JIT) composed of Australian, Belgian, Dutch, Malaysian, and Ukrainian experts.[1880] Soon after the crash, international media outlets and politicians voiced the suspicion that a separatist unit was behind the downing.[1881] Their first instinct proved right. The findings of the JIT investigators, the Dutch Safety Board (OVV), and several open-source investigators paint a clear picture. There is conclusive evidence that MH17 was shot down by a separatist unit using a Buk surface-to-air missile. While there is no evidence that Russia gave the order to launch the attack, Moscow had delivered the Buk anti-aircraft system to the rebels only days before. At this point, one can only speculate about the true

---

1877 Dutch Safety Board (OVV), 'Crash of Malaysia Airlines Flight MH17' (2015) 9.

1878 One of the first news outlet on site was Vice News. The documentary 'Russian Roulette – Dispatch 60' (Vice News, 18 July 2014) is available at <https://www.youtube.com/watch?v=Px2rfWBW4wg>.

1879 'MH17 Crash: OSCE Investigators Reach East Ukraine Site' (BBC, 18 July 2014) <https://www.bbc.com/news/world-asia-28361908>.

1880 Government of the Netherlands, 'The Criminal Investigation' <https://www.government.nl/topics/mh17-incident/achieving-justice/the-criminal-investigation>.

1881 See, for example, the statement by US President Barak Obama on 18 July 2014, available at <https://www.youtube.com/watch?v=iM-61K7l_mY>.

motives for shooting down a civilian plane. Most likely, the separatists mistook the Boeing for a Ukrainian An-26 military aircraft.[1882]

I will provide further detail on these findings when contrasting it with the Russian version of events. In terms of IHL, the downing represents a violation of the principle of distinction, since the civilian plane did not constitute a military target. In addition, the attack violated the principle of precautions, i.e. the obligation to gather sufficient reconnaissance on a target before attacking. Those directly responsible for the launch decision may be guilty of a war crime under IHL and/or murder under domestic criminal law.[1883] With regards to the Russian State, the provision of a powerful weapon like Buk to untrained hands raises the question of State responsibility.[1884] In the following, however, I will not attempt to answer this lush bouquet of legal questions. Rather, I will show how Russia tried to avoid *any* legal discussion by unleashing an impressive salvo of alternative facts.

3.2 Finding responsibility – Russia's barrage of alternative facts

Shortly after MH17 was shot down, the Russian Ministry of Defence held a memorable press conference. Moscow presented not only one, but a series of alternative – and contradictory – explanations for the crash. Firstly, spokesman Andrey Kartapolov implied that a *Ukrainian* jet had shot down the Boeing using an air-to-air missile and produced maps, pictures, and flight data supporting this theory. Secondly, he suggested that Ukrainian air control had deliberately deviated flight MH17 to lure it into the conflict region, in order to provoke a crash. Thirdly, Andrey Kartapolov insinuated that the plane may have been shot down by a Ukrainian Buk

---

1882 In the weeks before the downing of MH17, the Ukrainians had suffered considerable losses in the air. From April to August 2014 alone, the rebels shot down four Mi-24 helicopter gunships, two Mi-8 helicopter transports, six Su-25s, three transport planes, and four strike and air-superiority jets, see Galeotti, *Armies of Russia's War in Ukraine* (n 785) 16, 50.

1883 See the opening statement of the public prosecutor at The Hague District Court, available at <https://www.prosecutionservice.nl/topics/mh17-plane-crash/prosecution-and-trial/opening-statement>.

1884 Marieke de Hoon, 'Navigating the Legal Horizon: Lawyering the MH17 Disaster' (2017) 33 Utrecht Journal of International and European Law 90, 99; Marieke de Hoon, 'Pursuing Justice for MH17: The Role of the Netherlands' (2019) 49 Netherlands Yearbook of International Law 2018 245.

surface-to-air missile which was allegedly spotted nearby. He produced several satellite pictures and videos in support of this theory. At the same time, he firmly stressed that Russia has never delivered anti-aircraft systems – or any weapons for that matter – to the rebels in eastern Ukraine.[1885]

All of these theories were untenable. The renowned experts of the JIT and OVV, as well as open source investigators, disproved the Russian allegations one by one.[1886] The mysterious deviation from the plane's course was negligible and occurred due to bad weather. There was no other plane in the vicinity, which exposed the Russian evidence as a blatant lie.[1887] Rather, the investigators concluded that MH17 had been shot down by a Buk surface-to-air missile.[1888] This missile, however, was not of Ukrainian origin as Andrey Kartapolov had claimed. Rather it belonged to the 53rd Anti-aircraft Missile Brigade of the Russian Army stationed at Kursk.[1889] The Russian satellite pictures of a Ukrainian Buk near the crash site were likely to have been altered by Photoshop.[1890] The hand that "pulled the trigger" belonged to a pro-Russian separatist. The missile that brought down the Boeing was fired from rebel-controlled territory near the village of Pervomayskiy.[1891] In addition, the Ukrainian Secret Service (SBU) intercepted a phone conversation in which a separatist fighter informs a

---

1885 The full press conference is available at <https://www.youtube.com/watch?v=4b NPInuSqfs>.

1886 For a comprehensive summary of the events please see the excellent podcast series prepared by Bellingcat; especially episode 2 deals with the misinformation provided by the Russian government after the crash, 'MH17, Episode 2 Guide: A Pack of Lies' (Bellingcat, 24 July 2019) <https://www.bellingcat.com/resource s/podcasts/2019/07/24/bellingcat-podcast-mh17-episode-2-guide-a-pack-of-lies/>.

1887 Dutch Safety Board (OVV) (n 1878) 109.

1888 ibid 253–254.

1889 Both Bellingcat and the JIT confirmed the origin of the Buk. See Eliot Higgins, 'Who's Lying? An In-depth Analysis of the Luhansk Buk Video' (Bellingcat, 29 May 2015) <https://www.bellingcat.com/news/uk-and-europe/2015/05/29/wh os-lying-an-in-depth-analysis-of-the-luhansk-buk-video/>; Government of the Netherlands, 'The Criminal Investigation' <https://www.government.nl/topics/ mh17-incident/achieving-justice/the-criminal-investigation>.

1890 Bellingcat, 'Forensic Analysis of Satellite Images Released by the Russian Ministry of Defense' (2014).

1891 Pieter van Huis, 'The MH17 Trial Part 1: New Material From The Four Defendants' (Bellingcat, 20 April 2020) <https://www.bellingcat.com/news/uk-and-eu rope/2020/04/20/the-mh17-trial-part-1-new-materials-from-the-four-defendants/ >.

Russian GRU General that one of their units had shot down a civilian plane.[1892]

In sum, all independent investigations reached the same conclusion: Flight MH17 was shot down by a separatist unit. While there is no evidence that the Kremlin ordered the launch, it had delivered the weapons to the separatists and was informed immediately after the tragedy.[1893] Despite the compelling evidence, Russia continues to deny any involvement.[1894] Rather it embarked on the usual strategy of absolute and obstinate denial, even if on an unprecedented scale. Instead of presenting a coherent alternative version, Russia presented numerous incoherent theories calling into question every piece of evidence. In the words of Russian security expert Mark Galeotti: The Russians "do not have a clear alternative narrative [...] What they have decided to do is not to say we know the answer; but to say: *no one* knows the answer."[1895] Embarking on this road of absolute denial also means leaving IHL in the ditch.

The MH17 incident sent a shockwave through the international community. In its aftermath, many laudable attempts to unearth the truth and shed light on the legal issues of State responsibility and criminal accountability were seen. The Netherlands and Australia publicly announced that they hold Russia *as a State* responsible for the downing of MH17.[1896] In parallel, relatives of the victims have turned to the ECtHR to hold Russia responsible for the downing.[1897] Furthermore, Dutch prosecutors filed criminal charges against three Russians and one Ukrainian national in June 2019. Among them is former GRU officer Igor "Strelkov" Girkin,

---

1892 The intercepted phone conversations are available at <https://www.youtube.co m/watch?v=BbyZYgSXdyw>.

1893 Galeotti, *Armies of Russia's War in Ukraine* (n 785) 16.

1894 Luke Harding, 'Three Russians and One Ukrainian to Face MH17 Murder Charges' (The Guardian, 19 June 2019) <https://www.theguardian.com/world/2 019/jun/19/mh17-criminal-charges-ukraine-russia>.

1895 Mark Galeotti, 'MH17, Episode 2 Guide: A Pack of Lies' (Bellingcat, 24 July 2019) at minute 31:30 <https://www.bellingcat.com/resources/podcasts/2019/07 /24/bellingcat-podcast-mh17-episode-2-guide-a-pack-of-lies/>.

1896 Government of the Netherlands, 'MH17: The Netherlands and Australia Hold Russia Responsible' (25 May 2018) <https://www.government.nl/latest/news/20 18/05/25/mh17-the-netherlands-and-australia-hold-russia-responsible>.

1897 ECtHR, *Ayley and Others v Russia*, No 25714/16, lodged on 6 May 2016 and ECtHR, *Angeline and Others v Russia*, No 56328/18, lodged on 23 November 2018. The applicants argue that the strike can be attributed to Russia. Alternatively, they argue that Russia failed to prevent the downing, or was at least complicit in it. See ECtHR, Statement of the Facts for Applications Nos 25714/16 and 56328/18, communicated on 3 April 2019, para 57.

one of the leading figures of the separatists in eastern Ukraine.[1898] The criminal trial began in spring 2020 at The Hague District Court in absence of the four accused. However laudable these initiatives, Russia maintains its position of absolute denial and does not cooperate in any way – neither in evidentiary issues nor with regards to extradition.[1899] The Dutch prosecutors have even accused Russia of trying to thwart the criminal trial and stressed that key witnesses "fear for their lives."[1900]

4. Conclusion

These incidents send a clear message. In cases where its conduct might result in international condemnation for a violation of IHL, Russia choses to deny the facts instead of providing legal arguments. A legal argument can be countered or defeated. Worse still, it can be turned against you, whereas denying the facts stalls the discussion before it even starts. While this may be a common strategy in international relations, the scale of Russia's disinformation campaign defies well-established principles of *realpolitik*, namely that a lie is only effective if it cannot be proved wrong.[1901]

It is interesting to contrast this "alternative-fact approach" with the attitude of other States. For example, the Georgian authorities also stood accused of using cluster munitions in the 2008 war. Georgia stressed that "cluster munitions, had been used in full compliance with the applicable rules of international humanitarian law, in particular the principles of distinction and proportionality" and provided legal arguments.[1902] The US, for example, admitted amidst increasing public pressure that it was responsible for attacking an MSF hospital in Kunduz. The US representative

---

1898 See pp 255 et seq.

1899 Marieke de Hoon, 'Prosecuting MH17 and the Dutch and Australian Move on Russia's State Responsibility' (Australian Institute of International Affairs, 25 July 2019) <http://www.internationalaffairs.org.au/australianoutlook/prosecuting-mh17-the-dutch-and-australian-move-on-russias-state-responsibility/>.

1900 'MH17 Trial: Russia Keen to Thwart Investigation, Says Prosecutor' (The Guardian, 11 March 2020) <https://www.theguardian.com/world/2020/mar/11/mh17-trial-russia-keen-to-thwart-investigation-says-prosecutor>.

1901 Ivan Krastev and Stephen Holmes, *The Light That Failed: Why the West Is Losing the Fight for Democracy (Electronic Edition)* (Pegasus Books 2020) 282.

1902 IIFFMCG, 'Report of the Independent International Fact-Finding Mission on the Conflict in Georgia (Tagliavini Report) Volume III – Views of the Sides on the Conflict, Chronologies and Responses to Questionnaires' (n 960) 339.

in the UN Security Council expressed deep regret and promised to study "what had gone wrong."[1903]

To be clear: Neither Georgia nor the US are humanitarian angels. Georgia's use of cluster munitions was heavily criticised for its collateral civilian damage.[1904] The US tried to cover up their responsibility for the Kunduz attack and only reluctantly assumed responsibility for the erroneous attack.[1905] However, when confronted with irrefutable evidence these countries have either accepted their responsibility or tried to provide a legal justification.

Russia, on the other hand, follows a policy of complete and absolute denial that makes any legal discussion superfluous. The incidental casualty is IHL which has no role to play, neither before, nor during, nor after the violation. IHL's remaining role is reduced to a showcase rule – a rule that exists for others but does not apply to Russia. This confirms a trend we have seen in other fields of international law, where Moscow uses legal norms as "a language in which it is possible to lie."[1906] This allows Moscow to call Ukraine's use of cluster munitions "barbaric" while using them indiscriminately in Syria;[1907] to blame Kyiv for shooting down a civilian aircraft, while having supplied the anti-aircraft system to the rebels; to condemn the US attack on a hospital in Kunduz, while targeting medical installations in Idlib and Aleppo.

1903 Statement by US representative to the United Nations, Michele J Sison (3 May 2016), available at <https://www.un.org/press/en/2016/sc12347.doc.htm>.

1904 Human Rights Watch, 'Up in Flames – Humanitarian Law Violations and Civilian Victims in the Conflict over South Ossetia' (n 1180) 64.

1905 Glenn Greenwald, 'The Radically Changing Story of the U.S. Airstrike on Afghan Hospital: From Mistake to Justification' (The Intercept, 5 October 2015) <https://theintercept.com/2015/10/05/the-radically-changing-story-of-the-u-s-airstrike-on-afghan-hospital-from-mistake-to-justification/>.

1906 Mälksoo, *Russian Approaches to International Law* (n 6) 191. He argues that, for example, with regards to *ius ad bellum* Russia uses the law as "a language in which it is possible to lie."

1907 Landmine and Cluster Munition Monitor, 'Russian Federation' <http://the-monitor.org/en-gb/reports/2015/russian-federation/cluster-munition-ban-policy.aspx#fn7>.

Part III: Contrasting the Past and the Present

"As Saul journeyed, he came near Damascus, and suddenly a light shone around him from heaven. Then he fell to the ground, and heard a voice saying to him, "Saul, Saul, why are you persecuting Me?"

Acts 9, 3–4 (NKJV)

This episode from the Bible describes the moment when Saul's life changes. He recognises the Lord and starts to preach the word of Christ in the synagogues. Later, he will be called Paul and become one of the central figures of early Christianity. The story of his conversion has become a metaphor for radical betterment. In my introduction I have inversed this process and asked the question: Did Russia turn from Paul to Saul in terms of IHL? That is, from advancing the law to avoiding the law?

The first part of this thesis dealt with Russia's historical role, while the second part zoomed in on its current practice. The following (and last) part will merge Russia's history and its present conduct.[1908] We will take two steps back to look at the bigger picture before us.

As a *first* step, I will contrast Russia's historical and contemporary role. At first sight, the difference is staggering. In many aspects, Russia now holds the very opposite position; IHL has fallen out of favour. However, I am fully aware that a comparison spanning a period of 150 years bears the risk of being simplistic. Therefore, I will take a *second* step back and focus on three factors that might explain why the Russian attitude has changed so radically. For not only has Russia evolved over time. The laws of war have changed. Warfare itself has changed, and with it, Russia's attitude towards IHL.

1908 In the following, I will not use cross-references when referring to my findings above, so as not to overburden the text with footnotes, Rather, I will only use citations when I introduce new ideas or use verbatim quotes.

1. O tempora, o mores – contrasting Russia's approach to IHL

Russia has radically changed its position on IHL in numerous respects. First of all, this concerns its role in diplomatic relations. Russia once initiated the St Petersburg Declaration and the Hague Conferences of 1899 and 1907 that led to the first comprehensive code of warfare. Russia's most renowned diplomat, Fyodor Martens, was also an expert on the laws of war and managed to instil his knowledge into the discussions. Russia adopted IHL as a trademark in international relations and competed with the ICRC and Switzerland for the leading role in humanitarian affairs.

Today, Russia blocks numerous initiatives in the regulation of weapons. It did not sign any of the major treaties that innovated IHL after 1991, let alone initiate a treaty-making process. For instance, Russia never signed the treaties prohibiting anti-personnel mines and cluster munitions. It also strongly opposes the regulation of nuclear weapons, autonomous weapons systems, and white phosphorous. This cannot but appear like historical irony. The driving force behind the first-ever weapons treaty, the St Petersburg Declaration of 1868, is now leading the opposition against any further regulation. The fate of the Martens Clause serves to illustrate this change of heart. The ingenious Russian invention once allowed for a compromise between strong and weak countries at the First 1899 Hague Conference. The Clause acted as a fall-back rule that closed possible lacunas with the "laws of humanity, and the dictates of the public conscience."[1909] While the Clause has become a corner stone of IHL, Russia explicitly dismantled its own legacy in the ICJ *Nuclear Weapons Advisory Opinion* declaring that "today the 'Martens clause' may formally be considered inapplicable."[1910]

Secondly, Moscow neglects the implementation of IHL. This is exemplified by the poor State of its domestic war crimes legislation. Russia once contributed greatly to the development of international criminal law. It penalised misconduct in war as early as 1868.[1911] The Soviet Union pioneered in this field by prosecuting Nazi war criminals as early as 1943.

1909 See for this above at p 56.
1910 Letter from the Ambassador of the Russian Federation, together with Written Comments of the Government of the Russian Federation (19 June 1995) 13.
1911 Esakov (n 702) 372. The author quotes Art 267 and Art 273–275 of the Воинский устав 'О наказаниях' [Military Law 'On Punishments'] of 1868 that provided punishment for imposing an unauthorised indemnity on residents of localities occupied by the army, robbing dead or wounded soldiers, and pillaging.

Furthermore, the Soviet Union contributed immensely and helped to lay a milestone in ICL. Soviet scholars like Aron Traynin shaped the contemporary debates on international crimes. Today, international criminal law still remains a hot topic in Russian academic circles, but the discourse stops at the wall of the ivory tower. While the Russian Criminal Code contains provisions on war crimes, they are both dogmatically deficient and *de facto* a dead letter. The lack of a single conviction for war crimes under Art 356 CCRF effectively sanctioned the widespread IHL violations during the two Chechen Wars. Recently, Moscow withdrew its signature from the ICC Statute, shattering any hope that scholars and activists may have harboured of improving this faulty system.

Thirdly, and most importantly, Russia's *volte-face* is illustrated by its behaviour in recent wars. Rules of IHL that Russia had once fought for are now neglected, ignored, or evaded by denying the facts. Belligerent occupation provides a good example. Protecting the occupied territories had once constituted a central pillar of Martens' "favourite child," the Brussels Declaration of 1874. While the Declaration never achieved binding status, the Russian Empire *voluntarily* imposed these obligations on its own Army during the Russo-Turkish War (1877–1878). On the whole, the Tsar's Army kept these promises and respected the obligations in occupied Bulgaria and Turkey. In 1899, Russia initiated the First Hague Peace Conference where the rules on occupation were finally cast into a binding treaty. Finally, in 1949 the Soviet Union supported the ICRC's efforts to adopt a strong civilian convention that further reinforced the existing protection in occupation. It is safe to say that Russia has done more than any other State to carve out the rules in occupied territories.

Today, there are five different situations with Russian involvement that qualify as occupation under IHL. Crimea is the most obvious example. Transdniestria, Abkhazia, South Ossetia, and Donbas are at least partially occupied.[1912] Moscow does not recognise its role as an occupant in *any* of these cases. Applying IHL is out of question. Rather, the Russian discourse closely links the term "occupation" to the barbaric crimes of the Nazis during the Second World War which makes it an insult rather than a legal classification. It goes without saying that the atrocities committed by the Nazis against the Soviet people were particularly brutal. From a historical angle, it is understandable that occupation carries such an enor-

---

1912 I have not discussed the example of Donbas under the angle of occupation, but the context resembles Transdniestria, Abkhazia, and South Ossetia. For a case study of proxy occupation in Donbas see Gilder (n 1078).

mous emotional burden. Nevertheless, the Hague Regulations conceived occupation as a neutral legal term. It remains a common occurrence in war and does not represent an "anomaly."[1913] The Russian approach, however, has completely sidelined this framework. What Martens conceived as a neutral, clear definition in the 1899 Hague Regulations has become an emotionally charged insult that can never apply to Russia. The decision of the Constitutional Court on 'Law on Cultural Objects' (1998) illustrates this. The Court ruled that the Soviets were not bound by the framework of occupation when establishing control over Germany at the end of the Second World War, because the Germans had forgone these rights as citizens of an "aggressor" State.[1914]

The protection of non-combatants against the conduct of hostilities is another instance where Russia abandoned rules that it once helped to create. In 1868, the Tsar initiated the St Petersburg Conference that broke with the principle of an unfettered war. It enshrined the principles of humanity, proportionality, and the prohibition of unnecessary suffering in its preamble. This sowed the seed from which would sprout the entire framework of the conduct of hostilities. Implicitly, the St Petersburg preamble condemned violence against civilians, since it stated that the "*only* legitimate aim in war is to weaken the *military* forces of the enemy." The Hague Regulations elaborated on this protection. Finally, in 1949, the Soviet Union was the driving force behind the Fourth Geneva Convention that exclusively applied to civilians, as well as the introduction of Common Article 3 that extended the protection of civilians to non-international armed conflicts.

What is the legacy of these promises today? At times Russian troops did behave in an extremely disciplined manner in order to avoid civilian casualties. In Crimea this respectful behaviour earned them the nickname

---

1913 Dinstein (n 984) 1. Dinstein argues that belligerent occupation is not an "anomaly or even an aberration", but "when an international armed conflict breaks out, armies tend to be on the move on the ground whenever they have an opportunity to do so."

1914 Постановление Конституционного Суда Российской Федерации по делу о проверке конституционности Федерального закона, 15.04.1998, 'О культурных ценностях, перемещенных в Союз ССР в результате Второй мировой войны и находящихся на территории Российской Федерации' [Ruling of the Constitutional Court of the Russian Federation Concerning the Constitutionality of Federal Law, 15 April 1998, 'On Cultural Objects Relocated to the USSR as a Result of the Second World War Currently Located on the Territory of the Russian Federation'] para 4.

"polite people" by those sympathetic to the annexation.[1915] The majority of conflicts with Russian participation, however, saw a high civilian death toll. In the Chechen Wars, for example, Moscow denied the application of IHL for over ten years which adversely affected its soldiers' behaviour on the ground: civilian suffering was tremendous, and tens of thousands of civilians died in indiscriminate aerial bombings or artillery shelling. Today in Syria, we witness a Russo-Syrian bombardment campaign that deliberately attacks hospitals. In Georgia and Syria, Russia also used cluster munitions in densely populated areas in an indiscriminate way.

From these examples a more fundamental turnaround can be evinced. Russia used to advance, cite, and adhere to IHL in an almost ostentatious manner. In the 19th century, Russia displayed remarkable efforts in taking the law from the books and applying it on the battlefield. It issued a military manual – a revolutionary step at the time.[1916] Both in the Russo-Turkish War and the Russo-Japanese War, the Empire undertook enormous efforts to protect captured and wounded enemy combatants. It shaped good practice such as the communication of name and rank of POWs and wounded soldiers to the enemy power through a central agency. Most importantly, it took *pride* in its adherence to the laws of war. Today, this has changed dramatically. Moscow evades the application of IHL in numerous ways. By outmanoeuvring the threshold of application (Chapter III "The Paintbrush"), by outsourcing warfare (Chapter IV "The Apprentice"), or by simply denying facts that may point to IHL violations (Chapter V "The Sledgehammer"). While Russia still cites the rules in abstract resolutions and with regards to third countries,[1917] it has successfully "showcased" IHL. The laws of war have become rules that apply *in abstracto* or in relation to other nations, but do not restrict Russian conduct in war. Chapters III, IV, and V, illustrated in great detail how Russia has attempted to evade the application of IHL using a toolbox of factual denial, outsourcing, and legal loopholes.

1915 Galeotti, *Russian Political War* (n 1458) 73.

1916 There are few examples of earlier military manuals. One is the Lieber Code (1863) to the Union Forces of the US. Today, most countries have elaborated a military manual that explains their stance on the laws of war.

1917 See, for example, the Russian statements regarding the indiscriminate use of cluster munitions in South Sudan (n 1854), the application of the framework of occupation to the US in Syria and to Israel in the Golan Heights (n 1203 and 1204), or the Russian support to UN Security Council Resolution 2286 (2016) (n 1808).

Yet, it is not all black and white. In certain aspects Russia did not change. During the Soviet period especially, certain fault lines appeared that are still visible today. The Soviets already displayed a tendency to deny facts in order to evade the law. In the Afghan War (1979–1989) they never recognised the application of IHL to the Red Army. In other conflicts like Hungary (1956) they rejected the application of IHL with a mix of peculiar legal arguments and factual denial. While the Soviets favoured the development of international criminal law, it was out of the question to apply this framework to their own acts. This double standard culminated at Nuremberg where the Soviet prosecutor accused the Nazis of the massacre of Katyn – the most notorious war crime committed by the Soviets themselves.

Most importantly, Russia's resistance regarding external oversight stretches from Tsarist times to the present day. Russia has always objected to any meaningful external compliance mechanism. In the early days of IHL this can be seen from its sceptical attitude towards the ICRC. The Tsars harboured distrust for the Swiss organisation and tried to break its humanitarian monopoly on several occasions. At the Hague Conference of 1899, for example, Russia attempted to subordinate the Geneva Conventions to the Hague Law. Tensions with the ICRC flared up after the October revolution and relations reached an all-time low after the Second World War. David Forsythe, author of a comprehensive study on the ICRC, argues that the Soviets never cooperated with the organisation in a meaningful way throughout the Cold War.[1918] Russia's reluctance towards external oversight was not confined to the ICRC. The Soviets understood, better than most other imperial powers, that they could accept virtually any text as long as it did not infringe upon their sovereign discretion to refuse outside supervision.[1919] While they advanced the law, they slowed down its enforcement. At the 1949 Conference, the Soviets obstructed any meaningful enforcement initiative such as the proposal to strengthen the role of the Protecting Powers.

This freedom-loving, sovereignty-centric spirit still prevails in modern-day Russia. In the past years, Moscow has been eliminating all remaining compliance mechanisms one by one. In 2015, it stalled the talks about a universal periodic review mechanism that would have obliged States to report on their IHL compliance at regular intervals. In 2016, it withdrew its signature from the ICC Statute. In 2019, it left the IHFFC. It has become

---

1918 Forsythe (n 522) 53.
1919 van Dijk (n 507) 234.

clear that Russia's current sovereignty-centric conception of international law excludes any external compliance mechanism.

There is, however, one important difference between Russia's resistance to external oversight in the past and today. Of course, Tsarist Russia insisted on a strong concept of sovereignty – as did virtually all States in the late Westphalian system. However, this did not affect IHL because the law was held in high regard *internally*. As I have shown above, this Russian enthusiasm has long cooled. Given the current lack of intrinsic motivation to respect and advance IHL, the absence of an external compliance mechanism is painfully obvious.

To conclude, the contrast is stark. While the façade of IHL already began to fissure in Soviet times, the cracks have widened. When comparing Russia's attitude during Tsarist times and today we find little common ground except the long-standing resistance to external oversight. In all other areas, Russia's enthusiasm for IHL has withered.

2. Looking behind the obvious – why has Russia changed?

Having said that, my comparison would remain simplistic if it stopped here. Russia's turnaround is more than a historical fun-fact. The reasons behind it are as interesting as the phenomenon itself. If Saul had simply told his followers that he stopped hunting down Christians to become one himself, people would not have believed him. What made him credible, was his reason – he had received a sign from God on the road to Damascus. He was blinded before he converted. So, let me rephrase the question. Yes, Russia's attitude towards IHL changed. But can we identify the reasons that led to this changed behaviour? In the following, I offer three explanations as to why Russia's humanitarian fervour has faded: The changed character of IHL, the radical changes in warfare, and the resulting lack of benefits that IHL has to offer to a State like Russia today.

2.1 *O tempora, o leges* – IHL as a victim of its own success?

> *"Herr, die Not ist groß!*
> *Die ich rief, die Geister*
> *Werd' ich nun nicht los."*

> *"Wrong I was in calling*
> *Spirits, I avow,*
> *For I find them galling,*
> *Cannot rule them now."*

Johann Wolfgang von Goethe, 'Der Zauberlehrling' (1797)[1920]

Russia started promoting IHL when it was still in its infancy. At the time of the St Petersburg Declaration in 1868, IHL treaty law consisted of only ten Articles: the provisions of the 1864 Geneva Convention that protected wounded soldiers. Up until 1949, the Geneva Conventions mostly dealt with combatants and did not protect civilians *per se* apart from the regime of occupation.[1921] In addition, IHL only applied to inter-State armed conflicts.

Since the end of the Second World War we have witnessed what Theodor Meron called the "humanization" of the laws of war. This process is "driven to a large extent by human rights and the principles of humanity."[1922] This change is already evident from the semantics of the legal framework. Before 1949, States referred to IHL as "laws and customs of war."[1923] The term international *humanitarian* law was only introduced to describe the Four Geneva Conventions of 1949. Over time, it became the trademark for the entire framework applicable in armed conflict.[1924] The new name set the tone for the ensuing substantial changes. Today, the humanisation of IHL manifests itself in five aspects.

1920 Taken from Johann Wolfgang von Goethe's famous poem 'Der Zauberlehrling' [The Sourcer's Apprentice]. Translation by Paul Dyrsen (1878).

1921 Robert Heinsch, 'The International Committee of the Red Cross and the Geneva Conventions of 1949' in Robin Geiss, Andreas Zimmermann and Stefanie Haumer (eds), *Humanizing the Laws of War: the Red Cross and the Development of International Humanitarian Law* (Cambridge University Press 2017) 31.

1922 Theodor Meron, 'The Humanization of Humanitarian Law' (2000) 94 American Journal of International Law 239, 239.

1923 See e.g. the terminology used in the Hague Regulations (1907): "Regulations concerning the *Laws and Customs* of War on Land" (emphasis added).

1924 Meron, 'The Humanization of Humanitarian Law' (n 1923) 239. In Russia, scholars and practitioners mainly use Международное гуманитарное право [international humanitarian law] although Право вооруженных конфликтов is sometimes used synonymously. The US, Israel, and the UK, for example, continue to use the term law of armed conflict (LOAC).

Firstly, human rights law and IHL have converged. While both remain separate fields, they apply at the same time and mutually influence each other.[1925] In addition, IHL has borrowed substantial rules from human rights law. The adoption of the UDHR in 1948 greatly influenced the rules of the 1949 Geneva Conventions. From 1949 onwards, we see parallel protections in IHL and IHRL such as the prohibition of torture and cruel, inhuman, or degrading treatment and punishment, arbitrary arrest and detention, and fair trial rights.[1926] The ICTY has explicitly recognised this influence of the "impetuous development and propagation" of human rights on IHL after the Second World War.[1927]

Secondly, the delegates at the Diplomatic Conference of 1949 extended the scope of IHL. Until then, it applied only to inter-State conflicts. After the introduction of Common Article 3, IHL regulated internal conflicts as well. Since most of today's wars are NIACs, this represented a monumental leap forward. However, it also meant assimilating IHL to human rights law, because both fields now regulated internal situations that were formerly under the impermeable umbrella of State sovereignty. This "growing measure of convergence in [...] personal and territorial applicability" of human rights and IHL changed the perception of the law.[1928]

Thirdly, there is a growing trend to deduce individual rights from IHL norms. Initially, IHL represented classic inter-State law that conferred neither rights nor obligations onto individuals. After the Second World War, IHL was "drawn [...] in the direction of human rights law."[1929] The wording of the Geneva Conventions of 1949 and their *travaux préparatoires* suggest that they confer rights on individuals.[1930] In recent times, we have started to see more evidence for individual rights in IHL.[1931] Under Art 75 of the Rome Statute, for example, the ICC can award reparations to

---

1925 See Cordula Droege, 'The Interplay between International Humanitarian Law and International Human Rights Law in Situations of Armed Conflict' (2007) 40 Israel Law Review 310.

1926 Meron, 'The Humanization of Humanitarian Law' (n 1923) 245, 266–273.

1927 ICTY, *The Prosecutor v Duško Tadić* (IT-94-1-T), Decision on the Defence Motion for Interlocutory Appeal on Jurisdiction, 2 October 1995, para 97.

1928 Meron, 'The Humanization of Humanitarian Law' (n 1923) 245.

1929 ibid 244.

1930 Hill-Cawthorne (n 822) 1200.

1931 This development is not linear. Rather, it oscillated between an individual rights-based and a State-centric approach throughout the history of IHL. However, we can identify a trend towards a rights-based approach in recent years, see ibid 1211–1212.

individuals for violations of IHL. In addition, we increasingly see how classic human rights law mechanisms take part in enforcing IHL.[1932] The ECtHR, for instance, has rendered ground-breaking judgments regarding situations of armed conflict, e.g. the Chechen Wars, and even applied IHL *expressis verbis* in its later case law.[1933]

Fourthly, *non*-governmental actors play an increasingly important role in interpreting and developing IHL. While States used to be the "Masters of the Treaties" and their interpretation, today international organisations, NGOs, and civil society movements contribute to interpreting and developing IHL. NGOs like Human Rights Watch and Amnesty International, which originally emerged out of the international human rights movement, frequently accuse States of violating IHL.[1934] Furthermore, the ICRC Customary Study had a tremendous effect on the expansion of IHL in NIACs. While the study is based on State practice (*consuetudo*) and *opinio iuris*, the codification itself was not a State-driven initiative. At times, States felt uneasy and criticised the ICRC's methodology.[1935] Finally, even organs that were established by States themselves went on to develop IHL at an unforeseen level. The ICTY – an organ created by the UN Security Council – did not only apply but also developed IHL in crucial aspects. It went beyond the strict letter of the treaties, for example, by creating the category "internationalised armed conflicts" or by expanding the scope of protected persons under Art 4 GC IV.[1936]

1932 See Émilie Max, 'Implementing International Humanitarian Law Through Human Rights Mechanisms: Opportunity or Utopia?' (Geneva Academy of International Humanitarian Law and Human Rights 2019).

1933 See e.g. ECtHR, *Chigarov and Others v Armenia*, No 13216/05, 16 June 2015, para 96, where the Court pronounced itself on the question of belligerent occupation; see also ECtHR, Hassan v United Kingdom, No 29750/09, 16 September 2014, para 110; for the Chechen cases see p 204.

1934 See Human Rights Watch, 'Up in Flames – Humanitarian Law Violations and Civilian Victims in the Conflict over South Ossetia' (n 1180).

1935 The US, for example, has voiced its criticism. While it reiterated "its appreciation for the ICRC's continued efforts in this important area", it criticised the methodology of the study and challenged the customary status of certain rules, see John B Bellinger III and William J Haynes II, 'A US Government Response to the International Committee of the Red Cross Study *Customary International Humanitarian Law*' (2007) 89 International Review of the Red Cross 443.

1936 For internationalised armed conflicts see ICTY, *The Prosecutor v Duško Tadić* (IT-94-1-T), Appeals Chamber Judgment, 15 July 1999, para 131; for the scope of Art 4 GC IV see ICTY, *The Prosecutor v Duško Tadić* (IT-94-1-T), Decision on the Defence Motion for Interlocutory Appeal on Jurisdiction, 2 October 1995, para 70; for a detailed analysis of the *Tadić* Appeals Chamber judgment see

Fifthly, despite the chronic lack of enforcement mechanisms, IHL developed some gritty compliance mechanisms after the Second World War. After the Nuremberg Trials, individual criminal liability became an "explicit part of the law."[1937] The ICTY, ICTR, ICC as well as domestic courts prosecuting war crimes became the torchbearers of criminal accountability for IHL violations.[1938] Furthermore, the ICRC has become increasingly influential. During the Second World War, its headquarters were housed in the small Villa Moynier on Lake Geneva. Today it is the biggest humanitarian actor outside the UN with a budget of 2 billion Dollars and nearly 20 000 employees in more than 80 countries.[1939] Most importantly, IHL has received help from "outside." The UN Security Council, the General Assembly, and other UN institutions make frequent reference to IHL.[1940] Russia, for example, has had to face allegations for occupying Crimea in the General Assembly and justify its bombing campaign of Syrian hospitals in the Security Council.[1941] In addition, the number of humanitarian actors has exploded. Today, the public is sensitised to IHL violations that will be "shamed" by various NGOs that reach a wide audience.

There are two sides to this coin. From the victim's perspective, the increased protection is to be welcomed. From a State perspective, however, IHL has become more intrusive, rigid, and restrictive – in other words, a

---

Claus Kreß, 'Friedenssicherungs- und Konfliktvölkerrecht auf der Schwelle zur Postmoderne' [1996] EuGRZ 638.

1937 George Aldrich, 'Individuals as Subjects of International Humanitarian Law' in Jerzy Makarczyk (ed), *Theory of International Law at the Threshold of the 21st Century: Essays in Honour of Krzysztof Skubiszewski* (Kluwer Law International 1996) 853.

1938 See the recent special edition of the International Criminal Law Review that analyses this development, its advantages, and its challenges: 'Special Issue: National Prosecutions of International Crimes: Sentencing Practices and (Negotiated) Punishments' (2019) 19.

1939 ICRC, 'Where Does Your Money Go' <https://www.icrc.org/en/support-us/where-does-your-money-go>.

1940 Hans-Peter Gasser, 'The United Nations and International Humanitarian Law: The International Committee of the Red Cross and the United Nations' Involvement in the Implementation of International Humanitarian Law – International Symposium on the Occasion of the Fiftieth Anniversary of the United Nations' (ICRC 1995).

1941 UN General Assembly Resolution 71/205, UN Doc A/RES/71/205 (1 February 2017) 2; UN General Assembly Resolution 72/190, UN Doc A/RES/72/190 (19 December 2017) 2; UN General Assembly Resolution 73/263, UN Doc A/RES/73/263 (22 December 2018) 2; UN Security Council, 8589th meeting, UN Doc S/PV.8589 (30 July 2019).

framework very different from Russia's "golden age" in the 19th century. Stricter norms always bear the risk of non-compliance, or as Theodor Meron puts it: "Humanization may have triumphed, but mostly rhetorically."[1942] This development is exemplified by belligerent occupation. The framework was once a bone of contention and prevented consensus at the Brussels Conference in 1874. Today, too, occupation sparks heated debates. However, the common fear in 1874 and the challenges today could not be more different. In 1874 the delegates of smaller States feared that invading armies, seeking to benefit from the powers that the law granted to occupants, would declare occupation *prematurely* without actually controlling the area. At that time, occupation was considered an *advantage* to the occupant. When the rules for occupation grew stricter and it became more of a "burden than a boon" States shifted to avoiding the application of Art 42 HR.[1943]

The irony of this development is, of course, that it was Russia that sowed the seed of humanisation. Moscow had itself insisted on the ideal of "humanity" in the St Petersburg Declaration. In the words of Minister of War Dmitry Milyutin, humanity was the "one principle on which we all agree."[1944] Furthermore, Russia enshrined "humanity" as a safety net in the Martens Clause and the Soviet Union fought for the humanisation of internal armed conflicts. It seems, however, that the rapid development after the Second World War took States aback much like Goethe's "Sorcerer's Apprentice" whom I have quoted above. While Moscow contributed very little to the development of IHL after 1949, IHL evolved, nonetheless. Today, IHL belongs to the civil society as much as it belongs to the military. It is stricter, more codified, and it has increasingly merged with human rights law, from which Russia has grown equally estranged.[1945] It seems that Moscow called the "Spirits" of humanity, but "cannot rule them now."

1942 Meron, 'The Humanization of Humanitarian Law' (n 1923) 276.
1943 Benvenisti (n 990) 43.
1944 von Martens (n 44) 451.
1945 For Russia's difficult relationship with the ECtHR see n 1205 and Bowring, 'Russian Cases in the ECtHR and the Question of Implementation' (n 836); Mälksoo, *Russian Approaches to International Law* (n 6) 121; for Russia's attitude towards human rights law in general, see Anna Lukina, 'Russia and International Human Rights Law: A View from the Past' in P Sean Morris (ed), *Russian Discourses on International Law: Sociological and Philosophical Phenomenon* (Routledge 2018).

2.2 *O tempora, o bella* – IHL as a victim of "new wars"?

Not only has IHL changed dramatically since the middle of the 19th century. Warfare itself is entirely different. A battlefield in Syria looks nothing like the battlefield of Solferino. Is Russia's change of heart a reaction to the challenges posed by "new wars?"[1946] Is it harder to adhere to IHL today, than it was in the 19th century?

Thousands of pages have been written about war's ever-changing nature. The following description cannot do justice to the detailed works of political scientists, historians, and jurists on this issue.[1947] However, we cannot completely ignore war's changing nature, because it is the very thing IHL sets out to regulate.

Between 1868 and 1991 warfare evolved dramatically. The essential changes are obvious: first of all, wars are no longer exclusively a State affair. The State monopoly of violence has been broken ("de-statisation").[1948] The main actors of current wars feature militias, paramilitaries, criminal gangs, and loosely organised rebel factions fighting against or alongside well-structured armies.[1949] Secondly, fighting has taken an asymmetric shape ("asymetrisation").[1950] In Clausewitzian times the decisive battle [*Entscheidungsschlacht*] between two armies marked the culmination of a war.[1951] Today, large battles have disappeared, and front lines have vanished. Current wars are often fought between unequal opponents which means that the weaker belligerent has an interest in avoiding large bat-

---

1946 For the term "new wars" see Mary Kaldor and Basker Vashee, 'New Wars – Restructuring the Global Military Sector'; Herfried Münkler, *Die neuen Kriege* (6th edn, Rowohlt Taschenbuch Verlag 2015); Mary Kaldor, *New & Old Wars: Organized Violence in a Global Era* (Third edition, Stanford University Press 2012); the term new wars has attracted considerable criticism. On the one hand, it is true that elements of new wars can also be found in old wars and that there is no clear line separating these two kinds of conflict. On the other hand, the distinction between new and old wars is a useful tool to highlight the disjunction between many of the assumptions on which IHL rests and contemporary armed conflicts, see Nicolas Lamp, 'Conceptions of War and Paradigms of Compliance: The "New War" Challenge to International Humanitarian Law' (2011) 16 Journal of Conflict and Security Law 225, 227.

1947 See e.g. Münkler (n 1947); Christine Chinkin and Mary Kaldor, *International Law and New Wars* (Cambridge University Press 2017); Kaldor (n 1947); Lamp (n 1947).

1948 Münkler (n 1947) 10.

1949 Lamp (n 1947) 227.

1950 Münkler (n 1947) 11.

1951 Carl von Clausewitz, *Vom Kriege* (Werner Hahlweg ed, Dümmler 1980) 453.

tle-style clashes. Instead of combatants, violence is increasingly directed against civilians that make up 90 percent of the victims in current wars.[1952] Finally, new wars tend to drag on longer because State armies have lost the ability to start and end a war at any given moment ("autonomisation").[1953] The number of belligerents has exploded, for example in Syria where hundreds of armed groups appeared, dissolved, and frequently changed their allegiance. This decentralised command structure and the absence of a decisive battle inflicting a crushing defeat leads to protracted conflicts, increasingly blurring the lines between war and peace.

The phenomena of de-statisation, asymetrisation, and autonomisation pose serious challenges to IHL. Firstly, de-statisation undermines IHL's inherent compliance mechanism – reciprocity. The laws of war are designed to apply *equally* to *all* belligerents. Each party will benefit from the other party's observance. This reliable mechanism jams if a conflict involves a myriad of different actors that do not find themselves on equal footing. Members of armed groups, for instance, may be prosecuted for participating in hostilities, whereas regular soldiers enjoy combatant immunity. This inequality of belligerents creates a severe challenge for compliance.[1954]

Secondly, "asymmetric" wars do not sit well with IHL, a field of law originally tailored to inter-State conflicts. IHL relies on a hierarchical structure to implement the rules. Armed groups in asymmetric wars often lack such effective disciplinary systems.[1955] Furthermore, asymetrisation challenges the fundamental distinction of (legitimate) military targets and (protected) civilian persons and objects under IHL. Wars are not fought out in the open, but using guerrilla tactics where fighters blend in among the civilian population, do not distinguish themselves, use civilians as human shields, or even intentionally target them as a means of warfare.

Finally, the application of IHL is built on the dichotomy between war and peace. Naturally, the laws of war only regulate armed conflict. This threshold of application may be called the Achilles' heel of IHL and make the law vulnerable to evasion tactics as we have seen above.[1956] Therefore, "autonomised" wars that blur the lines between war and peace further expose IHL's weakness and undermine the law's very foundation,

---

1952 Rens Steenhard, 'The Body Counts: Civilian Casualties in War' (*Peace Palace Library*, 10 May 2012) <https://www.peacepalacelibrary.nl/2012/05/the-body-counts-civilian-casualties-in-war/>; Münkler (n 1947) 11.
1953 Münkler (n 1947) 24.
1954 Lamp (n 1947) 234.
1955 ibid 261.
1956 See p 212.

Like all major military powers, Russia had to adapt to the trends of de-statisation, asymetrisation, and autonomisation. While the Russian Army needed time to learn from the flawed campaigns in Afghanistan and Chechnya, the Russo-Georgian War (2008) marked a watershed in Russian military strategy. Russian forces operated alongside local militias and auxiliaries, in a politically choreographed operation designed to provide a degree of deniability.[1957] Since then, we can clearly identify that Moscow follows an "adaptive use of force" according to which it uses overt military confrontation as a last resort.[1958] Before resorting to large-scale open violence, Russia will use proxy actors and covert special forces that blur the lines between war and peace.[1959] Given the above, this form of waging war inevitably challenges the effectiveness of IHL.

Some even argue that Russia embraced the changing nature of warfare more quickly and more thoroughly than other military powers. They claim that Moscow developed a novel doctrine of "hybrid warfare."[1960] Is this true, and if so, how special is Moscow in this respect? Can the alleged doctrine of hybrid warfare explain its turnaround regarding IHL?

The debate about Russia's strategy of hybrid warfare was sparked by an article published by the Russian Chief of Staff General Valery Gerasimov in 2013. Gerasimov claimed that "new challenges require us to rethink the forms and ways of waging hostilities." He spoke of the increased importance of non-military means in military operations and stressed the need to carry out military operations only as a last resort. If possible, open force should be used covertly:

"The focus of the methods applied in conflict has shifted towards an ample use of political, informational, humanitarian, and other non-military means [...] All this is supplemented by military means of a hidden character including actions of informational conflict and actions of the special forces.

1957 Galeotti, *Russian Political War* (n 1458) 46.
1958 Jonsson (n 1784) 154.
1959 Gergely Tóth, 'Legal Challenges in Hybrid Warfare Theory and Practice: Is There a Place for Legal Norms at All?' in Sergey Sayapin and Evhen Tsybulenko (eds), *The Use of Force against Ukraine and International Law: Jus Ad Bellum, Jus In Bello, Jus Post Bellum* (TMC Asser Press 2018) 181–182.
1960 See Galeotti, *Russian Political War* (n 1458) 2, 27–28, who used to speak of a doctrine of hybrid warfare, but changed his view in his most recent book. He now speaks of "political war".

> *The open use of armed force [...] is only used at a certain stage in order to achieve the final success in the conflict."[1961]*

Gerasimov published his article in reaction to the role of the West in the aftermath of the Arab Spring in Libya and Syria (2011). After Russia's intervention in Ukraine (2014), however, Western commentators re-interpreted it as evidence that Russia has switched from conventional war to hybrid warfare.[1962]

The term "hybrid warfare" was originally coined by Frank Hoffman who defined it as a range of "different modes of warfare including conventional capabilities, irregular tactics and formations, terrorist acts including indiscriminate violence and coercion, and criminal disorder" conducted by States or armed groups.[1963] Such warfare is "hybrid" because it resorts to dubious, sometimes lawless actors and methods, as well as regular troops.

One feature of hybrid warfare is operating below the enemy's reaction threshold.[1964] In legal terms, this may affect *ius ad bellum*, for example by outmanoeuvring the obligation under Art 5 North Atlantic Treaty to assist another NATO member in case of an armed attack; or by undercutting the threshold of self-defence according to Art 51 UN Charter. It may also concern *ius in bello*, for example by circumventing the threshold of application of IHL. Aurel Sari argues that IHL makes an easy victim in hybrid conflicts:

1961 В.В. Герасимов [V.V. Gerasimov], 'Новые вызовы требуют переосмыслить формы и способы ведения боевых действий [New Challenges Demand to Rethink the Forms and Methods of the Conduct of Hostilities]' (2013) 8 Военно-промышленный Курьер [Military Industrial Courier] 2, 2.

1962 See Mark Galeotti, 'I'm Sorry for Creating the 'Gerasimov Doctrine' (Foreign Policy, 5 March 2018) <https://foreignpolicy.com/2018/03/05/im-sorry-for-cr eating-the-gerasimov-doctrine/>; AJC Selhorst, 'Russia's Perception Warfare: The Development of Gerasimov's Doctrine in Estonia and Georgia and Its Application in Ukraine' (2016) 22 Militaire Spectator 148, 148, Selhorst called Gerasimov the "architect of Russia's asymmetrical warfare"; see also Galeotti, *Russian Political War* (n 1458) 27–28.

1963 When Hoffman created the notion of hybrid warfare, he did not refer to Russia. Rather, he coined the term against the backdrop of the wars in Iraq (2003) and Lebanon (2006), Frank G Hoffman, 'Conflict in the 21st Century: The Rise of Hybrid Wars' (Potomac Institute for Policy Studies 2007) 36; James N Mattis and Frank Hoffman, 'Future Warfare: The Rise of Hybrid Wars' (2005) 131 United States Naval Institute Proceedings Magazine 18.

1964 Aurel Sari, 'Legal Aspects of Hybrid Warfare' (*Lawfare*, 2 October 2015) <https://www.lawfareblog.com/legal-aspects-hybrid-warfare>; see also Tóth (n 1960), who argues that there is "no longer any real distinction between war and peace."

> *"Hybrid warfare, at least of the type practiced by Russia, is [...] designed to operate 'under our reaction threshold.' [...] Consider the dividing lines between intervention, use of force, armed attack or between situations of internal disturbances and tensions, non-international armed conflicts or international armed conflicts. Or consider the distinction between overall control and effective control, or between combatant and non-combatant."*[1965]

Can this alleged "Gerasimov doctrine"[1966] explain Russia's reluctance to apply IHL? When Gerasimov speaks of "military means of a hidden character" it reminds us of Russia's outsourcing to Wagner, Cossacks, and the SOM as described in Chapter IV. When Aurel Sari speaks of "operating under our reaction-threshold" we think of Russia's attempts to evade the application of IHL in Chechnya or Ukraine as described in Chapter III. In this sense, my case studies provide evidence of what the literature terms "hybrid warfare."

At the same time, we should not ascribe Russia's reluctance to apply IHL entirely to hybrid warfare. Firstly, there is no agreed definition and the term lacks contours.[1967] Russian security expert Michael Kofman writes sarcastically that "if you torture hybrid warfare long enough it will tell you anything, and torture it we have."[1968] For this very reason, recent scholarship has started to abandon the term, because it is too vague and does not help in truly understanding Russia's military strategy.[1969]

1965 Sari (n 1965).

1966 Mark Galeotti, 'I'm Sorry for Creating the 'Gerasimov Doctrine'' (Foreign Policy, 5 March 2018) <https://foreignpolicy.com/2018/03/05/im-sorry-for-creating-the-gerasimov-doctrine/>.

1967 Frank Hoffman calls a conflict hybrid, because the warring parties resort to different *military* means – conventional and non-conventional. Other authors, however, have broadened the term to encompass military and *non-military* means. According to their reasoning, hybrid warfare would include anything from an open assault to a media misinformation campaign, see e.g. Heidi Reisinger and Alexandr Golts, 'Russia's Hybrid Warfare' (2014) 105 Research Papers of the NATO Defense College 1, 3.

1968 Michael Kofman, 'Russian Hybrid Warfare and Other Dark Arts' (*War on the Rocks*, 11 March 2016) <https://warontherocks.com/2016/03/russian-hybrid-warfare-and-other-dark-arts/>.

1969 Jonsson (n 1784) 9. The author either wishes to return to Frank Hoffman's original definition of hybrid warfare or suggests abandoning the concept completely.

Rather, the "doctrine" of hybrid warfare is misleading – simply, because it is not a "doctrine."[1970] Moscow has *not* given up on conventional warfare. On the contrary, it still places great emphasis on conventional military tactics beyond the hybrid. The mere fact that its recent exercises *Zapad* (2017) and *Vostok* (2018) involved hundreds of thousands of soldiers show that conventional war remains a sturdy pillar of the Russian defence strategy.[1971] We also see evidence for this in recent conflicts. In Georgia, Russian troops fought openly, and Moscow even recognised the state of war. In Syria the Russian Air Force bombed rebel strongholds while cameras broadcast the images in the evening news. Even eastern Ukraine is not a "typical" example of hybrid warfare, if there even is such a thing. In the later stages it became a classic conflict that was decided by Russian boots on the ground and artillery fire. It was a conventional war as much as it was a hybrid war.[1972]

To sum up, IHL faces enormous challenges in new wars. Changes in warfare are as visible in Syria, Ukraine, and Georgia as they are in Afghanistan, Iraq, and the Democratic Republic of Congo. In the 19th century, war was conceived as a "duel" between States.[1973] Today, it resembles a pub brawl. Such an environment takes its toll on the effectiveness of IHL, because it calls into question both the grounds of application and the reasons for compliance.

While this is a global trend, Moscow has readily adapted to the changes. On the one hand, we should resist the reflex to ascribe Moscow's bad IHL record entirely to a novel strategy of hybrid warfare. On the other hand, Russia has reacted to the changing nature of warfare and brought its military strategy in line with the *zeitgeist*. Now, it clearly follows a strategy of "adaptive use of force" and prefers to use proxies to its own soldiers.

1970 Galeotti, *Russian Political War* (n 1458) 27. I fully agree with Ruslan Pukhov who argues that hybrid warfare has become a "propaganda term" that simply refers to a real or perceived threat from Russia, see Руслан Пухов [Ruslan Pukhov], 'Миф о "гибридной войне" [The Myth of Hybrid War]' (Nezavisimaya Gazeta, 1 June 2015) <http://svop.ru/main/15547/>.

1971 Galeotti, *Russian Political War* (n 1455) 47. Around 70 000 soldiers participated in the Zapad exercise (2017). Between 150 000 and 300 000 soldiers participated in the Vostok exercise (2018).

1972 Galeotti, *Armies of Russia's War in Ukraine* (n 785) 63.

1973 For the influence of this concept on IHL see Robert A Nye, 'The Duel of Honour and the Origins of the Rules for Arms, Warfare and Arbitration in the Hague Conferences' in Maartje Abbenhuis, Christopher Ernest Barber and Annalise R Higgins (eds), *War, Peace and International Order? The Legacies of the Hague Conferences of 1899 and 1907* (Routledge 2017).

It tries to "blur the line between war and peace" and thereby undercut the threshold of application of IHL.[1974] Given the above, these changes in military strategy were bound to affect the respect for the laws of war.

2.3 *Do ut des* – does IHL lack an incentive for compliance for Russia?

The previous two sections dealt with the evolution of IHL and warfare itself. The current section will ask a final, simple, but crucial question: What can Russia *expect* from IHL in this changed environment? States' rational expectations are essential for compliance with the law. The effectiveness of international law depends by and large on the acceptance of the utility of the rules. Acceptance may derive from self-interest, for example from a desire to be accepted into an international organisation. It may also derive from reciprocity, or even from a belief in shared norms.[1975] To rephrase the question: why should a State like Russia prefer a world with IHL to a world without IHL?[1976]

It is worth recalling Russia's motives for promoting IHL during the 19th and early 20th century. I have discussed this issue above at page 61 and identified the following five reasons:

1) Idealism: The Tsars and central elements of their governments embraced the humanitarian *zeitgeist* of the 19th century. Saving Europe from an unfettered war was part of their "curious missionary ambition."[1977] In addition, outstanding jurists and diplomats like Martens managed to translate this vague humanitarianism into solid laws.

2) Diplomatic pride: IHL became a Russian trademark in diplomatic circles and enhanced Russia's standing on the international stage.

3) Military strategy: Russia had the biggest land army in Europe but lagged behind in military technology. Thus, it hoped to preserve this numeric advantage and protect its combatants.

4) Economic interest: Russia wanted to avoid an all-out total war to save money and rather focus on economic growth.

5) Russian ingenuity: Russia saw the advantage of promoting restrictions for everyone instead of lagging behind alone. In other words, it consid-

---

1974 Jonsson (n 1784) 154.
1975 Chinkin and Kaldor (n 1948) 124.
1976 Tanisha M Fazal, *(Kein) Recht im Krieg? Nicht intendierte Folgen der völkerrechtlichen Regelung bewaffneter Konflikte* (Hamburger Edition 2019) 79–91.
1977 Eyffinger (n 80) 19.

ered mutual limitation by means of international law a useful tool to secure its own interests.

Are these reasons still valid today? Let's address them one by one, starting with idealism. The humanitarian spirit of the 19th century was tied to leading figures in the Russian government: Alexander II "the Liberator," Alexander III "the Peacemaker," and Nicolas II, eager to fill their shoes. The Romanovs possessed a "curious missionary ambition."[1978] In addition, people like Martens – who had a similar, albeit more concrete vision of humanity – provided the legal know-how and the diplomatic skills to advance law-making. Such prominent figures are absent from Russian politics today. It is a commonplace that Vladimir Putin, who has led the country since 1999 is anything but an idealist. Nor is there a strong desire for an idealist among the Russian population. The woes of the 90s – crime, unemployment, secession wars, and plummeting life expectancy – fostered a yearning for stability among the Russian people.[1979] In the eyes of many, Putin kept his promise to prevent the further disintegration of Russia and make its voice heard.[1980]

Even if Russia were steered by a more idealistic leader, IHL would not make the most humane "bumper sticker" in today's world. We live in the era of human rights, where IHL is often regarded as too pragmatic, too permissive, and too lenient towards the military. Critics argue that IHL "introduces a hierarchy of lives" and "legalizes killing."[1981] Others see it as a framework that allows States "to conduct wars relatively uninhibited by humanitarian constraints."[1982] I do not share this criticism and I have described at page 390 how IHL has been "humanised" over the years. Yet, despite these changes, IHL *does* remain more pragmatic than human rights law which is considered the more humane framework. At the same time, human rights is a field in which Russia has never managed to shine. It can hardly be "considered to have been a global leader or katechon" in this

---

1978 ibid.

1979 Krastev and Holmes (n 1902) 184–188.

1980 See e.g. Vladimir Putin's speech in the State Duma (16 August 1999): "Russia has been a great power for centuries and remains so. It has always had and still has legitimate zones of interest [...] we should not drop our guard in this respect, neither should we allow our opinion to be ignored." Quoted from 'Vladimir Putin: The rebuilding of 'Soviet' Russia' (BBC, 28 March 2014) <https://www.bbc.com/news/magazine-26769481>.

1981 Chinkin and Kaldor (n 1948) 255–256.

1982 af Jochnick and Normand (n 13) 95.

sphere.[1983] With such a bleak record, even fully embracing IHL would do little to polish Russia's oxidised image as a "humanitarian" power.

Secondly, we might consider whether Russia's former pride in IHL, and its adoption of IHL as a method for distinction in diplomatic circles still carry influence in Russia today. Today as in the 19th century, Russia remains a power very concerned with its status.[1984] Yet, Moscow's humanitarian trademark has long faded. The world has forgotten about Russia's historical achievements in the development of IHL. In addition, IHL itself does not bear the most humane trademark anymore, as I have just described. For these reasons, Moscow seeks diplomatic recognition elsewhere. The only prominent exception are Moscow's aid programmes, e.g. in Syria or Ukraine. In this respect, Russia uses highly publicised relief operations to enhance its international status, win "hearts and minds", and sway public opinion in its favour.

At the same time, Russia's current standing in international relations does not depend on its humanitarian image anymore. What does Moscow need to prove? As one of the victorious powers of the Second World War, Russia is a permanent member in the UN Security Council. It is *the* central power in current conflicts like Syria and Ukraine. It is crucial to de-escalation in North Korea, Iran, and Venezuela. The phrase "there can be no solution without Russia" became a commonplace the West needed to get used to. Obama's clumsy assumption that Russia only represents a "regional power" seems to have only increased Russian ambitions.[1985] Today, Moscow has its place at the negotiation table thanks to its influence in the post-war UN system and its determination to create facts on the ground. It does not need to go down the humanitarian alley to be perceived as a key actor on the international stage.

Thirdly, IHL has lost some of the military perks that it could offer to Imperial Russia in the 19th century. Admittedly, Russia still has a large army of around one million soldiers, a third of them ground forces.[1986] Thus, it has a vested interest in a protective framework for its combatants. IHL could offer that. However, Moscow is not the military giant it used

---

1983 Mälksoo, *Russian Approaches to International Law* (n 6) 159; see also Lukina (n 1946), who argues that for political, historical, and ideological reasons Russia can only conform to the modern human rights "canon" to a certain extent.

1984 Anne L Clunan, 'Russia's Pursuit of Great-Power Status and Security' in Roger E Kanet (ed), *Routledge Handbook of Russian Security* (Routledge/Taylor & Francis Group 2019) 4–5.

1985 Galeotti, *Russian Political War* (n 1458) 17.

1986 ibid 21.

to be in the 19th century. Its population of 145 million is dwarfed by the NATO countries (937 million) and China's (1.39 billion) both of which have highly modernised armies.[1987] Compared to NATO, Moscow finds itself both outgunned and outnumbered. In addition, Russia struggles with an ageing population and will suffer from a lack of conscripts in the long run.[1988] Furthermore, the sheer size of the army is much less important than it was 150 years ago, as the world has moved beyond land warfare to a certain extent. While it remains an important component, the air force, unmanned drones, and cyber-capabilities have become similarly decisive tools. Therefore, the classic protection offered to POWs and wounded combatants – once a major incentive for Russia to promote IHL – are of limited relevance today.

Fourthly, what about the financial perks of IHL? Unfettered wars, protracted conflicts, and a global arms race cost money, a fact as true in 1868 as it is today. Once, the Imperial Minister of Finance, Sergey Witte, dreamt of a de-mobilised Europe that would "thrive in an unprecedented way and guide the best part of the globe."[1989] Today, however, Russia does not seek to reduce military spending. On the contrary, defence has been made a national priority. From 2000 to 2009, the defence budget grew by almost seven percent every year.[1990] Russia has launched the ambitious State Armament Programmes GPV-2020 and GPV-2027 which set out to modernise the entirety of Russia's weapons and equipment.[1991] In 2018, Russia spent 61.4 billion dollars on its military, amounting to 4 percent of its GDP.[1992] In relation to its GDP, Russia thus spends far more than an average NATO State and even outspends the US.[1993] In terms of nuclear weapons especially, Russia remains a superpower. Moscow still owns the

---

1987 See <https://www.worlddata.info/alliances/nato-north-atlantic-treaty-organizati on.php>.

1988 Galeotti, *Russian Political War* (n 1458) 20.

1989 Dillon (n 171) 276.

1990 Susanne Oxenstierna, 'Russia's Economy and Military Expenditures' in Roger E Kanet (ed), *Routledge Handbook of Russian Security* (Routledge/Taylor & Francis Group 2019) 100.

1991 GVP stands for *Государственная программа вооружения* [State Armament Programme], for details see Jennifer G Mathers, 'The Rebuilding of Russian Military Capabilities' in Roger E Kanet (ed), *Routledge Handbook of Russian Security* (Routledge/Taylor & Francis Group 2019) 149; Oxenstierna (n 1991) 101–102.

1992 SIPRI, 'Yearbook 2019' (2019) 7.

1993 Galeotti, *Russian Political War* (n 1458) 19.

largest arsenal with 6 500 nuclear warheads.[1994] Both Russia and the US have embarked on a "path of strategic nuclear renewal" and launched extensive and expensive programmes to replace and modernise their nuclear capabilities.[1995] While Putin recently seems to have slowed down his military build-up to address the root causes of Russia's slowing economy, the defence budget is expected to grow at a moderate pace in the future.[1996] While IHL might still be a "money-saver" today, saving money on the military is clearly not a priority in modern-day Russia.

Finally, what does "Russian ingenuity" mean in the 21st century? In the 19th century, Russia managed to solve internal problems and promote external interests by means of international law, notably by promoting IHL and global disarmament. Today, Russia is not absent from the stage of international law, but it follows a different script. It promotes a traditionalist reading of international law that revolves around State sovereignty.[1997] In his 2007 Munich speech, Putin stressed the importance of the principle of sovereignty enshrined in the UN Charter and warned of a world with "one master, one sovereign" hinting at the US and Western interventionist strategies.[1998] The current Russian 'Foreign Policy Conception' (2016) vehemently insists on the principle of sovereignty and aims to counter

> *"attempts by some States to arbitrarily interpret [...] principles such as the non-use of force [...] respect for sovereignty and territorial integrity of States."*[1999]

Similarly, the Russo-Chinese Joint Declaration on International Law (2016) identifies sovereign equality as "crucial for the stability of international relations."[2000] The recent constitutional reforms (2020) introduced

---

1994　SIPRI (n 1993) 11.
1995　ibid 1, 10.
1996　Oxenstierna (n 1991) 106.
1997　Mälksoo, *Russian Approaches to International Law* (n 6) 177.
1998　Vladimir Putin, Speech at the Munich Conference on Security Policy (10 February 2007). The speech is available in English at <http://en.kremlin.ru/e vents/president/transcripts/24034>.
1999　Para 26(b) of Foreign Policy Concept of the Russian Federation (approved by President of the Russian Federation Vladimir Putin on 30 November 2016); an English translation is available at <https://www.mid.ru/en/foreign_policy/off icial_documents/-/asset_publisher/CptICkB6BZ29/content/id/2542248>; for details on the current Foreign Policy Concept and the role of Foreign Policy Concepts in Russia see Butler (n 829).
2000　The Declaration of the Russian Federation and the People's Republic of China on the Promotion of International Law (25 June 2016) para 2. Available at

a clause that urges Russia to "take measures to prevent the interference in the internal affairs of the State."[2001]

Admittedly, the call for sovereignty has always been a pillar in Russian/Soviet legal thinking, but it did not prevent Russia from agreeing to limitations on warfare.[2002] Today, however, Moscow's call echoes even louder, amplified in an age of multilateralism. Anne Clunan argues that Russia harbours the hope that with the US decline, "sovereignty will automatically harden [...] and Russia's status as a great power will be assured."[2003] To Moscow, this call for sovereignty represents a counter-model to the Western concept based on human rights and multilateralism. Moscow feels betrayed by the "idealist rhetoric" which it sees as a pretext to push through Western realist motives.[2004] IHL, too, is perceived as a possible source of Western interventionism, rather than a way of realising Russian interests in today's world.

In sum, none of the motives that led Russia to promote IHL exist in the same way as they did in the 19th century. In today's Russia, there are no reasons on the horizon that could substitute them. Naturally, this absence of intrinsic motivation to develop, advance, and promote IHL will lead to a decline of the law's standing. After all, international law, too, follows the principle that the Romans applied to their Gods: *do ut des* – I shall make a sacrifice to you, but what will you give me in return? Given Russia's current course in world politics, it has little incentive to offer a sacrifice on the altar of IHL. Rather, it sacrifices IHL on the altar of sovereignty.

<https://www.mid.ru/en/foreign_policy/position_word_order/-/asset_publisher/6S4RuXfeYlKr/content/id/2331698>.

2001 See Art 79 of the modified Constitution.

2002 Under the Tsars, i.e. in the late Westphalian era, sovereignty naturally played a key role. The Soviet Union continued to promote a strong (albeit peculiar) concept of sovereignty. For an analysis of the Soviet concept of sovereignty and its exceptions see Bowring, *Law, Rights and Ideology in Russia* (n 548) 77–95.

2003 Clunan (n 1985) 12.

2004 Mälksoo, *Russian Approaches to International Law* (n 6) 176.

Final Conclusion

Russia has undergone a transformation from Paul to Saul. Its extreme change of heart and the reasons behind it led me to write this thesis. In doing so I wanted to tell *both* sides of this story and reconcile the Western with the Russian narrative.

On the one hand, the West has largely forgotten about Russia's humanitarian achievements of the 19th and early 20th century. Of course, a handful of distinguished experts in this field have done much more than I could ever do to unearth this truth.[2005] However, mainstream opinion remains unchanged. It does not regard Russia as a nation that *makes* international law but rather one that *breaks* international law. Instead, Western States, the ICRC, and a large part of scholarly literature have co-authored the following narrative: Modern-day IHL was started by Henry Dunant, advanced by the ICRC, Switzerland, and other like-minded Western States, until it culminated in the adoption of the 1949 Geneva Conventions.

This storyline is at best a one-sided tale and falls silent on an important aspect. Before 1949, the most comprehensive documents of the IHL were not "Geneva law" but "Hague law." The latter was advanced neither by ICRC nor by most Western States but by *Russia*. After the ground-breaking achievement of the 1864 Geneva Convention, it took almost 90 years until an ICRC-driven process added new fundamental rules to IHL.[2006] Even at the 1949 Conference, this initiative only succeeded thanks to support from the Soviet Union. While the ICRC has done extremely valuable humanitarian work ever since its creation in 1863, it was a handful of States – above all the Russian Empire – that pushed for the further development of IHL in the 19th and early 20th century. I hope that the first Part of the thesis convinced the reader that Russia's humanitarian commitment in this era was indeed remarkable.

2005 See e.g. Holquist (n 117); Mälksoo, *Russian Approaches to International Law* (n 6); Mälksoo, 'FF Martens and His Time' (n 90); Hirsch (n 475); van Dijk (n 507).

2006 Of course, there were minor additions. In 1906, the ICRC succeeded in updating the 1864 Convention on the Wounded and Sick. In 1929, the ICRC initiated the Convention relative to the Treatment of Prisoners of War that supplemented the existing Hague Regulations of 1907. Only the Geneva Conventions of 1949, however, added a whole set of new substantial rules to IHL.

On the other hand, we find the mainstream Russian narrative. It either focusses on the past, while completely ignoring the shortcomings in the present, or it falls completely silent on IHL. In the second Part of this thesis, I have described many instances where Russia broke the law. It is telling, however, that there is virtually no example where Russia directly *challenged* the law by providing legal counterarguments. It prefers to avoid, evade, or deny it. Russian politicians and the military reduce IHL to an empty shell that may be solemnly endorsed in abstract declarations or turned into a diplomatic weapon to be fired against third countries – but that may not restrict Russia's sovereignty or its conduct on the battlefield.

By merging these two contradictory narratives I have shown that Russia has come a long way from *advancing* the law to *avoiding* the law. The contrast is striking, more than for any other country in the world. Russia is often called a country of the extremes just like the biblical character Saul himself. This holds equally true for its attitude towards IHL. Through its radical change, however, Russia may serve as a barometer that indicates the changes in its surroundings. After all, the nature of warfare and the protective scope of IHL have evolved radically over the past 150 years. This change of weather flung the needle of the Russian barometer from one extreme into the other.

In conclusion, it hurts to see that IHL has lost one of its most fervent advocates. While Russia's change of heart is undoubtedly linked to the evolution of warfare and the humanisation of IHL, this cannot excuse today's attitude of evasion, avoidance, and obstinate denial. As in other fields of international law, Russia uses IHL as "a language in which it is possible to lie."[2007] This attitude not only damages Russia's own legacy, but erodes an essential field of international law.

2007 Mälksoo, *Russian Approaches to International Law* (n 6) 191.

Bibliography

Monographies

Russian-language Monographies

А.А. Ковалев [A.A. Kovalev] and С.В. Черниченко [S.V. Chernichenko], *Международное право [International Law]* (3rd edn, Омега-л 2008)

А.В. Наумов [A.V. Naumov], *Комментарий к уголовному кодексу Российской Федерации [Commentary to the Criminal Code of the Russian Federation]* (2nd edn, Юрист 1996)

——, *Международное уголовное право [International Criminal Law]* (2nd edn, Юрайт 2014)

А.И. Полторак [A.I. Poltorak] and Л.И. Савинский [L.I. Savinskiy], *Вооружённые конфликты и международное право [Armed Conflicts and International Law]* (Наука 1976)

А.Н. Вылегжанин [A.N. Vylegzhanin], *Международное право [International Law]* (2nd edn, Юрайт 2010)

А.Н. Трайнин [A.N. Traynin], *Уголовное ответственность гитлеровцев [The Criminal Responsibility of the Hitlerites]* (Юридическое Издательство НКЮ СССР [Legal Publishing House NKYu USSR] 1944)

Б.Л. Зимненко [B.L. Zimnenko], *Международное право и правовая система Российской Федерации [International Law and the Legal System of the Russian Federation]* (Statut 2006)

В.Д. Зорькин [V.D. Zorkin], *Комментарий к конституции Российской Федерации [Commentary to the Constitution of the Russian Federation]* (3rd edn, Norma 2013)

В.Л. Полушин [V.L. Polushin], *Генерал Лебедь – загадка России [General Lebed – A Russian Enigma]* (Внешторгиздат 1997)

В.Л. Толстых [V.L. Tolstykh], *Курс Международного Права – Учебник [A Course in International Law – A Textbook]* (Prospect 2018)

В.Н. Русинова [V.N. Rusinova], *Нарушения международного гуманитарного права: индивидуальная уголовная ответственность и судебное предследование [Violations of International Humanitarian Law: Individual Criminal Responsibility and Prosecution before Courts]* (Yurlitinform 2006)

В.П. Звеков [V.P. Zvekov], Б. И. Осминин [B.I. Osminin], *Комментарий к Федеральному закону 'О международных договорах Российской Федерации' [Commentary to the Federal Law 'On international Treaties of the Russian Federation']* (Спарк 1996)

В.Э. Грабарь [V.E. Grabar], *Материалы к истории литературы международного права в России 1647–1917 [Materials Concerning the History of International Law Literature in Russia 1647–1917]* (Зерцало 2005)

Г.В. Игнатенко [G.I. Ignatenko], *Международное право и общественный прогресс [International Law and the Progress of Society]* (Международные отношения [International Relations] 1972)

Г.И. Тункин [G.I. Tunkin], *Вопросы теории международного права [Questions Regarding the Theory of International Law]* (Gosyurisdat 1962)

——, *Теория международного права [Theory of International Law]* (Международные отношения [International Relations] 1970)

Г.М. Вельяминов. [G.M. Velyaminov], *Международное право: опыты [International Law: Essays]* (Statut 2015)

Е.А. Коровин [E.A. Korovin], *Краткий курс международного права – часть II [Brief Course on International Law – Part II]* (Военно-юридическая академия РККА [Military-legal Academy of the Red Army] 1944)

——, *Международное право переходного времени [International Law of the Transitional Time]* (1971)

Е.Ю. Гуськова [E.Yu. Guskova], А.Б. Мезяев [A.B. Mezayev] and А.И. Филимонова [A.I. Filimonova] (eds), *Международный трибунал по бывшей Югославии: Деятельность. Результаты. Эффективность. [The International Tribunal for the Former Yugoslavia: Actions. Results. Effectiveness.]* (Индрик 2012)

И.И. Лукашук [I.I. Lukashuk], *Нормы международного права в правовой системе России [Norms of International Law in the Legal Sytem of Russia]* (Спарк 1997)

И.И. Лукашук [I.I. Lukashuk], *Международное право – особенная часть [International law – Special Fields of Law]* (3rd edn, Volters Kluver 2010)

И.П. Блищенко [I.P. Blishchenko], *Антисоветизм и международное право [Antisovietism and International Law]* (Международные отношения [International Relations] 1968)

Исаев М.А. [Isaev M.A.], *История Российского государства и права: Учебник [The History of the Russian State and Law: A Textbook]* (Statut 2012)

К.А. Бекяшев [K.A. Bekyashev], *Международное публичное право [Public International Law]* (4th edn, Prospekt 2008)

Л.А. Моджорян [L.A. Modzhoryan], *Субъекты международного права [Subjects of International Law]* (Gosyurisdat 1958)

Н. Геворкян [N. Gevorkyan], Н. Тимакова [N. Timakova] and А. Колесников [A. Kolesnikov], *От первого лица – разговоры с Владимиром Путиным [From a First Person Perspective – Interviews with Vladimir Putin] (electronic version)* (Vagrius 2000)

Н.Н. Новичков [N.N. Novichkov], В.Я. Снеговский [B.Ya. Snegovsky] and А.Г. Соколов [A.G. Sokolov], *Российские вооруженные силы в чеченском конфликте: анализ. итоги. выводы [The Russian Armed Forces in the Chechen Conflict: An analysis. Results. Conclusions]* (Holweg Infoglob 1995)

Н.Ф. Кузнецовой [N.F. Kuznetsovoy], *Комментарий к уголовному кодексу Российской Федерации [Commentary to the Criminal Code of the Russian Federation]* (2nd edn, Зерцало 1998)

П.Н. Бирюков [P.N. Biryukov], *Международное право [International Law]* (3rd edn, Yurist 2006)

Ф.Ф. Мартенс [F.F. Martens], *Собрание трактатов и конвенций заключённых Россиею с иностранными державами [Collection of Treaties and Conventions Concluded by Russia with Foreign States]* (Типография министерства путей сообщения [Printing House of the Ministry of Communication] 1874)

——, *Восточная Война и Брюсселъская Конференция 1874–1878 г [The Eastern War and the Brussels Conference 1874–1878]* (Типография министерства путей сообщения [Printing House of the Ministry of Communication] 1879)

——, *Современное международное право цивилизованных народов [Contemporary International Law of Civilized Peoples]* (1st edn, Типография министерства путей сообщения [Printing House of the Ministry of Communication] 1882)

——, *Современное международное право цивилизованных народов [Contemporary International Law of Civilized Peoples]*, vol 1 (5th edn, Типография министерства путей сообщения [Printing House of the Ministry of Communication] 1904)

——, *Современное международное право цивилизованных народов [Contemporary International law of Civilized Peoples]*, vol 2 (5th edn, Типография министерства путей сообщения [Printing House of the Ministry of Communication] 1904)

Ю.М. Батурин [Y.M. Baturin] (ed), *Эпоха Ельцина: очерк политической истории [Yeltin's Epoch: An Essay of Political History]* (Vagrius 2001)

Ю.М. Колосов [Y.M. Kolosov] and Э.С. Кривчикова [E.S. Krivchikova], *Международное право [International Law]* (2nd edn, Юрайт 2005)

International Monographies

Bartov O and Weitz ED, *Shatterzone of Empires: Coexistence and Violence in the German, Habsburg, Russian, and Ottoman Borderlands* (Indiana University Press 2013)

Benvenisti E, *The International Law of Occupation* (2nd ed, Oxford University Press 2012)

Besson S, D'Aspremont J and Knuchel S (eds), *The Oxford Handbook on the Sources of International Law* (Oxford University Press 2017)

Boissier P, *Histoire du Comité International de la Croix-Rouge* (Institut Henry-Dunant 1978)

Boister N and Cryer R, *The Tokyo International Military Tribunal: A Reappraisal* (Oxford University Press 2008)

Bonafè BI, *The Relationship between State and Individual Responsibility for International Crimes* (Martinus Nijhoff Publishers 2009)

Bowles TG, *The Declaration of Paris of 1856* (Sampson Low 1900)

Bowring B, *Law, Rights and Ideology in Russia: Landmarks in the Destiny of a Great Power* (Routledge 2013)

Brierly JL and Clapham A, *Brierly's Law of Nations: An Introduction to the Role of International Law in International Relations* (7th edn, Oxford University Press 2012)

Bugnion F, *The International Committee of the Red Cross and the Protection of War Victims* (Macmillan Education 2003)

Butler WE (ed), *The Law of Treaties in Russia and the Commonwealth of Independent States: Text and Commentary* (Cambridge University Press 2002)

Calazans E, *Private Military and Security Companies: The Implications under International Law of Doing Business in War* (Cambridge Scholars Publishing 2016)

Cameron L and Chetail V, *Privatizing War: Private Military and Security Companies under Public International Law* (Cambridge University Press 2013)

Casey-Maslen S and others, *The Arms Trade Treaty: A Commentary* (Oxford University Press 2016)

Cassese A, *Self-Determination of Peoples: A Legal Reappraisal* (Cambridge University Press 1995)

Cassese A and Gaeta P, *Cassese's International Criminal Law* (3rd edn, Oxford University Press 2013)

Chinkin C and Kaldor M, *International Law and New Wars* (Cambridge University Press 2017)

Clapham A, Gaeta P and Sassòli M (eds), *The 1949 Geneva Conventions – A Commentary* (Oxford University Press 2015)

Collins H, *Marxism and Law* (Oxford University Press 1984)

Crawford J, *State Responsibility: The General Part* (Cambridge University Press 2013)

Czapliński W and others, *The Case of Crimea's Annexation under International Law* (Scholar 2017)

Dalos G and Zylla E, *1956: Der Aufstand in Ungarn* (Bundeszentrale für politische Bildung 2006)

Darczewska J, *Putin's Cossacks. Folklore, Business or Politics?* (Center for Eastern Studies 2017)

David É, *Principes de droit des conflits armés.* (6th edn, Emile Bruylant 2018)

De Zayas AM, *The Wehrmacht War Crimes Bureau, 1939–1945* (University of Nebraska Press 1989)

Dillon EJ, *The Eclipse of Russia* (George H Doran 1918)

Dinstein Y, *The International Law of Belligerent Occupation* (2nd edn, Cambridge University Press 2019)

Dodd CJ, *Letters from Nuremberg: My Father's Narrative of a Quest for Justice* (Three Rivers Press 2008)

Dörmann K and others (eds), *Commentary on the First Geneva Convention: Convention (I) for the Amelioration of the Condition of the Wounded and Sick in Armed Forces in the Field* (Cambridge University Press 2016)

Dülffer J, *Regeln gegen den Krieg? die Haager Friedenskonferenzen von 1899 und 1907 in der internationalen Politik* (Ullstein 1981)

Dunant H, *Un souvenir de Solférino* (1862)

Durand A, *From Sarajevo to Hiroshima: History of the International Committee of the Red Cross* (Henry Dunant Institute 1984)

Escudero Espinosa JF, *Self-Determination and Humanitarian Secession in International Law of a Globalized World: Kosovo v Crimea* (Springer Berlin Heidelberg 2018)

Evangelista M, *The Chechen Wars: Will Russia Go the Way of the Soviet Union?* (Brookings Institution Press 2002)

Evangelista M and Tannenwald N (eds), *Do the Geneva Conventions Matter?* (Oxford University Press 2017)

Eyffinger A, *The 1899 Hague Peace Conference: The Parliament of Man, the Federation of the World* (Kluwer Law International 1999)

Fazal TM, *(Kein) Recht im Krieg? Nicht intendierte Folgen der völkerrechtlichen Regelung bewaffneter Konflikte* (Hamburger Edition 2019)

Forsythe DP, *The Humanitarians: The International Committee of the Red Cross* (Cambridge University Press 2005)

Freedman L, *Ukraine and the Art of Strategy* (Oxford University Press 2019)

Freud S, *Civilisation, War and Death: Selections from Three Works by Sigmund Freud* (Hogarth Press and the Institute of Psycho-analysis 1939)

Fuller Jr WC, *Civil-Military Conflict in Imperial Russia, 1881–1914* (Princeton University Press 2014)

Galeotti M, *Spetsnaz: Russia's Special Forces* (Osprey Publishing 2015)

——, *Hybrid War or Gibridnaya Voina? – Getting Russia's Non-Linear Military Challenge Right* (lulu 2016)

——, *Armies of Russia's War in Ukraine* (Osprey Publishing 2019)

——, *Russian Political War: Moving Beyond the Hybrid* (Routledge 2019)

Gebhardt M, *Als die Soldaten kamen: Die Vergewaltigung deutscher Frauen am Ende des Zweiten Weltkriegs* (DVA 2015)

Gellately R, *Lenin, Stalin, and Hitler: The Age of Social Catastrophe* (Alfred A Knopf Incorporated 2007)

Geyer D, *Russian Imperialism: The Interaction of Domestic and Foreign Policy, 1860–1914* (Yale University Press 1987)

Gilligan E, *Terror in Chechnya: Russia and the Tragedy of Civilians in War (e-Book)* (EBSCO Publishing 2014)

Grant TD, *Aggression against Ukraine: Territory, Responsibility, and International Law* (First edition, Palgrave Macmillan 2015)

Grasselli G, *British and American Responses to the Soviet Invasion of Afghanistan* (Dartmouth Publishing Group 1996)

Grotius H, *De Iure Belli Ac Pacis – Libri Tres*, vol 3 (1625)

Haak J, *Die Wirkung und Umsetzung von Urteilen des Europäischen Gerichtshofs für Menschenrechte: ein Rechtsvergleich zwischen der Bundesrepublik Deutschland und der Russischen Föderation* (Lit 2018)

Hesse H, *Steppenwolf* (Creighton Basil tr, Bantham Books 1969)

Higgins AP, *The Hague Peace Conferences and Other International Conferences Concerning the Laws and Usages of War* (Cambridge University Press 1909)

Hirsch F, *Soviet Judgment at Nuremberg: A New History of the International Military Tribunal after World War II* (Oxford University Press 2020)

Hobsbawm E, *Age of Capital: 1848–1875* (Hachette UK 2010)

——, *Age of Empire: 1875–1914* (Hachette UK 2010)

——, *Age of Revolution: 1789–1848* (Hachette UK 2010)

Hobsbawm EJ and Cumming M, *Age of Extremes: The Short Twentieth Century, 1914–1991* (Abacus London 1995)

Holquist P, *The Russian Empire as a "Civilized State": International Law as Principle and Practice in Imperial Russia, 1874–1878* (National Council for Eurasian and East European Research 2004) <https://www.ucis.pitt.edu/nceeer/2004_818-06g_Holquist.pdf>

Houses of Parliament, *Correspondence Respecting the Proposed Conference at Brussels on the Rules of Military Warfare – Miscellaneous No 2* (Harrison & Sons 1875)

Hugo V, *Actes et paroles – depuis l'exil 1876–1880* (J Hetzel 1880)

Hussner M, *Die Übernahme internationalen Rechts in die russische und deutsche Rechtsordnung: eine vergleichende Analyse zur Völkerrechtsfreundlichkeit der Verfassungen der Russländischen Föderation und der Bundesrepublik Deutschland* (Ibidem 2005)

ILC, *Yearbook of the International Law Commission 1949 – Summary Records and Documents of the First Session Including the Report of the Commission to the General Assembly* (United Nations 1956)

Jaimoukha AM, *The Chechens: A Handbook* (2012 edition, Routledge 2012)

Jones FC, *Manchuria since 1931* (Royal Institute of International Affairs 1949)

Jonsson O, *The Russian Understanding of War: Blurring the Lines between War and Peace* (Georgetown University Press 2019)

Joosten SPA (ed), *Trial of the Major War Criminals before the International Military Tribunal*, vol 22 (IMT 1948)

Kadell F, *Katyn: das zweifache Trauma der Polen* (Herbig 2011)

Kaiser G, *Katyn: das Staatsverbrechen, das Staatsgeheimnis* (Aufbau Taschenbuch 2002)

Kaldor M, *New & Old Wars: Organized Violence in a Global Era* (Third edition, Stanford University Press 2012)

Kaldor M and Vashee B, 'New Wars – Restructuring the Global Military Sector'

Kalshoven F, *Belligerent Reprisals* (A W Sijthoff 1971)

——, *Reflections on the Law of War: Collected Essays* (Martinus Nijhoff Publishers 2007)

Kennan GF, *The Decline of Bismarck's European Order: Franco-Russian Relations 1875–1890* (Princeton University Press 1979)

Kolb R and Vité S, *Le droit de l'occupation militaire: perspectives historiques et enjeux juridiques actuels* (Bruylant 2009)

Krastev I and Holmes S, *The Light That Failed: Why the West Is Losing the Fight for Democracy (Electronic Edition)* (Pegasus Books 2020)

Kross J, *Professor Martens Abreise: Roman* (Hanser 1992)

Långström T, *Transformation in Russia and International Law* (Martinus Nijhoff Publishers 2003)

Lenin VI, *Collected Works*, vol 21 (Progress Publishers Reprint 2011)

Mälksoo L, *Russian Approaches to International Law* (Oxford University Press 2015)

Mälksoo L and Benedek W, *Russia and the European Court of Human Rights: The Strasbourg Effect* (Cambridge University Press 2017)

Margalit A, *Investigating Civilian Casualties in Time of Armed Conflict and Belligerent Occupation: Manoeuvring between Legal Regimes and Paradigms for the Use of Force* (Brill Nijhoff 2018)

Marochkin S, *The Operation of International Law in the Russian Legal System: A Changing Approach* (Brill Nijhoff 2019)

Materski W, *Katyn: A Crime Without Punishment* (Anna Cienciala and Natalia Lebedeva eds, Yale University Press 2007)

McCarthy J, *The Ottoman Peoples and the End of Empire* (Arnold; Oxford : Distributed by St Martin's press 2001)

——, *The Ottoman Peoples and the End of Empire: Historical Endings* (Arnold 2001)

McFate S, *The Modern Mercenary: Private Armies and What They Mean for World Order* (Oxford University Press 2014)

Mehn B, *Waffentechnische Innovationen in der ersten Hälfte des 19. Jahrhunderts und ihre Umsetzung in der bayerischen Armee (Master's Thesis)* (University of Würzburg 2011)

Meissner B, *Sowjetunion und HLKO – Hektographierte Veröffentlichungen der Forschungsstelle für Völkerrecht und ausländisches öffentliches Recht der Universität Hamburg* (1950)

Mérignhac A, *Les lois et coutumes de la guerre sur terre d'après le droit international moderne et la codification de la Conférence de La Haye de 1899* (Marescq Ainé 1903)

Meyendorff AF, *Correspondance diplomatique de M de Staal (1884–1900)*, vol 2 (M Rivière 1929)

Milanović M, *Extraterritorial Application of Human Rights Treaties: Law, Principles, and Policy* (Oxford University Press 2011)

Molotov V, *Soviet Government Statements on Nazi Atrocities* (Hutchinson 1946)

Müller K-D, Nikischkin K and Wagenlehner G, *Die Tragödie der Gefangenschaft in Deutschland und in der Sowjetunion 1941–1956* (Bohlau Verlag 1998)

Münkler H, *Die neuen Kriege* (6th edn, Rowohlt Taschenbuch Verlag 2015)

Neugebauer K-V, *Grundzüge der deutschen Militärgeschichte: Historischer Überblick*, vol 1 (Rombach Verlag 1993)

Nussbaum A, *A Concise History of the Law of Nations* (Macmillan 1947)

Nußberger A (ed), *Einführung in das russische Recht* (Beck 2010)

——, *The European Court of Human Rights* (Oxford University Press 2020)

Nußberger A, Schmidt C and Morščakova T (eds), *Verfassungsrechtsprechung in der Russischen Föderation: Dokumentation und Analyse der Entscheidungen des Russischen Verfassungsgerichts 1992–2007* (Engel 2009)

Nystuen G and Casey-Maslen S (eds), *The Convention on Cluster Munitions: A Commentary* (Oxford University Press 2010)

O'Keefe R, *International Criminal Law* (Oxford University Press 2015)

Osten P, *Der Tokioter Kriegsverbrecherprozeß und die japanische Rechtswissenschaft* (BWV 2003)

Pictet J, *The Geneva Conventions of 12 August 1949: Geneva Convention for the Amelioration of the Condition of the Wounded and Sick in Armed Forces in the Field* (International Committee of the Red Cross 1952)

——, *The Geneva Conventions of 12 August 1949: Geneva Convention Relative to the Protection of Civilian Persons in Time of War* (International Committee of the Red Cross 1958)

——, *The Geneva Conventions of 12 August 1949: Commentary on the Geneva Convention Relative to the Treatment of Prisoners of War* (International Committee of the Red Cross 1960)

——, *The Fundamental Principles of the Red Cross* (Henry Dunant Institute 1979)

Politkovskaja A, Burry A and Tulchinsky T, *A Small Corner of Hell: Dispatches from Chechnya* (University of Chicago Press 2007)

Pustogarov V, *Our Martens: FF Martens, International Lawyer and Architect of Peace* (William E Butler tr, Kluwer Law International 2000)

Remnick D, *Resurrection: The Struggle for a New Russia* (Vintage Books 1998)

Rey-Schyrr C, *From Yalta to Dien Bien Phu – History of the International Committee of the Red Cross, 1945 to 1955* (ICRC 2007)

Roberts A, *Is International Law International?* (Oxford University Press 2017)

Rogers HCB, *A History of Artillery* (Citadel Press 1975)

Rousseau J-J, *Collection complète des œuvres*, vol 1 (1782)

Sadat LN, *Seeking Accountability for the Unlawful Use of Force:* (Cambridge University Press 2018)

Sandoz Y, Swinarski C and Zimmermann B (eds), *Commentary on the Additional Protocols of 8 June 1977 to the Geneva Conventions of 12 August 1949* (Martinus Nijhoff Publishers 1987)

Sassòli M, Bouvier AA and Quintin A, *How Does Law Protect in War?* (3rd edn, ICRC 2011)

Scanlan JP, *Dostoevsky the Thinker* (Cornell University Press 2002)

Schindler D, *The Different Types of Armed Conflicts According to the Geneva Conventions and Protocols* (Martinus Nijhoff 1979)

Schmitt MN (ed), *Tallinn Manual on the International Law Applicable to Cyber Warfare* (Cambridge University Press 2013)

Schoen S, *Der rechtliche Status von Beutekunst: eine Untersuchung am Beispiel der aufgrund des Zweiten Weltkrieges nach Russland verbrachten deutschen Kulturgüter* (Duncker & Humblot 2004)

Schwarzenberger G, *International Law as Applied by International Courts and Tribunals: Volume II: The Law of Armed Conflict* (Stevens and Sons 1968)

Schweisfurth T, *Sozialistisches Völkerrecht? Darstellung, Analyse, Wertung der sowjetmarxistischen Theorie vom Völkerrecht 'neuen Typs'* (Springer 1979)

Scott JB, *The Proceedings of the Hague Peace Conferences: Translation of the Official Texts*, vol 1 (Oxford University Press 1920)

Smith BF, *The Road to Nuremberg* (Basic Books 1981)

Snyder T, *Bloodlands: Europe between Hitler and Stalin* (Vintage Books 2011)

Société genevoise d'utilité publique, *Compte rendu de la Conférence internationale réunie à Genève les 26, 27, 28 et 29 octobre 1863, pour étudier les moyens de pourvoir à l'insuffisance du service sanitaire dans les armées en campagne* (Imprimerie Fick 1863)

Solis GD, *The Law of Armed Conflict: International Humanitarian Law in War* (Cambridge University Press 2016)

Sommerbauer J, *Die Ukraine im Krieg: Hinter den Frontlinien eines europäischen Konflikts* (K&S 2016)

Souleimanov E, *An Endless War: The Russian-Chechen Conflict in Perspective* (Peter Lang 2007)

Stökl G, *Russische Geschichte* (Kröner Verlag 1983)

Streit C, *Keine Kameraden: Die Wehrmacht und die sowjetischen Kriegsgefangenen 1941–1945* (Dietz 1991)

Taylor T, *Nuremberg and Vietnam: An American Tragedy* (Bantam Books 1971)

Tkacz M, Kries D and Fortin E, *Augustine: Political Writings* (Hackett 1994)

Toman J, *L'Union Soviétique et le droit des conflits armés* (PhD 1997)

Tomson E, *Kriegsbegriff und Kriegsrecht der Sowjetunion* (Berlin-Verlag 1979)

Tonkin H, *State Control over Private Military and Security Companies in Armed Conflict* (Cambridge University Press 2011)

Traynin A, *Hitlerite Responsibility under Criminal Law,* (Hutchinson & Co, Ltd 1945)

Troubetzkoy AS, *The Crimean War: The Causes and Consequences of a Medieval Conflict Fought in a Modern Age* (Carroll & Graf 2006)

Tschetschenien-Komitee (ed), *Tschetschenien: Die Hintergründe des blutigen Konflikts* (Diederichs 2004)

Tsygankov AP, *Russia's Foreign Policy: Change and Continuity in National Identity* (4th edn, Rowman & Littlefield 2016)

van Herpen M, *Putin's Wars: The Rise of Russia's New Imperialism* (2nd edn, Rowman & Littlefield 2015) von Clausewitz C, *Vom Kriege* (Werner Hahlweg ed, Dümmler 1980)

von Frobel G, *Von Löbell's Jahresberichte über das Heer- und Kriegswesen XXXVI Jahrgang: 1909* (ES Mittler & Sohn 1910)

Walzer M, *Just and Unjust Wars* (3rd edn, Basic Books 2000)

Zaslavsky V, *Klassensäuberung: Das Massaker von Katyn* (Rita Seuß tr, 2nd edn, Wagenbach 2008)

Zimnenko B, *International Law and the Russian Legal System* (William E Butler tr, Eleven International Publishing 2007)

Book Chapters

af Jochnick C and Normand R, 'The Legitimation of Violence: A Critical History of the Laws of War' in Michael N Schmitt and Wolff Heintschel von Heinegg (eds), *The Development and Principles of International Humanitarian Law* (Routledge 2017)

Akande D, 'Classification of Armed Conflicts: Relevant Legal Concepts' in Elizabeth Wilmshurst (ed), *International Law and the Classification of Conflicts* (Oxford University Press 2012)

Aldrich G, 'Individuals as Subjects of International Humanitarian Law' in Jerzy Makarczyk (ed), *Theory of International Law at the Threshold of the 21st Century: Essays in Honour of Krzysztof Skubiszewski* (Kluwer Law International 1996)

Arnold R and Berger A, 'Artikel 17' in Bernd Wieser (ed), *Handbuch der russischen Verfassung* (Verlag Österreich 2014)

Ball A, 'Building a New State and Society: 1921–1928' in Ronald Grigor Suny (ed), *The Cambridge History of Russia*, vol 3 (Cambridge University Press 2006)

Barber J and Harrison M, 'Patriotic War, 1941–1945' in Ronald Grigor Suny (ed), *The Cambridge History of Russia*, vol 3 (Cambridge University Press 2006)

Bos A, 'Crimes of State: In Need of Legal Rules?' in Gerard Kreijen (ed), *State, Sovereignty, and International Governance* (Martinus Nijhoff Publishers 2002)

Boulanin V and Grip L, 'Humanitarian Arms Control' in SIPRI (ed), *Yearbook 2017: Armaments, Disarmament and International Security – Summary* (Stockholm International Peace Research Institute Solna 2017)

Bowring B, 'Russian Cases in the ECtHR and the Question of Implementation' in Lauri Mälksoo and Wolfgang Benedek (eds), *Russia and the European Court of Human Rights: the Strasbourg Effect* (Cambridge University Press 2017)

——, 'Who Are the "Crimea People" or "People of Crimea"? The Fate of the Crimean Tatars, Russia's Legal Justification for Annexation, and Pandora's Box' in Sergey Sayapin and Evhen Tsybulenko (eds), *The Use of Force against Ukraine and International Law: Jus Ad Bellum, Jus In Bello, Jus Post Bellum* (Springer 2018)

Brownlie SI, 'Comment' in Antonio Cassese and Joseph Weiler (eds), *Change and Stability in International Law-making* (De Gruyter 2010)

Butler WE, 'Some Reflections on the Periodization of Soviet Approaches to International Law' in DD Barry, William E Butler and George Ginsburgs (eds), *Contemporary Soviet Law: Essays in Honor of John N. Hazard* (Martinus Nijhoff 1974)

——, 'Foreign Policy Discourses as Part of Understanding Russia and International Law' in P Sean Morris (ed), *Russian Discourses on International Law: Sociological and Philosophical Phenomenon* (Routledge 2018)

Cherkasov A, 'The Chechen Wars and the Struggle for Human Rights' in Richard Sakwa (ed), *Chechnya: from Past to Future* (Anthem Press 2005)

Clunan AL, 'Russia's Pursuit of Great-Power Status and Security' in Roger E Kanet (ed), *Routledge Handbook of Russian Security* (Routledge/Taylor & Francis Group 2019)

Condorelli L and Boisson de Chazournes L, 'Quelques remarques à propos de l'obligation des États de respecter et faire respecter le droit international humanitaire en toutes circonstances' in Christophe Swinarski (ed), *Études et essais sur le droit international humanitaire et sur les principes de la Croix-Rouge en l'honneur de Jean Pictet.* (Comité International de la Croix-Rouge 1984)

Crawford J and Keene A, 'The Structure of State Responsibility under the European Convention on Human Rights' in Anne van Aaken and Iulia Motoc (eds), *The European Convention on Human Rights and General International Law* (Oxford Scholarship Online 2018)

Davis GH, 'The Life of Prisoners of War in Russia 1914–1921' in Samuel RJr Williamson and Peter Pastor (eds), *War and Society in East Central Europe Vol V – Essays on World War I: Origins and Prisoners of War* (Brooklyn College Press 1983)

del Mar K, 'The Myth of Remedial Secession' in Duncan French (ed), *Statehood and Self-Determination: Reconciling Tradition and Modernity in International Law* (Cambridge University Press 2013)

Dorsey MG, 'More than Just a Taboo: The Legacy of the Chemical Warfare Prohibitions of the 1899 and 1907 Hague Conferences' in Maartje Abbenhuis, Christopher Ernest Barber and Annalise R Higgins (eds), *War, Peace and International Order? The Legacies of the Hague Conferences of 1899 and 1907* (Routledge 2017)

Evangelista M, 'How the Geneva Conventions Matter' in Matthew Evangelista and Nina Tannenwald (eds), *Do the Geneva Conventions Matter* (Oxford University Press 2017)

Fuller Jr WC, 'The Imperial Army' in Ronald Grigor Suny (ed), *The Cambridge History of Russia*, vol 2 (Cambridge University Press 2006)

Geiß R, 'Common Article 1 of the Geneva Conventions: Scope and Content of the Obligation to "Ensure Respect" – "Narrow but Deep" or "Wide and Shallow"?' in Heike Krieger (ed), *Inducing Compliance with International Humanitarian Law* (Cambridge University Press 2015)

Greenwood C, 'A Critique of the Additional Protocols to the Geneva Conventions of 1949' in Helen Durham, Timothy LH MacCormack and Alan Gilbert (eds), *The changing face of conflict and the efficacy of International Humanitarian Law*, vol 2 (Martinus Nijhoff Publishers 1999)

Hanson SE, 'The Brezhnev Era' in Ronald Grigor Suny (ed), *The Cambridge History of Russia*, vol 3 (Cambridge University Press 2006)

Heinsch R, 'The International Committee of the Red Cross and the Geneva Conventions of 1949' in Robin Geiss, Andreas Zimmermann and Stefanie Haumer (eds), *Humanizing the Laws of War: the Red Cross and the Development of International Humanitarian Law* (Cambridge University Press 2017)

Higgins HE, 'The 1907 Hague Peace Conference as a Milestone in the Development of International Law' in Yves Daudet (ed), *Actualité de la conférence de la Haye de 1907, deuxième conférence de la paix* (Martinus Nijhoff Publishers 2008)

Kolb R, 'Protecting Powers' in Andrew Clapham, Paola Gaeta and Marco Sassòli (eds), *The 1949 Geneva Conventions – a Commentary* (Oxford University Press 2015)

Kramer M, 'Russia, Chechnya, and the Geneva Conventions, 1994–2006' in Matthew Evangelista and Nina Tannenwald (eds), *Do the Geneva Conventions Matter?* (Oxford University Press 2017)

Kreß C, 'The International Court of Justice and the Law of Armed Conflicts' in Christian J Tams and James Sloan (eds), *The Development of International Law by the International Court of Justice* (Oxford University Press 2013)

Lattanzi F, 'Humanitarian Assisstance' in Andrew Clapham, Paola Gaeta and Marco Sassòli (eds), *The 1949 Geneva Conventions – a Commentary* (Oxford University Press 2015)

Leach P, 'Egregious Human Rights Violations in Chechnya: Appraising the Pursuit of Justice' in Lauri Mälksoo and Wolfgang Benedek (eds), *Russia and the European Court of Human Rights: the Strasbourg Effect* (Cambridge University Press 2017)

Lesaffer R, 'Peace through Law: The Hague Peace Conferences and the Rise of the Ius Contra Bellum' in Maartje Abbenhuis, Christopher Ernest Barber and Annalise R Higgins (eds), *War, Peace and International Order? The Legacies of the Hague Conferences of 1899 and 1907* (Routledge 2017)

Liivoja R, 'Competing Histories: Soviet War Crimes in the Baltic States' in Kevin Jon Heller and Gerry J Simpson (eds), *The Hidden Histories of War Crimes Trials* (First edition, Oxford University Press 2013)

Lukina A, 'Russia and International Human Rights Law: A View from the Past' in P Sean Morris (ed), *Russian Discourses on International Law: Sociological and Philosophical Phenomenon* (Routledge 2018)

Mälksoo L, 'Case Law in Russian Approaches to International Law' in Anthea Roberts and others (eds), *Comparative International Law* (Oxford University Press 2018)

——, 'Friedrich Fromhold von Martens (Fyodor Fyodorovich Martens) (1845–1909)' in Bardo Fassbender and Anne Peters (eds), *The Oxford Handbook of the History of International Law* (Oxford University Press 2012)

——, 'International Legal Theory in Russia: A Civilizational Perspective, or: Can Individuals Be Subjects of International Law?' in Anne Orford and Florian Hoffmann (eds), *The Oxford Handbook of the Theory of International Law* (Oxford University Press 2016)

Mantilla G, 'The Origins and Evolution of the 1949 Geneva Conventions and the 1977 Additional Protocols' in Matthew Evangelista and Nina Tannenwald (eds), *Do the Geneva Conventions Matter?* (Oxford University Press 2017)

Marouda M-D and Perrakis S (eds), 'Application of International Humanitarian Law in Contemporary Armed Conflicts: Is It "Simply'a Question of Facts?"', *Armed Conflicts and International Humanitarian Law 150 Years after Solferino: Acquis and Prospects* (Edition Sakkoulas 2009)

Mathers JG, 'The Rebuilding of Russian Military Capabilities' in Roger E Kanet (ed), *Routledge Handbook of Russian Security* (Routledge/Taylor & Francis Group 2019)

Meron T, 'Common Rights of Mankind in Gentili, Grotius and Suarez' in Theodor Meron (ed), *War Crimes Law Comes of Age: Essays* (Oxford University Press 1998)

Meurant J, 'Anatole Demidoff: Pionnier de l'assistance aux prisonniers de guerre' in Jacques Meurant and Roger Durant (eds), *Préludes et pionniers: Les précurseurs de la Croix-Rouge* (1991)

Moore B, 'Prisoners of War' in Evan Mawdsley and John Ferris (eds), *The Cambridge History of the Second World War – Fighting the War*, vol 1 (Cambridge University Press 2015)

Nußberger A and Safoklov Y, 'Artikel 15' in Bernd Wieser (ed), *Handbuch der russischen Verfassung* (Verlag Österreich 2014)

Nye RA, 'The Duel of Honour and the Origins of the Rules for Arms, Warfare and Arbitration in the Hague Conferences' in Maartje Abbenhuis, Christopher Ernest Barber and Annalise R Higgins (eds), *War, Peace and International Order? The Legacies of the Hague Conferences of 1899 and 1907* (Routledge 2017)

Oxenstierna S, 'Russia's Economy and Military Expenditures' in Roger E Kanet (ed), *Routledge Handbook of Russian Security* (Routledge/Taylor & Francis Group 2019)

Raleigh DJ, 'The Russian Civil War, 1917–1922' in Ronald Grigor Suny (ed), *The Cambridge History of Russia*, vol 3 (Cambridge University Press 2006)

Ratner SR and Giladi R, 'The Role of the International Committee of the Red Cross' in Andrew Clapham, Paola Gaeta and Marco Sassòli (eds), *The 1949 Geneva Conventions – a Commentary* (Oxford University Press 2015)

Rosenne S, 'War Crimes and State Responsibility' in Yoram Dinstein and Mala Tabory (eds), *War Crimes in International Law* (Nijhoff 1996)

Sassòli M, 'Ius Ad Bellum and Ius in Bello the Separation between the Legality of the Use of Force and Humanitarian Rules to Be Respected in Warfare: Crucial or Outdated?', *International Law and Armed Conflict: Exploring the Faultlines* (Brill Nijhoff 2007)

Schimmelpenninck van der Oye D, 'Russian Foreign Policy: 1815–1917' in Ronald Grigor Suny (ed), *The Cambridge History of Russia*, vol 2 (Cambridge University Press 2006)

Schindler D, 'International Humanitarian Law: Its Remarkable Development and Its Persistent Violation' in Michael N Schmitt and Wolff Heintschel von Heinegg (eds), *The Development and Principles of International Humanitarian Law* (Routledge 2017)

Shearer DR, 'Stalinism, 1928–1940' in Ronald Grigor Suny (ed), *The Cambridge History of Russia*, vol 3 (Cambridge University Press 2006)

Skaridov A, 'The Sea of Azov and the Kerch Straits' in David D Caron and Nilufer Oral (eds), *Navigating Straits: Challenges for International Law* (Brill Nijhoff 2014)

Smith SA, 'The Revolutions of 1917–1918' in Ronald Grigor Suny (ed), *The Cambridge History of Russia*, vol 3 (Cambridge University Press 2006)

Stone DR, 'Operations on the Eastern Front 1941–1945' in Evan Mawdsley and John Ferris (eds), *The Cambridge History of the Second World War – Fighting the War*, vol 1 (Cambridge University Press 2015)

Thürer D, 'Current Challenges to the Law of Occupation' in Mark Vuijlsteke and Floricica Olteanu (eds), *Proceedings of the Bruges Colloquium* (Collegium 2006)

Tolstykh V, 'The Nature of Russian Discourses on International Law – a Contemporary Survey' in P Sean Morris (ed), *Russian Discourses on International Law: Sociological and Philosophical Phenomenon* (Routledge 2018)

Tóth G, 'Legal Challenges in Hybrid Warfare Theory and Practice: Is There a Place for Legal Norms at All?' in Sergey Sayapin and Evhen Tsybulenko (eds), *The Use of Force against Ukraine and International Law: Jus Ad Bellum, Jus In Bello, Jus Post Bellum* (TMC Asser Press 2018)

van den Herik L and Duffy H, 'Human Rights Bodies and International Humanitarian Law: Common but Differentiated Approaches' in Carla M Buckley, Alice Donald and Philip Leach (eds), *Towards Convergence in International Human Rights Law* (Brill Nijhoff 2017)

Vereshchetin V, 'Some Reflections of a Russian Scholar on the Legacy of the Second Peace Conference' in Yves Daudet (ed), *Actualité de la Conférence de la Haye de 1907, deuxième Conférence de la Paix* (Martinus Nijhoff Publishers 2008)

von Martens GF, 'Protocole I des Conférences militaires tenues à Saint-Pétersbourg Mémoire sur la suppression de l'emploi des balles explosibles en temps de guerre', *Nouveau recueil général de traités et autres actes relatifs aux rapports de droit international*, vol XVIII (Scientia Verlag 1873)

Wechsler H, 'The Issues of the Nuremberg Trial' in Guénaël Mettraux (ed), *Perspectives on the Nuremberg Trial* (Oxford University Press 2008)

Wylie N, 'Muddied Waters: The Influence of the First Hague Conference on the Evolution of the Geneva Conventions of 1864 and 1906' in Maartje Abbenhuis, Christopher Ernest Barber and Annalise R Higgins (eds), *War, Peace and International Order? The Legacies of the Hague Conferences of 1899 and 1907* (Routledge 2017)

Zakharova L, 'The Reign of Alexander II: A Watershed?' in Ronald Grigor Suny and William C Fuller Jr (eds), *The Cambridge History of Russia*, vol 2 (Cambridge University Press 2006)

Ziegler AR and Wehrenberg S, 'Domestic Implementation' in Andrew Clapham, Paola Gaeta and Marco Sassòli (eds), *The 1949 Geneva Conventions – a Commentary* (Oxford University Press 2015)

Journal Articles

Russian-language Journal Articles

В.В. Герасимов [V.V. Gerasimov], 'Новые вызовы требуют переосмыслить формы и способы ведения боевых действий [New Challenges Demand to Rethink the Forms and Methods of the Conduct of Hostilities]' (2013) 8 Военно-промышленный Курьер [Military Industrial Courier] 2

Г.И. Тункин [G.I. Tunkin], 'XXII съезд КПСС и международное право [XXII Congress of the Communist Party of the Soviet Union]' (1961) Советский ежегодник международного права [Soviet Yearbook of International Law] 15

Е.А. Коровин [E.A. Korovin], 'Международное право на современном этапе [International Law at a Current Stage]' (1961) 7 Международная жизнь [International Life] 2

И.И. Котляров [I.I. Kotlyarov], 'Вклад России в стоновление и развитие международного гуманитарного права [Russia's Contribution to the Formation and Development of IHL]' (2007) Российский Ежегодник Международного Права [Russian Yearbook of International Law] 62

——, 'Вклад Ф.Ф. Мартенса в прогрессивное развитие международного гуманитарного право (к 140-летию Брюссельской конференции 1874 г.) [The Impact of F.F. Martens on the Progressive Development of IHL (on the Occasion of the 140th Anniversary of the Brussels Conference of 1874)' (2014) 95 Московский Журнал Международного Права [Moscow Journal of International Law] 102

М.Д. Беляева [M.D. Belyaeva], 'Сёстры милосердия Крымской войны – основатели культурных традиций сестринского дела в России [The Sisters of Mercy of the Crimean War – Founders of the Cultural Tradition of Nursing in Russia]' (2015) 94 Молодой Учёный Научный Журнал [Young Scientist's Journal] 390

О.И. Тиунов [O.I. Tiunov], 'Современные проблемы международного гуманитарного права – к 100-летию второй Гаагской конференции мира [Current Problems of IHL – on the Occasion of the 100th Anniversary of the Second Hague Peace Conference]' (2007) Российский Ежегодник Международного Права [Russian Yearbook of International Law] 23

Bibliography

Р.М. Валеев [R.M. Valeyev], 'Роль России в проведении Гаагских конференций мира (к 100-летию II Гаагской Конференции Мира 1907г) [The Role of Russia in the Hague Peace Conferences (on the Occasion of the 100 Year Anniversary of the Second Hague Peace Conference of 1907)]' (2007) Российский Ежегодник Международного Права [Russian Yearbook of International Law] 52

Ф.И. Кожевников [F.I. Kozhevnikov], 'Вопросы международного права в свете новых трудов И.В. Сталина [Issues Regarding International Law in the Light of the Latest Works of I.V. Stalin]' (1951) 6 Советское Государство и Право [Soviet State and Law] 25

International Journal Articles

Abresch W, 'A Human Rights Law of Internal Armed Conflict: The European Court of Human Rights in Chechnya' (2005) 16 European Journal of International Law 741

Alexander A, 'A Short History of International Humanitarian Law' (2015) 26 European Journal of International Law 109

Allison R, 'The Russian Case for Military Intervention in Georgia: International Law, Norms and Political Calculation' (2009) 18 European Security 173

Ambrosio T and Lange WA, 'The Architecture of Annexation? Russia's Bilateral Agreements with South Ossetia and Abkhazia' (2016) 44 Nationalities Papers 673

Arimatsu L, 'Beginning of IHL Application: Overview and Challenges' (2013) 13 Proceedings of the Bruges Colloquium on the Scope of Application of International Humanitarian Law 71

Atrokhov WT, 'The Khasavyurt Accords: Maintaining the Rule of Law and Legitimacy of Democracy in the Russian Federation amidst the Chechen Crisis' (1999) 32 Cornell International Law Journal 367

Averre D and Davies L, 'Russia, Humanitarian Intervention and the Responsibility to Protect: The Case of Syria' (2015) 91 International Affairs 813

Baranec T, 'Russian Cossacks in the Service of the Kremlin: Recent Developments and Lessons from Ukraine' (2014) 153 Russian Analytical Digest 9

Bearden M, 'Afghanistan, Graveyard of Empires' (2001) 80 Foreign Affairs 17

Becker A, 'The Great War: World War, Total War' (2015) 97 International Review of the Red Cross 1029

Bellinger III JB and Haynes II WJ, 'A US Government Response to the International Committee of the Red Cross Study *Customary International Humanitarian Law*' (2007) 89 International Review of the Red Cross 443

Bernard V, 'Violence against Health Care: Giving in Is Not an Option' (2013) 95 International Review of the Red Cross 5

Berry JF, 'Hollow Point Bullets: How History Has Hijacked Their Use in Combat and Why It Is Time to Reexamine the 1899 Hague Declaration Concerning Expanding Bullets' (2010) 206 Military Law Review 88

Bílková V, 'The Use of Force by the Russian Federation in Crimea' (2015) 75 ZaöRV/HJIL 27

Black-Branch J, 'The Legal Status of Cluster Munitions under International Humanitarian Law: Indiscriminate Weapons of War' (2012) 4 Journal of International Law of Peace and Armed Conflict 186

Blank LR, 'Understanding When and How Domestic Courts Apply IHL' (2011) 44 Case Western Reserve Journal of International Law 205

Brehm M, 'The Arms Trade and States' Duty to Ensure Respect for Humanitarian and Human Rights Law' (2007) 12 Journal of Conflict and Security Law 359

Bugnion F, 'Guerre juste, guerre d'agression et droit international humanitaire' (2002) 84 International Review of the Red Cross 523

——, 'The International Committee of the Red Cross and the Development of International Humanitarian Law' (2004) 5 Chicago Journal of International Law 27

Bujard D, 'The Geneva Convention of 1864 and the Brussels Conference of 1874' (1974) 14 International Review of the Red Cross 527

Bush JA, 'The Supreme Crime and Its Origins: The Lost Legislative History of the Crime of Aggressive War' (2002) 102 Columbia Law Review 2324

Cameron L, 'The ICRC in the First World War: Unwavering Belief in the Power of Law?' (2015) 97 International Review of the Red Cross 1099

Carnahan BM, 'Lincoln, Lieber and the Laws of War: The Origins and Limits of the Principle of Military Necessity' (1998) 92 American Journal of International Law 213

Carron D, 'When Is a Conflict International? Time for New Control Tests in IHL' (2016) 98 International Review of the Red Cross 1019

Cassese A, 'The Martens Clause: Half a Loaf or Simply Pie in the Sky?' (2000) 11 European Journal of International Law 187

Chazournes LB de and Condorelli L, 'Common Article 1 of the Geneva Conventions Revisited: Protecting Collective Interests' (2000) 82 International Review of the Red Cross 67

Chinnappa AE, 'The United States and the Coalition Provisional Authority – Occupation by Proxy?' (2019) Leiden Journal of International Law 415

Cockayne J, 'Regulating Private Military and Security Companies: The Content, Negotiation, Weaknesses and Promise of the Montreux Document' (2008) 13 Journal of Conflict and Security Law 401

Crawford E, 'The Enduring Legacy of the St Petersburg Declaration: Distinction, Military Necessity, and the Prohibition of Causing Unnecessary Suffering and Superfluous Injury in IHL' (2019) 20 Journal of the History of International Law 544

Crawford J and Keene A, 'Interpretation of the Human Rights Treaties by the International Court of Justice' (2019) The International Journal of Human Rights 1

Danilenko GM, 'The New Russian Constitution and International Law' (1994) 88 The American Journal of International Law 451

——, 'Implementation of International Law in CIS States: Theory and Practice' (1999) 10 European journal of international law 51

Darcy S, 'The Evolution of the Law of Belligerent Reprisals' (2003) 175 Military Law Review 244

de Hoon M, 'Navigating the Legal Horizon: Lawyering the MH17 Disaster' (2017) 33 Utrecht Journal of International and European Law 90

——, 'Pursuing Justice for MH17: The Role of the Netherlands' (2019) 49 Netherlands Yearbook of International Law 2018 245

Dörmann K and Geiß R, 'The Implementation of Grave Breaches into Domestic Legal Orders' (2009) 7 Journal of International Criminal Justice 703

Dörmann K and Serralvo J, 'Common Article 1 to the Geneva Conventions and the Obligation to Prevent International Humanitarian Law Violations' (2014) 96 International Review of the Red Cross 707

Doswald-Beck L, 'New Protocol on Blinding Laser Weapons' (1996) 36 International Review of the Red Cross 272

Dowdeswell TL, 'The Brussels Peace Conference of 1874 and the Modern Laws of Belligerent Qualification' (2017) 54 Oosgoode Hall Law Journal 805

Draper GIAD, 'Military Necessity and Humanitarian Imperatives Studies: Seminar on the Teaching of Humanitarian Law In Military Institutions, Sanremo, 6–18 November 1972' (1973) 12 Military Law and Law of War Review 129

Droege C, 'The Interplay between International Humanitarian Law and International Human Rights Law in Situations of Armed Conflict' (2007) 40 Israel Law Review 310

Ellman M and Maksudov S, 'Soviet Deaths in the Great Patriotic War: A Note' (1994) 46 Europe-Asia Studies 671

Esakov G, 'International Criminal Law in Russia' (2017) 15 Journal of International Criminal Justice 371

Eyffinger A, 'The 1907 Hague Peace Conference: The Conscience of the Civilized World' (2007) Netherlands International Law Review 197

Fayet J-F, 'Le CICR et la Russie: Un peu plus que de l'humanitaire' (2015) 1 Connexe: les espaces postcommunistes en question 55

Felgengauer P, 'The Russian Army in Chechnya' (2002) 21 Central Asian Survey 157

Ferraro T, 'Determining the Beginning and End of an Occupation under International Humanitarian Law' (2012) 94 International Review of the Red Cross 133

——, 'The Applicability and Application of International Humanitarian Law to Multinational Forces' (2013) 95 International Review of the Red Cross 561

Focarelli C, 'Common Article 1 of the 1949 Geneva Conventions: A Soap Bubble?' (2010) 21 European Journal of International Law 125

Ford TK, 'The Genesis of the First Hague Peace Conference' (1936) 51 Political Science Quarterly 354

Fox GH, 'Eyal Benvenisti. The International Law of Occupation' (2013) 24 European Journal of International Law 453

Fujita H, 'The Advisory Opinion of the International Court of Justice on the Legality of Nuclear Weapons' (1997) 37 International Review of the Red Cross 56

Gaeta P, 'The Armed Conflict in Chechnya before the Russian Constitutional Court' (1996) 7 European Journal of International Law 563

Gal T, 'Unexplored Outcomes of Tadić: Applicability of the Law of Occupation to War by Proxy' (2014) 12 Journal of International Criminal Justice 59

Galeotti M, 'The Cossacks: A Cross-Border Complication to Post-Soviet Eurasia' (1995) IBRU Boundary and Security Bulletin 55

Gasser H-P, 'Internationalized Non-International Armed Conflicts: Case Studies of Afghanistan, Kampuchea, and Lebanon Conference: The American Red Cross-Washington College of Law Conference: International Humanitarian and Human Rights Law in Non-International Armed Conflicts (12–13 April 1983)' (1983) 33 American University Law Review 145

——, 'A Look at the Declaration of St Petersburg of 1868' (1993) 33 International Review of the Red Cross 511

Gerrits AWM and Bader M, 'Russian Patronage over Abkhazia and South Ossetia: Implications for Conflict Resolution' (2016) 32 East European Politics 297

Gerson A, 'Trustee-Occupant: The Legal Status of Israel's Presence in the West Bank' (1973) 14 Harvard International Law Review 1

Gilder A, 'Bringing Occupation into the 21st Century: The Effective Implementation of Occupation by Proxy' (2017) 13 Utrecht Law Review 60

Gillard E-C, 'The Law Regulating Cross-Border Relief Operations' (2013) 95 International Review of the Red Cross 351

Gillich I, 'Illegally Evading Attribution: Russia's Use of Unmarked Troops in Crimea and International Humanitarian Law' (2015) 48 Vanderbilt Journal of Transnational Law 1191

Ginsburgs G, 'Laws of War and War Crimes on the Russian Front during World War II: The Soviet View' (1960) 11 Soviet Studies 253

Gorbunova Y, 'Human Rights Abuses in Crimea under Russia's Occupation' (2014) 25 Security and Human Rights 328

Greenwood C, 'The Twilight of the Law of Belligerent Reprisals' (1989) 20 Netherlands Yearbook of International Law 35

Hafner G, 'The Intervention in Czechoslovakia – 1968' (2019) 21 Austrian Review of International and European Law Online 27

Heinsch R, 'Conflict Classification in Ukraine: The Return of the "Proxy War"?' (2015) 91 International Law Studies 323

Hershberg JG, 'New Evidence on the Soviet Intervention in Afghanistan' (1996) 8 Cold War International History Bulletin 128

Higgins N, 'The Application of International Humanitarian Law to Wars of National Liberation' (2004) Journal of Humanitarian Assistance

Hill-Cawthorne L, 'Rights under International Humanitarian Law' (2017) 28 European Journal of International Law 1187

Hirsch F, 'The Soviets at Nuremberg: International Law, Propaganda, and the Making of the Postwar Order' (2008) 113 The American Historical Review 701

Hoffman FG, 'Hybrid Warfare and Challenges' (2009) 52 Joint Force Quarterly 1

Holá B, Mulgrew R and van Wijk J (eds), 'Special Issue: National Prosecutions of International Crimes: Sentencing Practices and (Negotiated) Punishments' (2019) 19 International Criminal Law Review 1

ICRC, '20th International Conference of the Red Cross, "Proclamation of the Fundamental Principles of the Red Cross"' (1965) 5 International Review of the Red Cross 567

——, 'ICRC Q&A on the Issue of Explosive Weapons in Populated Areas' (2016) 98 International Review of the Red Cross 97

ILC, 'Draft Articles on Responsibility of States for Internationally Wrongful Acts, with Commentaries' (2001) 2 Yearbook of the International Law Commission 30

Ivanel B, 'Puppet States: A Growing Trend of Covert Occupation' (2016) 18 Yearbook of International Humanitarian Law 43

Kalshoven F, 'The Undertaking to Respect and Ensure Respect in All Circumstances: From Tiny Seed to Ripening Fruit' (1999) 2 Yearbook of International Humanitarian Law 3

Kapustin A, 'Crimea's Self-Determination in the Light of Contemporary International Law' (2015) 75 ZaöRV/HJIL 101

Keefer S, '"Explosive Missals": International Law, Technology, and Security in Nineteenth-Century Disarmament Conferences' (2014) 21 War in History 445

Khalidi NA, 'Afghanistan: Demographic Consequences of War, 1978–1987' (1991) 10 Central Asian Survey 101

Kleffner JK, 'The Applicability of International Humanitarian Law to Organized Armed Groups' (2011) 93 International Review of the Red Cross 443

Kolb R and Milanov M, 'The 1868 St Petersburg Declaration on Explosive Projectiles: A Reappraisal' (2019) 20 Journal of the History of International Law 515

Koroteev K, 'Legal Remedies for Human Rights Violations in the Armed Conflict in Chechnya: The Approach of the European Court of Human Rights in Context' (2010) 1 Journal of International Humanitarian Legal Studies 275

Kozhanov N, 'Main Drivers of Russian Military Deployment in Syria' (2017) 13 International Studies Journal 21

Kramer M, 'The Perils of Counterinsurgency: Russia's War in Chechnya' (2005) 29 International Security 5

Kreß C, 'Friedenssicherungs- und Konfliktvölkerrecht auf der Schwelle zur Postmoderne' (1996) EuGRZ 63

Kreß C, 'The Peacemaking Process After the Great War and the Origins of International Criminal Law Stricto Sensu' (2021) 62 German Yearbook of International Law 163

Kreß C and Mégret F, 'The Regulation of Non-International Armed Conflicts: Can a Privilege of Belligerency Be Envisioned in the Law of Non-International Armed Conflicts?' (2014) 96 International Review of the Red Cross 29

Lamp N, 'Conceptions of War and Paradigms of Compliance: The "New War" Challenge to International Humanitarian Law' (2011) 16 Journal of Conflict and Security Law 225

Lauder MA, 'Wolves of the Russian Spring': An Examination of the Night Wolves as a Proxy for the Russian Government' (2018) 18 Canadian Military Journal 1

Lauterpacht H, 'The Limits of the Operation of the Law of War' (1953) 30 British Yearbook of International Law 206

Lawless R, 'A State of Complicity: How Russia's Persistent and Public Denial of Syrian Battlefield Atrocities Violates International Law' (2018) 9 Harvard National Security Journal 180

Leach P, 'The Chechen Conflict: Analysing the Oversight of the European Court of Human Rights' (2008) European Human Rights Law Review 732

Lippman M, 'Nuremberg: Forty Five Years Later' (1991) 7 Conneticut Journal of International Law 1

Lott A, 'The Tagliavini Report Revisited: Jus Ad Bellum and the Legality of the Russian Intervention in Georgia' (2012) 28 Utrecht Journal of International and European Law 4

Lukashuk I, 'Das neue russische Gesetz über internationale Verträge und das Völkerrecht' (1997) 43 Osteuropa-Recht 182

Lustgarten L, 'The Arms Trade Treaty: Achievements, Failings, Future' (2015) 64 International & Comparative Law Quarterly 569

Mačák K, 'A Matter of Principle(s): The Legal Effect of Impartiality and Neutrality on States as Humanitarian Actors' (2015) 97 International Review of the Red Cross 157

Malek M, 'Russia's Asymmetric Wars in Chechnya since 1994' (2009) 8 Connections 81

Maley W, 'Afghanistan: An Historical and Geographical Appraisal' (2010) 92 International Review of the Red Cross 859

Mälksoo L, 'Soviet Genocide? Communist Mass Deportations in the Baltic States and International Law' (2001) 14 Leiden Journal of International Law 757

——, 'FF Martens and His Time: When Russia Was an Integral Part of the European Tradition of International Law' (2014) 25 European Journal of International Law 811

Marochkin S and Popov V, 'International Humanitarian and Human Rights Law in Russian Courts' (2012) 2 Journal of International Humanitarian Legal Studies 216

Marten K, 'Russia's Use of Semi-State Security Forces: The Case of the Wagner Group' (2019) 35 Post-Soviet Affairs 181

Marxsen C, 'The Crimea Crisis – an International Law Perspective' (2014) 74 ZaöRV/HJIL 367

Maslen S and Herby P, 'An International Ban on Anti-Personnel Mines: History and Negotiation of the "Ottawa Treaty"' (1998) 38 International Review of the Red Cross 693

Mattis JN and Hoffman F, 'Future Warfare: The Rise of Hybrid Wars' (2005) 131 United States Naval Institute Proceedings Magazine 18

Meltzer BD, 'Note on Some Aspects of the Nuremberg Debate, A' (1946) 14 University of Chicago Law Review 455

Melzer N, 'Keeping the Balance between Military Necessity and Humanity: A Response to Four Critiques of the ICRC's Interpretive Guidance on the Notion of Direct Participation in Hostilities Forum: Direct Participation In Hostilities: Perspectives on the ICRC Interpretive Guidance' (2009) 42 New York University Journal of International Law and Politics 831

Meron T, 'The Geneva Conventions as Customary Law' (1987) 81 American Journal of International Law 348

——, 'The Martens Clause, Principles of Humanity, and Dictates of Public Conscience' (2000) 94 American Journal of International Law 78

——, 'The Humanization of Humanitarian Law' (2000) 94 American Journal of International Law 239

Milanović M, 'Al-Skeini and Al-Jedda in Strasbourg' (2012) 23 European Journal of International Law 121

Milanović M and Papić T, 'The Applicability of the ECHR in Contested Territories' (2018) 67 International and Comparative Law Quarterly 779

Mitrokhin N, 'Infiltration, Instruktion, Invasion: Russlands Krieg in der Ukraine' (2014) 64 Osteuropa 3

——, 'Diktaturtransfer im Donbass – Staatsbildung in Russlands Volksrepubliken' (2017) 67 Osteuropa 41

Moussa J, 'Can Jus Ad Bellum Override Jus in Bello? Reaffirming the Separation of the Two Bodies of Law' (2008) 90 International Review of the Red Cross 963

Mullins CW, 'War Crimes In The 2008 Georgia-Russia Conflict' (2011) 51 British Journal of Criminology 918

Munoz Mosquera AB and Bachmann SD, 'Lawfare in Hybrid Wars: The 21st Century Warfare' (2016) 7 Journal of International Humanitarian Legal Studies 63

Myles E, 'Humanity, Civilization and the International Community in the Late Imperial Russian Mirror – Three Ideas Topical for Our Days' (2002) 4 Journal of the History of International Law 310

Nachtigal R, 'Seuchen unter militärischer Aufsicht in Rußland: Das Lager Tockoe als Beispiel für die Behandlung der Kriegsgefangenen 1915/16' (2000) 48 Jahrbücher für Geschichte Osteuropas 363

Nagan W, 'Simulated ICJ Judgment: Revisiting the Lawfulness of the Threat or Use of Nuclear Weapons' (2012) 1 Cadmus 93

Nase V and Kielsgard M, 'A Call for Legal Accountability in the Wake of the MH17 Tragedy' (2015) 80 Journal of Air Law and Commerce 639

Neumaier C, 'The Escalation of German Reprisal Policy in Occupied France, 1941–42' (2006) 41 Journal of Contemporary History 113

Newton MA, 'Contorting Common Article 3: Reflections on the Revised ICRC Commentary' (2016) 45 Georgia Journal of International and Comparative Law 513

Nollkaemper A, 'Concurrence between Individual Responsibility and State Responsibility in International Law' (2003) 52 International & Comparative Law Quarterly 615

Nußberger A, 'Der "Fünf-Tage-Krieg" vor Gericht. Russland, Georgien und das Völkerrecht' (2008) 58 Osteuropa 19

——, 'The War between Russia and Georgia – Consequences and Unresolved Questions' (2009) 1 Goettingen Journal of International Law 341

Oeter S, 'Civil War, Humanitarian Law and the United Nations' (1997) 1 Max Planck Yearbook of United Nations Law 195

Okowa P, 'The International Court of Justice and the Georgia/Russia Dispute' (2011) 11 Human Rights Law Review 739

Orakhelashvili A, 'Overlap and Convergence: The Interaction between Jus Ad Bellum and Jus in Bello' (2007) 12 Journal of Conflict & Security Law 157

O'Reilly K and Higgins N, 'The Role of the Russian Federation in the Pridnestrovian Conflict: An International Humanitarian Law Perspective' (2008) 19 Irish Studies in International Affairs 57

Pain E, 'From the First Chechen War Towards the Second' (2001) 8 The Brown Journal of World Affairs 7

Pain E and Love RR, 'The Second Chechen War: The Information Component' (2000) 80 Military Review 59

Pejic J, 'The Protective Scope of Common Article 3: More than Meets the Eye' (2011) 93 International Review of the Red Cross 189

Penter T, 'Local Collaborators on Trial. Soviet War Crimes Trials under Stalin (1943–1953)' (2008) 49 Cahiers du monde russe 341

Preliminary Peace Conference, 'Commission on the Responsibility of the Authors of the War and on Enforcement of Penalties' (1920) 14 American Journal of International Law 95

Prusin AV, '"Fascist Criminals to the Gallows!": The Holocaust and Soviet War Crimes Trials, December 1945–February 1946' (2003) 17 Holocaust and Genocide Studies 1

Quénivet N, 'The Moscow Hostage Crisis in the Light of the Armed Conflict in Chechnya' (2001) 4 Yearbook of International Humanitarian Law 348

Reeves S and Wallace DA, 'The Combatant Status of the "Little Green Men" and Other Participants in the Ukraine Conflict' (2015) 91 International Law Studies 361

Reisinger H and Golts A, 'Russia's Hybrid Warfare' (2014) 105 Research Papers of the NATO Defense College 1

Reisman WM and Silk J, 'Which Law Applies to the Afghan Conflict?' (1988) 82 American Journal of International Law 459

Reno W, 'African Weak States and Commercial Alliances' (1997) 96 African Affairs 165

Reuveny R and Prakash A, 'The Afghanistan War and the Breakdown of the Soviet Union' (1999) 25 Review of International Studies 693

Rey-Schyrr C, 'Les Conventions de Genève de 1949 : une percée décisive – première partie' (1999) 833 Revue Internationale de la Croix-Rouge 209

——, 'Les Conventions de Genève de 1949 : une percée décisive – seconde partie' (1999) 855 Revue Internationale de la Croix-Rouge 499

Rodenhäuser T, 'Strengthening IHL Protecting Persons Deprived of Their Liberty: Main Aspects of the Consultations and Discussions since 2011' (2016) 98 International Review of the Red Cross 941

Sassòli M, 'The Implementation of International Humanitarian Law: Current and Inherent Challenges' (2007) 10 Yearbook of International Humanitarian Law 45

Sayapin S, 'A Curious Aggression Trial in Ukraine: Some Reflections on the Alexandrov and Yerofeyev Case' (2018) 16 Journal of International Criminal Justice 1093

Scelle G, 'Quelques réflexions sur l'abolition de la compétence de guerre' (1954) 25 Revue Générale de Droit International Public

Schäfer R, 'The 150th Anniversary of the St Petersburg Declaration: Introductory Reflections on a Janus-Faced Document' (2019) 20 Journal of the History of International Law 501

Schatz VJ and Koval D, 'Russia's Annexation of Crimea and the Passage of Ships through Kerch Strait: A Law of the Sea Perspective' (2019) 50 Ocean Development & International Law 275

Selhorst AJC, 'Russia's Perception Warfare: The Development of Gerasimov's Doctrine in Estonia and Georgia and Its Application in Ukraine' (2016) 22 Militaire Spectator 148

Sellars K, 'Imperfect Justice at Nuremberg and Tokyo' (2010) 21 European Journal of International Law 1085

Senn AE, 'The Soviet Union's Road to Geneva, 1924–1927' (1979) Jahrbücher für Geschichte Osteuropas 69

Sloane RD, 'The Cost of Conflation: Preserving the Dualism of Jus Ad Bellum and Jus in Bello in the Contemporary Law of War' (2009) 34 Yale Journal of International Law 47

Socher J, 'Lenin, (Just) Wars of National Liberation, and the Soviet Doctrine on the Use of Force' (2017) 19 Journal of the History of International Law 219

Sorensont A, 'South Ossetia and Russia: The Treaty, the Takeover, the Future' (2016) 42 North Carolina Journal of International Law 223

Spearin C, 'NATO, Russia and Private Military and Security Companies: Looking into the Dark Reflection' (2018) 163 The RUSI Journal 66

——, 'Russian Military and Security Privatization: Implications for Canada' (2019) 19 Canadian Military Journal 4

Sutyagin I, 'Russian Forces in Ukraine' (2015) 9 RUSI Briefing Paper

Szpak A, 'Legal Classification of the Armed Conflict in Ukraine in Light of International Humanitarian Law' (2017) 58 Hungarian Journal of Legal Studies 261

Ticehurst R, 'The Martens Clause and the Laws of Armed Conflict' (1997) 37 International Review of the Red Cross 125

Toal G and O'Loughlin J, 'Inside South Ossetia: A Survey of Attitudes in a de Facto State' (2013) 29 Post-Soviet Affairs 136

Tolstykh V, 'International Humanitarian Law in Russia (1850–1917) (Transl.)' (2004) Russian Law 67

——, 'Three Ideas of Self-Determination in International Law and the Reunification of Crimea with Russia' (2015) 75 ZaöRV/HJIL 119

Tonkin H, 'Common Article 1: A Minimum Yardstick for Regulating Private Military and Security Companies' (2009) 22 Leiden Journal of International Law 779

Trumpener U, 'The Road to Ypres: The Beginnings of Gas Warfare in World War I' (1975) 47 The Journal of Modern History 460

Tuzmukhamedov B, 'The Implementation of International Humanitarian Law in the Russian Federation' (2003) 85 International Review of the Red Cross 385

Urse C, 'Solving Transnistria: Any Optimists Left?' (2008) 7 Connections 57

van Dijk B, '"The Great Humanitarian": The Soviet Union, the International Committee of the Red Cross, and the Geneva Conventions of 1949' (2019) 37 Law and History Review 209

Van Schaack B, 'Mapping War Crimes in Syria' (2016) 92 International Law Studies 282

Vité S, 'Typologie des conflits armés en droit international humanitaire: concepts juridiques et réalités' (2009) 91 Revue Internationale de la Croix-Rouge 69

von Pelet-Narbonne G, 'Die neueren Tendenzen der Militärpolitik' (1909) 2 Zeitschrift für Politik 440

Walker C and Whyte D, 'Contracting out War? Private Military Companies, Law and Regulation in the United Kingdom' (2005) 54 International and Comparative Law Quarterly 651

Westad OA, 'Prelude to Invasion: The Soviet Union and the Afghan Communists, 1978–1979' (1994) 16 The International History Review 49

Wiebe V, 'Footprints of Death: Cluster Bombs as Indiscriminate Weapons under International Humanitarian Law' (2000) 22 Michigan International Law Journal 85

Wilson P, 'The Myth of International Humanitarian Law' (2017) 93 International Affairs 563

Wither JK, 'Making Sense of Hybrid Warfare' (2016) 15 Connections 73

Wood B and Abdul-Rahim R, 'The Birth and the Heart of the Arms Trade Treaty' (2015) 12 The SUR File on Arms and Human Rights 15

Wright Q, 'The Outlawry of War and the Law of War' (1953) 47 American Journal of International Law 365

Reports

Russian-language Reports

Б.Е. Немцов [B.E. Nemtsov], 'Независимый Экспертный Доклад: Путин – Война [Independent Expert Report: Putin – War]' (2015)

Владимир Неелов [Vladimir Neelov], 'Частные военные компании в России – опыт и перспективы использования [Private Military Companies in Russia – Experiences and Perspectives of Their Use]' (2013)

Мемориал [Memorial], 'Всеми имеющимися средствами: Операция МВД РФ в селе Самашки, 7–8 апреля 1995 года [All Necessary Means: the Operation of the Russian Ministry of Interior in the Village of Samashki, 7–8 April 1995]' (1995)

——, 'Правовые аспекты чеченского кризиса [Legal Aspects of the Chechen Crisis]' (1995)

——, 'Условия содержания задержанных в зоне вооруженного конфликта в Чеченской Республике: Обращение с задержанными [Conditions of Detention in the Chechen War Zone – Treatment of Detainees]' (1995)

——, 'За спинами мирных жителей: Захват заложников и использование гражданского населения в качестве "живого щита" федеральными войсками России в ходе вооруженного конфликта в Чечне [On the Backs of Civilians: the Practice by the Russian Armed Forces of Taking Hostages and Using Civilians as "Human Shields" during the Armed Conflict in Chechnya]' (1996)

——, 'Россия – Чечня: цепь ошибок и преступлений [Russia – Chechnya: A Series of Mistakes and Crimes]' (1998)

——, '"Точечные удары": краткая хроника бомбардировок и обстрелов 1 ноября-4 декабря 1999 г. ["Punctual Strikes: a Short Chronic of the Bombardments and Shellings from 1 November-4 December 1999]' (1999)

——, 'Здесь живут люди! Чечня: хроника насилия, Часть 1 Июль – декабрь 2000 г [People Live Here! – Chechnya: a Story of Violence, Part I July–December 2000]' (2003)

International Reports

Amnesty International, 'Annual Report 1982 (POL 10/0004/1982)' (1983)

——, 'For the Motherland: Reported Grave Breaches of International Humanitarian Law (EUR 46/046/1999)' (1999)

——, 'Civilians in the Line of Fire – the Georgia-Russia Conflict (EUR 04/005/2008)' (2008)

——, 'Europe and Central Asia Summary of Amnesty International's Concerns in the Region, July–December 2007 (EUR 01/001/2008)' (2008)

Bellal A, 'The War Report – Armed Conflicts in 2016' (Geneva Academy of International Humanitarian Law and Human Rights 2017)

——, 'The War Report – Armed Conflicts in 2018' (Geneva Academy of International Humanitarian Law and Human Rights 2019)

Bellingcat, 'Forensic Analysis of Satellite Images Released by the Russian Ministry of Defense' (2014)

Canada, Office of the Judge Advocate General, 'The Law of Armed Conflict at the Operational and Tactical Levels' (2001)

Council of Europe, 'Opinion on the Provisions of the Law on Education of 5 September 2017 Which Concern the Use of the State Language and Minority and Other Languages in Education (CDL-AD (2017) 030-e)' (2017)

Crawford NC, 'Human Cost of the Post-9/11 Wars: Lethality and the Need for Transparency' (Watson Institute for International & Public Affairs 2018)

Czuperski M, 'Hiding in Plain Sight: Putin's War in Ukraine' (The Atlantic Council of the United States 2015)

Deutscher Bundestag, 'Drucksache 13/718 – Antwort der Bundesregierung, Verhalten der Bundesregierung zum russischen Vorgehen im Tschetschenien-Konflikt' (1995)

Deutsches Bundesministerium der Verteidigung, 'Zentrale Dienstvorschrift (Dv) 15/2 Humanitäres Völkerrecht in bewaffneten Konflikten – Handbuch' (2016)

DGO, 'Russlandanalysen Nr. 362' (Länderanalysen 2018)

Dutch Safety Board (OVV), 'Crash of Malaysia Airlines Flight MH17' (2015)

Ermacora F, 'Report on the Situation of Human Rights in Afghanistan Prepared in Accordance with Commission on Human Rights Resolution 1985/38 (UN Doc E/CN.4/1986/24)' (1986)

EU Parliament Subcommittee on Security and Defence, 'Russian Military Presence in the Eastern European Partnership Countries' (2016)

Fischer S, 'The Donbas Conflict – Opposing Interests and Narratives, Difficult Peace Progress' (Stiftung Wissenschaft und Politik 2019)

Gasser H-P, 'The United Nations and International Humanitarian Law: The International Committee of the Red Cross and the United Nations' Involvement in the Implementation of International Humanitarian Law – International Symposium on the Occasion of the Fiftieth Anniversary of the United Nations' (ICRC 1995)

Gillard E-C, 'Promoting Compliance with International Humanitarian Law' (Chatham House 2016)

Hoffman FG, 'Conflict in the 21st Century: The Rise of Hybrid Wars' (Potomac Institute for Policy Studies 2007)

Howse R, 'The Concept of Odious Debts in Public International Law (UNCTAD/OSG/DP/2007/4)' (United Nations Conference on Trade and Development 2007)

Human Rights Watch, 'Chechnya: Report to the 1996 OSCE Review Conference (D816)' (1996)

——, 'Backgrounder on the Case of Kheda Kungaeva – Trial of Yuri Budanov Set for February 28' (2001) <https://www.hrw.org/legacy/backgrounder/eca/chech-bck0226.htm>

——, 'Georgia/Russia: Use of Rocket Systems Can Harm Civilians' (2008) <https://www.hrw.org/news/2008/08/11/georgia/russia-use-rocket-systems-can-harm-civilians>

——, 'A Dying Practice – the Use of Cluster Munitions by Russian and Georgia in August 2008' (2009)

——, '"Who Will Tell Me What Happened to My Son?" Russia's Implementation of European Court of Human Rights Judgments on Chechnya' (2009)

——, 'Up in Flames – Humanitarian Law Violations and Civilian Victims in the Conflict over South Ossetia' (2019)

ICRC, 'Annual Report 1956' (1956)

——, 'Annual Report 1968' (1968)

——, 'Annual Report 1969' (1969)

——, 'Annual Report 1980' (1980)

——, 'Annual Report 1981' (1981)

——, 'Annual Report 1995' (1995)

——, 'International Humanitarian Law and the Challenges of Contemporary Armed Conflicts (31IC/11/5.1.2)' (2011)

——, 'Expert Meeting, Occupation and Other Forms of Administration of Foreign Territory' (2012)

ICRC/Swiss Federal Department of Foreign Affairs, 'Strengthening Compliance with International Humanitarian Law – Concluding Report of the 32nd International Conference of the Red Cross and Red Crescent (32IC/15/19.2)' (2015)

IHFFC, 'Report on the Work of the IHFFC on the Occasion of Its 20th Anniversary Constituted in 1991 Pursuant to Article 90 of Protocol I Additional to the Geneva Conventions' (2011)

IICI, 'Report of the Independent International Commission of Inquiry on the Syrian Arab Republic (A/HRC/33/55)' (2016)

——, 'Report of the Independent International Commission of Inquiry on the Syrian Arab Republic (A/HRC/34/64)' (2017)

——, 'Report of the Independent International Commission of Inquiry on the Syrian Arab Republic (A/HRC/43/57)' (2020)

IIFFMCG, 'Report of the Independent International Fact-Finding Mission on the Conflict in Georgia (Tagliavini Report) Volume I' (2009)

——, 'Report of the Independent International Fact-Finding Mission on the Conflict in Georgia (Tagliavini Report) Volume II' (2009)

——, 'Report of the Independent International Fact-Finding Mission on the Conflict in Georgia (Tagliavini Report) Volume III – Views of the Sides on the Conflict, Chronologies and Responses to Questionnaires' (2009)

ILC, 'The Obligation to Extradite or Prosecute (Aut Dedere Aut Judicare) – Final Report' (2014)

International Campaign to Ban Landmines, 'Landmine Monitor 1999' (1999)

——, 'Landmine Monitor 2004' (2004)

——, 'Landmine Monitor 2018' (2018)

International Crisis Group, 'Abkhazia: The Long Road to Reconciliation' (2013)

International Law Association (Committee on the Use of Force), 'Final Report on the Meaning of Armed Conflict in International Law' (2010)

Israeli Military Advocate-General's Corps Command, 'Rules of Warfare on the Battlefield (Second Edition)' (IDF School of Military Law 2006)

Klein M and Pester K, 'Kiew in der Offensive – Die militärische Dimension des Ukraine-Konflikts' (Stiftung Wissenschaft und Politik 2014)

Max É, 'Implementing International Humanitarian Law Through Human Rights Mechanisms: Opportunity or Utopia?' (Geneva Academy of International Humanitarian Law and Human Rights 2019)

Mines Action Canada, 'Banning Cluster Munitions – Government Policy and Practice' (2009)

——, 'Cluster Munition Monitor' (2010)

——, 'Cluster Munition Monitor' (2011)

OHCHR, 'Report on the Human Rights Situation in Ukraine (16 February – 15 May 2019)' (2019)

Organisation for Economic Co-operation and Development, 'Civilian and Military Means of Providing and Supporting Humanitarian Assistance during Conflict: A Comparative Analysis Note by the Secretariat (DCD/DAC(97)19/REV1)' (1998)

OSCE SMM, 'Latest from the OSCE Special Monitoring Mission to Ukraine, Based on Information Received as of 19:30, 24 May 2018' (2018) <https://www.osce.or g/special-monitoring-mission-to-ukraine/382531>

——, 'Spot Report by OSCE Observer Mission: Seventy-Sixth Russian Convoy of 17 Vehicles Crossed into Ukraine and Returned through Donetsk Border Crossing Point' (2018) <https://www.osce.org/observer-mission-at-russian-check points-gukovo-and-donetsk/386142>

——, 'Latest from the OSCE Special Monitoring Mission to Ukraine, Based on Information Received as of 19:30, 8 August 2018' (2018) <https://www.osce.org/ special-monitoring-mission-to-ukraine/390179>

OSCE/IHFFC, 'Executive Summary of the Report of the Independent Forensic Investigation in Relation to the Incident Affecting an OSCE Special Monitoring Mission to Ukraine Patrol on 23 April 2017' (2017) <https://www.osce.org/home /338361?download=true>

OSCE/ODIHR, 'Human Rights in the War Affected Areas Following the Conflict in Georgia' (2008)

——, 'Report of the Human Rights Assessment Mission on Crimea (6–18 July 2015)' (2015)

Østensen ÅG and Bukkvoll T, 'Russian Use of Private Military and Security Companies – the Implications for European and Norwegian Security' (Norwegian Defence Research Establishment 2018)

PACE, 'Recommendation 1600 (2003) – The Human Rights Situation in the Chechen Republic' (2003)

——, 'Legal Remedies for Human Rights Violations in the North-Caucasus Region: Report of the Committee on Legal Affairs and Human Rights to the PACE' (2010)

PAX, 'Crunch Time – European Positions on Lethal Autonomous Weapon Systems' (2018)

Peterke S, 'Regulating "Drug Wars" and Other Gray Zone Conflicts: Formal and Functional Approaches' (Hasow 2012)

Reynolds N, 'Putin's Not-So-Secret Mercenaries: Patronage, Geopolitics, and the Wagner Group' (Carnegie Endowment for International Peace 2019)

Rotar I, 'The Cossack Factor in Ukrainian War' (Jamestown Foundation 2014) <https://www.refworld.org/docid/53f49aeb4.html>

Schweizerische Eidgenossenschaft/ICRC, 'The Montreux Document on Pertinent International Legal Obligations and Good Practices for States Related to Operations of Private Military and Security Companies during Armed Conflict' (2008)

SIPRI, 'Yearbook 2019' (2019)

Syrian American Medical Society, 'The Failure of UN Security Council Resolution 2286 in Preventing Attacks on Healthcare in Syria' (2017)

Syrian Archive & Bellingcat, 'Medical Facilities under Fire – Systematic Attacks during April 2017 on Idlib Hospitals Serving More than One Million in Syria' (2017)

The Office of the ICC Prosecutor, 'Report on Preliminary Examination Activities 2016' (2016)

Tweede Kamer der Staten-Generaal, 'Kamerstuk 2008–2009, 31595 Nr. 2: Verslag Onderzoeksmissie Storimans' (2008)

UK Ministry of Defense, 'The Joint Service Manual of the Law of Armed Conflict (Joint Service Publication 383)' (2004)

UN General Assembly, 'Report of the Special Committee on the Problem of Hungary: General Assembly Official Records, 11th Session, Supplement No 18 (A3592)' (UN 1957)

US Department of Defence, 'DoD Law of War Manual Updated Version 2016' (2015)

Venice Commission, 'Opinion No 762/2014 on Whether the Decision Taken by the Supreme Council of the Autonomous Republic of Crimea in Ukraine to Organise a Referendum on Becoming a Constituent Territory of the Russian Federation or Restoring Crimea's 1992 Constitution Is Compatible with Constitutional Principles' (2014)

——, 'Opinion No 902/ 2017 on the Provisions of the Law on Education of 5 September 2017 Which Concern the Use of the State Language and Minority and Other Languages in Education' (2017)

Blog Posts

Aiesi MJ, 'The Jus in Bello of White Phosphorus: Getting the Law Correct' (*Lawfare*, 26 November 2019) <https://www.lawfareblog.com/jus-bello-white-phosphorus-getting-law-correct>

Arnold R, 'Whose Cossacks Are They Anyway? A Movement Torn by the Ukraine-Russia Divide' (*Ponars Eurasia*, January 2019) <http://www.ponarseurasia.org/memo/whose-cossacks-are-they-anyway-ukraine-russia-divide>

Azzarello C and Niederhauser M, 'The Independent Humanitarian Fact-Finding Commission: Has the "Sleeping Beauty" Awoken?' (*Humanitarian Law & Policy*, 9 January 2018) <https://blogs.icrc.org/law-and-policy/2018/01/09/the-independent-humanitarian-fact-finding-commission-has-the-sleeping-beauty-awoken/>

Caballero R, 'Les évolutions de la primauté de la souveraineté dans l'approche russe du droit international' (*Völkerrechtsblog*, 8 January 2018) <https://voelkerrechtsblog.org/les-evolutions-de-la-primaute-de-la-souverainete-dans-lapproche-russe-du-droit-international/>

Dunlap C, 'White Phosphorus Sometimes Can Be Lawfully Employed as an Anti-Personnel Weapon…but Should It Ever Be Used That Way? (Probably Not, but Maybe.)' (*Lawfire*, 29 September 2016) <https://sites.duke.edu/lawfire/2016/09/29/white-phosphorus-sometimes-can-be-lawfully-employed-as-an-anti-personnel-weaponbut-should-it-ever-be-used-that-way-probably-not-but-maybe/>

Fox AC, 'Battle of Debaltseve: The Conventional Line of Effort in Russia's Hybrid War in Ukraine' (*Benning*, 14 September 2016) <https://www.benning.army.mil/armor/eARMOR/content/issues/2017/Winter/1Fox17.pdf>

Fox GH, 'Ukraine Insta-Symposium: Intervention in the Ukraine by Invitation' (*OpinioJuris*, 10 March 2014) <http://opiniojuris.org/2014/03/10/ukraine-insta-symposium-intervention-ukraine-invitation/>

Galeotti M, 'Living in Cossackworld' (*Jordan Russia Center*, 2 October 2012) <http://jordanrussiacenter.org/news/living-in-cossackworld/#.Xa8IBOgzaUk>

——, 'Moscow's Mercenaries in Syria' (*War on the Rocks*, 5 April 2016) <https://warontherocks.com/2016/04/moscows-mercenaries-in-syria/>

Harwood C, 'Will the "Sleeping Beauty" Awaken? The Kunduz Hospital Attack and the International Humanitarian Fact-Finding Commission' (*EJIL Talk!*, 15 October 2015) <https://www.ejiltalk.org/will-the-sleeping-beauty-awaken-the-kunduz-hospital-attack-and-the-international-humanitarian-fact-finding-commission/>

Hoffman F, 'On Not-So-New Warfare: Political Warfare vs Hybrid Threats' (*War on the Rocks*, 28 July 2014) <https://warontherocks.com/2014/07/on-not-so-new-warf are-political-warfare-vs-hybrid-threats/>

Ioffe Y, 'The Amendments to the Russian Constitution: Putin's Attempt to Reinforce Russia's Isolationist Views on International Law?' (*EJIL Talk!*, 29 January 2020) <https://www.ejiltalk.org/the-amendments-to-the-russian-constitution-puti ns-attempt-to-reinforce-russias-isolationist-views-on-international-law/>

Issaeva M, 'A Nationalized Approach to International Law: The Case of Russia' (*Völkerrechtsblog*, 5 January 2018) <https://voelkerrechtsblog.org/a-nationalized-a pproach-to-international-law-the-case-of-russia/>

Joyner D, 'The Treaty on the Prohibition of Nuclear Weapons' (*EJIL Talk!*, 26 July 2017) <https://www.ejiltalk.org/the-treaty-on-the-prohibition-of-nuclear-weapon s/>

Kaina E, 'China's Strategic Ambiguity and Shifting Approach to Lethal Autonomous Weapons Systems' (*Lawfare*, 17 April 2018) <https://www.lawfareb log.com/chinas-strategic-ambiguity-and-shifting-approach-lethal-autonomous-we apons-systems>

Kofman M, 'Russian Hybrid Warfare and Other Dark Arts' (*War on the Rocks*, 11 March 2016) <https://warontherocks.com/2016/03/russian-hybrid-warfare-and-ot her-dark-arts/>

Kraska J, 'The Kerch Strait Incident: Law of the Sea or Law of Naval Warfare?' (*EJIL Talk!*, 12 March 2018) <https://www.ejiltalk.org/the-kerch-strait-incident-law-of-t he-sea-or-law-of-naval-warfare/>

Leach P, 'The Continuing Utility of International Human Rights Mechanisms?' (*EJIL Talk!*, 11 January 2017) <ejiltalk.org/the-continuing-utility-of-international -human-rights-mechanisms/>

Levin I and Schwarz M, 'At a crossroads: Russia and the ECHR in the aftermath of Markin' (*Verfassungsblog*, 30 January 2015) <https://verfassungsblog.de/crossroad s-russia-echr-aftermath-markin-2/>

Maresca LG, 'Nuclear Weapons: 20 Years since the ICJ Advisory Opinion and Still Difficult to Reconcile with International Humanitarian Law' (*Humanitarian Law & Policy*, 8 July 2018) <https://blogs.icrc.org/law-and-policy/2016/07/08/nucl ear-weapons-20-years-icj-opinion/>

Marten K, 'The Puzzle of Russian Behaviour in Deir Al-Zour' (*War on the Rocks*, 5 July 2018) <https://warontherocks.com/2018/07/the-puzzle-of-russian-behavior-i n-deir-al-zour/>

Marxsen C, 'Cleavages in International Law and the Danger of a Pull towards Non-Compliance' (*Völkerrechtsblog*, 31 January 2018) <https://voelkerrechtsblog. org/cleavages-in-international-law-and-the-danger-of-a-pull-towards-non-complia nce/>

Nuzov I and Quintin A, 'The Case of Russia's Detention of Ukrainian Military Pilot Savchenko under IHL' (*EJIL Talk!*, 3 March 2015) <https://www.ejiltalk.or g/the-case-of-russias-detention-of-ukrainian-military-pilot-savchenko-under-ihl/>

Poulopoulou S, 'Strengthening Compliance with IHL: Back to Square One' (*EJIL Talk!*, 14 February 2019) <https://www.ejiltalk.org/strengthening-compliance-wi th-ihl-back-to-square-one/>

Sari A, 'Legal Aspects of Hybrid Warfare' (*Lawfare*, 2 October 2015) <https://www.l awfareblog.com/legal-aspects-hybrid-warfare>

Sayapin S, 'Russia's Withdrawal of Signature from the Rome Statute Would Not Shield Its Nationals from Potential Prosecution at the ICC' (*EJIL Talk!*, 21 November 2016) <https://www.ejiltalk.org/russias-withdrawal-of-signature-from -the-rome-statute-would-not-shield-its-nationals-from-potential-prosecution-at-th e-icc/>

——, 'The End of Russia's Hybrid War against Ukraine?' (*Opinio Juris*, 4 January 2019) <http://opiniojuris.org/2019/01/04/the-end-of-russias-hybrid-war-against-u kraine/>

Schatz VJ and Koval D, 'Ukraine v. Russia: Passage through Kerch Strait and the Sea of Azov' (*Völkerrechtsblog*, 10 January 2018) <https://voelkerrechtsblog.org/u kraine-v-russia-passage-through-kerch-strait-and-the-sea-of-azov/>

Steenhard R, 'The Body Counts: Civilian Casualties in War' (*Peace Palace Library*, 10 May 2012) <https://www.peacepalacelibrary.nl/2012/05/the-body-counts-civili an-casualties-in-war/>

Selected Newspaper Articles

Russian-language Newspaper Articles

Бахтияр Тузмухамедов [Bakhtiyar Tuzmukhamedov] 'Как воевать по правилам?' [How Do You Wage War by the Rules?] (Nezavisimaya Gazeta, 15 February 2010) <http://www.ng.ru/dipkurer/2010-02-15/11_wars.html>

Владимир Галицкий [Vladimir Galitsky], 'Война в правовом вакууме [War in a Legal Vacuum]' (Nezavisimaya Gazeta, 16 June 2000) <http://nvo.ng.ru/concept s/2000-06-16/4_vacuumwar.html?id_user=Y>

Денис Коротков [Denis Korotkov] 'Повар любит поострее [The Cook Likes to Spice It up]' (Novaya Gazeta, 22 October 2018) <https://www.novayagazeta.ru/ar ticles/2018/10/22/78289-povar-lyubit-poostree>

——, 'Ландскнехтов в Сирию послал Петербург [St Petersburg Sent the Mercenar- ies to Syria]' (Fontanka, 30 October 2013) <https://www.fontanka.ru/2013/10/30 /099/>

——, '"Славянский корпус" возвращается в Сирию [The Slavonic Corpus Returns to Syria]' (Fontanka, 16 October 2015) <https://www.fontanka.ru/2015/10/16/11 8/>

——, 'За Башара Асада – без флага, без Родины [For Bashar Assad – without Flag and Motherland]' (Fontanka, 22 October 2015) <https://www.fontanka.ru/2015/ 10/22/144/>

——, 'Они сражались за Пальмиру [They Fought for Palmyra]' (Fontanka, 29 March 2016) <https://www.fontanka.ru/2016/03/28/171/>

——, 'Последний бой "Славянского корпуса" [The Last Fight of the Slavonic Corpus]' (Fontanka, 14 November 2013) <https://www.fontanka.ru/2013/11/14/060/>

——, 'Расшифровка года – Вагнер [The Decryption of the Year – Wagner]' (Fontanka, 3 January 2017) <https://www.fontanka.ru/2016/12/28/094/>

——, 'Умереть за Башара Асада [Dying for Bashar Assad]' (Fontanka, 24 January 2014) <https://www.fontanka.ru/2014/01/24/062/>

Екатерина Сергацкова [Yekaterina Sergatskova], 'Очень краткий путеводитель по комбатам сепаратистов [A short who's who of the separatist fighters]' (Colta, 16 March 2015) <https://www.colta.ru/articles/society/6649-ochen-kratkiy-putevoditel-po-kombatam-separatistov>

'Павел Лаптев: срок жизни Европейского суда может быть сокращен [Pavel Laptev: The Days of the European Court May Be Numbered]' (Kommersant, 31 May 2010) <https://www.kommersant.ru/doc/1378599>

'Частная армия для президента: история самого деликатного поручения Евгения Пригожина [A Private Army for the President: the History of the Most Delicate Mission of Evgeniy Prigozhin]' (The Bell, 29 January 2019) <https://thebell.io/41889-2/>

International Newspaper Articles

Andrew E Kramer, 'Russians Find Few Barriers to Joining Ukraine Battle' (The New York Times, 9 June 2014) <https://www.nytimes.com/2014/06/10/world/europe/russians-yearning-to-join-ukraine-battle-find-lots-of-helping-hands.html>

Christiaan Triebert et al, 'How Times Reporters Proved Russia Bombed Syrian Hospitals' (The New York Times, 13 October 2019) <https://www.nytimes.com/2019/10/13/reader-center/russia-syria-hospitals-investigation.html>

Evan Hill and Christiaan Triebert, '12 hours. 4 Syrian hospitals bombed. One culprit: Russia. (The New York Times, 13 October 2019) <https://www.nytimes.com/2019/10/13/world/middleeast/russia-bombing-syrian-hospitals.html>

Judy Dempsey, 'How Looted Art Haunts German-Russian Relations' (Carnegie Europe, 24 June 2013) <https://carnegieeurope.eu/strategiceurope/52181>

Michael Cruickshank, 'Investigating The Kerch Strait Incident' (Bellingcat, 30 November 2018) <https://www.bellingcat.com/news/uk-and-europe/2018/11/30/investigating-the-kerch-strait-incident/>

Pieter van Huis, 'The MH17 Trial Part 1: New Material From The Four Defendants' (Bellingcat, 20 April 2020) <https://www.bellingcat.com/news/uk-and-europe/2020/04/20/the-mh17-trial-part-1-new-materials-from-the-four-defendants/>

'"Putin's Cook" Set Out to Mine Gold in Africa' (The Bell, 5 June 2018) <https://thebell.io/en/putin-s-cook-set-out-to-mine-gold-in-africa/>

Simon Shuster, 'Armed Cossacks Flock to Crimea to Help Russian Annexation Bid' (Time, 12 March 2014) <https://time.com/22125/ukraine-crimea-cossacks-russia/>

Simon Shuster, 'Meet the Cossack 'Wolves' Doing Russia's Dirty Work in Ukraine' (Time, 12 May 2014) <https://time.com/95898/wolves-hundred-ukraine-russia-co ssack/>

Tim Lister, Sebastian Shukla, and Clarissa Ward, 'Putin's Private Army' (CNN, August 2019) <https://edition.cnn.com/interactive/2019/08/africa/putins-private -army-car-intl/>

'Wagner Mercenaries With GRU-issued Passports: Validating SBU's Allegation' (Bellingcat, 30 January 2019) <https://www.bellingcat.com/news/uk-and-europe/ 2019/01/30/wagner-mercenaries-with-gru-issued-passports-validating-sbus-allegat ion/>

Encyclopedia Entries

Baker B, 'Hague Peace Conferences (1899 and 1907)', *Max Planck Encyclopedia of Public International Law* (Oxford University Press 2009)

Charlesworth H, 'Universal Declaration of Human Rights (1948)', *Max Planck Encyclopedia of Public International Law* (Oxford University Press 2008)

Crawford JR, 'State Responsibility', *Max Planck Encyclopedia of Public International Law* (Oxford University Press 2006)

Forteau M, 'Regional International Law', *Max Planck Encyclopedia of Public International Law* (Oxford University Press 2006)

Gautier P, 'General Participation Clause (Clausula Si Omnes)', *Max Planck Encyclopedia of Public International Law* (Oxford University Press 2006)

Gebhard J, 'Militias', *Max Planck Encyclopedia of Public International Law* (Oxford University Press 2010)

Nachtigal R and Radauer L, 'Prisoners of War (Russian Empire)', *International Encyclopedia of the First World War* <https://encyclopedia.1914-1918-online.net/h ome.html>

Nesi G, 'Uti Possidetis Doctrine', *Max Planck Encyclopedia of Public International Law* (Oxford University Press 2018)

Nußberger A, 'Russia', *Max Planck Encyclopedia of Public International Law* (Oxford University Press 2009)

——, 'Abkhazia', *Max Planck Encyclopedia of Public International Law* (Oxford University Press 2013)

——, 'South Ossetia', *Max Planck Encyclopedia of Public International Law* (Oxford University Press 2013)

Treves T, 'Customary International Law', *Max Planck Encyclopedia of Public International Law* (Oxford University Press 2015)

Zimmermann A, 'State Succession in Treaties', *Max Planck Encyclopedia of Public International Law* (Oxford University Press 2015)

Court Decisions

Decisions by Russian Courts

Постановление Конституционного Суда Российской Федерации, 31.07.1995, N 10-П [Ruling of the Constitutional Court of the Russian Federation, 31 July 1995, No 10-P]

Постановление Пленума Верховного Суда Российской Федерации, 31.10.1995, N 8 'О некоторых вопросах применения судами Конституции Российской Федерации при осуществлении правосудия' [Resolution of the Plenum of the Supreme Court of the Russian Federation, 31 October 1995, No 8 'On Certain Questions of the Application of the Constitution of the Russian Federation by Courts when Adjudicating']

Постановление Конституционного Суда Российской Федерации по делу о проверке конституционности Федерального закона, 15.04.1998, 'О культурных ценностях, перемещенных в Союз ССР в результате Второй мировой войны и находящихся на территории Российской Федерации' [Ruling of the Constitutional Court of the Russian Federation Concerning the Constitutionality of Federal Law, 15 April 1998, 'On Cultural Objects Relocated to the USSR as a Result of the Second World War Currently Located on the Territory of the Russian Federation']

Постановление Пленума Верховного Суда Российской Федерации, 10.10.2003, N 5 'О применении судами общей юрисдикции общепризнанных принципов и норм международного права и международных договоров Российской Федерации' [Resolution of the Plenum of the Supreme Court of the Russian Federation, 10 October 2003, No 5 'On the Application of Universally Recognized Principles and Norms of International Law and International Treaties by Lower Instance Courts']

Постановление Конституционного Суда Российской Федерации, 06.04.2006, N 3-П [Decision of the Constitutional Court of the Russian Federation, 6 April 2006, No 3-P]

Постановление Конституционного Суда Российской Федерации, 28.06.2007, N 8-П по делу о проверке конституционности статьи 14(1) Федерального закона 'О погребении и похоронном деле' [Ruling of the Constitutional Court of the Russian Federation, 28 June 2007, No 8-P Concerning the Constitutional Review of 14(1) of the Federal Law 'On Burial and Undertaking']

Постановление Конституционного Суда Российской Федерации, 09.07.2012, N 17-П 'По делу о проверке конституционности не вступившего в силу международного договора Российской Федерации' [Ruling of the Constitutional Court of the Russian Federation, 9 July 2012, No 17-P 'On the Issue of the Constitutional Review of Treaties of the Russian Federation that Have not yet Entered into Force']

Decisions by the ECtHR

ECtHR, *Abakarova v Russia*, No 16664/07, 15 October 2015

ECtHR, *Abdulkhanov and Others v Russia*, No 22782/06, 3 October 2013

ECtHR, *Abuyeva and Others v Russia*, No 27065/05, 2 December 2010

ECtHR, *Akhmatov and Others v Russia*, Nos 38828/ 10, 2543/11, 2650/11 et al, 16 January 2014

ECtHR, *Al Skeini and Others v The United Kingdom*, No 55721/07, 7 July 2011

ECtHR, *Amuyeva and Others v Russia*, No 17321/06, 25 November 2010

ECtHR, *Anchugov and Gladkov v Russia*, Nos 11157/04 and 15162/05, 9 December 2019

ECtHR, *Angeline and Others v Russia*, No 56328/18, lodged on 23 November 2018

ECtHR, *Arkhestov and Others v Russia*, No 22089/07, 16 January 2014

ECtHR, *Aslakhanova and Others v Russia*, No 2944/06 et seq, 18 December 2012

ECtHR, *Ayley and Others v Russia*, No 25714/16, lodged on 6 May 2016

ECtHR, *Catan and Others v Moldova and Russia*, Nos 43370/04, 8252/05 and 18454/06, 19 October 2012

ECtHR, *Damayev v Russia*, No 36150/04, 29 May 2012

ECtHR, *Esmukhambetov and Others v Russia*, No 23445/03, 29 March 2011

ECtHR, *Georgia v Russia*, No 38263/08, 21 January 2021

ECtHR, *Gisayev v Russia*, No 14811/04, 20 January 2011

ECtHR, *Güzelyurtlu and Others v Cyprus and Turkey*, No 36925/07, 29 January 2009

ECtHR, *Ilaşcu and Others v Moldova and Russia*, No 48787/99, 8 July 2004

ECtHR, *Isayeva v Russia*, No 57950/00, 24 February 2005

ECtHR, *Ivanţoc and Others v Moldova and Russia*, No 23687/05, 15 November 2011

ECtHR, *Jaloud v The Netherlands*, No 47708/08, 20 November 2014

ECtHR, *Kerimova and Others v Russia*, No 17170/04 et al, 3 May 2011

ECtHR, *Khadisov and Tsechoyev v Russia*, No 21519/02, 5 February 2009

ECtHR, *Khamzayev and Others v Russia*, No 1503/02, 3 May 2011

ECtHR, *Kononov v Latvia*, No 36376/04, 17 May 2010

ECtHR, *Kushtova and Others v Russia*, No 21885/07, 16 January 2014

ECtHR, *Malika Dzhamayeva and Others v Russia*, No 26980/06, 21 December 2010

ECtHR, *Mangîr and Others v the Republic of Moldova and Russia*, No 50157/06, 17 July 2018

ECtHR, *Maskhadova and Others v Russia*, No 18071/05, 6 June 2013

ECtHR, *Mezhidov v Russia*, No 67326/01, 25 September 2008

ECtHR, *Mozer v Moldova and Russia*, No 11138/10, 23 February 2016

ECtHR, *OAO Neftyanaya Kompaniya Yukos v Russia*, No 14902/04, Judgment Just Satisfaction, 31 July 2014

ECtHR, *Olujic v Croatia*, No 22330/05, 5 February 2009

ECtHR, *Sabanchiyeva and Others v Russia*, No 38450/05, 6 June 2013

ECtHR, *Sadykov v Russia*, No 41840/02, 7 October 2010

ECtHR, *Sargsyan v Azerbaijan*, No 40167/06, 16 June 2015

Bibliography

ECtHR, *Taysumov and Others v Russia*, No 21810/03, 14 May 2009

ECtHR, *Turluyeva v Russia*, No 63638/09, 20 June 2013

ECtHR, *Umayeva v Russia*, No 1200/03, 4 December 2008

ECtHR, *Yandiyev and Others v Russia*, Nos 34541/06, 43811/06, and 1578/07, 10 October 2013

ECtHR, *Zalov and Khakulova v Russia*, No 7988/09, 16 January 2014

Decisions by the ICJ

ICJ, *Accordance with International Law of the Unilateral Declaration of Independence in Respect of Kosovo*, Advisory Opinion, ICJ Reports (2010) 403

ICJ, *Legal Consequences of the Construction of a Wall in the Occupied Palestinian Territory*, Advisory Opinion, ICJ Reports (2004) 13

ICJ, *The Legality of the Threat or Use of Nuclear Weapons*, Advisory Opinion, ICJ Reports (1996) 226

ICJ, *Application of the Convention on the Prevention and Punishment of the Crime of Genocide (Bosnia and Herzegovina v Serbia and Montenegro)*, Judgment, ICJ Reports (2007) 43

ICJ, *Application of the International Convention on the Elimination of All Forms of Racial Discrimination (Georgia v Russian Federation)*, Preliminary Objections, Judgment, ICJ Reports (2011) 70

ICJ, *Armed Activities on the Territory of the Congo (Democratic Republic of the Congo v Uganda)*, Judgment, ICJ Reports (2005) 168

ICJ, *Military and Paramilitary Activities in and against Nicaragua (Nicaragua v United States of America)*, Merits Judgment, ICJ Reports (1986) 14

ICJ, *United States Diplomatic and Consular Staff in Tehran*, Judgment, ICJ Reports (1980) 3

Decisions by Other International Courts

ICC, *Situation in Georgia* (ICC-01/15–12), Pre-Trial Chamber I, 27 January 2016

ICC, *The Prosecutor v Jean-Pierre Bemba Gombo* (ICC-01/05–01/08), Decision Pursuant to Art 61(7)(a) and (b) of the Rome Statue on the Charges of the Prosecutor Against Jean-Pierre Bemba Gombo, 15 June 2009

ICC, *The Prosecutor v Thomas Lubanga Dyilo* (ICC-01/04–01/06–2842), Trial Chamber Judgment, 14 March 2012

ICTY, *The Prosecutor v Duško Tadić* (IT-94-1-T), Appeals Chamber Judgment, 15 July 1999

ICTY, *The Prosecutor v Duško Tadić* (IT-94–1-T), Decision on the Defence Motion for Interlocutory Appeal on Jurisdiction, 2 October 1995

ICTY, *The Prosecutor v Fatimir Limaj et al* (IT-03–66-T), Trial Chamber Judgment, 30 November 2005

ICTY, *The Prosecutor v Ivica Rajić* (IT-95–12-R61), Review of the Indictment pursuant to Rule 61 of the Rules of Procedure and Evidence, 13 September 1996

ICTY, *The Prosecutor v Ljube Boškoski and Johan Tarčulovski* (IT-04–82-T), Trial Chamber Judgment, 10 July 2008

ICTY, *The Prosecutor v Milan Martić* (IT-95–11-A), Appeals Chamber Judgment, 8 October 2008

ICTY, *The Prosecutor v Mile Mrkšić et al* (IT-95–13/1-T), Trial Chamber Judgment, 27 September 2007

ICTY, *The Prosecutor v Mladen Naletilić and Vinko Martinović* (IT-98–34-T), Trial Chamber Judgment, 31 March 2003

ICTY, *The Prosecutor v Ramush Haradinaj et al* (IT-04–84-T), Trial Chamber Judgment, 3 April 2008

ICTY, *The Prosecutor v Tihomir Blaškić* (IT-95–14), Trial Chamber Judgment, 3 March 2000

ICTY, *The Prosecutor v Vlastimir Đorđević* (IT-05–87/1-T), Trial Chamber Judgment, 23 February 2011

ICTY, *The Prosecutor v Zejnil Delalić et al* (IT-96–21-T), Trial Chamber Judgment, 16 November 1998

ICTY, *The Prosecutor v Zoran Kupreškić et al* (IT-95–16-T), Trial Chamber Judgment, 14 January 2000

ITLOS, *Case concerning the detention of three Ukrainian naval vessels (Ukraine v Russian Federation) Request for the prescription of provisional measures (Case No 26)*, Order, 25 May 2019

PCIJ, *France v Turkey (Lotus Case)*, 7 September 1927, 1927 PCIJ (Ser A) No 10